CHALLENGER REVEALED

An Insider's Account of How
the Reagan Administration
Caused the Greatest Tragedy
of the Space Age

RICHARD C. COOK

THUNDER'S MOUTH PRESS
NEW YORK

CHALLENGER REVEALED:
*An Insider's Account of How the Reagan Administration
Caused the Greatest Tragedy of the Space Age*

Published by
Thunder's Mouth Press
An imprint of Avalon Publishing Group, Inc.
245 West 17th Street, 11th Floor
New York, NY 10011
www.thundersmouthpress.com

AVALON
publishing group incorporated

Library of Congress Cataloguing-in-Publication data is available

ISBN-10: 1-56025-980-9
ISBN-13: 978-1-56025-980-0

Designed by Pauline Neuwirth, Neuwirth & Associates, Inc.

10 9 8 7 6 5 4 3 2 1

Printed in the United States of America
Distributed by Publishers Group West

CONTENTS

INTRODUCTION   vii

PART I | PRE-DISASTER   1

1 "WE GOT YOU CHEAP"   3
How I Arrived at NASA

2 "THINK AND TALK POSITIVE"   16
My Introduction to the Space Shuttle Program

3 "TWO-MINUTE RIDE"   31
The Dangers of the Solid Rocket Boosters

4 "THE CENTAUR IS THE ONLY VEHICLE"   49
Politics in the Space Shuttle Program

5 "GIVING AN HONEST ESTIMATE"   60
Things Go Wrong with the Centaur

6 "FLY AS IS"   70
NASA Ponders the Centaur Problems
as Challenger Looms on Pad 39-A

PART II | HISTORY   89

7 "FIRST YOU HAVE TO GET THE HORSE"   91
How America Decided to Build the Space Shuttle

8 "GET OUT OF OUR WAY"   109
Operating the Shuttle Like a Scheduled Airline

9 "A VISION OF THE FUTURE"   128
Weapons in Space

10 "WE'LL END UP RULING THE WORLD"   149
The Right Wing Subverts NASA's Leadership

11 "LESSON FROM SPACE"   169
A Brief History of Shuttle Missions

PART III | LEAKS   187

12 "DON'T LET ANYBODY SAY ANYTHING"   189
The Cover-ups Begin

13 "THIS IS GOOD STUFF"   209
How the New York Times *Came to Disclose the O-ring Papers*

14 "AN UNPLEASANT, UNFORTUNATE SITUATION"   228
The Commission Meets Behind Closed Doors

15 "WHAT IS HE DOING TO THEM?"   254
My Appearance Before the Commission

16 "LOWER TEMPERATURES AGGRAVATE THIS PROBLEM"   283
The Commission Changes Direction

17 "THE TOOTH FAIRY"   314
The World Hears the Thiokol Engineers' Story

18 "AFRAID THAT THE MESSENGER MAY BE SLAIN"   359
The Commission Moves Ahead—Sort of

PART IV | RESPONSIBILITY 379

19 "SHOCKINGLY SPARSE CONCERNS FOR 381
   HUMAN LIFE"
   The Commission's Flawed Report

20 "IT IS NOT GOING TO FAIL BECAUSE OF ME" 400
   The Senate and House Hearings

21 "THEY THINK YOU'RE CLOSE TO THE TRUTH" 418
   My Work with Senator Ernest Hollings

22 "NO ONE EXPECTED CHALLENGER 438
   TO BE LAUNCHED"
   *The House Report Closes the Government's
   Book on Challenger*

23 "NO SUCH THING HAS EVER TAKEN PLACE" 448
   Did President Reagan Order the Challenger Launch?

POSTSCRIPT 478
NASA'S SHUTTLE MATRIX ORGANIZATION
   ON JANUARY 28, 1986 480
ACKNOWLEDGEMENTS 481
GLOSSARY 483
NOTES 491
INDEX 504

INTRODUCTION

T**HIS IS A** book that tells an insider's story of why the space shuttle Challenger blew up just over one minute after launch on January 28, 1986. It took twenty-one years for me to complete the narrative. To ask why it took so long is legitimate, though books are constantly being published on historical events which took place decades or even centuries ago, bringing new perspectives, evidence, and arguments. So a new book on one of the signature events of the 20th century may itself be a contribution to the historical literature.

But the real reason had more to do with my own personal circumstances. I wrote much of the book by 1991 from a massive archive of notes, interviews, documentary sources, and my own published articles on the subject. But at that point, I was still a government employee. I felt I owed it to my family not to jeopardize my position. I put the archive away in boxes and placed them in the attic.

More years passed. My views of the Challenger story developed. By now I had reached the thirty-year mark of my tenure with the federal government, so I was eligible for retirement. I had always known that the book had to be written so that the public could see beyond the official accounts. I also had a personal story to tell. And the Challenger saga sheds light on today's crisis in government, where the honesty of public officials in explaining the true rationale for events and decisions is so much in question.

So an urgent need to finish the book had appeared. For six months I wrote every night and weekend, seeing new connections and clarifying points and issues that had been obscure. Again I read the record of the Presidential Commission's hearings and the House and Senate hearings and reports. Finally, I was satisfied that I had explained the disaster as completely as I could, including my own role as the NASA analyst who had documented engineers' concerns about a possible catastrophe before it took place and their judgment afterward that it had been a preventable accident. The experience of writing the book was also personally cathartic, allowing me to relive those trying days and make sense of them to myself, my family, and as many others as I would be able to reach through publication.

The space shuttle Challenger disaster and its aftermath were devastating to me personally. The event deeply shocked our nation and the world. But the complete story of what happened to cause it, and how various parties within the government, including the Presidential Commission, tried to gloss over critical aspects of it, has never been told.

My book is an attempt to correct that omission. A factor which gave my effort impetus was my belief that during the mid-1980s, when the disaster occurred, our country began to walk a dangerous path from being the world's leading industrial democracy to what is starting to resemble today a military imperial state. As my book shows, the underlying causes of the Challenger tragedy were the militarization of the U.S. manned space program by the Reagan administration and the political imperatives of top-down management. The disaster should have provided an early warning about what was going on during the military build-up of those days. But it did not, because the official investigations made it appear that the problems were "communications," "schedule pressure," and "technical decision-making" and that the incident itself was an "accident." These representations were far from accurate.

The writing of the book was extraordinarily painful, as the reading of it may also be to sensitive readers. But it was also a healing experience. After suffering for almost two decades from various wounded feelings, I ultimately realized that every person involved in the tragedy and subsequent events only did what seemed right to them at the time. While the results of their actions were harmful in the extreme, a careful analysis of all pertinent and available facts disclosed the wisdom of something I heard a wise man say many years ago: "There is no conscious evil."

Today public policy has become more a matter of emotion, prejudice, and politics than intellect and analysis. There is often a chasm between the managers who bow to the political and financial bosses and the people who do the work day in and day out. This is why it is so important that the causes of Challenger be identified, understood, and assimilated. The Challenger disaster was not an isolated incident. It was a symbol of our era and a parable for our times that calls for an informed, enlightened—and apolitical—public sector.

PART I

PRE-DISASTER

"WE GOT YOU CHEAP"

—How I Arrived at NASA

JANUARY 28, 1986, 11:41 a.m. EST. I am sitting, stunned, in a large conference room. It's called the news auditorium, though it's just a tile floor with folding chairs and a narrow wooden stage at the back. The room is on the sixth floor of the headquarters building of the National Aeronautics and Space Administration at 400 Maryland Avenue, S.W., in Washington, D.C. In the front of the room, a large, lonely TV monitor tuned to NASA Select television keeps vigil. I have just witnessed the explosion of the space shuttle Challenger.

Two blocks to the north is the Smithsonian Institution's Air and Space Museum, the most visited museum in the world. The crowds there will soon learn that their universe has changed. My own life too will never be the same. Just how, I will start to learn over the next few days.

I was interested in this launch mostly because of Christa McAuliffe, the Teacher-in-Space. She was an exceptionally fresh, bright, and articulate young woman. I had walked over to the conference room from my office, about two minutes away, to witness the start of her journey to space, which she called the "Ultimate Field Trip." Now she and the other six Challenger astronauts were gone. The words from the broadcast are echoing in my mind: "Obviously a major malfunction. . . . We have no downlink. . . . We have a report from the flight dynamics officer that the vehicle has exploded."

Impossible. But I hear the words again. Yes, I knew it could happen, and it did happen, but why today? I see in my mind's eye the clouds of puffy white vapor streaming away from Challenger in the deep blue Florida sky, as two errant solid rocket boosters fish-tail into oblivion.

I work in the office of the NASA comptroller. I am an experienced government analyst, having worked for the U.S. Civil Service Commission, the Food and Drug Administration, and the Carter White House. Now I analyze budgets for the space shuttle's external tank, solid rocket boosters, and Centaur upper stage.

Worried-looking people from all over the building are walking briskly into the room. A couple of women are slumped in their chairs, sobbing. The TV has been switched to CBS News. Senator John Glenn is on the air. No one could have more credibility than the former Mercury astronaut. He says in a thoughtful voice, "First light seemed to come from a solid rocket booster."

After watching the broadcast for a few minutes, I walk back to my office and phone my wife long-distance at home. The phone rings for a while before she picks up.

"The space shuttle blew up," I say. "They are all dead."

"My God," Phyllis answers. She rushes to turn on the TV, then comes back to the phone. Yes, all the networks are covering the story.

"It's not May yet," she says grimly.

"No," I answer.

She is referring to a project I had been working on. For several months I had been studying the Centaur. This was a rocket fueled by supercooled hydrogen and oxygen, which the shuttle's orbiter was to carry in its payload bay. Once the orbiter had been launched and was circling the Earth, the payload bay doors would open, and the Centaur would emerge. It would then ignite and blast through space toward its destination. It would be launched on two shuttle missions in May 1986. I had been following the building of the Centaur closely. Just ten days earlier, I had returned from two intensive days of meetings at the Kennedy Space Center in Florida.

The Centaur was so dangerous, and there were so many problems with its design and construction, that the astronauts and the Houston managers at mission control believed it was unsafe. They called it "the bomb in the bay." There was no time to fix some of the most serious problems before the May missions. So Centaur was scheduled to "fly as is."

There were other shuttle safety problems, of course. They seemed to show up more often on Challenger than the other orbiters in the fleet. For example, a main engine had shut down due to a sensor flaw on the July 1985 flight, where a catastrophic ditching into the Atlantic Ocean seemed possible.

Then there were problems in another of my hardware areas, the solid rocket boosters. The SRBs are the two huge solid-fuel rockets that burn for the first two minutes of a shuttle flight in order to assist the orbiter in breaking free of Earth's gravitation. In 1983, a near-burn-through of the lining of one of the rocket's nozzles had placed Challenger seconds from possible disaster on only its second flight.

The solid rocket boosters are built in segments to permit reusability, and the joints in-between are protected by O-rings and putty. Flames from burning fuel during several shuttle flights had caused heat damage to the O-rings. On one flight in April 1985, the primary O-ring in a joint was completely eaten through and the secondary O-ring eroded. In February, only a couple of weeks from now, an improved joint design called the "capture feature" would be tested, which engineers were hoping would solve the problem. I was planning to fly to Utah as part of the official group to witness the test at the factory of the manufacturer, Morton Thiokol.

At 4:30 that Tuesday afternoon, I join my vanpool, take my usual seat behind the steering wheel, and set off on the long drive through southern Maryland, across the Potomac River bridge, to rural Virginia, where I live with Phyllis and our two young children. Fred is a baby—seven months old. Adele has just turned three. Phyllis is an at-home mother. I have two other kids, Nat and Tim, who live with their mother, Barbara, my first wife, in Maryland.

On the drive home, I listen to the news. They are broadcasting a press conference from Kennedy where Jesse Moore is speaking. He is the associate administrator for space flight, the top operations manager at NASA. Moore is the one who gives the launch order for the shuttle, but he doesn't have much to say. NASA hasn't ruled out anything as a cause. The weather was windy, he says, but otherwise not a problem. That was about it.

"They have to know more than that," I think.

During the afternoon, Phyllis had recorded some of the TV news broadcasts. One was of a CBS News special with Dan Rather, where a guest analyst named Leo Krupp was narrating a video of Challenger. He said there were "flame leaks" coming out of one of the solid rocket boosters, and the videos look like he was right. I remember that afternoon at NASA when Senator John Glenn was on TV saying "first light" seemed to be coming from a solid rocket booster. . . . Could it be?

I am agitated when I get to work the next day. I walk briskly through the outer area of our suite to my office and say good morning to Alice, the secretary, and Carol, my office mate. I start to scramble through the files in a drawer of my gray metal government-issue desk. I am anxiously looking for a memo I wrote on the solid rocket booster O-rings.

I think it was last July, not too long after I started to work at NASA. I had walked over to the other headquarters building where Jesse Moore and the engineers for the Office of Space Flight worked. I had talked at length to two of the propulsion engineers—Paul Wetzel, the solid rocket booster branch chief, and Paul Herr, the engineer for the solid rocket motors. They told me that the O-rings were. . . .

Here it is, stuffed in a large file folder with some of the other memos I had written about the SRBs. The memo is addressed to my supervisor and dated July 23, 1985. As I read, my hands are shaking, and beads of sweat break out on my forehead. The memo says:

> Earlier this week you asked me to investigate reported problems with the charring of seals between SRB motor segments during flight operations. Discussions with program engineers show this to be a potentially major problem affecting both flight safety and program costs.
>
> Presently three seals between SRB segments use double O-rings sealed with putty. In recent shuttle flights, charring of these O-rings has occurred. The O-rings are designed so that if one fails, the other will hold against the pressure of firing. However, at least in the joint between the nozzle and the aft segment, not only has the first O-ring been destroyed, but the second has been partially eaten away.
>
> Engineers have not yet determined the cause of the problem.

Candidates include the use of a new type of putty (the putty formerly in use was removed from the market by EPA because it contained asbestos), failure of the second ring to slip into the groove which must engage it for it to work properly, and as yet unidentified assembly procedures at Thiokol. The Marshall Space Flight Center is trying to identify the cause of the problem, including on-site investigation at Thiokol, and the Office of Space Flight hopes to have some results of their analysis within thirty days. There is little question, however, that flight safety has been and is still being compromised by potential failure of the seals, and it is acknowledged that failure during launch would certainly be catastrophic. . . .

The potential impact of the problem depends on the as yet undiscovered cause. If the cause is minor, there should be little or no impact on budget or flight rate. A worst case scenario, however, would lead to the suspension of shuttle flights, redesign of the SRB, and scrapping of existing stockpiled hardware. The impact on the FY 1987-88 budget could be immense.

It should be pointed out that Code M [Office of Space Flight] management is viewing the situation with the utmost seriousness. . . .

God, they knew all about it. They told me it was being fixed. But they kept on flying. Why? What happened?

———

I GREW UP in Midland, Michigan, and Williamsburg, Virginia, where we moved when I was thirteen. My father worked for Dow Chemical, and my mother was a nurse and a tour hostess for Colonial Williamsburg. I had three sisters.

When I was in the tenth grade, I became fascinated with rockets. It was 1961, and the U.S. manned space program was just starting. I learned how to make gunpowder using ingredients from the drugstore, but found it a little too dangerous after a friend and I shook up the neighborhood by blowing a hole in our garage wall with a homemade pipe cannon.

So I settled on match head rockets. I stuffed the match heads in paper tubes rolled from newspapers, then ignited the rockets with a fuse and sent them sailing above the trees. Sometimes I taped a transparent plastic pill container on the end and placed Japanese beetles inside to be my space travelers.

As I went through high school and beyond, NASA's Mercury, Gemini, and Apollo programs were an ongoing adventure that became part of the background of life.

I also learned something about mechanics. My parents bought me a 1950 Plymouth for $100 that I drove throughout high school. It was a great car. Under the hood was the engine, an air filter, a starter motor, a distributor, some spark plug wires, and the radiator, but not much else.

I also became interested in politics. I handed out campaign literature around Williamsburg for John F. Kennedy in 1960 and heard Robert Kennedy speak for his brother's candidacy one night at the Williamsburg courthouse. When President Kennedy was assassinated on November 23, 1963, one of my high school teachers called me to the office, where I listened to the terrible news on the radio. I wrote an article for the school newspaper, saying how bad this was for America, that it was a sign of a violent, deranged society.

I was also strongly affected by the violence in the South against blacks and the young Northerners who took part in the civil rights movement. I told some friends I was going to introduce a motion in our high school student council in favor of integrating the public schools in Williamsburg. But the school administration heard about it and had me removed from the council. They said my resolution would cause an upcoming school bond issue to be voted down. But soon after my class graduated, the Williamsburg/James City County schools were integrated.

After a couple of years of traveling around the country, I returned to Williamsburg, enrolled at the College of William and Mary, and settled down to study. I made straight A's, read constantly, founded an improvisational theater group that gave some well-attended performances, and was elected to Phi Beta Kappa.

I went to college on loans from the National Defense Education Act and soaked up the beauty and atmosphere of the William and Mary campus, where Thomas Jefferson was the most famous alumnus. My favorite philosopher was Plato, and my favorite book was Plato's *Republic*, which was what got me interested in government. The *Republic* showed the way it was supposed to be done. The Guardians were the ones who should govern a nation—selfless, rational, disinterested, educated, scientific. That was the ideal, and I knew then that I really was an idealist in the philosophical sense of the term. Plato said that the world we see in our everyday consciousness is only the shadow of the world that exists in reality. I knew he was right and that this was why the world of everyday life often seemed so unreal. I also read Bishop Berkeley, who said the world is an idea in the mind of God.

The Vietnam War was now raging. I was in college and wasn't drafted, but boys I had known in high school were killed, including two I had played with on the football team—Talmadge Alfin, who lived on my street, and Terry Palm. And the father of another boy, Gene Michelli, was killed. I hated the Vietnam War. I saw it as a power grab by the military-industrial complex that Eisenhower had warned against.

I took part in the 1969 March on Washington against the Vietnam War. Yet I was not against the government, as such. I watched the Apollo 11 moon landing on July 20, 1969, with fascination. I loved NASA and the space program. Why couldn't our government do more things like this instead of the Vietnam War?

As graduation from William and Mary approached, I was sick of being broke and wanted to earn a living. I got hold of a catalogue of federal government jobs and applied for several.

The job that looked the best was as an employee development specialist with the Bureau of Training at the U.S. Civil Service Commission at 1900 E Street, N.W., in Washington, D.C. I started as a GS-7 earning $7,500 per year. While the war in Vietnam was raging, I was given meaningful assignments working for the civilian side of government.

At the commission, I was assigned to design and write the 1970 report on *Employee Training in the Federal Service*. Another assignment was to write a regulation authorizing upward mobility training for lower-graded federal employees. The men I worked for were real professionals. They liked and respected me, and the feeling was mutual. They knew I had taken part in anti-war marches, but they were broad-minded and weren't bothered by it, including some who were military veterans.

I worked three blocks from the White House. They gave out tickets to attend ceremonies where President Nixon would welcome foreign heads of state. Standing on the White House south lawn, I felt like I really belonged. I was part of something important, and I had found my calling as a civil servant.

But the Vietnam War loomed over everything. It was now the fall of 1970. The decade of the1960s had been a momentous one for the U.S., and people who were not growing up then will always find it difficult to understand the effect it had on those who did.

I worked for the U.S. Civil Service Commission for two years, but my interest was drifting. I had met many new people in Washington and felt I needed a different kind of challenge.

So I decided to take a chance and teach at a new private secondary school that was starting up on the second floor of an old two-story office building a couple of blocks up Connecticut Avenue from Dupont Circle. It was called the Field School. I had a friend who would be teaching English there, and I was hired as the history teacher. The work was exhausting, the pay was less than my government job, but I learned an extraordinary amount. My wife Barbara gave birth to our first son, Nathaniel, just after I started to work at the school in September 1972. We rented an apartment near the National Zoo, but while I was still teaching, we bought a small house in Kensington, Maryland, and I began to commute to work by bus.

The Field School was one of several small, progressive private secondary schools that had sprouted up in Washington, D.C., in the area around Rock Creek Park. The students were extremely bright. Most were children of Washington professionals, including the son of South Dakota Senator James Abourezk, the grandson of former Secretary of Defense Clark Clifford, and the daughters of attorney Max Kampelman, later President Reagan's lead arms negotiator.

From the school I returned to the U.S. Civil Service Commission, but now I was the program evaluation officer for the Bureau of Training. I had been promoted to a higher level due to my teaching experience.

I now became a supervisor in charge of evaluating all the bureau's Washington and regional training centers. One time I found that a $300,000 deficit had been run up in a reimbursable training program because they were late in sending out course announcements. The center director yelled at me for making him look bad. I sat calmly and listened, then filed my report. I was 29 years old.

I worked daily with the bureau's top managers and traveled throughout the U.S. The bureau director, Jim Beck, told me I would likely become a "super grade" someday; i.e., a top career executive. Jim had previously been director of the Federal Executive Institute in Charlottesville, Virginia, where the University of Virginia and Jefferson's Monticello were.

I switched jobs, and for the next three years worked at the Food and Drug Administration. We had a second son, Timothy, but my wife and I divorced. I then moved on to the U.S. Office of Consumer Affairs within the Jimmy Carter White House. While there, I met the woman I would soon marry, Phyllis Menge, who had been a stewardess for United Airlines and lived in Old Town Alexandria, across the Potomac River in Virginia.

But political upheaval in America was looming that would change my life, along with the lives of millions of other people. The early 1970s had seen the collapse of the American military adventure in Southeast Asia. Saigon fell in 1975, we retrenched militarily, and President Carter angered many people by signing the Panama Canal Treaty in 1977 that would eventually return the canal to the Panamanian people. In 1978–79, the Shah of Iran was overthrown by militants during the Iranian Revolution, and in November 1979, sixty-six American hostages were seized and made prisoner at the U.S. embassy in Tehran. There had also been the Soviet invasion of Afghanistan and President Carter's decision to protest by canceling U.S. participation in the 1980 summer Olympic Games in Moscow.

The 1970s saw the steepest peacetime inflation in American history. It seemed to have been caused not by the rise in gasoline prices, as some believed, but by low unemployment and rising wages and salaries. Skilled workers were in demand. These might have been positive developments for working families if productivity hadn't been lagging and prices could have been kept under control. Nixon had tried wage and price controls in the early 1970s, but they could not be enforced, and there were no other government mechanisms to stem inflation as long as interest rates remained at low to moderate levels. Housing prices led the surge, with the cost of a home doubling over a five-year period. Government planners at the federal, state, and local levels did not object, because tax revenues are pegged to incomes, capital gains, and other measures of economic activity.

These events made it difficult for Carter to be reelected, and he had a formidable opponent in Ronald Reagan, former film actor and governor of California, who had the backing of powerful forces.

The stage had been set for Carter to be voted out of office in November 1980. His was now a lame-duck administration. Just after the election, Phyllis and I married and rented a townhouse in the Yates Gardens section of Old Town Alexandria, where my sons Nat and Tim would sometimes visit from Annapolis. I had a lot of time on my hands, and it was a pleasant hiatus for us, but much would be changing in Washington, D.C., and in our own lives.

I was offered a job interview with the Office of Management and Budget but decided to stay with the U.S. Office of Consumer Affairs. Our suite in the OEOB was now needed for the incoming Reaganites, so we were ordered to vacate the premises. I reported to work at an office in the Reporter's Building at 7th and D Streets, S.W., near the national headquarters of HUD, the Department of Transportation, the Department of Education, and NASA.

At work I kept reasonably quiet about my political views, and it was strange to find that I was being given consumer-related correspondence addressed to President Reagan to answer and was assigned speech-writing duties for Virginia Knauer, the new head of the Office of Consumer Affairs. I guess she liked me, because at one conference where she spoke, she introduced me from the podium as her press secretary, so I stood up and waved to the applauding Republican faithful.

Meanwhile, the American economy was crashing. Paul Volcker, chairman of the Federal Reserve, had decided to wring the inflation out of the economy. This was accomplished by raising bank interest rates to the twenty percent range. It caused the worst economic decline since the Great Depression.

Reagan made huge cuts in income tax rates for the upper brackets while starting a major military escalation. He financed both, while covering losses in tax revenues from the recession, through massive Treasury Department borrowing. The national debt soared due to the largest federal budget deficits in history. The recession not only drove down wages and raised unemployment, it also gutted the American economy and led to long-term deterioration in America's industrial base and physical infrastructure. Small businesses were hit hard, and entire industries, such as steel, were devastated.

Once again I had a growing family. Our daughter Adele was born in December 1982. By now, Phyllis and I had decided to leave Washington. In March 1983, I resigned from the government, and we moved to a small mountain farm in Monroe County, West Virginia, not far from Lewisburg and White Sulfur Springs.

I intended to become a writer and worked on a novel about life in Washington during the transition between the Carter and Reagan administrations. I also did carpentry, yard work, and odd jobs for some of our neighbors. I learned to use dynamite to remove tree stumps, and we had a large garden, raised goats and chickens, and made maple syrup from the sugar maples on our property.

Running out of money, we sold the farm and moved to an estate in Virginia across the James River from Williamsburg in Surrey, where I worked for a few months as a farm manager for a wealthy couple. But I still had child support to pay for my two sons who were now 10 and 13, and Phyllis was pregnant again. With Nat, Tim, Adele, and one coming, that would be four kids.

In January 1985, in the middle of a snowstorm and with the help of my father and my brother-in-law Don Hutton, we left the estate and put our furniture into storage. We drove back to Washington. Friends on home leave to New Zealand—he worked at the World Bank—offered to let us housesit at their home in Arlington, Virginia. I was back in the nation's capital, unemployed and desperately poor, with many mouths to feed.

We needed income right away, so to at least generate a paycheck, I visited the Norrell temporary job agency next to the Alexandria, Virginia, metro station and took a typing test. The next day, Norrell called and asked me to report to a job site for the TRW Defense Systems Group.

The TRW facility was in the midst of a checkerboard of low-rise industrial and office buildings separated by a maze of access roads and parking lots. There were no signs or markings on the outside of the building except for a street number. Inside was a top-secret factory, where I was to work in the computer room, actually a sealed bank-like vault.

I was a data entry clerk but soon was promoted to word processor. This allowed us to rent a two-bedroom apartment in Alexandria at a complex on U.S. One. At TRW I had a "blue badge" clearance, which entitled me to work in the vault and type part numbers from engineering drawings into a computerized database. We were automating the design of—something; I was not told what. Once, however, I passed through what they called the "high bay," where there was a tractor-trailer being outfitted with computers and other electronic devices.

What we were building was mobile military command, communication, and control—"C3"—units that would roam the highways of America during military exercises or war. It was part of the Reagan military build-up, preparation for World War III. I was in the midst of true believers. In the parking lot I saw an employee's pick-up truck with a bumper sticker that said, "I'd Rather be Killing Communists."

I continued to get pay raises, moving quickly up the ladder. The manager I worked for, who saw me as smart and reliable, offered me a permanent job. But I had continued to apply for federal jobs and hoped eventually to return to the government, so I turned it down.

When I resigned from the government two years earlier, I had been a GS-13. I was now applying for every federal job I thought I had a shot at down to GS-9. At that level, I would at least be making as much as I was with overtime at TRW. Around the first of May, I was selected for a GS-12 job at the Department of the Treasury. Phyllis and I thought that our troubles were finally over, but at the last minute the personnel office at Treasury canceled the vacancy because of a budget shortfall. It was a grievous disappointment.

I continued to apply for jobs. We were anxious to start getting health insurance, with the baby due around the Fourth of July, since there was none with the TRW job. We were joking about having a "Yankee Doodle Baby," but the cost of the delivery—we were using a midwife service, but it was still expensive—was a serious matter. I applied for jobs with over a dozen federal agencies, including several Defense Department units as well as NASA, though the NASA job looked remote.

One day as I sat working in the TRW computer vault, I got a call from a woman who asked me to come downtown to NASA headquarters for a job interview for a GS-9 analyst position. I took time off, drove into Washington, and found a parking space on the Mall near the Air and Space Museum. NASA headquarters was nearby on Maryland Avenue, so I walked through the museum to get there. I was a little early for the interview, so I stopped to look at the Mercury and Gemini space capsules, the Apollo lunar landing vehicle, and some of the other NASA displays. I began to feel excited.

The job interview was with the comptroller's office on the sixth floor, down the hall from the NASA news auditorium. I met with two men—

one I'll call the supervisor and the other the division director. It was a resource analyst job with responsibility for reviewing the shuttle plans and budgets submitted by the Office of Space Flight to NASA's administrator, James Beggs. The job for which I was being interviewed oversaw the budget for the shuttle's external tank—the ET—and the solid rocket boosters—the SRBs. Later, the Centaur upper stage was added to my portfolio.

The interview was cordial. The division director seemed relaxed and friendly, though the supervisor was stiff and distant. I said that it sounded like a great job. They offered me the position at the GS-9 level, but said promotion was to GS-15, perhaps the highest grade in the government for a non-supervisory analyst. The pay once I reached that level would be equivalent to being an attorney or M.D. at other federal agencies. It looked like a once-in-a-lifetime opportunity. Later, the supervisor told me they hired me because "we got you cheap." He meant they had picked up someone with an excellent resumé and many years of government experience for practically entry-level pay. But I was glad to be back in the government and excited to be part of the U.S. manned space program.

I called Phyllis after the interview. "I can't believe it," I said. "I'm going to be working on the space shuttle."

"That is really great," she said. "Congratulations."

———

IT WAS GOOD for life to seem normal again. Phyllis and I had been through a long ordeal with my departure from the government, life on the farm, and the return to Washington, followed by the brief but desperate struggle with poverty while I tried to get my career on track. But we were back and could start looking for a house. We even had our Yankee Doodle Baby—Fred was born on July 8, a week after I began to work at NASA.

"THINK AND TALK POSITIVE"

—My Introduction to the Space Shuttle Program

WHEN I WENT to work for NASA in July 1985, the agency's head-quarters occupied office space in two federal office buildings. The administrator's and comptroller's offices, the public affairs office, the news auditorium, and some other administrative divisions, were at 400 Maryland Avenue, S.W., a building NASA shared with the U.S. Department of Education. A couple of blocks north was Independence Avenue, with the entrance to the Air and Space Museum directly opposite the Maryland Avenue building. Situated on Independence Avenue slightly to the west was another federal building that housed NASA's program offices—Space Flight, Space Science, and Space Station, plus a bookstore, library, cafeteria, health unit, credit union, procurement office, and public exhibits in the lobby. The two NASA headquarters buildings were a short walk from L'Enfant Plaza, where there was a metro station to which I rode from the Huntington station in Alexandria.

When I joined the staff of the Resources Analysis Division, NASA was at a hiatus in its planning and budgeting cycle, though there was still plenty of work to do just to track what was happening in the program offices. NASA had no organized training on its history or on what was called the Space Transportation System. But I was expected to grasp the financial minutiae of the space shuttle as quickly as possible. And of course there were hundreds of acronyms to remember as I began to learn NASA-speak.

I saw that the best way to approach the learning process was to break down the subject into its component parts and master each of them methodically. I had always had mechanical aptitude. Now I had to apply it to the most complex machine ever built. My job was to understand what each component of the system cost and the variables that could cause these costs to change. An example was costs of raw materials; for instance, the shuttle's budget was affected by worldwide shifts in the prices of metals such as aluminum.

But the most important variable, overshadowing everything else, was the flight rate. How often would the shuttle fly in a given year? The number of flights was increasing, but not as much as planned. The target, I was told, was two flights per month, twenty-four in a year. But NASA in 1985 was a long way from achieving that goal.

The major subdivisions at NASA headquarters had code letters. Code "A" was the Office of the Administrator, who was the distinguished and aloof techno-aristocrat James Beggs. At present there was no deputy, since Dr. Hans Mark had left to become chancellor of the University of Texas.

Code "E" was the Office of Space Science, which was in charge of NASA's scientific payloads, including the planetary exploratory missions, which had revolutionized the world's consciousness of the complexity and beauty of our solar system. But how they got Code E out of space science was beyond me.

Code "M" was the big one. That was the Office of Space Flight, headed by the man who was arguably the most important person in NASA, Jesse Moore, the associate commissioner for space flight. It was Code M that built and launched the space shuttle. Moore was the man who personally gave the launch command each time the shuttle lifted off. It was an awesome responsibility.

Code M also loosely supervised the NASA field centers that were in charge of the design and development of the shuttle, as well as of launch and mission control. These centers were world renowned—the Lyndon B. Johnson Space Center in Houston, Texas, home of the astronaut corps; the George C. Marshall Space Flight Center in Huntsville, Alabama, the world's premier center for rocket science; and the John F. Kennedy Space Center at Cape Canaveral, Florida, the nation's space-port and launch site for every U.S. manned mission in history.

Code "B" was the Comptroller's Office, where I was assigned. This one was easy. "B" stood for "bean-counters," said people in Code M with a smirk. This was because the analysts of Code B were always breathing down their necks for spending so much money. At NASA, you see, getting to the moon was one thing. Controlling costs was impossible.

Code B was headed by the comptroller, Thomas Newman. His deputy was Thomas Campbell. Newman gave the air of a kindly old gentleman, very tall with short hair and glasses, but he did not seem to take part in managing the everyday business of the budget office.

In the face of a program as complex as the space shuttle, NASA had decided to set up an entire division within Code B staffed by program analysts. This was the Resources Analysis Division. They had brought in my supervisor from an Army base in Michigan, where he had managed costs for combat tank development. He said that resource analysts should treat the program staff as "adversaries." On his office wall were his official commendations and several photos of the Army tank he had spent much of his career bird-dogging.

The program analysts in the Resources Analysis Division were expected to learn the technical details of their assigned pieces of space hardware, investigate resource problems in those areas, attend meetings at the program office, travel to the field centers, make recommendations on funding, and find soft spots in the budget to challenge.

The Resources Analysis Division had within its purview all NASA programs. But it was lopsided, in that most of its work concerned the space shuttle. By now, the shuttle was by far NASA's predominant activity, eclipsing space science and aeronautical research. While a space station office had been established, it largely involved talk and conjecture between NASA and the European Space Agency.

My mentor in studying the craft of NASA resource analysis was Jim Brier. Using his office blackboard and large quantities of chalk, Brier gave me a rapid-fire orientation to the external tank and the solid rocket boosters. Brier was an industrial engineer, while I was mainly a technical writer and analyst. But I understood machines, so our discussion sessions were productive.

Brier focused on the segmented construction of the solid rocket boosters. He described how the powdered aluminum perchlorate fuel for the booster flight segments was poured in casting pits at the plant of the booster contactor, Morton Thiokol, Inc., headquartered in Brigham City, Utah. The segments were then shipped cross-country by rail to the Kennedy Space Center on the Florida coast. At Kennedy, the segments were assembled into flight units and the joints between the segments sealed. The rockets were then fitted with nosecones and frustrums, the part of the nosecone that held the parachutes which eased the boosters' fall into the sea after a shuttle launch. Following the shuttle lift-off, the solid rocket boosters burned for about two minutes. They fell to the ocean and were towed to shore by recovery ships, broken down again into segments, then shipped back to Utah for refurbishment. The key to shuttle cost-control was the ability to reuse the flown segments of the solid rocket boosters.

Brier also taught me about the external tank. This was the giant brown tubular structure, shaped like a big cigar, which sat underneath the shuttle and contained the liquid hydrogen and oxygen that fueled the three space shuttle main engines housed in the orbiter's tail section. Space shuttle propulsion was far more complex than the gigantic one-shot staged rockets of Apollo days. The shuttle orbiter was a big hunk of hardware to shoot into space and get moving fast enough to balance the earth's gravity. At lift-off, the solid rocket boosters did just what their name implied—gave the shuttle a boost. But it was the main engines, consuming the fuel from the external tank, that finished the job. As the shuttle approached orbit, the external tank was jettisoned. Unlike the solid rocket boosters, it was not recovered. Instead, it broke up over the Indian Ocean and came down in harmless aluminum fragments halfway around the world. The external tank was the only major shuttle component that was not reused.

My third area of responsibility, after the solid rocket boosters and the external tank, was the Centaur upper stage. The Centaur would be carried aloft in the orbiter's payload bay and was being adapted from its former use as the upper stage of the unmanned Atlas and Titan-Centaur.

I was starting to see that my image of NASA before I went to work there was impressionistic, romanticized, and largely based on public affairs displays of its greatest triumphs. Now, at NASA headquarters in Washington, this imagery was brought down to earth by mountainous heaps of technical documents with space program budgets, page after page of figures on residual development, production base versus surge hardware deliveries, touch labor costs versus overhead, and data on cost-plus-incentive-fee and cost-plus-award-fee contracts. This information was contained in dozens of large black notebooks that filled Code B's filing cabinets and bookshelves.

I quickly saw that there was an unusual degree of tension at NASA headquarters. The space shuttle was having serious mechanical problems that were discussed mainly behind closed doors. The plan for the shuttle looked great on paper—steadily increasing flight rate, tons of money that would come in from shuttle launch customers, reusable shuttle hardware that would fly over and over again—but it wasn't quite working out that way. Nerves were often on edge. Even in Code B there were some people who were quite tense and angry.

Still, I worked hard. I was a quick learner, especially after I began to spend time attending meetings and talking to engineers at Code M.

Code M was located on the fourth floor of the Independence Avenue building. Tourists passing by would never have guessed it, but inside this nondescript cement and glass block was the central managing unit that launched NASA's manned space shots. Thus it was one of the focal points of the hopes and dreams of the human race in the late 20th century.

But several shuttle missions had dangerous hardware glitches. Another problem was that Administrator James Beggs had a strategy of transforming the manned space program, which had always been viewed as one of the frontiers of pure technological research, into a Space Transportation System, to be run like a chartered airline. This had far-reaching implications. For instance, headquarters staff devoted to planning and oversight had been cut, and money to fix the hardware glitches had not been budgeted. The staff at Code M was overworked, and many doubted that the operational goal of twenty-four flights per year could be achieved. Some thought, and some even said, that the hardware problems were so serious, especially with the main engines, that "sooner or later" there had to be a catastrophe.

Code B resource analysts made frequent appearances at Code M, sitting in on meetings, talking to the budget analysts in Code M's budget shop, and sometimes snooping around for information about cost problems that Code M preferred to keep to itself. Code B had two main interests. One was finding fat that could be cut. This marked them as potentially hostile outsiders. The other was reshuffling funds from one program area to another, where new problems had to be investigated or fixed. Much of the shuffling was done from the ET and SRB budgets into the main engines. Since the anticipated shuttle flight rate had not materialized, this meant that money for the postponed flights was freed-up for other purposes. "Stretching out" project budgets was a time-honored NASA tool for funding overruns in areas with the most problems.

Code M displayed the ubiquitous posters and high-quality prints of the space shuttle that could be found throughout the headquarters complex. Signs taped to the walls were intended to boost morale and said things like, "Look Sharp." Or, "Think and Talk Positive."

The problem with "thinking and talking positive" was, about what were you thinking and talking? If it was a general admonition to support the overall goals of the program, fine. But if it was to repress pertinent information that could call those goals into question, what then? At Code M, this was sometimes the case. There was pressure to mouth the party line and pretend things were in a lot better shape than they were. It was a culture that could produce a lot of "yes-men."

Code M's engineers were brilliant and were experts in their fields. But they lacked authority, because they were only staff advisers to the associate commissioner for space flight, Jesse Moore. This meant that they were merely second-guessers, with the meat of the technical work being delegated to the field centers. After James Beggs became administrator in 1981, he promised the centers that they would not be "micromanaged" from headquarters. In my own areas, the external tank and the solid rocket boosters were managed from the Marshall Space Flight Center in Huntsville, Alabama, while the Centaur was managed from the Lewis Research Center in Cleveland, Ohio.

Early in my employment at NASA, I flew to Huntsville for a tour and discussions with their budget officials. On the way to the Marshall center, you passed by the immense Redstone Army Arsenal, the U.S. Army's rocket research facility. It was natural to build Marshall next door when NASA was set up by the National Aeronautics and Space Act of 1958. From 1960 to the early 1970s, Marshall's Director was the world-renowned German rocket scientist, Wernher von Braun, who was supported by a cadre of German engineers and technicians and their American counterparts. Von Braun was one of the remarkable men of the 20th century, and it was his engineering and organizational genius that was the bedrock on which the U.S. manned space program was built.

But von Braun was "shipped out" to a desk job in Washington at the start of the shuttle era. His successor from 1973 to 1974 was Rocco Petrone, a NASA engineer, who later figured in the Challenger disaster as the Rockwell executive who said his company could not guarantee a safe launch due to ice on the shuttle launch tower.

Following Petrone was William Lucas, an engineer who had worked on the Apollo program and who rose through the ranks to become deputy director in 1971 and director in 1974. It was said that Lucas personally supervised the engineering design of many of the shuttle components. He controlled an enormous research and development budget and was reputed to be the second most powerful man in Alabama, after Governor George Wallace. His formal supervisor at NASA was Jesse Moore, which was odd when you considered Lucas's longevity and institutional pedigree compared with that of Moore, who had been in his job less than two years. This was reflected in the status of the Marshall "POP," the annual program operating plan. Each year, Marshall would submit a draft POP to Code M, which would modify it and alter the funding allocations. Marshall would then stick the POP from Code M in a filing cabinet and manage to their own. Lucas reportedly made it clear to everyone that the Marshall POP was the "real" POP.

Lucas had a formidable reputation. A man who had been to many meetings with Lucas at Marshall told me that senior staff members trembled in his presence. And after the Challenger disaster, when Marshall took the brunt of the blame from the Presidential Commission for the flawed launch decision and Lucas retired, some employees wept that the stern but beloved father-figure was gone.

When I visited Marshall, the budget officials were dressed immaculately in moderately-priced suits, spoke quietly and articulately, said nothing unusual or controversial, and had pronounced southern accents. The visit was pleasant, but I learned little that you couldn't find in print at headquarters.

Despite tension between Code M and such field centers as Marshall,

Associate Administrator for Space Flight Jesse Moore seemed on good personal terms with everyone. Moore was a slender man who wore slacks and a sport coat, glasses, and white long-sleeved dress shirts with a narrow tie as was then the fashion. His speech was quiet, focused, and informal. He had come to headquarters from NASA's Jet Propulsion Laboratory in Pasadena, California, so he was not a manned spaceflight veteran. He had been General James Abrahamson's deputy associate administrator for space flight before stepping into the number one slot. Sometimes he was funny, though I don't remember what he was referring to when he said, "We might be in deep kimche."

I saw Moore operate in several major technical meetings at Code M, including two days of meetings at the Kennedy Space Center on the shuttle-Centaur program in January 1986. I was impressed by his knowledge and his wit, though he seemed more interested in keeping flights on schedule than delving into technical issues. He was polite and respectful when speaking to people. He asked direct questions. But he had to juggle a massive amount of programmatic detail and was facing some deeply troubling issues, including the problems in the main engine systems that were showing up on the 1985 shuttle flights.

Moore was viewed as overworked. He had his own personal "shuttle"; namely the NASA-One jetliner that ferried him back and forth between Washington and the Kennedy Space Center, where he oversaw each space shuttle launch. But he was bailing out of the Washington scene. In December 1985 it was announced that he would be leaving headquarters to become director of the Johnson Space Center in Houston. On paper, this was a demotion. At Code M, he was the supervisor of the Johnson director. But in Washington, D.C., Moore was just another high-ranking career official with too much on his plate. In Houston, he would be a big fish in a much smaller pond. The Challenger disaster, however, overtook Moore's plans. Following the tragedy he left for Houston earlier than planned but left the government in early 1987.

Moore's meetings took place in Code M's huge fourth floor conference room in the Independence Avenue building. On one wall of the room were the colorful logos of each completed space shuttle mission—trophies of the Space Transportation System. At the front of the room was a large, horseshoe-shaped conference table with microphones that were linked to a teleconference system connecting Code M to the field centers. At Moore's meetings, the room was often packed with thirty to forty people, mostly white men in shirt sleeves, many with pocket protectors containing pens and other paraphernalia.

Reflecting NASA's aging workforce, the men in the room were mostly middle-aged or older. At 38, I was a youngster by comparison, and I was a stranger. A couple of times they looked at me as if to say, "Who the hell are you?" But overall, they were a congenial group who loved to gab, though their language was heavily dominated by space age acronyms.

At one of the first Code M meetings I attended, in early August 1985, Moore conducted a teleconference that included officials from Kennedy and Johnson. At the meeting he personally set the day and time of landing for the currently space-borne Challenger, then flying mission 51-F. I almost had to pinch myself to see if I was dreaming. Wow, I just saw the biggest decision being made in my whole federal career! I felt I had arrived.

This awe was not shared by everyone at NASA. One hard-bitten space program veteran told me that the quality of NASA's management had deteriorated and that there was "no way the present bunch could have put a man on the moon." But another said that in spite of all the problems, "We're the best federal agency. Not perfect, but the best."

NASA's shuttle launch system had its own set of reviews and meetings that Moore attended. These included the Level I flight readiness reviews preceding each shuttle launch. Moore was Level I. If he went to a meeting, it was a Level I meeting, as he was the head of the Space Transportation System. For shuttle launch meetings, Administrator James Beggs might also attend, but I never saw Beggs at a Code M meeting in Washington, even when major decisions were made. The only time I saw Beggs was when I was named by the Resources Analysis Branch to be the office contact person for the annual federal charity fund-raising drive. This duty fell each year to the newest employee. Beggs gave a pep-talk for the drive at a meeting I attended with other agency representatives.

The STS hierarchy had three other levels under Moore. Level II referred to Arnold Aldrich, national STS director at the Johnson Space Center in Houston. On paper, he coordinated the various elements of the NASA system that took part in each shuttle launch, but he was not necessarily privy to all of the information flow that passed from the centers to headquarters outside the formal launch process.

Level III referred to the shuttle elements at the different centers, such as the Shuttle Projects Office at Marshall, managed by newly-appointed Stanley Reinartz. Though Reinartz was supposed to report to Aldrich at Level II at shuttle launch time, it was Marshall Director Willliam Lucas who filled out his performance appraisal. This made Lucas his organizational superior, causing Reinartz and the other Level III managers at Marshall to have split reporting channels. Today this would be called a "matrix" team. Such teams are always subject to divided loyalties and confusing channels of communication.

Finally, Level IV was the contractor in charge of a shuttle component, such as Morton Thiokol for the solid rocket boosters, Martin Marietta for the external tank, Rockwell for the orbiter, and General Dynamics for the shuttle-Centaur.

Moore's deputy was Michael Weeks, whose title was "deputy associate administrator for space flight (technical)." Weeks was in charge of reviewing and overseeing technical decisions concerning manned space flight hardware. Although he presided over management meetings in Moore's absence, he and Moore were not interchangeable in terms of authority or scope of responsibility. Still, he had been around a long time and everyone knew him. Weeks was a short, stocky man who dressed in baggy brown suits and often brought a sandwich to meetings. He had worked in the aerospace industry and often cracked jokes.

Weeks was associated with three major decisions about space shuttle hardware that may have involved pushing the technical envelope too hard, too fast, and too far. At the risk of getting ahead of ourselves in the story, it seems necessary to recount these, because all three programs were in the works while I was at NASA during the months before Challenger.

One was the decision to continue flying the shuttle with known solid rocket booster O-ring joint design defects. The decision grew out of an August 19, 1985, meeting at NASA headquarters involving Marshall and Thiokol. It was Mike Weeks who presided at this meeting, because Jesse Moore was occupied with main engine issues. At the meeting, Thiokol recounted the history of O-ring charring and erosion during previous shuttle missions and presented alternative designs to fix the problem.

One of these designs was to be tested at a firing at the Thiokol plant in Utah in February 1986.

But, based on the recommendations of Marshall and Thiokol, NASA decided the shuttle would keep flying. Weeks was familiar with the details of the O-ring joint, because in 1983, he had signed a waiver for a redundancy requirement that called for effective performance of both a primary and a secondary O-ring in each booster field joint. These were joints that were mated in "the field"; i.e., at the launch site at Kennedy, not the factory in Utah. The reason a waiver was needed was that the secondary O-ring was lifting off the metal surfaces when the rockets fired and the joints expanded through a phenomenon known as "rotation." The waiver allowed the shuttle to continue to fly, even though the secondary O-ring might not seal and prevent the type of catastrophic flame leaks that destroyed Challenger. Later it came to light that the astronauts had never been told about the waiver.

The second instance of questionable decision-making was for NASA to utilize the Centaur cryogenic rocket as a shuttle-borne upper stage. Following congressional inquiries, this decision was confirmed in a technical report written by Weeks in 1981. After the Challenger disaster, NASA cancelled the $1 billion Centaur project as unsafe.

The third instance was the program Weeks was helping to oversee to build the "filament wound case." This was a lightweight graphite-epoxy solid rocket booster casing to be used for military shuttle flights that were to be launched from Vandenberg Air Force Base in California. The lighter weight was deemed essential, because with the regular steel booster casings, the shuttle was too heavy to have enough lift capacity for the huge military satellites that the Air Force placed in polar orbit from Vandenberg. Shuttle launches from Vandenberg were due to begin in 1986, but were cancelled after the Challenger disaster. Later, the facility was mothballed due to a major design defect. The filament wound case was never used in a shuttle flight and was also cancelled.

The main organizational subdivision I dealt with at Code M was the Division of Propulsion. This division handled the rocketry for the shuttle—main engines, external tank, solid rocket boosters, filament wound case, upper stages, etc. Because the design, development, and fabrication of much of this hardware was managed out of Marshall, the engineers and resource analysts in the Propulsion Division were in close touch with their counterparts there. But in trying to keep track of Marshall, the handful of engineers was outnumbered and lacked organizational clout.

———

OF MY THREE areas of responsibility, the solid rocket boosters and the Centaur upper stage became the most time-consuming, since they had the most problems. I'll discuss these in later chapters. By comparison, the external tank, which supplied liquid hydrogen and oxygen to the shuttle main engines, seemed to be causing little trouble. The main problem was that too many were being built, since the anticipated shuttle flight rate had not materialized.

Nevertheless, the external tank had challenges. First it was big—154 feet long—half the length of a football field—and 28 feet in diameter. Then, unlike earlier expendable liquid-fuel tanks used for manned and unmanned space flight, the external tank separated in flight from the reusable main engines it powered. Engineering a safe separation from the shuttle orbiter was no joke. It required explosive separation bolts, and anything that explodes can do so too early, too late, or not at all. There was also a need for a complex system of valves that could provide an unimpeded flow of fuel to the main engines during ascent, but allow a perfect disconnect when the fuel was used up. These disconnect, or "flapper" valves, received attention following the Challenger disaster when astronaut John Young pointed out their flaws as a potential source of another catastrophic shuttle failure.

Construction of the external tank required an assembly line operation that could turn out an increasing number of flightworthy units at a steadily decreasing unit cost. The work was done by the Martin Marietta Corporation, whose headquarters was in the Washington, D.C., suburb of Bethesda, Maryland. Martin Marietta had developed the external tank under the direction of Marshall, and built it at a giant NASA-owned factory at Michoud, outside New Orleans, in Louisiana. Once built, the tanks were loaded onto barges in a canal at the factory site, floated down the Mississippi River to the Gulf of Mexico, then shipped around the tip of Florida to the Kennedy Space Center.

A major challenge in building the external tank was turning out a massive number of trouble-free welds to knit together the hydrogen tank at the base of the unit, the oxygen tank at the top, and the inter-tank that connected the two in the middle. The external tank was per-haps the world's greatest monument to the welder's art, because the primary danger in the external tank and its plumbing system was leaks of the invisible but explosive hydrogen fuel. You could then have a Hin-denberg on your hands. In NASA's "failure modes effects analysis" sys-tem, which documented the numerous ways the shuttle could fail, fuel leaks were among the most ominous. Such failures could result in "loss of vehicle, mission, and crew."

I visited Michoud one autumn day in 1985 with a small headquar-ters team. We stayed in a motel near the airport and had a long drive in a rental car to the factory, located by an inlet of the ocean east of downtown New Orleans. I was struck by how flat the terrain was and by the bodies of water stretching in every direction. I could understand why people who lived in New Orleans were apprehensive every hurri-cane season, fearing that "the big one," if it ever came, could be the last. Of course catastrophe finally struck with Hurricane Katrina in 2005.

At the factory in Michoud, most of Martin Marietta's assembly line was devoted to welding operations. The welds had to result in a tank structure that would not leak—not only sitting in the factory or on a barge, but when the shuttle blasted off. The stresses resulting from the thrust of the main engines and solid rocket boosters firing in unison at lift-off were tremendous. Added to these were environ-mental stresses, such as wind shear coming in waves high above the launch site and rapid changes in surrounding temperatures. The prob-lems were complicated by fact that the aluminum walls of the fuel compartments were so thin they had to be pressurized when empty so the sheets would not buckle.

Martin Marietta was well ahead of the "flow" requirements for plac-ing completed external tanks at the shuttle assembly facility at the Kennedy Space Center, and the company expected to meet the require-ments for the accelerating flight rate during 1986-7 with ease. It's not easy to find a shelf big enough for an external tank, but the extra ones were being stored on the premises, and a new building was coming up for that purpose.

Another impressive operation at Michoud, besides the welding, was the towering chambers where machines sprayed the welded aluminum tanks with the foam insulation that kept ice from forming while the tank was on the launch pad. Without insulation, too much ice could form, crack off at lift-off, and damage the tiles on the surface of the orbiter. Another purpose of the insulation was to reduce the rate of cryogenic boil-off after the tank was filled. When the job was done, the sprayed tanks had a frothy appearance, with the brownish insulation displaying a pattern of concentric circles, owing to the circular movements of the external tanks on the spraying stand.

The insulation looked similar to what is used on the ceilings of some school gymnasiums. But it could be brittle. Long after the Challenger disaster, it was a piece of external tank insulation that damaged the tiles on the leading edge of the left wing of shuttle Columbia in January 2003. The wing burned through, and the orbiter broke up and was destroyed at reentry, killing the crew. When the shuttle returned to flight with the Discovery launch in July 2005, there were again fears of tile damage from another piece of foam insulation, though this time the crew got home safely.

Built in 1985, there was little worry in the Division of Propulsion about providing a steady flow of external tanks. As the months wore on, I began to see why Code M had such a blasé attitude about this particular piece of hardware. It was because most of the experts doubted that NASA could ever achieve its ambitious goals for the shuttle flight rate, for reasons that had nothing to do with whether the factories could keep up. The real bottlenecks were in much more elusive areas: the capacity of the staging and launch facilities at Kennedy; the time and capacity to train astronauts at Houston; and spare parts for the orbiters. Consequently, the Code M engineers were not worried about external tanks in flow. NASA insiders referred to the expectation that the desired flight rate would never materialize as "betting on the come." This also related to the underlying sense I mentioned earlier that the shuttle had so many problems that "sooner or later" a disaster would halt flights.

The external tank was a big moneymaker for Martin-Marietta. Even though the shuttle was supposedly "operational," a new, lucrative sole-source contract was in the works. When a Code M resource manager raised the question of possibly excessive profits on the external tank contract at a meeting I attended in October 1986, another manager said, "I don't care how much the profit is, as long as they deliver good hardware."

"TWO-MINUTE RIDE"

—The Dangers of the Solid Rocket Boosters

THE SHUTTLE'S SOLID rocket boosters were a large, dangerous experiment. A 1979 NASA publication, *The Space Shuttle at Work*, gave the following description:

> Standing 45.5 meters from nozzle to nose, and 3.7 meters in diameter (150 ft. by 12 ft.), the boosters are attached near their ends to the external tank, slightly taller and twice as fat, which in turn is attached to the orbiter. A shuttle booster is the largest solid-fuel rocket ever flown, the first built for use on manned spacecraft, and the first designed for reuse.
>
> For launch, the propellant—500,000 kilograms (1,100,000 lb.) in each booster—is ignited by a small rocket motor. Flame spreads over the exposed face of the propellant in about 0.15 second, and the motor is up to full operating pressure in less than half a second. . . . The two boosters' thrust of 5,200,000 pounds augments the 1,125,000-pound thrust of the orbiter's three main engines through the first two minutes of ascent.

The boosters burned for two minutes. Once ignited, they could not be shut down. If they malfunctioned, neither the astronauts nor ground controllers could separate them from the rest of the shuttle. And there was no way for the crew to escape from the orbiter. As a NASA manager said to me after the Challenger tragedy, "It's a two-minute ride."

Code M's solid rocket booster project office was part of the Division of Propulsion. The chief engineer was Paul Wetzel, who reported to the acting director of the Division of Propulsion, David Winterhalter. Under Wetzel was Paul Herr, the engineer for the solid rocket motor contract handled by Morton Thiokol. The O-ring joints were within Herr's area of surveillance.

Also under Wetzel was Irv Davids, who oversaw the booster assembly contract carried out at the Kennedy Space Center by U.S. Booster Industries. USBI assembled the equipment on top of and at the base of the solid rocket boosters, including the parachutes that eased their fall to the ocean surface after flight, as well as the nozzle assembly and the auxiliary power units that swiveled the nozzles.

The other solid rocket engineer in the Division of Propulsion was Russ Bardos, who was in charge of oversight for the filament wound case.

I felt comfortable with Wetzel and Herr. Talking to them was part of my education at NASA, and while they didn't volunteer a lot of information, they always answered my questions. Each of them had a private office, and if they wanted to tell me something without being overheard, they would pull the door three-quarters shut. They were both well-educated and interested in the world around them, and Herr always had a copy of the *Washington Post* in his office.

I met other people in Code M and spent time talking to them in their offices. When I left my office to go to Code M, I would tell our clerk-typist Alice that I was going "across the street." So whenever I passed her desk she would say, "Going across the street?"

Wetzel and I frequently discussed project costs. Like the external tank, costs for the solid rocket boosters were below budget, and for similar reasons. It was because the flight rate for the shuttle, while increasing, was growing at a slower rate than projected, so certain budgeted expenditures could be deferred. NASA's goal, as put forth by Administrator James Beggs, was twenty-four flights per year by 1991. But NASA's production contracts were geared to a production base of eighteen, with the balance to be met by "surge" deliveries if and when the higher rate came about. The deadlines for ordering surge hardware came and went and nothing was done. As I indicated before, the assumption made by space flight managers that the flight rate goal could not be achieved was known as "betting on the come."

Yet there were funds budgeted by the agency and approved by Congress for the twenty-four-per-year "mission model." This meant that money for six or so flights—the differences between the production and the budget figures—could be cut. But beyond these expected reductions, Marshall and Code M siphoned off additional tank and booster funding to cover deficiencies elsewhere in the shuttle budget, mainly for the orbiter's main engines.

Unbudgeted contingency funding for the solid rocket boosters had been reduced for the same reason—the main engines were having such big problems. Reductions had also been made by deferring purchases of raw materials needed for booster production from 1985-86 to 1987, from postponing manufacture of some flight units of the filament wound case, and from compensating for previous miscalculations in assuming more inflated production and overhead costs than actually occurred. These reductions eliminated funding for the solid rocket boosters that might have been used to resolve hardware design problems that were a growing concern throughout 1985.

I quickly began to learn about technical and safety issues in addition to financial ones. In November 1984, a Code M meeting agenda had listed the solid rocket boosters as a "no problem" program area, though the same document cited charring of O-rings in the segment joints as a "major issue." At NASA, something could be okay and not okay at the same time. My informal discussions with the propulsion engineers—Wetzel, Herr, Davids, and Bardos—resulted in a lot of information that I documented in memos to my supervisor.

Another thing I learned about was a problem that resulted in an instance of near-catastrophic flame erosion on STS-8 in 1983 that occurred in the lining of a solid rocket motor nozzle. While there had been no significant nozzle damage since then, a costly redesign and testing effort was underway that consumed much of the remaining developmental funding for the solid rocket boosters. Developmental funding, which in past years had been a major expense, had been whittled down to a minimum. This was because the boosters, except for the filament wound case, were now, by definition, flawless; i.e., they were "operational" and could no longer even be referred to as developmental hardware.

By 1985, the worst problem with the SRBs was the O-rings, the synthetic rubber rounded washers, identical to what you can buy in a hardware store except much bigger, that sealed the joints connecting the booster segments and prevented the escape of fiery gases during ignition and launch of the shuttle. At this time, the average person would have had no idea that there were O-rings used in the shuttle. A few months later, shuttle O-rings would be a household word. Paul Wetzel and Paul Herr made it clear to me from the beginning that Code M was watching the O-ring situation carefully and that a redesign of some major defects was in the works.

I began to learn about O-rings after being on the job for only three weeks. One hot summer day in July 1985, my supervisor said to me, "I want you to go over and find out what the problem is with the O-rings."

I went across the street to the Independence Avenue building to visit the engineers. This was my first meeting with Wetzel and Herr. Of course, after the Challenger disaster, much was said and written about the SRB joints and the O-rings. NASA claimed in testimony before the Presidential Commission, to the House Science and Technology Committee, and in statements to the press that it never saw the O-ring joints as a "safety of flight" issue. The Commission said that NASA should have grounded the shuttle and fixed the O-ring joint design before flying again, but it never sufficiently challenged the contention that the seriousness of the problem was not recognized at the highest management levels. In fact it was, and NASA was concerned all the way to the top.

Still, the complete story was never told on the NASA side, the way it was through the testimony of the Thiokol engineers about what was going on at Morton Thiokol. At NASA, neither of the headquarters experts, Wetzel or Herr, was called to testify publicly, though the Commission interviewed them behind closed doors. Instead, the investigators took extensive public testimony from managers at the Marshall Space Flight Center about the debate over O-ring joint safety with the Thiokol engineers the night before the disaster, but only heard perfunctory accounts of what had been talked about at headquarters throughout 1984-85.

Wetzel and Herr gave me a frank assessment of the O-ring concerns, which I documented in the later-famous memo I wrote on July 23, 1985, and which was cited in the lead *New York Times* story on Sunday, February 9, 1986, twelve days after the Challenger explosion.

Although I was new on the job, the technical details that Wetzel and Herr described were understandable, the topic was important, and I knew how to ask questions of experts. My words were practically quotes from these senior engineers. The memorandum I wrote was quoted in its entirety at the beginning of this book. The key statement, which reflected what Wetzel and Herr told me, was, "There is little question, however, that flight safety has been and is still being compromised by potential failure of the seals, and it is acknowledged that failure during launch would certainly be catastrophic."

I knew as I talked to Wetzel and Herr that I had come across real trouble. I asked what would happen if the O-rings failed. Herr said quietly, "The shuttle would blow up." Later in the conversation he said, "We hold our breath every time this thing goes up."

Wetzel and Herr made it clear that Code M management was thoroughly apprised of this frightening situation. So I went back to my office to write down my findings. I had been trained as an analyst and knew how to document issues. I knew this one was important enough that I should take care with my wording and stick as closely as I could to what was actually said. Nothing in the memo was speculative or went beyond what the two senior engineers told me.

I gave the memo to my supervisor but not to Wetzel and Herr. This was an informal report, not audit findings where the source of the information may be given an opportunity to comment. After the Challenger disaster, my supervisor told the Presidential Commission and the press that he thought I had overstated the concerns.

Obviously, the concerns I portrayed were not overstated, as they accurately predicted the cause of the Challenger disaster. Afterwards, some people called the memo "prophetic." If it was, this was only because Wetzel and Herr were top-flight professionals who had a keen sense of what could happen and a deep understanding of how the solid rocket boosters worked and how they could fail. And I had the ability of a good analyst to capture the thoughts of technical experts and express them in clear, understandable language. My supervisor said nothing to me about the memo—he never answered it either verbally or in writing.

Back in Code M, the agenda for every one of Jesse Moore's monthly reviews listed O-ring erosion as a major problem. After each shuttle flight, the Division of Propulsion gave Moore and other Code M officials a detailed written analysis of any O-ring charring that occurred. But even with all this, Wetzel once told me in quiet, almost conspiratorial tones, "They're not going to stop flying."

I continued to report what I was learning about the situation. In a memo dated September 10, 1985, I wrote:

> . . . Marshall has been ordered to study the cost of installing a "capture feature" which would mechanically interlock the booster segments, so that even if O-ring failure occurred, segments would not be forced apart in flight. Marshall will examine the impact of installing the fix on new segments, as well as a retrofit on existing hardware. Costs of new installation should be available within the next two weeks and for the retrofit within a month to six weeks.

Wetzel told me that he was the one who thought of the capture feature, though after the Challenger disaster, when the agreed-upon repair of the booster joints was to incorporate it, the Hercules Corporation took credit. They were the contractor for the filament wound case. Because the test of the capture feature in February 1986 was to be done on an FWC unit, it was subsumed under that portion of the budget.

One day Wetzel drew a diagram of the capture feature for me. It was a rim machined into the bottom of a solid rocket motor segment that would slip onto the top of an adjoining segment and lock the two together. As I reported to my supervisor, the purpose was to keep booster segments from being forced apart in flight. Such "rotation," which occurred at engine ignition, could unseat the secondary O-ring and allow catastrophic flame leaks to burst out of the side of the boosters during the two-minute ride if the primary O-ring failed.

Wetzel told me that the O-ring erosion problem was "being taken care of" by the capture feature. He said that the developmental budget was adequate.

The solid rocket booster production budget was being augmented so that the Marshall SRB project office headed by Larry Mulloy could purchase seventy-two new booster cases from the Rohr Corporation, a Thiokol subcontractor, and that an order had been placed for segments that would contain an extra thickness of steel on the case rims. This would allow the capture feature to be machined if the 1986 test regime proved successful.

Unfortunately, and despite Wetzel's assurance of adequate funding, the removal of production and contingency funds and the scaling back of the developmental budget meant there was no money for major joint redesign. After the Challenger accident, I learned that NASA had even told Thiokol to avoid a "radical design change." Such a change would have required reinstatement of the developmental budget, would have contradicted the dogma that the STS was a fully operational system, and could even have halted flights. Consequently, NASA and Thiokol were looking for a "quick fix," which is what the capture feature was. Later, a member of the Presidential Commission characterized it as "a Mickey Mouse on a Mickey Mouse." The solid rocket booster joint redesign that was eventually implemented after the Challenger disaster was more thorough and has stood the test of time.

In the latter part of 1985, the production costs for solid rocket booster flight units were close to half a billion dollars per year. While the developmental budget was pegged at $50 million for FY 1986, most of it was for the filament wound case, with a smaller amount for the nozzle erosion project. There were no funds separately identified for O-ring joint redesign.

NASA had known, of course, that the O-ring problem could end up costing money. Not only did the Code M monthly management meeting agendas going back to mid-1984 list O-ring charring as a problem area, it was also listed as a "budget threat." Even though Administrator James Beggs later told the Presidential Commission he had "no concerns" about the O-ring joints, the phrase "budget threat" was also used in a 1985 budget document that I saw, which was created for a meeting between Moore and Beggs. Still, NASA was dealing with the funding for the redesign quietly, which assured that the O-ring problem would not be documented in budget reports going to the Office of Management and Budget or Congress. Despite this, all the key players at headquarters, all the way up to Beggs, were informed.

Wetzel did not tell me what he thought NASA would do to assure safety during the 1986-87 flights while the capture feature was being prepared for installation on solid rocket booster flight units. I saw no indication that there was such a plan, nor did anyone tell me whether the precise cause of the O-ring charring and erosion had been isolated. So I gathered that the capture feature was supposed to take care of all contingencies. In the meantime, to use a NASA phrase I heard applied to Centaur, the space shuttle would "fly as is."

There was another funding problem with the O-ring joints. As I wrote in my July 23 memo, the putty used in the joint system was the primary suspect as to why O-ring erosion seemed to be getting more frequent. The putty was forming tiny blow-holes that were seen in eroded areas after post-flight inspection. When the hot gas of burning propellant slammed against the putty, these holes, which sometimes extended all the way through to the O-rings, could produce a blowtorch effect.

The Code M engineers told me that a new type of putty was needed. But to develop and flight-qualify a new putty would cost $4-5 million. The solid rocket booster developmental budget didn't have a dime for this. The engineers were nonplussed when I pressed them for an answer about what they were going to do, but they had no idea where the money could come from. In meetings, all the Code M managers were told that the 1987 budget had no room for "new activities." Again, the shuttle was "operational."

———

NASA HAD A big problem with the filament wound case. This was a lightweight solid rocket booster substitute being developed for Thiokol by a subcontractor, Hercules. It was made of graphite-epoxy fiber. Case segments were spun on giant spinning machines, like a butterfly's cocoon. The case was to be flown on military shuttle missions out of the Air Force's launch site at Vandenberg Air Force Base in California, once the shuttle began to be launched from there in March 1986. Vandenberg was about 120 miles northwest of Los Angeles on the Pacific Coast.

The case used the same type of O-ring joint system as the regular steel-case SRBs. As with the SRBs, the case was managed for NASA by Marshall, with oversight from Code M's Division of Propulsion.

When the space shuttle was designed, major decisions were made to allow it to be used for military missions. These included a large, sixty-foot orbiter payload bay, with enough capacity to carry the giant military reconnaissance satellites. Payload weight capacity for military missions was supposed to be 65,000 pounds. To reach that meant weight minimization for the shuttle itself, including the external tank and the solid rocket boosters.

The main driver for weight minimization was to allow the shuttle to loft heavy military satellites into polar orbit from Vandenberg. The filament wound case would help accomplish this feat. The reason for the polar orbit, instead of the customary east/west latitudinal orbit for conventional satellites, was to maximize the time the military spy satellites would spend over the Soviet Union.

North-south polar orbits could not be executed from the east coast launch site at the Kennedy Space Center, because the shuttle's rockets would be firing over populated areas. But launch physics dictated that the thrust required for successful launch from Vandenberg be much greater than from Kennedy, because rockets fired on a north-south axis could not take advantage of the extra "oomph" derived from launching in conjunction with forces from the eastward rotation of the Earth. You could get more thrust from Vandenberg by weight reduction—hence the filament wound case—and by cranking up the throttle on the space shuttle main engines, which was also part of the plan.

Another problem with Vandenberg was that its average temperature was lower than at Kennedy. Because there were several minimum temperature constraints for shuttle launches, this could also become an issue for getting off military flights on schedule.

The issue with the filament wound case was whether it could be made safe enough to fly. Graphite-epoxy is prone to crack. In fact, the case had failed a major safety test in 1985. This happened when a full-sized test model, known as the structural test article, or STA, burst when it was filled with water, then pressurized. This was called a hydrostatic test, a word for pumping water into a closed vessel and seeing what happened. The test was to simulate the forces the case would encounter when loaded with propellant and fired. The rupture occurred below the margin of safety needed to certify the case for safe usage on the space shuttle. I wrote a report for the October 9, 1985,

Resources Analysis Division staff meeting that stated: "Failure of FWC STA much worse than thought. Design problem indicated. Cannot at this time risk failure of another STA. Second STA is not completely funded anyway." A rupture at lift-off would blow up the shuttle on the launch pad, causing engineers in Code M to tell me that the filament wound case should be abandoned.

Whether NASA liked it or not, the STA failure meant that the test had to be redone. This would use up another case, since STA testing meant that you pumped up the pressure until the unit ruptured. If the pressure at the point of rupture was greater than the calculated pressure for a live launch, plus a margin of safety, you were okay. If the rupture point was below that, you were not.

Now we had a budget problem. The cost of the STA test was $10 million. As I indicated in my report to Code B, use of a second STA was underfunded. To cover the cost, Marshall wanted once again to raid the SRB operational budget. Code M said they couldn't do that because it was too risky to the planned shuttle flight rate. So it was decided to fund the next STA hydrostatic test by using most of the remaining contingency dollars from the SRB development line. This meant that no funding remained for future redesign of any part of the solid rocket boosters if flight experience disclosed problems that required engineering attention. Code M would be gazing into a dry hole.

Because of NASA's cuts in reserve funding for the external tank and solid rocket boosters in the 1985 budget to cover shortfalls elsewhere, there was almost no contingency funding left anywhere in the shuttle program. NASA treated these reductions as "internal reprogramming," thereby escaping disclosure to OMB or Congress. In agency documents, the cuts were referred to euphemistically as "management challenge," or "undersupport."

I wrote in a memo:

> Of course Code M says the FWC *has* to fly because of the commitment to the Air Force. But there are doubts as to whether the test program between now and January is adequate to dispel all concerns about FWC safety and flightworthiness, doubts which have been fed by adverse off-the-record comments to the program office [at Marshall] by Langley (Langley being the experts on composite materials) [i.e., NASA's Langley Research

Center in Hampton, Virginia]. Unfortunately, MSFC is not talking to Langley about these concerns. From a budget standpoint, MSFC came in with a $6.1 million augmentation to cover the STA, versus previous estimates of $14 million. Unfunded is $1-2 million to cover the replacement of the instrumentation islands [i.e., tubes on the flight article that provided a conduit for the electrical wiring] for the first VAFB [Vandenberg] flight. Code M now admits the $8 million APA [reserve funding] which they formerly said had irreversible liens against it, could now be used to cover both the STA and the islands. The trouble is, no one in the program office believes the $6.1M figure, and they have said so to MSFC. The program office also realizes that there will be no way to come up with additional money if the FWC development cost exceeds the budget figure of $41.1 million for FY 86. There is supposed to be a full-blown technical review at Code M on November 18. Until then, everything is up in the air. Should the FWC not fly out of Vandenberg in March, the KSC flight model is endangered because of a resulting shortage of steel cases if diversion of hardware to DoD for their missions is required.

This memo clearly documented the pressure within NASA to meet schedules and how this pressure could raise major safety issues, particularly when there was a commitment to the Defense Department for military flights.

On November 18, 1985, I attended the flightworthiness review for the filament wound case led by Jesse Moore in the Code M conference room. This was a big, important meeting. A crowd of Marshall managers and engineers had flown in from Huntsville, and the Kennedy and Johnson Space Centers were live on the telecom speakers. The purpose of the meeting was to determine whether NASA would move forward with its plans to launch the filament wound case in the first Vandenberg launch in March 1986. If so, it would be the first graphite-epoxy rocket launch in the history of spaceflight.

This meeting stood out for me because it was the one time before the Challenger disaster that I saw Larry Mulloy in action. Mulloy was the head of the solid rocket booster project office at Marshall. A heavy-set man with graying hair who always wore a dark baggy suit, Mulloy became known after the Challenger disaster for having been the NASA official who was alleged in testimony to have pressured the Thiokol engineers who thought the weather on January 28 would be too cold for the O-rings to perform as they should. They were afraid the O-rings in the SRB joints would lack the resiliency to seal properly, which is what happened when Challenger exploded seventy-three seconds after lift-off. It was Mulloy who said to them over the telecom hookup, "When do you want me to launch, Thiokol, next April?" After this, the Thiokol managers overruled their own engineers and approved the launch.

As I observed Mulloy, it was clear that he had one objective: to sell headquarters on flying the filament wound case on the first Vandenberg launch. It was what NASA called a "pitch." Mulloy repeatedly asserted, without offering data, that despite the STA failure, the case was safe and would be proven so when retested. Also at the meeting were engineers from Marshall's Science and Engineering Directorate, which was organizationally separate from the Shuttle Projects Office to which Mulloy reported. One engineer, in a detailed presentation, questioned Mulloy's assertions and said that concerns with the FWC had not been resolved.

Here is the memo I wrote on the meeting:

> Yesterday Code M conducted a flightreadiness review with representatives of the Marshall Space Flight Center (MSFC). The meeting was called because of growing concern over NASA's ability to supply a fully-qualified filament wound case (FWC) flight set for the first Vandenberg launch in March 1986. This concern was triggered by the failure of the FWC structural test article (STA), which failed in compression testing at a 125 percent factor of safety.
>
> In yesterday's review, MSFC asserted that the next STA test, now scheduled for January, will demonstrate the required 140 percent of safety and that the current launch schedule can be met. Larry Mulloy, chairman of the design certification review committee for space shuttle mission 62-A, also stated that the FWC design has been certified as meeting all flight requirements.
>
> Still, concerns remain. MSFC's George Brown gave a report on the current testing program for the FWC, and stated that some design changes would definitely be indicated if the program were starting all over. However, Brown also made the following points:

- The next STA is stronger than the first, but based on analysis and coupon testing, only has a probable factor of safety of 1.39;
- This estimate is probably conservative;
- Tightening of the forward solid rocket booster/external tank attach point tolerance is in progress and will reduce FWC load at the failure point by about two percent, leading to a revised factor of safety of 1.42.

A number of questions were raised about the coupon testing and analysis that led to these conclusions, including the limited number and size of the coupons, certain unexplained inconsistencies in the test data, and uncertainty about the load at which delamination of the STA initiates. Michael Weeks seemed to catch the mood of the meeting by stating that the analytical approach was very theoretical and that only when the next STA shows a factor of safety of 1.4 in actual testing, could the analysis be believed. Jesse Moore stated that as much testing as possible should be done to assure the safety of the FWC. Moore also addressed the question of whether to stack the FWC segments, which can begin as early as this Wednesday, by stating that stacking can start, so long as it is understood that this is not an absolute commitment to flight, since de-stacking can also take place if necessary.

The Johnson Space Center (JSC) then entered into the conversation via telecom to discuss the load alleviation options. The purpose of this analysis was to recommend ways to reduce the maximum load build-up, which occurs during the fourth second after space shuttle main engine ignition.

JSC noted that all options involve some undersupport of the flight schedule, so that a launch delay may in fact have to be accepted. Further, the possible success of some of the options is questionable. Discussion of the various options followed, with MSFC asserting with some overconfidence that no load alleviation is required beyond the shimming needed to lighten the attach point mentioned above.

Note the difference between the Marshall and Johnson perspectives. Johnson, home of the astronauts, wanted an additional margin of safety and was willing to slip the Vandenberg military launch schedule to get it. Marshall was opposed. To continue:

Nevertheless, Jesse Moore instructed JSC to take the measures of placarding west wind velocity at launch and increasing the stagger of SSME firing to about two seconds between engines.

The reference to "placarding" meant that Moore was talking about putting up a gigantic billboard to shield the shuttle from the wind.

According to JSC's preliminary analysis, this measure has the greatest potential for reducing bending load for a given level of cost and effort and will serve as a safety valve in case this additional load relief is in fact needed at the time of lift-off. Staggering is also an attractive option in that it will cost only about 200 pounds in payload performance.

Two additional load reduction measures were rejected. These were to reduce SSME thrust to ninety-four percent of full throttle until after lift-off and to change the cant on the SSME nozzles. A major reason for rejecting these options was reluctance to make further changes in a launch configuration, including computer software, which had produced success on previous flights. Also, the probable load alleviation would be much less than by changing the engine staggering.

Jesse Moore noted that a lot of work is still needed before anyone can get comfortable with the FWC. He will also attend a meeting coming up at Vandenberg toward the end of the week where more precise scheduling will be done.

From a resource perspective, it should be noted that no mention was made of possible costs of expanding the testing program or implementing the load alleviation options. MSFC's operating plan has come in at $6.1M over the budget mark for STA work, but the program office doubts that even this figure is high enough. FWC costs have already increased because of the removal of the instrumentation islands on VLS-1 which were improperly installed because of a contractor error. This removal is complete, but was done with a significant labor cost which should show up in the December cost reports.

As a result of yesterday's meeting, Code M has given marching orders on FWC testing without any specific limitations on cost—an effort which has the appearance of being more rigorous and costly than what MSFC would have done if left entirely to their own devices. And as stated, JSC will be incurring its own costs for work on the load alleviation problem. By next week a new schedule should be in place for the remainder of the FWC testing program, and it would seem reasonable at that point to ask Code M to revise its estimate of what the bill will come to and how any possible overruns will be funded.

The pressure on Moore to approve the use of the filament wound case was immense. A major portion of NASA's future budget depended on reimbursements from the Defense Department for military missions, including testing for the Strategic Defense Initiative. These missions would also carry into orbit the huge reconnaissance satellites that were the backbone of America's ability to track military developments in the Soviet Union. The security of the United States would be riding on the filament wound case. In retrospect, it seems incredible that NASA was placing so much reliance on untried, and possibly unsafe, hardware which veteran engineers told me should be cancelled. The FWC saga also showed how militarization of the shuttle produced additional safety risks.

Another problem with the SRBs had to do with the segment attrition rate, and reflected the fact that the solid rocket boosters were designed for reuse.

Each solid rocket booster consisted of eleven weld-free steel segments joined together. A flight set of two boosters consisted of twenty-two segments. Each segment was supposed to have a lifetime of twenty shuttle flights. But NASA realized that, on occasion, a segment would be damaged beyond repair and would have to be discarded and replaced. This was "attrition."

The STS budget assumed that when the shuttle reached its projected annual flight rate of eighteen to twenty-four per year, solid rocket booster case attrition would be running at a rate of 5.4 percent of flown segments. Unfortunately, no one had any experience on which to base this figure. The number meant that on the average, of the twenty-two segments flown on a shuttle mission, one unit would have to be discarded after a single use.

But the attrition rate from the first shuttle mission through the end of 1985 was nearly fifteen percent, almost three times the target. This figure comprised segments damaged in flight, one that was damaged in a handling accident for which repair was questionable, and two complete booster rockets that sank after a shuttle flight. According to Wetzel, sinking was not just a one-time stroke of bad luck. He said it would happen now and then. In fact, during the countdown for Challenger's last mission, the high seas in the recovery area made the loss of one or two boosters possible. If the ships that were supposed to pick them up couldn't reach them, they'd be gone.

Also, segments could corrode as they sat "on the shelf" at the Thiokol plant in Utah. "Why couldn't you just lather up the cases with Vaseline?" I asked Wetzel. He said the SRB casings were made of high-carbon steel that was unusually susceptible to corrosion. Thiokol was experimenting with various anticorrosive coatings, but none of them worked very well.

Damage at water impact was also a worse problem than had been anticipated. Even with parachutes, the SRBs floated down a long way before they hit the surface of the ocean. Damage occurred particularly through the formation of cracks at the stiffener ring bolt holes, as well as on the aft skirt, just above the nozzle. The cracks were difficult to detect through visual inspection. But soon after the shuttle began to fly, NASA decided to cut costs by eliminating the practice of 100 percent X-raying of flown booster segments and resorting instead to sampling. According to Paul Herr, one cracked segment that had previously been flown and that went undetected ruptured in a subsequent test pressurization. This would have been catastrophic in flight.

Finally, attrition was not balanced among types of segment. The aft segments seemed to be damaged more than those in the mid and upper sections of the SRB. Thiokol's manufacturing schedule had not been adjusted accordingly. So even putting together complete matched sets was starting to be recognized as a potential schedule threat.

Another problem was turnaround time. The turnaround issue— how long it took to get a shuttle component that had flown ready for the next flight—was a problem not only for the SRBs but also for the orbiter and the main engines.

After their two-minute burn, the SRBs separated from the external tank and fell to the sea. Parachutes that were deployed from the frustrums broke their fall. After landing in the ocean, they were towed by the recovery ships back to the Kennedy Space Center. They were then broken down into segments, scrubbed to remove the highly-corrosive salt water, inspected for damage, and shipped back to Utah by rail for refurbishment. They were then inspected for cracks, subjected to pressurization to determine post-flight structural integrity, and stored.

When the segments were pulled off the shelf for their next use, insulation was applied to the interior surface, and the fuel poured in casting pits. Then they were sent back to Kennedy by rail for the next shuttle mission. The period it took for this transcontinental operation to be accomplished was the turnaround time.

In late 1985, turnaround time for a given SRB segment was eight to ten months. When the shuttle was flying only nine times a year, this was not too bad. There was even the luxury of having some segments wait in storage. But it was twice the four to five-month turnaround that would be required once the accelerated flight schedule was in place by 1987-88. The phase that was most out-of-whack was post-flight processing at the Kennedy Space Center. I discussed this with a Marshall manager stationed at Kennedy named George Duke when I visited KSC in January 1986 for the meetings on the shuttle-Centaur.

The problem, said Duke, was that he did not control the ground transport of the segments while they sat at Kennedy after being recovered from the Atlantic Ocean. He said his work crew often had to wait until trucks were available to haul the segments from one operation to the next. Unfortunately, the different phases of handling and transport were done by different contractors. Theoretically, coordination of the work was to be done by Lockheed, which had been awarded a giant shuttle processing contract at Kennedy a year earlier. But it wasn't working.

Neither the attrition nor the turnaround problems would have been so bad for a shuttle program that had the flexibility to launch when it made sense to do so rather than on an airline-type schedule. But they were serious issues for an operational Space Transportation System.

The more time I spent on the SRBs, the more problems appeared. Just as I thought I understood what was going on, another surprise would jump out from my talks with Wetzel, Herr, Bardos, Davids, and others. I finally concluded that this was a program in serious trouble. There also seemed to be a desire to keep word of this trouble from getting out. Of course, to have admitted to the SRB problems openly would have blown the dogma that the Space Transportation System was operational, or even reliable. NASA had "customers" who depended on it for "assured access to space." That this access was not assured was the secret NASA felt anxious to protect.

I was pleased with the progress I had made toward understanding the solid rocket boosters. I had uncovered, analyzed, and documented some major issues and their budget implications. I was not alarmed about these issues, because I knew that managing hardware this complex was not easy. But my experience as an analyst had taught me that you cannot solve problems unless you first identify them. Perhaps naively, I had also accepted Paul Wetzel's assurances that the capture feature would "take care of" the O-ring joint problem.

The aspect of the solid rocket booster program I knew least about was the flight readiness reviews that took place before each shuttle launch. These were conducted at the Kennedy Space Center, and I would not visit there until January 1986. I was not in the loop on any discussions of the O-rings that might be taking place at those reviews or about the imposition or waiver of launch constraints by Marshall that came to light during the Challenger Commission's hearings. Plus I had heard nothing about how cold temperatures might affect the resiliency of the O-rings.

——

Now it was autumn in Washington, the days had become cooler and there were frosts at night. It was perhaps the most beautiful season of the year in our region. Phyllis and I, with our two kids, had just moved into a house in the country in King George, Virginia, and were unpacking and putting things away. After all our travels the last three years, having a home that seemed permanent was a huge relief. Where we lived, the colors of the autumn leaves were stunning. And we loved seeing the brightness of the stars at night from our yard.

Our first big job outdoors would be to put up wire fencing around the property plus the sections of white picket fence we'd bought to surround the house. I had filled the fifteen seats on the vanpool I was operating with commuters to the city, and though the drives to and from Washington on U.S. 301 through southern Maryland were long, the weather was gorgeous, and it gave me a chance to listen to the radio or just be alone with my thoughts. Life was starting to seem good again.

"THE CENTAUR IS THE ONLY VEHICLE"

—Politics in the Space Shuttle Program

AFTER A COUPLE of months at NASA, I was assigned to write a history of the shuttle-Centaur program. The Centaur upper stage was my third piece of shuttle hardware, along with the external tank and solid rocket boosters. I began by reviewing documents from Code B's legislative files that focused on the politics of NASA's decision to build Centaur. It was a fascinating story.

Centaur was scheduled to be launched on two shuttle missions in May 1986. The Centaur rocket would be fueled by supercooled hydrogen and oxygen and carried into orbit inside the shuttle orbiter's payload bay. The rockets would then be released from the bay, ignited, and directed into space to deploy the Galileo and Ulysses planetary spacecraft.

But Centaur was viewed as extremely hazardous. Until Challenger exploded, many viewed the Centaur missions as the leading candidates for the first U.S. in-space disaster. NASA's managing engineers, especially at the Johnson Space Center in Houston, were wary. So many waivers and compromises with safety had been made on the Centaur that the astronauts called it "the bomb in the bay." Following the Challenger disaster, it became the first rocket ever built in the manned space program to be canceled as unsafe. The billion dollar shuttle-Centaur never flew.

As NASA's development of the space shuttle began in the mid-1970s, engineers debated over how to transfer heavy scientific or military payloads from the shuttle's low-earth orbit either to a higher orbit, including geosynchronous rotation, where a satellite remains fixed over a particular point on earth, or to the expanse of space beyond earth's gravity. The latter could include scientific probes to other planets or exploratory spacecraft placed in their own circuits around the sun.

To meet these demands, the shuttle orbiter would become a launch pad for the high energy upper stages needed to support the defense, scientific, and commercial customers NASA planned to service. The shuttle would replace all expendable launch vehicles (ELVs), such as Atlas-Centaur, Titan-Centaur, and Delta, which had launched military satellites and such successful payloads as Voyager and Viking I and II to Jupiter, Saturn, and Mars. The problem was that any upper stage held a huge store of rocket fuel. Safely transporting the fuel in a manned space vehicle carried unique risks.

The shuttle was designed with a large payload bay—sixty feet long. Even then, it was questionable whether the bay was large enough to hold a solid-fuel rocket with enough power to propel the big military satellites or the largest unmanned scientific spacecraft. With the military satellites the issue was weight—an upper stage needed a lot of thrust. With the scientific spacecraft it was distance—the upper stage had to burn for a long time to allow a spacecraft to escape earth's gravity.

The alternative to a solid-fuel upper stage was a more hazardous and complicated rocket powered by cryogenics—liquid hydrogen and oxygen under pressure, the same fuel that powered the shuttle's main engines. But with the main engines, the fuel was carried in the external tank, outside the orbiter. With a cryogenic upper stage, the fuel would be inside a rocket in the payload bay.

Early in the shuttle program, NASA viewed cryogenics as too dangerous for a shuttle-borne upper stage. Liquid hydrogen and oxygen can leak through the tiniest gaps, then vaporize and explode. By contrast, solid fuels are difficult to ignite—a heavy-duty detonator is required.

At the time Challenger blew up, the Centaur was being prepared to launch the two 1986 planetary missions. Along with the Hubble Space Telescope and the Astro-1 Halley's Comet observer, the Galileo and

Ulysses planetaries were the basis for what NASA was promoting as the "Year of Space Science."

Once Galileo was released from Atlantis, the spacecraft would cruise through the asteroid belt beyond Mars before it settled into orbit around Jupiter. There it would measure and photograph the giant planet for almost eight years.

Ulysses had been known as the International Solar Polar Mission— ISPM—and was co-sponsored by NASA and the European Space Agency. Ulysses was to be deployed by Challenger after returning from the 51-L mission scheduled for January 1986. The purpose of Ulysses was to investigate the structure of the sun's magnetic field and the pathways of the solar wind. It was to be inserted into its unusual solar polar orbit by using Jupiter's gravity as a giant slingshot that would allow it to break the plane of the solar system's planetary ecliptic and circle the sun above and beneath its poles.

NASA would be relying on Centaur for the success of the Galileo and Ulysses flights. But in the early days of the shuttle's upper stage program, Centaur and the solid-fuel inertial upper stage (IUS) had been in competition for the duty of the planetary missions. In fact, IUS had been the initial selection.

In April 1978, the Defense Department announced the award of a $265 million contract to the Boeing Aerospace Company for development and production of the Air Force/NASA inertial upper stage. As with so many other elements of the space shuttle program, NASA and DoD would be partners.

This joint military/civilian procurement reflected the fact that when President Richard Nixon approved the space shuttle in 1972, its purpose was to consolidate all space activities of the U.S. into one program, using a single manned vehicle. This was a fundamental departure from the Mercury, Gemini, and Apollo programs, where NASA's civil space missions, while supported by military personnel and facilities, had their own scientific and exploratory objectives.

The first two-stage IUS was to be delivered to NASA in April 1980, with the launch of Galileo then scheduled for January 1982. NASA would also use IUSs to launch tracking and data relay satellites (TDRS) from the shuttle. TDRS was the space-based communications system that would allow NASA to maintain radio contact between mission control in Houston and the shuttle orbiter and dispense with its expensive network of ground stations. The Defense Department, meanwhile, would initially mate its IUSs to unmanned Titan booster rockets but later fly them in the shuttle.

The Galileo spacecraft would utilize a "twin-spin" IUS specially designed for the high thrust requirements for planetary missions. Using a slow spin to stabilize a spacecraft is an alternative to fins, which don't work in the vacuum of space. The risk with the IUS was that the projected weight of the interplanetary spacecraft was approaching its maximum lift capacity.

This was an obvious yellow flag. It meant that design changes to the IUS or to the planetary spacecraft, or even variations in launch schedules or mechanics, could push the payload weight out of range. Thus the ability of the IUS to meet NASA's objectives was marginal from the start.

By 1979, serious budgetary problems had emerged in the IUS program. By the end of the year, the Air Force was studying cost and schedule issues that were causing the Air Force Systems Command to talk about canceling the project. The Air Force was not abandoning the idea of using the shuttle as a booster for military satellites but was looking at alternatives.

There was also trouble with NASA's schedule. Slippage in the projected launch date of the first shuttle mission had caused NASA to postpone the Galileo flight to a date when different relative positions of the Earth and Jupiter rendered the IUS's lift capacity insufficient. NASA's space scientists now sat pondering at their desks the fact that the IUS could not carry their Galileo probe to Jupiter.

NASA told Congress about the problem at a November 1979 hearing of the House Appropriations Subcommittee on HUD and Independent Agencies, chaired by Congressman Edward Boland. This was the subcommittee that approved NASA's budget. Testifying for NASA were its administrator, Dr. Robert Frosch; William Lilly, the NASA comptroller; and Dr. Thomas Mutch, associate administrator for space science.

The hearing was on the Galileo mission. Dr. Frosch highlighted its scientific importance by saying that Galileo was the only U.S. mission to Jupiter planned for the foreseeable future. If American scientists wanted to study Jupiter, Galileo had to succeed.

Dr. Frosch explained to the subcommittee that Galileo could not be launched as planned because the IUS lacked the thrust to carry the combined weight of both parts of the spacecraft—the orbiter, which would circle Jupiter and map its magnetosphere, and the probe, which would descend and transmit scientific data about its atmosphere's chemical composition.

To solve the launch problem, said Dr. Frosch, NASA was thinking about dividing Galileo into its two components and deploying the orbiter and probe on different IUSs during separate shuttle missions. NASA had already rejected the option of resuscitating an expendable launch vehicle—the Titan-Centaur—which had been discontinued after the 1977 Voyager launches.

The other alternative was to take the cryogenic Centaur upper stage from the Atlas-Centaur, modify it to be stowed in the shuttle orbiter's payload bay, then utilize its extended burn time to deploy the combined Galileo orbiter/probe on a single shuttle launch.

The following year, 1980, was the crossroads for NASA's space shuttle upper stage program. The shuttle had not yet flown, but by the end of the year, NASA was laying the groundwork for a decision to abandon the IUS in favor of Centaur for Galileo and ISPM. The IUS would be retained for lighter-weight payloads, such as TDRS. The stated motives in the decision to use Centaur were the rapidly escalating IUS overruns—an additional $100 million for FY 1981-82—plus avoiding the extra cost of flying the shuttle on dual missions to compensate for the IUS's weight-lift shortfall.

By now, NASA was worrying that there might be no robust shuttle-compatible vehicle for future planetary and deep space exploration. With the phasing out of ELVs, such an outcome could be disastrous for American space science. In January 1981, with President Jimmy Carter leaving office, NASA decided that Centaur, manufactured by the General Dynamics Corporation, was to be the planetary workhorse.

FROM THE EARLIEST days of space shuttle design, the builders of Centaur at General Dynamics had their eye on adapting it for shuttle use. The shuttle would be making the company's Atlas-Centaur obsolete, along with the other expendable launch vehicles in America's spaceflight stable. But General Dynamics was determined not to be left out of the shuttle era. If the shuttle was to become a manned reusable launch platform, why not use a proven, dependable upper stage for high-earth orbit and the space science planetaries? After all, Centaur had been successful in launching all America's planetary missions in the decade of the 1970s. The only time it had ever blown up was on a long-ago 1965 test flight.

The managers, engineers, and astronauts at NASA knew, of course, that the design requirements of the manned space environment were vastly more complex than for expendable launch vehicles. The objection to Centaur was the hazard of carrying pressurized liquid hydrogen and oxygen in the orbiter's payload bay, with the possibility of explosions from leaks.

General Dynamics lobbied hard with Congress. Centaur's credentials were skillfully portrayed by company spokesmen in a May 1980 meeting with Congressmen Donald Fuqua and Bill Nelson, both ardent space program supporters. According to a NASA document, General Dynamics held as one of the main points in its favor that, "Titan-Centaur is the only vehicle in the U.S. inventory that has the boost capability to fly Defense spacecraft designed for the shuttle." In addition, the company said that NASA had commented favorably on Centaur's safety. But this was a preliminary and theoretical determination, not even close to a thorough evaluation by the Johnson Space Center. General Dynamics also claimed that NASA agreed on the ease of integrating Centaur with the shuttle orbiter, though this too was a preliminary judgment. As important as anything else was the promise of "firm costs" at a time when the expense of the IUS had gotten out of hand.

NASA decided to go with Centaur in January 1981. Funny things can happen in Washington in the waning days of presidential administrations. As late as January 8, Frosch had been urged in a letter from Senator Howell Heflin to delay any decision to alter the planetary program until a new NASA administrator came on board. A request to delay the upper stage decision was also made to Frosch in a January 9 letter from Dr. Hans Mark, then secretary of the Air Force. The Air Force was NASA's partner in the IUS venture.

According to documents in its legislative files, NASA held a top-level management meeting, on whether to use Centaur, the next day—

January 10. Two days later, on January 12, Dr. Alan Lovelace, NASA's deputy administrator, sent a memorandum to several NASA executives asking for the data needed to make a decision on Centaur. At this point in my research, I consulted the NASA Historian's Office and learned that Frosch's last day on the premises at 400 Maryland Avenue was January 16, only four days after Lovelace sent the data call and four days before President Jimmy Carter's last day in office and the inauguration of Ronald Reagan.

The record showed that the decision to use Centaur rather than the IUS for the planeteries had been made within another week, by January 23, 1981. On that day, John Yardley, associate administrator for space transportation systems—Code M—issued instructions to NASA's operational centers to phase out the IUS for the planetary missions and prepare to switch over to Centaur.

Lovelace had become NASA's acting administrator upon Frosch's departure and held this position until July 10, 1981, when James Beggs took over as President Reagan's nominee. Lovelace then left NASA to become head of the General Dynamics Space Systems Division. There he would be the executive in charge of the shuttle-Centaur program. So the man who evidently decided that NASA would use Centaur left the agency to build it.

The Lewis Research Center in Cleveland, Ohio, which became the NASA field center responsible for overseeing Centaur conversion, gave the following justification in a "fact sheet" to Congress:

- Centaur capability to geosynchronous orbit is 13,500 pounds vs. 5,000 with the IUS.
- Centaur has demonstrated reliability of ninety-seven percent while IUS has never flown.
- The program would utilize the existing government/industry team which has managed the successful Centaur expendable launch vehicle program.
- Modifications to Centaur are minimal and relatively low risk, and only those required for safety and adaptation to the shuttle will be made.
- Safety reviews by the Johnson and Kennedy Space Centers have concluded that Centaur integration is safe.

- Centaur has more mission flexibility, including multiple burn/restart and low-thrust capability.
- Centaur would cost only $49.8 million for a 1986 launch, compared to $71.4 million for the IUS. Total cost for development, integration, production, and launch of Galileo and the International Solar Polar Mission would be $634 million, less savings from not having to utilize the IUS.

Some members of Congress opposed NASA's decision to go with Centaur. In reporting on the FY 1982 NASA authorization bill, the House Committee on Science and Technology demanded a study of alternative upper stage systems. Acting Administrator Lovelace, who had not yet left for General Dynamics, proposed a joint NASA/Department of Defense study to be completed within ninety days. Lovelace did not conceal what he thought the outcome of the study would be by writing in an internal memorandum that "it would let us continue to proceed with planned Centaur procurement activities. . . . Any substantial delay would threaten our ability to meet the 1985 launch window."

In June, before the study began, NASA awarded contracts worth up to $11 million to General Dynamics and several Centaur subcontractors. The contracts set forth an option of developing three shuttle-Centaur flight vehicles, with actual award of a development contract to be made by the end of the year.

By September, the General Accounting Office had supported NASA's award of sole-source preference to General Dynamics, following a protest by McDonnell-Douglas. GAO ruled that NASA had acted properly in making the judgment that if Centaur or something like it were to be developed, it could only be done in a timely and economical manner by General Dynamics.

The study was completed, and on November 2, 1981, NASA/DoD sent it to Congress. The report had a single recommendation:

> In order to satisfy the national mission requirement needs of both the DoD and NASA, the Air Force should continue development and production of the IUS, and NASA should develop the Centaur.

NASA's main contributor to the report was Michael Weeks, later Jesse Moore's deputy associate administrator for space flight (technical).

By the time the report was sent to Congress, Columbia had flown its first orbital mission, STS-1, with commander John Young and pilot Robert Crippen at the controls. The shuttle blasted off for the first time on April 12, 1981.

As the winter of 1981-82 approached, budget officials throughout the federal government wondered what changes President Reagan's new team at OMB might bring to the federal budget process. No doubt about it, some federal programs would be in trouble. The new OMB director, former Congressman David Stockman, was an unknown quantity.

As NASA's planners went forward with delivering the administration their space budget for FY 1983, Stockman had a surprise for them. He cancelled the Centaur program.

OMB's rationale was that the near-term cost of building the Centaur was too high, despite the projected lifetime savings NASA was claiming of $63 million over the IUS. OMB ignored NASA's contention that Centaur was necessary for deep space exploration in the coming decade. This non-quantifiable benefit was swapped by OMB for an estimated near-term savings of $165 million in FY 1982-83.

David Stockman had administered NASA's managers a smack in the face. NASA's executives upheld the reversal, justifying what was now the administration's official position in subsequent budget hearings before Congress. Administrator James Beggs admitted that the Air Force did not have an immediate need for a high energy upper stage, meaning that the only missions that absolutely had to have Centaur were Galileo and ISPM. It followed, Beggs said, that OMB was right and that the higher short-term expenditure on Centaur could not be justified.

Previously, some members of Congress had questioned NASA's decision to replace the IUS with Centaur. Now Congress came to Centaur's defense by questioning OMB's reversal. The hearings made it clear that some of the scientific results of the Galileo mission would be lost as a result of the decision. The switch from Centaur back to an IUS would also result in additional risk of spacecraft damage or failure, since it would have to fly thirty months longer in making the trip to Jupiter. And the scientific "encounters" of the Jupiter orbiter would be reduced from eleven to six, with a ten percent loss in scientific data.

Congressional criticism also focused on the lack of coordination between NASA and the Department of Defense, though no one mentioned that the difficulty of obtaining such coordination proved the wisdom of the National Aeronautics and Space Act of 1958 in keeping civilian and military space operations separate.

The debate over Centaur continued after the budget hearings. Everyone was now seeing that if Defense agreed to take part in the development and share the costs, Centaur would make sense. Defense did in fact seem to need a high-energy shuttle-based upper stage, if not immediately, at least in the future. In a memorandum sent by Under Secretary of the Air Force Edward C. Aldridge, Jr., to the military vice chief of staff of defense, DoD now put forward the point that it needed to build its own high energy upper stage even as NASA's plans to do the same thing were being cancelled.

The Aldridge memorandum got to Capitol Hill and was cited by Senator Harrison Schmitt, himself a former astronaut, in a February 23, 1982, hearing of the Senate Subcommittee on Science, Technology, and Space. Schmitt scolded NASA Administrator James Beggs:

> Now, how in the world can we here in the Congress look at the relatively modest costs of building both a short and long Centaur upper stage compatible with the shuttle and see the Air Force recommending the independent development of something else that provides essentially the same capability in a longer timeframe. . . . I am very disturbed by it. . . . I just do not understand why Congress should be expected to see the capability lost for shuttle activity when the Air Force and everyone else concerned admits they are going to need that capability and then expect somebody to come in from the other side, the DoD side, and ask for funds in order to build a high energy upper stage, whether it includes Centaur subsystems or not. It doesn't make any sense. . . .

Congress decided to reverse OMB's cancellation of Centaur. While on April 30, 1982, NASA headquarters issued termination orders for the shuttle-Centaur program, by July Congress had passed the Urgent Supplemental Appropriations Act of 1982. A provision of the act instructed NASA to reinstate Centaur and terminate funding for any other upper stage for Galileo and the International Solar Polar Mission.

President Reagan signed the Urgent Supplemental into law on July 16, 1982. This was only three days after NASA Administrator Beggs and Secretary of the Air Force Orr sent a joint letter to the congressional leadership with the administration's last-ditch appeal that its decision against Centaur be upheld. Of course the letter was ignored.

The issue continued to smolder during the following weeks. OMB Director David Stockman complained that the congressional mandate on Centaur undermined the administration's budgetary goals, but he did not take a forceful stand against it. The Air Force similarly pointed out that congressional action in favor of Centaur contradicted its own flexibility in planning for future space missions. But again, the objections were mild. Despite Beggs's on-the-record support of OMB's cancellation decision, insiders at NASA and General Dynamics, with their supporters in Congress, had won the battle.

"GIVING AN HONEST ESTIMATE"

—Things Go Wrong with the Centaur

I HAD FILLED all the seats on my vanpool, but it was a long commute, and by the time I got started in the morning, there was a lot of traffic, especially after crossing the Potomac River into Charles County, Maryland. I said to Phyllis, "It would be nice if I could get an earlier start."

She said, "Why don't you ask if you can change your work hours a little?"

I went to the NASA personnel office and asked what the policy was for changing work schedules. They said changes were routine and that supervisors were expected to grant them. So I gave my supervisor a request in writing to change from 8-4:30 to 7:30-4.

He came into my office and handed back the request with his initials approving it. But he said quietly, "I got really upset when I saw this." Then he walked away. Changing your work schedule was evidently out of line in Code B.

———

I CONTINUED WRITING my Centaur history, which eventually was more than 100 pages long. I wondered what Code B would do with it when it was done. They didn't seem to handle my memos on SRB

O-rings and other issues too well. After I gave them to my supervisor I never heard anything further.

For two years after the final decision to build Centaur, silence shrouded the project. Now General Dynamics, its subcontractors, NASA's Lewis Research Center, and the Air Force got to work.

The contract called for development of two Centaur "G-prime" vehicles for Galileo and Ulysses and two "G" stages for the Defense Department. Later contracts covered launch operations to be carried out by General Dynamics at the Kennedy Space Center and the building of an additional vehicle to launch NASA's Venus Radar Mapper.

While General Dynamics saw the Centaur upper stage as a familiar friend, it was a dangerous machine in the manned space environment. It held 45,000 pounds of cryogenic fuel and was to be supported in the orbiter's payload bay by the Centaur integrated support system (CISS). This was an aluminum alloy cradle that rotated on pins and was to release the rocket into space, along with the attached spacecraft, when the doors of the orbiter payload bay opened. The Centaur and the CISS would be mated to form a single unit during shuttle lift-off. Once in orbit, the Centaur with its payload would separate from the CISS by means of explosive charges in a patented separation ring known as "Super Zip."

Following the activation of Super Zip, twelve large springs would give the now-weightless Centaur a gentle push. The rocket, with its spacecraft, would float out of the orbiter bay into the zero-gravity vacuum of space. Then, after Centaur had drifted a safe distance from the orbiter, its two Pratt-Whitney RL-10 engines would fire. The launch sequence for Centaur would be initiated not by the astronauts, but by NASA's mission control at Houston, and would proceed by means of computers located on the CISS. Though the deployment was automated, the astronauts would have to be vigilant to deal with contingencies or emergencies.

For instance, if Centaur's deployment were aborted, causing launch of the planetary spacecraft to be abandoned, the crew would dump the enormous cryogenic load into space to avert the danger of a catastrophic explosion when the orbiter returned to Earth. In no case would they travel any longer or further than necessary with the highly volatile fuel and oxidizer still in the payload bay.

If a fuel dump were incomplete, the astronauts would don their space suits, leave the orbiter cabin, and by means of an EVA—extra-vehicular activity—jettison the Centaur and its attached spacecraft overboard. No such feat had ever been attempted in manned spaceflight.

Obviously, a Centaur mission would require a lot of astronaut training. And the contingencies were so varied and complex that no additional shuttle payloads or activities would be scheduled for a Centaur mission. Following deployment or an abort, the orbiter would immediately return to earth. Even if the fuel were dumped in an abort, the orbiter would return to Earth with a heavy load—the vehicle, the CISS, and the planetary spacecraft. Under no scenario would the orbiter attempt to land with any liquid hydrogen or oxygen still aboard.

The CISS and Centaur vehicle subsystems were complex. The flight operations plan was exacting and unprecedented. But none of it was represented by General Dynamics or NASA's Lewis Research Center as presenting serious technical problems. The same procedures to weld the stainless steel cryogenic fuel tanks would be used as on earlier Centaur expendable launch vehicles. The engine-mounted hydraulic system that supplied power to gimbal—i.e., swivel—the engine nozzles would also be the same on the new Centaur as the old.

On the bulkhead were the pneumatic storage and supply system and the tank vent system that modulated tank pressurization levels. Tank pressurization was established and maintained by a computerized system. The avionics system consisted of a 16-K core memory digital computer unit, a four-gimballed platform inertial measurement group, a sequence control unit, a servo inverter unit, two remote multiplexing units, two signal conditioners, multiple pyrotechnic initiator control units to fire Super Zip, an associated instrumentation system, a propellant utilization and level-sensing system, a telemetry system, and an electrical power system with batteries.

None of these systems was new.

According to General Dynamics, all that was new were "a few minor component changes to the Centaur D-1A avionics system." These included the addition of a dual-failure-tolerant arm/safe sequencer, which precluded premature arming of the Centaur firing mechanisms, and spacecraft deployment functions.

Unfortunately, during the two seemingly peaceful years of 1983-84, the several thousand engineers, technicians, administrators, and skilled workmen who were assigned by General Dynamics and its subcontractors to work on Centaur discovered that adapting it for manned space flight was enormously more difficult and complex than NASA and the company's management had led Congress and OMB to believe.

The fact was that you couldn't simply take the old Centaur upper stage off an Atlas booster, make it a little fatter, and bolt it into the shuttle orbiter payload bay. A staggering number of engineering changes had to be made. The old materials were now seen as insufficient to ensure safety. New welding specifications had to be developed. The question had not been satisfactorily thought through as to how the dangerous liquid hydrogen/oxygen propellants could be dumped in an abort.

Also, the seals on the premier cryogenic valves in the aerospace industry failed when tested for shuttle use. Later, in 1985, the redesign of the Centaur's fuel tanks was revealed as much more difficult than expected when the hydrogen test tank sprung a leak and required a new testing protocol. This alone cost the developmental phase two months and added $2 million to the cost estimates.

As fabrication and testing slipped, crash work schedules with multiple shifts and extensive overtime were ordered. Sixty-hour work weeks for technicians became the norm. Additional incentive fees had to be paid to subcontractors to supply needed parts to meet the accelerated schedules. NASA ordered unexpected engineering changes, as developmental revisions were still being made to the shuttle orbiter. These required corresponding modifications in Centaur's design. Of course, NASA had to pay for them.

Further, General Dynamics' archaic materials-handling system suffered a near-breakdown. The Convair Division's first strike in its history idled 4,200 members of the hourly workforce. During the strike, the company tried to carry on with less than fully-skilled workers, but some of their work later had to be torn out and redone.

In short, a fiasco was in the works at Kearney Mesa in San Diego.

In early 1984, General Dynamics declared a small overrun of $16.5 million on the prime contract. But this was slight compared to the $70.6 million overrun in January 1985, which, combined with a new estimate of $35 to $40 million over plan for production and launch services, showed a total overrun of more than $100 million. This assumed no more surprises before launch time. When the figures were revealed, NASA appeared to be taken by surprise.

What had gone wrong? And why did it take NASA so long to find out? After General Dynamics disclosed the overrun, NASA dug in its files to identify and analyze earlier contractor reports. These showed that through December 1984, 300,000 more man-hours than planned had been charged to the Centaur contract. 54,000 of these hours were in design engineering and were attributed by General Dynamics to an inexperienced team of structural engineers, draftsmen, and stress analysts. Unfortunately, the old Centaur team had been broken up when production of the Atlas-Centaur and Titan-Centaur expendable launch vehicles had been discontinued.

Also to blame were extensive and unexpected modifications to the Centaur due to new Johnson Space Center safety requirements, extra time spent on procurement paperwork for the new parts and materials, design improvements to reduce the weight of the vehicle and alter its insulation and radiation shield, changes to the test schedule, late definition of the temperature extremes the vehicle was expected to undergo in the orbiter bay, and changes to accommodate unanticipated pressures on the redesigned vehicle at shuttle lift-off from high G-forces.

There had also been errors that took extra man-hours to correct. One was a mistake in the General Dynamics avionics laboratory that I had been told of when I visited Kearney Mesa in August 1985. Assembly of Centaur's electronic flight units was delayed by a month when a conductive epoxy that potentially allowed the disaster of random closing of electronic circuits was used to secure electronic parts to the aviation boards. This problem came to light when it was discovered that a thermally-conductive epoxy that acted as a heat sink also became electrically conductive at certain voltages. This commonality should have been tested beforehand but was not.

Thousands of unexpected design and manufacturing changes had to be made. Each change drove up costs through increased labor, new parts and materials, and additional paperwork. Each new direct cost carried its own burden of company overhead.

Estimates for the launch support contract—work General Dynamics would be doing at the Kennedy Space Center when Centaur went up in the shuttle—were driven up by similar causes. Included were

10,000 more hours than planned for parts engineering, 7,000 for scheduling, 130,000 for "increased program support complexity over Atlas/Centaur experience," and 120,000 for "improved understanding of Centaur integration tasks."

A General Dynamics document from this period dissected the overrun into further minutiae. Cited were labor charges from higher-than-expected employee turnover, the lack of experienced computer-aided design operators, and the need to provide the procurement staff with "detailed drawings of substitute fasteners."

There were also extra staff meetings, redesign of an equipment module and stub adaptor to save fifteen pounds at shuttle lift-off, unexpected weaknesses upon creasing of the materials that made up the insulation and radiation shield, redesign of package mounts to provide shock insulation, study of the effect on the Centaur vehicle of the "high velocity of air" rushing past the shuttle orbiter's cryogenic dump valves, a high scrap rate in the production process caused by poor workmanship and inadequate fabrication techniques, test failure of round washers and their replacement with square ones, etc.

The problems were constant, serious, and costly. Above all, they proved that the contractor was not simply adapting a familiar vehicle but designing a new one with unique characteristics. Thus the judgment, claims, and assurances of General Dynamics and NASA had proven wrong, though it took almost two years for anyone at management levels to say so.

Congress wanted to hear about it too. On May 21 and 23, 1985, Congressman Bill Nelson, whose home district included the Kennedy Space Center, and who was later a passenger on the January 1986 flight of Columbia, chaired a hearing of the House Subcommittee on Space Science and Applications. Nelson called as the principal witnesses two familiar faces in the Centaur story—Administrator James Beggs and General Dynamics executive and former NASA deputy and acting administrator Dr. Alan Lovelace.

Nelson's first order of business was to place in the record a statement by the subcommittee's ranking Republican member, Robert S. Walker, who cited the apparent causes of the overrun as governmental indecision, contracting delays, schedule pressure from inflexible launch windows, and breakdown of the engineering and management systems of both NASA and General Dynamics. Walker faulted NASA's "no problem" approach, which he said:

> . . . takes the stand that we have had problems in other programs, but we have already learned all the answers, so we will encounter no problems on this program and therefore don't have to plan extra time, or budget extra money, to cover contingencies.

Walker's statement also cited a second and perhaps more serious problem, which was "the failure of NASA to understand how difficult it would be to integrate a very complex upper stage filled with liquid hydrogen and oxygen into the shuttle payload bay."

Beggs admitted that NASA underestimated the requirements of integrating the Centaur into the shuttle but said the agency had completed a major review that gave confidence Centaur was a safe vehicle for manned spaceflight. He did not explain why it took two years for NASA to determine that the engineering problems at Kearney Mesa led to a cost overrun estimated at $100-110 million.

Accompanying Beggs at the hearing were Jesse Moore, by now the successor to General James Abrahamson as associate administrator for space flight, Andrew Stofan, director of the Lewis Research Center, and Larry Ross, director of space flight systems at Lewis. In the questioning that followed, it was evident that this group, particularly Stofan, agreed that the expense of the job had been underestimated, but that little would have been managed differently in the technical approach to design, testing, and fabrication had the program been viewed as new development instead of adapting an existing piece of hardware.

This view is difficult to reconcile with the General Dynamics overrun analysis that several months earlier gave the impression that many of the technical problems were surprises. It is also notable that the tone of the NASA executives was to justify what had been done and to deny that actions which may have had untoward cost consequences were mistakes. This frame of mind seemed to reflect an institutional attitude, though Beggs admitted some of the costs contributing to the overrun had been "swept under the rug."

Beggs was not sympathetic to Congressman Walker's complaint about the "no problem" approach. To Beggs, the attitude was natural. He said:

Now, the over-optimism, I don't think you can do anything about. I will be very candid with you. I don't think the Congress, you can stand up here and make speeches and hold hearings and do anything you want. When a young engineer or program manager is trying to sell a program, he is going to be optimistic. And you can haul him up here and rake him over any kind of—through any kind of torture chamber that you want to rake him through, he will be optimistic, because that is his bread and butter, that is what he lives on is that new program that he is going to be optimistic about.

Beggs ended his appearance by admitting that "earlier in the process" NASA should have challenged General Dynamics' billing. But the hearing came to an end without any criticism of General Dynamics' internal manufacturing practices or the competence of its management. Except for Beggs' remark about the company sweeping costs under the rug, NASA avoided calling attention to performance deficiencies on the part of General Dynamics or its subcontractors.

————

I HAD A chance to view the situation at Kearney Mesa in San Diego firsthand in August 1985, when I accompanied Assistant Comptroller Mal Peterson on an on-site financial review. The internal reports that resulted never reached Congress or the public, but contained such comments as:

> The readiness of the workforce in terms of experience and training seems questionable. Although GD worked for an extended period of time on letter contract and should have benefited from that in terms of task definition, the financial planning (manpower and material) was poor. . . . There may be reason to be concerned about the cost motivation of the contractor in a fee environment where launch success is the only motivator.

Other reports noted that General Dynamics' claim of instituting cost control measures was not happening. During the review, the company said it would save $3 million by bargaining down fee claims made by materials subcontractors at a time when the subcontractors were demanding additional fees for expedited deliveries. By late 1985, for example, the Fairchild Corporation, a major Centaur subcontractor, was showing alarming overruns on cryogenic valves, and an issue had developed over how much of the cost General Dynamics would refuse to accept and how much would be passed on to NASA and the taxpayer. By January 1986, new overruns were showing up in NASA's accounting records, confirming the doubts of analysts that the company's claims of cost savings would be realized.

During the August review, General Dynamics informed the NASA team that Dr. Alan Lovelace, former NASA deputy administrator and now a General Dynamics vice president, had ordered labor reductions of 100,000 hours in engineering manpower and 50,000 in quality control. The quality control reductions were to be accomplished without any sacrifice of product quality, which raised the question of why these hours had been budgeted in the first place if they were not needed. But again, by the first of the year, new overruns were appearing, including hours in engineering manpower, one of the categories Lovelace reduced. Regarding these and other issues, Peterson said that Lewis and General Dynamics "appear to be saying all the right things" but that their assurances gave little confidence.

The review team also noted problems with the quality of workmanship and the process of inspecting completed flight hardware. Peterson discussed conditions in the Kearney Mesa plant with the resident staff members of DCAS, the Defense Contract Audit Service of the Defense Supply Agency. Following his questions to DCAS, as well as to Analex, a technical support contractor to the Lewis Research Center, Peterson wrote of "questionable procedures" and that the General Dynamics operations group was working under such strong scheduling pressure "that the QC [quality control] inspectors for GD are being 'encouraged' to buy off on work that is of lesser quality. The DCAS personnel . . . are having to operate as policemen to prevent GD from proceeding with next level assembly tasks until the quality discrepancies are cleared."

NASA's reviewers from the Lewis Research Center noted that delays had occurred because engineers were kept busy with make-work alterations to the hardware. Lewis's reviewers also criticized the materials handling system at General Dynamics, and sometimes engineers from the Lewis resident office at Kearney Mesa would go on search expeditions to the factory floor to find missing parts that were urgently needed for assembly projects. On one occasion they found a critical electronics part that had been missing for several weeks after it fell off the back of a table in the reviewing inspection room and appeared to have been lost.

Lewis also noted a lack of sufficient hourly manpower, especially in parts handling and vehicle assembly. In the latter case, General Dynamics, which seemed so lavish with its use of engineers, was reluctant to assign more people to the skilled labor tasks for fear of worsening the overrun.

The situation was so bad that Mal Peterson said the only way the Galileo and Ulysses missions could fly as scheduled in May 1986 would be through catch-up work performed by the more capable and motivated General Dynamics crew at the Kennedy Space Center. This crew could set to work once the flight hardware was shipped from San Diego.

As time passed after I returned to Washington from the General Dynamics inspection, Centaur looked more and more like a botched program. Later I would see that mission control in Houston, along with the astronauts, thought so too.

"FLY AS IS"

—NASA Ponders the Centaur Problems as Challenger Looms on Pad 39-A

THE ALARMING CONTRACTOR performance that so many observers noted at Kearney Mesa had reached its low point in June 1985. General Dynamics had shipped the Centaur integrated support structure that would hold the SC-1 Galileo Centaur vehicle in Atlantis's payload bay to the Kennedy Space Center. Kennedy and NASA headquarters staff reacted to the condition of the CISS with dismay. The reviewing staff engineer in Washington wrote in a memorandum: "The systems are incomplete, the workmanship and cleanliness . . . are poor, and documentation, including inspection buyoffs, is incomplete."

General Dynamics had lived up to a promise Dr. Lovelace made to Congress by shipping the CISS on schedule. Unfortunately, it was lacking 1,400 parts, and the plan for procuring the missing parts was inadequate. The reviewing engineer at headquarters told me that the CISS was in "worse shape than any major piece of contractor hardware ever delivered to the NASA space program."

The paperwork did not show inspection stamps to indicate that installation of components had been done in accordance with blueprint specifications, so the CISS had to be disassembled and rebuilt. The CISS had poor workmanship on its rivets, misaligned ducts and loose fittings, missing and mislocated brackets, inadequate clamping of harnesses, and miswired connectors. It was dirty, with metal particles in the purge system tubing, air bubbles and other contaminants under the gold tape, and cigarette ashes, metal shavings, and pieces of plastic and other debris on the metal surfaces.

The reviewing engineer said that General Dynamics was clearly giving the shuttle a low priority compared to the Defense Department's cruise missiles that were also being manufactured at Kearney Mesa. The engineer also noted that the condition of the CISS would probably delay its mating to the Centaur vehicle, which he said might finally bring home to NASA's upper management the seriousness of General Dynamics' performance problems. He concluded his written report by stating:

> An all-out effort to improve parts deliveries, quality verification, and work standards at General Dynamics must be made. If the SC-1 vehicle is shipped to ELS [eastern launch site; i.e., Kennedy] in the CISS condition, the launch schedule is in jeopardy. Some discipline *must* be injected into the San Diego operation.

By this time, NASA's "no problem" attitude was crumbling, even at headquarters. It was unbelievable to many observers that after provoking so much frustration and embarrassment over the cost overrun, General Dynamics could let a debacle like the CISS delivery take place.

To avoid repeating the embarrassment of the CISS delivery, General Dynamics shipped the additional flight hardware, including the Centaur rocket itself, more complete, but late. "Bank time" in the launch schedule was slipping away, parts shortages were continuing to impede assembly, and NASA headquarters was worried about launching on time. The launch schedules could be achieved only if final hardware assembly and testing at Kennedy disclosed no major problems that required engineering redesign.

The overrun was on the move again by the end of 1985, as design problems emerged in the testing program and the bills for the parts that were finally arriving at Kennedy were paid. NASA wanted to finance the overrun without returning to Congress for more money. Still, the word got up to Capitol Hill, where NASA's friends in Congress quietly slipped the agency a $40 million supplemental appropriation for Centaur for fiscal year 1985. It was probably the easiest $40 million NASA ever picked up. The remainder of the overrun was covered by deferrals in the Venus Radar Mapper and the TDRS communications satellite programs. Funding for the VRM and TDRS upper stages was, to use NASA's phraseology, "moved to the right" on the budget charts; i.e., deferred to the budgetary out-years.

The agency drew the line at the suggestion of one Lewis manager that some of the overrun in the development budget be disguised by shifting charges to the operations account. Both Code M and Code B rejected the illegal option when it was presented at a Code M management meeting.

Another type of shifting seemed to take place, however. A January 23, 1986, report signed by a General Dynamics official documented the charging of $1.182 million for replacement of Centaur computing unit relays, not as an overrun to NAS3-22901, to which the action in question belonged, but as a fee-bearing charge against NAS3-23439, which was a smaller project support contract. A colleague showed me the document. When I said it looked improper, he answered, "So what else is new?"

Even without illegal cost shifting, in an eight-year period, vehicle costs for the upper stages for the two planetary missions had grown by more than 800 percent. But until Challenger blew up, what had been bothering NASA most about Centaur was not the cost overruns as much as the hardware and software problems growing out of the late deliveries and test failures. The number one issue at the start of 1986 was safety.

During the early testing, failure of Centaur components occurred that NASA engineers declared would have been catastrophic in flight, now only a few months away. Predictably, these failures occurred in components that had not been part of Centaur when it was flown as an expendable launch vehicle atop the Titan and Atlas boosters, but were new ones that were added when Centaur was adapted for manned spaceflight on the shuttle.

The chief problems were failures of a Fairchild cryogenic dump valve that would be used if the astronauts had to discard propellant if the mission aborted, and of relays in the computing units—CUs—the central electronic brain of the rocket. General Dynamics had never built

CUs of this type, which, because of the many new systems and sub-assemblies, were much more complex than those in the unmanned version of the rocket.

The implications of these failures were ominous. If a dump valve failed to open during an abort, the astronauts would not be able to get rid of more than twenty-two tons of explosive cryogenic fuel and oxidizer. The astronauts would then have to suit up, perform an EVA, and manually jettison the Centaur and its scientific payload, costing hundreds of millions of dollars, into the graveyard of space. During this sensitive manual operation, Centaur's fuel tanks would be bubbling away with hazardous cryogenic fuel.

If the CUs on the Centaur failed, the situation could be even worse. As a stroke can render a human victim paralyzed and helpless, CU failure in a spacecraft can disable essential flight systems. Electric power could be knocked out, the Centaur could lose its ability to separate from the shuttle orbiter, or pressurization of the tanks or fuel lines could be lost. The Centaur could be reduced to an inert mass of metal sitting in the orbiter bay, again with twenty-two tons of destructive fuel and leaks a virtual certainty over time.

When the test failures occurred, NASA's engineers realized immediately that there was not enough time before the May launches to fix the valves or the CUs properly. In an ordinary developmental program, the failed components would be redesigned and requalified for flight. But so much of the Galileo/Ulysses schedule had been eaten up by contractor delays that temporary fixes had to be engineered.

In its internal meetings, the ones behind closed doors that the press or Congress never heard about, NASA's managers acknowledged these decisions to be compromises with flight safety. Even if the launch schedule could be slipped for a few weeks, relief could be sought. But the May launch windows were inflexible, due to the need to optimize the relative positions of the sun, the Earth, and the planets. For Galileo, a delay past the close of the window would mean a thirteen-month postponement until Earth and Jupiter reached a similar alignment.

Thirteen months may not have seemed worth risking people's lives over in terms of exploring a universe created eight billion years ago, but NASA was in a hurry. The cost to repeat the pre-launch tests and preparations, as well as to store the vehicles and spacecraft for a year, would add more than $50 million in costs. Also, NASA would lose face with the Air Force, the European Space Agency, Congress, the public, and itself.

Other problems emerged during testing, though none were so disturbing as the valve and CU failures. A set of large, spherical bottles that held helium under pressure were clamped to the Centaur integrated support structure. These are a familiar sight in photos of space vehicles. The helium would be forced into the Centaur's ductwork to purge the lines of moisture and of gaseous hydrogen and oxygen that boiled off from the fuel tanks. Helium was also used to pressurize the tanks and actuate the vent and dump system valves. Manufactured by the Arde Corporation, the twenty-two-inch bottles were coated with Dupont-manufactured Kevlar overwrap, which had become streaked with oil from a leak in Dupont's winding machines. The oil weakened the bottles, creating the danger that they might burst under pressure. The most heavily-streaked bottles had to be discarded, and tests had to be performed to qualify the more lightly-streaked bottles for flight. Again, this qualification was for the May 1986 flights only. There was also a tight schedule for the completion of CU flight software, after which General Dynamics would send it to the astronaut training facility in Houston to be installed in the Johnson Space Center's mission training simulator.

All this time, the House Appropriations Committee's survey and investigations staff was traveling from one NASA installation to another conducting its own quiet analysis of the mounting problems. It turned out they hadn't swallowed the line put out in the May 1985 hearings by NASA and General Dynamics that everything was going to be okay.

General Dynamics finally decided to do something to salvage the situation. From San Diego, the company reported "corrective actions," including improved "management presence/visibility in manufacturing areas." The purpose was to engender better work by hourly employees through the oddball solution of positioning senior managers in booths to scrutinize the men and women at work on the factory floor. This might also have implied an attempt to place the blame for deficiencies on the faceless workers, whereas virtually all the Centaur problems could be laid at management's feet in the first place. General Dynamics also now spoke of "improving coordination [among] engineering, planning, and production control."

By November 1985, the Johnson Space Center, which many at NASA felt had never wholeheartedly supported the shuttle-Centaur program, and which had hoped, it was believed, that the program would just go away, now began to take it seriously. Johnson had started to realize that in a few months its astronauts would climb into the shuttle orbiter and haul the Centaur vehicle to orbit, where, perhaps, they could blow up. The astronauts were calling Centaur "the bomb in the bay." This was just two months before the Challenger explosion.

On November 20-21, 1985, NASA conducted a Level I design certification review board at Kearney Mesa. Because Level I referred to the office of the associate administrator for space flight, the meeting was chaired by Jesse Moore, who had the final say on all important decisions. People could try to persuade Moore, but they could not overrule him.

Attending the review were the top NASA managers and engineers in charge of the shuttle-Centaur program and the Galileo/Ulysses missions. The board focused on the valve and CU problems, and the extensive modifications being done on the Challenger and Atlantis orbiters. The board also discussed the work underway at Kennedy to accelerate completion of a second shuttle launch pad—39-B—and to equip both pads for cryogenic loading of fuel onto both the Centaur and the external tank.

At the meeting, representatives of the Johnson Space Center laid their cards on the table. JSC made it clear that the Galileo/Ulysses flights carried a higher cargo risk than any previous space shuttle mission because of the presence of explosive fuel, the complex interactive hardware and software systems, and the numerous waivers to customary safety standards that were being made to allow the Centaur to fly at all.

NASA had no choice but to view certain hardware shortcomings as virtually hopeless. They would become "acceptable risks" for the Galileo/Ulysses missions. But a Johnson representative wrote in a briefing chart:

> Recent actions to "fly as is" on planetaries and fix for future missions indicates schedule pressure is forcing solutions which might otherwise be rejected.

After the review, in a December 11, 1985, memorandum to board members that transmitted minutes of the meeting, Jesse Moore recounted:

> The board concluded that, indeed, there is cause for concern, and the "fly as is" decisions on the flight hardware for our first two missions must be monitored very closely. Deviations and waivers must be judged not only on a one-to-one basis, but on a cumulative basis as well, to assure minimal risk to the STS and crew. . . . The S/C [i.e., shuttle-Centaur] team should be made aware and sensitive to the potential for increased safety risk due to the individual acceptance of these "fly as is" hardware decisions, as well as the overall increased risks in general.

This memo is an expression of the fact that, even before Challenger, whatever impression NASA tried to convey of having a "safety first" policy was a myth. Safety is shown in Moore's statement as a factor in the decision process at NASA, but one that is clearly weighed in the balance against schedule pressures. Even in the days of Mercury, Gemini, and Apollo, safety first may have been more an ideal than a reality, as was shown by the hardware deficiencies that resulted in the 1967 Apollo 1 fire when astronauts Grissom, Chaffee, and White were killed.

But by 1985, the "fly as is" policy, where safety was knowingly compromised to meet schedules, seemed to be the new standard. Following the Challenger disaster, both the Presidential Commission and the House Science and Technology Committee noted that schedule pressures had compromised safety. But neither took the further step of pointing out that "fly as is" was a deliberate NASA policy, as the Centaur documentation indicated.

Then, on January 16-17, 1986, as Challenger loomed on Pad 39-B prior to its scheduled launch less than two weeks away, NASA conducted the most important meetings yet on the shuttle-Centaur missions. I attended these meetings with Mal Peterson as a Code B representative.

The January meetings took place in the main administration building at the Kennedy Space Center. The weather was mild and cloudy, but pleasant. Since we were on the ocean, there was a sea breeze. The Kennedy Center complex was huge, and I was looking forward to a tour the afternoon of the 17th before returning home.

Also attending the meetings were Richard Smith, director of the Kennedy Space Center; Andrew Stofan, director of the Lewis Research Center; Lewis's shuttle-Centaur program managers, led by Larry Ross; Code M's managing engineers for the Centaur project; Code M budget analysts; representatives of the Johnson Space Center, the Marshall Space Flight Center, and NASA's Jet Propulsion Laboratory; headquarters engineers from the Office of Space Science in charge of the Galileo spacecraft; a European Space Agency delegate responsible for the Ulysses spacecraft; leaders of the Air Force Space Systems Command; and astronauts Richard Hauck and David Walker, flight commanders for the Galileo and Ulysses missions. Interestingly, no one was there from General Dynamics or any other contractor. This was strictly a government meeting.

During the nine hours of briefings, which lasted two days, every aspect of the shuttle-Centaur program was analyzed. The meeting began with an almost gleeful report by the Lewis Research Center team on the successful tank test then underway for the SC-1 Galileo vehicle, during which the cryogenics were loaded and drained to demonstrate the functioning and interaction of ducts, valves, and pressurization subsystems.

But the safety issues rushed to the forefront. No one, especially the Johnson representatives, was in the mood for a NASA program office "pitch." Participants repeatedly emphasized what had been obvious for years but was always glossed over—that the shuttle-Centaur was a new vehicle that had never flown before. It had never even had a test firing. For it to succeed, a large number of complex, untried systems had to work perfectly the first time they were used, and in the presence of a live crew.

The Johnson delegates bore down on the temporary repair to the five-inch dump valve, which had been changed to a single-point-failure mode by realigning actuators in a Wright three-way solenoid valve. Usually in a spacecraft, the most vital safety systems were built with redundancy when possible, so that if a system failed, an identical back-up would kick in to perform the disabled function. In the interests of time, however, redundancy had been sacrificed in the five-inch dump valve, so that a single failure could now prevent the crew from carrying out a fuel dump in case of an abort. This was the scenario that could lead to the unprecedented decision to jettison a fully-loaded vehicle in orbit—again, an operation that would be performed by hand labor through an astronaut EVA.

A Lewis Research Center manager said, and the briefing hand-outs repeated, that the decision to fix the valve by creating the single-point failure mode had been the "best of two bad choices." But JSC was adamant that were the Centaur "our bird," the single-point failure would be changed. Jesse Moore then ordered Lewis to find out if any means of doing so remained. Someone said it might be possible to create redundancy by revising the switches that controlled the valve system. But Johnson answered that this would require changes to the CU software that General Dynamics was supposed to deliver to Johnson for astronaut simulation training by the end of January, which was less than two weeks away.

What if the training software were delayed? Johnson made it clear that if this happened, NASA could write off both Centaur missions. The schedule had no room for delivery slips in training software. The flight crew workload was now set at a minimum of sixty-three hours per week for the eleven weeks preceding flight and was certain to increase. The astronaut training schedule was viewed by Johnson as almost impossible to achieve and was threatened with disruption, as Johnson was changing its training contractor while trying to assure that the new one employed some of the more experienced people who had been writing software under the old contract.

Commander Richard Hauck then dramatized the gravity with which the flight crew was viewing the situation by telling the group that not since Apollo 11, the first moon landing, had NASA flown a mission without a rookie aboard. Further, each of the two flight crews would recieve only 100 hours of flight simulation, a mere twenty-five hours more than for the much less complex IUS flights. Also, said a Johnson Space Center spokesman, General Dynamics had made changes to previous versions of the flight software that would require old procedures to be unlearned. Anomalies in the software were still being clarified, one of which would cause initial alerts of Centaur system malfunctions to mask subsequent failures of the same systems.

Participants at the meeting examined several other problems which, if not solved, could halt the May missions and force the dreaded thirteen-month delay. One of the most disturbing problems was constraints on Kennedy Space Center facilities and equipment. These included, most critically, the mobile launch platforms (MLPs), the tractor-like devices used to carry the space shuttle to the launch pad from the Vehicle Assembly Building (VAB), where stacking of the orbiter, the solid rocket boosters, and the external tank took place. It was not until a shuttle lifted off from an MLP that the unit could be rolled back to the VAB for stacking of the next shuttle flight set.

Also, until the SC-1/Galileo vehicle completed its tank test with full cryogenic loading in Kennedy's Complex 39, the SC-2 Ulysses rocket could not be hauled in for its test. NASA was now in the midst of a rapid acceleration of the shuttle launch schedule, shifting from nine flights in 1985 to fifteen in 1986. Flight schedules were periodically listed in a published manifest, and in a briefing paper handed out by a Kennedy official, the attempt to juggle the vast amount of shuttle components and launch equipment required to meet the 1986 launch schedule was jokingly termed "Manifest Bingo."

The Kennedy Space Center officials emphasized that for them to process the shuttle components and payloads for the Galileo and Ulysses missions, hardware had to work as it was supposed to, launches had to take off and land reasonably close to schedule, and cooperation and support were required from NASA's other centers. Specifically, for Ulysses to meet its launch window, Challenger would have to return on time from its 51-L mission, and the orbiter Atlantis, scheduled to fly the Galileo mission, would have to move through its pre-launch stacking and checkout routine promptly and efficiently.

At the time, Challenger was scheduled for launch on Thursday, January 23. When it exploded just after lift-off on January 28, it was already five days late. At the meeting, the Kennedy staff members handed out a "Preliminary January Manifest/KSC Assessment" prepared on January 10 that showed Challenger back at Kennedy from its seven-day mission by January 30 to start the flow in preparation for the May 15 Ulysses launch. Landing was scheduled for the runway at Kennedy to avoid lost time from having to ferry Challenger cross-country following an Edwards Air Force Base landing in California.

These charts would make it appear that NASA may have launched Challenger in freezing temperatures on January 28 in order to meet the deadlines of Manifest Bingo. Certainly, this situation had to contribute to a sense of pressure. But to some extent, the Kennedy planners were deliberately trying to build a feeling of urgency in order to make a point. At the conference table, the Kennedy delegates departed from their prepared briefing charts and, turning to Jesse Moore, said in reassuring tones that despite the tight deadlines on paper, there was still leeway in the schedule before the plans for the May launch opportunity for Galileo were irretrievably lost. My notes from this meeting read: "Maximum contingency time in KSC launch schedule—four weeks. . . . four weeks + means scrub."

This meant that the Challenger launch could have slipped even further than it finally did. Also, a month earlier, Moore had given the mission 61-C astronauts and the KSC launch crews the Christmas and New Year holidays off. This was during the multiple launch delays for the Columbia flight that preceded Challenger. Thus there was still enough slack in the schedule for NASA to show mercy to its teams of overworked employees. Manifest Bingo was not the cause of NASA's flawed decision to launch Challenger on January 28, 1986.

Yet another problem had emerged at the January 16-17 meetings because of the complex abort contingencies for the two May flights. Kennedy was already behind schedule in writing its operational management instructions, each OMI comprising a thick volume, and faced the difficult task of preparing its launch and rescue teams for the numerous malfunctions that could occur during or after shuttle lift-off.

The orbiters themselves were having technical problems in being readied for the planetary missions. With a fully-tanked Centaur onboard, they would be carrying an unusually heavy load. Special analyses and precautions were needed to assure the crew could maintain control in flight, particularly in case of an abort or fuel dump. If a dump occurred, the orbiter could require 500 more pounds of fuel than usual for its maneuvering engines to be able to counteract the roll torque exerted by Centaur's cryogenic fuel spraying into space from the lateral dump vents. Such an event could transform the orbiter into a spinning top if the crew lost control.

The orbiter's hydrogen vent had been poorly located, creating the danger of a mechanical reaction that could result in overheating and buckling of the Centaur fuel tanks. And to support the weight of full tanking of the Centaur for the Galileo mission, the main engines had to fire at 109 percent of rated power, a thrust level never before attempted in a shuttle lift-off. Without this extra thrust, 2,375 pounds of Centaur fuel would have to be off-loaded, and the number of Galileo deployment opportunities during the orbital phase of the shuttle's mission would be reduced by almost 75 percent. This would magnify the chance of missing the launch window if malfunctions prevented Atlantis from lifting off precisely on schedule. At a break in the meeting, one of the headquarters managers, with a knowing smile, said to another attendee, "I'll bet you Marshall goes with the 109 percent even if the qualifications tests fail."

The 109 percent thrust level had formerly been considered the "emergency" power level to be used only to abort the shuttle to orbit or to return to the launch site. From 1981 to 1985, there had been five main engine test failures on the ground at Marshall's Bay St. Louis, Mississippi, test facility. All failures were at 109 percent or greater throttle settings, and all would have been catastrophic in flight. Here was another potential "fly as is" situation, where NASA might have been forced to add to the already uncomfortable risk of main engine failure.

Further, a temporary fix might have to be made to the orbiter's main engine low pressure fuel duct to increase the number of times orbiter fuel could be reloaded if repeated launch delays occurred on the pad during countdown. Under the flight rules, such reloading could only occur on two consecutive days before a full day's recess was required to inspect the stressed cryogenic fuel lines and determine if temperature extremes had damaged them. This was primarily an "ovality" check to determine out-of-roundness. The rule would be a handicap if repeated stops and starts of the countdown required frequent fuel reloadings to meet the launch window.

Another issue that emerged during the mid-January meetings was concerns of the Johnson Space Center with modifications being made to Centaur's helium system plumbing and the fact that the "water hammer effect"—i.e., the momentary surge exerted on ductwork when a valve opens and allows fluids under pressure to rush into a line of tubing—would produce pressure spikes of 400 pounds per square inch on lines that had been proofed only to 150. When Johnson's representatives raised this point, Jesse Moore looked around and asked who at NASA was working on the problem, but no one in the room knew whether anyone was or not.

Johnson's representatives also expressed concern with the effects of shock on the Centaur valves when Super Zip fired and separated the vehicle from the CISS in the orbiter bay. Further, they pointed out how difficult it would be for Centaur to be cleared for launch once it had reached the pad. At that point, 400 mechanical checks had to be made on the vehicle, of which 2-300 were "redlines"—i.e., points where, if a readiness standard were not met, the launch would be called off. This was twice the number of redlines for an IUS launch, such as Challenger's 51-L mission scheduled for lift-off within a few days. Challenger would be carrying a TDRS satellite mounted on an IUS.

The Galileo scientific spacecraft that was to fly to Jupiter, bristling with measuring devices of various kinds, had its own problems, though most had been resolved prior to the January 16-17 meetings. For instance, a massive retrofit had been done on the memory circuits of the spacecraft's brain—its command data system. More than 600 parts had been replaced, with the work being done under alcohol to avoid damage to the circuits from static electricity.

The group also heard an alarming tale of the tardy status of clearances for the Galileo/Ulysses nuclear energy sources. These were the RTGs—plutonium-powered radioisotope thermoelectric generators, ingenious devices for long-term electricity-generation in space. If an accident occurred during either mission—missions which, due to the presence of cryogenics in the orbiter bay, would already be the most dangerous shuttle missions yet flown—hazardous radioactive fuel could be left in low-earth orbit, possibly to re-enter the earth's atmosphere later, where it could be inhaled by human beings. Worse, if the shuttle had a catastrophic failure, Centaur's plutonium fuel could be strewn across populated areas. Whether anyone at NASA believed this could happen or not, responsible planning meant that the contingency had to be accounted for.

A number of clearances had to be obtained. Before RTGs could be flown on the shuttle, for example, the Department of Defense had to approve the safety of the mission. It was basing its clearance on the assumption that explosion of the orbiter was not a "credible failure mode."

Office of Space Science representatives then reported that flight safety was also under review by the Interagency Nuclear Safety Review Panel, which included the Departments of Energy and Defense, along with NASA. The panel would be preparing a confidential report for White House clearance that would be sent to the Office of Science and Technology Policy in the Executive Office of the President. The report was expected to reach the White House only two weeks before launch. Meanwhile, NASA planned to publish an environmental impact statement that would give the public the opportunity to comment on the safety issues and possibly seek a court injunction to halt the Galileo and Ulysses missions. It would then be up to a federal judge, likely in the District Court of the District of Columbia, to decide if the risk to the public was excessive.

At this point, Jesse Moore asked why, with a program in the works for years, had NASA waited until the last minute to obtain the essential White House clearance and to issue an environmental impact statement with a mandatory public comment period?

This question was met by silence. After a few awkward moments, the Office of Space Science representatives spoke up. They assured Moore that all would go well, because a draft of the Safety Review Panel's report would be given to the White House for advance review. They also produced a letter from Department of Defense Under Secretary William Howard Taft IV to Administrator James Beggs. In the letter, Taft promised his "personal assistance" in expediting the required clearances, because, as he wrote, the Department of Defense wanted to clear the way for its own use of radioactive devices in space under the Strategic Defense Initiative (SDI) program. I realized when I heard this that Taft was not writing about RTGs. What SDI planners were contemplating was nuclear weapons in space.

The two days of meetings closed with a commentary by Jesse Moore on the large amount of work yet to be done and the need for maximum cooperation among the NASA centers. Then came a final discussion of safety. My notes from earlier in the day read, "Fully aware of dangers. Fully accepted by crew and NASA centers."

Now, in retrospect, after the Challenger disaster of January 28, 1986, followed by the cancellation of Centaur, the cancellation of the filament wound case, the abandonment of the Vandenberg military launch site, the decision by the Clinton administration to cease use of the shuttle for military missions and for the launch of commercial satellites, and, eventually, the loss of Columbia in the re-entry disaster of

February 1, 2003, can it be said that the attitude of "fully accepting" the dangers posed by the kind of situation NASA faced in the Centaur program—can it be said that this was truly a responsible attitude?

The answer has to be it was not. It is not responsible for anyone, even astronauts whose lives are at risk, to court that risk if it is based on bad decisions. It is irresponsible and immoral to risk other people's lives, or even your own, in order to meet objectives based merely on politics, or scheduling expediency, or face-saving, or career advancement, or fear of being ridiculed, or saving money, or any similar reason that itself is not a matter of life or death. Life is too valuable to be trivialized in this way. And that is what was going on in this meeting. The risk was being trivialized. In no way was it a matter of life or death to anyone that Galileo and Ulysses launch on the current schedule.

This was shown by what Jesse Moore said next. Looking around the room, he remarked:

> KSC, JSC, and Lewis all have to work safety. I'm not sure we're not doing a lot of arm waving. We need to get everything on the table. It needs a much sharper focus. There are major open safety questions right now.

For the top man in the manned space program to label the previous nine hours of serious, sober discussion as "arm waving" sent a clear message to me and perhaps others.

Moore was answered by a JSC representative, who said bluntly, "I think we have a serious problem."

Again, Moore answered. "But the wagons are loaded."

Mal Peterson, who was also representing Code B at the meetings, turned to me at one point and said, "When Centaur is launched and it's a success, all will be forgiven." To Peterson, a Centaur failure was simply incomprehensible, even though he had been tracking and reporting on the hardware problems for months.

It was then agreed that the next major review of the status of the two Centaur launches would take place at Kennedy in March. Nothing was said about how, in the meantime, the multitude of serious problems would be tracked or reported. But even as many of NASA's top managers discussed the safety and hardware issues that threatened Centaur, the forces were gathering by which Challenger, waiting on launch pad

39-B, would be destroyed. Somewhere in far-away Canada a wintry pocket of frigid air was forming that in less than two weeks would envelope Florida in an unseasonable cold spell.

For me to have attended the two days of meetings at Kennedy was the high point of my NASA tenure, but I noticed something that sent chills down my spine. When I walked out of the conference room in the executive suite, I saw a photograph of William Graham hanging on the wall. Graham had arrived just weeks ago as deputy to Administrator James Beggs. But within days, Beggs had been indicted for alleged proprieties on a military procurement contract he had supervised while an executive at General Dynamics.

In December, Beggs took a leave of absence from NASA in order to prepare his defense in his expected trial. This was a shocking event to everyone at NASA. Beggs was not viewed as a great manager—he was too aloof and distant to be seen as that—but he was a graduate of the Naval Academy, a space program veteran, and, to all appearances, a man of integrity. Graham was now acting administrator, but he was someone with no space program experience, whose background was in the more obscure aspects of nuclear weapons research, and whose appointment by the White House Beggs was known to have opposed.

Early in the morning of both the 16th and the 17th of January, Mal Peterson and I rode with some other headquarters visitors to the shuttle landing strip to watch Columbia return from orbit on the 61-C mission. Both times Columbia was waved off due to forecasts of turbulent weather. Out on the runway, it was windy, and the clouds looked unsettled, but there was no rain either day. Columbia was forced to land at Edwards Air Force Base in California early on the morning of the 18th. I did not know it at the time, but the Edwards landing also forced a delay in the Challenger launch.

My visit to Kennedy included a tour on the afternoon of Friday, January 17, of the Vehicle Assembly Building where the shuttle orbiters were mated to the external tank and solid rocket boosters before being rolled out to the launch pad. I then was taken on a drive by one of the NASA site managers around both the Kennedy Space Center and the adjacent Air Force base on Cape Canaveral. We stopped for a walk-through of the buildings where the SRBs were broken down into their component segments after being recovered from the ocean following a shuttle launch. The site manager told me of the difficulties he faced in getting timely support in moving the SRB segments from place to place from Lockheed, the overall shuttle flow contractor.

I returned to Washington, D.C., on NASA-One, the agency's executive jet. We flew from the shuttle runway and reached home in a couple of hours. On the plane, I sat with a genial group from the Office of Space Science. We drank ginger ale and ate peanuts, as I perused their interesting letter from William Howard Taft IV promising help in getting the nuclear generators for Galileo and Ulysses into space.

By Friday evening, I was back at National Airport, where I had parked the family car. I had an alternate driver for my vanpool, who had been in charge of getting my passengers to and from work while I was away. In a couple of more hours I was back home in King George looking forward to the weekend in the country.

Our family had now been living in the house on Round Hill Road for almost three months. We were in an isolated neighborhood with about eight other houses. Though the houses were small, they each had a good bit of land, while across the road was a huge expanse of forest and marsh that extended to the next county in the direction of the town of Colonial Beach and the Potomac River. Down the road toward the King George courthouse area there were small farms with horses and other livestock. The courthouse was about seven miles distant, with the Southern States feed and hardware store on the way.

I spent the next week at work bringing my Centaur history up-to-date, with details from the January 16-17 meetings at Kennedy. Then came another pleasant weekend at home, which included watching the Super Bowl on Sunday where the Chicago Bears defeated the New England Patriots at the Superdome in New Orleans.

Now it was Tuesday, January 28, and I sat working at my desk, with lunch not far off. I was talking to one of the resource analysts at Code M and had asked him the number of the contract to which General Dynamics had improperly shifted the overtime charges I had heard about.

"I don't have it right in front of me," he said. "I'll get it, though. Do you want to hold on?"

There was a shuttle launch that morning, so I said, "Why don't we take a break? I want to watch the launch. I'll call you back this afternoon."

"Okay," he said, and we hung up.

I walked down the hall and around the corner to the news auditorium. I had been particularly interested in this launch because of Teacher-in-Space Christa McAuliffe. Both NASA and the press had been giving her flight a lot of publicity, much more so than other recent shuttle launches, which were starting to seem almost routine. I liked Christa. She seemed like a great person, and she had come to the Washington, D.C., area the same time I did in 1970 to teach school. Later she had moved to New Hampshire. With her going aloft I'd even had my own fantasy about someday being the first resource analyst in space.

There were about twenty people in the auditorium watching the countdown on NASA Select television. Three or four of them were from my division. The TV monitors showed Challenger sitting on the pad.

I sat down and watched the remaining countdown. I had not been following the run-up to the launch and so had not heard anything the networks were reporting about the cold snap that had hit Florida overnight.

I had arrived just in time for the launch. The shuttle lifted off. It was an emotional sight as the announcer spoke. This was what it was all about, why everyone here worked as hard as they did. "Lift-off. Lift-off of the twenty-fifth space shuttle mission, and it has cleared the tower."

I watched as Challenger rose in the sky. It looked huge and silent. Watching a U.S. manned space launch was a moving experience.

After about a minute, the camera angle shifted—NASA had planes up there with cameras to track the shuttle until after the solid rocket boosters separated. Suddenly there were hissing and popping noises, like firecrackers. The screen filled with what looked like smoke.

"Oh my God!" shouted someone in the room.

That's just the boosters separating, I thought. But I was wrong. "Stuff" of some kind was flying around in the sky. I could not believe what I was seeing. A few seconds more and the voice came: "Obviously a major malfunction. We have no downlink." Then: "We have a report from the flight dynamics officer that the vehicle has exploded."

PART II

HISTORY

"FIRST YOU HAVE TO GET THE HORSE"

—How America Decided to Build the Space Shuttle

THE U.S. MANNED space program, as it developed from the time NASA was established by the National Aeronautics and Space Act of 1958 to the last Apollo mission, the joint American-U.S.S.R. Apollo-Soyuz orbital flight in July 1975, was based on single-use capsules launched by gigantic one-shot rockets. This changed dramatically with the space shuttle.

But years before the reusable shuttle was created, rocket scientists saw the advantages of someday being able to retrieve manned vehicles from space to be used again. As in so many areas, the foremost pioneer was Dr. Wernher von Braun, the German rocket scientist who became the director of NASA's new rocket engineering facility, the Marshall Space Flight Center, at Huntsville, Alabama, in 1960.

By then, von Braun had already described a three-stage system that would service an Earth-orbiting space station. The third stage, resembling the future shuttle orbiter, would be a winged spaceship that would land on an airstrip at the end of its mission and carry six crew members. Ocean-going ships would recover its spent booster stages for reuse. The similarities between von Braun's early conception and NASA's eventual space shuttle were striking.

Meanwhile, the brief epoch of expendable manned spacecraft reached its apogee on July 20, 1969, when NASA made good on President John F. Kennedy's 1962 pledge that the U.S. would place a man on the moon and return him safely to Earth before the end of the decade. But moon shots were expensive. Each Apollo lunar mission cost the U.S. taxpayer a billion dollars. Even a single launch of a Saturn V moon rocket cost $300 million.

By the late 1960s, NASA's spaceflight managers were aware that the White House and Congress would soon stop writing blank checks for space extravaganzas. The Mercury, Gemini, and Apollo programs had been conceived and born in a mood of national ebullience—Kennedy's New Frontier and Johnson's Great Society—but they were overtaken by the massive U.S. commitment to an Asian land war in Vietnam. By the time Neil Armstrong set foot on the moon, the bubble was about to burst. The Vietnam War divided the nation and cost the Democratic Party the presidency. Lyndon Johnson, who was instrumental in providing the congressional support for NASA in the first place, was gone. The Republicans under President Richard M. Nixon were now in power.

Even before the 1969 Apollo 11 moon landing, President Nixon had appointed a Space Task Group to study the future of U.S. manned spaceflight. It filed its report in September 1969, only two months after Apollo 11 touched down on the lunar surface. Few informed observers outside NASA took its prime recommendation seriously. It was for a gargantuan follow-on to Apollo that would create a fifty-man Earth-orbiting space station, along with a second but smaller station to circle the moon and service a manned lunar base. Ambitious though the plan was, it was merely a prelude to the more far-reaching objective described in the report, which was a manned mission to Mars by 1985. Service vehicles would include a reuseable cargo carrier to "shuttle" between the Earth and the space station and a "space tug" to journey back and forth from the Earth-orbiting station to the moon base.

Mars was the goal, with the shuttle and space station as steps toward getting there. Whatever NASA's ups-and-downs in the years to come, the recommendation of the Space Task Group for a manned voyage to Mars would remain. In 1988, two years after the Challenger disaster, former NASA administrator and Space Task Group member Thomas Paine would say, "There's no question that Mars is the great destination of humanity for the 21st century." And when in September 2005, NASA described the manned program to succeed the shuttle, Mars was still the objective.

The Space Task Group described a "Space Transportation System" as a means to "carry passengers, supplies, rocket fuel, other spacecraft, equipment, or additional rocket stages to and from orbit on a routine, aircraft-like basis." This would be "a low unit-mission-cost transportation system that would make Earth-moon space easily and economically accessible to man for his use for exploration, applications, science, and technology research."

But when President Nixon answered the Space Task Group in a White House message in March 1970, his choice was much less ambitious. Nixon agreed that a goal of the U.S. space program should be to reduce the cost of space operations and that NASA would study proposals for the space station and shuttle. But there would be no specific exploration projects, and there would be no Mars expedition.

Nixon's public formulation of his space policy did not mention military priorities. Behind the scenes, however, a different scenario was unfolding. NASA and the Nixon administration were already viewing the not-yet-approved shuttle as a large, versatile spacecraft for both civilian and military uses. This policy was a substantial departure from the separation of civilian and military functions mandated by the National Aeronautics and Space Act of 1958 and supported by Presidents Eisenhower, Kennedy, and Johnson. The Act established NASA as a research and development agency to serve a highly idealistic mission. Section 102(a) stated, "The Congress hereby declares that it is the policy of the United States that activities in space should be devoted to peaceful purposes for the benefit of mankind."

The Act made a clear demarcation between the responsibilities of NASA and those of the Department of Defense. Section 102(b) stated:

> The Congress further declares that such activities shall be the responsibility of, and shall be directed by, a civilian agency exercising control over aeronautical and space activities sponsored by the United States, except that activities peculiar to or primarily associated with the development of weapons systems, military operations, or the defense of the United States (including the research and development

necessary to make effective provision for the defense of the United States) shall be the responsibility of, and shall be directed by, the Department of Defense.

The act provided for research conducted by NASA to be utilized for military purposes, but during the Mercury, Gemini, and Apollo programs NASA's flights did not carry military payloads. This practice would change with the space shuttle and was a major contributing factor to the Challenger disaster.

The decision by the Nixon administration to combine civil and military functions in a single space vehicle under central NASA management was a major compromise of U.S. space policy, one which institutionalized Cold War politics at the agency. Congress debated but never acted on the militarization issue, even though under the National Aeronautics and Space Act of 1958, Nixon's actions could have been challenged as unwise, if not illegal.

The Defense Department, chiefly the Air Force, had to be forced by the White House to support the new policy of combining civilian and military payloads in the same manned vehicle. So it was not surprising that in the early conceptual stages, NASA drastically altered the shuttle's design to meet military performance requirements.

NASA needed the Air Force more than the Air Force needed it, particularly when it became evident in the cost-conscious environment of the 1970s that the only way to justify a major new manned spaceflight program was to spread costs over a large number of flights. NASA aimed its sales pitch at the Air Force by promising higher performance than expendable rockets.

This gave the Air Force leverage when it came to shuttle design. In fact, the NASA/Air Force bargain had already been struck by the time the Space Task Group met in 1969. The agreement was outlined by Mike Yarymovych, deputy assistant secretary of defense for space:

NASA needed Air Force support, both for payloads and in Congress. I told Mueller [i.e., George Mueller, NASA's associate administrator for manned space flight] we'd support the shuttle, but only if he gave us the big payload bay and the cross-range capability, so we could return to Vandenberg after a single orbit. Mueller knew that would mean changing

Max Faget's beloved straight-wing design into a delta wing, but he had no choice. He agreed.

If the Air Force was to be forced by political and financial pressure to utilize the shuttle, it wanted to launch it into polar orbit from Vandenberg Air Force Base on the California coast. The shuttle would also have a large payload bay—15 x 60 feet—sufficient to deliver a big spy satellite to orbit. The performance implications of these decisions were severe and led to major changes in NASA's plans. Besides changing the shape of the orbiter from a straight-wing to a delta—i.e., triangular—wing design, the added weight would make it more difficult to deflect the enormous temperatures generated when the orbiter reentered the Earth's atmosphere. This would mean a higher performance threshold on the orbiter's heat-shield, making the thermal protection system—TPS—a virtual Achilles heel.

Extra demands would also be placed on the propulsion systems. The shuttle would have to be bigger, faster, heavier, and bulkier than it would be just for civilian uses. So it would be less safe. The changes to support military missions also added twenty percent to the cost of shuttle development and operations.

In 1971, Thomas Paine stepped down as NASA's administrator. Paine had shared with Dr. Wernher von Braun the conviction that the destiny of the space program lay with manned interplanetary travel. Paine's successor, Dr. James Fletcher, held a doctorate in physics from the California Institute of Technology and had been president of the University of Utah since 1964. But characteristic of the shift in NASA's direction during the Nixon administration, Fletcher had specialized in military weapons research for several major aerospace firms. He started his career at Hughes Aircraft in 1948 and worked in the 1950s on ICBM development. He held ninety-nine patents in sonar devices, guided missile systems, and other aerospace specialties and had published extensively on such topics as underwater sound, explosive yields in standard soils, radar scattering, ground clutter, and missile guidance analysis.

Fletcher served as NASA's administrator during the remainder of the Nixon-Ford years. Later, as a consultant to the Reagan administration, he led a study on the feasibility of a space-based missile defense system that was the starting point for the Strategic Defense Initiative—

"Star Wars"—program. Finally, Fletcher returned to head NASA in 1986 after the Challenger disaster.

Fletcher's tenure at NASA was another indication that conversion of the manned space program to military purposes was in the works. Following his arrival at NASA in 1971, Fletcher continued the effort to hold onto Air Force support of the shuttle. In a December 11, 1971, letter to Deputy Secretary of Defense David Packard, he wrote:

> The shuttle could be maintained on ready alert, making possible rapid responses to foreseeable and expected situations and greatly increase flexibility and timeliness of response to military or techno-logical surprises, such as: a) rapid recovery and replacement of a faulty or failed spacecraft essential to national security; b) examination of unidentified and suspicious orbiting objectives; c) capture, disable-ment, or destruction of unfriendly spacecraft; d) rapid examination of crucial situations developing on earth or in space whenever such events are observable from an orbiting spacecraft; and e) rescue or relief of stranded or ill astronauts.

Fletcher had already adopted a version of the new space vehicle known as the thrust-assisted orbital shuttle—TAOS—with an externally-mounted fuel tank for the orbiter's main engines and two unmanned strap-on booster stages. TAOS was essentially the shuttle that exists today. According to studies by Mathematica, a consulting firm NASA hired to analyze the economics of shuttle construction, the system could be built for $6 billion—OMB agreed to fund $5.5 billion—with a cost per launch of only $6 million.

Unfortunately, this cost per launch was based on a wildly exaggerated flight rate—a total of 714 flights during the planned 1978-90 "payback" period. This would come to fifty-nine flights per year, more than one per week. To arrive at this number, NASA would have to fly the shuttle for every conceivable use, including civilian and military satellites, space launches for other nations, orbital space science research, planetary probes like the Mariner spacecraft, and such commercial projects as space-based manufacturing and electrical power generation. After the Challenger disaster, Dr. Richard Feynman, a member of the Presidential Commission on the Space Shuttle Challenger Accident, labeled

NASA's projections from the early 1970s a "fantasy." But at least NASA would get its "horse." As space scientist, author, and publicist Jerry Grey is reported to have said, "First you have to get the horse, then you decide where to ride him."

There was a final hurdle for NASA to clear before President Nixon gave the shuttle the final go-ahead. Staffers at the Office of Management and Budget had been impressed with how quickly and creatively NASA cranked out alternative shuttle designs when presented with reduced cost options. What would happen, OMB now wondered, if development costs were cut even further, say to $3 to $4 billion? This would have meant a smaller orbiter with a 14 x 45 foot payload bay, an option Administrator Fletcher seemed willing to accept. After all, it would have been a safer, more flexible machine.

But such changes in shuttle design would have eroded military capability to an unacceptable degree. The Air Force, for instance, would have to retain the unmanned Titan 2 to launch its largest reconnaissance satellites. It was time to lock the OMB staff back in their cages, when OMB Director George Schultz came out in favor of the larger payload bay. So, reportedly, did National Security Adviser Henry Kissinger, Domestic Policy Adviser John Ehrlichman, and the president himself.

Later, Ehrlichman recalled that "a strong influence was what the military could do with the larger bay in terms of the uses of satellites," and "the capability of capturing satellites or recovering them." Still, Nixon reportedly told Fletcher that the civilian side of the shuttle should be played up. The president also liked the idea that with the benign shuttle design, making the flight to orbit an easier ride than with single-use capsules, ordinary people would now be able to go to space, not just professional astronauts. These approaches to characterizing the shuttle continued until the Challenger disaster.

On January 5, 1972, ten months before running for reelection, President Nixon inaugurated the shuttle program by declaring:

> The United States should proceed at once with the development of an entirely new type of Space Transportation System designed to help transform the space frontier of the 1970s into familiar territory, easily accessible for human endeavor in the 1980s and 90s. . . . It will revolutionize

transportation into near space by routinizing it. . . . It will take the astro-
nomical costs out of astronautics. . . .

The system will center on a space vehicle that can shuttle repeatedly
from Earth to orbit and back. . . . It will go a long way toward delivering the rich benefits of practical space use and the valuable spinoffs from
space efforts into the daily lives of Americans and all people. . . .

This is why commitment to the space shuttle program is the right
next step for America to take in moving out from our present beachhead
in the sky to achieve a real working presence in space. It will make the
ride safer and less demanding for the passengers, so that men and
women with work to do in space can commute aloft without having to
spend years in training.

Nixon did not mention military uses of the shuttle, though the
shuttle he approved was heavily influenced by political and military
considerations, not just technical ones. And the $5.5 billion funding
level would hold NASA to a rigid developmental budget inadequate for
thorough design and testing. This would ensure a running battle
between NASA and OMB and Congress that continued until Challenger blew up, along with deep cuts to space science to fund overruns.
With design compromises, underfunding, and the disingenuous promises of more than one shuttle flight per week, NASA, under the direction of President Richard Nixon and Administrator James Fletcher, dug
a hole it never climbed out of, one that in the long run produced a
national fiasco.

———

NASA NOW MOVED to gain congressional approval of the final shuttle design. On November 6, 1972, agency officials told the House Committee on Science and Astronautics that the first manned orbital flight
would take place in March 1978, following the first atmospheric glide
tests in mid-1977. The shuttle fleet would be "operational" by 1979, they
said. Flight rate figures had been revised upward so that between 1980
and 1991, the shuttle would fly 581 times at a cost of $43.1 billion.
NASA said the same missions using expendable rockets would cost
$48.3 billion.

NASA's new associate administrator for manned space flight was Dale Myers, former Apollo manager for North American Aviation, the Apollo prime contractor. Myers gave Congress the remarkable assurance that the shuttle could be built with no new technological breakthroughs. It was the same script NASA and General Dynamics would read from several years later when they sold Congress on the shuttle-Centaur.

But there were four areas where groundbreaking technological development would soon be underway.

First, NASA was planning a rocket engine radically different from its predecessors. The space shuttle main engines (SSMEs) would burn liquid hydrogen with liquid oxygen as the oxidizer. These fuels had never been fired at ground level before—in earlier manned space flights, cryogenics were used only for the upper stages. With cryogenics there was greater danger of explosion when fired on the launch pad than with rockets powered by liquid fuel at ambient air temperature.

The new engines would boast extremely high thrust for their size, so that the thrust-to-weight ratio—"specific impulse"—would be the highest ever. Three of these monsters would be shoehorned into the shuttle orbiter's tail section. The result would be enormous internal operating pressures—3,000 pounds per square inch in the combustion chamber—the highest of any engine ever developed. The engine's high-pressure pumps would be capable of emptying an Olympic-size swimming pool in twenty-five seconds.

The SSMEs had to be lightweight and reusable, though no rocket engine had ever been used more than once. They would be built for fifty-five flights, firing eight minutes each time. This was an engine life of seven-and-a-half hours, a figure then unheard of.

The second innovation was the solid rocket boosters. The most decisive factor in designing and building any type of rocket is what kind of fuel it will use. Making this choice has critical implications for vehicle weight, performance capabilities, length and control of burn, relative safety, and other factors. When the decision was made to build the space shuttle, NASA had not yet decided how the strap-on booster rockets would be powered. They would be needed only for the first two minutes of flight, yet were indispensable for the manned vehicle to reach the velocity required for orbital insertion. Three types of rocket could meet the thrust requirements. These were a liquid-fuel kerosene-based stage; a more complex cryogenic stage fueled, like the SSMEs, by supercooled hydrogen and oxygen; or large military-style solid rockets like those on the Titan 3.

The first two could be shut down if something went wrong, so they would be safer. They would also be cheaper to operate. But the solids would be simpler and less costly to develop. This would appear to offer a short-term advantage to a program squeezed for funds from the start. There was also an advantage to the solid-fuel rockets in that it was more likely the casings could be recovered and reused. Liquid-fuel rockets would be more difficult to refurbish for future flights because the complex plumbing would be more prone to damage upon ocean impact. A complication from any type of reusable rocket would be that they could only be made practicable if they were built in segments. Otherwise they would be too bulky to move from one place to another as they were being refurbished and refueled. Ominously, segmentation would require some kind of joint sealing system to prevent burnthroughs.

NASA officials said they decided to use solid rocket boosters because this would cut development costs for the shuttle almost in half. NASA wrote in a 1979 publication, "in the face of tight budgets, the decision seemed obvious." The choice was made by Administrator James Fletcher in March 1972. Thiokol, Inc.—later Morton Thiokol—which made the solid rocket boosters, was located in Fletcher's home state of Utah, where the company manufactured solids for the Minuteman and Trident missiles. During the contractor selection process, NASA's staff evaluators ranked the Thiokol product third among all competitors in technical design. But it was the lowest-priced bid.

The decision to use solid rocket boosters was not supported by Wernher von Braun, who had been moved out of the directorship of the Marshall Space Flight Center to a desk job in Washington, D.C., in 1971. Von Braun had guided NASA's rocketry for a decade, during which there had not been a single primary propulsion failure on a manned space launch.

NASA transferred von Braun out of Marshall around the time the agency was retrenching under Fletcher to the $5.5 billion shuttle. Fletcher made von Braun the deputy assistant associate administrator for planning at headquarters. In the federal government, such a title is immediately recognizable as a non-job for someone they hope will go away, which von Braun did within a year.

Von Braun retired from NASA in 1972 to become a vice president of Fairchild Republic, an aerospace firm. He died of cancer in June 1977, a few weeks before the first atmospheric gliding test of Enterprise, the shuttle prototype. Following the Challenger disaster, in the wake of the horrendous publicity blanketing the Marshall Space Flight Center, some who had worked with von Braun moved quickly to extinguish any suggestion that he or his team may have played a part. On June 13, 1986, the *Huntsville Times* printed the following letter from a man named Erich Hartmann:

> Your June 8 article entitled "Tragic Price" was disturbing to me, because it seemed to imply that somehow the original von Braun group shares responsibility for the Challenger disaster. Such an insinuation is not only incorrect, but shameful.
>
> As you will recall, in 1971, von Braun was promoted to a higher position in Washington, and, as a result, no longer had any control of the Marshall Center. This move was disastrous, because within two years almost all the original German scientists had been forced into retirement. NASA officials politely called it "early retirement."
>
> The Rogers Commission states that the booster problems go back as early as 1973. I can also tell you that many of those "old" scientists were glad to have left NASA, since many objected, and were overruled by managers, to the initial booster design.

The third innovation on the space shuttle was a new type of thermal protection system (TPS) to shield the orbiter from atmospheric reentry temperatures approaching 3,000 degrees F. The ablative materials that charred away and protected the astronauts during reentry in the earlier manned space capsules were not suitable for a reusable vehicle. It would cost too much to give the orbiter a new coating each time it flew.

The fourth new and challenging requirement was for a computerized flight control system that would allow the shuttle to be flown during reentry like an airplane. With the absence of atmospheric flight engines, though, the shuttle pilots would be making what is called in avionics a "dead-stick" landing. In other words, you only get one chance to hit the runway, because you cannot pull out of a descent and try again.

The design challenge that was never solved was crew escape. The plan President Nixon approved in 1972 was the first U.S. manned space vehicle without an escape system. During the shuttle's first four experimental flights in 1981-2, the two-man crew would have ejection seats, but even these could be used only after the shuttle lifted off from the launch pad. These seats were removed for subsequent flights, because it would be unconscionable for the commander and pilot to eject to safety in case of a mishap while the rest of the crew rode to their deaths. Ejection seats would also make the vehicle too heavy, especially for flights with big military satellites.

But having no plan is itself a plan. Greg Easterbrook pointed this out in his 1980 article, "The Spruce Goose of Outer Space," in the *Washington Monthly*, an article intensely critical of the shuttle program and design. Writing of the solid rocket boosters, he noted that given the shuttle design there was no way the crew could escape if the boosters malfunctioned. "What is the plan?" he asked. "The plan is, you die," which is exactly what happened with Challenger.

North American Rockwell, selected as the prime contractor, started building the prototype shuttle in mid-1974. This was Enterprise, the ship that would be used in the 1977 gliding tests. The shuttle program was now virtually invisible to Congress and the public, which was losing interest in manned spaceflight anyway. In 1972, Apollo 17 had made the last voyage to the moon, ending the lunar exploration program. In 1973 came the three successful manned Skylab missions that set new records for human endurance in space, followed by Apollo-Soyuz, the orbital docking operation between U.S. and Soviet spacecraft, the last U.S. manned mission prior to the shuttle. With the hiatus in manned voyages, NASA placed its focus on unmanned planetary probes to Jupiter, Saturn, Venus, and Mercury, the spectacular photographs and scientific data sent back from Mars by Viking 1 and 2, and the birth of the new science of comparative planetology. But NASA's early golden age of manned space exploration was over.

Shuttle development and testing now seemed to be going well, or so NASA said. There were sporadic cost overruns, but they were obscured by reshuffling funds within the NASA budget and by reductions of testing in areas that seemed to be going smoothly.

NASA ran into numerous testing problems during the early development period, but managed to downplay them. By January 1977, the space shuttle was a Carter administration program—and problem—and

Dr. Robert Frosch succeeded James Fletcher as NASA's administrator. Frosch was a physicist with degrees from Columbia University and former director of Columbia's Hudson Laboratories, which performed research under contract to the U.S. Navy. When Frosch arrived, NASA and the shuttle program were in trouble. The General Accounting Office had reported to Congress:

> The space shuttle is being developed under a different management philosophy. In order of priority, cost had become one of the most important concerns, and, as a result, test programs have been curtailed. Previous NASA programs contained more extensive and timely testing, and other management factors, including mission accomplishment, had priority over cost.

Publicly, shuttle development seemed to be rolling along. In 1977 the test prototype Enterprise was carried aloft over the California desert by NASA's Boeing 747 and cut loose for the first free-flight gliding tests. Space shuttle Enterprise was so named by President Gerald Ford because of a clamor by Star Trek fans to have the first orbiter be a salute to their TV heroes.

Despite this success, problems with the main engines were retarding the project. As early as May 1975, a report by a NASA advisory panel had pointed to the unique technical requirements that NASA had glossed over in reports to Congress. By September 1975, NASA had completed only thirteen of the 964 engine tests required for flight certification. The agency was still holding to a March 1979 launch date for the first orbital mission, but engine development costs were starting to overrun.

Under the 1971 plan, the main engines were to be operational by the first suborbital test flights. They were not. From March 24, 1977, to November 4, 1979, there were fourteen engine test failures. The engines had problems with faulty seals, uneven bearing loads, cracked turbine blades, cracked fuel injector posts, broken heat exchangers, valve failures, and hydrogen line ruptures. In several cases, engines exploded. Eight failures resulted in fires on the test stand. The first time three engines were fired together, they all blew up. NASA had to double the number of test engines it ordered from Rocketdyne. The company had no problem complying with the demand for more hardware and sending NASA and the taxpayer the bill.

For a while in 1978, NASA believed it might be getting back on schedule. On July 21, 1978, a three-engine cluster similar to what might actually be fired on the shuttle ran for the first time for 100 seconds. There were three successive firings at 100 percent of rated power, and on October 23 an engine ran for 823 seconds. This was how long a single engine would have to fire at shuttle lift-off if the two others failed and still leave hope of a safe launch abort. By the end of fiscal year 1978, total engine test time was 34,810 seconds compared to the 80,000 needed for certification for orbital launch. But further test problems stalled the program again.

Engineers were now calling the test program "hardware starved," as schedules slipped further. By the winter of 1978, it was clear that the first orbital flight could not take place before November 1979. Soon engineers were convinced that the shuttle would not be ready until well into 1980. Some were afraid the engine pumps would have to be redesigned, but money had run out. Administrator Frosch and his deputy, Dr. Alan Lovelace, were beginning a series of treks up Independence Avenue to Capitol Hill to ask Congress for supplemental appropriations to cover the overruns.

Design problems had also been disclosed with the external tank, leading to more delays and cost overruns. The only major piece of shuttle hardware that seemed relatively trouble-free at this stage was the solid rocket boosters. Problems did arise at one point in the design of the nozzle lining that would later cause a near-catastrophe on the eighth shuttle mission, but for now that concern seemed to have been resolved. O-ring heat effects in the joints between the solid rocket booster case segments would later start showing up as early as the second shuttle mission, but these did not occur in the development or qualification test firings. These firings, however, did not fully replicate launch pressures and conditions, including potential low temperatures at launch.

The unexpected but potentially alarming loss of joint redundancy where primary and secondary O-rings were situated inside the joints occurred in a 1977 hydroburst test. But all but a few engineers at the Marshall Space Flight Center ignored its significance. Later, this flaw would be a chief contributor to the Challenger explosion, but it did not prevent the design from being accepted.

Then there was the TPS. NASA had decided on two types of orbiter tile. The surfaces that would experience the greatest heat—approaching 3,000 degrees F—were the nose tip and the leading edge of the wings. These would be covered with a material called "carbon-carbon," a graphite cloth embedded in pyrolitic graphite, one of the most heat-resistant substances known to man, and coated with silicon carbide. The other surfaces would be coated with more simple tiles made of silica fibers with a film of borosilicate glass—roughly, hardened sand. 31,000 tiles would be glued onto each orbiter, each tile of a slightly different shape to conform to the curves of the fuselage.

The tiles were exceptionally difficult to manufacture and install, and NASA's fear was that they would fall off under the tremendous dynamic stresses encountered at lift-off or be damaged by falling debris, including ice, insulation, or contaminants in the atmosphere or space. This could leave the orbiter circling the earth with a hole in its shield and the prospect of burning and breaking up as soon as it reentered the atmosphere. Even a small burnthrough could penetrate the crew cabin and cause a fatal depressurization. Once the shuttle began to fly, a burnthrough did in fact occur, though on a relatively harmless section of the wing. But the possibility of a catastrophic incident was foreseen from the beginning. Such an event destroyed the orbiter Columbia on February 1, 2003, seven years after the Challenger disaster.

More main engine problems now appeared. In the fall of 1979, a hydrogen leak and other problems caused tests to be postponed for six months on the main propulsion test article, a three-engine cluster to be fired for final flight qualification. On November 4, the engines cut off on a test after only nine seconds, when excessively high pressure in an oxygen pump led to a fire following rupture of a hydrogen line. NASA found that the cause was "improperly-dimensioned" welding wire due to a supplier's mistake. All the engines in inventory had to be inspected for the same problem, including the three installed in Columbia. It was found that these engines also had the smaller welding wire. They had to be removed from Columbia's tail section, shipped back to Rocketdyne in California, and repaired.

1980 brought more engine troubles. While the ninth three-engine firing at Marshall's National Space Technology Laboratory in Bay St. Louis, Mississippi, was a success, the tenth failed in July when a preburner was eaten through, which shut down the cluster. Overheating and a nozzle burnthrough aborted the next three-engine test in November.

But by late 1980, NASA seemed to be turning the corner in getting the shuttle ready to fly. A 1981 launch looked feasible. On November 24, 1980, less than three weeks after Ronald Reagan defeated Jimmy Carter for the presidency, Columbia was rolled out of the orbiter processing facility at the Kennedy Space Center and moved to the refurbished Vehicle Assembly Building to be mated to its external tank and solid rocket boosters.

No space vehicle in history had taken so long or cost so much to develop. More than a decade had passed since studies began in 1969. Many of the workers who were now bringing Columbia to the launch pad had been children when America first went to space twenty years earlier.

But the main reason the problems with the development of the shuttle had not resulted in its cancellation was its planned military uses. By 1978, test programs, delays, and cost overruns connected with the program were so bad that some on Capitol Hill tried to finish it off for good. That challenge had been deflected in large measure by the Carter administration's claim that the shuttle was needed to carry up additional spy satellites for the Pentagon during SALT II arms control negotiations with the Soviets.

The Defense Department's position was expressed by Dr. William J. Perry, undersecretary of defense for research and engineering (later a secretary of defense under President Clinton), who told a June 1979 hearing of the House Subcommittee on Space Science and Applications:

> The Defense Department is becoming increasingly dependent, first of all, on space and as time goes by, on specifically the shuttle. Our dependence on space for navigation, communications, early warning, surveillance, and weather forecasting [will become] increasingly greater in the decade of the 80s. We [will begin] in 1982 to transition to the shuttle vehicle, and ultimately we will be conducting all of our space operations with the shuttle.

Perry said that in the next ten years, the Defense Department foresaw 113 shuttle launches in order to meet its needs and that the number would reach fifteen per year by the end of that period. Defense would replace all expendable rockets with the shuttle and would be totally dependent on it for satellite launches by the mid-1980s. To maintain control and security over shuttle launches, the Air Force would have its own consolidated space operations center—CSOC (pronounced "See-Sock")—that it was building at Colorado Springs, Colorado, at a cost of $500 million. CSOC would also provide back-up in case NASA's mission control at the Johnson Space Center in Houston were disabled or attacked in wartime. The 100,000 square-foot CSOC facility would be encased in steel so the Soviet Union could not intercept its computer signals.

But the career military officers in charge of the Air Force's unmanned reconnaissance communications satellite systems viewed the official shuttle policy with disgust. They saw the shuttle—and NASA—as offering neither reliability nor economy. One of these was Dr. Robert Bowman, then a lieutenant colonel in charge of what the Reagan administration later made the Strategic Defense Initiative— "Star Wars"—program. Later director of the Institute of Space and Security Studies in Chesapeake Beach, Maryland, and an actor in the post-Challenger controversy over politicization of the shuttle program, Bowman wrote after retiring in 1984:

> The peacetime nature of our space assets was reinforced by the decision to compel the Air Force to design all its new satellites for launch on the space shuttle. Over the vehement opposition of the military, the space shuttle was crammed down the throats of the program offices responsible for operational satellite systems. At the time, this was deemed necessary in order to justify the shuttle financially. And indeed, later in the development of the shuttle, the political and financial support of the Air Force was the only thing that saved it from cancellation. Time and again, Congress was forced to ante up more money to complete the shuttle development because of the total dependence of the Air Force on it— a dependence that had been thrust upon the Air Force to create just this situation. The shuttle, of course, is so vulnerable that it is inconceivable that the U.S. could launch any new or replacement satellites once any

hostilities had broken out. . . . Similarly vulnerable is our capability to communicate with the shuttle and get data back from it or any of our other satellites.

NASA pushed the policy of becoming, in effect, a military contractor in order to maintain its manned presence in space. The policy, starting with the Nixon administration, was confirmed and extended by the Carter administration to assure continued funding at the time of delays and overruns. Then it was the Reagan administration that put the policy into operation.

"GET OUT OF OUR WAY"
—Operating the Shuttle Like a Scheduled Airline

I T WAS A time in American life when people believed that the job of Management, with a capital "M", was to set imaginative goals that organizations would then heroically strive to achieve. Top-down "management
by objectives" and its derivatives were the result. The business schools produced thousands of management consultants to implement such ideas.

A by-product seemed to have been a parting of the ways within
organizations, where managers became that class of people who
believed the hyperbole in the "strategic" and "tactical" plans. Meanwhile, the rest of the organization struggled to keep up, while
laughing—or crying—behind management's backs. And when a man
left the professional or technical ranks to "put on a management hat,"
funny things could and did happen. So it was with the space shuttle.

From STS-1 [STS stands for "Space Transportation System"], the first
orbital flight of Columbia that lifted off from the Kennedy Space Center
on April 12, 1981, to the explosion of Challenger in the 51-L mission on
January 28, 1986, NASA launched the space shuttle twenty-five times.

Prior to the first shuttle mission and again before the fifth, which was
the first to be designated as "operational," every NASA project and technical manager was required to sign a "verification completion notice,"

certifying that each piece of shuttle hardware met design and test specifications and was ready for use. There were problems everywhere you looked, including SRB O-ring erosion on the second shuttle flight. But the party line was that the shuttle was so safe it could be managed like a commercial airliner. It had been spoken of that way since the Space Task Group first recommended a shuttle in 1969. Why should reality now get in the way?

Starting with the first flight, the shuttle was a Reagan administration program. In July 1981, James Beggs became NASA's administrator, and it was Beggs, more than any other person, who became the driving force behind the operational strategy. He served until December 1985, when he was indicted for alleged procurement fraud from years earlier when he was an industry executive, on charges later dropped as baseless.

When Ronald Reagan became president, James Beggs was one of the nation's most experienced technology managers. As one of his first major personnel appointments at NASA, he named Major General James Abrahamson as his associate administrator for space flight, the top operational post. Beggs was a firm, distinguished executive and Abrahamson a positive-talking can-do manager, and both were determined that the space shuttle program would fully meet expectations. But even by the time of the first flights, when NASA was averaging over 100 days to prepare the shuttle to go into space for the next mission, it was clear that the decade-old goal of someday flying more than one mission per week was somebody's pipedream.

Even before becoming administrator, Beggs in 1980 had commissioned Dr. Robert Bowman to study NASA's space shuttle flight rate projections. As late as 1979, NASA was still claiming that the shuttle, when operational, would fly 472 times by 1994 at an average cost of $18 million per flight.

Beggs asked Bowman to calculate what really could be expected. Bowman's estimated flight rate was shockingly lower and projected costs much higher—200 flights by 1994 at $200 million each. For the near term, while NASA's projection was for 116 flights through December 31, 1985, Bowman foresaw only twenty-four for the same period. Remarkably, the actual number was twenty-three and would have been twenty-four had mission 61-C, the flight preceding Challenger, been launched on time instead of slipping for a month.

Clearly something had to be done. The pressure was on General Abrahamson to run through the experimental regime of the first four shuttle missions as quickly and efficiently as possible. The four experimental flights were completed on July 4, 1982, when flight commander Thomas Mattingly and pilot Henry Hartsfield, returning from the 112-orbit STS-4 mission, touched down on a dry lake bed at Edwards Air Force Base in California in front of President and Mrs. Reagan, a crowd of dignitaries, and 500,000 spectators. Also that day, the energetic General Abrahamson was promoted from major- to lieutenant-general.

In addition to NASA's urgency to make the Space Transportation System operational, another factor came into play that day as an influence on flight decisions. This was political pressure. For in order that the president and spectators would not have to arrive too early at Edwards, NASA departed from its flight plan by causing Columbia to kill time through flying an extra orbit.

Beggs now focused on implementing the operational system as quickly as possible. One of the first things NASA did was adopt a controversial pricing policy for the launch of shuttle payloads. The Space Transportation System would be a government-run business; i.e., space socialism. If a private company wanted a satellite launched, they would have to pay, though they had already been doing so with expendable government-launched rockets. But the possibility had existed of a private launch industry starting up. Now, prices on the shuttle would be so low that private companies would be excluded for good. NASA would be assured of the launch monopoly it needed to fend off assaults on its budget from OMB and Congress.

But NASA never came close to cost recovery or to meeting White House objectives of cost-effectiveness. From that standpoint, the space shuttle program has been one of the great public policy failures of modern times. But NASA tried, and in trying pushed the system beyond its capabilities, just as a balloon—or an ego—will burst if overinflated.

To recover as many costs as possible, along with the need to support the growing military flight rate promised to the Air Force, Beggs was trying at least to force the system to reach the scaled-down goal of twenty-four flights per year. According to CBS News reporter Robert Schakne, Beggs's last instruction to his managers at NASA before he left was that the goal of twenty-four flights per year must be achieved.

Beggs was clear to Congress about his intentions. At a congressional hearing he stated the obvious: "The larger number of times you fly, the more you can spread . . . a fixed cost." This cost included what NASA called the shuttle's "standing army" of 29,500 federal and contractor employees. One who was not convinced was Congressman Donald Fuqua, who had monitored space programs from Capitol Hill for two decades. Fuqua told the *Washington Post* that he knew the shuttle really wasn't operational. "Every time Beggs said that to me," he said, "I chuckled."

President Ronald Reagan was also pushing the system forward. In an August 1984 visit to NASA's Goddard Space Flight Center, he boasted that through the utilization of space and other uses of advanced technology, "America would create a bounty of new jobs, technologies, and medical breakthroughs surpassing anything we have ever dreamed and imagined . . . if the doubting Thomases would just stand aside and get out of our way."

But even if NASA achieved the desired flight rate, it was doubtful that there was enough civilian business to run to full capacity. Space-based manufacturing, for instance, was an industry that never got off the ground, so to speak, despite early well-publicized experiments such as growing crystals, making perfect tiny latex spheres for medical use, or conducting materials processing experiments in the microgravity vacuum of space.

Even early projections of commercial satellite launches overestimated the demand. As *Jane's Spaceflight Directory* reported:

[In 1985], NASA's own forecasts showed that the demand for comsat [i.e., commercial satellite] launchings would total only sixteen to eighteen per year through 1991, a level much too low to support both shuttle and Ariane [the French unmanned rocket launched from Guyana in South America], and ignoring competition from private launch companies and the growing pressure from the Soviet Union and China to carry their proportional "share" of international communications satellites.

Jane's also noted that even at scaled-down flight rate projections, there would be excess shuttle launch capacity until space station operations began in 1992. In fact, the first twenty-four shuttle missions ran nowhere near capacity, consumed hundreds of millions of dollars in operational costs, and while launching a number of commercial satellites, focused chiefly on tests and maneuvers to demonstrate shuttle capabilities, along with numerous small-scale scientific experiments involving physiological and materials behavior in the weightless environment.

Starting in 1982, NASA stepped out to implement Beggs's goal of creating an operational support system for the shuttle. The agency would now be managed more like a business with decentralized divisions than the research and development institution it had always been.

Beggs promised the far-flung NASA centers that they would not be "micro-managed" from headquarters. This was in contrast to the Apollo program, where strong managerial coordination and control was exerted from Washington. From 1980 to 1985, employment at headquarters was cut more than ten percent, and the number of NASA scientists and engineers dropped twenty percent. This continued a decade-long trend that had seen agency employment plummet from 36,000 at the height of the Apollo program to 22,000 in the 1980s, along with a seventy-one percent reduction in safety, reliability, and quality assurance personnel. Staff reductions under Beggs were carried out by retirements, hiring freezes, and transfers to the space station and other projects.

At a September 26, 1979, House Space Science and Applications Subcommittee hearing, NASA disclosed its plan to strip headquarters of all technical oversight responsibilities. This meant that headquarters would have no one to watch over the safety and engineering status of the shuttle system and no ability to monitor flight trends, anomaly patterns, or redesign requirements. The assumption of a perfect, trouble-free system was astounding.

All headquarters would be left with was "business management" and "user services," essentially an accounting and sales staff. Within the context of standard federal government operating procedures, this would have been a shocking abdication of policy direction and control by Washington. In fact, NASA did move in this direction, and by 1985 the Office of Space Flight's propulsion engineers were begging for more help because of poor contractor performance and dubious quality control practices.

Treating the shuttle as operational also meant that design changes to its hardware components would be minimized. As noted earlier, one of Beggs's first actions after taking over as administrator in 1981 was to "freeze" shuttle design. As reported after the Challenger disaster by the House Science and Technology Committee, this was documented in an August 21, 1981, memorandum to Beggs from Marshall Space Flight Center Director William Lucas, entitled, "ET/SRB Producibility/Cost Reduction." Lucas wrote:

> I wholeheartedly agree with your statements that shuttle performance requirements and design should be frozen so that we can concentrate all efforts on bringing the system to a cost-effective operational status.

Here we are looking at questionable management behavior. Freezing performance requirements could make sense, because at some point you have every right to declare the output of a machine "good enough" and plan your service levels accordingly. But if you discover flaws in the design that could be compromising performance or that could degrade safety or efficiency, you then have an obligation to weigh the factors involved in doing a redesign. To prohibit such considerations, or to force the system into a "quick-fix" as problems are discovered, is fraught with danger. "Management by objectives" increases the temptation to do just this.

During the early shuttle flights, and especially after STS-5, weight was reduced and performance increased on the main engines, external tank, and solid rocket boosters to augment the shuttle's payload capacity. The reason for these changes was that as the shuttle orbiters were coming into service out of the Rockwell plant in Downey, California, they were failing to reach the 65,000 pound lifting capability that had been promised to the Air Force. Freezing shuttle design proved impossible, especially with the main engines, where near-catastrophes had occurred on shuttle missions.

In accordance with the operational strategy, NASA also tried to establish routinized launch procedures at the Kennedy Space Center. Thus the agency announced in September 1983 that the Lockheed Space Corporation would manage a new shuttle processing contract to coordinate all pre-launch activities. NASA also tried to pattern shuttle payload bookings after the management of charter airline flights and used the American Airlines organization chart as a model in creating its headquarters customer service operation. Booz, Allen, Hamilton, and other consultants also studied the notion of turning all shuttle operations over to a private company to operate on a for-profit basis, though Beggs had previously come out against this idea in a study he led before becoming administrator. But it was a sign of the times, when privatization of government services was becoming a hot topic in Washington and elsewhere.

Centralization of shuttle operations also took place at the Johnson Space Center, where an STS operations contract was awarded to Rockwell. The contract consolidated the work of sixteen different contractors and would take care of most of the activity at JSC in support of shuttle flight preparations, crew training, and flight operations. The contract was worth $685 million over four years and was viewed as compensating Rockwell for loss of its dominant position at KSC when the shuttle processing contract was awarded to Lockheed.

The doctrine of the operational Space Transportation System also found expression in NASA's public relations approach and its selection of astronauts.

The space shuttle was a public relations bonanza for NASA and the Reagan administration. The romance and glory of manned spaceflight had returned, and the orbiters looked a lot more like the spaceships of the movies and TV than did the stubby little capsules of Apollo days. NASA made certain that the right people saw the shuttle in action. A 1984 study carried out by the General Accounting Office at the request of Senator William Proxmire found that NASA spent more than $780,000 flying 2,226 special guests to witness the first twelve shuttle launches. The agency used both charter flights and its own executive jets to transport VIPs to the viewing stands at the Kennedy Space Center.

Early shuttle launches and landings were carried on live network TV, and all were covered by NASA Select, the agency's own TV system that could be patched into the networks. President Ronald Reagan did not attend any launches—there was always too much uncertainty about whether a scheduled launch would actually take place on time. But the president frequently phoned the shuttle astronauts as they orbited the Earth, and both he and Vice President George Bush visited mission control at Houston during flights.

NASA also set up a space camp for schoolchildren, and America's space journalists wrote a small library of books about the shuttle. Their natural competitiveness took on steamy proportions when NASA announced that one of them would be picked to ride the shuttle on a 1986 flight. Artists were flown in to create original oil paintings of shuttle launches. These were often of museum quality. NASA also capitalized on the idea of "routine" spaceflight by colorful posters about "Going to Work in Space" and by publicizing the Getaway Specials and student science experiments to be flown at low cost to scientists, universities, and industrial sponsors.

The shuttle astronauts were often different too. True, the men in charge of flying the orbiter were still top-ranked military pilots, but now there were mission and payload specialists, including the first paying passengers to go to space, mainly foreign nationals of countries for which NASA was launching satellites. And a large number of the new class of astronauts were civilians. Then there was the Teacher-in-Space program announced by President Reagan at the start of the 1984 presidential campaign.

Few were able to formulate their misgivings precisely, but many people within the NASA system were aware that James Beggs's operational strategy was a house built on sand.

A 1985 report of NASA's Aerospace Advisory Panel was polite about it. After all, its members served at NASA's invitation and were paid for their trouble. But its critique struck at the heart of the matter:

> NASA management would be well advised to avoid advertising the shuttle as being "operational" in the airline sense when it clearly isn't. . . . The continuing use of the term "operational" simply compounds the unique management challenge of guiding the STS through this period of "developmental" evolution.

As early as 1981, soon after the shuttle began to fly, it became clear that a major constraint on achieving the desired flight rate was the higher-than-expected turnaround times needed to process the shuttle for the next launch. So corners were cut. For example, in the August 2, 1981, memorandum from Lucas to Beggs on freezing the shuttle's design, Lucas was already speaking of reducing the "mandatory government inspection requirements for solid rocket booster processing by Thiokol at the Kennedy Space Center." Similar pressures to cut turnaround times existed for other shuttle components besides the solid rocket boosters, such as a waiver of structural inspections for the orbiter fleet.

Due to problems with processing times and to hardware-caused delays for some of the early flights that sometimes stretched into months, the shuttle was able to fly only twice in 1981, three times in 1982, four times in 1983, and five times in 1984.

By September 1984, following the twelfth shuttle mission, Jesse Moore, who had succeeded General Abrahamson as associate administrator for space flight, was able to declare the program back "on schedule." By this he meant that NASA would be aiming for one flight per month during 1985, though when 3,800 tiles on Challenger began to come unglued and Discovery was damaged in a processing accident, only nine could be achieved.

But even this number of flights was stressing both orbiter hardware and shuttle support systems, especially spare parts. Other constraints were providing enough astronaut training time in the shuttle simulators and the Gulfstream training planes, as well as Johnson and Kennedy flight development, processing, and launch facilities. Dr. Hans Mark, a former secretary of the Air Force and NASA's deputy administrator under Beggs from 1981 to 1984, said after the Challenger disaster that "NASA is a first-class engineering development organization, but it was never intended to be the agency for the long-term operation of a Space Transportation System."

There was also a paradox in the operational strategy in that success depended on happy paying customers. Yet to make them happy NASA felt it had to make constant changes to the launch manifest and flight programs to accommodate their needs, even if the customers wanted last-minute changes.

Changes in flight plans were initiated by NASA itself through the scheduling of short-notice satellite retrievals, late additions of payload specialists, including Senator Jake Garn and Congressman Bill Nelson, and changes to low priority scientific experiments. NASA also had to adapt to payload hardware malfunctions, such as an early failure of the inertial upper stage, one of the satellite-bearing rockets launched from the orbiter's payload bay. This had a domino effect, causing the cancellation of three subsequent payloads for which satellite deployment using the IUS had been planned.

The uncertainty in scheduling pointed to the fact that the effort to increase the flight rate, so necessary for cost-effectiveness, was contradicted by the need for flexibility in making the Space Transportation System viable. From this viewpoint, the shuttle was a system at odds with itself.

The frequent changes to the shuttle manifest showed how sensitive and susceptible NASA was to outside pressures and influence, despite the denial made later by the Presidential Commission that such pressures might have been brought to bear by the Reagan White House and perhaps played a part in the decision to launch Challenger in dangerous weather conditions on January 28, 1986.

NASA's problems also involved its relationships with its contractors. Clearly, the operational Space Transportation System could succeed only if the NASA-industry partnership that James Beggs liked to speak of worked. But one of NASA's better-kept secrets had always been the cracks in that relationship that pointed to the agency's failure to bring the discipline and accountability to bear on contractors that I had wondered about as soon as I went to work at NASA in July 1985. Indeed, a primary cause of the shuttle-Centaur fiasco was NASA's inability to apply firmness in its dealings with General Dynamics.

The primary authorities in charge of monitoring NASA's dealings with its contractors were its Office of Inspector General and the General Accounting Office, which operates under the direction of Congress. By the time the shuttle was being built, there were only two employees serving as contract monitors at the Johnson Space Center, which supervised the building of the shuttle orbiters, compared to twenty-eight during the Apollo program. According to IG and GAO auditors, Rockwell, acting under JSC's direction, had spent $20 million on orbiter propulsion systems without having agreed with NASA on a price. At times, more than $750 million in work was being done without price agreements, and one audit report stated, "The budget and planning cost estimates prepared by Rockwell International Corporation are often inaccurate and unreliable."

On another occasion, auditors asked Rockwell to examine 1,800 parts on Challenger, which found that a number of them could not be certified as properly built. According to the *New York Times*:

> But the company suggested that the Challenger "fly as is," because of the "high design margin" and "noncritical" function of the parts. It suggested repeated inspections and limits on the use of the parts because of possible "crack growth." One part carried the warning, "May yield under load, but no catastrophic failure."

Auditors also cited numerous cases of contractor fraud, as well as price markups exceeding 1,000 percent on parts purchased from vendors and resold to NASA. Fraudulent records submitted by contractors and employees at times led to arrest, conviction, and imprisonment. NASA settled one $10 million contractor overcharge by collecting only $2.4 million. Cases were repeatedly cited in audit reports, particularly in regard to Rockwell, where the company had illegally charged NASA for work it was doing for the Defense Department. NASA was also cited for paying Rockwell's Rocketdyne Division $120 for $3.28 bolt assemblies, $315 for three-cent metal loops, $80 for a $1 washer, $86 for a $2 clamp, and $1,621 for a $78 bolt.

NASA also paid for contractor "idle time"; i.e., for contractor employees to do nothing. This included, in one audit, thirty percent of the time charged by Rockwell's engineers. Repeated instances of on-the-job drug use were also noted, including narcotics use at the Johnson Space Center. There was also theft of government equipment, including precious metal supplies, and a potentially dangerous instance of falsification of quality.

Contractor work quality eroded at the Kennedy Space Center with the Lockheed processing contract. On March 8, 1985, the orbiter Discovery was damaged so badly in a processing accident that the shuttle mission scheduled for that month had to be cancelled. The accident occurred when a work platform crashed into the payload bay, breaking a technician's leg and cutting two large gashes in the orbiter's side. Worker overtime and fatigue also became factors, and fatigue was cited as a cause of a near-mishap on the January 6, 1986, scrub of the 61-C mission of Columbia. In that instance, a tired contractor worker mistakenly drained 18,000 pounds of liquid hydrogen from the external tank, which controllers noticed through a change in tank temperature. Lift-off in such conditions could have resulted in a tank collapse and a gigantic explosion.

———

IT WOULD BE naïve to assume that "safety first" can ever be an absolute value in any line of human endeavor. Otherwise, why get out of bed in the morning? Since the inception of the U.S. space program, NASA sought a blend of safety, schedule, and cost considerations. It never was and never could be "safety first" 100 percent of the time. In practice, the agency recognized that none of the three values is absolute—that total safety is unattainable, that the nation expected a challenging schedule to be met, and that money was not unlimited. But at certain times, a better job was done of maintaining balance than at others. There were times when NASA really did try to make the equipment it had to work with as safe as it could be.

After the fatal 1967 Apollo 1 fire, NASA put a robust safety system in place that prevented further loss of astronaut life through completion of the Apollo program. But by the start of shuttle flights, NASA's safety apparatus was defunct, and what remained was understaffed, organizationally feeble, and primarily devoted to paper-based hazard analysis exercises. As we have seen, hardware testing for shuttle components had been underfunded, and the flight qualification and certification process had led to the acceptance of borderline equipment.

There was also the ever-looming absence of an adequate launch-pad escape system. This came up in a rare congressional discussion of flight safety at a 1979 Senate budget hearing led by Senator William Proxmire. The senator wanted to hear about a report by three NASA consultants who recommended that President Carter be informed of "narrower-than-Apollo" safety margins, because "the shuttle bears the burden of being a significant part of the image of U.S. technical capability." Proxmire asked NASA Administrator Robert Frosch, "If you delay the shuttle further, could you buy more safety?" Frosch answered:

I don't think so. . . . What I want to do is to continue to look at a more stringent test and certification program, which is what we are doing. We will not fly before we have accomplished it.

In tones of disbelief, Proxmire then read aloud from *Aviation Week and Space Technology* magazine:

The primary abort mode in the event of a pad emergency such as a propellant explosion is to run quickly from the vehicle.

Frosch answered, "It does not have an escape. . . . We have not found any way to deal with that problem."

It was questionable that even NASA's run-like-hell escape plan would do much good. If the shuttle blew up on the pad, it would have the force of 3.15 kilotons, or 630,000 pounds of TNT. The burning fuel of the solid rocket boosters would spread toxic fumes to a radius of 3.5 miles. Later, NASA tried to ease the launch pad escape problem by installing baskets on slide wires leading from the orbiter crew cabin to a bomb-proof bunker.

Proxmire later told the *Washington Post* that it was NASA's "military overtones" that caused Congress to overlook safety problems. He said, "You don't ask the Pentagon about safety either."

NASA received many warnings of the drastic safety effects of cost and schedule pressures on such a complex machine as the space shuttle. As early as 1978, Herbert Grier, chairman of NASA's Aerospace Safety Advisory Board, told a congressional subcommittee that:

We feel one of the important safety considerations is the effect of the schedule driving technical people to make "fixes" rather than engineer a solution to the problem.

Later, in 1983, the same board observed that "the pressure of schedule seems to relax the rigor" of safety certifications of inspected equipment. The board also criticized NASA's management for "a continuing strong bias" that emphasized schedule over safety.

Was the board crying wolf? By the end of 1984, NASA had flown fourteen shuttle missions without any evident life-threatening emergencies, at least any that were highly visible to the press and public on the scale of, say, Apollo 13. Nine more flights lifted off and returned to Earth in 1985. Fifteen were planned for the big push in 1986.

Few outside NASA realized that from the start, the shuttle program had seen a multitude of hardware malfunctions that were never publicized, some with new equipment being used for the first time, but some with equipment that had been used on earlier space vehicles and was viewed as thoroughly understood and reliable.

Behind the tapestry, the shuttle was exactly what former astronaut Frank Borman called it: "experimental gear." There were several true flight emergencies, but smaller annoying glitches—sometimes in flight-critical hardware—were also constant. Some problems, such as main engine component failures and the solid rocket booster nozzle lining near-burnthrough, delayed flights for weeks or even months at a time.

The problems were maddeningly diverse. For instance, malfunctioning main engine hydraulic actuators twice caused engine shutdown just prior to lift-off (missions 41-D and 51-F).

There were numerous failures of main engine temperature and pressure sensors. On flight 51-F, this resulted in premature shutdown of a good engine during flight. When malfunctioning heat sensors threatened to shut down a second engine, an event that would have resulted in a catastrophic ocean ditching, controllers disabled the sensors in flight to prevent such an outcome.

Main engine turbine blades and sheet metal parts often developed cracks, leading to premature replacement of components.

On STS-8, excessive erosion of the solid rocket booster nozzle lining placed the shuttle seconds away from a potentially disastrous failure.

On fourteen of twenty-three flights where the solid rocket boosters were recovered, there was evidence of heat distress on the O-rings in the seals between segments.

There were several instances of anomalous behavior or failure of the orbiter's on-board flight computers.

Solid rocket booster thrust varied more than expected, producing orbiter ascent trajectories that were too high or too low.

There were at least seventy-eight instances of anomalous behavior of the orbiters' communications and tracking equipment, including an unexplained three-channel shutdown on STS-3 that was "the worst communications failure in the history of U.S. manned spaceflight."

At least sixty-three instances of anomalies took place in the reaction control system, which was a set of forty-four small rockets that provided thrust for orbiter velocity changes and attitude control (pitch, yaw, and roll). The RCS thruster propellants were nitrogen tetroxide oxidizer and monomethyl hydrazine. These burnt hypergolically; i.e., on being mixed in the combustion chamber. A nitrogen tetroxide spill on Columbia's nose prior to STS-3 delayed flight for several weeks.

There were at least forty-eight instances of anomalous behavior of the three on-board auxiliary power units (APUs). Each APU was a 138-horsepower turbine engine weighing eighty-five pounds and powered by liquid hydrazine. The APUs drove hydraulic pumps which operated the orbiter's elevons, rudder, and other aerosurfaces, as well as the swiveling mechanism on the main engine nozzles and the landing gear. On STS-9, two APUs failed when the orbiter landed, then exploded several minutes after the vehicle had come to a stop on the runway and the crew had exited.

Of particular concern were the brakes, since high-speed lock-up with catastrophic consequences was a constant danger. There was brake damage on fifteen of the first twenty-three shuttle flights, caused mainly by cracking and break-up due to hot spots, dynamic load, and vibration. Flight 51-D had low speed wheel lock-up and a blown tire, and 61-C almost had lock-up. According to the House Science and Technology Committee report on the Challenger disaster:

> The pilots were given the astounding instructions to never release a brake once applied because if the brake is reapplied, the loose fragments will destroy it and cause seizure.

Chief astronaut John Young commented to the Presidential Commission, "We don't believe that astronauts or pilots should be able to break the brakes." The problem occurred because there was little or no design margin in the brakes, which were created for a lighter vehicle than the orbiter turned out to be. When the weight of the orbiter grew during the design phase, NASA simply lengthened the runway landing from 10,000 to 12,000 feet rather than improve the brakes. The

Aerospace Safety Advisory Board supported a brake redesign, but management opposed it because of budget constraints. Also unfunded were improvements in tires and landing gear, which, along with wheels and nosewheel steering, were operating at their design limits.

The brake and landing gear problems were potentially far more dangerous for landings at the Kennedy Space Center than at Edwards Air Force Base in California. The purpose of the KSC landings was to reduce orbiter turnaround times in preparing for upcoming shuttle missions. Otherwise, to ferry an orbiter back from Edwards to Florida on the 747 added four days to a week. KSC landings were more dangerous because of the notoriously unpredictable and violent weather along the Florida coast. One aspect of the weather problem was that cross-winds could suddenly come up that would produce excess lateral stress and blow the tires. Another was possible loss of visibility from fog sweeping in. A third was that landing in the rain could damage the orbiter tiles from the velocity of the raindrops and cause greater turnaround times because of the ensuing tile replacement and repairs.

There were constant problems with the heat-resistant tiles, including in-flight loss of tiles, de-bonding of thermal blankets from the surface of the orbiter, chemical decomposition of the "screed" layer beneath the tiles, and deterioration of the tile adhesive that on one occasion delayed flight for several weeks. Of constant concern was damage from ice and insulation falling from the external tank of the type that would lead to the loss of Columbia in 2003. It was the danger of ice tumbling from the launch tower that caused postponement of a 1985 flight and later caused Rockwell to question the launch of Challenger on January 28, 1986.

Tiles were damaged on another occasion as an orbiter was being ferried back to KSC on the 747 and flew through a rainstorm. On STS-4, prelaunch rain had seeped into the space between the tiles, causing the orbiter to pitch and roll in flight. On mission 41-D, there was a thermal protection burnthrough on an elevon cove at the tip of the wing that penetrated the skin and exposed the gridwork of the wing's interior structure.

Other shuttle hardware failures included a support strut collapse on the forward RCS oxidizer tank during STS-1, early termination of STS-2 because of a shutdown of a fuel cell, a type that had been used on manned spacecraft since Gemini days, and collapse of a 17-inch orbiter/external tank disconnect flow liner on STS-4.

When shuttle flight anomalies are assembled in this manner, the commercial airline analogy vanishes. It may be argued, of course, that it is easy to compile such a list in hindsight. Nevertheless, these problems were all known to NASA management either when they happened or soon afterwards. In some cases, efforts were made to fix them, in others equipment was replaced, and in others, the anomalies became an "acceptable risk," the decision being to "fly as is."

A few of these problems became known to the press, but most NASA kept to itself. Internally, as I saw in the solid rocket booster and shuttle-Centaur programs, these problems were a source of intense anxiety. But the official curtain NASA drew across the shuttle program never faced any serious scrutiny from outside the agency, including the White House, Congress, or the press. All had dutifully swallowed the fiction of the operational Space Transportation System.

Unfortunately, anyone at NASA who might have wanted to raise safety issues, even the astronauts, faced a crippling disadvantage in the absence of quantitative estimates of risk attached to specific hardware components. NASA used a failure modes effects anaysis— FMEA—system that identified a general level of criticality for all shuttle hardware items. But no one could give a numerical degree of risk for a given type of possible failure using the FMEA methodology. Risk could not be quantified because the shuttle testing program tested few components to the point of failure. Consequently, no one knew what the outside tolerances were.

An objective system for assessing risk simply did not exist. This undermined the value of the shuttle's critical items list and reduced it to a paper exercise. No one ever paid any attention to it. In fact, NASA's shuttle safety system was practically useless. So the managers of the shuttle were left with nothing to rely on but their own subjective judgments, which could obviously be clouded by such factors as funding, politics, personal preference, fear of being a Chicken Little, or even the bravado of having the "right stuff." Of course it was the astronauts' lives, not the managers' that were at risk.

Nevertheless, there had been times when various parties had attempted to calculate the probabilities of a catastrophic failure either of the space shuttle or of manned spaceflight vehicles in general. The question was whether these calculations were compatible with NASA's definition of the shuttle as an operational system. At a June 12, 1986, hearing on the Challenger disaster by the House Science and Technology Committee, Congressman James Scheuer (D-N.Y.) said:

> We had the testimony just yesterday of George McKay, a project engineer at the Marshall Space Center, who said that twenty years ago, Marshall safety engineers predicted a flight failure in every twenty or twenty-five flights. And he said, "We didn't tell anybody about it at that time because it would have scared the hell out of everybody."

Back in 1977, NASA commissioned the Wiggins Group to conduct a study of failure probability for the space shuttle then in development to determine the likely risk to the population near the Kennedy Space Center from a catastrophic failure at lift-off. By examining data for all previous space launches, a likely failure rate of one in fifty-seven was derived, a similar order of magnitude to the prediction of the safety engineers at Marshall.

But NASA complained that many of the launch vehicles the Wiggins Group included were not similar enough to the shuttle to be part of the database. So Wiggins changed the probable failure rate to one in 100.

There were other studies, giving wildly varying estimates, though a study conducted for the Air Force placed the likely failure rate for the shuttle in a similar range to the Wiggins analysis, and a 1984 study placed the failure rate for the solid rocket boosters alone at one in thirty-five. None of these studies was publicized, and most of newspaper reporters who covered NASA probably never heard of them. But the underlying message was that something bad could happen sooner rather than later.

The time arrived, however, when NASA was forced to come up with an official number. This happened in 1985 in the circumstances I have already described in connection with the planned 1986 launches of the Centaur upper stage for the Galileo and Ulysses missions.

Each of the spacecraft would get its electrical power from a small plutonium-powered nuclear power plant, a radioisotope thermonuclear generator, or RTG. If the shuttle blew up at lift-off, the plutonium in the RTG could be spewed across populated areas on the Florida coast, producing a possible cancer risk to the people below. This was why federal regulations required NASA to publish an environmental impact statement followed by a public comment period. NASA was also required to gain approval for launch of nuclear devices from an interagency committee that included the Energy and Defense Departments. Final approval had to come from the White House. In its documentation for these approvals, NASA was required to show a figure defining the probable shuttle failure rate.

The figure NASA gave was one in 100,000. This estimate was developed by the agency's chief engineer. At a rate of twenty-four launches per year, this meant that NASA expected the shuttle to fail catastrophically only once every 4,167 years.

"A VISION OF THE FUTURE"

—Weapons in Space

THE ELECTION OF Ronald Reagan as president in 1980 can be analyzed from many perspectives. From one point of view, it clearly represented a successful power play by what President Dwight D. Eisenhower had warned against in his 1961 farewell address—the growing power of a permanent "military-industrial complex." Reagan had already enjoyed the backing of this element when he ran for election and won as governor of California in 1966 and 1970.

Reagan seemed to thrive in the role of commander-in-chief. One of his heroes was British World War II Prime Minister Winston Churchill. Reagan's supporters loved his "great power" rhetoric. Yet he was not willing to repeat the disastrous experience of Vietnam by engaging in another major land war. Instead, wars were to be fought by proxy—this was the "Reagan doctrine"; i.e., the support of anti-communist military movements in third world countries. There was also an expansion of CIA covert action under Director William Casey. The prime example of Casey's influence was the creation of the Contra army by CIA operatives in Nicaragua starting in 1981, a by-product of which was the Iran-Contra scandal six years later.

As far as overt military action was concerned, the Reagan administration seemed to prefer easy targets, as in the invasion of the tiny

Caribbean island of Grenada in 1983 or the bombing of Libya in 1986. One U.S. deployment backfired when the Marine barracks in Beirut were destroyed in 1983 by a suicide bomber, with the loss of 220 American lives.

But behind every target, the specter of the Soviet Union loomed. In its approach to the perceived Soviet threat, the U.S. remained a nation expecting total war.

The great minds within the military industrial complex were still trying to figure out a way that a full-scale nuclear conflict with the Soviet Union could be won. Results were the decision to build the MX missile, able to retaliate after a Soviet first strike, and the B-1 bomber, useful only in total war. In an article in *Foreign Policy*, Colin S. Gray and Keith Payne wrote that with the proper strategy, U.S. losses would be "maybe as few as twenty million deaths."

Such men had more power in the early days of the Reagan administration than at any time since the Vietnam escalation of the 1960s. A key element of their strategy had become the use of space for military purposes. This included the intention to repeal the Anti-Ballistic Missile Treaty to allow the development of spacebased weapons systems.

The impact on NASA would be profound, even though President Reagan himself seemed to have scant interest in the details. Former NASA Administrator James Beggs later said of him:

> He was almost technically ignorant. Not quite, but almost. He grasps a few of the broader concepts, but when you start talking in any kind of detail about the broader aspects of the program, his eyes glaze over.

As his administration began to be organized, Reagan played little part in setting space policy. But the direction was clear. Barbara Honegger was a White House aide at the time, who attended meetings where NASA's space program was discussed by OMB Director David Stockman and other officials. "The whole thing," she told me, "was to make it military."

In 1982, the year after Reagan took office, the Defense Department, now run by Secretary of Defense Caspar Weinberger, created the Air Force Space Command to consolidate space programs, including military shuttle operations. At NASA, high-level appointments reflected the shifting orientation. General James Abrahamson became associate administrator for space flight, in charge of space shuttle operations. Former Air Force chief of staff General Lew Allen was named director of NASA's Jet Propulsion Laboratory in Pasadena, California. In 1979, Allen had said:

> Whatever else the shuttle does and whatever other purposes it will have, the priority, the emphasis, and the driving momentum now has to be those satellite systems which are important to national security.

Under Allen's direction, the emphasis at JPL reportedly shifted from unmanned planetary probes to military and commercial projects.

In another major appointment, Dr. Hans Mark was named NASA's deputy administrator. After working as a nuclear physicist at the Lawrence Livermore Weapons Laboratory, Mark headed NASA's Ames Research Center at Moffett Field, California, from 1969-77. He was undersecretary of the Air Force from 1977-79 and secretary of the Air Force from 1979-81. A nuclear weapons specialist, Mark gave particular emphasis at NASA to such military support projects as the filament wound case and the shuttle-Centaur upper stage.

As early as 1982, the General Accounting Office reported that at least one fourth of NASA's budget was devoted to military projects. Meanwhile, the Pentagon's civilian and uniformed leadership continued to raise the specter of Soviet power. At the September 1982 Air Force Association National Convention, Air Force Undersecretary Edward C. Aldridge told the audience that for the Soviet Union the "space medium" was a priority, "a vital fourth dimension to those of air, land, and sea." The communists were intent on exploiting space to the best of their ability. It was integral to their strategies for political success over the West.

Lieutenant General Richard C. Henry told the convention that space is "a theater of operations. It is now time that we treat it as a theater of operations." Speaking in terms that past generations might have reserved for the divine, Henry said that the military space mission is to deliver:

> from on high to our operational forces, the electronic bit stream—a written message, an oral conversation, a picture or a navigation signal

wherever they need it, whenever they need it, and with total certainty.
. . . Our future in space, in terms of scientific, economic, and national
security needs, is limited only by our imagination.

Given such ambition, it was not surprising that the military was
unhappy with its dependence on NASA. The need to satisfy the military, along with NASA's other customers, made it critical that the operational shuttle strategy succeed. But while NASA Administrator James
Beggs saw the role of the military as important in space program planning, he did not view it as the only priority. He described the agency's
position in the Winter 1983 edition of *Directors and Boards*:

> We are running a business and facing the competitive pressures
> that all businesses face.
> NASA provides transportation to space for commercial, military, gov-
> ernment, and foreign payloads on the space shuttle and on expendable
> launch vehicles. We sell space on a shuttle the same way a business
> would sell space. We collect the money and at some point we hope we
> will break even—and even make money.

Beggs's strategy was to serve three more or less equal "customers"—
the commercial sector, space science, and the military. One of those
who saw the military as more than a mere customer of NASA, however,
was President Reagan's science adviser, George Keyworth III.

In 1981, Keyworth was a forty-one-year-old physicist who worked for
the government's Los Alamos Scientific Laboratory in the remote
uplands of northern New Mexico. He was virtually unknown to the
nation's scientific community. He had graduated from Yale University
in 1963 and received a PhD from Duke in 1968.

Keyworth was politically well-connected. He had a marked advantage in stepping into the White House in that he was vigorously backed
for the job by Edward Teller, known as the scientist behind the hydrogen bomb and former director of the Lawrence Livermore lab. He also
had the support of Harold Agnew, president of the General Atomics
Corporation and a former director of Los Alamos. Another backer of
Keyworth was William Wilson, President Reagan's special envoy to the
Holy See and a member of the President's so-called Kitchen Cabinet.

Keyworth viewed Teller as his "intellectual father." In fact, in an interview with *Barron's*, he referred to Teller as "my dad. He is sort of a second father." It was said that when the White House was searching for a science adviser, support for what later became the Strategic Defense Initiative was a requirement. Keyworth qualified. He was also a strong supporter of the military in space in other respects besides SDI. Keyworth also opposed NASA's plan to create a launch monopoly for the space shuttle, and after his appointment he reportedly argued that the shuttle should be turned over to the Air Force.

Though he was now the nation's top scientist, he wanted NASA's space science program cut back. He told *Barron's*:

Oh . . . people wanted to see us go ahead with a large program to continue to explore the planets, like the Voyager II mission last year that showed us the beautiful rings of Saturn. That cost $500 million. The next mission would have cost $800 million, and the next one a billion. It would be $2 billion each very soon, the cost rising much faster than inflation, because of the complexity.

We said, "Whoa!" We can't afford this any more. Let's retrench and see if we can't make missions for only a few hundred million dollars, like to go and look at the surface of Venus.

Regarding NASA's space station, Keyworth said he was "extremely skeptical." He said:

. . . I have asked ever since I came to this office for people to tell me what we will do with the space station. Neither NASA nor the space community has been able to define what those men would do who would be up on that space station. . . . NASA has just set up a huge inter-industry panel to try to identify what they would do.

Keyworth favored the use of unmanned rockets to launch communication satellites, a business NASA was trying to monopolize for the shuttle. He also favored greater involvement of the private sector in space ventures, a position that was supported by such conservative groups as the Heritage Foundation, which criticized NASA for trying to be the "sole arbiter of space." Regarding the role of the military in space, Keyworth said, "It is extremely competent, sophisticated, and professional."

Keyworth's lukewarm support for space science had its effects. Ever since NASA was founded in 1958, it had been difficult for space science to hold its own in a budgetary environment dominated by massive funding for manned spaceflight. By the time the Apollo program was peaking in the late 1960s, the competition for funds within NASA had become intense. Space scientists looked with dismay on NASA's plans for a major new post-Apollo manned program, and many testified against the shuttle in congressional hearings. One of the shuttle's most notable opponents was Dr. James Van Allen, America's most eminent space scientist, who believed, as Keyworth did later, that space science was better served by cheaper unmanned launches.

If commercial applications and satellite launches were not meeting expectations and space science was falling from favor, where was the shuttle program headed? The answer within the White House was that the future of the shuttle lay with the military. This was Reagan administration policy, and in developing it, George Keyworth was a dominant figure, along with the National Security Council.

After his appointment as science adviser, Keyworth headed an interagency group to draft a policy statement on space affairs. Members comprised NASA, Defense, the CIA, the National Security Council, and the Department of Energy. The group produced President Reagan's speech at the completion of the fourth space shuttle mission on July 4, 1982, when he declared the shuttle operational.

In his speech, Reagan said that the United States was committed to "the exploration and use of space by all nations for peaceful purposes and the benefit of mankind." He added, however, that a primary goal of the space program was to "strengthen the security of the United States," though he did not indicate how this would be done. That day the White House also issued a "fact sheet," indicating that the president's speech would "set the direction of U.S. efforts in space for the next decade." While the fact sheet repeated Reagan's statement that the nation was committed to the exploration and use of space "for peaceful purposes," it added that "'peaceful purposes' allow activities in pursuit of national security goals."

This definition would essentially allow the government to use the space shuttle for any military-related activities it desired. It would also appear to be a serious compromise of the intent of the National Aeronautics and Space Act of 1958, in that it essentially made NASA subservient to national security priorities. In fact, the shuttle flight that President Reagan witnessed on July 4, 1982, carried the first major defense payload.

Interestingly, the Air Force had begun to picture the space shuttle on its recruitment ads in *National Geographic* and other magazines, and eventually, the orbiter Discovery was to become a vehicle dedicated solely to Air Force missions. According to an article in *Industrial Research and Development* in October 1982, Air Force Secretary Vern Orr "was quoted as remarking during a tour of the Johnson Space center, 'Most people in the Air Force think far enough downstream, we will probably be running the shuttle.' "

But the professional officer corps of the Air Force never swallowed the idea of sole dependence on the shuttle, especially when it became evident that launch of the shuttle would require 6,000 ground support personnel at Vandenberg, compared to 600 for an expendable launch vehicle. Finally, even the Air Force's top echelons had enough, and in 1985 obtained White House agreement to order a new series of ten unmanned rockets for satellite launch.

More bad news for NASA came when the National Oceanic and Atmospheric Administration stated its own preference for discarded Titan II ICBMs to launch its future weather satellites. In a panic, NASA appealed to the White House for help, which responded by requiring the Air Force to commit to a program of one-third shuttle utilization, or a minimum of eight launches per year, based on a mission model of twenty-four flights per year by 1991. It was in return for this agreement that the White House allowed the Air Force to order the ten Titan 34D-7 booster rockets.

Thus the shuttle's space launch monopoly had been broken by the time Challenger blew up. Still, it seemed as though the basic program of having a third of all shuttle payloads dedicated respectively to the military, space science, and commercial and foreign satellites remained viable. But by 1985 a new element had appeared that caused military requirements for the shuttle to increase. This new element, radical both in its origins and implications, was the Strategic Defense Initiative.

The Strategic Defensive Initiative—"Star Wars"—was conceived, sold, and promoted to the U.S. public by the Reagan administration as a defensive system, intended to destroy ICBMs launched against the United States by the Soviet Union. It would thus deliver us from the fear of nuclear war caused by the supposedly outmoded presence of a threat of mutually assured destruction; i.e., "MAD." But SDI still meant that weapons would be built. Its supporters acknowledged that SDI could become the largest research and development program in history. The revenues and benefits to the military-industrial complex would be staggering. And the knowledge gained would certainly be transferable to offensive weapons as well.

By the beginning of the 1980s, the breakneck pace of technological development, especially in aerospace, where the U.S. had retained a lead it had lost to Japan and other nations in consumer product engineering, caused policy makers to look to space to ensure worldwide military dominance, whether it was "offensive" or "defensive."

On May 6, 1981, Dr. Hans Mark, NASA's newly-appointed deputy administrator, told the students and faculty of the Naval War College, "One could create a long list of things in which the United States enjoys a technological lead that could be exploited to enhance its position in the world."

Mark said of lasers:

Perhaps the most interesting development in the past twenty years, from the viewpoint of real and potential military applications, is the laser. Low-power lasers have already found a number of important applications in fire control and target designation. The question now is whether high-intensity lasers can be turned into practical weapons systems capable of doing real damage to military targets.

Mark, now the number two man in the civilian space agency, said lasers could be used as an airborne weapon to shoot down surface-to-air or air-to-air missiles, or to shoot down ballistic missiles launched from submarines. He continued:

Once airborne weapons are fielded, the next step is to see what might be done with space-based lasers, for which there is also no propagation problem. . . . Therefore the possibility of placing such lasers on orbiting spacecraft has been considered.

Mark also said that new technological developments make "a non-nuclear antiballistic missile system possible now, whereas it was clearly impossible to create such a system ten years ago." It was seriously being asked whether lasers could be harnessed to incinerate enemy cities, and by 1984, the Defense Department had already spent $2 billion on laser research. Another exotic weapon that was undergoing research was the electromagnetic railgun, whereby a small object could be shot earthward from space with the same devastating impact as a meteorite. From this point of view, what was soon to become the SDI program was another step in the arms race and part of the ongoing search for military supremacy.

Speaking of military surveillance and communication, Mark said, "There is every reason to believe that great strides will be made in this area once the new space shuttle becomes operational."

Others went well beyond Mark in envisioning weapons in space. One of these was Allan D. Simon, a Washington, D.C., consultant who had been director of air warfare in the Office of the Secretary of Defense and a member of numerous Pentagon advisory boards. In a 1982 article, Simon set out to "predict the politico-military situation in the year 2032." He wrote, "there will be at least a dozen greatly powerful nations . . . technologically capable of putting satellites into orbit." He continued:

> The U.S. will recognize the inescapable fact that it cannot compete militarily by the use of large quantities of men and equipment, that only advanced technology will continue its military preeminence.

Simon speculated that the nations of the world would place their "doomsday weapons . . . in the oceans, in Antarctica, and in deep space." The technological systems Simon described would have the same quality of omnipotence that was projected at the 1982 Air Force Association national convention described earlier. He wrote:

> We must have total and instantaneous surveillance of the entire world. Although we have made good use of space systems, we need to

move forward in a much bolder manner to take and preserve the high ground of both near-earth and deep space. . . .

We must drive toward invincible C3, totally dependable command, control, and communications—a concept crucial to all thee other concepts. . . .

Weapons fifty years from now must *all* be emplaced remote from their targets, yet be capable of surgical delivery to any point on Earth in quick time.

Control of space would be the key. Simon wrote:

Warfare scenarios in 2032 will be quite different than those with which we are familiar. A major change will be our movement to the high ground of space. There will be a U.S. force that conducts military operations from space.

A key weapons platform used by the U.S. space force will be the space battle station. In 2032, at least three of these space battle stations, nuclear-powered, should be in geosynchronous orbit. Each battle station would contain a crew of about 1,000 people and sufficient supplies to operate autonomously for a few years. Each would be fortified against attack and equipped with offensive and defensive systems to insure its own protection and that of escorts and ancillary spaceships.

Simon's article, written for the most prestigious of aerospace journals, and presented as a serious contribution to contemporary thought, has a feverish quality reminiscent of something out of *1984*. In the last paragraph of his article, Simon wrote:

To get to this "brave new world" will take brave new people in the decision-making jobs in the government. They must be capable of fencing off large sums of money to move in these bold new directions. If not, we will likely try to arm ourselves with products of new technology but fight with outmoded concepts and tactics—the most dangerous course of all!

President Reagan presented his plans for SDI to the American public in a speech on March 23, 1983. Politically, SDI was supported most vehemently by the extreme right wing. As Dr. Robert Bowman wrote in *Star Wars: Defense or Death Star*:

> For many years, there had been a few on the "lunatic fringe" who warned of the imminent deployment of Soviet laser battle stations and urged us to go beyond our prudent research program into a crash development of our own "Star Wars" system. Fortunately, these few were kept in check by the majority of career military professionals, who understood the technical and strategic realities. They knew that the Soviets were even less capable than we of putting up a militarily meaningful "Star Wars" system, and that for us to attempt to do so would be counterproductive for our overall national security effort. . . .

With Reagan's election, the extreme right-wingers had a measure of power, though they were forced to compete for influence within the administration with the more traditional elements of the Republican Party and with the entrenched bureaucracies of the federal executive agencies, including Defense and State. They had acquired, however, a new respectability. They were known now as the Conservative Movement, or simply "The Movement." Reagan was their agent of destiny, whom they idolized, and on whom they were dependent for their political power.

The focal point of space weaponry was Edward Teller. In 1966 he had met Reagan for the first time, shortly after Reagan's election as governor of California. In 1967, he convinced Reagan to visit his home base, the Lawrence Livermore National Laboratory near San Francisco. Reagan was briefed on the laboratory's programs, including "an upcoming test in Alaska of a large, ground-launched nuclear weapon that was designed to destroy incoming Soviet missiles." According to Teller, Reagan asked "maybe a dozen questions" and "got along with everybody."

Over a decade passed. In 1979, while seeking the Republican Party nomination for president, Reagan visited NORAD headquarters in Colorado with an aide, Martin Anderson, who later became a domestic policy adviser in the new administration. Anderson told Hedrick Smith, *New York Times* reporter and author of *The Power Game*, that Reagan was dismayed when told that if the U.S. learned a Soviet ICBM was headed toward an American city, the only possible response would be to call city officials and tell them that they would be bombed within fifteen or so minutes.

In 1980, Reagan ran for president on a platform that included "vigorous research and development of an effective antiballistic missile system, such as is already at hand in the Soviet Union, as well as more modern ABM technologies." The platform also called for new offensive missiles and an "overall military and technological superiority over the Soviet Union."

A few days after Reagan was elected in November 1980, the Lawrence Livermore Laboratory detonated a nuclear weapon underground in Nevada that tested a new concept: the so-called X-ray laser, later revealed publicly by George Keyworth in a January 14, 1983, speech at Livermore. The device was a prototype of what Teller was calling a "third-generation" nuclear weapon, the first two being the A-bomb and the hydrogen bomb.

The X-ray laser was intended to be a space-based weapon system, where a hydrogen bomb would be detonated in space and pump a tremendous wave of energy through a laser rod. X-ray laser beams with very short wavelengths would result which would then be directed at enemy ballistic missiles after they were launched against targets in the U.S.

The feasibility of the concept was never demonstrated, but the political implications of the X-ray laser and other kinds of possible space-based nuclear weaponry were severe. Within the closed circles of government policymakers, the X-ray laser test was a source of great excitement that added to Teller's influence and prestige. From the first days of the Reagan administration, Teller lobbied for a commitment to anti-ballistic missile research and testing that would focus on lasers and other new developments coming out of the Livermore lab.

The masterminds of this next leap forward in the arms race began to move their project ahead as soon as Reagan was inaugurated in January 1981. Early in the Reagan administration, Teller began to meet with Reagan's Kitchen Cabinet. The meetings were facilitated by presidential advisers Edwin Meese, future attorney general, and William C. Clark, who later became national security adviser after the resignation of Richard Allen.

The meetings took place at the Heritage Foundation, then a fledgling conservative think tank located a few blocks from the Hart Senate Office Building on Capitol Hill. The foundation was created in 1973 by Edwin J. Feulner and Paul Weyrich, both congressional aides, with money provided by Joseph Coors. When Reagan won the 1980 presidential election, the foundation quickly asserted its power by filling key policy-level jobs with candidates it deemed appropriate. According to a September 22, 1985, *Washington Post* article, T. Kenneth Cribb, counselor to Meese, said, "Having an endorsement from Heritage is important. It's almost like shorthand. It cuts through the inquiries that would have to be made otherwise." Later, the Heritage Foundation was instrumental in placing William Graham as deputy administrator at NASA.

The goal of the Kitchen Cabinet—extraordinary for a non-official body—was, in the words of William Broad, writing in his 1985 book *Star Warriors*, "to formulate a plan for creating a national system of defense and to convey that plan to the newly elected president." The group liked Teller's plan based on nuclear-powered X-rays. The Kitchen Cabinet acquired security clearances so they could be let in on the secrets of third-generation weapons research emanating from Livermore.

According to Broad, "The group's first meeting with the president took place in January 1982, followed by two other White House visits prior to the 'Star Wars' speech of March 1983." With Reagan now on board, the planners needed an official sponsor. This requirement was met by Deputy National Security Adviser Robert "Bud" McFarland, who later took over as NSA from Judge William Clark in late 1983 when the latter replaced James Watt as Secretary of the Interior. The Strategic Defense Initiative—SDI—now became a pet project of the National Security Council and—like the later Iran/Contra arms deals—was planned in utmost secrecy. The federal agencies with the functional authority, technical expertise, and the most direct interest in policy formulation and implementation—Defense and State—were excluded from the planning stages, though the subject was broached in a 1982 meeting of the Joint Chiefs of Staff attended by the president.

The next requirement after an internal sponsor was the selling of the program. This became the job of President Reagan himself, and he did so in a characteristic manner. He went directly to the public with a televised speech on March 23, 1983, with virtually no prior consultation with anyone in his administration or Congress. Reagan wrote much of the speech himself at Camp David.

The astonishing thing was that Reagan succeeded, and the Strategic Defense Initiative—"Star Wars"—was born. In his March 23 speech, he said:

> ... If the Soviet Union will join us in our effort to achieve major arms reductions we will have succeeded in stabilizing the nuclear balance. Nevertheless it will still be necessary to rely on the specter of retaliation—on mutual threat, and that is a sad commentary on the human condition.
>
> Would it not be better to save lives than to avenge them? Are we not capable of demonstrating our peaceful intentions by applying all our abilities and our ingenuity to achieving a truly lasting stability? I think we are—indeed, we must! After careful consultation with my advisers, including the Joint Chiefs of Staff, I believe there is a way. Let me share with you a vision of the future which offers hope. It is that we embark on a program to counter the awesome Soviet missile threat with measures that are defensive. Let us turn to the very strengths in technology that spawned our great industrial base and that have given us the quality of life we enjoy today.

The president gave some indication that he was aware his program would be viewed as a huge escalation of the arms race by saying:

> I clearly recognize that defensive systems have limitations and raise certain problems and ambiguities. If paired with offensive systems, they can be viewed as fostering an aggressive policy, and no one wants that.

Toward the end of his speech, Reagan said, "We seek neither military superiority nor political advantage." But the chosen means—"defensive technologies"—had been steadfastly rejected by all responsible parties—scientific, military, and political—since it was first broached in the early 1960s. No one had ever been able to demonstrate satisfactorily that once either the U.S. or the Soviet Union launched its nuclear arsenal of ICBMs, the other side could shoot them down, even had the ABM

Treaty not existed. And while there may have been some technological justification for research into ground-based defensive systems, a space-based capability always seemed out of the question.

If the president's proposal meant what it said, he was, only halfway through his first term, staking the security of the U.S. on an idea with virtually no chance of success and with massive potential liabilities.

After Reagan's speech, the White House stepped out to publicize the new program. A leading figure in the promotional effort was George Keyworth, who now began to push SDI with the science community and Congress. According to a November 11, 1985, article in the *National Journal*, Keyworth, who had in his portfolio all the scientific issues facing the U.S. government, spent "roughly one-half his time on SDI." In a 1985 interview with Daniel Greenberg, editor of *Science and Government Report*, Keyworth said, "I believe like a religion, almost, that strategic defense against ballistic missiles is feasible, necessary, and stabilizing."

On November 7, 1983, Keyworth made a speech in favor of testing a laser anti-satellite system. He wanted the U.S. to show the Soviets that we had "an important part of the technology for an ABM system . . . and that development was more a matter of time than breakthroughs at that point." He added that this "would pressure the Soviets to take our arms reduction proposals much more seriously than they do now." Later in 1983 he said he wanted the U.S. to develop a larger anti-satellite (ASAT) capability, "not because that is the best way to do the ASAT mission, but because it will give us the technology to do the ABM mission." And connected with Keyworth's effort to sell the SDI program to university researchers, the Pentagon awarded a number of highly-visible contracts, most notably to researchers at the California Institute of Technology, Carnegie-Mellon, and MIT.

For a presidential science adviser to become the prime spokesman for the largest military weapons program in history showed the degree to which science had compromised itself within U.S. government circles. As a result of the pressures exerted by Keyworth and other partisans, acceptance of SDI quickly became a political litmus test of loyalty to the president. Top officials within the administration who had been shocked when the March 1983 speech was proposed quickly fell into line as backers of the proposal.

Congressional Republicans, as well as many Democrats, also fell into formation. One reason was that perhaps the most powerful lobbying group in the U.S. viewed SDI as a bonanza. According to one defense analyst, Wolfgang H. Demisch of the First Boston Corp:

> The traditional defense budget clearly isn't going to grow much in the near future. Every company is on notice that, if they want to be a long-term player, they can't let SDI get away.

The primary beneficiaries were in fact the big west coast aerospace firms that formed the backbone of President Reagan's constituency. By late 1985, the TRW Corporation, based in Redondo Beach, California, led in SDI contracts with awards of $424 million. Boeing had awards of $217 million, and Lockheed had $192 million. And these were just the initial "project definition" studies. The firms involved in SDI viewed with foreboding the possibility that at some point the program would go on the table as a bargaining chip in arms-control talks with the Soviet Union. This was one reason that both the Reagan administration and the contractors were anxious to sink so much money into SDI that no future presidential administration could undo it.

Support for SDI had also been firmed up by the fact that Soviet Premier Mikhael Gorbachev reacted to it with such apparent alarm during the months preceding the 1985 Geneva Summit. He might have done better by laughing it off. But SDI seemed like an easy target of Soviet efforts to portray Reagan as a warmonger. This played into Reagan's hands, making him seem like a strong leader who was facing down the head of the communist "evil empire."

Soon the Pentagon had established a Strategic Defense Initiative Office (SDIO) directly under the Secretary of Defense. The White House also convened three major panels for feasibility studies that essentially were to ratify and justify decisions that had already been made.

One of these panels was led by former—and future—NASA Administrator James Fletcher. The "Fletcher Commission" had the official name of the Defense Technologies Study Panel. The other two panels dealt with missile defense strategy. As Dr. Robert Bowman wrote, Fletcher's panel:

> . . . attempted to identify the technology hurdles to be overcome in pursuing a "Star Wars" system capable of intercepting 99.9% of ICBMs

launched against us. The fifty-person panel worked for four and a half months and produced a voluminous classified report which included a good bit of skepticism.

There was a vast difference, however, between the body of the report and what the president and the public read. As Jerome Wiesner and Kosta Tsipis wrote in the *New York Times*:

> In an effort to counter the incredulity generated by [the president's March 23, 1983, speech], the White House appointed a committee of experts under James Fletcher . . . to decide ex post facto whether Star Wars would be technically feasible. The panel produced a pessimistic report, curiously prefaced by an enthusiastic and optimistic introduction, the only part of the report usually read by most non-experts. Asked about this, Mr. Fletcher made the astounding statement that it had not been written by anyone on the committee. By whom, then? "Somebody in the White House," he replied.

Statements like this made it clear how dubious Reagan's SDI program really was. An alert Congress easily could have questioned the president for throwing away taxpayer money on a boondoggle. But the worst was yet to come, because we are following a trail of events that led directly to the Challenger disaster.

In March 1984, General James Abrahamson returned to the Pentagon from NASA, where he had spent three years directing the space shuttle program, now becoming director of the Strategic Defense Initiative Office. Abrahamson's first task was to define what kind of missile defense shield could and should be built. By year's end, he had awarded the first ten major study contracts. Even at this stage, it was already apparent that the immediate objective would be to build a smaller system to protect the U.S. land-based nuclear arsenal, as opposed to a shield that could spare the civilian population from a nuclear attack. Thus within a year of the president's speech, his vision of "changing the course of human history," by saving civilians from attack, had already been discarded.

But space weapons research was alive and well. Ten percent of the SDIO budget was for space-based nuclear weapons research. SDI had

quickly become a limited ABM system, and Abrahamson acknowledged that within a few years the program would cross the boundary
of legal activity allowed by the ABM Treaty. The program he eventually
outlined bore scant resemblance to President Reagan's scheme to
remove the threat of nuclear war. Rather it was an extension of
deterrence—mutually assured destruction. Critics called the plan
"madder than MAD."

These permutations did not put a damper on the enthusiasm exhib-
ited by the aerospace industry toward SDI. The same firms which had
been selected for the definition studies were the ones that would be bid-
ding on the hardware contracts to build whatever system was designed.

SDI research and development proceeded, with various groups and
individuals lining up for or against. Among the groups against SDI were
the Union of Concerned Scientists, the Institute for Space and Security Studies, the Federation of American Scientists, the Brookings
Institution, and the MacArthur Foundation. The assumption that a
defensive strategic system was feasible was also criticized by the congressional Office of Technology Assessment.

The technical critique of SDI had two principal focuses. One was
that a leak-proof shield would be unbelievably complex and expensive.
The other was that a missile defense that was feasible to build would
be almost useless, in that it would defend against perhaps ten percent
of Soviet ballistic missiles and not at all against intermediate-range missiles or manned bombers.

Dr. Robert Bowman later wrote in the *Orlando Sentinel*:

. . . Consider what a Star Wars system is. It would be five or so layers of chemical laser battle stations, electromagnetic railguns, particle
beams, nuclear-weapons-generated X-rays, orbiting mirrors, etc. Besides
these many fists (kill mechanisms), it would have arms (pointing systems), a few eyes (sensors), and ears (discriminators), a brain (battle
management computer), and central nervous system (communications network).

This complex organism could be rendered totally useless by dis-
abling any one critical element—many of which are extremely vulnerable, particularly those based in space. It could be penetrated with
ease by employing any of several countermeasures already available.

And, like any Maginot line, it could be skirted with delivery systems that do not go through space.

Still, the initial experiments went forward, including one aboard the shuttle Discovery. This made 1985 a turning point in U.S. military history by seeing a test of space weaponry on a manned space vehicle launched under the authorization of the National Aeronautics and Space Act of 1958. The political pressure to press forward with SDI projects was immense, and the shuttle was to play an ongoing role.

Regarding the free-flowing money tap, at an industry seminar in Rosslyn, Virginia, in 1986, Air Force Colonel George M. Hess, Jr., director of survivability, lethality, and key technologies at SDIO, spoke of making satellites less vulnerable to attack. He said, "We can get any amount of money out of General Abrahamson we want to invest in survivability for anybody who's got a good idea."

In the process of spending, some questionable practices emerged. On December 3, 1985, *New York Times* columnist Flora Lewis reported that a March 23, 1985, test of the X-ray laser, timed to commemorate Reagan's SDI speech two years earlier, had failed so badly that it demonstrated, in the words of one scientist in the program, "instead of a weapon we have a toy." One problem was that the instruments that measured the laser were unreliable and greatly exaggerated the brightness of the beam. Lewis wrote:

> Undaunted, Mr. Teller went to Mr. Reagan and wangled another $100 million for the project, including this month's test, which will probably cost $30 million. Participants urged a delay until the measuring problem could be solved, which would take six months to a year. That was rejected on the grounds that loss of momentum would be politically unfavorable, even though the test is almost certain to be futile in the circumstances.

The resemblance between the political pressure to show progress in SDI to NASA's need to push forward with the "operational" shuttle is striking. Both shared the common fault of elevating image above reality. Flora Lewis concluded that:

The hyper-selling of "Star Wars" has gone far beyond the childish crayola spot aimed at the general public on TV, beyond the vague claim made to businessmen and allies by the program director, Lieut. Gen. James A. Abrahamson, of progress at an "incredible pace." It has gone to the point of covering up scientific failure in a way that endangers the honesty of research.

The willful distortion of research is a scandal, reminiscent of Stalin's support for Trofim Lysenko's phony theories of genetics because they were politically pleasing. The result set Soviet biology back a generation.

Meanwhile, General Abrahamson moved ahead. He had admitted publicly by now that even without SDI, the U.S. led the Soviet Union in anti-missile technology. A similar statement had been made to Congress in 1984 by Defense Advanced Research Project Director Robert Cooper. These statements by top U.S. military planners contradicted a decade-and-a-half of alarmist right-wing propaganda, but were necessary to instill confidence within Congress that those who were asking for ever-increasing amounts of money had the know-how to put it to good use.

By November 1985, the SDIO had disclosed plans for a seven-layered space defense system consisting of thousands of orbiting armed satellites. It was understood that the space shuttle would play the key role in the testing and deployment of this array, which would be many times as complex as the shuttle itself. According to the party line, the now-operational shuttle worked great. Why shouldn't SDI work just as well?

After the Challenger disaster, SDI planners became more realistic. By 1988, plans had been scaled-back to a mere $69 billion system, virtually nothing compared to what had been proposed. Under the new plan, the system would be mounted on a few space reconnaissance platforms, a plan that was criticized in Congress as much less capable than had been promised and easy to shoot down by an enemy attack. And when the Soviet Union collapsed, most of the SDI scheme was put in mothballs.

But in 1985, things looked promising indeed, for faith in the technology was high. The career military had long been skeptical of technological solutions that excluded the human element, but the space weaponry technocrats were on a roll. Unfortunately, it was the shuttle itself that now stood as the weak link. With so much of the Pentagon's new wave of military planning dependent on the shuttle, how could it be that it was in such unreliable hands: i.e., that of NASA and its luke-warm technocratic leadership headed by James Beggs, a political moderate? NASA never quite fit in with the Conservative Movement's vision, but events were moving along to correct that flaw.

"WE'LL END UP RULING THE WORLD"

—The Right Wing Subverts NASA's Leadership

IN THE LATE 1960s, the U.S. concluded that there was no immediate military requirement for manned spaceflight. This led to cancellation of all projected manned Air Force programs. When the Carter administration decided in the late 1970s to use the shuttle for all civilian and military space launches, the only immediate military uses were for the launch of spy and communication satellites and for small-scale experiments in manned surveillance and photography of foreign military sites.

Planned military use of space was to change in a big way with the Reagan military build-up, with advances in space communications and weapons technology, and with the Strategic Defense Initiative. SDI viewed the shuttle as a platform for testing of weapons technology, with early tests being readied to measure laser beams, practice aiming lasers at objects in space, and fire subatomic particles.

In early 1985, the Pentagon said that initial shuttle tests in tracking and targeting enemy missiles from space would start within two years. General Abrahamson told *Aviation Week and Space Technology* in February 1985 that, "The key point is that I am trying to get people to understand that the flexibility of the space shuttle offers some good ways to get additional data." He said that starting in 1987, there would be SDI experiments on two shuttle missions per year.

The first test was conducted earlier than that, taking place on Discovery on June 20, 1985. The test was an attempt to bounce a laser beam off Discovery from the ground, but it failed when controllers sent instructions to the crew in nautical miles instead of feet, causing Discovery to be out of position. The test was conducted successfully two days later, but the contrast between elementary human error and the pretensions of SDI planners regarding a system of cosmic complexity made NASA and the shuttle program look ridiculous. The fiasco was worsened by the fact that DoD had given the test an extraordinary level of publicity, obviously to impress people with how far the SDI program had advanced.

There had been other SDI payloads before the Challenger disaster, but soon the military was to have its own shuttle launch capability. The first shuttle flight out of Vandenberg Air Force Base in California, and also the first that would use the lightweight filament wound case booster rocket, was scheduled for mid-1986. It would also be the first time the space shuttle main engines would run at 109% of rated power. Aboard for this mission would be Under Secretary of the Air Force Edward Aldridge, the Pentagon's first civilian passenger, imitating the previous VIP astronauts Garn and Nelson. To support SDI and other military projects, NASA also added eight military officers to the astronaut corps in mid-1985 out of a total of thirteen new members selected.

One particularly important SDI tracking and pointing experiment that would use a large laser beam had been planned for a late 1986 shuttle mission, though it had to be cancelled after the Challenger disaster. It was reportedly an experiment growing out of what had been called the Talon Gold project. According to Dr. Robert Bowman, who directed the project while with the Air Force:

> The end result of the restructured Talon Gold program will be a pointer-tracker system that can be combined with the other two elements of the DARPA triad to form a prototype laser battle station. The import of this program is that it represents the first publicly acknowledged use of the space shuttle for large-scale space weapons tests.

Plans to use the shuttle for SDI testing accelerated, though NASA's spaceflight chief Jesse Moore said publicly, as did James Beggs, that the agency viewed DoD's Strategic Defense Initiative Office as simply one of several "customers." Unfortunately for NASA, when the Department of Defense played the role of a "customer," it was accustomed to calling the shots. So why should NASA be different? DoD viewed the shuttle as its primary means of carrying into space the equipment needed for the space-based battle stations that were the core of the planned SDI system. In the longer term, as SDI matured, the shuttle could be used to repair SDI satellites and to carry out command, control, communications, and intelligence activities (CI3), including battle coordination, guiding the delivery of nuclear warheads, electronic snooping, target selection, etc.

Later, depending on how far SDI proceeded, shuttle-mounted weapons such as laser cannons were envisioned to shoot down enemy satellites or missiles, or, when the technology became available, could conceivably attempt to incinerate enemy cities. Offensive and defensive weapons could be launched into space, and there was even talk of sending the president into orbit in wartime, allowing him a haven from which to guide military operations. Unfortunately, the utility of the shuttle for these purposes would disappear once war broke out, as, without a maze of defensive space weapons to protect it, the spacecraft would be easy to shoot down. The shuttle's launch facilities were also an easy target for attack or sabotage.

Some SDI schemes required a degree of shuttle utilization that crossed well over into the realm of fantasy. The so-called chemical laser, for instance, was to be powered by hydrogen and fluorine. Commentators estimated that to put the components in orbit for a fleet of laser battle stations would take the shuttle one hundred years. Ashton Carter, in a well-known 1984 Office of Technology Assessment background paper entitled "Directed Missile Defenses in Space," placed the estimate higher—1,400 shuttle flights—two hundred years at the 1985 launch rate, assuming no interference from any civilian missions.

According to General Abrahamson's seven-tiered missile defense system announced in November 1985, the SDI hardware to be placed initially into orbit included one-shot "kinetic" weapons, relay mirrors, laser radars, large multi-shot directed energy weapons, satellite-based tracking sensors—all in low-orbit, the maximum the shuttle could reach—and battle-management satellite computers boosted with shuttle-borne upper stages to a 22,300-mile geosynchronous orbit. Most of this was to be lofted into space by the shuttle or its planned successor vehicles, including an unmanned space transport and a manned spaceplane to be developed jointly by DoD and NASA. At a June 17, 1986, Senate Space Subcommittee hearing, Senator John D. Rockefeller IV said, "It has been suggested by SDI people that there would have to be literally 50,000 launches at the current rate to get SDI working." 50,000 launches would cost $3.5 trillion in operational costs, assuming a perfectly working shuttle with no accidents and no other payloads.

While such a launch rate was inconceivable, it was clear that somehow the U.S. was going to have an awful lot of SDI "stuff" to put up there and that far more shuttle flights would be needed than the eight per year the Air Force agreed to in meetings with NASA and the White House in 1985. This was at the time the White House agreed to allow the Air Force to purchase ten new Titan 34D-7 unmanned launch rockets. Military anxiety was fed that year by a National Research Council study which warned that a "generic failure" in the shuttle fleet—i.e., a failure resulting from a design flaw—"could shut down the nation's ability to conduct space launches." The study also noted that the shuttle had never met the 65,000-pound capacity required for the largest military payloads.

During 1985, the military lobbied for more shuttle payloads simply because it had no choice, given the numbers it was facing and the political pressure from the White House to push SDI forward. While the White House order of March 1985 committed the Air Force to eight shuttle flights per year, a number NASA used as the basis for its reports to Congress, Under Secretary Aldridge was reported as foreseeing an average of ten military shuttle launches per year through 1995. But even this number was too low.

On July 23, 1985, the day I wrote my O-ring memo at NASA on a possible shuttle catastrophe, Major General Donald Kutyna told Representative Bill Nelson and the combined House Armed Services and Science and Technology Committees that "excluding Strategic Defense Initiative requirements, we anticipate launching nine to twelve shuttle-equivalent payloads per year through the 1990s." General James Abrahamson told the committees that the long-term flight rate for the SDI program "by itself would equal or significantly exceed the current and projected national launch capability" of the space shuttle.

Whatever figures are taken, Pentagon planning for the shuttle, with SDI added, was now well beyond the eight flights per year of the 1985 White House order, a fact that aroused considerable anxiety within Congress. Among others, Congressman Bill Nelson was pushing for a fifth shuttle orbiter to be built to provide what he called "assured access to space."

James Beggs was no SDI zealot. Beggs favored a balanced program of space science, exploration, commercial experimentation in space manufacturing, and the launching of commercial and foreign satellites, along with national defense. With the shuttle flight rate likely to top out at eighteen to twenty-four launches per year, this meant no more than six to eight flights for each of the primary business lines for the foreseeable future. There was no chance SDI could be implemented, given these figures.

Beggs also persisted in attempting to fend off competition from unmanned launchers operated by private competitors. This continued to anger political conservatives, who favored the privatization of as many government functions as possible. Beggs was willing to entertain eventually spinning off the shuttle to the private sector, but he also saw NASA's destiny in the traditional terms of building the stepping stones to new adventures in manned exploration of the solar system. His immediate program was to create an operational space shuttle as a step toward a permanently manned International Space Station. As always, Mars beckoned. Beggs's vision was a continuation of the dominant themes at NASA since the space agency was created, but it did not correspond to that of the right-wing partisans who backed SDI. So Beggs had to go. But the president didn't like to fire people.

———

UNDER THE REAGAN administration, the political right wing achieved its strongest measure of political power up to that time. Calling itself the Conservative Movement, or just the Movement, among its primary objectives was to place certified conservatives in policy-level jobs within the executive branch. Among the key players in this operation was Edwin Meese, Reagan's chief of staff during his California governorship. Meese became a key adviser to the president, and with Michael Deever and James Baker part of the "triumvirate" that ran the White

House during Reagan's first term. Meese was a leader of the administration's Movement faction and the top White House conservative. Later he was appointed attorney general of the U.S. in 1984.

Another major Movement figure was John Herrington, the White House personnel director. Herrington was a California lawyer and real estate developer who had worked as an advance man for Reagan since his successful 1966 campaign for the California statehouse. In 1985, Herrington was named secretary of energy, placing him over the Lawrence Livermore lab, as well as U.S. facilities for the manufacture of nuclear weapons. He thus became a central figure in the SDI program by being in charge of the research and testing of third-generation nuclear weapons such as the X-ray laser that were integral to Edward Teller's vision of the American future in space.

As in the early days of the Reagan administration, when it hosted the meetings of the Kitchen Cabinet with Teller that led to President Reagan's SDI speech, the Heritage Foundation was again a catalyst in assuring that federal appointments went to the right people. It was said, for instance, that foundation president Edwin Feulner cleared every appointment to the U.S. Information Agency. The foundation was also able to use vigorous lobbying to place conservative Danny J. Boggs as deputy secretary of energy, another post with authority over nuclear weapons development. The foundation also took part in an informal group, including CIA Director William Casey, which sought to place Movement people in State Department jobs. The group failed, however, to overcome control of State by the career foreign service.

Another major lobbying organization that supported SDI was the Committee on the Present Danger (CPD). The CPD was founded in 1976 at the end of the Ford administration and included conservative members of both political parties, including, once again, Edward Teller. CPD's policy statement began:

> Our country is in a period of danger, and the danger is increasing. Unless decisive steps are taken to alert the nation, and to change the course of its policy, our economic and military capacity will become inadequate to assure peace with security.

The best-known CPD alumnus was Ronald Reagan, whose election threw open the doors of government to its members. By November 23,

1981, ten months after Reagan's inauguration, thirty-two of CPD's 182 members had been named to major federal government policy positions. The *Washington Post* reported:

> Alumni of the committee are sprinkled throughout the highest levels of the government, amounting to a virtual takeover of the nation's national security apparatus.

Two members of the CPD's executive board played major roles in the Challenger history and investigation. One was William Graham, who became NASA's deputy, then acting administrator, in November 1985. The other was Washington, D.C., attorney David Acheson, a member of the Challenger Commission who headed the sub-group in charge of investigating the circumstances of the flawed launch decision.

As members of the CPD executive board, Graham and Acheson contributed to setting policy for the organization. In 1982, CPD published a pamphlet that chided the Reagan administration, whose massive military build-up would become the largest in peacetime history, on the grounds that "the administration's defense program is a minimal one." Instead, CPD advocated a huge additional increase in defense spending, one that could lead to fifty-five percent growth in Navy shipbuilding over the Reagan program, a doubling of strategic airlift capability, and a restoration of the military draft as part of "a program to mobilize the nation's human resources." CPD also said, "The U.S. should reconstitute its lost capabilities for industrial mobilization." In other words, the CPD wanted to place the U.S. economy and government on a full wartime footing.

CPD staunchly supported the SDI program. An October 1986 CPD statement written by Edward Teller termed SDI "an attempt to find out what is already known in Russia." This was in contrast to statements to Congress by General Abrahamson and others that the U.S. had a ten-year lead over the Soviet Union in space weapons technology.

Both the Heritage Foundation and the Committee on the Present Danger supported the move to place William Graham at NASA. These organizations were allied with elements of the White House staff, where the most conservative unit was considered the Office of Communications. Within this office was the speechwriting group, where the 1986 State of the Union address, which was to mention Teacher-in-Space

Christa McAuliffe aboard Challenger, was written. Director of Communications at the White House was Patrick Buchanan, hired by Chief of Staff Donald Regan in 1985. The top White House speechwriter was Anthony Dolan, a former investigative journalist and author of Reagan's famous "evil empire" speech. In September 1985, Dolan said of the Conservative Movement, "I get the feeling that we'll end up ruling the world. I wonder if I'm wrong."

During 1985, the Conservative Movement decided to take over NASA. According to conversations I had after the Challenger disaster with Christine Dolan, political news director of the Cable News Network, a group was set up that included Edwin Meese, John Herrington, and figures with the Heritage Foundation. Dolan told me this group met at a restaurant in Georgetown to decide their strategy. They were encouraged by their belief that the prospects of budget cuts under the new Graham-Rudman-Hollings budget control legislation would make NASA more dependent on Defense Department reimbursements, and thus more compliant in emphasizing military over civilian priorities.

According to Christine Dolan, the Meese/Herrington/Heritage Foundation group decided to "fix" NASA by placing William Graham in the deputy administrator's job that Dr. Hans Mark had vacated in 1984 when he left to become chancellor of the University of Texas.

Graham had been an adviser to Ronald Reagan in the 1980 presidential campaign. He was a member of the administration's transition team and was later named chairman of the General Advisory Council on Arms Control and Disarmament. This committee advised the Arms Control and Disarmament Agency, which, contrary to its name, was one of the forces behind the Reagan military escalation. The agency was headed by Kenneth Adelman, another CPD member. Graham was also the favored candidate of George Keyworth for deputy administrator of NASA. Prior to his designation, Graham had a standing invitation to join the Reagan administration in a policy-level post.

Graham had a B.S. in physics from the California Institute of Technology and an M.S. and PhD from Stanford. He had spent three years at Hughes Aircraft and three more at the Air Force Weapons Laboratory in Albuquerque, New Mexico. There he became a nuclear weapons "effects" expert. Graham then spent six years as a staff scientist at the RAND Corporation in Santa Monica, California, but left to become a co-founder of

R&D Associates in Marina Del Rey. There he was senior associate, corporate program manager, and assistant to the company president.

When in 1985 Graham's name came up as a choice to be NASA's deputy administrator, the appointment was strenuously opposed by James Beggs. In order to allay fears in Congress that his appointment meant the further militarization of NASA, the administration portrayed Graham as "just a technician."

Regarding Graham's firm, R&D Associates, Thomond O'Brien of the Institute of Space and Security Studies wrote:

> A study by R&D Associates was made public in May 1985 detailing the offensive capabilities of lasers being developed under the SDI program. The study reported, "In a matter of hours, a laser defense system powerful enough to cope with the ballistic missile threat can also destroy the enemy's major cities by fire. The attack would proceed city by city, the attack time for each city being only a matter of minutes. Not nuclear destruction, but Armageddon all the same." The report went on to state, "After spending hundreds of billions of dollars we would be back where we started from: deterrence by retaliation. Our cities would be hostage to lasers instead of nuclear weapons." One such laser is the free electron laser being developed at the Lawrence Livermore National Laboratory.
>
> Dr. Latter of R&D Associates said that he and Dr. Marinelli, co-authors of the report, were under pressure not to release the study and that people at SDIO were very unhappy to see reports like this become public. Each stated that it was a "very touchy subject."

The R&D Associates study was one of many indications that President Reagan's March 1983 SDI speech was really not a proposal for a defensive shield but rather a radical escalation of the arms race with offensive as well as defensive capabilities. The R&D study was reported by Robert Scheer of the *Los Angeles Times*, who also quoted Theodore A. Postol, former adviser to the chief of naval operations, who said that such lasers could create "mass fires of enormous scale and ferocity." And in an article in *Physics and Society*, Argonne National Laboratory physicist Caroline L. Herzenberg wrote that massive urban fires started by lasers could cause the same effects as "nuclear winter."

While the R&D Associates study could be read as questioning the basic premise of SDI as a defensive system, it also showed that William Graham's think tank was at the heart of the space weapons community and well understood the implications of what was underway with the SDI program.

The problem within the Reagan administration in placing Graham at NASA was that James Beggs did not want him. In early 1985, Beggs interviewed the slate of candidates offered by the White House for the job and said he would take any of them but Graham. He said Graham had no management experience and was unqualified. But the White House insisted that Graham was the man. Beggs protested to Chief of Staff Donald Regan, who agreed with his assessment of Graham's lack of qualifications but said he couldn't help. He told Beggs that Graham had support from the "west coast."

Finally, just before John Herrington left the White House personnel office to head the Energy Department, he and Meese reportedly went into the Oval Office with an order for Graham's appointment. Reagan signed. Beggs had to give in, though he viewed the appointment as the prelude to turning the shuttle over to the Air Force. Graham's name was sent to the Senate for confirmation, and he took office on November 25, 1985.

Eight days later, Beggs was indicted by a California grand jury for fraud in General Dynamics' handling of an Army weapons contract. Evidence for the indictment had been developed by the Justice Department under extremely peculiar circumstances, and suddenly Graham was now elevated to the position of acting administrator. The indictment charged Beggs and three other General Dynamics executives with trying to cover-up cost overruns on a fixed-price Army contract awarded in 1978 to build prototypes of the Sergeant York anti-aircraft gun. The project had been cancelled before the gun went into production. Beggs had not worked directly on the contract but had overseen it while he was an executive vice president at General Dynamics' St. Louis headquarters. The defendants were charged with concealing the overruns by shifting the costs to research and bid preparation for other project work.

Problems of this type were normally worked out administratively between the government and the contractor. No one had ever been indicted, much less convicted, on these sorts of charges before, and there were indications that the contract in question actually permitted such billing to be done.

To the public, however, it appeared that the Reagan administration had taken a step to crack down on defense procurement fraud. General Dynamics had been the recent subject of highly-publicized government investigations. In a December 4, 1985, editorial, the *New York Times* called Beggs "a surprising victim," but added that "indicting General Dynamics for misattributed costs is a welcome step."

Here the *Times* misspoke. It was not General Dynamics that was indicted. It was Beggs and his colleagues. They, not General Dynamics, were in danger of having their careers and reputations destroyed and of being sentenced to a federal penitentiary. The *Times* went on that "even a leave of absence would be an embarrassment to the president he serves," urging Beggs to resign. "The charge," the *Times* said, "involves the plain and squalid crime of mugging the taxpayer."

The White House gave Beggs the opportunity to resign. On December 4, the day after the indictment, spokesman Larry Speakes said President Reagan believed Beggs "will do the right and proper thing . . . whether it is to continue or not to continue—whatever he does, in our view, will be the right and proper thing." But Beggs would not quit. He asked for a leave of absence, to which President Reagan, ever loath to fire anyone, agreed.

Just before Beggs' leave began, NASA's top twenty-seven managers sent Congress and the White House a statement praising him as "an individual with the highest standards of integrity which have earned him the esteem and respect of his colleagues." Beggs made a defiant statement to NASA's employees that:

> There is nothing that I did in the case involved that I would not do again, if I had to do it over again. We acted in an entirely ethical, legal, and moral sense. The charges are therefore baseless, they are outrageous, ridiculous, and I feel confident that once this is brought to trial I'll be completely exonerated of the charges.

To the chagrin of Graham, Beggs refused to vacate his office, stubbornly continuing to frequent the premises at 400 Maryland Avenue. He was there when Challenger blew up.

. . .

Following the Challenger disaster, after I learned the details of the Beggs case from CNN's Christine Dolan, I located the attorney at the Justice Department who had been in charge of the initial investigation. "I reported," he told me, "that there was nothing that had been done that was criminal in nature." He added that cases of this type "take a lot of work and investigation. You don't continue beyond the point where it looks like a crime was not committed. You don't keep spinning your wheels for the sake of spinning your wheels."

The attorney then took a transfer from Justice's Criminal to its Civil Division. He said that the transfer was voluntary and not related to his finding of no criminal activity in the General Dynamics case. His successor, however, carried what had been viewed as a non-existent case to the federal grand jury in Los Angeles, which dutifully handed down the indictment.

The attorney said that because the head of a federal agency was involved, the case could not have been carried forward unless Attorney General Edwin Meese had been informed. "I would be amazed," he said, if the decision memo on the case "was not passed up the line" to Meese. If this were true, it would then have been Meese's decision whether to proceed with an indictment of Beggs on charges that were known at the time to be spurious, or whether the matter should be pursued as a civil or administrative matter, or even not at all.

Meese's latitude in the matter would have been enhanced by the lack of clear guidelines for Justice to follow in the area of defense procurement fraud, where the statutes were unclear and case law practically non-existent. The indictment made the Justice Department look good to the press and created the impression that the Reagan administration was attacking procurement fraud so vigorously that it was willing to sacrifice one of its own top officials. Beggs' career was ruined in the process. Later, the Justice Department admitted it had no case and that there had been no wrongdoing. The charges against Beggs and the other defendants were dismissed in federal district court on June 19, 1987, and Edwin Meese apologized. But Beggs had successfully been removed from NASA. For that, a trial and conviction were not needed. The indictment was enough.

William Graham could not conceal his delight at his good fortune in taking over the leadership of the fabled National Aeronautics and

Space Administration. In an article entitled, "New NASA Chief is on Top of the World," Richard Corrigan of the *National Journal* reported three days before Challenger was lost:

> They say you can tell the age of the boy by the price of the toy. William R. Graham suddenly finds himself in charge of billions of dollars' worth of high technology gear as acting chief of the nation's space agency, and, at age 48, he's as giddy as a kid at Disney World.
>
> "This is the greatest job in the world," said Graham, acting administrator of NASA, saying he feels sorry for Ronald Reagan. "If I were president," Graham said, "I'd take the NASA job" and let somebody else run the White House.

Having no experience himself at managing large organizations, Graham named Philip E. Culbertson, NASA's space station director, to the newly minted post of general manager.

Graham did not follow the customary administrator's protocol, in that he skipped the launch of the oft-postponed 61-C mission carrying Congressman Bill Nelson, which lifted off on January 12, 1985, and it was said he was spending time lobbying NASA's overseers in the House and Senate to support his hoped-for designation as Beggs's permanent successor. Graham also told Jesse Moore's Office of Space Flight to accept no more commercial customers on the shuttle. This reversed one of Beggs's most cherished policies, opened the door to the privatization of spaceflight by encouraging private companies to enter the launch business, and fueled speculation that a higher degree of military utilization of the shuttle was on the way.

Then, on January 23, 1986, just five days before Challenger blew up, Jesse Moore signed a new agreement with Secretary of the Air Force Edward Aldridge for a military flight rate significantly higher than what NASA had told Congress. Publicly, NASA had said the military would fly eight shuttle-equivalent missions per year, or one-third of projected shuttle capacity when the goal of twenty-four flights per year was reached around 1990. The new Moore/Aldridge plan, however, listed a fiscal year 1991 military flight rate of 11.533—i.e., eleven and a half shuttle-equivalent payloads, with reimbursements totaling $982,504,000. Though Graham's name did not appear on the document, this was the first major agreement signed between NASA and the Air Force during his tenure. It represented a major departure from Beggs's balanced program of equal shuttle utilization for science, commerce, and defense.

With the agreed-upon priority NASA was to give military missions and the expectation within the agency that a realistic shuttle flight rate would be closer to eighteen per year than twenty-four, it would have been possible that by 1991 well over half of all shuttle missions would have been military. Unquestionably, the increased number of flights was for SDI payloads, since many of DoD's conventional satellites would be going into orbit on the new unmanned 34D-7 Titans now on order.

Later I mentioned the Moore/Aldridge agreement to a journalist, who asked a congressional staff aide if they were aware of it. The aide said that Congress was not. He added that had they known, it would have been viewed as a violation of the National Aeronautics and Space Act, which stated that only DoD was to fly military missions. (The aide did not explain why 11.5 flights per year would be a violation while the previous number of eight was not.)

Thus on the eve of the Challenger launch, it is a fact, which was not generally recognized in the literature on the disaster, that NASA was in the throes of the greatest leadership crisis in its history. James Beggs, the driving force behind the shuttle's operational policy, pined in his office, without authority or official standing, indicted by the Justice Department for non-existent crimes. William Graham, a Conservative Movement ideologue, was without space program experience, had little knowledge of shuttle technology, and had no political constituency outside the radical right. And there was no deputy administrator who could help out once Graham was elevated to the acting position. Further, Jesse Moore had just been selected as the new director of the Johnson Space Center, where he was to report after the May 1986 planetary shuttle missions. Moore was in no position to rock the boat, as he had much to lose if he did anything to jeopardize his transfer to Houston.

The right-wing putsch to gain control of NASA had succeeded, and the agency lay at the feet of the SDI zealots. But the turmoil that resulted cost the lives of seven astronauts, including Christa McAuliffe, the Teacher-in-Space.

We are told that President Reagan did not like to make decisions. The day Challenger went down, the *San Jose Mercury-News* printed a story that quoted Assistant Secretary of Defense Richard Perle:

> "There has been a lot of infighting. One reason for that is that the president doesn't give strong direction. He lets every issue ventilate until it bubbles up and forces a decision. On the other hand, there hasn't been a disaster, so maybe Reagan's system works."

The disaster that took place at the Kennedy Space Center that morning was partly a result of the type of infighting Perle described, by which the right-wing faction within the administration had sown confusion at NASA.

But the president understood the art of publicity quite well. It was in this area alone that NASA and the White House had forged an effective partnership. Federal agencies are constantly making proposals to the White House for the president to participate in agency-sponsored events and thereby publicize their activities. But Reagan had come to the presidency by running against the Washington bureaucracy. One of the few agencies he paid attention to was NASA, perhaps in part because the space shuttle program that was commencing when he took office offered him media exposure.

Under circumstances totally ignored by the Presidential Commission, President Reagan used the manned space program as a political backdrop more frequently and effectively than any other president. This was done primarily through tightly scripted phone calls from the president to the shuttle. There was also a visit by Reagan to mission control in Houston, his attendance and speech at the landing of Columbia at Edwards on July 4, 1982, and calls and visits by Vice President Bush. The contacts declined by 1985, because shuttle flights were becoming more routine and because of the limitations imposed by such circumstances as the two classified DoD missions and the hijacking of a TWA airliner at the Beirut airport which coincided with the shuttle's Arabsat mission. At the time of two other 1985 flights, the president was undergoing intestinal cancer surgery. There was also the Spacelab mission in 1985, which was managed mainly by West Germany.

The Teacher-in-Space program, however, guaranteed an opportunity for massive mutual P.R. between NASA and the president. The return of manned spaceflight with the shuttle era opened a new chapter in NASA's self-promotional annals. The human interest stories connected with the variety of shuttle astronauts going to space also allowed President Reagan to be part of the action.

As the shuttle program unfolded, NASA decided to seize on one of the more promising avenues of publicity, that of placing an "ordinary citizen" on a manned space mission. NASA had been frustrated because none of the professional astronauts who had been to space seemed to be able to express his or her experience in a way that allowed the public to understand how wonderful it all was. The fact that the books that were written, for instance by Apollo astronaut Michael Collins, were widely read, showed the potential. Still, the space program had not produced any truly great literature. So NASA decided to run a competition to select a journalist as the first "ordinary" astronaut.

But in 1984, presidential politics intervened. In the contest between Reagan and Minnesota Senator Walter Mondale, the president was being portrayed, with some success, as anti-education. In August, the National Education Association enthusiastically endorsed Mondale. In response, the White House and NASA decided that the first ordinary citizen in space would be a schoolteacher.

Reagan reportedly took a strong personal interest in the Teacher-in-Space program, and, during the several months of Christa McAuliffe's training, the White House and NASA worked together on her presentation, most notably the televised broadcast that was ultimately set for day four of the mission. This program, along with the Challenger launch, would be presented over closed-circuit TV to the nation's schools. NASA also set aside alternative times during the flight for presidential phone calls similar to Reagan's calls to the shuttle on many earlier flights. After she died aboard Challenger, one of Christa's closest friends from her hometown of Concord, New Hampshire, told me, "Christa felt Reagan was using her, but she felt that what she was doing benefited education."

When William Graham took over the top job at NASA in December, he was said to be excited about the Teacher-in-Space program. After the

Challenger disaster, he announced the program would continue, though it was put on hold when James Fletcher returned as administrator and was never reinstated. Was Graham using the Teacher-in-Space as cover for the diversion of NASA's long and proud mission of scientific and civil space exploration to becoming a virtual branch of SDI? Putting ordinary citizens on vacant space shuttle seats seemed easy and promising. It appeared cheap, painless, and popular, and the ratio of minutes of TV coverage to agency expenditure was vastly higher with someone like Christa McAuliffe aboard than for space science experiments or planetary fly-bys.

Meanwhile, the White House was crafting the 1986 State of the Union address to be delivered by President Reagan to a joint session of Congress on Tuesday, January 28, 1986.

The speech as originally written contained a pause where the president would halt and introduce, as he had done in the past, an American hero. In the past, the hero had sat in the gallery with Mrs. Reagan, but when the speech was finally given on February 4, after being postponed from the night Challenger blew up, there was no hero. The day after the disaster, the *Washington Post* printed an article by Lou Cannon—later a Reagan biographer—saying that aides told him Teacher-in-Space Christa McAuliffe was to have been mentioned in the speech. Without doubt, she was to have been the hero, though after the disaster, the White House tried to suppress any suggestion that there was a connection between Christa and the Challenger mission, and the president and his speech.

———

FEW OUTSIDE NASA seemed to grasp how ambitious the 1986 shuttle launch schedule was. Fourteen flights were listed. When the 61-C flight with Congressman Bill Nelson slipped past the Christmas and New Year holidays, the number was up to fifteen. The workload would be staggering.

As the Manifest Bingo charts showed—the ones that were passed around Director Richard Smith's conference room at KSC during the January 16-17 Centaur meetings—NASA's ability to meet the schedule depended on the measured progress of shuttle components—orbiters,

ETs, SRBs, upper stages, and payloads—through the maze of storage and processing facilities, into final assembly inside the Vehicle Assembly Building. In the VAB the shuttles would be stacked on one of the two mobile launch platforms, then slowly rolled out on railroad tracks to the distant launch pads. For the first time in the shuttle era, one of the old Apollo pads—39-B—would again be in use. The first launch from the refurbished 39-B would be the January 51-L Challenger mission.

Several, if not most, of the 1986 missions were more crucial to NASA's objectives than 51-L. One was the inaugural flight from the Vandenberg military complex with the filament wound case, now moved back to June. Two others were the May scientific missions—Galileo and Ulysses—to be deployed from the Atlantis and Challenger orbiters by the new Centaur upper stage. Another was the flight carrying the Hubble Space Telescope. The March flight of Discovery would carry ASTRO-1, the U.S.'s only major instrument for the observation of Halley's Comet, which would be visible for the first time in seventy-five years and to which the European Space Agency was giving far greater attention than NASA.

The Challenger 51-L mission was not of major significance from a scientific, commercial, or military standpoint. Its primary payload, the TDRS-2 communications satellite, was the second in the series of NASA's geosynchronous satellites to link the shuttle and its payloads with ground controllers in Houston. But TDRS was just space program infrastructure. The only thing that made 51-L unique to the politicians, the press, and the public was the Teacher-in-Space.

By now James Beggs was on leave-of-absence, and William Graham was making the major decisions. The rumor was that with so many delays, NASA might have canceled the previous mission, 61-C on Columbia, except for the presence of Congressman Bill Nelson. Nelson was a key figure in Graham's effort to gain political support as Beggs's permanent successor, obviously not a man to offend or embarrass.

Once NASA decided to go ahead with 61-C in the face of a record seven flight postponements, Challenger's launch date was jeopardized, because several important spare parts had to be removed from Columbia after its return to Earth and installed on Challenger. NASA's flight directors therefore were determined to land Columbia at the Kennedy Space Center so the cannibalization could take place quickly. The 61-C flight was even cut short so this could be done.

But the weather at KSC during much of January 1986 was bad—rainy and cold. On two successive days—January 16 and 17—forecasts of turbulent weather forced Columbia to be waved-off in the early hours of dawn. The landing finally took place 3,000 miles away at Edwards on Saturday the 18th. The required parts were then pulled from Columbia and flown back cross-country. As a result, Challenger's launch date was postponed from the 23rd to Sunday, January 26.

The launch couldn't slip much further. For NASA to meet its spring schedule, Challenger had to lift off soon, so it could be brought back for modifications to prepare it for the March Galileo mission. This included mounting of the cradle in the payload bay to hold the Centaur upper stage. Perhaps as important, Challenger had to vacate its mobile launch platform so the MLP could roll back to the VAB for stacking of the March ASTRO-1 mission aboard Discovery. Meanwhile, the weather continued to be unsettled, with weather fronts and more cold and rain heading toward Florida from the American continental land mass to the northwest. But, as we were told at the January 16-17 Centaur briefings, the schedule still had some slack.

Again, it was the Teacher-in-Space, a presidential initiative, which made 51-L of the utmost importance. For NASA, it was another opportunity to be associated with the president and to please the president. For a chief executive who knew little of space technology and took scant interest in the details of government, the first private citizen in space—a teacher, mother, and likeable personality—spoke a language he and the mass media could easily understand.

The television networks had stationed sizable crews at the Kennedy Space Center for live coverage of the Teacher-in-Space launch. This was the first time there had been live network coverage since the shuttle's early days, before shuttle launches had become routine. It was costing the networks a lot of money to sit at the Cape just waiting.

Sunday the 26th came and went, but NASA didn't launch. They said it was because of threatening weather, but the weather that day was perfect for a shuttle launch. The Presidential Commission never asked anyone about it, though it was William Graham who made the decision.

Graham and the White House may have preferred the launch to take place on Monday, a school day, when live television could broadcast the event to thousands of classrooms. Or maybe it was because they didn't want the launch to compete with the Super Bowl being played Sunday afternoon. Christa McAuliffe reportedly said that the astronauts were glad their launch wouldn't interfere with the fans' enjoyment of the game. Or perhaps, as I later surmised, there were less obvious reasons.

Monday, January 27, was also a good day to launch, but a bolt got stuck in a hatch door. The TV networks howled with scorn.

The next day was Tuesday, January 28, with the president's State of the Union address scheduled for that evening. On Monday night, as the Thiokol engineers in far-away Utah told NASA and their own company managers it would be too cold to launch because the SRB O-rings might freeze, Christa McAuliffe phoned Eileen O'Hara, her closest friend in New Hampshire. O'Hara later told me that Christa said NASA "was determined to go the next day—no matter what."

"LESSON FROM SPACE"
–A Brief History of Shuttle Missions

MANY CHRONICLES OF space shuttle missions have been written over the years, so some of the details of flights one through twenty-five will be familiar to many readers. But a careful review of the missions prior to the Challenger disaster reveals certain trends. The four most notable were:

- The unpredictable nature of equipment problems, which showed the shuttle was an experimental, not an operational, vehicle.
- Mounting problems with the solid rocket booster O-ring joint seals that Morton Thiokol, the Marshall Space Flight Center, and NASA headquarters failed to deal with adequately.
- The extent to which the president and NASA used the shuttle program to promote their political and public relations agendas.
- The militarization of the shuttle and how that may have influenced decision making.

It was these four elements coming together in a witch's cauldron of circumstances and fate that produced the greatest tragedy of the Space

Age. But beyond this characterization, there may be even deeper levels of meaning which make the Challenger disaster a parable of our civilization or even of the human condition.

The U.S. manned space program started as a vision of innocence, whereby mankind, through science and technology, would leave the confines of Earth to explore the universe beyond. This vision was linked through the Apollo moon voyages—a name which evoked the sun god himself—to themes of idealism, daring, and transcendence—a quest undertaken for the spiritual nourishment of the entire human family. But the space shuttle was being turned into a machine of warfare and politics.

———

FOLLOWING IS A very abbreviated, selective history of the first twenty-five shuttle flights, with particular emphasis placed on trends that I believe pointed to inevitable disaster:

It was on the second shuttle mission that post-flight inspection revealed O-ring damage. When Shuttle Mission 2 was over on November 14, 1981, disassembly of the right solid rocket booster showed that a primary O-ring had been eroded. Four years and two months later, a similar O-ring flame leak, made worse by stiffening of the O-rings due to cold weather, destroyed Challenger.

In 1982, on Shuttle Mission 4, Columbia carried the orbiter's first classified Defense Department payload, the cryogenic infrared radiation instrument for shuttle, or CIRRIS. This was an infrared radiance telescope designed to detect Soviet missiles and aircraft against the background radiation of earth. Its identity was supposed to have been kept secret but had already been disclosed by DoD at a congressional hearing.

On Shuttle Mission 6, when Challenger landed at Edwards Air Force Base on April 9, 1983, for the second time post-flight inspection revealed O-ring damage on the SRBs, when both nozzle-to-case joints showed a hot gas path through the sealing putty that was supposed to protect them, with an indication of heat distress on the primary O-ring. A month earlier, heat erosion had occurred on a nozzle O-ring during a qualification motor test firing at the Thiokol plant in Utah. The

STS-6 Challenger flight had been the first to use new steel booster rocket casings that were 4,000 pounds lighter than their 185,000-pound predecessors. The casings' thinner metal walls gave a greater possibility of distortion under the pressure of ignition, a phenomenon called "joint rotation" that engineers believed could weaken the seals by lifting the O-rings off the metal inside the joints.

Post-flight inspection indicated that Challenger had come close to blowing up at launch on Shuttle Mission 8, August 30–September 5, 1983. Examination of the recovered left SRB showed a near-burnthrough of the carbon-cloth insulation in the nozzle that courted catastrophe. The purpose of the three-inch-thick ablative lining was to slowly char in the heat of the 5,600 degrees F. flames from the burning solid fuel and deflect the heat away from the aluminum of the nozzle casing. In this case, a hole had burned in the nozzle to within 0.2 inches of the metal. At a later press conference, Marshall's solid rocket booster project manager said the lining would have burned through in 16–17 more seconds had not booster separation occurred first. A crew member reportedly said it was four seconds, and other reports said two seconds.

For Shuttle Mission 9, Columbia lifted off at 11:00 a.m. EST on November 28, 1983. It was the first flight of Spacelab, a large pressurized laboratory with breathable oxygen that was built in Europe by the European Space Agency. On Day Eight, President Reagan and West German Chancellor Helmut Kohl placed a joint telephone call to Columbia. Reagan spoke from the White House and Kohl from Athens, where he was paying an official visit to Greece. An incident occurred in connection with this call that demonstrated the pains taken by the White House and NASA to orchestrate the president's public interaction with the shuttle. As reported in *Jane's Spaceflight Directory*:

> A live TV hook-up with the U.S. president, the German chancellor, and the crew demonstrated how little is known nowadays of what is really going on. During a TV test, Garriott, Parker, and Shaw lined up in Spacelab covering their eyes, ears, and mouth in a "see, hear, and speak no evil" demonstration. It was a protest against a White House "script" for the hookup, which had decreed that only Young, Lichtenberg, and Merbold were to appear, and even telling them what they should say and when.

After the success of the Spacelab mission, Columbia's return was marred by several serious computer failures. During the descent, two leaking auxiliary power units caught fire and smoldered, then exploded after the crew hurriedly vacated the ship on the runway. The APU fires occurred when a deformed O-ring in a fuel control valve allowed hydrazine fuel to leak into a motor compartment.

Challenger's troubles continued during Mission 10, when flight 41-B suffered what General Abrahamson called a "major disappointment" through the failure of two payload assist modules (PAMs) upper stages intended to launch communications satellites into geosynchronous orbit. Touchdown came on February 11, 1984. On landing there was significant damage to the right main landing gear. Despite the payload problems, 41-B appeared to be a relatively trouble-free flight as far as shuttle primary hardware was concerned, except that a chunk of ice had formed on Challenger in orbit then broke off, damaging one of the orbital maneuvering system pods. On disassembling the SRBs, engineers discovered that two separate O-rings had experienced heat damage, one on the nozzle joint of the right booster and one on the forward field joint of the left booster. ("Field" joints are so-called because the segments they connect are put together in the "field"; i.e., at the Kennedy Space Center rather than at the Thiokol factory in Utah. It was a burnthrough in a field joint that destroyed Challenger.)

At a calculated launch temperature of fifty-seven degrees F., the O-rings were colder than on any previous shuttle flight. NASA did not correlate this to the increased damage, but Thiokol engineers in Utah soon noted the connection. It was also the first time the field joints had been subjected to a prelaunch pressure of 200 pounds-per-square-inch in a test designed to check for leaks in the seals. The procedure may have created holes in the joint putty that produced a blowtorch effect in transferring the heat of burning rocket propellant at launch ignition. Prior to the Challenger disaster, NASA engineers viewed the putty problem as a possible contributor to damage of the SRB O-rings at launch.

Despite some concerns about stiff high-altitude winds above the launch site, Shuttle Mission 11, 41-C , lifted off on schedule on April 6, 1984. The main goal of the mission was to repair the solar maximum mission satellite—Solar Max—launched by NASA on an expendable launch vehicle in 1980 to observe solar flares at the peak of their 11-year cycle known as the "solar maximum." Challenger landed at Edwards on April 13, 1984, at 5:38 a.m. PST after a mission of six days, twenty-three hours, and forty minutes. Challenger's bad luck with the O-rings continued. Post-flight inspection showed that for the first time, three SRB O-rings had signs of heat distress.

Shuttle Mission 12, 41-D, was the maiden flight of the new orbiter Discovery when it lifted off on August 30, 1984. The launch followed a series of delays and payload reshufflings that began when the first launch attempt of 41-D was halted at T-minus-nine minutes when Discovery's back-up computer malfunctioned. The next morning was the first time a shuttle launch was scrubbed following main engine ignition, when the main fuel valve on engine #3 failed to open properly. Next, several small fires that had started in Discovery's tail section were doused by water from the booster rocket sound suppression system, and for a time it appeared to controllers that the crew might have to flee the cabin by using the emergency basket and slide-wire system. While the #3 engine was being changed, NASA decided to cancel mission 41-F and move its payloads to 41-D. Earlier, planned flight 41-E had also been canceled. The next launch attempt on August 29 was delayed for a day. This was to correct a single-point failure contingency in the Discovery's master events controller box that created a timing problem, which in turn could have prevented the SRBs from being jettisoned after lift-off. The shuttle had flown with this problem on all previous missions, but, amazingly, the astronauts had just learned of it and insisted to the Marshall Space Flight Center and NASA headquarters that it be fixed before they flew again. Post-flight inspection showed primary O-ring erosion in field and nozzle joints and blow-by in the same nozzle joint and an igniter joint.

Mission 15, January 24-27, 1985, was the first dedicated to secret Defense Department payloads. The payloads originally had been scheduled for December 1984 on Challenger, but were shifted to the January Discovery flight when 3,800 of Challenger's heat shield tiles had to be replaced. NASA postponed the first launch attempt on January 23 because of freezing Florida temperatures—what some newspapers called "the freeze of the century"—that damaged ninety percent of the citrus crop. NASA feared that ice forming on the external tank and launch tower could crash onto Discovery at lift-off and damage its tiles.

Also susceptible to freezing were launch pad water lines and the water baths for the booster rocket sound suppression system. It was the first time cold weather had forced the postponement of a space shot from the Kennedy Space Center—although NASA launched Challenger in worse ice conditions on January 28, 1986. Discovery's was the shortest mission since the STS-2 flight in November 1981. Following disassembly of the solid rocket boosters, engineers were alarmed to find heat distress on a record five O-rings, and studies were ordered to determine whether the unusually cold pre-launch temperatures might have been a cause. The calculated temperature of the O-rings at lift-off was fifty-three degrees F. Thiokol's engineers soon concluded that temperature-induced stiffening of the O-rings, which reduced "resiliency" could indeed be a significant hazard.

NASA's one-a-month flight plan for 1985 did not hold up. At the Level I flight readiness review for 51-E, Marshall Space Flight Center managers would not allow Thiokol to mention the link they had found between cold launch temperatures and O-ring heat distress on the previous mission. The reason, stated in hallway conversations, was that any resulting launch commit criterion for O-ring temperature might interfere with military flights from Vandenberg, where the weather was cooler than in Florida.

For Shuttle Mission 16, 51-D, April 12-19, 1985, Discovery's launch had been delayed from March 28, when technicians from the Lockheed shuttle processing contract accidentally dropped a 2,500 pound work platform on the payload bay doors. Finally, launch came with only fifty-five seconds remaining in the launch window, despite threatening weather. For the fifth time, landing was at the Kennedy Space Center. After Discovery was waved off due to rain clouds near the runway, landing came in a stiff crosswind, causing lateral pressures, which may have contributed to the locking of both sets of wheel brakes and a tire blow out. There had also been some tile damage caused by external tank insulation that had broken loose at launch. Tile damage on the elevon area of the left wing tip resulted in the first significant burnthrough of the orbiter's surface, with damage to the underlying wing structure. Inspection also revealed heat distress on four SRB O-rings, for a total of nine distressed O-rings on the last two flights.

Because of the brake and tire problems on the previous flight and the added weight of Spacelab, there was no attempt to land at Kennedy for Shuttle Mission 17, flight 51-B. Touchdown came at Edwards Air Force Base on May 6, 1985. Heat damage was found on Challenger's right orbital maneuvering system pod as a result of a loosened insulation blanket, and about twenty tiles needed replacing. Still, Associate Administrator for Space Flight Jesse Moore said NASA was "pleased with the shape of the tiles and the tires," and the agency's scientists said a "spectacular" amount of scientific data had been recovered from the mission. Inspection of the SRBs, however, showed erosion that one engineer later called "terrifying." Three O-rings showed heat distress, and one, the primary O-ring on the left-hand booster nozzle joint, had been breached completely. The secondary O-ring in the joint had held, preventing catastrophe, but it too had been partially eaten away by hot gases.

After a three-day delay caused by problems with a satellite antenna, Shuttle Mission 18, 51-G, Discovery lifted off on June 17, 1985. During ascent, flight controllers warned the crew that thrust levels were low at SRB separation. 51-G was the first shuttle mission to deploy four satellites and the first to carry a major experiment for the Strategic Defense Initiative. "We're going to be carrying a lot of these experiments in the future," said Jesse Moore at the end of the flight. Discovery landed at Edwards and came to an abrupt halt when its left landing gear dug six inches into the lakebed. NASA announced that landings would continue at Edwards while brake work was done and studies completed on the uneven surface of the Kennedy Space Center runway. Heat distress was observed on three O-rings.

The shuttle shut down on the launch pad following main engine ignition for the second time during Shuttle Mission 19, causing an abort of Challenger's July 16 launch attempt—just three seconds before the SRBs were to fire. Water sprays were turned on to prevent the type of launch pad fires that occurred after the 41-D abort eleven months earlier. The 51-F mission was postponed to July 29. Upon lift-off on that day, after only five minutes and 45 seconds, engine #1 shut down when a temperature sensor showed the engine chamber overheating. A premature engine shutdown had never happened on a U.S. manned spaceflight. Acting swiftly with the aid of ground controllers Commander Fullerton switched Challenger's controls to an "abort-to-orbit" sequence. The next day, NASA officials said the shutdown was caused by two heat sensors that showed excessively high readings, but that the sensors, not the engine, were at fault. NASA also disclosed that the heat sensors in a second engine had failed, threatening to shut that one down too. Had this occurred, a flight director told the press, "Challenger would have been in the water," certainly a catastrophic event. The faulty sensors that had threatened to destroy the shuttle were simple in concept, essentially two thin pieces of wire mounted in the engine flame path. The incident raised the engineering design issue of whether a device whose only purpose is safety should itself have the ability to cause a catastrophic accident if it malfunctions. Post-flight inspection showed heat damage on a solid rocket booster nozzle O-ring. Soon after the flight, on August 19, 1985, Thiokol presented its plans for redesign of the joints to NASA headquarters. Implementation was to take more than two years, during which the shuttle would continue to operate.

As Discovery awaited lift-off for its sixth mission, Shuttle Mission 20, a series of launch delays took place that again showed the shuttle's susceptibility to the weather, to seemingly minor hardware problems, and to constrained launch windows caused by payload and mission requirements. Launch was first scheduled for August 24, then canceled because of threatening weather. Lift-off was rescheduled for the next morning, but with the astronauts again strapped into their seats, Discovery's brand-new back-up flight computer began to register errors, and again lift-off was canceled. The launch was postponed for two full days, to Tuesday, August 27. Post-flight inspection of the SRBs showed two instances of heat erosion on a nozzle joint primary O-ring.

Atlantis, NASA's newest orbiter, was launched on its maiden voyage, Shuttle Mission 21, on October 3, 1985. It was the space shuttle's second classified Defense Department mission. All the crew members were military officers, and lift-off time was kept secret, as were the payloads and the planned mission duration. The secrecy of the mission was widely criticized. The Federation of American Scientists noted:

> The current U.S. policy of not announcing military shuttle payloads does not prevent the Soviets from identifying those satellites, even as it has not prevented us from doing so with public sources alone. This policy only inhibits public awareness and discussion of U.S. military activities in space.

Throughout the flight, communications between Atlantis and mission control were blacked out to outsiders. It was reported in the press, however, that the primary payload was a pair of DSCS-3—defense satellite communication system—satellites designed to relay messages among U.S. military forces around the world. *Jane's Spaceflight Directory* reported that among the Atlantis payloads may have been a reflight of CIRRIS—the cryogenic infrared radiance instrument for shuttle. It had been flown on STS-4, but failed to work because a lens cap had become stuck. For the first time in seven flights, and the only time between November 1984 and the loss of Challenger, postflight inspection mystified engineers when it showed no damage to the SRB O-rings.

The launch of Shuttle Mission 22 on October 30 was observed by NASA's Teacher-in-Space designee, Christa McAuliffe, who in less than three months would die on Challenger. The West Germans showed their resistance to the type of politicization of manned spaceflight that had taken place under the Reagan administration. The incident, reported by *Jane's Spaceflight Directory*, had to do with a planned phone call from the West German chancellor:

> Determination at GSOC—the German space operations center—to put science first was illustrated by the decision of the mission manager there, Hans Ulrich Steimle, to cancel the in-flight broadcast between German Chancellor Helmut Kohl and the Spacelab crew so that repairs to the mono-ellipsoid mirror heating facility in the material science double rack could be completed. The decision was reminiscent of Dr. Charles Berry's refusal to allow President Nixon to have dinner with the Apollo 11 crew the night before they set out for the moon. "I don't know what the repercussions will be, but I felt the mission science was more important than a VIP broadcast," said Steimle. "If there are any problems afterwards, they will be on my shoulders."

On reentry, there was a return to SRB O-ring heat damage after its absence on the previous flight. This time, three O-rings had erosion or blow-by, one on the nozzle joint of the right-hand booster and one each on two left-hand booster field joints.

The next-to-last flight before the loss of Challenger, Shuttle Mission

23, came on Atlantis, flying its second mission. Lift-off was on schedule on November 26, 1985. It was the shuttle's second nighttime launch. On Day Four of the mission, astronauts conducted the first of two EVAs to build two large framework structures in space. The work was of interest not only to space station designers, for, as *Jane's Spaceflight Directory* reported, "SDI's director of survivability, lethality, and key technologies later expressed interest in more such work in cooperation with NASA." Post-flight inspection showed erosion on the nozzle joint O-rings on each of the SRBs. The day Atlantis landed, Administrator James Beggs was indicted. William Graham, NASA's recently-appointed deputy administrator, took over as acting administrator.

Mission 61-C was the first shuttle flight on William Graham's watch. It was a fitting prelude to the Challenger disaster. Hampered by bad weather, launch was delayed seven times. Two of the delays were for potentially catastrophic equipment malfunctions, one caused by human error. The mission was to have been cut short because of constraints from the delays leading into the accelerated 1986 launch schedule, but after some on-board experiments had been terminated, bad weather led to an unprecedented two-day landing delay. The weather also forced the landing to be shifted from KSC to Edwards, leading to further scheduling problems and delaying the pending Challenger launch because of the need to transfer spare parts from Columbia cross-country. There were two SDI experiments.

Prior to the Challenger flight that exploded ten days later, there was not enough time for disassembly and inspection of the SRBs used on the 61-C flight. Later inspection showed heat distress on three O-rings, one each on both nozzle joints and a third on the aft field joint of the left-hand booster.

On January 28, 1986, Flight 51-L, space shuttle Challenger, the shuttle's twenty-fifth mission, carrying Commander Francis R. Scobee, Pilot Michael Smith, Mission Specialists Ellison Onizuka, Judith Resnik, Ronald McNair, and Payload Specialists Christa McAuliffe and Gregory Jarvis, blew up seventy-three seconds after launch, and the crew died. It was the greatest tragedy of the Space Age.

Flight 51-L was the second but final shuttle launch overseen by NASA's Acting Administrator William Graham. The mission was most notable due to the presence of Teacher-in-Space Christa McAuliffe. On

Day Four of the flight, McAuliffe was scheduled to deliver a nationwide "lesson from space" called the "Ultimate Field Trip" to the nation's school children. She was also to videotape six science demonstrations on the effects of weightlessness on plant growth, simple machines, effervescence, magnetism, chromatography, and Newton's laws of gravity. NASA had requested time during McAuliffe's presentation for President Reagan to place a phone call to Challenger. Two other times during the flight were also included by NASA in their request for a presidential phone call. The Teacher-in-Space mission was to be featured in President Reagan's State of the Union address the evening of Tuesday, January 28, though the White House denied it.

Gregory Jarvis, an engineer from Hughes Aircraft, had won a company competition to ride the shuttle along with a Hughes satellite, but had been bumped from two previous shuttle missions to make room for politicians-in-space Senator Jake Garn and Congressman Bill Nelson. Jarvis was placed on the 51-L mission at nearly the last minute, through the Hughes satellite he was to accompany had already been deployed during the Discovery mission six months previously. He was along for the ride to meet NASA's commitment to his employer and was given the task of conducting a fluid dynamics experiment.

The seven member crew which included two women—Resnik and McAuliffe— McNair , an African-American—and Onizuka, an Asian-American—was NASA's most diverse shuttle team to date. The presence of Teacher-in-Space McAuliffe arguably made the launch the most newsworthy manned space lift-off since the first shuttle flight in 1981 or even since Apollo days. To cover the event, the commercial TV networks stationed substantial crews at the Kennedy Space Center.

On January 15, three days after launch of the Columbia 61-C mission, and while Columbia was still in orbit, NASA conducted a flight readiness review at Kennedy, which declared that Challenger was "all systems go" for a January 23 launch. Past O-ring heat damage on solid rocket booster joints was not mentioned at the review. Previously, the Marshall Space Flight Center had removed the O-ring problem from the pre-flight safety system by giving it a waiver and declaring it an "acceptable risk." Meanwhile, Marshall was moving ahead with its plans to test a redesigned rocket joint on a test article firing at the Thiokol plant in Utah in February. If the redesign was deemed successful, it would take more than two years to implement while the shuttle continued to fly with the existing design on the solid rocket boosters.

The previous flight, 61-C on Columbia, landed at Edwards in California on January 18. On January 22, NASA officials said they were postponing the launch of Challenger, scheduled for the 23rd, to Sunday, January 26, because of a forecast for dust storms at the emergency landing site in Dakar, Senegal. This explanation was absurd on its face, since the Challenger astronauts were not even in Florida at the time. They were still in Houston, so could not possibly have flown as scheduled on the 23rd. Along with the delay to the 26th, NASA shuffled the in-flight schedule by moving Christa McAuliffe's Teacher-in-Space broadcast to Day Four of the mission so it would take place on a weekday when schools would be in session, not on a weekend.

The real reason for the delay from the 23rd to the 26th was that the weather-enforced landing of Columbia at Edwards on January 18 meant that the spare parts from Columbia that needed to be installed on Challenger had to be flown by NASA cross-country from California. Thus Challenger would not be mechanically ready for launch for a few more days.

The following day, January 23, the Challenger astronauts arrived at Kennedy and gave a brief press conference on the tarmac of the shuttle landing strip, with Christa McAuliffe the featured respondent.

At 10:30 p.m. on the evening of Saturday, January 25, NASA announced a decision by Acting Administrator William Graham that the launch of Challenger scheduled for the next morning had been canceled. Vice President Bush had made tentative plans to fly to Kennedy to witness the launch. NASA said that the reason for the cancellation was a forecast for rainstorms at the launch site the next day. But because the weather at Cape Canaveral is so unpredictable, in all past cases involving questionable weather forecasts, NASA had boarded the astronauts to await a possible launch opportunity, and in fact had launched the shuttle at least twice through breaks in rain clouds.

At launch time on Sunday, January 26, it was sunny and warm at the Kennedy Space Center, a perfect day for a shuttle launch. James Beggs later said of Graham's postponement, according to the *Washington Monthly*, "That was a bad decision." But NASA never disclosed the reason the decision was made, and Graham was never asked for an explanation by the Presidential Commission or Congress.

The astronauts boarded Challenger for the first time on Monday, January 27. At 12:36 p.m., the launch was canceled due to a stuck bolt that prevented the hatch to the crew cabin from being closed. The astronauts exited the vehicle and were transported back to their quarters. NASA's alleged incompetence in dealing with this problem was mocked by TV commentators on the network evening news shows.

Two hours later, around 2:30 p.m., reports began to circulate at the Kennedy Space Center that a severe cold front would be moving into the vicinity overnight, bringing a predicted low temperature of eighteen degrees F. In Utah, following the request of NASA officials at the Marshall Space Flight Center, Thiokol engineers who worked on the solid rocket boosters were alerted. Robert Ebeling, the leader of a Thiokol seal task force formed in 1985 to recommend a redesign of the O-ring joints, convened a meeting at the Brigham City plant with Roger Boisjoly and other company engineers. They were to assess the possible effect of the cold weather on the solid rocket booster joints, which they had known for two years could degrade sealing performance and create the danger of catastrophic flame leaks and burnthroughs.

Ebeling phoned Thiokol's solid rocket motor project director Alan McDonald at the Kennedy Space Center, who informed Ebeling that the predicted air temperature at launch was twenty-nine degrees F.

This was followed by a short teleconference, lasting only fifteen minutes, from 5:45 to 6:00 p.m. Based on the consensus of Boisjoly and the other Thiokol engineers, Thiokol's vice president for engineering, Robert Lund, recommended to NASA in writing that the launch be delayed until noon or later, when temperatures would be expected to rise. Judson Lovingood, NASA's deputy manager of shuttle projects at Marshall, recommended to Stanley Reinartz, his supervisor, who was at Kennedy, that Reinartz inform Arnold Aldrich, STS manager, and Jesse Moore, associate administrator for space flight, of the possibility of a delay. Plans were then readied to reconvene the teleconference that evening.

At 6:30 p.m., Reinartz and Larry Mulloy met with Marshall Director William Lucas and Director of Engineering James Kingsbury in Lucas's room at the Merritt Island Holiday Inn. The topic was the upcoming teleconference with Thiokol. Reinartz and Mulloy left the motel room and proceeded to the evening teleconference. The Presidential Commission never questioned any NASA official in detail about what was said in the meeting.

That evening at KSC, the Challenger astronauts enjoyed their traditional pre-launch dinner with a cake and refreshments, although, with the cold weather blowing in, they did not believe NASA would launch. The Astronaut Office was preparing to fly them back to Houston to resume training exercises until the front had passed through. But the evening wore on, and the launch was not canceled.

At 8:45 p.m, EST, the second teleconference began between Thiokol and NASA's managers and engineers at Marshall in Hunstville, Alabama, and at the Kennedy Space Center in Florida. Also at Kennedy was Thiokol's solid rocket motor manager, Alan McDonald. Thiokol's engineers held to their unanimous conclusion that it was not safe to launch at a joint temperature below fifty-three degrees F., which was the calculated O-ring temperature at the January 1985 launch of Discovery when a record five O-rings showed heat distress. The reason was the likelihood that the solid rocket booster O-rings had lost resiliency; i.e., they would be hardened so much by the cold weather that they could not effectively seal the joints between the rocket segments, especially with the design flaws that caused joint rotation and separation between the secondary O-rings and the surface of the booster metal casings.

At 10:00 p.m., after more than an hour of discussion, Thiokol executive Joe Kilminster recommended against the launch. In sharp distinction from their attitude at the first teleconference, which took place prior to the motel room meeting with Marshall Director William Lucas, NASA's managers now sharply challenged Thiokol's position, maintaining that the data were inconclusive. George Hardy at Marshall in Huntsville said he was "appalled at the Thiokol recommendation," but that he would not recommend launching over a contractor's objection.

Speaking from KSC, Marshall's Larry Mulloy said that "the eve of a launch is a hell of a time to be generating new launch commit criteria. . . . When do you want me to launch, Thiokol, next April?"

Kilminster asked for a five-minute recess to go off-line and caucus. Engineers Arnie Thompson and Roger Boisjoly continued to argue against the launch. The top Thiokol executive in the meeting room then told the engineering manager to "take off your engineering hat and put on your management hat." He then asked for a vote, and all four managers present voted to approve the launch. None of the engineers present was asked to vote.

The five-minute caucus had lasted half an hour. Kilminster called NASA back at 11:00 p.m. and told them that Thiokol had reversed its position and believed it was safe to launch. Reinartz asked over the line if there were any disagreements, but no one participating from any of the three locations spoke up. Larry Mulloy then told Kilminster to put Thiokol's final decision in writing and fax it to Reinartz and himself at Kennedy.

At KSC, Thiokol's Alan McDonald continued to argue with Reinartz and Mulloy for a delay or cancellation, stating that if they wouldn't stop the flight for the O-rings, they should do so because of the stormy seas in the booster recovery area and the ice that was forming overnight on the launch pad. He was told these were "not your concern." McDonald then asked Mulloy and Reinartz how they could rationalize launching at a temperature "below what the motor was qualified to"; i.e., 40 degrees F. He added that, "If anything goes wrong on this flight, I wouldn't want to have to be the person to stand up in front of a board of inquiry and explain why I launched this thing outside of what the solid rocket motor was qualified to."

At 11:30 p.m., Kilminster's fax recommending the flight arrived at Kennedy. After the disaster, Jesse Moore, Arnold Aldrich, and other top NASA launch officials said they were told nothing about the teleconference with Thiokol or the engineers' objections to the launch.

NASA's overall launch commit criteria—conditions that had to be met prior to lift-off for there to be a "go for launch"—prohibited launch of the space shuttle at an air temperature at the launch pad below thirty-one degrees F. This was a constraint that applied to the entire space shuttle system.

At 11:39 p.m., mission control in Houston, evidently acting with no knowledge of the Marshall-Thiokol O-ring debate, requested permission from launch control officials at Kennedy to waive the thirty-one degree prohibition. Permission for this total system waiver, the first ever in the U.S. manned space program, was granted at 12:09 a.m. Also during the night, launch officials waived a separate temperature launch constraint for the external tank of thirty-one degrees F. They granted authority to launch the external tank down to a temperature of ten degrees.

From 1:30 to 3:00 a.m., NASA's ice team at Kennedy, with inspectors from Rockwell, the orbiter contractor, inspected the launch pad facilities and found huge quantities of ice on the launch tower, the mobile launch platform, and the launch pad apron. Some of the ice was shown in photographs that later appeared in the press and in the report of the Presidential Commission. Some of the statements made by the NASA ice team and Rockwell personnel appeared in the report of the House Science and Technology Committee, such as:

"It looks like something out of Dr. Zhivago."

"Ice looks bad, yeah."

"Sounds grim."

"The big concern is that nobody knows what the hell is going to happen when that thing lights off and all that ice gets shook loose and comes tumbling down, and what does it do then? Does it ricochet? Does it get into some turbulent condition that throws it against the vehicle? Our general input to date has been basically that there's vehicle jeopardy that we're not prepared to sign up to."

"This is going to be a tough one."

"We are still of the position that it's still a bit of Russian roulette. You probably make it. Five out of six times you do, playing Russian roulette."

Charles Stevenson, the leader of the NASA ice team, rendered his judgment to launch control. He said, "Well, I'd say the only choice you got today is not to go."

In the middle of the night, James Harrington, a NASA manager who worked for Jesse Moore, went to the launch pad to inspect the ice. Around daybreak, the astronauts ate breakfast together. Normally, they were joined for their meal by NASA launch officials, including the associate administrator for space flight who gives the launch command. This was Jesse Moore, who later told Presidential Commission interviewers that he skipped the breakfast because he was coming down with a cold.

At 7:00 a.m., the representative at Kennedy for Rockwell, the shuttle orbiter contractor, called Rocco Petrone, president of Rockwell's Space Transportation Division, at his home in California and reported the results of the ice team inspection. Petrone was one of the nation's most experienced space technology managers, with a long and productive career at NASA before he retired in 1975 to join Rockwell. Petrone told his project manager at Kennedy, Robert Glaysher, "Make sure NASA understands that Rockwell feels it is not safe to launch."

At 8:30 a.m., astronauts Scobee, Smith, Resnik, McNair, Onizuka, Jarvis, and McAuliffe rode the elevator up the launch tower. When they got off, a technician handed schoolteacher McAuliffe a bright red apple. She smiled graciously. The astronauts were not told that there was a sheet of ice on the astronauts' escape platform outside the Challenger crew cabin, which they would have to cross in making an emergency exit.

The astronauts were strapped into their seats for the three-hour wait prior to launch. The main topic of jokes and conversations as recorded and later released by NASA in a transcript was the frigid temperatures. The ice still hanging on the launch facility was also visible to spectators in the viewing stands, including Christa McAuliffe's parents. Press reports later stated that there was disbelief both among the astronauts and their friends and families who had come to watch that NASA would launch in such conditions. The news announcers broadcasting on live TV gave a running commentary on the ice and cold air.

At 8:50 a.m., Rockwell's Robert Glaysher told Arnold Aldrich, NASA's second-in-command behind Jesse Moore, that "Rockwell cannot assure that it is safe to fly."

At 9:00 a.m., NASA's mission management team, including Jesse Moore, Arnold Aldrich, William Lucas, Larry Mulloy, Stanley Reinartz, and others decided to launch. They had decided to postpone lift-off for two hours while attempts were made to clear some of the ice debris from the launch pad and to allow the air to warm up a little. The members of the mission management team were never questioned by the Presidential Commission about what was said among them leading to the launch decision, except that Moore and Aldrich said they never heard about the teleconferences with Thiokol where the company engineers opposed the launch. Nevertheless, at least some members of the NASA team were aware that key individuals from two contractors were against it.

Normally, NASA's administrator would be present for the launch. William Graham, however, was now back in Washington, D.C. That morning he was on Capitol Hill meeting with congressmen, reportedly continuing his lobbying for the NASA administrator's position. James Beggs, officially on leave-of-absence, sat in his office at headquarters on Maryland Avenue. NASA's ranking official at Kennedy was Philip Culbertson, Graham's choice for general manager.

At 11:23 a.m., mission control in Houston gave its final go-ahead for launch. At 11:38 a.m., Challenger's main engines ignited. Massive quantities of ice from the tower came crashing down. The solid rocket boosters fired six seconds later. At NASA headquarters, a top official in the Office of Space Flight, having just received a phone call, rushed into a conference room where the launch was being televised and shouted, "My God! I hope we don't lose them!"

Within less than a second of ignition, cameras recorded a puff of smoke emerging from the side of the right-hand solid rocket booster at the aft field joint near a strut attaching the rocket to the external tank. Investigators later determined that the incipient burnthrough was likely clogged by combustion debris which broke up when wind shear hit the shuttle during ascent. Fifty-eight seconds into the flight, a flame appeared at the same location on the SRB and continued to grow. Pieces of the SRB later recovered from the Atlantic Ocean showed a hole in the booster at the aft field joint large enough for a man to pass through.

Forty-eight thousand feet above the Atlantic, the Challenger exploded. After being burned through, the strut attaching the solid rocket booster to the external tank broke loose. There was a huge fireball as the hydrogen and oxygen from the external tank ignited in the sky. Pilot Michael Smith could be heard to say, "Uh oh" before ground contact with Challenger was lost. Technicians at mission control in Houston stared into their monitors with disbelief as the shuttle broke up and the two solid rocket boosters flew off wildly into the morning sky.

The orbiter had broken into pieces, with the crew cabin emerging intact and plummeting toward the ocean, with the astronauts possibly surviving the initial break-up. Within two minutes and forty-five seconds of the explosion, the cabin hit the surface of the ocean at 200 miles per hour. Four minutes after shuttle engine ignition, the waters of the Atlantic Ocean gently washed over the spot where the cabin went down. During the fall, NASA later reported, at least three of the astronauts activated their individual emergency airpacks supplying air to their spacesuits. Death for some likely occurred from the force of water impact or else soon afterwards from drowning. NASA recovered the crew remains but did not release autopsy results.

PART III

LEAKS

"DON'T LET ANYBODY
SAY ANYTHING"

—The Cover-ups Begin

HAD NEVER met or heard of Roger Boisjoly, the engineer from Morton Thiokol in Brigham City, Utah, where the solid rocket boosters were
made. It was Boisjoly who led the Thiokol engineers in arguing against
the launch of Challenger during the teleconference the night before.

Having lost the battle, Boisjoly and the other Thiokol engineers
could only watch and hope the next morning. Later he described his
experience:

> The next morning I paused outside Arnie Thompson's office and told
> him and my boss that I hoped the launch was safe. But I also hoped that
> when the booster joints were inspected we would find all the seals
> burned almost all the way through the joint, and then maybe we could
> get someone with authority to take a stand and stop the flights.
>
> Later, I was walking past the room normally used to watch the
> launches, when Bob Ebeling stepped out to invite me to watch the launch.
> At first I refused . . . but he encouraged me to enter. The room was filled,
> so I seated myself on the floor close to the screen and leaned against Bob's
> legs . . . . The boosters ignited, and as the vehicle cleared the support tower,
> Bob whispered to me that we had just dodged a bullet. The reason Bob

made this statement was that the propellant experts had told us that the boosters would explode at ignition if we developed a leak in the case.

At approximately T+60 seconds, Bob again whispered to me that he had just completed a prayer of thanks to the Lord for a successful launch. Just thirteen seconds later, we both saw the horror of destruction as the vehicle exploded. We all sat in stunned silence for a short time. Then I left the room and went directly to my office, where I remained in shock for the rest of the day. Two of my seal task team colleagues inquired about my condition at the office, but I was unable to speak to them and hold back my emotions, so I just nodded, yes, I was okay.

———

How soon did NASA's managers know that a burnthrough had occurred in a solid rocket booster O-ring joint?

Immediately after the explosion, all NASA's top managers except William Graham, who was still in Washington, were called to an urgent meeting in a large conference room near the firing area at KSC launch control. According to press reports based on interviews with anonymous meeting participants, there were NASA officials in the room who, like their Thiokol counterparts in Utah, knew almost immediately that the explosion they witnessed was caused by failure of the O-ring seals on a solid rocket booster. According to published reports, within two hours of the tragedy, William Graham had been informed it was an SRB burnthrough.

In its report, the Presidential Commission said nothing about how soon NASA's top managers knew what had happened. Much later, as I was poring through the Commission's records at the National Archives, I came across a memorandum from investigator John R. Molesworth to Presidential Commission Executive Director Alton G. Keel, Jr., which stated that in the meeting at launch control, NASA's managers viewed a film of the launch. According to Molesworth's memo, "The film showed smoke and flame coming from either the SRB or external tank. [Gene] Thomas recalled somebody stating, 'We've got a burnthrough.'"

Within the next couple of days, evidence of the SRB burnthrough mounted. According to author Richard Lewis, writing in *Challenger: The Final Voyage*, on January 29, the day after the disaster, George Hardy, deputy director of science and engineering at the Marshall Space Flight Center, had evidence that showed the SRBs thrusting unevenly. The right booster's deficit grew to 85,000 pounds when the shuttle exploded.

Other telemetry data showed the right-hand booster swinging away from the external tank. Further data showed steering corrections by the main engine nozzles, when Challenger began to veer off-course, and a drop in liquid hydrogen pressure in the external tank.

Later, Jesse Moore told the House Science and Technology Committee that either the day after the disaster, or the next day, he was meeting with Marshall and other NASA managers and engineers on the massive Thiokol briefing package from the August 19 O-ring meeting at NASA headquarters. This was the meeting presided over by Moore's deputy Michael Weeks.

Thus, within two to three days of the tragedy, the entire series of events, anomalies, and decisions concerning the O-ring joints, was being examined in detail by NASA's launch managers and officials.

———

THE MORNING AFTER the explosion, January 29, I got off my van on 6th Street, across from NASA headquarters. From there, my alternate driver would drive the van to the parking lot. I bought a copy of the New York Times. The huge banner headline read, "The Shuttle Explodes."

To me, the explosion of Challenger was an event of enormous significance. Certainly the press and the public were treating it as a monumental occurrence. Later, a public opinion poll rated the accident and its aftermath as the leading news event of 1986.

But when I took the elevator to the sixth floor, I was surprised that the people in the hallway and the Code B offices looked, talked, and acted like it was any other day. No one was even discussing the disaster.

As related earlier, I dug out my July 23 warning memo about the O-ring joints and read it, my hands shaking.

> There is little question . . . that flight safety has been and is still being compromised by potential failure of the seals, and it is acknowledged that failure during launch would certainly be catastrophic.

After I read the memo and was sitting at my desk staring into space, my supervisor came into the room. Almost casually he asked me to prepare estimates of how much it would cost to replace the solid rocket booster segments that were lost in the catastrophe. After the shuttle had broken up in the skies over the Atlantic Ocean, the range safety officer had detonated the explosive charges and destroyed them. His tone of voice seemed to express the feeling that this was just more budget data. I became angry at being told to start scouring what I called sarcastically "Code B's big black notebooks" for budget details at a time like this. "Don't you have anything to say about the disaster but that?" I asked him. He just walked away.

Returning to my memo, I hadn't the slightest doubt that what destroyed Challenger was exactly the type of O-ring failure the Code M engineers told me they "held their breath" about. I made several copies of the memo along with some others. For whatever reason, I was fearful that something could happen to the many memos I had written while at NASA if I didn't secure them and make copies to take home. This included my Centaur paper, which I continued to work on, since there was nothing much to do other than pull together the data on the lost booster segments that my supervisor wanted. I made an appointment to talk to the engineers at Code M about this later in the day.

As I was at my desk, I got a call from a manager at the U.S. Treasury Department. Before coming to NASA, I'd been interviewed for a GS-12 job which, at the last minute, was cancelled for budgetary reasons. The manager commented that we must all be in shock over Challenger. He wanted to know if I was still interested in the job at Treasury.

"I think I am," I heard myself answering.

"Bad news, though," he said. "They won't give you a GS-12. They said if you come you have to take a lateral at GS-9."

This was bad news indeed. I would soon be promoted to GS-11 at NASA. "How long would I be at the GS-9 level?" I asked.

"I don't know," he answered. "We'll promote you as soon as we can, but I can't promise anything."

I took a deep breath. "Yes, I'm interested," I said quietly. I felt that knowing what I knew, having written all that I had, and what could be going on at NASA in the aftermath of Challenger, it might be difficult to stay.

But in making the choice I did, the long-term result was that I ruined my government career. All my hopes and dreams of making it to the top were shattered.

This was not, however, an official call offering me the job. The manager said that would come from the personnel office at Treasury "in a few days."

Later in the morning I went to talk to the engineers at Code M. The first person I encountered was a resource analyst I had worked and traveled with. I asked her pointedly if the solid rocket boosters had failed. "No!" she answered vehemently. "The guys over here have been looking at the videotapes over and over. It looks like an ET strut failure."

But she didn't sound convincing. Everyone at Code M knew the dangers of the O-ring joints. Her talk of the strut failure was wishful thinking, though later it was disclosed that a strut had been severed by the SRB burnthrough. But I had no desire to argue.

In another office, two women were talking. "At least they died suddenly," one said of the Challenger astronauts. "They didn't suffer. They were at the peak of their emotion."

So, they got blown up, I thought, but died with smiles on their lips? Even if it were true, it seemed like a horribly self-serving viewpoint. But this too was wishful thinking, as months later NASA disclosed that at least some of the astronauts had not died in the initial shuttle breakup but may even have survived until the crew capsule hit the ocean surface.

I reached Paul Herr's office. "Did a booster fail?" I asked.

"I don't know," he said quietly.

We talked for a while, and though it was clear that Herr suspected an SRB malfunction, he had no more information about the accident than was in the newspapers. I was astonished that the leading solid rocket motor engineer at NASA headquarters was not privy to the early stages of the investigation then underway at KSC and had not flown to the Cape to participate. What the hell is going on here? I wondered.

But again I said nothing. I wanted to remain a fly on the wall at Code M and learn what I could. I felt I had to be careful. I got the data my supervisor wanted about the lost booster segments, then turned to leave Herr's office. "Wait," he said and lowered his voice. "We were called at home last night from the Cape. Two contractors opposed the launch." This was shocking news.

Herr invited me to go with him to a Code M conference room. "They've put the 1986 shuttle schedule on hold," he said. He told me that the previous afternoon, James Beggs had told Graham he'd better get down to Kennedy, which Graham did after leaving the White House where he'd gone right after the disaster. Graham flew down with Vice President George Bush and Senators John Glenn and Jake Garn, who had gone to try to comfort the families of the dead astronauts.

Graham had stayed at Kennedy for meetings and a press conference, which was now coming on over NASA Select on the TV monitor in the conference room. Also on the dais at KSC were Jesse Moore, KSC director Richard Smith, and Lieutenant Commander James Simpson of the Coast Guard, who was directing the initial search for debris off the Florida coast.

As Graham began to speak, I felt shivers up my spine. What did this man know? It was all just too weird. He said:

> I want to assure you, as others have, including the president of the
> United States, that this loss will not stop us Americans from exploring
> the frontiers of science and the frontiers of space.

It was just the wrong thing to say. What about the astronauts? What about their families? How can you sit there and say it's business as usual? Graham then announced that on Friday the 31st, two days from now, NASA would conduct a memorial service for the Challenger crew in Houston which President and Mrs. Reagan would attend.

The questions from the press began. The first one was about the cold weather. Herr turned and looked at me but didn't say what he was thinking.

Graham referred the question to Moore and Richard Smith. Moore replied, "There were a series of technical meetings yesterday morning about the ice on the pad." Already Moore had contradicted his statement in the previous day's press conference that there were no unusual weather conditions. He now continued:

> The ice team went out, did an inspection early in the morning, very
> early in the morning, and then came back and reported. And the

technical people did sit down—all the NASA people involved as well as the contract people involved—and did feel that the conditions were acceptable for launch and basically recommended that, you know, we launch.

Moore turned to Richard Smith to ask if he had anything to add to the account. "No," Smith said,

> I think that is the case. It was very thoroughly assessed, and the indications were that there was a very low risk involved.

This was the first I had heard of the ice. But what about the solid rocket boosters?

Now Bill Braden of the *New York Times* said that compared to Challenger's projected ascent timeline made available to the press, the actual altitudes called out after lift-off made the rate of climb appear slow. Braden asked,

> Were there any unusual anomalies whatsoever, significant anomalies in that period up to the point of explosion that you know of?

Moore replied:

> Not that I have heard, quite frankly. . . . I have not heard of any significant anomalies during that period of time. Like I said, my inputs as of now indicate that the flight was normal up to that point in time. Now, I have not looked at the data in detail. We have not gone back and run the analysis on all the flight trajectory data in great detail. That's what we're trying to set up and make sure we've got a mechanism to do that . . . and just as soon as we understand that and we can talk on a conclusive basis as opposed to a speculative, I think we'll be able to come forward.

Moore also said that no requirements had been waived to launch in the cold weather, but months later it was revealed in the reports of the Presidential Commission and the House Science and Technology Committee that temperature requirements had been waived for the external tank and for the entire shuttle system.

I went back to my office. Acting Administrator William Graham had ordered all NASA employees not to "speculate" on the cause of the Challenger disaster. According to press reports, Graham told his aides, "Do not let anybody say anything until we are sure it is correct." NASA also told contractor employees and former agency officials not to talk to the press.

The bunker mentality had set in. According to later reports, journalists were now finding that their carefully-cultivated NASA sources who, prior to the disaster, had freely answered their questions, were silent. "Nobody will answer that," became the standard reply at Marshall to questions about shuttle propulsion systems or the status of the investigation. At Kennedy, NASA seized all camera equipment used by the news media to photograph the launch. When the press protested, NASA admitted that the seizure may have been illegal, but officials claimed they needed to preserve possible clues of the cause of the mishap.

At home that night, I was in agony. I felt I was caught up in an event that could destroy me. I showed Phyllis my July 23 O-ring memo. Without looking at the "To" and "From" lines, she read the text. "They knew!" she said. "I'm not surprised!"

"Look who wrote it," I said.

"You!"

I told her Treasury would likely be offering me a job but only at the GS-9 level. She felt in as much mental conflict as I did over the possibility that I might have to take it.

Two days after the disaster, Acting Administrator Graham formalized the existence of an interim review mishap board that Jesse Moore had convened. Moore, who gave the launch order and had been in charge of briefing the press, was to remain the head. Other members were William Lucas, Arnold Aldrich, Richard Smith, and NASA consultant Walter Williams. Williams was formerly a NASA launch director with the Mercury and Gemini programs and later NASA's chief engineer. James Harrington, headquarters director of STS integration, would be executive secretary to the board.

Soon, two astronauts were added: Robert Crippen and Joseph Kerwin, who was director of space and life sciences at the Johnson Space Center. Serving as ex-officio members of the board were John O'Brien, NASA's general counsel, and Chief Engineer Milton Silviera.

NASA seemed to have it all figured out, I thought. We know what caused the disaster. We have imposed a total press blackout and placed a gag order on all employees and contractors, including the ones who Paul Herr said opposed the launch. And we've set up a board headed by the man who gave the launch order.

In naming the board, Graham said its work could take months. Named as the board's press spokesman was Chuck Hollinshead, public affairs director at KSC. He would release information to the public, Graham said, "as needed," after clearance by Jesse Moore. It was striking how little involvement NASA headquarters would have in the investigation. As with the Code M engineers, the headquarters public affairs office was excluded.

But while NASA was building a boat to ferry its management team across the swamps of disclosure and exposure, press reports, fed by leaks, were increasingly turning to the solid rocket boosters and the possibility of a torch-like burnthrough of hot gas at 5,600 degrees F. On Thursday the 30th, NBC radio reporter Jay Barbree was called by a NASA official who insisted on anonymity. The official said that NASA's investigation was focused on a flame leak in a joint of the right-hand solid rocket booster, a report which other unnamed sources confirmed.

Employees at Code M were indignant at the press reports. "It's not fair!" one analyst shouted at me when I went back across the street to visit the SRB engineers. "They just don't know what happened—it's all speculation!" screamed another. She was parroting the party line, I realized, but it was more wishful thinking. Later I read in the *New York Times* that they were saying the same things at Thiokol in Utah, where a former plant worker said, "It isn't fair! Why does the media come up with these things and try to place blame? They want to attack and find guilt." People were becoming hysterical.

Back in Paul Herr's office, we talked about the likelihood of an SRB failure due to the flawed O-ring joint. Herr looked at me grimly. "I hate to say this, but this is starting to look more and more like a preventable accident." He said that the accelerating NASA flight rate was "politically motivated." We agreed that this was why NASA kept flying the shuttle while the SRB joint was being redesigned.

As I was leaving Herr's office, I saw Irv Davids standing next to one of the secretary's desks. Davids, like Herr and their supervisor Paul Wetzel, was also stuck here in Washington, excluded from NASA's so-called investigation.

Davids had a couple of pieces of paper in his hand. He gave me a
knowing look and held them out. It was a two-page memo that contained a detailed report on a visit to Marshall made by Davids and
another engineer named William Hamby, where they received a series
of briefings on the history of the O-ring problems and an analysis of the
probable causes. The memo began:

> As a result of the problems being incurred during flight on both case-
> to-case and nozzle-to-case O-ring erosion, Mr. Hamby and I visited
> MSFC on July 11, 1985, to discuss this issue with both project and S&E
> [Science and Engineering] personnel.

The memo contained a lengthy history of problems with the O-ring
joints. The only thing that was not mentioned was any effect of cold
temperatures. Davids and Hamby had been at Marshall less than two
weeks before I wrote my July 23 memo, which was based on my talk
with Herr and Wetzel. So the whole group of headquarters SRB engineers had been hot on the trail of the O-ring problem at the same time.

I did not yet know about the August 19 meeting, when headquarters
brought in Marshall and Thiokol to explain what they were going to do
about the problem. Later, when I understood the chronology, I saw that
the Davids/Hamby trip may have been one of the preludes to that
meeting.

David's memo demonstrated further the accuracy of my July 23
memo in summarizing the main concerns of the headquarters engineers. It showed how well-documented the details of the probable
failure were at headquarters, and I repressed my excitement as I read
it, handed it back to Davids, then left Code M for my own office. I had
already told my supervisor that I was talking to the Code M engineers
about the possible role of the solid rocket boosters in the Challenger
accident. Now I caught up with him outside his office. I told him that
I had been talking to Wetzel's staff and that whether or not the SRBs
were the cause of the disaster, the O-ring problem had to be resolved.
As I talked, he nodded.

Back in my own office, I was so agitated I couldn't sit down. I felt I
had to get hold of a copy of Irv David's memo. I returned to Code M and,
as casually as I was able, asked him for it. To my surprise, he readily

agreed, ran a copy, and gave it to me. Davids didn't ask why I wanted it, and I didn't offer an explanation.

I now went back to Paul Herr's office and asked him—also without explanation—if he had any further documentation on the O-rings. By now, Herr was starting to glance around when he saw me coming to see if anyone was watching him talk to me. He gave me several reports relating to the O-ring problems that had been prepared for meetings with Jesse Moore and one for a meeting with James Beggs. The reports went back to November 1984.

"Actually, we had it on the agenda earlier than that," Herr said. "I think in March. Some of the guys at Marshall called and said the program office [headed by Larry Mulloy] wasn't taking this seriously enough. I had to push to get it on the agenda for the A.A. [i.e. associate administrator] meetings. So-and-so [he gave me a name] controlled the agendas and said that it shouldn't be in writing, but I pushed and got it on. Even so, we didn't get anywhere while so-and-so [he gave me another name] was division director. He'd never let problems like this get anywhere."

I was amazed—a division director at NASA headquarters who would not allow potentially catastrophic hardware problems to be written down. I asked Herr, "How many engineers at NASA do you think would be able and willing to talk honestly about this if they were asked?"

"Maybe half a dozen," he said.

But neither Herr nor any of these engineers was called to testify publicly before either the Presidential Commission or the House Science and Technology Committee. And their knowledge of the O-ring issues and how they kept Code M management informed were not included in either report.

It had been a long day for me. It was clear that Herr and Davids, and likely others, saw the Challenger catastrophe as preventable, though officially NASA was maintaining the claim that no possible cause was being excluded from the investigation. At home that night, I showed Phyllis the Davids and Herr documents, and we agreed that NASA's cover-up was coming along nicely. I also brought home several copies of each document in case something happened to the ones I was carrying in my briefcase. I had begun to feel that my growing collection of O-ring papers was getting rather "hot."

. . .

On Friday, January 31, President Reagan flew to the Johnson Space Center in Houston for the memorial service for the seven Challenger astronauts. The New York Times that morning carried a confirmation by an "expert close to the investigation" that the explosion might have resulted from an SRB burnthrough.

At Code B, my supervisor conducted a regularly-scheduled staff meeting, where we each were to report on our program areas. I said that the Code M engineers were viewing an O-ring joint failure as the likely cause of the Challenger explosion.

"We knew we had a design problem," the supervisor said. He told me to continue to gather information, realizing as we all did that a joint redesign could have major budgetary implications. I told him that I planned to turn in some of my conclusions in writing on Monday.

I was relieved that I was not pulled back from my investigation or questioned too closely about the information I was gathering. I did not tell anyone at Code B about the documents I'd gotten from Davids and Herr. Also, I had indicated to my supervisor that I'd likely be leaving NASA and that he could expect a call from the Treasury personnel office as they checked out my references. He said he was not surprised to hear that.

As I walked back to my office, the resource analyst for the main engines came up and said to me, "You know, the main engine boys were surprised it wasn't their piece of hardware that went first!"

After the staff meeting, I went over to Code M and joined Davids, Herr, and some other analysts and engineers who were discussing the latest news reports. Davids took me aside and asked, "Have you shown that memo I gave you to anyone in the comptroller's office?"

"No," I said.

"I shouldn't have given it to you," he went on. "I need you to give it back to me!"

What is going on here? I wondered. Who told him to retrieve the memo and why? I stared hard at him and said nothing, and he seemed to understand he wasn't going to get it. "At least don't let Graham see it," he said quietly, turning away.

A few minutes later, Code M's deputy director for resources came into the room where the group was talking. He looked around to see who was there, then asked, "If we redesign the boosters to use the capture feature, can we still use the segments we already have?"

The engineers in the room said not to worry, all the existing segments could still be used. The resource manager breathed a sigh of relief and left. This was interesting, I thought. NASA had not made any official statement about the cause of the accident, but they've already decided on the likelihood of doing a redesign with the capture feature.

We all then went over to the large Code M conference room. The TV monitors were tuned to NASA Select, where, at Houston, President Reagan had arrived for the memorial service. I was annoyed by a man who sat near the screen announcing the names of the senators and congressmen who were there and by a woman in the room who was loudly chattering away.

What struck me most about the memorial service was how President Reagan had been thrust into the situation as the center of attention. As I sat watching, I felt it was strange that while the president was presuming to console the nation, his employees in Washington were secretly making plans to fix the problem they knew had killed the astronauts but weren't telling anyone about.

Against the background of NASA's secret planning to fix the problem which they knew had killed "our astronauts," I found Reagan's performance that day to be a tragic spectacle. I felt that way even more, years later, when I learned that Reagan himself had been part of the flawed launch decision.

That same day, Thiokol formed a failure investigation team that included Roger Boisjoly and Arnie Thompson, the company's two top O-ring seal experts. According to Boisjoly, the team was immediately sent to the Marshall Space Flight Center in Huntsville. The purpose was to examine the evidence for the joint failure. The next day, Gilbert Moore, a Thiokol spokesman, was quoted by the New York Times saying that they were cooperating, they didn't know what had gone wrong, they had been asked to speculate what caused the accident—and they wouldn't.

I spent most of the next weekend writing and rewriting a memo to my supervisor on my findings from the past week. I realized that this was my last chance to place on record my views on the disaster and its causes.

That Saturday, NASA released photographs and videotapes of Challenger's ascent after launch that showed what they were calling on TV a "plume" of flame on the booster's aft segment, starting about ten seconds before the explosion. A NASA spokesman said, "The cause is still unknown and neither the board nor NASA will speculate as to the cause or effects of this observation."

The tapes of the plume were shown at a briefing in Washington given by Acting Administrator William Graham to about fifty congressmen and congressional staff members. A source told the *Washington Post* that "the flame appeared to spout from a point near the base of the booster on the right side of the large main tank [external tank]."

When I saw the press reports Sunday morning, I felt Graham was being set up by NASA's launch managers in a very dangerous way. If Irv Davids had asked me for his memo back on Friday because Code M was trying to keep information from Graham, then what they were doing was sending him out to brief Congress with a burnthrough videotape and a script about what to say, but with no real information. "Good God," I thought. "When everything about the O-rings comes out, this guy has had it."

That day the *New York Times* reported the observation George Hardy had made to the NASA board that there was a sudden drop in power on one of the solid rocket boosters just before the explosion. It was at this point in the flight that the plume reported in the press on Saturday had appeared on the side of the SRB. The report also said that the engine nozzles had swiveled to compensate for the thrust imbalance. One of the NASA spokesmen at Houston said, "None of these things happened." But the *Times* also quoted a source as saying that, "Officials believe that the most plausible explanation for the power drop would be flames burning through the side of the right-hand rocket."

To Phyllis and me it was agonizing to see the news media dancing around what was so obvious—that an O-ring joint had failed. It was even harder to watch William Graham on the Sunday morning interview programs, especially with the O-ring documents from NASA, including my July 23 memo, spread out on the kitchen table and tomorrow's report for Code B sticking out of the electric typewriter.

We were sure that many other people from NASA were either laughing or groaning as Graham tried to explain away the plume video. He seemed to be saying that the SRBs simply could not have failed. Graham told Lesley Stahl of CBS's *Face the Nation*:

These solid rocket boosters are some of the sturdiest parts of the entire shuttle system . . . [and] are considered primary structure and not susceptible to failure. Of course we designed them that way. They were designed with great care and great thought.

"Not susceptible to failure . . ."? What planet was he from? Graham added that, "There were certainly no corners cut. We never compromised on safety. We never compromised on reliability."

On NBC's *Meet the Press*, Graham said:

Certainly not within the range of the engineering judgment and detailed analysis and extensive testing that had gone into the construction and operation of this system up to flight twenty-five was there any reason to believe there would be an anomaly of the sort that you saw on the tape and there was therefore no reason to have a specific instrumentation to deal with that.

Graham was so adamant in declaring that the accident was not a possible scenario—he insisted that failure of a solid rocket booster was not a "credible failure mode"—that he was asked by one reporter if he was saying the accident didn't happen. But Graham also said on one of the Sunday programs that the plume in the videotape "appears to grow at the area where it is occurring, and finally, it goes to the explosion point." Thus there seemed to be no doubt in at least one corner of his mind that a booster rocket had in fact failed. I was not the only one at NASA who was incredulous as Graham spoke. Some days later, on February 12, Bill McCarty, a NASA quality assurance and risk analyst, told the *Wall Street Journal* that, "We consider the boosters as the one system most prone to failure." He said he "would not go as far as Dr. Graham" in assessing SRB reliability.

I finished typing my memo Sunday night. It was blunt and, I realized, could possibly even get me fired. But I didn't care. At this point, neither Phyllis nor I could take what NASA was dishing out.

When I got to work on Monday I retyped the memo I had written

over the weekend and dated it February 3, 1986. It was addressed to my
supervisor and read as follows:

> There is a growing consensus that the cause of the Challenger explosion
> was a burnthrough in a solid rocket booster at or near a field joint. It is also
> the consensus of engineers in the Propulsion Division, Office of Space
> Flight, that if such a burnthrough occurred, it was probably preventable and
> that for well over a year the solid rocket boosters have been flying in an
> unsafe condition. This has been due to the problem of O-ring erosion and
> loss of redundancy caused by unseating of the secondary O-ring.
>
> The technical details of the O-ring problem were described in the
> attached memorandum from Irv Davids to the associate administrator
> for space flight in June 1985. Also attached is a copy of the memoran-
> dum I wrote on the subject on July 23, 1985, in which I stated: "There
> is little question . . . that flight safety has been and is still being com-
> promised by potential failure of the seals, and it is acknowledged that
> failure during launch would certainly be catastrophic."
>
> Even if it cannot be ascertained with absolute certainty that a burn-
> through precipitated the explosion, it is clear that the O-ring problem
> must be repaired before the shuttle can fly again.
>
> It is not clear, however, how long this will take or what it will cost.
> The facts are:
>
> - The capture feature to be tested further on the filament wound
>   case is not yet a demonstrated fix to the problem and has not
>   been accepted by the Marshall Space Flight Center for use on
>   steel SRB cases.
> - It is clear that the field joint putty plays a significant role in O-
>   ring erosion. It must be replaced in any case, because it con-
>   tains asbestos and is a potential health hazard to workers.
>   Flight qualification of new putty is recognized to be a major
>   unbudgeted cost item.
> - The effects of environmental and weather factors on the putty
>   and O-rings may have design implications which require fur-
>   ther investigation.
> - Currently eight SRB flight sets are in manufacturing flow.
>   Segments of these flight sets must either be retrofitted with the
>   capture feature, or field joint segments must be reengineered

and replaced. In either case, the propellant must be removed, either by hand-scraping under carefully controlled conditions or by static firing. One million pounds of propellant per flight case must be removed, at a cost for propellant alone of $2 million per flight set.

- Five flight sets of hardware remain on the shelf at Thiokol, but should not be loaded until the O-rings are repaired. Consequently, we are looking at a probable factory shutdown.

- A further potential safety hazard has been identified which can take away O-ring redundancy. If the leak test ports between O-rings are not properly capped before flight, a small leak in the field joint can result if the primary O-ring is eroded. Consequently, procedures to assure proper capping must be reassessed. Further, the instance of case rupture during a test following failure to detect a crack at the stiffener ring bolt hole must call into question Thiokol's safety procedures and orientation. It should be determined whether this situation has any implications for the current negotiations for the third production buy regarding failure penalties.

- Given the known O-ring problem, it could be construed as negligent not to have installed sensors on the surface of the SRB which could have detected a burnthrough or to provide a system to jettison the SRBs when loss of control is detected such as was apparently the case with 51-L. Videotapes show the burnthrough commencing twelve to twenty-five seconds before the explosion, and I understand that loss of SRB control was evident eight seconds before the explosion. Correcting this situation will require a considerable investment to revise instrumentation, software, and launch and training procedures.

- It is possible that the capture feature will fail to be flight-qualified for steel segments and that reengineering of the field joints will be required. In this case, three of every eleven SRB segments will have to be discarded, and reengineered segments manufactured by Rohr. Manufacturing lead time would be thirteen months after successful acceptance testing.

- The attrition rate of SRB segments following flight has been far higher than the planning projections and has been made even worse by the loss of both boosters in flight 51-L. More intensive inspection for cracks and other anomalies will probably lead to further unanticipated attrition. It seems clear that the planning assumptions are unrealistic and must be revised. This will have major budgetary implications.

- The filament wound case project now needs to be reassessed, as there is an opinion among staff engineers that it should be discontinued for safety reasons. It is essential that such misgivings now be taken seriously.

Given these facts, it is my considered opinion that NASA is facing a suspension of shuttle flights due to SRB problems of a minimum of nine months and possibly as long as two years or more. This assumes that the agency makes a rapid decision to proceed with the required SRB improvement program, along with improvements in Thiokol's safety management. The financial planning assumptions also need to be redone. The commencement of this program does not depend on the outcome and final conclusions of the Challenger investigation, since it would have to be done even if the explosion were due to some other cause. The delay could be longer, of course, if additional findings require reengineering of the external tank or other hardware.

It is also my opinion that the Marshall Space Flight Center has not been adequately responsive to headquarters concerns about flight safety, that the Office of Space Flight has not given enough time and attention to the assessment of problems with SRB safety raised by senior engineers in the Propulsion Division, and that these engineers have been improperly excluded from investigation of the Challenger disaster. For these reasons, I recommend that the SRB reassessment be led, tightly controlled, and adequately staffed at the headquarters level. I also recommend that the acting administrator [i.e., Graham] be informed of the history of the SRB problems as outlined in this report.

When I finished the memo, I looked to see if my supervisor was in his office. When I saw he was not, I placed the original on his chair and also left a copy for Jim Brier. Not wishing to stay around for the reaction, I left the office to visit Paul Herr at Code M.

Herr still had no definitive information from his friends at Kennedy about the exact cause of the disaster. He was looking at a copy of that morning's *Washington Post* with the "plume" photo. The only question was whether the plume was coming from the lower field joint where the O-rings were located, or higher up on the rocket's casing where a burnthrough might have resulted from some other cause, such as a crack in the propellant. In the photo, the rocket was tilted away from the camera. "It seems to be above the joint," Herr said of the plume.

"That's because of the foreshortening effect," I replied, speaking of the distorted perspective caused by the camera angle.

Herr pondered for a moment, went to his files, and pulled out some more paper. "This is the 'Death Document,'" he said, and handed me some documents from 1982-83 that defined the criticality and waived the redundancy requirement for the SRB O-ring joints. The documents stated that the result of an O-ring joint failure would be "loss of vehicle, mission, and crew due to metal erosion, burnthrough, and probable case burst resulting in fire and deflagration." The waiver, formally known as a "Space Transportation System Level I Change Request," was dated March 28, 1983. "Death Document" seemed an apt description, as it described accurately what seemed to have happened to Challenger.

Then Herr added grimly, "It's probably going to be the little guys that get fried for this." I hoped he wasn't thinking of himself.

When I returned to the office, the secretary told me that Jim Brier wanted to see me. She said he'd come to her and asked if she knew of anyone else I had given "that memo" to. I went to Brier's office, and he said to come in. He seemed very upset and told me that the supervisor wanted him to talk to me.

"This is an explosive memo," Brier said as I sat down. Holding the memo, he began by calling my contentions "unsupported." We discussed his objections, and I methodically explained the basis for each statement. It was a reasonable discussion, but at length I became exasperated and said, "There is nothing there that I wouldn't swear to under oath."

I didn't realize that in eight days I would be required to do just that in testimony before the Presidential Commission. Brier now became more conciliatory. By the time we finished he said, "You know, in the short time you've been here, you've learned more about the engineering side of this stuff than I did in all the years I worked on the SRB."

I had always liked Brier, and by now our conversation was quite cordial. The discussion turned to the fact that I would soon be leaving NASA. Not wanting to discuss the deeper reasons for my departure, I told Brier that I couldn't work while I was constantly under pressure to put in unpaid overtime and that the supervisor never responded to the analyses I gave him.

"Well, I'd agree with that," Brier said. "But I really think you should consider staying. After this accident, the SRB analyst will really be in the limelight!"

As we talked, I felt sick over the conflicts I was experiencing inside. I wanted to stay at NASA, but I felt I had to leave. Now my memo had been confiscated, I was marked as a complainer, and my last attempt to document and deliver critical though unwelcome information to NASA headquarters had been suppressed.

"THIS IS GOOD STUFF"

—How the *New York Times*
Came to Disclose the O-ring Papers

THE LEAD STORY on the Monday night news was that President Reagan had appointed a Commission to examine the Challenger disaster. Phyllis and I were excited. We'd seen the daily drama of NASA's stonewalling, claiming that they were examining all possible causes and had no idea why Challenger blew up. We hoped, perhaps naively, that the new Presidential Commission would expose the cover-up. There was speculation in the news reports that creating the Commission was a slap in the face to NASA, but the record shows that the Commission was not intended to balance or offset NASA's own internal investigation.

It was White House Chief of Staff Donald Regan who decided on creating the Commission. In his memoir, *For the Record: From Wall Street to Washington*, Regan wrote:

Plainly an investigation of the tragedy would be necessary. I told the president as we watched the coverage that no ordinary investigation would be adequate, that he must appoint a blue-ribbon group to probe every aspect of the situation.

Why did Donald Regan think that "no ordinary investigation would be adequate"? He proposed a Commission to the president almost instantly. Could the White House have had something to hide?

In his book, Donald Regan noted that National Security Adviser John Poindexter, along with NASA and its supporters in Congress, "wished to leave the investigation in the hands of the space agency." This would have been in line with the precedent of NASA's internal Apollo review board, created in 1967 to investigate the launch pad fire that killed astronauts Grissom, White, and Chaffee.

Something strange was going on. If the Commission had been set up to protect national security secrets, Poindexter and Congress would have supported it. But they were evidently not aware of Regan's motivations for controlling the Challenger investigation from the White House. During the week following the Challenger disaster, President Reagan was receiving daily briefings on the aftermath of the accident. It was he who made the final decision. Donald Regan wrote:

> On the way back to Washington from Houston after the memorial service for the lost astronauts, the two points of view [i.e., a NASA investigation vs. a Presidential Commission] were put to the president, and he opted for an independent Commission. Reagan accepted my suggestion that he ask William P. Rogers . . . to serve as chairman.

It is notable that Donald Regan did not explain why the president made this critical decision against all advice except for that of his chief of staff.

It is also pertinent that William Rogers was Regan's personal friend and business associate. Rogers had been President Nixon's first secretary of state. Now he was a senior partner in the firm of Rogers and Wells, and his clients included Merrill Lynch, the giant Wall Street brokerage firm whose former president was Regan himself.

Why then was the Commission on Challenger created? Was it to protect President Reagan, Donald Regan, and the White House from public knowledge that the president himself may have been involved in the order to launch Challenger?

The news reports we watched that night showed Rogers and Commission Vice Chairman Neil Armstrong, first man to set foot on the moon, at the White House. Rogers' remarks implied anything but a critical attitude toward NASA. He said:

> I think we're going to work very closely with [NASA]. We're not going to rely solely on that investigation [i.e., the one being conducted by NASA's board]. And because the president felt there should be an overall Commission that made the final recommendations and the final report, we're going to make it. We're going to make some recommendations. We're going to make the inquiry. Now that is not adversarial as far as NASA is concerned.

Rogers had made it clear his Commission would supplement but not replace NASA's review board. He then said:

> We are not going to conduct this investigation in a manner which would be unfair, unfairly critical of NASA, because I think, we think, I certainly think NASA has done an excellent job, and I think the American people do.

My heart sank when I heard Rogers say this. I turned to Phyllis and spoke the word that flashed through my mind: "Whitewash."

Neil Armstrong himself seemed puzzled about why the Commission he was to help lead had been set up, as he said from the White House podium, "Based on my experience, I would not have doubts about NASA being honestly able to conduct [its own] investigation."

When I heard that the Commission was being convened, I thought at first that I should hand over the O-ring documents to it, including my July 23 memo. But hearing the rest of what Rogers had to say, I began to suspect that his Commission and NASA were going to be working together to manage the news. I went to bed depressed, feeling that the hand of power had shown itself.

At work the next morning, February 4, I continued writing my history of the shuttle-Centaur. I was including references to the Challenger disaster in the introduction, stating that proceeding with Centaur could lead to another catastrophe, which would be due to the same "fly as is" mentality that NASA demonstrated by continuing to launch the shuttle when they knew of the defects in the SRB O-ring joints.

My office mate was not there, so I got up, closed the door, returned to my desk, and phoned the White House. I had no reason to believe anyone was monitoring my calls, and I asked the operator to connect me with any person who was working with William Rogers on the Challenger Commission.

Eventually I was put through to Rogers' personal secretary at his law office. "I can't tell you my name," I said, "but I need to know what the Commission will do if anyone at NASA brings them information about what really happened to Challenger."

I wanted to find out if people who came forward would be protected from reprisals by NASA's management. Despite my misgivings, I saw the Commission as the proper recipient of my memos and the O-ring documents I had collected from Paul Herr and the other engineers.

The secretary misunderstood me. I was looking for protection for myself. But she jumped to the conclusion that I was asking if NASA's officials who admitted to mistakes would be assailed.

"Don't worry," she said. "Mr. Rogers is not going to be hard on any-body. He's a very nice man. Besides," she laughed, "He'd much rather be playing golf!"

I thanked her and hung up.

I was not going to trust my career, my safety, and the public inter-est to a political operative who would rather be playing golf. But I did-n't know what to do. The documents I had were explosive. They proved that NASA knew how dangerous the O-rings were, yet it kept flying.

I had an appointment that morning with my prospective supervisor at the Treasury Department, who had told me that the official job offer from their personnel office was imminent. I took the metro across town to the Treasury Annex, near the White House and Lafayette Park.

After a brief meeting, the supervisor introduced me to another man who was a division director to whom I would eventually be assigned fol-lowing a reorganization that was in the works. We talked, but my guts were churning over my dilemma about what to do with the O-ring doc-uments I was carrying in my briefcase.

I wanted the advice of a lawyer, but with the recent purchase of our house, the costs of moving in, child support payments, and debt, we were broke. There was no way I could afford legal representation in dealing with NASA. But maybe I could go the political route.

I left the Treasury Annex and located a pay phone on the other side of Lafayette Park within sight of the White House, got a number from the information operator, and called the office of Joseph Califano. He was a powerful and combative Washington attorney who had been secretary of health, education, and welfare under President Carter.

His secretary answered. I said, "I work for NASA and I've got some very important documents pertaining to the Challenger disaster. I wonder if I could speak to Mr. Califano."

"Mr. Califano is extremely busy right now with an important legal case," she said.

"I need to talk to him," I persisted.

The secretary was annoyed. "I'm sorry, he can't talk to you now," she answered.

I hung up without saying anything more.

Back at the office, I passed two NASA managers. They were discussing a meeting that was about to take place with staff members of the Congressional Budget Office who wanted to discuss the impact of the Challenger disaster on the space shuttle budget. "Don't tell them too much," I heard one manager say. By now, nothing I heard at NASA would surprise me.

I spent the rest of the day working on the Centaur paper. When I reached home that night, I talked to Phyllis about the documents—the Davids memo, the reports from Paul Herr on the Code M meetings, Herr's "Death Document," my January 23, 1985, memo, and the memo on the SRBs I had turned in to Code B on Monday.

These documents were far different from the hearsay and press leaks that were going on, which indicated NASA was looking at the solid rocket boosters as a likely cause of the accident. It would be easy for NASA to explain away this kind of piecemeal information. It would be a matter of stretching out the disclosures over time, talking a bunch of rocket science obfuscation, and hoping that eventually the whole thing would blow over.

"But it shouldn't blow over," I said to Phyllis. "What they are ignoring is that the public has a right to know what happened."

Surely, I said, someone will go public and say that NASA knew all along that the cause of the disaster had been anticipated, feared, and documented and that with each flight America's astronauts were being sent aloft in full public view on dangerously flawed machinery.

"Who is going to do it?" she asked.

After a long pause, I said, "I have to give the documents to the press." She nodded.

This was more a realization than a decision. It was starting to seem like fate. We were sitting here in our little house out in the country with the hottest collection of incriminating documents since the start of the Space Age.

"Why me?" I asked. I didn't want to be a whistleblower. I hated the word. I had always been a team player. At FDA, my boss had called me a "model employee." And he was right; I was. I tried to be one at NASA too, despite the conflicts that seemed to be driving me out. Then the Treasury job offer appeared. It might be a safe haven. At least it would be harder for the government to get at me there. NASA would fire me if they thought I leaked—Treasury might not.

There was only one issue. What was the right thing to do? I was an American. I believed in the public interest. I believed the government should work for the people, not just the powerful. I believed in truth, honesty, and open government. Hadn't Watergate taught us anything? This was NASA's Watergate. I had not come to Washington after college in 1970 to be part of a cover-up.

"We have to decide which newspaper to talk to," I said to Phyllis.

We discussed which one to call. The New York Times had been way out in front with coverage of the disaster so far. It also had a certain distance from the Washington power culture. "It's pretty late in the day," I said, "but maybe they're still open."

I got the number from information and called the New York Times' Washington, D.C., bureau. As with the other calls I had made that day, a secretary answered. I said, "My name is Richard Lee, and I have some information about the Challenger disaster."

"Thank you, Mr. Lee," she replied. "I'll have someone call you." Great, I thought as I gave her my number, another clerical dead end.

Within a couple of minutes the phone rang. The voice on the other end was brisk and sounded like it belonged to a northerner. "I'm Phil Boffey," said the voice, "and I'm the science reporter for the New York Times in Washington. Mr. Lee?"

"Yes," I said, feeling awkward. The great crusader lying about his name.

"I've got the NASA phone directory, and I can't find your name."

I was already being drawn in deeply. "All right," I said. "My name is Richard Cook." I felt this could be the beginning of the end of my career and maybe my family's livelihood.

"Okay, here it is," said Boffey. "In the Resources Analysis Division?"

"That's right."

I gave him a summary of the documents. He was cautious. "I'll need to sit down with you and look at everything before we can decide what to do. Are you available tomorrow morning?"

"Yes," I said.

"9:00 a.m.?"

"That'll be all right."

"Do you know where we are?"

"No."

He gave me directions and we hung up. I was still hoping to keep my name out of it.

———

I LEFT MY office for the meeting with Phil Boffey. It was Wednesday, February 5.

As I walked to the metro, I realized that it would be easier to explain to Boffey the workings of the solid rocket booster joint system if I had a good diagram. I doubled back to Code M to ask Paul Herr for one, which he quickly pulled out of his files. By now Herr seemed to suspect what I was up to.

"Don't give this stuff to the newspapers," he said. I looked hard at him. "Not yet anyway," he said. I did not respond and left.

I took the metro to the Farragut North station and walked to the *New York Times'* office at Connecticut Avenue and K Street. I took the elevator to the newsroom. Phil Boffey came out of a back room and introduced himself. He was a slender man with graying hair and wore a white dress shirt with the sleeves rolled up. He was cordial and upbeat but seemed in a hurry.

We went around a corner to a conference room, and I explained what I did at NASA. At first Boffey seemed skeptical and asked me to show him the photograph on my NASA identification badge. He consulted the NASA phone book again.

He was apologetic. "I'm sorry I have to do this," he said. "I have to be careful that you're a real source."

I said I had no problem with that and showed him my collection of O-ring documents, including my own memos—the one I wrote the previous July that warned of a catastrophe and the one from earlier in the week about the disaster being a preventable accident. I did not view my memos as being important except as providing background information. I felt the critical ones were the Davids memo, the Code M meeting documents, and the Criticality 1 waiver that Paul Herr called the "Death Document." Boffey said, "This is really interesting. I need to go over all of it."

"I have to emphasize," I said, "that I don't want my name brought into this."

"I understand," he said. "I guarantee that your identity will be protected. *New York Times* reporters will go to jail before disclosing their sources. You can count on it."

"Good," I said. "I appreciate that."

"Let me read through everything, and I'll call you." We shook hands and I left.

I decided to walk around outside for a while and let my emotions unwind. I felt relieved that in Boffey I had found someone who understood the significance of what was going on.

Back at NASA, a memo was circulating from the comptroller, Thomas Newman. Dated that day, February 5, it listed the space shuttle's flight priorities, placing the military ones first. A few days before, I had read that a Pentagon spokesman said, "The Defense Department will not abandon its role as the financial mainstay of the shuttle."

Newman's memo, which was stamped "Sensitive," displayed three "standdown options." The first assumed that the shuttle would be inoperative for four months, the second for eight months, and the third for twelve months. This was irritating, because Code B was obviously paying no attention to the assessment in my February 3 memo that the shuttle could be grounded for two years or more. But I was right, and NASA was wrong. The shuttle in fact did not fly again for two years and eight months.

The memo placed DoD payloads at the top of each list. The four- and eight-month options stated, "All DoD (Dedicated and Shared) Flight

Requirements Satisfied." For the twelve-month standdown, "All DoD Dedicated Missions Accommodated; Shared Payloads Slip Six-Fifteen Months." Also for this option, commercial payloads would slip three to nine months, while, "Most Major NASA Payloads Encounter Slips of Nine-Twenty-four Months." An exception would be the Hubble Space Telescope, which would retain a high priority; otherwise, space science would come last.

That night Phil Boffey called me at home. "This is good stuff," he said. He wanted to discuss the O-ring documents in detail.

"I can come by tomorrow afternoon. The Presidential Commission is holding a public hearing in the morning, and I want to see it."

"Okay," he said, "but we can't delay on this."

"All right," I replied. "How about 1 p.m.?"

The Presidential Commission's first public hearing was held in the National Academy of Sciences auditorium on Constitution Avenue on Thursday, February 6, and was shown on Cable News Network and NASA Select TV. I settled down to watch in the NASA sixth floor news auditorium, where I had seen Challenger blow up.

The Commission was what White House press secretary Larry Speakes called "a stellar group." Besides Chairman William Rogers and Vice-Chairman Neil Armstrong, the panel members were: David C. Acheson, former vice president and general counsel, Communications Satellite Corporation, currently a partner in the Washington, D.C., law firm of Drinker, Biddle, and Reath; Dr. Eugene E. Covert, professor and head, Department of Aeronautics and Astronautics, Massachusetts Institute of Technology; Dr. Richard P. Feynman, professor of theoretical physics, California Institute of Technology, and recipient of the 1965 Nobel Prize in physics; Robert B. Hotz, former editor-in-chief of *Aviation Week and Space Technology*; Major General Donald J. Kutyna, U.S. Air Force, director of Space Systems Command; Dr. Sally K. Ride, physicist, astronaut, and first U.S. woman in space; Robert W. Rummel, aerospace engineer and former vice president of Trans World Airlines; Joseph F. Sutter, aeronautical engineer and executive vice president of Boeing; Dr. Arthur B. C. Walker, Jr., astronomer and professor of applied physics, Stanford University; Dr. Albert D. Wheelon, physicist and executive vice president, Hughes Aircraft; and Brigadier General

Charles "Chuck" Yeager, U.S. Air Force retired, former experimental test pilot and first person to break the sound barrier.

William Graham, NASA's acting administrator, and Jesse Moore, associate administrator for space flight, opened the meeting with prepared statements. Graham said, "NASA continues to analyze the system design and data, and as we do, you can be certain that NASA will provide you with its complete and total cooperation."

Graham now introduced Moore, who talked about the launch delays preceding the January 28 lift-off. Probably not aware of the Pandora's Box he was opening, Chairman William Rogers asked Moore:

> Well, in that connection I noticed in a press report that one of the contractors said that they had made—gave a warning of some sort about the cold weather. Could you deal with that, please?

Moore answered:

> We had a fairly lengthy meeting, with the only concern being expressed that the weatherman had predicted the temperatures were going to be fairly cold that evening, down into the mid-twenties, and the main concern was the water systems of the support systems on the launch pad, were these pipes going to freeze. And that was the major concern that the system had at that point. . . . The other problem we were concerned about during this discussion was ice. We were concerned about ice on the launch tower and that particular ice doing some damage to the orbiter surfaces and the orbiter tiles.

Rogers pressed the point.

> I thought that the report I read about temperature referred not to the outside of the spaceship but the booster rocket. The claim was, according to the newspaper, that there was concern that the cold temperature might have affected the booster rocket inside, not outside.

Moore replied:

That may be. The one paper article I remember seeing, Mr. Chairman, was the article on the effects on the orbiter and so forth. And I'll ask the people here who were in charge of the solid rocket booster to talk about any discussion that went on relative to that.

Chairman Rogers: What I referred to is not a rumor, or just gossip. It was a statement by one of the contractors that was a quote that was issued.

Mr. Moore: Yes, sir.

In response to another question, Moore repeated, "I did not have any concerns about the temperature expressed other than a concern on the launch complex."

Moore remained head of the NASA board for only three more weeks. Once the Commission found out that the Thiokol engineers had advised against the launch, Moore and all other NASA officials who had a role in what the Commission by then was viewing as the "flawed" launch decision were barred from further participation in the Challenger investigation.

As the hearing went on, Rogers asked Space Transportation System program manager Arnold Aldrich from Houston the same question he had asked Moore: "Do you remember any warning from, I guess it was Morton Thiokol, that there might be a problem with the temperature on the booster?"

Aldrich answered, "I do not recall such a warning at that time. . . . We had no concern for the performance or safety of the flight articles at that time [i.e., the time of the launch], nor do I even at this time."

Aldrich's statement was the first in a long series of claims by NASA officials, including Moore and those at Marshall, that they never saw the problems with the solid rocket booster seals as a "safety of flight" issue.

At this hearing, the O-rings were mentioned publicly for the first time. The existence of O-rings was so little known that the New York Times hearing transcript published the next day referred to them in one place as "old rings."

The discussion drifted to another topic but came back to the solid rocket booster joint seals when Air Force Major General Donald Kutyna said to Marshall manager Judson Lovingood, "Jud, do you have a slide of the joints where these segments are joined? Do you have a technical description of that?" The discussion proceeded as follows:

Dr. Lovingood: No, I had planned to have some detail as back-up, but we didn't have back-up for this briefing. That is the normal way we do things, and I thought it might come up.

General Kutyna: Have you looked at these post-mission, after you've recovered them from the ocean, to see if there's any leakage at those joints from the previous flights?

Dr. Lovingood: We have seen some evidence of what we call blow-by of these seals. The primary seal. We have never seen any erosion of a secondary seal, but we have seen evidence of soot in between the two seals.

General Kutyna: Was that any cause for concern?

Dr. Lovingood: Oh, yes, I mean that's an anomaly, and that was thoroughly worked, and that's completely documented on all the investigative work we did on that, and we can get that for you.

But what Lovingood said was not accurate. There had been alarming secondary seal erosion on a previous Challenger flight, launched on April 29, 1985. This erosion was on a secondary O-ring in a nozzle joint, while the Challenger disaster resulted from breach of a seal in a field joint.

It was an awkward moment in the hearing. Watching the proceedings, I wondered if Lovingood would succeed in getting out of the tight spot Kutyna had put him in. Perhaps sensing the tension, Chairman Rogers tried to smooth things over, saying:

If a committee or a subcommittee of the Commission visits your operation, would you have the information there that you could answer specific questions about this more conveniently, and particularly about the Challenger as distinguished from the overall operation?

Lovingood seemed relieved. Rogers had let him off the hook. Lovingood said:

Yes, we would have more data there that we could get, plus we would have our experts in these areas that could talk much more intelligently than I can on the subject.

Chairman Rogers: Well, we do not expect you—I mean, we understand that you didn't have much notice, and that you were to give an overview, so you don't have to be apologetic, but we are just trying to figure out how to get the information ourselves, and that certainly would be one way we could do it, isn't it?

Dr. Lovingood: Yes, I think that would be a way.

Chairman Rogers: Thank you.

Clearly Kutyna knew, everyone there from NASA knew, and I certainly knew, that a critical subject had been broached. But did Rogers know? At this key moment, he backed off. He seemed confused. Perhaps he thought that it was not a discussion to have in public.

As Lovingood and others spoke, I took careful notes. Then I realized I was being watched. I turned around and saw my supervisor walk away.

After the hearing, I went back to my office and began to type the notes. As I worked, my supervisor came up behind me.

"What are you doing?" he asked.

"Making some notes on the hearing."

He paused, then said sternly, "People's careers are at stake," and walked away. It was a warning, but about what? Not to talk to the Commission? And how did he know that people's careers were at stake? Whose careers? His? What about my career, which I felt had been ruined?

That afternoon, I left the office and went back uptown to the *New York Times*. During this visit, Phil Boffey seemed more relaxed. We spent about two hours going over the O-ring documents. Boffey was a science writer with a solid grasp of technology, but still it was difficult to explain the workings of the O-ring joints. I wasn't certain of all the details myself, but as we proceeded we both became more confident about what we were examining.

I told him again that I didn't want my name to be used or my own memos to appear in the news reports. But I said I was expecting a job offer from Treasury that might make it easier on me if I had to be drawn into events.

We finished our meeting, and again Boffey said he would be in touch. He said he now had to talk about the story with his editors. It was exhilarating to see how interested the *Times* was and that they did in fact believe the documents were important to understanding Challenger. I had been walking a lonely road, with Phyllis the only person I could talk to. Boffey's eagerness validated my own sense of the significance of what I was doing. Still, I was afraid of the possible repercussions if NASA found out.

It was now Friday, February 7. As fate would have it, the personnel office at Treasury called to make the official job offer, one that was legally binding. My first day on the job there would be Monday, February 17. I accepted the offer with mixed feelings—sadness over having to leave NASA and the setback to my career, but relief at having escaped what was feeling almost like a death sentence.

Again I mention fate. I had begun to feel like an actor in a drama, reading the lines, playing a role assigned by an unknown director. My only choice was to play it well or poorly. The role was that of the one person who knew about the history of the O-ring joints and was at liberty to disclose that knowledge.

And what would happen if I failed to act? Sooner or later, NASA would get around to disclosing a minimal portion of what happened, and the information would come out piecemeal. No one would ever get the full horror of what had been done, that NASA's management was launching people on badly flawed machinery to meet politically motivated objectives.

Probably many of the details would never be disclosed. The Commission would find some way to make it all go down in a politically acceptable way, with nothing ever really changing. I wondered about the millions of school children who had watched the deaths of Christa McAuliffe and the other Challenger astronauts. Shouldn't they know the truth?

Boffey called again and asked me to come back for a third meeting. When I arrived, he said, "My editors want to publish the story this weekend—on Sunday. We've got to hurry. The *Orlando Sentinel* is coming out with a story tomorrow where they talk about the O-rings."

"All right," I said.

"The *Times* wants it to be the lead story Sunday morning. We'd do it sooner, but I have to spend some time tomorrow calling NASA's management and getting their comments."

All this sounded fine.

"Now," he said. "The documents are coming from you. We'll protect your identity, but if you want to back out we'll return everything and act as though you never came here."

"That's very admirable," I said, but "the story needs to be written."

"Yes, it does," said Boffey, "but there's one more thing. We think it's very important to publish your July 23 memo. It's your warning that explains it all and ties everything together."

"All I did was report what the engineers said," I replied.

"But you put it into words everyone could understand. And if we quote from it we'll need to say it was Richard Cook who wrote it."

As I heard Boffey say this, I was starting to feel dizzy. My worst fears were coming true. I couldn't hide or escape. I had to play my part, even if it was an overwhelming one.

"I don't want to do it," I said. He just looked at me. I had told him about the Treasury job and that if I got it I would be out of NASA. "This morning I got the job offer from Treasury," I said.

"Wow! That is really great!" Boffey seemed genuinely elated. "You're safe."

He wanted me to come with him to talk to the chief of the Washington bureau, Bill Kovach. When we walked into his office, Kovach was on the phone, and Boffey said he was talking about the O-ring story with the *Times'* publisher, Arthur O. Sulzberger, in New York.

When Kovach hung up, we shook hands and chatted for a few minutes. He was in his 40s and courteous and friendly. As we talked, I felt that both he and Boffey understood my fears as well as my sense that what I was doing was not for fame or notoriety but to advance the public interest. Kovach gave me his home phone number and said to call him there or at work any time.

The last thing Boffey and I did together that day was talk about how the article would describe the source of the material. He said that he needed to say something in print about who had made the disclosures. We decided that he would refer to an unnamed "solid-fuel rocket analyst" early in the article, while naming me later in the text as the author of the memo which pointed to a possible catastrophe.

Boffey and I shook hands. He seemed excited about the story. He said cheerfully, "If it turns out this is what caused the accident, you're going to look like a genius."

That night as I drove home to King George it was dark by the time I pulled into the driveway. I walked into the house both fearful and excited. I said to Phyllis, a little sheepishly, "I'm going to be famous."

She was upset. "Why?"

"They're going to print my memo with my name attached to it."

"They can't do that."

"I gave permission."

We talked for a long time and finally agreed that for the O-ring papers to have the impact they should, my memo was needed. I was the one who gave voice to the engineers' concerns that failure of the O-ring seals could be catastrophic. Mine was the one document that delved behind the engineers' jargon to the way they actually felt and spoke about the problem. When I went to sleep that night, my stomach was in knots.

Thank God it was now the weekend. Saturday was a day for chores— bringing in firewood and stacking it by the woodstoves in the front and back of the house, emptying ashes, brushing the flues, hauling trash to the landfill, and working on putting up fencing around the property. I had phoned my parents to let them know what was going on. My mother lived in Williamsburg and my father in Newport News. My father was planning to visit on Sunday and said he would stop and pick up a copy of the *New York Times*.

The main thing I felt now was fear. No matter how hard I tried, I couldn't get it out of my mind. It was just there, and it was also in my body—through tension, a knot in my stomach, shallow breathing, and a growing pain in my lower back. The back pain got worse through the morning, and when I stood up from the lunch table and walked toward the laundry room, I fell to the floor in agony. I lifted myself to all fours, but could not stand up without the pain becoming overwhelming. So I just crouched there on the floor for a while. Then, using crutches, I was able to stand, though barely.

Obviously it was fear and tension that had manifested itself in this way. I found some relief lying on an electric heating pad and taking aspirin. But the fear was still there, and it was painful to try to get up off the bed. Finally I went to sleep. After that, over the years, the same agonizing back pain returned periodically. My lower back was yet another casualty of the Challenger disaster.

. . .

On Sunday morning, February 9, my mother called to say that the story had appeared on the front page of the *Richmond Times-Dispatch*, reprinted from the *New York Times* news service. My name was in the article. Soon my father arrived with the *Times* and we gathered around the dining room table to read it.

It was the lead article on the front page. The headline said: "NASA HAD WARNING OF A DISASTER RISK POSED BY BOOSTER."

The sub-headlines said: "ENGINEERS FEARED LEAKS" and "Internal Reports Cited Erosion of Rocket Seals—Agency Declines to Comment."

The article began:

WASHINGTON, Feb. 8—The space agency was warned last year that seals on the space shuttle's solid-fuel booster rockets might break and cause a catastrophic accident, according to documents from the agency's files.

The documents show that engineers at the headquarters of the National Aeronautics and Space Administration and its Marshall Space Flight Center in Huntsville, Ala., were concerned that leaks might occur where segments of the booster rockets are mated.

The next section of the story had the sub-headline "A Stark Warning" and spoke about my July 23 memo:

One NASA analyst warned in an internal memorandum last July that flight safety was "being compromised by potential failure of the seals." He added: "Failure during launch would certainly be catastrophic." A 1982 "Critical Items List" for the booster also warned that if the seals should fail the results could be "loss of vehicle, mission, and crew due to metal erosion, burnthrough, and probable case burst resulting in fire and deflagration," or rapid, intense burning.

The article said that those NASA officials who were contacted about the story declined to comment, including Jesse Moore, Michael Weeks, and David Winterhalter.

Then Boffey wrote that the leading theory for the explosion "is that a plume of flame emerged from one side of a booster and set off an explosion of the shuttle's giant external fuel tank." The article cited William Graham's statement on a news program the previous Sunday that the plume "did appear to happen at least near a seam."

Next Boffey wrote about Thursday's meeting of the Presidential Commission, where NASA admitted it had consulted with Thiokol about cold weather concerns. But, Boffey reported, "Judson A. Lovingood, deputy manager of shuttle projects at Marshall, indicated that Thiokol said the launch should proceed. Lovingood also acknowledged that there had been concern after previous shuttle flights about erosion damage to some of the seals, but he indicated that this problem had been thoroughly investigated. . . ."

The article then described how the O-ring seals were supposed to work, "much as a rubber washer on a faucet seals tight to prevent water from leaking." It then noted that the one area of concern that was not addressed by the documents was the effect of cold temperatures.

Now the article addressed my July 23 memorandum in more detail:

> Mr. Cook warned that "the charring of seals," which had been observed on recent shuttle flights, posed "a potentially major problem affecting both flight safety and program costs." In the joint between the nozzle section of the rocket and the adjoining segment, the memorandum said, "not only has the first O-ring been destroyed but the second has been partially eaten away."

My statement that "the second has been partially eaten away" was an accurate description of the erosion of the secondary O-ring on a nozzle joint on flight 51-B of Challenger, April 29–May 6, 1985. This was the erosion I later heard a Thiokol engineer call "terrifying." Boffey then summarized Irv Davids' memorandum. The article pointed out that Davids also wrote of secondary seal erosion, stating that:

> Both this observation and Mr. Cook's memorandum appear to contradict Mr. Lovingood's assertion that no erosion of a secondary seal had been observed.

The article noted that Davids' memo had described the "jetting effect" from the joint putty and the "lifting off" or "unseating" of the secondary O-ring due to joint rotation, a problem that "has been known for quite some time." Also mentioned was the proposal to use the capture feature to eliminate the problem.

The article then made references to the various Code M briefing documents, including the one that referred to the O-rings as a major budget threat, and closed with another mention of Paul Herr's "Death Document," the 1982-1983 waiver from the critical items list that cited the problem with joint rotation and how it compromised O-ring redundancy.

It was a spectacular article. There had been other news leaks from NASA in the days since the disaster, but this was the first time actual documents had appeared in the press. Phil Boffey later received the Pulitzer Prize, and he certainly deserved it. I had studied and taught history, and there were no other instances I could think of where an insider had worked with the press to break open a major federal government cover-up in this way, by disclosing a whole series of key documents which, in effect, had predicted a catastrophe.

Pretty good work, I thought to myself. I had no doubt, nor did Phyllis or my father, that I had done the right thing. We were satisfied that we had acted in the public interest. NASA would never be able to credibly deny that they knew this could happen.

We had expected phone calls that day from the news media, but none came. I was glad of that, because I hadn't known what I would say. As far as I was concerned, my role in the drama was over. Later we learned that as new residents far out in the country we were not listed in the Washington, D.C., telephone information system.

I was still hobbling around the house on crutches, and it seemed my back pain gave me a perfect excuse to take the week off on sick leave before reporting to Treasury on Monday, February 17. "You can't do that," Phyllis said. "They'll know for sure you were the leaker." She was right. I decided to go to work the next day.

The question now was what they were going to do to me. Probably nothing, I guessed. I was hoping for a quiet week. Then I would report to Treasury the following Monday and get on with my life and my career. I wanted the whole situation to go away, now that I had done my professional and moral duty. But my life would never be the same. William Rogers took care of that.

"AN UNPLEASANT, UNFORTUNATE SITUATION"

—The Commission Meets Behind Closed Doors

DURING THE MORNING of Saturday, February 8, Phil Boffey had phoned NASA's officials, asking for comments on his article. I was at home in King George, with my stomach tightening in a knot of tension and my lower back starting to hurt. After the public hearing on Thursday and one the next day in executive session, members of the Presidential Commission had been dismissed by Chairman Rogers to go about their business. Their only instructions were to show up at the Kennedy Space Center the next Thursday.

The Commission member who most avidly wanted to play an active role in the Challenger investigation was the legendary Dr. Richard Feynman, under cancer treatment at the time. Feynman was a professor of theoretical physics at the California Institute of Technology, where William Graham had been one of his students. He said that when Graham phoned him to serve on the Challenger panel he didn't know who he was. Feynman had worked on the atomic bomb at Princeton University and at the Los Alamos Laboratory in New Mexico. He was a recipient of the 1965 Nobel Prize in physics. He was also a bongo drummer and a talented painter. He died a year later in 1987.

In downtown Washington, Feynman was talking to Graham, the

head of the agency that was supposedly under investigation, pleading for some real investigative work to do.

Graham told Feynman that maybe he could fly to Houston, where Commission member Sally Ride had returned, and talk to NASA flight control personnel about the disaster. Just to be on the safe side politically, Graham phoned his friend and political crony, Commission member David Acheson, to ask what he thought of this.

Also playing it safe, Acheson phoned William Rogers. When Acheson called back, he told Feynman, as recounted in Feynman's own written recollections, "I think it's a great idea, but I can't convince Rogers. Rogers refuses to say why he's against it, and I just don't know why I can't convince him that you should get started."

Feynman's trip to Houston was off. Graham next told Feynman that he would bring in some people to talk to him there at headquarters. He got Rogers on the phone, but Rogers vetoed that idea too. Rogers told Graham he didn't want Feynman going off on his own.

Feynman now got on the phone with Rogers. As he wrote later, "I complained that we had several meetings by now, but we hadn't yet discussed who was going to do what, or how to get started on the investigation."

Rogers said, "Well, do you want me to bother everybody and bring them together again for a meeting on Monday to discuss this?" This was odd. Why would he bring the entire Commission together to discuss Feynman's request? Was he using it as a ploy to get Feynman to back off?

Feynman said, "Yes!" He had called Rogers' bluff.

Rogers now relented and said, "Okay, go to NASA. It's okay."

Feynman took a cab to NASA headquarters, where he was met by Michael Weeks. By now, Rogers had phoned General Donald Kutyna, the member of the Commission who represented the Air Force, to get him to talk Feynman out of going to NASA. But it was too late, as Feynman had already left his hotel.

At NASA headquarters, Weeks expanded on a summary of the O-ring problems Feynman had already been given at NASA's Jet Propulsion Laboratory before leaving California for Washington. Feynman later wrote that Weeks explained that the problem with the O-ring joints had been discovered early on and noted on "flight after flight," but that flight readiness reviews cleared the shuttle to fly nonetheless. Weeks showed the briefing charts presented by Thiokol and Marshall at the August 19, 1985, meeting at NASA headquarters. Feynman wrote:

> At the end of this long report on the problem of the seals, there was a page of recommendations. This is how all information is communicated in NASA—by writing everything down behind little black circles, called "bullets."
>
> When I looked at the recommendations, the thing that struck me was the contradiction between two of the bullets. The first one says, "The lack of a good secondary seal in the field joint is most critical. Ways to reduce the effects should be incorporated as soon as possible to reduce criticality." Then, further down the page, it says, "Analysis of existing data indicates that it is safe to continue flying with existing design." . . .
>
> I pointed out this contradiction and said, "What analysis?" It was some kind of computer model. A computer model that determines the degree to which a piece of rubber will burn in a complex situation like that—is something I don't believe in!

Feynman concluded that NASA had decided that if a seal leaked "a little" but the flight got off the ground, the problem wasn't serious. To him, it was as though NASA were playing Russian roulette with the shuttle. Feynman wrote that at the end of his briefing, Weeks referred to "a rumor that the history of the seals problem was being leaked."

The next day, Sunday, Feynman got a call at his hotel from General Kutyna. As disclosed months later when transcripts were released, at the Commission's closed hearing the previous Friday, Arnold Aldrich had noted that serious O-ring erosion had been observed on the previous cold-temperature flight in January 1985. Now, someone had alerted Kutyna, as Feynman put it, that "there was information, somewhere in the works of NASA, that the O-rings had no resiliency whatever at low temperature, and NASA wasn't saying anything about it."

Kutyna told Feynman over the phone, "I was working on my carburetor, and I was thinking, you're a professor. What, sir, is the effect of cold on the rubber seals?"

Feynman wrote that he immediately understood the implications of Kutyna's question. The shuttle had launched at twenty-nine degrees on January 28; the previous coldest launch was fifty-three degrees. Next, Feynman read about my memo:

That weekend, the *New York Times* put out an article about a man named Cook, who was in the budget department of NASA. Mr. Cook had written a letter to his superior a year earlier, saying that the engineers knew there was something wrong with the seals, that they might have to fix the problem, and it might be expensive. Mr. Cook was working out the budget and recommended that NASA prepare for the contingency that it would suddenly need a big load of money to fix this problem of the seals.

Feynman also wrote, "Mr. Cook's story sounded like a big exposé, as if NASA was hiding the seals problem from us." This was a rather dubious statement from someone as intelligent as Feynman. The purpose of my *New York Times* news leaks was not to bring the history of the O-ring problems to members of the Commission. It was to inform the nation and the world.

Feynman's commentary, in which he also disclosed that the Commission members were sent away for several days with nothing to do, suggested that the Commission did not exist to investigate the disaster. Rather its purpose seemed to be to manage the flow of information to the press.

Rogers reacted to the Sunday *New York Times* article by calling the Commission into closed session on Monday, February 10, at the Old Executive Office Building next to the White House, where I once worked for Esther Peterson and the U.S. Office of Consumer Affairs in the Jimmy Carter White House. It was a cold, dreary morning, as the members trudged through the rain to the meeting. A number of NASA's managers and engineers had been called to attend, including William Graham. Thiokol managing engineer Alan McDonald, who lived in Utah, reportedly heard about the meeting and showed up uninvited.

The transcript of this meeting, which was not printed until months later, is a strange one. Nothing appears to preoccupy the participants so much as Sunday's news disclosures and the importance of discrediting the idea that NASA had prior knowledge that the flawed seals could blow up the shuttle.

But here an important correction needs to be made to the public record. In his book on his experience with the Commission, Feynman stated that I attended this meeting. He wrote, "That afternoon we had our emergency closed meeting to hear from the guy whose story was in the *New York Times*. His name was Mr. Cook."

It was unclear whether this was an error or a willful misstatement, and there was no way to find out because Feynman died from cancer a year later. Of course it would have been better and more honest if Rogers had invited me to the meeting. Instead, he used the meeting to plan the attack he would carry out against me the next day. I am making this correction, because Feynman's error found its way into other books about the Challenger disaster.

Another point to bear in mind is that the Commission's published transcripts of its meetings were incomplete. They deleted information that was deemed too sensitive or embarrassing. So in recounting the hearings, including closed sessions, I have added some of the deleted material to which I later gained access.

The February 10 meeting was never reported in the press, as it was an executive session. And it was never discussed in detail in any book written after the Challenger disaster. During the hearing, Commission members for the first time engaged NASA's launch managers in a discussion of key issues, but that discussion was forgotten in the next day's charade, where Rogers and his NASA collaborators tried to pillory me.

Rogers opened the February 10 closed hearing by announcing that a public meeting would be held the next day and that NASA had been asked to produce all documents pertaining to the solid rocket booster seals. Rogers then said:

> I think it goes without saying that the article in the New York Times and other articles have created an unpleasant, unfortunate situation. There is no point in dwelling on the past. The important thing is to be sure that the Commission has all the appropriate documentation and all the appropriate information. It may well be that we have learned a lesson from this, that as much as possible we would hope that NASA and NASA's officials will volunteer any information in a frank and forthright manner. We don't want to be in a position that we have to ask for everything in advance.

Rogers was expressing disappointment that the Commission had to find out through the media the existence of relevant documents and facts. To be certain no one at NASA had to be afraid he would affix any serious blame for anything that had been done, he added:

This is not an adversarial procedure. This commission is not in any way adversarial, and we hope that in the future, as much as it is humanly possible, when you think information has been developed that we should know about, that you will volunteer to give us that information.

Rogers now was contradicting his own statement the previous Friday, when he told Jesse Moore and other NASA officials in closed session:

But I just think that the fewer documents we have in our possession until we get ready to do something with it, the better off we are.

Rogers might have said that the explosion of Challenger and the NASA "investigation" in process had created the "unfortunate situation." Instead, he focused the blame on news leaks. In fact, his attitude toward NASA seemed apologetic. It seemed clear that his intent was to work with NASA to produce a favorable public impression with which the published reports unfortunately interfered. NASA was being chastised, not for having produced what was ever more clearly an accident caused by factors that should have been anticipated, but for not having given the Commission incriminating documents before they appeared in the press. The transgression of NASA's managers was that they were making the Commission's job of protecting them—and the Reagan administration—more difficult.

William Graham spoke next. He said that from now on, all NASA testimony would be "reviewed on a word-by-word basis by a knowledgeable NASA technical review team" and corrected for the record. He acknowledged that "it is possible for NASA to occasionally misspeak or to delete something inadvertently."

Rogers then asked Graham if anyone in NASA had been working on the "preparation" of the New York Times story. Graham said no. Rogers then acknowledged the pertinence of the story to the investigation. He said:

I guess what concerns me a little bit about it, and I hope we don't have any further discussion publicly about it, is that this seemed to go right to the heart of the matter, and it seemed to be related to the "plume" that was . . . shown to the public, and it occurred to us that there must have been a good deal of thought in NASA about how serious a story it would be if it appeared, and therefore I would have thought that there would have been an eagerness to present it to the Commission on Thursday, and particularly on Friday, in the private session.

Graham replied, "Yes, sir, I share your view of that." Rogers then made a statement that was deleted from the official transcript and is being printed here for the first time:

Is there anything that you would like to tell us now that we should know about that it would not be wise to disclose to the public at this time? It might be useful to you to send me a letter as to these priorities, if there should be another newspaper story to that effect. I can say we're working on it. . . . Write us a letter saying you are preparing [information]. . . . Then if there's a newspaper story, I will say, NASA is apprised of the fact. We have every confidence we are going to get all the information. We don't want what we are doing here to interfere with your investigation as long as it doesn't appear that we are trying to cover things up.

Graham replied, "We will certainly do that, and you will have that within the day." Again, this statement by Rogers suggested that the Commission was not created to investigate anything but was brought into being to manage the news.

Then, astonishingly, William Graham, the acting head of the agency, left the meeting, leaving General Manager Philip Culbertson in charge. Throughout the entire course of the hearings, Graham was remarkably disengaged.

Jesse Moore then introduced the NASA personnel, including Paul Wetzel, Paul Herr, Irv Davids, William Hamby, and Russ Bardos, the whole group of headquarters SRB engineers. There was also Michael Weeks and David Winterhalter, the Division of Propulsion director. From Marshall there was the director, William Lucas, Larry Mulloy, and a couple of others. Then there was the uninvited guest, Alan McDonald of Thiokol.

Moore then turned the discussion over to Michael Weeks, who quickly made my July 23 memorandum the main topic of discussion. He said:

As was spoken to, and it is in your document there, the first one is the Cook memorandum, and that is a memorandum that was written on the 23rd of July, and it was prepared by the financial analysts over in the financial department, and the person is a financial type person and not too knowledgeable of the whole program situation . . . and I guess I would suggest to you that that is a less clinical analysis of this whole situation, because the young chap came aboard about the first of July and was just picking up things in a hallway, and wrote this to his immediate supervisor.

Chairman Rogers: Is he here today?

Mr. Weeks: No, he is not.

Mr. Moore: We could bring him, Mr. Chairman.

Chairman Rogers: We didn't expect him. I was just asking. He is still employed by NASA?

Mr. Weeks: Yes, he is. . . .

Chairman Rogers: Just so you don't go too fast, let's focus for a moment on the Cook memorandum. As I understand it, you are saying that he was just hired and was in a department where he really didn't have much knowledge of what was going on?

Mr. Weeks: I would believe that you should discount this to a fairly great extent, because as you will see in the next memorandum of Mr. Irv Davids, who has been with our program for at least a decade, and is thirty years with the agency, it is a very careful and thoughtful response to his memo. His memo was created because we had a failure in April of 1985 in which it is the first time in all of the program that we had the secondary seal have any difficulty, and the only time, whereas the other erosions were all in the primary seal, the primary being the one that first sees the pressure, the secondary being the one that is backing it up.

Weeks' strategy in discussing my memo was clear—"not too knowledgeable," "young chap," "picking up things in a hallway," "discount this to a fairly great extent." Typical shoot-the-messenger stuff. Also, Davids did not write his memo in response to mine. He had never seen my memo.

But some Commission members, to their credit, wanted to know if what I was saying was true.

Mr. Hotz: Mr. Weeks, could you tell us whether there are any errors of fact in this memo, and if so, would you point them out?

Mr. Weeks: Which one?

Mr. Hotz: The first memo, the Cook memo.

Mr. Weeks: Would you help me out on that?

Mr. Moore: We can get Mr. Cook here if you would like, Mr. Chairman.

Chairman Rogers: Yes, we would like that, but let's just go ahead.

Mr. Moore: We will get an answer to that.

Chairman Rogers: Just so we understand. I think Mr. Hotz and I asked the same questions. All right. This says: You have asked us or me to investigate reported problems, and then he says, discussions with program engineers show that these are potentially major problems affecting both flight safety and program costs. My question is, is what he set forth there accurate, and didn't he talk to the engineers and deduce this information? Isn't this information he got from the engineers?

Mr. Weeks: I think that his statement in here where he says that it might be catastrophic I think is overstated.

Overstated? The problem was indeed catastrophic. This was what blew up Challenger, and Weeks knew it.

Chairman Rogers: Well, that may be.

Mr. Moore: I think the best thing for us to do, Mr. Chairman, is to think about getting Mr. Cook here, and then we can ask Mr. Cook to sit down and try to answer your questions on this thing.

Chairman Rogers: Yes, but we want to ask questions as we go along.

Mr. Hotz: We would also like your opinion of whether this is accurate or not—

Chairman Rogers: This is a case where you are saying, in effect, that you didn't have much confidence in this fellow because he was in the wrong department and had been there just a short time, and so we are asking is the material that he reported on accurate?

Mr. Weeks: If I may, I would like to pore over every word and come back to you.

Chairman Rogers: Well, is it substantially accurate?

Mr. Weeks: I think it is substantially accurate.

It took a while, but under the pressure of questioning, Michael Weeks, NASA's top space shuttle technical expert, finally admitted that the memo written by the young budget analyst who had been on the job for three weeks was "substantially accurate."

Dr. Eugene Covert closed the sequence of questions by saying:

I think the other thing, Mike, when you go through it, try to go through it from the point of view of a rather naïve sort of guy who hears the words and doesn't necessarily understand all the nuances but gets an overall picture of things. It has been my experience that sometimes people have amazing insight.

The discussion then moved to the Davids memo. Weeks introduced it by referring to the "secondary erosion on the flight of the 29th of April" as the event that triggered sending Davids and Hamby to Marshall, "because we were concerned about this being the first case of any erosion on the secondary seal." The discussion did not reference statements the previous week by Judson Lovingood that there had never been any secondary seal erosion.

As the meeting progressed, Chairman Rogers returned to my memo. He cited the statement that "Code M is viewing the situation with the utmost seriousness" and that future budgets should provide for solution of the seal problem. Rogers now asked:

Now, that memorandum either had not received much attention, on the one hand . . . or it was followed up, and some decisions were made on it, and I guess that is what I think we have to keep in mind.

Mr. Moore: Mr. Chairman, let me just add one quick point to that, if I might. In the case of a situation that Mr. Cook describes, we have been following up, and we have been following up this O-ring concern for some time. In fact, you will see a program laid out that we have had underway leading up to some tests that are scheduled for the month of February. So he is right in that particular aspect, and he is also right in the sense that it did represent in his common knowledge a budget threat, that we may come over and ask for a substantial amount of money in the budget request.

Chairman Rogers: I think that is the answer to my questions.

Mr. Moore: You will see, Mr. Chairman, the program that we have laid out has been underway for some time in this whole question about O-rings.

Moore's reference to "the program that we have laid out" was the capture feature. The first time the Commission had heard about that was in the Davids memo in the *New York Times*. In fact, as one reads the meeting transcript, it is increasingly clear that the *New York Times* article served the purpose of launching Rogers' Commission into what would eventually resemble a legitimate investigating body.

Now, astronaut Sally Ride, who had been silent, weighed in. Unlike all the NASA managers who had been speaking, not to mention all the members of the Commission except Neil Armstrong, she and her blue-suited colleagues had to ride the deeply-flawed shuttle into space. She said:

Can I ask you a question? . . . You've got this SRM [solid rocket motor] O-ring charring listed as a potential budget threat [i.e., in a Code M budget document cited in the *New York Times*]. What sort of a threat was it being considered as? In other words, were people thinking of it as a threat because they needed lots more O-rings, or were they thinking of it as a threat because there was a potential redesign of the solid rocket? In other words, how serious a safety consideration was this, and what kind of budget implications did it have? I mean, when people were briefing this were they saying we may have a solid rocket design or redesign, or were they saying we need more O-rings?

Jesse Moore answered:

Let me try and answer the question from a budget threat point of view. What we had underway, we did not have a safety of flight concern in our program area that said we should not fly the shuttle at this point in time.

Moore did not answer Ride's question about whether there was a potential redesign. Instead, Moore used the phrase "safety of flight." This phrase would be repeated by other NASA officials throughout the investigation. Moore gave the phrase an exact definition. It meant we did not feel we should ground the fleet. Sally Ride was not satisfied. Her questions showed how little the astronauts had been told about the issue. She continued:

> I guess what I'm concerned about is, you're saying you might want a potential re-design, because you were concerned at some level about erosion of the seals, and if there's any concern if the O-rings go you've lost the solids, and if you've lost the solids you've lost the flights. So it seems like a fairly serious consideration.
>
> Mr. Moore: It was a serious consideration, and in the analysis that will be presented by Larry Mulloy and the Marshall people here this afternoon it was given a very serious look, and everybody in the program felt that we did not have a safety of flight concern and that we should stop flying the program.

Rogers asked if there was any discussion of stopping flights. Moore answered:

> To my knowledge—and anybody else in the room can address the question that you asked. To my knowledge, there was no concern on the part of anybody here who said we should stop flying because of the budget threat potential and so on.
>
> Chairman Rogers: Was there anybody who said we ought to stop for a little while and slow down and take the following corrective steps before we fly?
>
> Mr. Moore: No, sir.

Sitting in the room that day at the Old Executive Office building were the men who told me, "We hold our breath whenever that thing goes up." Now these men were silent. And what about the obvious question—that if failure of the O-ring joints caused the Challenger disaster, maybe it should have been a "safety of flight" concern? Maybe NASA was horribly, tragically wrong? And if they were wrong, why?

Eventually, the Commission said NASA should have stopped flights after the August 19 briefing at headquarters, but they were not there yet in their thinking. And NASA was not giving them any help.

Now Neil Armstrong asked a question:

But what I'm trying to understand here, this charring item on the chart is on there, and that says that there was a concern of some sort, and Mr. Moore is telling us that it wasn't a safety of flight concern. And what I am trying to understand is, what might have made it a safety of flight concern? What is the difference? What is the dividing line that puts it on this, and what is the dividing line that would put it into a safety of flight concern?

At last someone asked the critical question, the one the entire investigation could turn on. Neil Armstrong, besides being the most famous astronaut in history, was a scientist. It was a scientist's question, demanding a scientist's answer. But Moore did not answer. Instead he said:

I will ask Dave Winterhalter here, who is head of that division [Division of Propulsion] to tell you of his perceptions on this fine line of the safety of flight concern, and also the concern we had about the O-ring.

Winterhalter addressed the Commission :

Firstly, if I thought at the time that that was a real safety of flight issue that it wouldn't have been a budget threat. It wouldn't have appeared on this list. It would have appeared as a mandatory change, a make-work change, that we would say we don't do any more flying, we don't do any more testing, until we make some changes. What we were talking about in this instance was we had seen some erosion on the O-rings. We had taken some action to take a look at some changes in designs, et cetera. However, we hadn't completed that evaluation to the point where we had scoped it money-wise to say, okay, it's going to take maybe $5, $10 million worth of extra testing and improvement in order to bring that on later in the program. But we listed it as a budget threat, something that maybe would use up some of our APA, whatever reserve we had in the program. Now, obviously if we had a whole list of things there that would also have the same effect on the budget. If they were an overrun, they weren't determined to be a budget threat.

You can hear the disgust in Sally Ride's voice as you read the transcript. She asked:

What amount of erosion would have given you a problem to call it a safety of flight issue?

Mr. Winterhalter: Well, we had test results on this and, even with the erosion on the secondary ring, which was the only instance we saw, we had a safety factor of over two to one in our tests.

What tests? Sally Ride continued asking about the timing of the sealing action at ignition: "What does that mean in terms of the amount of time?"

Larry Mulloy jumped in: "That is probably best explained with some charts that I have in my briefing."

Michael Weeks seemed to sense that this sequence of questions and answers wasn't going too well: "Sally, I don't think that you should get the idea that we weren't deeply concerned about that first instance of the secondary O-ring having erosion."

Vice Chairman Armstrong: "I find myself not really understanding the feeling of the people that were involved in this." He still wanted an answer about what was deemed safe and what was not.

Chairman Rogers wanted to know how the safety of flight issue was resolved: "What is it that shows how you resolved your concerns?"

Weeks didn't want to talk about it any more:

Well, I think that if we could proceed and get past the New York Times thing and get into the genuine chronology, I think that would come through a lot better.

Now General Kutyna jumped in:

Before you do, Mr. Chairman, I would like to call your attention to page seventeen. And when we look at the Cook memo you have a statement that the failure of the seal would certainly be catastrophic, and it was stated that that was overstated. And if you look on page seventeen, here's another group saying the same thing. It says: "failure mode and causes," and then about the fourth or fifth box down, "failure effect summary."

Mr. Weeks: Now, this is the document that is the December 1982, and that is when it was signed by myself, on the 28th of March in 1983. The critical items list was changed from a 1-Redundant to a Criticality 1 period, which means the redundancy was to some degree compromised.

General Kutyna: My problem is the *New York Times* kind of problem. Here it is said that Cook says it's going to be catastrophic and here is another guy who says loss of mission, vehicle, and crew. Somehow we've got to explain away in the open session tomorrow why this is different from what you've said.

Larry Mulloy then stated flatly, the "[joint] design is safe." Rogers then said:

Yes, what I was suggesting is we want to be careful that NASA doesn't suggest by [Mulloy's] answer that nothing has changed. [i.e., that it didn't change anything back in 1982-1983 when the O-ring seals were reclassified from Criticality 1R—redundant, to Criticality 1—no backup safety feature in case of a primary system failure.] That would be a devastating comment. I think the answer to that is: "We're not sure yet. That is what we are studying."

Here, William Rogers, a former attorney general and secretary of state of the United States, and now head of a prestigious Presidential Commission convened to find the cause of a national tragedy, appears to be coaching a key witness on how to avoid making a "devastating comment" in the next day's planned public hearing, and is telling him what he should say instead when questioned under oath.

Next, Larry Mulloy briefed the Commission , starting with an explanation that in 1982 they tested the SRB joints and:

. . . We did determine that we did not have redundant seals, which was the initial design intent. . . . The simple fact of the matter is that, due to this joint rotation, which I will explain, one of the seals is not effective, in that it is essentially lifted off its sealing surface. . . . And if you can't make it redundant, is it a reasonable risk to continue with the single failure of the system leading to a catastrophic failure?

Mr. Walker: Can I ask a question?

Mr. Mulloy: Yes, sir.

Mr. Walker: Does that mean it's a single point failure, Category 1?

Mr. Mulloy: Loss of mission and life.

Mr. Walker: It doesn't necessarily mean it has a negative connotation?

Mr. Mulloy: That is correct. It simply means you have a single point failure with no back-up and the failure of that single system is catastrophic.

How extraordinary: possible "loss of mission and life" doesn't have a "negative connotation." The reason Mulloy agreed with Commission member Walker that it does not have a "negative connotation" is likely that it had been deemed an "acceptable risk." Unfortunately, there had never been any criteria for defining an "acceptable risk," as shown by NASA's non-answers to Neil Armstrong's question about what would produce a determination to suspend flights. An "acceptable risk" was whatever someone at NASA said was an "acceptable risk," for whatever rationale they happened to come up with. This was a by-product of using a failure modes effects analysis system without quantitative risk measures.

As I had in my July 23 memo, and Irv Davids did in his memo, Mulloy also described the problems with the putty:

What has been happening to us is, you might get a very small hole through the putty. So during that ignition transient when you're coming up to pressure, you essentially have a jet, a hot gas jet here.

Mulloy then explained that the erosion they had seen on the O-rings had been only a half to a third of what they could safely sustain. He said they had been looking for "what causes some O-rings to erode and others not to." He did not say why they were confident that an O-ring could not erode beyond the presumed safety allowances, if they had not yet determined the cause.

Dr. Covert asked, "How about temperature gradient?"

Mulloy said, "I can't answer that."

A discussion of joint temperature followed, with several Commission members participating. Mulloy said, "The launch commit criteria is that the vehicle can be launched in a thirty-one degree ambient environment." He did not mention the higher forty-degree specification for the solid rocket motor that was brought up by Alan McDonald of Thiokol in the Challenger pre-launch debate.

Mulloy also now told the Commission that the "mil spec" [military specification] of the Viton rubber they used for the O-rings was "that it operates at minus 50 to 500 degrees F." It was on the basis of the mil spec that Mulloy now claimed the O-rings could be safely operated in freezing temperatures, though a mil spec was never mentioned during the arguments prior to the Challenger disaster.

Further, Mulloy did not mention bench tests conducted by Thiokol after the January 1985 cold-weather flight that had resulted in five - heat-damaged O-rings. These bench tests, done in March 1985, showed that the O-rings began to stiffen as low as seventy-five degrees F. and lost their resiliency altogether at fifty degrees. Thiokol had briefed these test results at Marshall with Mulloy and Director William Lucas present, along with other Marshall officials. The tests were well-known at the working levels but had never been briefed to the astronauts or to Houston mission control. The extent to which the resiliency tests had been briefed at headquarters is one of the enduring mysteries about the Challenger disaster and will be discussed later in this book.

Mulloy, master of the NASA pitch, went on about technical joint details until he was interrupted by Chairman Rogers, who wanted to wrap up the meeting and talk about the next day's open session. Rogers now repeated to Moore the question he had asked at the start of the meeting:

> Is there anything that you would like to tell us now that we should know about that it would not be wise to disclose to the public at this time? We want to try to be sure that we don't do anything which injures or impairs your investigation, but, on the other hand, we want to disclose as much as we can in the public session. Is there anything that we should not disclose tomorrow, as far as you know?

Moore had nothing to suggest but turned to Marshall Director William Lucas, who said:

> I would suggest, if I might, that out of Larry's presentation you might want to skip over to the actions that we began talking in about June of 1985. . . . [i.e., when the capture feature was proposed].

Chairman Rogers: I think that would be very helpful. . . . So if you could give the explanation as you go along and say what this means and that when we were told about this particular problem that we did the following things, and these are the reasons why we decided that.

Mr. Moore: I don't know what your thoughts are specifically on tomorrow, but I thought we would go back this afternoon and try to put a textual story together to give you some context, and then probably ask Larry to go through some of this stuff that he is doing here tomorrow.

Chairman Rogers: I think that is good. Well, let's go ahead and you do whatever you think. . . . But you can make it a bit briefer tomorrow. What we would really like to acknowledge—and I think we're getting a lot of very useful information in the chronology of things that concerns you—how you dealt with those concerns, who made the judgments about what went on. And I think that if you can do that it will alleviate a lot of the problems that have developed.

Sally Ride now jumped into the discussion:

Is there any internal correspondence on potential concern over the operation of the O-ring or the joint? Because I think that is probably the next thing. Since we've dealt with erosion, that's going to be the next thing.

Mulloy went back to the issue of O-ring temperatures:

There are documents that are test results that are even now in progress of some tests that have been done previously to understand the resiliency of O-rings at various temperatures.

Marshall Director William Lucas now seemed to feel it was time to talk about the teleconference on the O-rings held the night before the disaster. He said, "I believe also, Larry, that there was a discussion in close proximity between you and other people and Thiokol." Mulloy then gave his version of the teleconference:

At about seven on the evening of the 27th, I received a phone call from Stan Reinartz, who is my immediate supervisor, Stanley Reinartz, who is the manager of the Shuttle Projects Office at the Marshall Space

Flight Center, who works directly for Dr. Lucas, and he had been informed by our resident manager that Thiokol had looked at the conditions for the solid rocket motors and wanted to discuss the situation as they saw it for launch and what they are looking at. . . . Thiokol presented to us the fact that the lowest temperature that we had flown an O-ring or a case joint was fifty-three degrees, and they wanted to point out that we would be outside of that experience base. . . . After hearing the discussion, we all concluded that there was no problem with the predicted temperatures for the SRM, and I received a document from the solid rocket motor project manager at Thiokol to that effect that there was no adverse consequence expected due to the temperature on the night of the 27th.

Neither Mulloy nor anyone else mentioned other critical details—there had been an earlier teleconference, after which Lovingood told Reinartz to expect a launch delay; a meeting between the two teleconferences that was held in William Lucas's motel room; or Mulloy's reported pressuring of Thiokol to approve the launch. Also, Mulloy was rewriting history when he said, "We all concluded that there was no problem with the predicted temperatures," because the Thiokol engineers never agreed with that conclusion. But Rogers was satisfied with Mulloy's explanation, and the meeting had already gone on a long time.

Now Rogers raised the point that he'd heard "someone from Rockwell called and expressed concern about the icing conditions." He asked Moore if he had any recollection of that call and who made it. Without saying anything about the lengthy series of inspections and meetings on the issue of ice on the launch tower, along with Rockwell's statement that they could not assure a safe launch, Moore said:

Rockwell did express some concern initially at that point about some ice that may be coming off the launch platform and impacting the tiles on the orbiter—and that is the only tie that we have been able to find out that Rockwell may have had a concern.

Rogers answered:

Well, I'm not sure it's essential [to have someone from Rockwell at the meeting], but I think it is important that we have an answer to that.

If Rockwell was the one that raised the concern, then we want some-body from Rockwell to say I raised the concern, we talked it over, and my concern was satisfied and we said go ahead. As long as we still have that concern on the part of Rockwell, if you testify or someone testifies from NASA that there was the meeting and everybody was reasonably satisfied, then someone from Rockwell comes along and says that's not so, we told you not to go ahead and you went ahead anyway, that is the kind of thing we want to try to deal with at these meetings.

By "these meetings," Rogers meant the closed executive sessions. This fully expressed his intention to "work with" NASA. But Feynman now went back to the joint temperature issue. He said:

I just want to go back to something that I would need to know in order to help me to determine what caused the accident. . . . When you were giving the thermal data, I've seen some thermal data which may be the same as you are talking about, about the O-ring response to the compression set at different temperatures [i.e., the Thiokol bench test data on the O-rings]. But the obvious question is how fast did it return [i.e., how fast did the O-ring return to its round shape after being squeezed at different temperatures], and I didn't see any data that told me it was milliseconds, a second goes by, how much do temperatures vary. I mean, that is typically what a temperature does, is it changes an apparent viscosity, and I would like to get some idea if the low tem-perature could have made it so that when things separated temporar-ily that the joints moved, that it did not do the usual thing and close the gap so quickly so as to let the gas go through.

Mulloy said he would "collect those test data." Rogers told Mulloy to give the data to Feynman who would then brief the Commission. Finally, Feynman had an official assignment.

Now, for the first time, Alan McDonald, Thiokol's managing engi-neer at the Kennedy Space Center, spoke up about the teleconference the night before the launch. He said:

That meeting was called by Thiokol. . . . The recommendation at that time from the data that was sent out from Thiokol was not to launch below fifty-three degrees F., because that was our lowest acceptable experience base and did demonstrate some blow-by from a year ago, and also we had some data that indicated the poor resiliency of response of the Viton seal to low temperatures, so that was the first transmittal of information saying you should be aware of that, and where the data was discussed.

General Kutyna: You said not to launch below fifty-three, and what was the actual temperature?

Mr. Mulloy: The actual temperature predicted at that time, based upon Thiokol's calculations, was twenty-nine degrees.

Chairman Rogers: Could you stand up again and say that a little louder so we could hear it? I'm not sure we all understood what you said.

The discussion continued, with Armstrong, Covert, Kutyna, and Mulloy commenting. Finally Rogers said:

Am I hearing you say that you recommended against launch and never changed your mind?

Mr. McDonald: No, I did not say that. We did change our mind afterwards.

McDonald did not mention that Roger Boisjoly, Arnie Thompson and the other Thiokol engineers never changed their minds, believed Challenger would blow up, and were not surprised when it did. Rather it was four company managers in the room at Thiokol who caved in to the pressure from NASA and voted in favor of the launch.

Rogers asked, "What brought you to that decision?" McDonald answered:

Well, the data that was reviewed, NASA concluded that the temperature data we had presented was inconclusive, and indeed a lot of the data was inconclusive because the next worst blow-by we had ever seen in a primary seal in a case-to-case field joint was about the highest temperature we had launched at, and that was true—the next worst blow-by. . . . We did not calculate the effect of all that from the data that we had, but we did have some data that indicated that the timing function of the O-ring seal was going in the wrong direction, in the direction of badness. The O-ring was getting harder. The grease in there was getting more viscous. The time to seat the O-ring took longer and it would be more difficult to extrude it because of the hardened O-ring. We didn't know exactly where the right temperatures were that would make it so it could not seal, but it was in the wrong direction. And the temperatures that were being reported for the 51-L were so much away from our experience base that we didn't feel comfortable operating that far away.

Other Commission members now joined the discussion of why Thiokol changed its mind. Feynman said:

In other words, to make it absolutely transparent to me, you are saying that you said, at least at that time, that you didn't want to launch if the O-rings were below fifty degrees and, secondly, you made an estimate, in view of the history of the weather, that the temperature of the O-rings might be as low as twenty-six or thirty degrees?

Mr. McDonald: That is correct. . . .

Chairman Rogers: I still don't understand your explanation. Did you change your mind?

Mr. McDonald: Yes. The assessment of the data was that the data was not totally conclusive, that the temperature could affect everything relative to the seal. But there was data that indicated that there were things going in the wrong direction and this was far from our experience base.

Now, for the first time, McDonald was indicating that there was pressure being exerted by NASA for Thiokol to change their minds:

The conclusion being that Thiokol was directed to reassess all the data because the recommendation was not considered acceptable at that time of the fifty-three degrees. NASA asked us for a reassessment and some more data to show that the temperature in itself can cause this to be a more serious concern than we had said it would be. At that time, Thiokol in Utah said that they would like to go off-line and caucus for about five minutes and reassess what data they had there or any other additional data.

The caucus lasted half an hour, after which the Thiokol managers came back on-line and said they would approve the launch. NASA asked for a fax saying so, which Thiokol sent to McDonald at Kennedy. Both Lovingood and Arnold Aldrich had mentioned the teleconference at the previous week's closed hearing, but this was the first time the Commission had been told that Thiokol had changed their recommendation.

Rogers by now was concerned with having to get on with the planning for the next day's open session. He apparently felt that his first priority was to dispel the impression the *New York Times* article had created in the minds of the press and the public that NASA had been negligent. He said to McDonald:

> Well, I think in view of the very serious nature of this and the fact that it will be scrutinized for years that we should have precisely what the data was before we present it.
>
> Mr. McDonald: I have that in my notes, sir.
>
> Chairman Rogers: Well, you are just conveying information that pertains to a decision somebody else made.
>
> Mr. McDonald: I have the faxes that were distributed at both these meetings in my book that were transmitted, all of the charts from the original meeting and the one afterwards.
>
> Chairman Rogers: Who made the decision from Thiokol?
>
> Mr. McDonald: I do not know who made the final decision. I do know that the fax was signed by Mr. Joe Kilminster, my boss, the vice president.
>
> Chairman Rogers: I'm sure you can see the logic of what you're saying. You recommended against a flight on one night and then you have meetings with NASA people and they seem anxious to go ahead, or at least they were asking questions about it . . . and you got word back from the home office to go ahead because the evidence is inconclusive. . . . I would express the caution that it's hearsay as far as you're concerned. We really want to get the people before the Commission who made the decisions and ask them why did they appear to change their minds and ask them specifically. Unfortunately, you are just conveying information.

Rogers was expressing lawyerly caution, but he was only partially correct. It wasn't just "hearsay." McDonald had been a participant in all of the teleconference except the final off-line caucus at Thiokol where the company's managers reversed themselves. He also was carrying the relevant documents in his briefcase.

Rogers was through with this topic for the day. He turned to Moore, who asked Mulloy to finish his briefing. But first, Rogers called a recess. There is no record of whom he may have talked to during the recess or what was said about McDonald's revelations.

Now the meeting resumed for the final discussion, which was on the subject of Larry Mulloy's presentation of plans to install the capture feature to cut down on joint erosion. It was an all-purpose fix, since NASA still didn't understand the reasons the joints failed to work properly. But it had been a long day. Rogers wrapped it up with a final bit of coaching:

> We will have plenty of time to study the other things you have been doing to improve things, but I think the focus of attention is going to be what caused this accident. . . . What you are saying is we have conducted extensive tests of this type and that type, and we have concluded as follows, and these are the recommendations, but anybody there is going to be interested in what are the things that happened that relate to 51-L. I mean, others are going to say this is a filibuster. Now, you have told us now, and we will have a chance to ask a lot of further questions, but if we appear to be ducking the issue, the issue is what happened prior to the launch of 51-L.

Before the meeting broke up, Chairman Rogers told the Commission members to feel free to ask the same questions the next day.

> I tell you, I liked the questions that were asked today, and I wouldn't hesitate to ask the same questions tomorrow, because it shows that members of this Commission have a lot of background on this subject, and I don't think we should hesitate to ask these questions again, and I thought they were all good.

In short, the next day's public hearing would be play-acting.

————

I was feeling sheepish the morning of Monday, February 10, as I limped through the cold drizzle on crutches into the offices of the

Resources Analysis Division and glanced away from the stares of my colleagues. I walked past the division director's office, looked at him, and shrugged. On my desk were phone messages from Robert Hager of NBC News and other TV and newspaper journalists. There was also a copy of a *Wall Street Journal* article someone had left me to read. It said:

> In a memo written in July, Richard Cook, who works in NASA's comptroller's office, said a back-up seal had been "partially eaten away" during a launch and warned that a seal failure could have catastrophic consequences. But in an interview yesterday, Mr. Cook's superior said that Mr. Cook had been working at the agency for only two weeks when he wrote the memo and that, "Frankly, I wasn't happy with it because it had a lot of questions in it."
>
> Nevertheless, the superior said, the agency was so concerned about the seals that even before the Cook memo it had conducted a full-scale review. As a result, he said, there "were process changes and materials changes, so obviously, we thought it was safe to fly."

This was the first I had heard that my "superior" "wasn't happy with" my memo or with anything else I had written at NASA. Also, I had never heard of a "full-scale review." If he had been talking about the August 19 meeting, which I never knew about, that took place after I wrote my memo. Finally, even if NASA did think it was "safe to fly," their judgment obviously was wrong.

I threw the phone messages from the news reporters into the wastebasket. I had nothing more to say and didn't want to talk to anyone. In another week I would be at the Treasury Department. Now I hobbled out of my office and told the secretary I was going over to the health unit at the Code M building.

This was a place where I felt safe. The health unit was in the basement, which you entered through a pair of swinging doors at the end of the building where they kept the trash dumpsters. The doctor was very friendly, though she didn't know I had been in the news about Challenger.

"So what are they saying happened?" she asked.

"They think there was a burnthrough on a solid rocket booster."

"Well, they'll fix it and keep going, I guess."

"I guess."

She decided to put me into the whirlpool bath, which I entered gingerly, and where I gratefully spent the entire day. Here was one more thing I liked about NASA. I was sure the health unit at Treasury would not have a whirlpool bath. I called the office secretary and told her where I was. "Enjoy yourself!" she said cheerfully, and I was glad to hear a friendly voice. I also phoned Phyllis and said I was hiding out.

By the afternoon, when I emerged from the hot water with prune-like skin, I was surprised at how much better my back felt. I could stand up without crutches, though my torso was still a little crooked. I was relieved that my positive response to the bath treatment indicated that the pain was muscular and not something worse. Of course I knew that the pain was a physical manifestation of the fear I had been feeling because of the *New York Times* article. But I had gotten through Monday without repercussions. Only four more days to go. I could return to the health unit tomorrow, or, if my back was well enough for me to walk, maybe I could go over to the National Gallery of Art. I certainly was not going to hang around NASA.

That night at home, I was starting to relax for the first time since the disaster, when my supervisor called. "It's your boss," Phyllis said. I felt the knot in my stomach return.

"The Commission is going to meet tomorrow, and Jesse Moore wants you to attend," my supervisor said. He did not say I would be placed on the witness stand or that I should prepare testimony.

"I don't think I'll be coming to work tomorrow," I replied.

He sounded low-key as he tried to reassure me that it was no big deal and that he really thought I should come in. Of course both he and I knew that with my transfer coming up to Treasury, I was no longer entirely under his control.

But I was now feeling that perhaps I would have to be there. I said, "Well, I don't know if I want to say anything without having a lawyer present."

"You can have a lawyer if you want."

It was a bluff, of course. I didn't have a lawyer, and there was no time to find one, though I would have been far better off to have gotten on the phone and engaged a lawyer to accompany me.

"All right, I'll be there," I said fatalistically.

Then he said, "Jesse wants to talk to you before the meeting. He wants to know how you feel about things."

"WHAT IS HE DOING TO THEM?"
—My Appearance Before the Commission

AFTER THE COMMISSION'S executive session on Monday, February 10, someone from NASA gave Feynman the bench test resiliency data referred to by Al McDonald. This was data that Roger Boisjoly and the other Thiokol engineers had generated almost a year ago, had briefed to Marshall, and used in the Challenger pre-launch cold weather debate to argue that the O-ring joints in the SRBs might not seal.

Feynman wrote that these data were in the middle of a large stack of papers, "just like a sandwich," but "was of no use" in determining how the joint would behave in "fractions of a second during launch when the gap in the field joint is suddenly changing."

Feynman did not like the way the Presidential Commission was proceeding and was wondering what he could do about it. He was frustrated with the information he'd gotten from NASA about the Viton rubber O-rings, and decided to intervene at the Commission's meeting the next day with an experiment in which he would deliberately disrupt William Rogers' staged melodrama. He wrote:

> Later I'm feeling lousy and I'm eating dinner. I look at the table, and there's a glass of ice water. I think, "Damn it, *I* can find out about that

rubber *without* sending notes to NASA and getting back a stack of papers. All I've got to do is get a sample of the rubber, stick it in ice water and see how it responds when I squeeze it! That way, I can learn something new in a public meeting."

That night, Feynman phoned his NASA contacts and asked for a piece of O-ring rubber but was told it was impossible to get. He then called William Graham, who said that the model of the field joint that NASA would be using in the meeting the next day contained real O-ring rubber.

The next morning, Feynman left his hotel early and took a cab to a local hardware store to buy "some screwdrivers, pliers, clamps, and so on, because I wasn't sure exactly what I'd need." He then went to Graham's office at 400 Maryland Avenue and took the model apart. He wrote that Graham was "very cooperative, as always." He then took the piece of O-ring, dipped it in ice water, and found that it stiffened as expected.

——

ELSEWHERE IN THE Maryland Avenue building, I had arrived at work. My back was somewhat better, though I continued to use the crutches. I also wore my business suit to the office that day.

After I had sat in my office for a short time reading the newspaper, my supervisor came in.

"Let's get going. We're going over to Code M," he said.

This was the start of a strange sequence of events. I had no idea that the Commission had met the previous day, and so had no clue what an elaborate charade was in the works. I picked up my briefcase in which I had my two O-ring memos along with newspaper articles, put the crutches under my arms, and left the office. I did not know that I would never return and would never see anyone I worked with in the branch or division again. The people in the office suite of the Resources Analysis Division stared at me as we departed. No one said a word.

It was an overcast, chilly morning after the rain of the previous day. When we were outside on the sidewalk near some magnolia trees, my supervisor stopped. "Were you the one who leaked the documents?" he asked abruptly.

Odd as it may seem, I had not thought about how to answer this question if asked and had not discussed it with Phyllis.

"No," I said without thinking much about it. My supervisor still had the power to fire me or blackball me with Treasury. It wasn't just my career anymore, it was my family's livelihood—I had four children to support.

The supervisor did a double-take. He'd evidently expected me to answer otherwise. "I'm surprised," he said. "I've been really angry at you, because I thought you were the one. Over at Code M, they've been looking hard for whoever it might have been."

I pictured Paul Herr, Paul Wetzel, and Irv Davids being grilled.

"You know," he continued, "this may have destroyed my branch." He said it in almost a lighthearted way. This guy tried so hard never to show emotion—never to really care about anything. But I could hear the tension in his voice.

At this point I didn't care about his branch. His branch was part of a NASA machine whose faulty workings had killed people. I changed the subject: "I really didn't appreciate what you said about me to the *Wall Street Journal*. You never answered my July 23 memo, and you know what I wrote was true."

My supervisor still tried not to betray any emotion. "You've got to understand," he said, "that the press just wants to sell newspapers."

I didn't answer, but I wondered if this was what our First Amendment rights had come down to. That the government can justify any kind of concealment by saying the press just wants to sell newspapers?

"After we talk to Jesse we're going to the Commission meeting at the State Department," he said. "If anyone asks you, tell them that the concerns you raised in your memo were reviewed and that the problem was being taken care of."

There might have been a time when I would have said just that, because Paul Wetzel did tell me that with the capture feature, the problem was "being taken care of." But now it was obvious that the problem was never taken care of and that the decision to "fly as is" while the capture feature was being tested and retrofitted on the SRBs was a tragic mistake. Why couldn't NASA just say that? How simple it would have been. We were wrong. We'll fix it. Then move on. That's what NASA did with Apollo 1. Why not now? What was wrong with these people?

We arrived at the Independence Avenue building. Usually my

supervisor walked up the back stairway two steps at a time while his staff members hustled to keep up with him. But because of my crutches, we took only single steps to the fourth floor and entered Jesse Moore's spacious suite of offices.

Moore was sitting behind his desk. He looked gaunt, tense, and tired. We sat saying nothing. What, I wondered, was I supposed to say?

Remembering my supervisor's concern about the future of his branch, I said, "I hope this doesn't reflect badly on Mike and that they can still do their jobs."

They just stared at me. Had I admitted I was the leaker? All right then. I looked hard into Moore's eyes. I said, "Everything about this is going to come out."

Moore sounded flustered as he repeated, "Uh, yes, everything is going to come out."

There were a few moments of silence, then Moore got up and grabbed his overcoat from the coat rack. Neither of them said another word to me. As we left the building, and I got into a chauffeured government station wagon with them, I felt as though I were being kidnapped. We arrived at the State Department on Virginia Avenue and 21st Street, N.W., entered through the C Street entrance, and after some confusion at the guard station about who we were, we were allowed in. We found our way through the back corridors of the building to the Dean Acheson auditorium. My supervisor escorted me into an adjacent conference room and walked away.

As I looked around the room, it was striking that both the NASA officials and Commission members, whom I recognized from TV, had gathered together in the conference room and were sitting around chatting with each other like old friends. "One of these groups is investigating the other?" I wondered. "You'd never know it." A couple of the members of the Commission were reading newspapers. People looked up at me when I entered the room, but no one spoke as I leaned on my crutches, waiting.

Word came that the hearing would be starting, so those of us in the conference room filed into the auditorium. The Commission members took their places behind long daises in front of the room. They had name plates and microphones. The room was buzzing with news reporters, and cameras were lined up facing the stage.

William Rogers looked comfortable sitting behind the dais in a building where he had once been in charge as secretary of state. He now opened the meeting by stating what was news to me, that:

> Yesterday we had a meeting in executive session, at which time the NASA officials and others produced documents at our request, and memoranda, dealing principally with the O-rings and seals on the booster rockets. They complied fully with the request that we made and were very forthcoming in discussing all aspects of it that we were able to discuss at the meeting. This morning we will start the meeting with officials from NASA, particularly dealing with the matter of seals on the booster rockets. And I would like as much as possible to limit our discussions today to that one subject matter.

Rogers gave no hint that the hearing which was now underway had been rehearsed and that every actor had been given his lines except me. William Graham next spoke, saying NASA planned to review all testimony for accuracy and make corrections as needed.

Rogers then began the type of performance he had evidently perfected as an attorney who was practiced in the art of asking leading questions:

> Chairman Rogers: Now, there is no feeling on the part of NASA that the work of the Commission is in any way interfering with the disclosure of information, I hope?
> Dr. Graham: No, sir. In fact, the work of the Commission is very much in accord with the work that NASA is undertaking and conducting internally, and we find these to be in general complementary.
> Chairman Rogers: In fact, you asked me to have this public session today in order to make it clear that NASA was not trying to brush anything under the rug, isn't that right?

As I sat in the auditorium watching the performance unfold, the hair was starting to stand up on the back of my neck.

Dr. Graham replied:

> Yes, sir, I suggested to you that you consider having a public session today on specific characteristics of the SRBs, the solid rocket boosters,

and any other matters you saw fit to question the NASA officials concerning.

Chairman Rogers: I assume that there are thousands and thousands of documents that you are now considering for purposes of the investigation and for purposes of this Commission, is that right?

Dr. Graham: Yes, sir, a large number of internal documents that we have in review and consideration. We plan to release to the press today at the conclusion of this discussion the material that will be presented to you today. And then tomorrow NASA will have a press briefing, and at that time we plan to release the entire bulk of the material that was released and presented to the Commission yesterday. The amount of material alone is a stack probably three inches high, and that is just a small part of the total data that we are reviewing and preparing for transmission to you and to release.

Chairman Rogers: In light of the memorandum which has appeared in the press, written by Mr. Cook to Mr. Davids—and incidentally, those gentlemen are here today and will appear and testify—I assume that there are a lot of other documents of that nature, which make suggestions about how matters should proceed, pointing out risks that were involved in launches, et cetera, is that correct?

I am going to testify? As soon as I heard Rogers say that, I pulled out a copy of my February 3 memo, turned it over, and began to make notes for a statement. It was time to organize my thoughts. I was not going to stand up there and be crucified while having nothing to say. The staged dialogue continued:

Dr. Graham: Yes, sir. In any highly sophisticated technical operation such as the operation of the space shuttle system, there has to be a continuing dialogue within the agency that is responsible for operating it concerning the performance of the system, the characteristics, how well the design is behaving in comparison with the operational data and the design expectation of the system. All that is being constantly cross-checked and reviewed and re-analyzed, and you will find that there is a substantial volume of information that documents that process inside NASA, and we will make that available to you as soon as we have a chance to accumulate it and put it together in a form that is comparable.

Chairman Rogers: The point I'm making is it's not unusual in an agency like yours to have employees make critical comments, suggest dangers that might be involved in the program. That is the way the system works, isn't it?

Dr. Graham: Yes, sir. It is very, very important, in fact, for the system to be somewhat self-critical, and in the process of operating these systems to constantly review the issues, the engineering decisions, the performance. That internal self-criticism is in fact one of the strongest characteristics of NASA and one of the things that makes it in my view such a high quality technical operation.

I tried to keep listening as I was writing my notes. Hearing Graham, I thought to myself, "Too bad NASA never did any of that. If they had, they might not have blown up Challenger."

Chairman Rogers: And if we focus today on, to some extent on the seals and O-rings and memoranda that are written by Mr. Cook and others dealing with that subject, the fact that we focus on it doesn't mean that it is the only area of concern as far as you're concerned or as far as the Commission is concerned, is that right?

Dr. Graham: No, sir, it is not the only area where we will find memoranda expressing engineering issues and engineering concerns. And it certainly doesn't mean that the NASA internal analysis has singled out any area at this point—the O-rings, the seals, the field joints, or any other specific area as a unique source of concern and analysis. We are still looking across a broad range of issues to try to establish what actually occurred in the Challenger accident.

Next came Jesse Moore, who now gave the kind of filibuster Rogers warned against the previous day. He talked and talked and talked.

We plan to cooperate very fully with the Commission. . . . we are preparing a list and setting up a group of panels . . . we are continuing our salvage operations . . . our primary consideration is to try to reconstruct a mission events timeline . . . were there any unusual set of circumstances? . . . weather is certainly an issue that we're going to be working very hard . . . all these will be looked at in very great detail . . . it is critical to understand the pedigree of this hardware . . . another element that is very important in this particular launch is the launch pad . . . we were carrying some cargo on-board this flight . . . no stone will be left unturned . . . we are putting together failure scenarios. . . .

Chairman Rogers decided to assist a little:

> Jesse, based upon what you told us before, though, you have been doing that each time, haven't you? I mean, this analysis is not new to 51-L?
> Mr. Moore: We have failure modes and effects analysis for all elements of the shuttle, and that has been done and documented, and we're using these failure modes and effects analyses that are in the program as starting points for the kind of analysis that we're doing right now, Mr. Chairman.
> Chairman Rogers: Good, because we wouldn't want to leave the impression that you're doing it just because of this accident. Your records indicate you have been doing this on a regular basis.
> Mr. Moore: Yes, sir. . . .

Moore continued by saying, "The solid rocket booster is obviously one area that we are focusing very heavily on," then said, "We're also going to discuss seals."

Next came Larry Mulloy. The transcript of his presentation, along with questions from Commission members and his answers, takes up twenty pages in the record—another filibuster. Throughout the hearings, neither Mulloy nor anyone else from Marshall ever backed off the statement that they believed then and now that the solid rocket boosters were safe to fly.

But now Feynman jumped in. He began bearing down on Mulloy on the subject of O-ring resiliency at lower temperatures. As much as powerful people think they can always dictate how everything is going to happen, life has a way of going in other directions. Feynman was departing from Rogers' script, as he and Mulloy had this dialogue:

> Dr. Feynman: Can I ask a few questions in succession to help explain how this thing works?
> Mr. Mulloy: Yes, sir.
> Dr. Feynman: This rubber thing that is put in, the so-called O-ring,

that is supposed to expand to make contact with the metal underneath so that it makes a seal, is that the idea?

Mr. Mulloy: Yes, sir. In the static condition it should be sealed to—it should be in direct contact with the tang and the clevis of the joint, and be squeezed twenty thousandths of an inch.

Dr. Feynman: And if it weren't there, if it weren't in contact at all and there was no seal at all, that would be a leak. Why don't we take the O-rings out?

Mr. Mulloy: Because you would have hot gas expanding through the joint and destroy—

Dr. Feynman: Pushing the putty through, and so on?

Mr. Mulloy: Yes. You will always push the putty through, because the motor pressure is 900 psi nominally, 1,000 psi at max, and that putty will sustain about 200 psi.

Dr. Feynman: Now, we couldn't put instead of this some sort of material like lead, that when you squash it, it stays? It has to be that it expands back, because there is a little bit of play in this joint and it has to be able to come back. I mean, it is a rubber material, so that it comes back when you move a little, and it stays in contact, is that right?

Mr. Mulloy: Yes, sir, that is the purpose of the putty, as a thermal barrier. In the data that we have presented to the Commission, as you noted yesterday, we have looked at other alternatives, some of those alternatives are things like—

Dr. Feynman: I'm talking about the rubber on the seal?

Mr. Mulloy: I'm sorry?

Dr. Feynman: In the seal, in order to work correctly, it must be rubber, not something like lead?

Mr. Mulloy: Yes, sir.

Dr. Feynman: Because when the seal moves a little bit when there is vibration and pressures, it would lift the lead away, while the rubber expands in place?

Mr. Mulloy: Yes, sir.

Dr. Feynman: So it is important that it have this property of expansion and not be plastic like lead. And I think you call that resilience, right?

Mr. Mulloy: That is correct. It has to have resiliency, and that is why we use an elastomer.

Dr. Feynman: If this material weren't resilient for say a second or two, that would be enough to be a very dangerous situation.

Mr. Mulloy: Yes, sir.

Feynman was now explaining why Challenger blew up, and he knew it. It was because the O-rings had gotten stiff in the cold temperature, just as the Thiokol engineers had argued. He was setting the stage for his ice water experiment later in the morning.

Next, General Kutyna asked Mulloy for a history of O-ring erosion, and here the solid rocket booster manager from Marshall made some unusual claims. Mulloy said:

> The thing of interest here is what we have seen in the O-rings. Now, the fact is, before 51-L, we hadn't seen any anomalous erosion for about a year. The O-rings had been performing very well. The last time we had seen any erosion on O-rings was the January launch the year before. But we were very sensitive to it, mainly because of the activity that we've had going on in the last year to try and improve the margin in that joint, we had been very sensitive to how that was going on, and we were continuing to look very carefully at the previous flights to assure that nothing had changed in that area that would change our rationale that we had developed for continuing to fly in light of the erosion we were seeing on the O-rings. We considered that in 51-L, and concluded, particularly since we had not seen any significant erosion in the last year, and we had no test data that changed our rationale, then the same rationale then applied for 51-L as it applied to the last year in the flight readiness review. . . .
>
> Chairman Rogers: Could I say on that that the only thing you say that you have had a history of one year's success with the O-rings previous to flight 51-L?
>
> Mr. Mulloy: Yes, sir.

When I heard this exchange between Mulloy and Rogers, I was startled. There had been a lot of O-ring erosion and other kinds of heat distress during 1985. When I had entered the auditorium at the start of the hearing, I noticed Paul Herr and had taken a seat a few rows away from him on the right hand side of the room facing the stage. I now slipped into a chair behind him and leaned over and asked, "There was erosion in 1985 wasn't there?"

He answered, "I think so." I did not want to embarrass him by having people see me talking to him, so I got up to return to my seat. He turned to me and said quietly, "Watch out. They really hate you over at the agency. Watch out! The Commission's trying to set you up."

Rogers and Mulloy had seriously departed from the historical record by telling the world that NASA "had a history of one year's success with the O-rings previous to flight 51-L." But Feynman was ready when Rogers called a recess. With news reporters gathered in front of the stand on which Commission members were sitting behind their daises, he placed the O-ring he had cut out of the model in Graham's office that morning in a glass of ice water. When he pulled it out, it was stiff. Feynman had given a dramatic image of how Challenger was destroyed. This was how he later described the incident:

> I kept wanting to do my experiment all during the meeting, but General Kutyna, who was sitting next to me, gave me advice. He had given me advice before. At the first public meeting he had leaned over and said, "Copilot to pilot: Comb your hair." So now he was saying, "Copilot to pilot: not now!"
>
> So when he told me, "Now!" I did it, and everything went all right. As you probably know, I demonstrated that the rubber had no resilience whatsoever when you squeezed it at that temperature, and that it was very likely a partial cause of the accident. We all agreed later that, in fact, was true.

Chairman Rogers soon reconvened the hearing. Feynman now said:

> This is a comment for Mr. Mulloy. I took this stuff that I got out of your seal, and I put it in ice water, and I discovered that when you put some pressure on it for a while and then undo it, it doesn't stretch back. It stays the same dimension. In other words, for a few seconds at least and more seconds than that, there is no resilience in this particular material when it is at a temperature of thirty-two degrees. I believe that has some significance for our problem.

But Rogers didn't want to discuss O-ring resiliency. Instead he said, "I would like to ask Mr. Cook to come forward."

I stood, picked up my crutches, and hobbled onto the stage and behind the podium set up for witnesses. I was sworn in, promising to tell the truth. I was grimly determined not to give in to Rogers' bullying, not to back down from what I felt was right, but to try to play the role of a budget analyst trying to report the facts. When it was all over, I felt I had made some points but was disappointed in myself. I did not want to fight with the Commission or NASA, but felt that perhaps I should have.

Rogers began the session by saying:

> Mr. Cook, the Commission asked you to appear today because of recent stories concerning particularly a memorandum which you wrote on the 23rd of July, 1985, and we will let you make whatever comments you would like to make on that memorandum. And we will of course make the memorandum available to the press. You told me before the meeting was reconvened that you would like to make some preliminary comments, and of course you may go right ahead and say anything you want to.

I had written out several pages of notes, taking advantage of Moore's and Mulloy's long-winded remarks, feeling I had as much right as any other witness to make as lengthy an opening statement as I desired. By this time, I was not feeling afraid of William Rogers or anyone else in the room. I began by telling them my background at the Civil Service Commission, the FDA, the White House consumer office, and TRW. I was determined to do what I could to counter the claims by my supervisor and others at NASA that I was just a new analyst who didn't know anything. I continued:

> . . . The reason that we do things like this is because we have to prepare the budget for NASA. We have to cost out what things are going to require, particularly if we have engineering questions that come up that are going to require some kind of additional funding or some kind of change in the funding profile, to be able to pay for it.

So for this reason, we have to keep pretty much in touch with the project people in the Office of Space Flight, and we also go on field trips down to Marshall or Kennedy or other places to try to keep as informed as we can. And then, when issues arise that look like they might be budget threats, we have got to report back on it and try to come up with some kind of estimate with the program office of what it's going to cost to repair this type of thing.

And it became apparent to me that there were some real concerns with the O-ring problem at that time, concerns from an engineering standpoint, which, as I understood it from what I discussed with people, had flight safety and potentially major budgetary concerns, because with something like this, as I understood it, if you fix something like this you've got quite a range of cost implications.

. . . And we felt that the O-ring problem—and I think it was our impression from the Office of Space Flight—was a potentially major budget hit. When we went through the monthly briefings over at the Office of Space Flight, the O-ring problem was one of the—there was a list of budget threats that was printed each month.

Every month the O-ring problem or O-ring charring problem was on that list. Sometimes it was first on the list, sometimes it wasn't. But I don't think that necessarily reflected priority. But there was no question that the O-ring problem was considered a potential budget threat month after month and on into the fall.

I had noted nothing had been said in the hearings so far about any information having gone to the administrator about the O-ring problem, whether James Beggs, or after Beggs had taken leave of absence, William Graham. So I now pointed out:

And I understood it was, even when it went up to the administrator in August, with the annual budget review to the administrator, it was also listed on that presentation as a budget threat.

I reported back to my management monthly on the assessment I was getting from across the street on what the O-ring situation was. And I know I'm not an engineer. I can't talk in engineering detail. I think I understand the basics of joint configuration and all that stuff, although I certainly couldn't comment on an engineer's analysis of it. But there were some things that were being factored into my analyses that I think have some bearing on this.

For instance, it was mentioned that an effort was going to be made to keep the secondary O-ring from unseating in flight or at least from breaking the seal in flight. Now the secondary O-ring, as I understand it, we went back a couple, three years, when they first started to discover that this rotation, this joint rotation, was unseating the secondary O-ring, and that was reducing or eliminating in some cases the redundancy feature on that joint.

And so there was a lot of concern about how we could get redundancy back in that joint without having to throw away half a million dollar SRB segments and starting all over again with redesigning them and recasting them. There was a thirteen month lead time if you wanted to order a new segment from the manufacturer, and so if you had to throw this stuff out you had a problem.

And so we were looking for ways to get the thing taken care of in a reasonable manner. And as I understand it, the capture feature was going to be on the QM-5 firing, which had been scheduled this week, but I think has been postponed. . . . As I understand it, if the O-ring— the capture feature got through the review, the QM-5 firing, and whatever other reviews Marshall and the Office of Space Flight were going to do, we were going to try to get that on the booster segments around January of 1988. . . .

There was another issue that came up on the leak test port. It was my understanding that the leak test port had been mentioned as a problem back when the redundancy requirement was reviewed for the unseating of the secondary O-ring, because at that time, as I understand it, there was no good test for checking the pressure on it once you plugged that thing back in down at Kennedy. . . .

Now, I do have one question, and I'm certainly not competent at all to comment on Mr. Mulloy's presentation this morning. I won't even attempt to do that. But from my own perspective as the guy who is supposed to be watching this issue for the comptroller's office, it was my understanding that there was at least some erosion going on in 1985 on the O-rings. I understand, I have been told there is a Thiokol document from August 19 that documents it. I know I have seen in my own files a report from Code M indicating some erosion on a flight, I believe in August.

I then suggested the Commission go back and get the monthly reports of the Propulsion Division and talk to some of the engineering staff there. The person I had in mind was Paul Herr, my primary source for my reports on the SRBs. But Herr was never put on the witness stand, though he was interviewed by the Commission privately. I closed by saying:

> But I must say that I take full responsibility for what I said in my memo of last summer. I realize that what I was saying in there was of some concern. I felt it my obligation to report to my management.

My speech did nothing to deter William Rogers from his agenda. The main purpose of the February 11 meeting seemed to be to attack my credibility, which he tried to do through the following exchange:

> Chairman Rogers: Thank you Mr. Cook. I would like to ask you a few questions. First your memorandum was sent to Mr. Mann. He was your superior?
> Mr. Cook: Yes, sir.
> Chairman Rogers: And your focus of attention was primarily budgetary. Is that correct?
> Mr. Cook: Yes, sir.
> Chairman Rogers: And, to summarize it, you were, I gather, thinking about whether, if changes were required for safety reasons or any other reason, you had to think about how much it would cost?
> Mr. Cook: Yes.
> Chairman Rogers: And therefore your questioning of people in NASA was in connection with that budgetary matter?
> Mr. Cook: Exactly.
> Chairman Rogers: You didn't, I assume, make any attempt to weigh budgetary considerations and safety considerations, did you?
> Mr. Cook: Not at all.
> Chairman Rogers: You weren't qualified for that?
> Mr. Cook: No, sir.
> Chairman Rogers: And you assumed other people were doing that?
> Mr. Cook: Yes.

Rogers , an experienced courtroom attorney, made me feel like I was backpedaling. Obviously in my July 23 memorandum, I was commenting on safety issues, though I was summarizing and paraphrasing what I had been told by Paul Wetzel and Paul Herr. I should have said so. But I was not certain enough of myself and my grasp of the facts. I was trying to survive the ordeal, not to fight and win. But this was just the beginning. Rogers had stuck in the knife. Now he drove it deeper:

> You had no reason to think the other people were not qualified to do that, or you had no reason to think that people who were weighing those considerations were not qualified to do it?

But I tried to rally:

> I had no reason, except I would have to qualify that not from the standpoint of criticizing anybody, but it relates to something that I said earlier—and I know that I have the highest regard for the professionalism in NASA; I worked in several agencies, and it is the most professional agency I have worked for—as far as the depth in which these things are analyzed.
>
> And so I wouldn't want to reflect at all on that, and particularly in the comptroller's office. But going back to what I said earlier, we had a developmental budget for the SRBs that was coming to an end. We have a budget, a developmental budget, which is divided into three parts. We have the filament wound case, which is, as you know, the substitute lightweight solid rocket booster that is being developed right now. We have the tooling, which is mainly based upon an effort to get the tools in place at the factories, so that when the flight rate got up to twenty-four per year we could support that flight rate.
>
> And the third thing is residual development. But that budget was coming down very steeply, and, at the same time, the flight rate was going up very rapidly. And, to me, that creates a very difficult situation where a lot of judgment is required to figure out what you're going to spend your developmental money on.
>
> I had no reason to question anybody's—the way that was weighed. All I am saying is that it puts the agency, it put me, having to analyze it

and make recommendations, in a spot where you just had to use real good judgment to say what was needed and what you were going to do if a surprise came up and you had to come up with a whole lot of money to cover one of these things.

What I should have said was that the capture feature was a quick fix. NASA wanted to do it cheaply, because there was no money to do it better. And had William Rogers been more thorough, he would have followed up with questions to NASA on whether a shrinking developmental budget influenced the choice of the capture feature as the method of fixing the O-ring problem. But he returned to grilling me, and I continued to backpedal.

> Chairman Rogers: But still, what you've just said relates to the budgetary considerations. My question was did you have any reason not to rely on the recommendations of the people who were highly qualified to make recommendations insofar as safety was concerned?
>
> Mr. Cook: No, sir.
>
> Chairman Rogers: So you don't now and you never have said that you distrusted or were unable to rely on those people who were primarily responsible for the safety features?
>
> Mr. Cook: Not at all, no, I didn't.
>
> Chairman Rogers: And so you felt that to perform your job in terms of the comptroller's office you were anxious to find out, if you could, what plans were being made that might impact on the budget?
>
> Mr. Cook: That's right.
>
> Chairman Rogers: And you didn't feel that you were in a position or should you make those decisions about what should be done with the space program?
>
> Mr. Cook: That's right.

By now in his eight-day old investigation, Rogers knew that engineers within NASA had questioned the safety of the solid rocket boosters. He knew that contractor engineers had opposed the launch. He knew that NASA had concealed these facts from the press and the public. Yet he was attacking me, the one person who had brought this information into the public arena, like a prosecuting attorney. The other members of the Commission and the NASA officials present who knew better, including Wetzel and Herr, were silent, and I was caving in. If I had ever needed legal representation, it was now. An attorney would never have allowed Rogers to pursue this barrage of leading questions, nor would a conscientious judge. He continued:

> And so that memo, which has been given a great deal of attention, sort of suggests that you were taking issue with the people who were highly qualified to make those judgments, when in fact you weren't at all. You were looking to see how much it might cost if certain changes had to be made. Is that right?

At this point I at least had the presence of mind to stop the bleeding and get back to the real issues. I referred to the statement in my July 23 memo that, "It should be pointed out that Code M management is viewing the situation with the utmost seriousness." I tried to move the discussion back to the 1985 chronology:

> And I had no reason to doubt that, and I didn't as time went on. In fact, in the fall the reports I was getting, because every time I had to make my monthly report I would ask the program people about the situation and about the O-rings, what was happening with the O-rings, and in fact we were seeing, as I understand it, there was erosion, according to the records I was given in the summer of 1985.

Rogers continued:

> I think the Commission and I certainly understand what you are saying. As you were reporting back to the comptroller's office, and to perform your job on budgetary considerations, and you were picking up information from different sources as to what they might be thinking about. You were not passing judgment, though, yourself on what they should or should not be doing, were you?
>
> Mr. Cook: Not at all. In fact, I was new to the program and I felt I was hearing things that I expected. I wasn't the only one that was hearing in the comptroller's office. I had no reason to believe that. But I felt for my own education and for my own professional judgment that I would

write it up as I heard it, and that is what I did. I was not passing judgment.

Chairman Rogers: Since the time of the accident—well, let me withdraw that. Well, since the accident occurred have you had discussions with people about your memorandum of July 23, 1985?

Mr. Cook: Yes, particularly since it showed up in the newspapers.

Chairman Rogers: Did you have discussions with people before it showed up in the newspaper?

Mr. Cook: I had given it to my boss just as a matter of documentation.

Chairman Rogers: But no one else?

Mr. Cook: Someone else? Well, my boss and the other, the former SRB analyst that I worked with very closely.

Mr. Rogers: Anyone out of the office?

Mr. Cook: No.

Rogers then referred to my February 3 memo.

Chairman Rogers: Since the accident have you written another memorandum in connection with the accident?

Mr. Cook: Yes.

Chairman Rogers: What prompted that?

Mr. Cook: The heat of the moment. I did write another memorandum and what I was saying essentially was that, given all of the information that was coming in, I felt at that time that, number one, it had not been demonstrated what caused the accident. The evidence that points to the SRB is either circumstantial or interpretations of photographs.

My backpedaling continued. Now I was not even able to back up my own February 3 memorandum. I had said, "It has not been demonstrated what caused the accident," when we all knew what caused the accident. All through my life I had trouble standing up for myself when attacked by a bully. Now a bully was mauling me, and I just wanted to be left alone. But this only egged the bully on. Now I tried to turn and make some kind of a stand:

But I felt that the problems that I had been apprised of during the

WHAT IS HE DOING TO THEM?" | 273

course of, now it wasn't just the first weeks on the job, it was several months, ought to be looked at seriously enough so that whatever happened this needed to be taken care of, the O-ring problem needed to be taken care of before we could look at the shuttle program as being completely resolved. And we had some other major budgetary issues that came up in that connection.

Chairman Rogers: You were still doing it in terms of the budget? I mean, was that the purpose of writing the memorandum after the accident?

Mr. Cook: Yes.

He knew, and I knew, that this wasn't the reason I wrote the memorandum. I wrote it because I wanted to set the record straight about what NASA really knew. So again, why couldn't I say that? The strange thing was, this memo was not cited in the *New York Times* article, even though I had given it to Phil Boffey. So the audience in the auditorium didn't know it existed. Now, Rogers was bringing it out in the open. He obviously was angry about what I had written.

Chairman Rogers: Did you have reason to think that efforts would not be made after the accident to investigate it thoroughly?

Mr. Cook: No. In fact, I knew that across the street they were doing the same analyses we were doing.

Chairman Rogers: Then will you explain again why you wrote the memorandum?

Mr. Cook: To document what I felt were all of the budgetary implications of the situation.

Chairman Rogers: Only budgetary? Was there any other purpose?

He waited for me to answer, but I felt things had gone far enough. I was not going to attack NASA or the Commission directly and get caught in an argument that would touch on who was to blame for the Challenger disaster or whether there was a cover-up. On the other hand, I was tired of being forced to undermine myself. So I said nothing.

Chairman Rogers: Well, if you'd rather not answer, that's all right. I'm just curious about why you wrote the memorandum. I mean, it doesn't sound as if you have budgetary implications in mind. It sounds differently. But I just wanted you to have an opportunity to tell the Commission why you wrote it.

Now I answered in a tone of exasperation:

I wrote it because I felt that it was a serious enough situation that I didn't think that until these various issues were resolved with the SRBs that I had been involved with, that they had to be taken care of before the shuttle could safely continue.

Now he'd gotten what he wanted. I'd fallen into the trap and was making safety judgments. Now he brought out the sarcasm.

Did you think your engineering experience, based on the short time you had been with NASA improved your ability to pass judgment on what others had decided?

Again I just stared at him.

Well, here again, I really don't want to press you. Do you have anything else to tell the Commission?

I took a drink of ice water and said nothing. Was it over, I wondered? Evidently not. Rogers said:

I just received a copy of the memorandum that I referred to previously, which is dated February 3, 1986, and the other Commission members have not had a chance to look at it. I would propose to let them take a look at it during the lunch hour, and then we can resume and they may have some questions to ask and you may have some comments to make.

It was lunchtime. I felt badly beaten but not quite dead. I had a misplaced sense of relief that I was not forced to admit that I was the leaker, but I did not realize how much my feeling of shame for backing down so much would eat away at me for years to come. When I stepped off the podium, I was surrounded by a swarm of reporters, but did not feel like answering questions. One of the faces I recognized was Bob Schieffer of CBS News. Someone said, "Let him go to lunch," so I left the room and went downstairs to the cafeteria.

After lunch, on the way back to the auditorium, I stopped at a pay phone and called Phyllis.

"How did I do?" I asked.

"You did great. You sounded like you knew what you were talking about, and he sounded like a grouch."

That made me feel a little better. "Okay, well I have to go back on."

"Good luck—you'll be fine."

I realized going back to the auditorium that in the Commission's only public hearing, last Thursday, they said almost nothing about the details of the SRBs and the O-rings. Mulloy's briefing this morning was so technical and confusing that probably no one could figure out what he was talking about. So thus far, between the *New York Times* article and what I said this morning, I was the leading public source about what had happened to Challenger. So maybe things weren't as dark as they seemed.

I returned to the auditorium and sat down to wait for the hearing to resume. At this point, William Rogers came over and sat next to me. Later, someone said to me that observers had told him how he was losing the media battle through his undisguised aggression.

Rogers told me that he heard during lunch that I had not written the February 3 memo on my own initiative but that I had done so because of an assignment. My supervisor had known I was talking to the SRB engineers and had told me to keep gathering information, so I told Rogers that was correct.

Later, I was told that Rogers had put his arm around my shoulders. For many years I had no recollection of that, but it was so. I do remember having a certain feeling of warmth toward Rogers. He had a quality of earnestness and charm that probably went a long way toward his success in the world of Washington politics. Though I resented what he had done to me, I was more angry and disappointed with myself than with him.

The first thing Rogers did when the afternoon session began was ask if I wanted to sit down, since I was still going around with crutches. I said, "I am much more comfortable just to stand up."

Chairman Rogers: Well, let me begin by saying that I had a chance to talk a little bit with Mr. Cook during lunch and learned that he had in fact been asked to prepare a memorandum subsequent to the accident on budgetary matters, and Mr. Cook pointed out, and we discussed the fact that the initiation of the memo included some material in there that did not strictly come within the budgetary request that was made.

Nevertheless, he said in his testimony this morning that he did it in the heat of the moment, and I thought maybe, Mr. Cook, you would want to follow up on the discussions we had about how you relate to the engineers in NASA and the others in terms of their ability and their qualifications.

By now, Rogers had changed his tone. He had pointed out that my February 3 memorandum, the one that didn't get into the *New York Times* article, was an official document prepared in connection with an assignment. He had also acknowledged, without complaining about it, that I included material that went beyond just the budget issues. In fact, I had reported that the engineers viewed the Challenger disaster as a preventable accident.

What he now did, perhaps to improve the negative image he had generated of himself and his Commission during the morning session, was to give me a platform to express the concerns I had written about. Here again, I was acting as the leading public source of information about the problems that led to the tragedy. So I spent several minutes paraphrasing the key facts about the SRB problems that I outlined on February 3.

I had given the Commission a blueprint of issues to examine when looking at the overall solid rocket booster program. But Rogers was not ready to give up.

. . . Summarizing your first memo, of July 23, 1985, as you have said several times, it was done for budgetary considerations that you did not intend to pass judgment on any of the engineering features as such. You were looking at it for budgetary purposes?

Mr. Cook: Absolutely. That was all I was, that was all I was able to do.

Chairman Rogers: And you were satisfied with the performance and ability of the engineers you dealt with at NASA?

I was getting very tired of all this. But I now saw an opportunity to remind the Commission to turn its attention to working-level people like Wetzel and Herr as the people they should talk to.

Mr. Cook: Yes, and I would say particularly the fellows in the Propulsion Division at headquarters. I thought it was an extremely professional group. It was a great deal of help to me particularly getting on-board and getting up to speed on all of these things. And I thought they were an excellent team that had the interest of NASA and the program entirely in mind, and I had complete confidence in the information I was providing.

Chairman Rogers: Thank you very much. Now I asked you this morning about the reason for the memorandum subsequent to the accident, which is dated February 3, 1986. And it subsequently turns out that you were asked to provide a memorandum to the effect along the lines of your summary just now. In other words, you were asked to do that by Mr. Mann?

Mr. Cook: Yes, sir.

Chairman Rogers: And the memorandum that is dated February 3 that you have just summarized was in response to that request, and I think your summary of the memorandum is very good and it explains to the Commission your motivation.

I would just like to ask one question about the memo. You say at one point when you are referring to the engineers, I believe you say—well, let me read the whole thing. "It is also my opinion that the Marshall Space Flight Center has not been adequately responsive to headquarters concerns about flight safety and that the Office of Space Flight has not given enough time and attention to the assessment of problems with SRB safety raised by senior engineers in the Propulsion Division."

Now this is that part I want to ask about. "And that these engineers have been improperly excluded from the investigations that are being conducted now at Kennedy." Are you still of that view?

I said:

Frankly, I was amazed that when this incident occurred the engineers in Washington were over there in their offices getting the data on the investigations from the newspapers and the media, and now and then phone calls from guys down at Kennedy about what was being found.

These were the top propulsion engineers who prepared reports for the Office of Space Flight and for the administrator and for us. I just couldn't understand why that group wasn't down there going through the data and looking at the photos and everything else. Frankly, and I will be honest with you—and I'm not intending to explain why that was or criticize anybody—I was just, in a way I was glad because I could go over and talk to them and get my information from them.

But I just couldn't understand why the headquarters propulsion office didn't have their guys down taking part in that.

I was feeling that I had escaped Rogers and that I had gained the initiative in the dialogue. But I couldn't bring myself at the end of the day to openly assault NASA or the Commission, cover-up or not. All I could do was to point them to the people they needed to talk to.

The only thing that I would urge would be that as much as you can to get just the ordinary working guys, such as me and the engineers and the guys from the Marshall S&E lab, and if you can get them in from Thiokol, just the ordinary engineers who break these things down [i.e., the O-ring joints], who look at them, who call each other on the phone and say, hey, look what I found here, you've got to take a close look at this. And that is what I hope will be included. And I think that if everybody who has firsthand knowledge and experience and feels they can come up and talk freely, I think that you will have a good investigation.

Chairman Rogers: . . . You also mentioned this morning that you wrote the [February 3] memo in the heat of the moment, and I assume you were, like everybody else in the country was, terribly disturbed and upset by the accident, and it was in that spirit or at that time when you wrote the memorandum. You didn't really mean to adversely criticize for public consumption your associates or people around you, did you?

Mr. Cook: No, I didn't, but I must say, I didn't say anything in there that I didn't feel I had—that I couldn't back up and wouldn't stand by.

Chairman Rogers: No, I understand. I am really not asking you to back down at all. I think to understand the contents of the memo, it is helpful to have you say what you have said. I just mean that it was done in the heat of the moment, and I think that has helped to understand the memo.

The ordeal had ended. I stepped down from the stage and took a seat. I paid little attention to the rest of the hearing. There were two other speakers who had been called to further place my memos in "context," though their statements were now anticlimactic after all that had happened during the day. Then Jesse Moore made some more remarks, and the Commission brought Larry Mulloy back for one last curtain call.

So here we were, almost at the end. Remember how much hand-wringing the Commission did in its closed session the previous day over how to explain that NASA was trying so hard to fix the O-rings when it wasn't a "safety of flight" concern? Now Vice Chairman Armstrong decided to try to do just that with acting director of the Division of Propulsion David Winterhalter on the stand:

> Vice Chairman Armstrong: Was it the view of your division, the propulsion group, that the seal design, as it was installed and operating in the shuttle system was safe and adequate?
>
> Mr. Winterhalter: It was.
>
> Vice Chairman Armstrong: But it was further your group's view that the margins on the seal design were not such that it would not benefit from improvement. Is that correct?
>
> Mr. Winterhalter: That is correct. We felt like it could be improved. We weren't happy with the situation the way it was. We understood that the testing had been done, the margins, etc., but as you are well aware, we are always striving to make things more perfect.

So the O-ring joints were perfect, and all NASA was doing was trying to make them "more perfect"? The hearing was clearly coming to an end, but Dr. Richard Feynman was angry. In his subsequent writings on the subject, he seemed to see the whole day as a waste of time, perhaps even political manipulation. Now he said to Winterhalter:

> If the matter of Mr. Cook is more or less covered, I would like to ask some detailed questions about seals either from you or anyone else you wish to call, like Mr. Mulloy.
>
> Mr. Winterhalter: I would just as soon that Larry came up and talked about seals since he did such an adequate job this morning. . . .
>
> Dr. Feynman: We spoke this morning about the resiliency of the seal, and if the material weren't resilient, it wouldn't work in the appropriate

mode, or it would be less satisfactory, in fact it might not work well. I did a little experiment here, and this is not the way to do such experiments, indicating that the stuff looked as if it was much less resilient at lower temperatures, in ice. Does your data agree with this feature, that the immediate resilience, that is, within the first few seconds, is very, very much reduced when the temperature is reduced?

Mr. Mulloy: Yes, sir, in a qualitative sense. I just can't quantify it at this time.

Dr. Feynman: Then you would say that I would conclude from that and the various things that you told me about the need for resilience and the lack of resilience within the first few seconds, and of course, it comes back very slowly, isn't it true, then, that the temperature at a low temperature increases the chance of a joint failure?

Mr. Mulloy: The low temperature increases the time that would be required for the O-ring to extrude into the gap, and that would allow greater erosion on the O-ring, yes, sir.

Feynman and Mulloy repeated some of the dialogue from Monday's closed hearing about the temperature at which the O-rings could not seal properly, ending with Mulloy's statement:

Mr. Mulloy: There were data presented, as we have discussed, by some—by Thiokol engineering that there was a suggestion that possibly the seals shouldn't be operated below any temperature that it had been operated on previous flights.

This seemed to set off alarm bells in the minds of Chairman Rogers and some of the other Commission members. The Commission wasn't supposed to go there today. Rogers cut Feynman off. Looking at the other members, he said: "Are there any further questions?" David Acheson immediately jumped in with an irrelevant question about engine tests. Rogers then said:

Unless everybody is really eager to press on, I think it would be helpful if we considered this in detail and carefully at the next session, and I would hope that we could ask individual questions when we are at Kennedy.

Larry Mulloy, however, had a piece of unfinished business. He now spoke up to "clarify" his testimony from the morning, stating that there had in fact been some O-ring erosion in 1985, as I had pointed out. Later documentation showed there had been eighteen instances of erosion. The hearing was now over. Rogers said:

> I just want to add to what I said before, that at the hearings that we have that will deal with temperature effects, and weather and environmental effects and so forth we will want the Thiokol people there. Yesterday we had a representative from Thiokol there [Al McDonald], but he did not have as much firsthand information as we would like, and so we want to be sure at that hearing to have firsthand information and a chronology of all of the events preceding the launch that dealt with weather and environmental problems.

One of the most memorable hearings in U.S. government history was over. It was not so memorable to the Commission, however, as they didn't even mention it in the list of public and private hearings in their final report. Feynman was so upset with what had been done that when the hearing was over he told people he was through. He was going back to California. But General Kutyna and some of the other members talked him out of it. They told him that they now knew enough to begin to address real issues, starting with the trip that was planned for Commission members to make to Kennedy later in the week.

Phyllis later told me that during the afternoon session, as she watched the hearing on TV, my father had called her from his home in Newport News, VA. Distraught, he asked her, "What are they doing to him?"

"You mean, what is he doing to them?" she replied.

Later in the week, Bill Kovach, head of the *New York Times'* Washington bureau, told me that my disclosures had forced the Commission to start focusing its attention on the right issues. Then on Friday, as I was riding in a taxi, the subject of the Challenger disaster came up. The driver said, "Yeah, I think it was them O-rings that made that thing blow up." I realized that thanks in part to what I had done, O-rings were now a household word. Maybe now, I thought, some of the harm that had been inflicted on the nation by the Challenger disaster could begin to be repaired.

I didn't know what the future held for me, but it helped a little a few days later when I got a letter from a woman in Vermont:

Dear Richard,

I am writing you this letter because I have a message for you. In every system God puts someone to break the system. You are the one that God put in the system. How do you break the system? By not going along with it. You will be challenged to do something that is wrong and against your system. Stand up for right and God will be with you. This is the time to stand up and be counted.

God's plan is for everyone to experience the good way and the bad way then choose which way you want to go. The good way promises nothing and gives you everything. The other way promises you everything and gives you nothing but despair. God is for everyone. The other way benefits no one.

God knows you can do it. You have been tested many times and have come through for good ways. God knows there are good teachings mixed in with bad teachings, and we are confused. That is why He sends a guardian angel when we are in a bind. We know that fear knocks out God and this is what will be used on you. When you feel this coming on, ask for God's help. He will send help from above. A guardian angel.

You will be opening the door for good ways to come in and the young to come in and help. They are strong in God and will show us the way.

We will be rooting for you to come through. We love you for hanging in there when the going got tough. As the saying goes, when the going gets tough, the tough get going.

God bless you and take care. We will be praying for you. Pray that God's way comes through.

"LOWER TEMPERATURES AGGRAVATE THIS PROBLEM"
—The Commission Changes Direction

THE DAY AFTER the February 11 hearing, NASA released the massive briefing package presented by Thiokol at the August 19, 1985, meeting at NASA headquarters which Marshall had set up in response to the Davids/Hamby visit. This was the meeting after which the Presidential Commission said in its report to the president that NASA should have stopped flights and fixed the O-ring joints. Interestingly, no one from the Johnson Space Center had been invited to attend that meeting, so the astronauts had no way of knowing about it.

The August 19 meeting took place after I wrote my July 23rd memo, but I did not know about it either. The meeting seemed to have been a well-guarded secret, which suggests something about how NASA viewed the information as being sensitive.

The Commission's final report described the meeting as follows:

On August 19, 1985, Thiokol and Marshall program managers briefed NASA headquarters on erosion of the motor pressure seals. The briefing paper concluded that the O-ring seal was a critical matter, but it was safe to fly. The briefing was detailed, identifying all prior instances of field joint, nozzle joint, and igniter O-ring erosion. It recommended an "accelerated pace" to eliminate seal erosion but concluded with the recommendation that "it is safe to continue flying existing design as long as all joints are leak checked with a 200 psig stabilization pressure, are free of contamination in seal areas, and meet O-ring squeeze requirements."

A briefing chart entitled "General Conclusions" described what was in fact the cause of the Challenger disaster: "The primary O-ring in the field joint should not erode through but if it leaks due to erosion or lack of sealing the secondary seal may not seal the motor." This was from the same package of charts Dr. Richard Feynman was shown by Michael Weeks at NASA headquarters on Monday, February 10, which led Feynman to make his ice water demonstration at the open hearing the next day.

The first item on the chart on "Recommendations" stated: "The lack of a good secondary seal in the field joint is most critical, and ways to reduce joint rotation should be incorporated as soon as possible to reduce criticality." This was what the capture feature was intended to do— reduce joint rotation. "As soon as possible" turned out to mean in practice that the shuttle was to "fly as is" for over two more years.

Now, here is an interesting fact about these briefing charts. Months later, when the Commission had completed its work, I went through its records in the National Archives. I found a document that was an alternative to the "General Conclusions" chart from the August 19 briefing. On this version of the chart, after the line cited above, there appeared in bold black letters this sentence: "Data obtained on resiliency of the O-rings indicate that lower temperatures aggravate this problem."

Was this bold-print statement originally part of the Thiokol August 19 briefing? If so, both NASA headquarters and Marshall were far more concerned about the possible hazardous effect of cold weather on the O-rings than anyone ever disclosed.

———

AFTER MY FEBRUARY 11 testimony, I never returned to my office but for the rest of the week rode into Washington with my vanpool. I spent most of the time traveling around town by metro giving media interviews. I was the only participant in events relating to the Challenger disaster who at that moment was able and willing to speak freely and for the record about what had happened. Later, Alan McDonald did give a key interview to the *New York Times*. Also, after he left Thiokol, Roger Boisjoly wrote and spoke about his experience. But for over a year, I was the main insider news source. I gave more interviews to the media than I could count.

All this took place while I was employed as an analyst at the U.S. Treasury Department, gradually working my way back up through the bureaucracy. It was a long time before I again was working at the same level of responsibility that I had at NASA or my previous government jobs.

During the three days following my appearance as a witness at the Commission's February 11 hearing, I gave several media interviews that stood out in my recollection. One was again with Phil Boffey for an article that appeared in the *New York Times* on Friday, February 14, entitled, "Analyst Who Gave Shuttle Warning Faults 'Gung-Ho, Can-Do' Attitude":

> Mr. Cook said today that after the shuttle disaster NASA was "gripped in a climate of fear," in which his immediate superiors and colleagues asked him to return a memorandum that they described as too "explosive." The memorandum, written six days after the shuttle explosion, said that the shuttle had been flying "in an unsafe condition" for more than a year and that the accident "was probably preventable."
>
> Mr. Cook also charged that the space agency and the Presidential Commission investigating the accident had combined in an effort to discredit him and his concerns. He was referring to a public hearing Tuesday at which NASA witnesses cast doubt on his competence to judge the safety of the seals and where William P. Rogers, the Commission's chairman, asked a series of aggressive questions probing Mr. Cook's motives, frame of mind, engineering competence and whether he had given his July memorandum of potential catastrophe to anyone outside the agency.

In the article, I spoke about my meetings with Paul Herr and Paul Wetzel:

> "They said to me, almost in a whisper in my ear, that the thing could blow up," he continued. "I was shocked." In his July memorandum,

Cook explained, "I was simply paraphrasing what this engineering group was telling me. I was not making it up that flight safety was being compromised and the results could be catastrophic. I didn't put it in my memorandum, but one of them said to me, 'When this thing goes up, we hold our breath.' "

Bill Kovach, the *Times'* Washington bureau chief, told me that this interview was "probably the most important article yet" on the Challenger disaster. Overall, the press coverage was running strongly against NASA and the Commission. It had already irritated a lot of reporters and news organizations that NASA was being so secretive, and now the Commission was being seen as trying to intimidate the one person who had raised safety issues. The Commission's credibility had been compromised.

Another interview was with the *Orlando Sentinel*. The *Sentinel*, which viewed NASA's Kennedy Space Center, only twenty-five miles away, as its home turf, threw a large number of reporters at coverage of the accident and its aftermath. The day after the February 11 hearing, *Sentinel* reporter Chris Reidy appeared unexpectedly at our house in King George. He came to the front door, which we usually unlocked only to bring in firewood.

"How did you find us here?" Phyllis asked when she opened the door to let him in. Round Hill Road was a lonely stretch of rural pavement, and hardly anyone in the area knew us.

"It's my job to find you," said Reidy.

As a result of Reidy's visit, I phoned the *Sentinel's* Washington bureau and arranged to meet reporter Tim Smart in Washington on Friday. Phyllis had asked me to purchase some Valentine's Day candy for our daughter, so I asked Smart if he would be willing to talk to me as we walked to a candy shop on Connecticut Avenue. He agreed, and we completed the interview there over coffee.

The article was entitled "NASA Critic Says Job Binds Him to Truth, not Agency." It was sympathetic, and began:

> Richard Cook, the NASA budget analyst who claims engineers "held their breath" at every shuttle launch, insists he is not a whistleblower.
> He is, he says, simply a public servant who refuses to compromise

standards. He sees his job as telling the truth, even if that truth is unpleasant and brings unwanted celebrity and attention.

Another interview was with Jim Lehrer of the PBS McNeil/Lehrer News Hour and took place on Friday evening, February 14. The night before, I had dinner at a hotel on M Street in Georgetown with McNeil/Lehrer producer Lee Koromvokis and TV news correspondent Elizabeth Brackett. I gave them copies of several documents from the January 1985 Centaur meetings at the Kennedy Space Center, including Jesse Moore's "fly as is" memo and the statement from the JSC briefing chart that, "Recent actions to fly as is on planetaries and fix for future missions indicate schedule pressure is forcing solutions which might otherwise be rejected."

I also told Koromvokis and Brackett that once the Commission began to have public hearings on all the Challenger issues, they would resemble "Soviet-type show-trials with lower-level officials taking the hit." This turned out to be an accurate prediction.

The interview with Lehrer took place at a studio across the Potomac River in Arlington, Virginia. It was preceded by a news report by Brackett, where she displayed the Centaur "fly as is" document. She had also done a phone interview with the author of the charts at JSC who "said he remains concerned that the pressure of the schedule kept the level of risk on the Centaur missions too high."

When the interview with Lehrer began, I was startled to find that they had arranged for Jerry Grey of the American Institute of Aeronautics and Astronautics to debate me on the air. Grey was one of the foremost astronautical engineers and space program publicists in the world—in fact, one of his books is a source for Chapter 7 of this book—and he was speaking remotely over a TV monitor from a hook-up in New York. Since I had not been told this would happen, I became tentative in my responses, which disappointed Koromvokis and Brackett, who hoped I would be as outspoken on the air as I was over dinner at the hotel.

Lehrer was trying to get me to say whether schedule pressure had compromised safety. After Grey said that the kind of waiver NASA made on O-ring redundancy in 1983 was common, Lehrer asked me, "Mr. Cook, is it your position that no safety waivers should ever be granted?" How should I know? I wondered. But I was able to compose myself.

Mr. Cook: No, sir. But I'd like to speak for just a minute about the waivers on the O-rings. I looked today for the first time in detail at the Thiokol report that came out on August 19th, and this was the one that NASA had requested to come up with alternatives for solving the O-ring problem. And the language that was used in that report was in some ways similar to the language that I was using last summer. It was stated that it was a critical need to have redundancy on those field joints. It was stated that it was essential that as soon as possible the redundancy problem be taken care of. And that plan that NASA had in effect was to repair that feature by January of 1988. So that essentially we would have been flying for over two years in the face of a situation which Thiokol themselves were using critical language to describe.

Speaking impromptu, I had described the same issue that the members of the Presidential Commission had wrestled with on Monday in the closed session about how they were going to get NASA to explain away this obvious contradiction at Tuesday's open hearing. Now Jerry Grey would get his chance to explain what NASA or the other Commission members couldn't: why should you fix something you say isn't broken?

But Jerry Grey didn't do any better than anyone else. He described what NASA did—kept using the system "that isn't ideal"—point A—until they were able to install the new system—point B. The trouble is that between points A and B, Challenger blew up. So they made a bad decision, one that they were doing their best to keep secret, even within the organization. Lehrer then asked me if I believed there was some "kind of dereliction of duty, some kind of political decision." This was a good question, but I was not yet there in my thinking.

The reasons NASA did not stop flights to fix the O-rings were twofold.

One was what Elizabeth Brackett was getting at in her report on Centaur, that Centaur, along with the O-rings, were two major problems where NASA had chosen the "fly as is" route. Others were the main engine problems, as well as external tank flapper valves and other hardware issues later disclosed by astronaut John Young and others. So the whole shuttle system was in a "fly as is" mode. This was why people in Code M were sure that "sooner or later" there would be a disaster, why they were "betting on the come." But no one could say for sure which major piece of hardware would go first.

The second reason was political, which I didn't understand very well at this point. I still didn't know that NASA didn't take the issue of cold O-rings seriously because they did not want to interfere with future Vandenberg military launches. The increasing military flight rate, which I had become aware of, had something to do with having always to "fly as is," but I hadn't yet thought through the militarization issue. Also involved were the politics of the commercial launch marketplace and commitments to the European Space Agency. Plus the shuttle had been a great political back-drop for President Reagan. And NASA had to look good to itself, Congress, the public. The list of political aspects was a very long one.

What I said to Lehrer was that there was "significant disagreement among the engineers" going back to the previous summer about whether the shuttle should fly or not before the O-ring problem had been addressed. But Lehrer pressed on. What motivated the decision to fly? This was the key question. But I didn't know. I did point out, however, that the program plan had zoomed up to twenty-four flights a year, and that there was "tremendous pressure to meet that flight rate."

That night, McNeil/Lehrer paid for a sixty-five-mile cab ride through the darkness of night to my home in King George. It was now late Friday night, the weekend was upon us, and I was exhausted. It was strange to go home to our little house in the country, where we were struggling to survive financially, after the heady experience of being in the news all week. Of course our kids, Adele and Fred, were too young to be aware of what was going on, though I tried to keep my older sons Nat and Tim in Annapolis informed, and they were able to see me a couple of times on TV. Now my life would be undergoing a big change as I tried to prepare myself mentally to report to the U.S. Treasury Department on Monday.

———

THE New York Times O-ring disclosures were the first of two major jolts that shook the Presidential Commission out of its complacency. The second was revelations about the pre-launch teleconference involving

Thiokol and Marshall, where engineers argued against the launch but were overruled by their own managers after pressure from NASA.

The Commission had begun to hear about this from Alan McDonald at its closed session on Monday the 10th. At the public session on the 11th, Dr. Feynman was dramatizing the effects of cold temperature on the O-rings but did not know about the teleconference as the point in the launch sequence where predictions of these effects came into play. Later in the week, on Friday the 14th, the Commission met at the Kennedy Space Center in Florida and heard the story from the Thiokol engineers at a closed session. It was the testimony of the engineers, after some inconsequential presentations by NASA the previous day, that transformed the Commission's role into that of an investigative body rather than NASA apologist. The *New York Times* article on February 9, with my memo and the other O-ring documents, had started the ball rolling.

NASA's hierarchy was starting to be shaken up. After the *New York Times* story, Acting Administrator William Graham stripped General Manager Philip Culbertson of his duties, because, as I was told by *Chicago Tribune* reporter Storer Rowley, Graham had not been informed of the existence of the O-ring documents that I had leaked.

According to Rowley, Culbertson, when confronted, told Graham that he thought "everyone knew" about the history of the O-ring problem. This related to what Irv Davids said to me after he gave me a copy of his own O-ring memo, that I should not let Graham see it. So there seemed to have been a deliberate attempt to hide the details of the O-ring history from him. By Friday, Graham had issued a memo stating that, "Effective immediately, the specific responsibilities delegated to the position of general manager for the following offices are withdrawn." The memo then listed all six of NASA's major program areas. Culberstson said he was left only with "running the Xerox machine." Not too long after, he retired from the government.

Events were now moving at a rapid pace. Hints had already appeared in the press that something had gone wrong during the launch process. Word about Rockwell's opposition to the launch due to the ice situation had appeared within a day of the disaster and had been the subject of several questions directed to NASA's managers during their early press conferences.

Coinciding with the release of documents on February 12th, Marshall Director William Lucas and SRB chief Larry Mulloy gave a press conference in Washington, D.C., where they denied that Challenger had been launched over Thiokol's objections. It was now Marshall that represented the NASA hardcore. Mulloy was asked, for instance, why Thiokol employees had first opposed the launch, then changed their minds. He said:

> It is not an accurate statement to say that Thiokol recommended against launching. There was an engineering discussion in which the engineering element of Thiokol pointed out that we would be operating 51-L outside of our experience base. . . . That discussion led to a conclusion on the part of the program manager at Thiokol, which was concurred in by NASA, that there was no direct correlation [i.e., between temperature and seal performance].

But this flies in the face of written documentation. Thiokol had presented a written statement not to launch at the temperatures predicted for the next morning. It was this recommendation from Vice President for Engineering Bob Lund that Thiokol's managers reversed, following pressure from NASA, during the evening teleconference.

Despite the turmoil of the past few days, William Graham was trying to project a business-as-usual image. On February 13, he announced that the Teacher-in-Space program would continue and that Christa McAuliffe's back-up, Barbara Morgan, would be offered the chance to become the first ordinary citizen to fly on the space shuttle.

On February 13 and 14, the Commission made its scheduled trip to the Kennedy Space Center for two days of closed hearings. As with the hearing on the 10th, the ones held at Kennedy were to be preliminary sessions to review information the Commission would later release to the public. The Commission was still trying to manage the news, as shown by Chairman Rogers' opening remarks referring to the previous day's Lucas/Mulloy press conference. As you read the following account, bear in mind that the transcripts for the meetings on the 13th and 14th were not made public until months later. Rogers opened by saying to Jesse Moore:

I would like to suggest that, in view of the story this morning in the *New York Times* resulting from yesterday's briefing [i.e., the Lucas/Mulloy press conference], that you get the appropriate people to start thinking about this Criticality 1 problem, because it came through in the newspapers as if the waiver was of tremendous significance, and it appears as if the waiver only applied to this particular flight and this particular problem.

So now Rogers was going back to the problem from Monday about how to spin the fact that NASA was trying to fix something that wasn't broken and how routine it all was.

And so I think we may want to, after we've had a chance to talk to you about it, pointing out that this is not all that unusual, that it is not a waiver as such [?!], that you've isolated a criticality problem and then you've thoroughly considered whether that should result in the stopping of flights or not or whether it was something that was an important factor and you had done all you could about it, but you decided to proceed.

Now, if you can show that that is also not an unusual circumstance, the same papers and the same documentation would show a lot of other aspects of the shuttle program, that would help you.

If you saw the paper this morning, it sounds very serious, just as in the case of the O-rings, and you waived something that was dangerous. So give some thought to how we might handle that possibly this afternoon.

Mr. Moore: Yes, sir. Let me just comment on that. We started an action yesterday going back through the entire program looking at Category 1 items, and there are a number in the program, and I think we will put that particular situation in context.

Moore was evidently trying to humor Rogers. It was clear that in fact the O-ring waiver was serious, was dangerous, and that there were no comparable situations with other pieces of shuttle hardware.

The first presentation at the February 13 closed session was by Dick Kohrs of the Johnson Space Center, a manager who worked for Arnold Aldrich, the STS program manager—Level II—from Houston. Kohrs led off what became a long, rambling discussion involving various

NASA managers and Commission members on the subject of the weather—winds, rainfall, weather forecasts, and temperatures.

There were a few highlights that are worth noting, including the fact that when Challenger was launched, the predicted wind shear at high altitude over the launch pad was the most severe for any shuttle launch. Also, the wind shear was the strongest at the altitude where the plume appeared on the right-hand solid rocket booster fifty-eight seconds after lift-off. This later led to the conclusion that the wind shear probably broke the joint open after it had been re-sealed from combustion products early in the launch sequence. In fact, Kohrs said that the wind shear probably was a contributor to "this failure scenario [i.e., the SRB field joint burnthrough] that is being developed."

Kohrs then talked about the forecast for freezing temperatures in the low twenties the night of January 27, 1985, and how NASA decided to let the water trickle on the launch pad to keep the lines from freezing. This was what resulted in the massive build-up of icicles on the launch tower, as well as a sheet of ice covering the astronauts' escape platform outside the orbiter. The sheet of ice was not mentioned by NASA in the hearings but was revealed in the Commission's final report.

Next, NASA engineer Horace Lamberth talked about temperature readings taken on the launch pad the night of January 27th. He disclosed that readings on the right-hand solid rocket booster were as low as seven degrees F. on the nozzle, while the left-hand SRB had readings in the twenty-three to twenty-five degree range. Lamberth said the low readings on the right booster may have resulted from some kind of effect from the clear night sky. Remember, it was the right-hand SRB that failed. Later during the investigation, this temperature reading was re-calculated at sixteen degrees, which was still extremely low. Even with this reading, the O-rings would have frozen as hard as rocks. As stated by Roger Boisjoly, "it was like trying to shove a brick into a crack rather than a sponge."

William Rogers was concerned about the temperature readings. He said:

> Just because we are in closed session, I don't want to be unpleasant, but—and maybe I am being unpleasant, but it would seem to me that if the temperature at that time you've got down there was in the low twenties at two o'clock in the morning and it had been in the low twenties for

approximately eleven hours, and everybody knew that that would probably have some adverse effect and there were some limits of some kind about that, why that wasn't a matter of major concern?

I can see why your team that was primarily concerned about ice and damage to the orbiter and the facility, whether the water faucet was working and that stuff—but I would think that that would have been a major concern to everybody. And it would be helpful in this closed session, because you're going to be struck with it in public. What was it?

No one could offer a satisfactory answer to Rogers' question, but Arnold Aldrich and General Kutyna knew what he was getting at. Aldrich said:

> Mr. Aldrich: At no time during this period was I aware of a concern for the temperature of the SRB within the ranges as we had from the weather forecaster. . . .
> General Kutyna: . . . And yet in previous testimony we heard somebody say don't launch [the SRB] outside of forty to ninety degrees.

George Hardy of Marshall was at the hearing, so Chairman Rogers asked him:

> . . . the coldness of the weather really wasn't of concern as far as the solid-fuel boosters were concerned?
> Mr. Hardy: Absolutely correct.

Hardy's response, of course, was nonsense. Sally Ride pursued the point:

> Dr. Ride: . . . I guess the question would really be what launch commit criteria there are related to cold temperature.

She was talking about criteria for the entire space shuttle system, not for the solid rocket boosters or any other component.

> Mr. Aldrich: I was just trying to fit that in if I got the floor again, Mr. Chairman and Sally. The launch commit criteria for cold temperature is to launch at an ambient outside temperature at launch time of thirty-

one degrees or greater. Now the prediction was for [it] to be greater than that, and that in fact is how the data turned out. . . .

The final report read that:

> The ambient air temperature at launch was thirty-six degrees F. measured at ground level approximately 1,000 feet from the 51-L mission launch pad 39B. This temperature was fifteen degrees colder than that of any previous flight.

The Commission later discovered a fact that appeared prominently in the report of the House Science and Technology Committee, which was that mission control at Houston had requested a waiver of the thirty-one degree requirement, so was prepared to launch at a lower temperature if necessary. It seems impossible that Aldrich would not have known of this at the February 13 hearing, because it would have been coordinated through the mission management team. Whether or not he knew, he did not mention it.

> Dr. Ride: So the assumption is that, back when the solid rocket boosters were, to pick an example, were qualified and built and certified for launch on the shuttle flight, they had to prove that if the ambient temperature was thirty-one degrees, all parts of the solid rocket were go for launch?
> Mr. Aldrich: That would be implied, and it has been for a series of launches.

Actually, as Alan McDonald argued the night before the disaster, the solid rocket motor had been qualified only down to forty degrees, so Aldrich was mistaken. No launch or test had ever taken place at or below that temperature until Challenger.

Now Rogers asked about the Thiokol recommendation not to launch.

> Mr. Lamberth: Mr. Chairman, their concern that they raised at that time—and we will give you a full discussion of that, and Thiokol will also explain their position. But it was related to the O-rings, was the only point for consideration that they raised in that discussion on the potential lower temperatures.

Chairman Rogers: Of the O-rings?

Mr. Lamberth: Of the O-rings, and the possibility that you might have increased erosion due to the lower temperature.

Chairman Rogers: Well, we will come to that later.

Mr. Walker: But there is no such written requirement? That is just something they brought up and were concerned about, and it is not written down and it is not a checklist item?

Mr. Lamberth: That was not a checklist item against the launch procedure.

Now Kohrs began to show photographic slides of the soon-to-be famous black puff of smoke coming from the right-hand SRB at ignition. Other slides of the Challenger ascent followed.

At this point in the hearing, Commission member Joseph Sutter, an executive at Boeing, went off in a tirade at NASA. Earlier in the hearing, he expressed exasperation that NASA was not doing any testing of the possible failure scenarios, such as whether the substances in the SRB joint would actually produce black smoke when set on fire. Now he said:

I didn't appreciate it when I was lying home in bed sick, and after the last goddamned airplane left for the east coast, I was asked to be at a meeting at two o'clock on Monday [February 10], and I couldn't make it because I don't have my executive jet. But I am glad I wasn't there, because that was nothing more than to reply to a leak, and there are going to be leaks. I am not complaining about leaks, but I think it was important that we discuss these theories [of what caused the accident], and we discuss every damned thing you know, and when you tell us what the hell you are going to do so that when the press hears about the black smoke, which they will, the Commission will say, hell, they've told us everything they know about it, they have told us what the hell they are going to test for, and we will let NASA tell you about it. We have already told them what the hell we expect out of them. I would rather help you guys investigate this, rather than have the goddamned *New York Times* or *Washington Post* do it.

Mr. Moore: We are with you 1,000 percent on that, and if we can stay ahead of the press, we are a lot better off.

As a result of the discussion, NASA and the Commission agreed to release the photos of the black puff of smoke that evening, Thursday, February 13. It was the clearest evidence yet that a booster rocket had failed. Worse, the failure evidently began at lift-off, making it seem even more calamitous that the astronauts had no warning of impending catastrophe nor any means of escape.

When the Commission members went back to their motels the night of February 13, they had little idea of what awaited them the next day. They had heard the names of Roger Boisjoly and Arnie Thompson. Finally they would learn what these two front-line SRB engineers had to say. But the engineers had almost no time to prepare. Boisjoly wrote:

> I was given very little notice that a hearing would be held on February 14. I had approximately two hours total by myself prior to the hearing and was struggling to organize a set of notes to aid me during my testimony, while [Thiokol] management had their publications department prepare a formal set of professional viewgraphs for their version of the events leading up to the launch decision. Meanwhile, at a pre-hearing meeting with management, the company attorneys advised us to answer all questions with only "yes" or "no" and not to volunteer anything freely. This advice was not followed by me nor Arnie Thompson and Al McDonald, and there were obvious tense feelings between management and us after the testimony session.

Thus the crucial pre-launch teleconference, where NASA pressured Thiokol to overrule its engineers and approve the Challenger launch, is known to us today only because Boisjoly, McDonald, and Thompson defied the Thiokol attorneys.

The February 14 meeting did not have a detailed pre-planned agenda. It started by Chairman Rogers asking the Commission's executive director, Alton Keel, an OMB associate director, to review the record from the February 10 closed meeting where Al McDonald tried to explain the teleconference and which Rogers called "hearsay."

Rogers now said that the February 14 meeting underway was an "investigation," not a hearing, so that witnesses did not have to be sworn. He said they should tell the truth, but that the meeting would be "informal," just a "discussion."

Stanley Reinartz of Marshall then jumped in and proposed that Larry Mulloy "give you the background that led up to the discussion we had with Morton Thiokol." They would then give Morton Thiokol the opportunity to speak.

Rogers said, "Sure."

Mulloy had prepared slides and went through a quick account of the events following the 1:00 p.m. scrub of the January 27 Challenger lift-off due to the faulty orbiter hatch handle.

Mulloy told the Commission that the first discussion relative to predicted cold temperatures rolling into Kennedy overnight was at 5:15 p.m. on the 27th. Arnold Aldrich interrupted to say this was not true. He called attention to a two p.m. meeting of the mission management team, which Mulloy attended, where the temperatures were discussed.

At this point, Rogers changed his mind and decided to swear in all the Thiokol participants. There were nine. He did not swear in the NASA representatives. Thus only the Thiokol people could have been charged with perjury if they had lied.

There actually had been two teleconferences held on the 27th. Mulloy further misspoke by saying that Thiokol initiated the concern with cold temperatures on the SRB. He omitted the fact that it was Marshall in Huntsville, Alabama, who asked them to take a look at it. Thus it was NASA, not Thiokol, which first raised the issue of cold O-rings.

Also, at the first teleconference on the day before the disaster, which Mulloy did not attend, Judson Lovingood at Marshall advised that his boss, Stanley Reinartz, tell Arnold Aldrich that Thiokol opposed the launch on the 28th and that Aldrich should be prepared for a recommendation against it.

Mulloy admitted, however, that at the later conference that evening:

> The bottom line of that, though, initially was that Thiokol engineering, Bob Lund, who is the vice president and director of engineering, who is here today, recommended that 51-L not be launched if the O-ring temperatures predicted at launch time would be lower than any previous launch, and that was fifty-three degrees.

Mulloy said he then asked Joe Kilminster, Thiokol's program manager for the booster program, what his recommendation was and that Kilminster "stated that, based on that engineering recommendation, he could not recommend launch."

Mulloy questioned the Thiokol position. He now told the Commission that he explained to Thiokol that his rationale of why the seal would be effective was based on their own engineering data. He said that his boss, Stanley Reinartz, then asked George Hardy, deputy director of science and engineering at Marshall, what he thought. Hardy said he agreed with Mulloy, but that he "also stated on the telecom that he certainly would not recommend launching if Thiokol did not."

So at various times, four management officials, Lund and Kilminster of Thiokol and Lovingood and Hardy of Marshall, said not to launch. It was not just the staff engineers. Mulloy now said Kilminster requested a five-minute caucus off-line back in Utah. After thirty minutes, Kilminster came back on and said Thiokol was recommending a launch.

Mulloy now introduced Jerry Mason, senior vice president of the Wasatch Division, head of the SRB operation. Rogers knew a critical moment had arrived. He warned Mason:

> Mr. Mason, might I suggest in your discussion with us today that you please disclose anything that you know about that may turn up. If you have documents that we don't know about that would be embarrassing to you, tell us about them now. We don't want to have to pry information out of you. You know what's there. Tell us the whole story, if you will.

Mason pointed out, contrary to Mulloy's statement, that it was NASA at Marshall and Thiokol's own people at Kennedy who asked the Utah staff to look at the possible effect of the predicted cold temperatures on the SRBs. He said:

> There were differing opinions within the group, and the only opinion that survived everyone was to launch at fifty-three degree O-ring temperature or higher.

Mason also pointed out that when a pre-launch leak check is done on the SRB's O-ring seals, air pressure is forced between the primary and secondary O-rings. This pushes the primary O-ring toward the center of the motor, away from the position it must assume at ignition. (Later in the investigation, astronaut John Young raised a vigorous objection to this obvious design flaw.) Therefore, the concern was that if the O-ring has lost resiliency and cannot move into its proper position fast enough, hot gas might get through. Then, if joint rotation has pulled the secondary O-ring off the casing metal, there could be a burnthrough.

Several Commission members now asked Mason and the other Thiokol managers to what minimum temperature the O-ring joints were qualified and what tests had been done to assure the standard was met. The astonishing answer was that there was no minimum temperature and no testing program.

Joe Kilminster, the SRB program manager, now said they once had a successful ground firing of a test SRB in a horizontal position with the O-rings at forty-seven degrees. General Kutyna asked how Thiokol reconciled the statement that they had only tested to forty-seven degrees with the fact that the entire shuttle was cleared to fly at an air temperature of thirty-one degrees.

> Mr. Kilminster: The only explanation I have is that we felt that we had a margin because of the material being capable down to minus thirty as identified in the [military] specifications.
> Dr. Wheelon: Capable of what?
> Mr. Kilminster: Capable of functioning.

Commission members made it clear that a military specification—MIL spec—didn't even come close to a valid test of how the O-rings in an actual SRB seal would perform under the variety of stresses and conditions of a shuttle launch.

Mason then returned to the fact that Thiokol's "best conclusion was to stay within our experience base" and launch only at fifty-three degrees or higher. But he said that then "we received a number of comments on the net." These comments were from NASA. Mason said:

> The ones that I looked upon as being of consequence were that we were reminded that there really wasn't a good correlation between temperature and blow-by.

Mulloy had argued that there had been hot gas getting by the primary O-ring at medium-range temperatures and a launch where there had been none. So Thiokol couldn't say simply that it was cold temperatures that caused the O-ring problems.

But Kutyna pointed out:

> But the worst blow-by you had was at the lowest temperature, which was 51-C [i.e., January 1985, with five distressed O-rings]. Did that not give you a strong correlation?
>
> Mr. Mason: That was the exact discussion we had. . . . Instinctively we felt that the cold would make it somehow worse.

Rogers wanted to know more about how the decision was made to change Thiokol's recommendation:

> Chairman Rogers: Mr. McDonald testified, at least I thought he did, that the recommendation was not to launch, Thiokol's recommendation was not to launch. Who—at one point, who was involved in that discussion . . . ?
>
> Mr. Mason: All of us that were in the meeting, we were gathered, and we were reviewing the data. . . .
>
> Mr. Rogers: Now, could you give us, without being too precise, the nature of the arguments against launch? Tell us what was being said. . . .
>
> Mr. Mason: [The engineers] were saying, we're going to be outside of our data base to go colder than fifty-three degrees, and we're concerned about whether the O-ring will move fast enough to seat and seal before the joint opens up [due to rotation]. And that was the thrust of the issue, is not knowing exactly how long it would take for the O-ring to move into position.

Mason was now asked a technical question he could not answer about the length of time after ignition it took for the O-ring seals to activate, so he turned to Roger Boisjoly, who began to spill the beans:

> Mr. Boisjoly: That was one of my concerns, and I addressed that as a timing function to seal. And I believed, and I still believe, and I believed that night that there isn't anybody on the face of this earth

that can tell you exactly the mechanism that happened in that joint . . . and [the O-ring] is eroding at the same time it is trying to seal, and it is a race between, will it erode more than the time allowed to have it seal.

The world's leading expert had just said that no one knows how the mechanism worked. Boisjoly continued:

> And that was the major concern, because SRM-15 [51-C, January 1985] showed erosion and hot gas blow-by at a low temperature, and that was the major issue on the table at that time.
> Chairman Rogers: Did you change your mind?
> Mr. Boisjoly: No, sir, never.
> Mr. Mason: . . . So our final conclusion was reached by me having a review with the vice president of engineering, the program manager Lund, Kilminster, and the general manager Wiggins, and my own opinion. . . . And we have brought with us today the people that had objections. In fact, Roger, as you just noted, is one who says he didn't change his mind. But it was one of those where it becomes the responsibility of management to make we think a rational decision, and that is what we did.

Now came an astonishing assertion:

> Mr. Lund: There was much data, and I will present that data to you in a little bit, that is both ways. Some say it's okay, some say it's not. So each engineer that was there reached his own conclusion from the data that was presented, and so there is a diversity of opinion.

But later in the investigation, Boisjoly said that the engineers unanimously opposed the launch and never backed down. Regarding the management people, Mason said:

> . . . we had a unanimous opinion among the key people reporting to me.

So it was the managers reporting directly to the big boss who were the ones who unanimously agreed.

Mr.Rogers: Very good. Thank you.

But Rogers had been listening and thinking. He gave the following summary of where things now stood, and as you read this, remember again that this was a closed meeting and that what the Commission was hearing about the teleconference was new to them.

Mr. Rogers: Could I put the case and oversimplify it a bit, because this is a good opportunity to be argumentative, if you will, on why you changed your mind. First, it was a Criticality Item 1, so that meant that if it was a failure, the mission was a catastrophe, one there had been discussion about that, a lot of it.

Note that the Commission had possession of and understood the redundancy waiver on the O-ring joints because the waiver, the so-called Death Document, was published in the *New York Times* five days previously. As a result of the article, the Commission held the February 10 and 11 hearings, which forced NASA to release the briefing materials for the August 19 meeting, where the loss of redundancy was highlighted. It was also on February 10 when Al McDonald first spoke up. So one thing led to another, but the entire sequence, from the *New York Times* leaks, to where the Commission was now on Friday the 14th, should be viewed as one organic chain of events, with the leaks being the catalyst. Rogers continued:

. . . Then you made a decision . . . to recommend against launch for this very reason, that you were concerned. And then Mr. McDonald, in describing what happened, said that Thiokol had notified NASA that they should in effect not launch in conditions that were not appropriate for launch, however you want to say it.

And then there was a phone call and he [Mulloy] said, the conclusion being that Thiokol was directed to reassess all the data because the recommendation was not considered acceptable, in that—he was a little unclear about what he said, but anyway the recommendation was not considered acceptable.

And then you were supposed to have a five minute phone call caucus, which lasted thirty minutes, and you changed your mind.

Now that, you know, it is hard to explain to an average outsider. You would think that that was one of the more critical things you can imagine in this program, and it had been so considered by NASA for a long time, and you obviously knew it.

What caused you to change your mind? Try to explain it. The impression is that you were directed to do it, that there was so much pressure to get this launch off that you were directed to do it, and you did it.

Now, if that is not the case, try to explain it in language that the public will understand why you changed your mind and how you did it so quickly?

Two points should be noted. One is that Rogers stated that "there was so much pressure to get this launch off." It implied that he did not know at this time that such pressure may have existed, whether from the White House or any other source. He also pointed to the remarkable speed of Thiokol's reversal of its no-launch recommendation.

Though Rogers did not know it, at one moment every single person from Thiokol who had an opinion recommended against launch. Thirty minutes later the company was for it.

This was unclear because Thiokol's managers had claimed the engineers were divided on whether to recommend against the launch. So Rogers swallowed the bait and asked:

> In the final telecom, did you or anybody from Thiokol let NASA know that the engineers were reasonably evenly split on whether to launch or not to launch?
>
> Mr. Mason: No, we did not.

Now astronaut Robert Crippen, part of NASA's investigating team, made a statement that would reverberate through the rest of the Commission's inquiry:

> Mr. Chairman, if I may make an observation. Since the earliest days of the manned space flight program that I've been associated with and Mr. Armstrong has been associated with, our basic philosophy is: "Prove to me that we're ready to fly." And somehow it seems in this particular instance we have switched around to: "Prove to me that we're

not ready to fly." I think that was a serious mistake on NASA's part, if that was the case.

Commission member Joseph Sutter now wanted to know why mission control officials from Houston were not involved in the teleconference. Stanley Reinartz immediately answered:

> Mr. Chairman, I might answer that directly. The item that was being considered was an SRB item, a Level III item. . . . We treated it as a Level III matter. It did not violate any of our—it did not require any waivers for our hardware and did not violate any launch commit criteria that we were made aware of by Thiokol. And on that basis, we did not bring in the Level II organization into that discussion.

Arnold Aldrich now spoke. He acknowledged that Houston, Level II, had concurred in the 1983 redundancy waiver for the O-ring, but:

> This meeting that we're discussing here, . . . where that was discussed as it pertains to the cold or the performance of the seal on the actual flight day of 51-L, is a meeting that was held only at Level III, as Stan just discussed. And not only the synopsis of the points considered in that meeting, but the fact that the meeting was held, was not known to myself or to the Level I organization, Jesse Moore, above it until subsequent to the event of the launch day.

The discussion now went back to why Marshall did not alert Arnold Aldrich, at Level II, and Jesse Moore, at Level I, of the engineers' concerns. Stanley Reinartz continued to argue that there was no requirement to do so once the matter was settled at Level III, which he was in charge of for the SRBs. Both Reinartz and Aldrich confirmed that such action was allowable under the launch rules and that no requirements or procedures were violated.

Neil Armstrong then expressed amazement that a vehicle designed to fly on winter mornings over twenty years was not able to handle conditions "down around freezing certainly if it is going to be operational in that category." Sally Ride concurred, and cited the von Braun-era NASA philosophy that "it is supposed to be 'prove to me that it works under these conditions.' " Of course, as Ride pointed out, there was "no data and no tests that indicate, that give you any confidence that the joint would be expected to operate at 31 degrees."

Chairman Rogers now called a recess and decided, with Alton Keel, the executive director of the Commission, to change the agenda for the rest of the day in order to give time for the Thiokol engineers to speak. First, one more Thiokol manager testified. This was Robert Lund, vice president for engineering. He was one of the four managers who voted to reverse the company's engineering recommendation and approve the launch.

During Lund's testimony there was a lot of technical discussion of how the O-ring joints behaved and the type of temperature testing done on O-ring resiliency which showed a rapid increase in hardness at seventy-five degrees and below. Dr. Richard Feynman said that hardness increases exponentially as temperature drops. "Temperature," he said, "has such enormous effects."

During the discussion, Lund indicated how concerned Thiokol had been about the O-ring problems, though, as Boisjoly's testimony and documents later showed, not nearly concerned enough. But Lund now said, "We have been working on this problem of this whole O-ring leakage scenario for some time." He also stated that as a result of the testing which had been done, "We concluded that at about fifty degrees F., blow-by could be experienced in those case joints." Lund also said that before the mid-teleconference caucus he opposed the launch, as did his staff engineers. No one asked him why he changed his mind.

But Thiokol was clearly on the spot. As Armstrong and others had indicated, NASA expected that they should be able to launch the shuttle down to thirty-one degrees F. James Beggs was planning to fly the shuttle twenty-four times a year. On the average, that would mean six winter launches.

It was time at last to hear from the real expert, Boisjoly. His few minutes of being questioned were enough to change everything. Boisjoly said he first heard of the cold temperatures at 1:00 p.m. on the 27th, after the Monday launch scrub. "So we spent the rest of the day raising the concerns about the effect of the cold on the O-rings." He said that he felt "successful" and "pleased" up until the early evening because the initial conclusion was not to fly. This was at the afternoon teleconference. But when the evening one began:

I was asked then on the net to support my position with data, and I couldn't support my position with data. I had been trying to get data since October on O-ring resiliency, and I did not have it in my hand.

He talked about the NASA pressure:

Listeners on the other line seemed not very pleased with the rec-ommendation. In fact, somebody asked Mr. Hardy what he thought about it, about our recommendation, and Mr. Hardy said he was appalled at MTI's decision. However, he would not go against our rec-ommendation not to fly. If the contractor recommended not to fly, he would not go against that. He would recommend not to fly also.

Boisjoly said that during the five-minute caucus that extended to thirty minutes, he and Arnie Thompson continued to argue against the launch, but gave up when it became clear that Thiokol's managers weren't listening. He said:

I basically had no direct input into the final recommendation, and I was not polled. I think Astronaut Crippen hit the tone of the meeting exactly right on the head when he said that the opposite was true of the way the meetings were normally conducted. We normally have to absolutely prove beyond a shadow of a doubt that we have the ability to fly, and it seemed like we were trying to prove . . . that we couldn't fly at this time, instead of the reverse.

Next, Arnie Thompson testified. He pointed out that with the 51-C launch at fifty-three degrees in January 1985, the blow-by in one O-ring seal covered an arc of 180 degrees—halfway around the circumference of the SRB. But Chairman Rogers was still trying to get at the consensus of engineers on the Challenger launch.

Chairman Rogers: Were there other engineers that would take issue with you on this matter, when it came to the launch question of whether to go or not to go? Did you have others who opposed your point of view?
Mr. Thompson: No, sir. I have twenty-four, twenty-five people, gals and guys, working for me, and I know none of them that would have

opposed this viewpoint that are involved in the case, the case/nozzle joints.

Chairman Rogers: All of these people would have said, "No," to the launch?

Mr. Thompson: My judgment is yes, that is true.

The hearing was near its end. Chairman Rogers still didn't understand why Thiokol's managers decided to approve the launch.

> Mr. Rogers: I mean, here you have a lot of warning, and you've all been discussing the O-rings and seals, and you've all had concerns, and it's all over the newspapers. All you have to do is look at it, as we have, and you can see that it's been a major concern. And now you have a situation where . . . a lot of your people expressed a negative vote, and our people in NASA don't even know about it. I mean, that is unbelievable to me. . . .
>
> Mr. Sutter: I just don't understand it. And I have listened for two hours and I still don't understand it. . . . It's sort of a hell of a way to run a railroad. . . .

The Commission saved the best for last. When Al McDonald had spoken up at the closed meeting on Monday the 10th, he had tiptoed around what had happened the night before launch. Not anymore.

McDonald had been Thiokol's senior representative at Kennedy. So far, Larry Mulloy had gotten off lightly, as the Thiokol engineers explained their perception of the pressure NASA was applying to get them to back off their recommendation. But at Kennedy, McDonald and Mulloy had been sitting together as the pre-launch teleconference proceeded. McDonald now said:

> Besides the comment being made that NASA was appalled by our recommendation, but they said they wouldn't fly without our concurrence, Larry Mulloy jumped in and said you guys are trying to establish new launch commit criteria, and you can't do that on the spur of the moment.

McDonald now talked about his understanding that the solid rocket motor was qualified to launch only from forty to ninety degrees F. and that the predicted launch temperature would be below that. Mulloy said the forty to ninety degrees was the mean bulk temperature of the propellant in the SRB. McDonald said he didn't believe that, because it was clear that the flight range for the filament wound case was clearly forty to ninety degrees atmospheric temperature and that it had to be the same for the SRBs. McDonald said:

> I made the statement that if we're wrong and something goes wrong on this flight, I wouldn't want to have to be the person to stand up in front of a board of inquiry and say that I went ahead and told them to go ahead and fly this thing outside what the motor was qualified to.

The night before the disaster, McDonald now said, he had not been satisfied when Thiokol came back on the intercom and reversed themselves with a recommendation to launch. He said he asked NASA for "one more reconsideration." He said the original launch schedule called for a launch at 3:45 in the afternoon of January 28.

McDonald did not speculate on why the time had been changed to the morning, though today we might ask whether the launch was moved back to 9:38 a.m. in order to have the astronauts settled when President Reagan gave his State of the Union address that night. Still, McDonald wondered why couldn't they wait for at least a few more hours.

McDonald then said to Mulloy that if what the Thiokol engineers said about the O-rings was not enough to stop the launch, there were two other good reasons: high seas in the booster recovery area would prevent the recovery ships from reaching the designated area with the possible loss of a substantial amount of hardware, and the ice all around the launch area could damage the orbiter.

Mulloy answered. According to McDonald:

> I was told that, you know, these are not your concerns. And I said, well, I am concerned about all of these, and I think those combined should be absolute criteria not to launch the thing because if I were the launch director, I wouldn't do it. That is what I told them.
>
> Well, I was waiting for the fax to come back [from Thiokol in Utah] because when the final recommendation was made by Thiokol to fly, they were told to put that in writing. I told Mr. Mulloy I wouldn't sign

that, it would have to come from the plant, because normally I am responsible for telling whether the flight goes or not.

So McDonald refused to approve the launch. Mulloy now told McDonald to go fetch the Thiokol fax when it came in, so McDonald left the room to walk to the other end of the building where the fax machine was. When he came back with the fax, Mulloy was sitting at a speaker phone talking to Arnold Aldrich, who was elsewhere in the Kennedy complex. Mulloy was telling Aldrich that because of the high seas they would likely lose some SRB equipment, but that they still would have enough on hand to support future flights. Aldrich said okay, but don't risk the SRB recovery ships by sending them into danger. It was extraordinary and showed extraordinary urgency to launch that Aldrich was prepared to lose two complete SRBs at a cost of $22 million.

Next, McDonald heard Mulloy and Aldrich discussing the issue of ice on the tower. He said, "I heard some comment basically that that was considered earlier and discussed." Then McDonald told the Commission:

> But I didn't hear anything about the O-ring discussion, and I presumed that the discussion happened while I was down at the fax machine, waiting for the fax to come in.

Now Aldrich jumped in. He said there had been a phone call to him about the "status of the launch facility with respect to the temperatures [i.e., ice]" and about the recovery ships. He said, "That was the total content of that discussion." He added that later on he determined that the seas had subsided and that the recovery ships would be in the proper position.

This was one of the critical moments of the Presidential Commission's investigation. What did Aldrich, at Level II, know about the O-ring teleconference? McDonald assumed he had to know, because he heard two issues that he considered less critical being discussed. And if Aldrich knew, then the question would be, what did he tell Jesse Moore at Level I?

So what did Chairman Rogers do?

I would like us, if there is no objection, I would like to recess the meeting now, and I think the Commission should consider the testimony that we have heard this morning very carefully and then decide our next step. We will be in touch with you as we make some decisions.

Alton Keel had one last question for Alan McDonald:

Mr. Keel: The inference, Mr. McDonald, from your testimony is that you were under pressure, perhaps unusual pressure, from NASA officials, to go ahead with the launch. Is that an accurate inference?

Mr. McDonald: That is an accurate inference, yes.

Chairman Rogers: And did I understand, too, that you did not sign off on this one?

Mr. McDonald: No, I did not.

Chairman Rogers: Was that unusual?

Mr. McDonald: I believe it was, yes.

Sources told the press that Chairman William Rogers was "appalled" by what he heard from Thiokol's engineers on Friday, February 14. It was clear, an unnamed Commission member said, that what happened the night of January 27 "did not conform to any previous NASA flight procedures."

The Commission now faced a crisis. Obviously, NASA had made a serious mistake, the depth and implications of which the Commission had only begun to fathom. Just as obvious was the fact that NASA's team investigating the disaster had not leveled with them about how vigorously the Thiokol engineers, including Alan McDonald, had opposed the launch, and how much pressure NASA had applied to get company management to overrule them.

Until now, Rogers had been NASA management's foremost apologist. He had advised them on what to say in hearings, tried to help them manage the release of information to the public, gone easy on them while they were being questioned. His experience showed him, and he had said so to Jesse Moore and the rest, that sooner or later, everything that happened would become public. Now it was clear that NASA was going to sink like a stone. Facing the Commission was the question of whether it would continue to front for the NASA management team and go down with them.

At the end of the hearing on the 14th, Rogers sent the NASA and Thiokol witnesses out of the conference room and conducted his own private caucus with Commission members. No account was published, but afterwards, Rogers said he phoned President Reagan to tell him there was a problem. No doubt Donald Regan would have been involved in this call as well.

The next day, Saturday, February 15, the Commission announced that:

> In recent days, the Commission has been investigating all aspects of the decision making process leading up to the launch of the Challenger and has found that the process may have been flawed. The president has been so informed.
>
> Dr. William Graham, acting administrator of NASA, has been asked not to include on the internal investigation teams at NASA persons involved in that process.
>
> The Commission will, of course, continue its investigation and will make a full report to the president within 120 days.

Thus NASA's investigating board lasted seventeen astounding days. I believe that indications show that the board intended to impound and conceal all documents pertaining to the history of the O-rings seals. This was strongly suggested by the fact that Irv Davids told me not to let his memo get to William Graham. If the board was going to conceal documents from Graham, it surely would have concealed them from the press and the public. Also, I believe that the board may also have intended to conceal the fact of the pre-launch teleconference and the opposition of the Thiokol engineers. Even with the Presidential Commission, it took the persistence of Alan McDonald in raising the matter, along with the fact that Boisjoly, Thompson, and McDonald courageously defied the gag order of Thiokol attorneys to get the facts of the teleconference aired in a closed Commission meeting.

I believe that my leaks to the *New York Times* may have been what really led to the cascading revelations before the Commission on February 14. Without these leaks, the history of the Challenger investigations and aftermath would have been very different.

The question that now faced the Commission was why did NASA do what they did? It was clear enough at this point that Thiokol could be faulted for failing to deliver a product that could operate during a year-round schedule of flights that would include some winter launches. But it was also clear that NASA and Thiokol together were flying a dangerous SRB system that should have been repaired. When the crunch came, the Thiokol engineers said "don't fly" at a time when a delay of a few days or even a few hours could have made the difference in the margin of safety. Why then did NASA pressure them to go ahead?

"THE TOOTH FAIRY"

—The World Hears the Thiokol Engineers' Story

ON MONDAY, FEBRUARY 17, 1986, I reported to work at the Financial Management Service, U.S. Department of the Treasury, at the Treasury Annex building on the corner of Pennsylvania and East Executive Avenues. The front door of the Annex faced Lafayette Park, which lay across Pennsylvania Avenue from the White House.

I was wondering if anyone at Treasury would be aware of who I was, and it didn't take long to find out. My new supervisor was angry. After sending me to the personnel office for completion of the required paperwork to bring me on-board, he took me to an office that I would share with another analyst who was not there at the moment.

He had a scowl on his face from the moment I first saw him. When I set my briefcase down on the desk and took off my suit jacket, he asked "Are you a professional whistleblower?"

"No," I said.

I had already started to realize that where I now would be working was buried so deeply within the bowels of the federal bureaucracy that there was nothing to blow the whistle on and no one to blow it to. Very few people had ever heard of the Financial Management Service, though if you got a federal check or a direct deposit, they were the ones who sent it to you.

"We have to go talk to public affairs," the supervisor said. "I'll be back in a few minutes."

He left, returned shortly, and took me to a conference room on the same floor. There was a woman from the agency and a short man with a mustache, gray hair, and suspenders who was from what was called "Main Treasury"; i.e., departmental headquarters. He introduced himself as Andy. Also sitting at the table was my division director. Finally, there was a woman named Christine. She was a senior specialist on the staff, had been one of those who interviewed me for the job, and became a good friend over the years.

"You're pretty well known," said Andy, who said he worked in the department's public affairs office. He introduced the woman as Suzy, who was from the Office of Legislative and Public Affairs for the Financial Management Service.

"I suppose so," I said.

The only one who seemed perturbed was my supervisor. The rest seemed not at all hostile.

Andy continued. "We're getting all kinds of press calls for you. I've never seen anything like it."

"Well, I can't help it," I said.

After a pause, Andy said, "What do you want us to do with all these?" He held out a handful of message notes from the news media.

I thought about it for a moment. No use giving these people a hard time, and it looked like Andy wasn't out to get me fired.

"Why don't you just give them to me, and I'll answer them on my own time."

"Okay by me," said Andy. "Anyone have a problem with that?" He looked around the table.

The woman from the bureau's public affairs office, Suzy, shook her head. "I don't mind," she said.

"I'm okay with it," said the division director.

"It'll be okay, Dan," Christine said to my supervisor as he sat there steaming. I guess he was hoping someone would try get rid of me.

"I assume you came here to work?" Andy said, closing out the discussion.

"Yes, sir," I said, as we all stood up. I shook hands with him, Suzy, and the division director as they turned to leave the room.

"Good luck to you," Andy said with a chuckle on the way out.

Suzy said, nodding toward Andy, "He's worked here a long time."

That left Christine, our supervisor, and me in the room. I tried to think of something to say. "I bet they have a pretty good library here at Treasury," I said.

"I don't know what you'd want with that," said the supervisor, walking out the door.

Christine stood and smiled. "Did NASA try to do anything to you?" she asked.

"No, but they tried to make me look bad in the press."

"They're not going to try to shoot you, are they?" she laughed.

I laughed too. "No, I don't think they'd do that."

"Don't mind Dan," she said. "He's got another job. He'll be leaving soon."

She was right. In a few weeks Dan, the supervisor, was gone. Later in the day, Christine came around with some government regulations on federal disbursing for me to read. It was nice to see a friendly face at work for a change. I felt that things here would probably work out.

The fact that they sent Andy, a man from Treasury headquarters, to meet with me showed that the political levels within the department and perhaps the White House would be keeping an eye on me. But a decision had evidently been made that they would leave me alone if I behaved myself. Still, I did not give up my involvement in the Challenger aftermath.

———

WITH PRESS REPORTS swirling in reaction to the Commission's announcement of a possibly flawed launch process, Chairman Rogers, Vice Chairman Armstrong, and NASA officials William Graham and Jesse Moore appeared on Capitol Hill for a hearing on Tuesday, February 18, before the Senate Subcommittee on Science, Technology, and Space. This was the first time since the disaster that Congress had convened to review what was going on with the investigation. The space subcommittee, chaired by Senator Slade Gorton (R-WA), was part of the Senate Committee on Commerce and Transportation, chaired by Senator John Danforth (R-MO). The ranking Democratic member was Senator Ernest Hollings (D-SC), who had been asking for Senate hearings almost since the accident.

The night before the Senate hearing, I wrote a letter to Chairman Rogers, and on the morning of the 18th, took the metro to Capitol Hill to deliver it. Once inside the Russell Senate Office Building, I gave the letter to a Senate committee staff member who said she would give it to Rogers.

I was not aware that the previous Thursday and Friday the Commission, in its meeting behind closed doors, had delved further into the history of the disaster. In the letter, I suggested to Rogers that the Commission interview the engineers at Marshall's Science and Engineering Lab who brought the O-ring problem to the attention of headquarters as early as 1984, as well as the Thiokol engineers who may have recommended that flights be suspended until the O-rings were fixed. At this point, I still had never heard of Roger Boisjoly.

My letter also discussed some of the NASA/Thiokol documents that were released after the February 11 hearing and suggested that the Commission investigate the possible effects of cold weather on the joint putty, as well as on the O-rings, which it later did; whether the field joints had been properly assembled and leak-tested prior to the 51-L launch, which it also did; and whether the Centaur schedule that had been discussed at KSC on January 16-17 contributed to the urgency to launch Challenger. I attached the Manifest Bingo charts, though I later concluded that this was not a factor in the Challenger launch and said so to Commission investigators.

When I delivered the letter to the Senate hearing room, the place was swarming with dozens of newsmen and TV cameramen. The atmosphere was one of pandemonium, with crowds of people trying to get in as spectators and uniformed police trying to control the foot traffic. Some of the news people recognized me and came over to talk. One of them asked me on camera if I felt "vindicated" by news leaks that NASA overrode engineers' safety warnings in order to launch. "I knew I was right," I replied. "I didn't need to be vindicated."

As the hearing got underway, Chairman Rogers said he was certain that "we're going to be able to determine what happened." He said that the right-hand solid rocket booster "appears to be the area where the trouble started," but that it would be a "mistake to focus all attention" on it. He said that NASA faced an "unpleasant" period of public scrutiny, though he was not questioning "the trustworthiness or integrity of the people involved." Finally, he said he was reluctant to draw conclusions. He said:

> Our intensive review to date had indicated that the decision making process may have been flawed. We have not said that the decision was flawed. We have said that the process may have been flawed, and we base that on testimony taken in executive session.

Rogers had the following exchange with Senator Albert Gore Jr. (D-TN):

> Senator Gore: Has the Commission uncovered a lack of regard for flight safety in the procedures followed by NASA?
>
> Chairman Rogers: I don't re—what's the question?
>
> Senator Gore: Has the Commission uncovered a lack of regard for flight safety?
>
> Chairman Rogers: Well, well, senator, we are not going to make any conclusion of that kind now. We have just been in operation for twelve days, and I think it's unfair to keep asking us to draw that kind of conclusion.

Gore pressed the issue by asking whether there was arguing the night before the launch. But Rogers refused to answer:

> Chairman Rogers: I don't want to get involved in those types of speculative questions. At the moment, I'm not going to answer any of those questions.

Senator Hollings then said that it was "an avoidable rather than an unavoidable accident." Hollings asked William Graham about the press accounts of the Thiokol opposition to launch and whether there was any evidence to support the report that engineers strongly or unanimously recommended against launch because of low temperatures on the SRB O-ring seals.

Graham said he could not give a "simple yes-or-no," because "quite a number of officials were involved." But he concluded that, "No, senator, the evidence is in the other direction." A few days later, Hollings said he had been deceived and called for Graham's resignation.

The following exchange took place among Rogers, Armstrong, and the subcommittee chairman, Senator Slade Gorton:

> Senator Gorton: You have concluded that there was a failure in one of those seals but not whether that was the first failure?
>
> Vice Chairman Armstrong: I have not concluded there was a failure in the seals.
>
> Senator Gorton: I gather that you are seriously investigating the effect of the extreme cold temperatures. That it is at least a suspect in having played a major role?
>
> Chairman Rogers: One of our members [Dr. Richard Feynman] is at Kennedy trying to get precise details about the weather. It's not as easy as you think to find out precisely what the weather conditions were. All the facts will be made fully public.

Jesse Moore then testified that top NASA officials had not been informed of unusually low temperature readings from the right solid rocket booster during the hours before lift-off. Moore admitted to Senator Gore, "There were discussions at Thiokol, discussions between Thiokol and the Marshall Space Flight Center." All he said about the teleconference was, "In the final analysis, the Thiokol management signed-off on a recommendation to launch."

The Senate hearing ended without Rogers giving any indication of when and how more information would become available. To the Thiokol engineers who testified on Friday, it must have been frustrating to see Rogers and the others gloss over the critical issues. After all, Boisjoly, Thompson, and McDonald had defied company orders and risked their careers by disclosing to the Commission the facts of what had happened the night before the disaster. Now, William Graham had even gone so far as to tell the senators that "the evidence is in the other direction." Was this a betrayal?

The next morning, Wednesday the 19th, saw another front-page *New York Times* article that made NASA and the Commission look like they had much to hide. This was an interview with Alan McDonald, who spoke from his home in Utah to reporter David Sanger. The story began:

The top Morton Thiokol engineer present at the Kennedy Space Center before the January 28 lift-off of the space shuttle Challenger said tonight that he had argued for hours with space agency officials not to launch the craft because of low temperatures.

He said that he persisted even after his own superiors had overruled him and given the agency a go-ahead.

McDonald said that he argued primarily with Larry Mulloy. He said that:

> The low temperatures make the O-ring seals much harder, stiffer, and it caused them to shrink. It is hard to quantify, but qualitatively that is what happened.

Again, an insider speaking to the press had torpedoed what still amounted to a cover-up. Again the Commission tried to counter the disclosure, this time by announcing later that day that "at least three key NASA officials" were not informed prior to lift-off of the engineers' objections to the cold-weather launch. So the Commission did not deny McDonald's account but tried to shield the higher-ups from being incriminated.

The next morning, at a press conference at NASA, Jesse Moore said that he was one of those who had not been informed. In another newspaper article, Commission member Robert Hotz claimed that Jesse Moore and other managers did not learn of the engineers' opposition until the Commission's February 14th closed meeting. Hotz said, "They were there at the dramatic moment when we all found out."

But the statement by Moore seems puzzling to me in light of the fact that Paul Herr told me that he and other headquarters engineers were phoned from Kennedy the night of the explosion and were told two contractors recommended against the launch. These engineers were on Jesse Moore's staff. Is it likely that they had been told at this early date if Moore had not known? I felt strongly at the time that the Commission was bending over backwards to portray Moore, and possibly Aldrich, as less well-informed than I thought they were—that perhaps they were being protected and the blame pushed down the management chain. This sense that the Commission may have been shielding the top brass grew in my mind in the days and weeks to follow.

Moore was now to leave Washington ahead of schedule to report as director of the Johnson Space Center in Houston. On Thursday, February 20, William Graham replaced Moore as associate administrator for space flight with Navy Rear Admiral Richard Truly, one of NASA's most experienced astronauts. Most recently, Truly had headed the Naval Space Command at the Naval Surface Weapons Center in Dahlgren, Virginia, where he managed the Navy's program of communication satellites. Truly would take over NASA's Challenger investigation, now called the design and data analysis task force.

At NASA, the few officials who would talk to the press continued to focus attention on Thiokol by emphasizing that the company had signed off on the launch. There was no mention of the fact that never in manned space flight history had a last-minute written recommendation been required of a contractor. On Friday, February 21, William Graham produced a copy of the telefax signed by Thiokol Vice President Joe Kilminster. The fax concluded that, even though the O-rings would be harder and take longer to seat, "MTI recommends STS 51-L launch proceed on 28 January 1986." But on the 22nd, the *Washington Post* reported that, "One Thiokol manager told the magazine *Science* that his management caved in because they felt 'a lot of pressure from our biggest client.'"

Now National Public Radio got in on the leak business. NPR reported on February 20 that the night before launch, Larry Mulloy had reacted to the cold weather warnings of the Thiokol engineers by exclaiming, "My God, Thiokol, when do you want me to launch, next April?" This was a detail the Commission had not yet heard.

NPR also reported on a detail the Commission had known about but had not disclosed publicly—that George Hardy, Marshall's deputy director of science and engineering had said, "I am appalled by your recommendation" not to launch. Finally, NPR broadcast another interview with Alan McDonald, who described in more detail how NASA had argued against the Thiokol engineers' no-launch position.

By the end of the week of February 17-21, the Commission was losing control of the public agenda. Commission members themselves seemed to be leaking, and Al McDonald was speaking openly whenever the media phoned him. What, then, was the Commission going to do?

By now, some of the Commission members had dispersed on their own official fact-finding trips. As William Rogers had told the Senate,

Feynman had stayed in Florida to find out more about weather factors. General Donald Kutyna had flown to Huntsville, Alabama, to continue the meetings with Roger Boisjoly, Arnie Thompson, and others from Thiokol. Boisjoly gave this description of the encounter:

> During this meeting, I handed a packet of memos and activity reports to a Commission member [Kutyna] as a response to one of his questions, and this action upset our company attorney. I sensed quite clearly from this time on that I had not endeared myself with MTI management, since my memos would clarify the true circumstances leading to the disaster and would also counteract both NASA and MTI managements' attempt to discredit our testimony up to that point. I thought it was unconscionable that MTI and NASA management wouldn't tell the whole truth so that the program could go forward with the proper corrective measures.

The memos Boisjoly was referring to were written by him during the latter part of 1985, expressing frustration that the task force to investigate and redesign the SRB seals was meeting with bureaucratic delays and had little management support. Probably the best example was a memo he wrote on July 31, 1985, eight days after I wrote my own July 23 warning memo at NASA headquarters. The memo was addressed to Robert Lund, vice president for engineering:

> This letter is written to insure that management is fully aware of the seriousness of the current O-ring erosion problem in the SRM joints from an engineering standpoint.
> The mistakenly accepted position on the joint problem was to fly without fear of failure and to run a series of design evaluations which would ultimately lead to a solution or at least a significant reduction of the erosion problem. This position is now drastically changed as a result of the SRM 16A nozzle joint erosion which eroded a secondary O-ring with the primary O-ring never sealing.
> If the same scenario should occur in a field joint (and it could), then it is a jump ball as to the success or failure of the joint, because the secondary O-ring cannot respond to the clevis opening rate and may not be capable of pressurization. The result would be a catastrophe of the highest order—loss of human life.

An unofficial team . . . with a leader was formed on 19 July 1985 and was tasked with solving the problem for both the short and long term. The unofficial team is essentially non-existent at this time. In my opinion, the team must be officially given the responsibility and the authority to execute the work that needs to be done on a non-interference basis (full-time assignment until completed).

It is my honest and very real fear that if we do not take immediate action to dedicate a team to solve the problem, with the field joint having the number one priority, then we stand in jeopardy of losing a flight along with all the launch pad facilities.

Even the language was similar. I used the word "catastrophic"; Boisjoly wrote "catastrophe."

The situation now tumbled further out of control when McDonald, responding to a request from several senators on the space subcommittee, flew to Washington, D.C., for what he thought would be a private meeting. The press had been alerted to his arrival, and when he reached the Capitol building, Senator Hollings wanted him to appear immediately on television to tell his story. Instead, McDonald slipped into a small Senate conference room, locked the door, sat down, and refused to come out. The situation had become almost comical. Several senators, including Hollings, phoned McDonald in the room and asked him what he wanted.

While this was going on, Senator Gorton, the space subcommittee chairman, phoned William Rogers and told him that the Commission had to allow McDonald to tell his story publicly. Rogers acquiesced. McDonald now said he wanted to go home, and he returned to Utah on a Thiokol company jet.

Since Hollings was unable to get information out of the Commission, he now demanded, along with Democratic Senators Riegle and Gore, another Senate hearing to question William Graham and Marshall's managers. Commerce Committee Chairman John Danforth then accused the Senate Democrats of "grandstanding" and "premature NASA-bashing."

Senator Gorton said that more hearings would create a "race rather than a sober investigation into the facts." But it was clear that the Presidential Commission and NASA were spared an immediate Senate investigation only by the fact that the Senate was under Republican control. The White House press office went so far as to accuse Hollings of trying to use Challenger to further his 1986 reelection campaign.

In the House of Representatives, the Democrats had the majority, but the space agenda was controlled by two vehemently pro-NASA Florida congressmen. One was Donald Fuqua, chairman of the House Science and Technology Committee, and the other was shuttle politician-in-space Bill Nelson, chairman of the House Space Subcommittee. Both said they would allow the Commission to finish its work before stepping in.

The lone voice in the House calling for immediate action was Representative Edward Markey (D-MA), chairman of the House Energy and Commerce Subcommittee, with jurisdiction over the radioisotope thermonuclear generators to be flown on the May 1986 Centaur missions. Quoted in the February 12 *Washington Post*, Markey said:

> There's been a systematic pattern of confusion, misstatements, and obfuscation by NASA. Whether there is a cover-up or plain, outright incompetence is impossible to determine, but that is the question. The credibility of the agency is now in question. We need the same kind of inquiries that were made after Watergate and Three Mile Island. That means by the executive branch and both the House and Senate.

Suddenly, everyone who had been closely following the events of the last four weeks was riveted by word going around Washington that NASA had launched Challenger in response to White House pressure in connection with President Reagan's State of the Union address, scheduled for the night of the lift-off. On Sunday, February 23, *New York Times* reporter Steven Roberts wrote, "Did the agency feel pressure to launch the vehicle with Mrs. McAuliffe aboard before President Reagan gave his State of the Union address that evening?"

The rumor had two parts: a) that as part of the State of the Union address, President Reagan had planned to introduce Christa McAuliffe and talk to her by phone. Simultaneously, TV coverage would show a split picture of Reagan with McAuliffe and the other Challenger astronauts; and b) reacting to the delays in the launch, Chief of Staff Donald Regan had ordered his aides to "tell them to get that thing up."

No good explanation had yet been given of why Thiokol had been pressured to approve the launch. It was Monday, February 24, when Christine Dolan, political director of CNN, phoned me at work at Treasury and asked, "Have you heard what they're saying? Is it plausible?"

I said, "Yes, it's plausible. There has to be a reason NASA made Thiokol change its mind."

But no news source had enough information to challenge the denials that were coming out of the White House. Despite some digging, most of the White House press corps had been unable to find anyone in the administration who would discuss the topic.

The exception was CNN. Dolan now told me that CNN had heard about phone calls between NASA and the White House prior to the launch. CNN had been told by Richard Davis, deputy cabinet secretary to Albert Kingon, that NASA had requested a phone call from the president to Challenger. Kingon was a former aide to Donald Regan when Regan had been Treasury secretary and was William Graham's contact on input NASA was said to have prepared on the State of the Union address.

Later, CNN reporter John Holliman told me that they had heard from White House sources that there was truth to Davis's statement, but that these corroborations were not specific enough to constitute the second source CNN needed to broadcast the story.

Now, three days of public hearings had been announced by the Commission. They took place back at the Dean Acheson Auditorium at the State Department on February 25, 26, and 27.

We can only speculate how the Commission made its decisions on how to handle these events. There would have been meetings on what to do, but not necessarily of the Commission itself. The meetings would have involved at least William Rogers and Donald Regan, White House chief of staff.

One time-honored method of managing a government crisis is to create a scapegoat. If the scapegoat is too highly placed, it could become embarrassing if he is hauled into court, sworn in, and forced to testify.

I can't prove this is how it happened. But it's how I think it had to happen. Dr. Mark Maier of Chapman University in Orange, CA., is one of the world's leading academic experts on Challenger. In an article for

Journal of Management Inquiry, Maier recounted a conversation he had with Leland Dribin, aerospace counsel for Thiokol. Dribin told him that the night before the start of the February 25-27 open hearings:

> Chairman Rogers summoned the contractor lawyers to his hotel room that evening and blandly asserted, "I have an American hero in Alan McDonald," adding, "I'm not interested in anything but making a public scapegoat out of Larry Mulloy and Thiokol management. This will be a public performance."

Evidently Rogers' plan was to let McDonald, along with Boisjoly and Arnie Thompson, talk as long as they wanted and get as much publicity as the press was willing to give them. Why?

Rogers was creating and elaborating a theory of the disaster. This theory was that flawed men—Mulloy and the rest from Marshall, plus the Thiokol managers—overruled the good and brave contractor engineers, and so blew up Challenger, while meanwhile the NASA higher-ups, specifically Jesse Moore and Arnold Aldrich, went about their launch routines in ignorance of what was percolating down below.

The issue would not be broached of why Mulloy did what he did or what pressures he was under. It was, simply, that he had failed. And there was likely a degree of truth to Rogers's theory, which is what made it so powerful.

By now, the real issue, of course, was, did the White House pressure NASA to launch? Was that where the pressure was coming from? It was that question that Rogers seemed determined to defuse.

Rogers likely felt safe in letting McDonald go public, because he was certain that no one from NASA told anyone in Thiokol where the pressure was coming from. Thiokol indeed felt pressure, but never knew why. There were no off-line comments or phone calls that let anyone from Thiokol in on whatever secrets were being preserved, or if there were, that information was reliably suppressed.

Rogers also likely felt certain that no one from NASA would spill the beans if there had been White House pressure. Such pressure would have come through William Graham. Obviously he was safe. Graham would never be called to testify. Moore and Aldrich had already shown through their behavior during the open and closed meetings that they were discrete. Rogers had no interest in having Moore and Aldrich, and probably even the Marshall managers, say anything in a closed or open session that could land them in court, either as defendants in a civil suit, or to face criminal charges. If that happened, circumstances could quickly get out of control if the defendants tried to save their own skins by fingering the political brass.

Despite Chairman Rogers's manipulation, some new information did come out in the February 25-27 hearings. To start the inquiry, which CNN carried live, Rogers gave a broad-ranging introduction. Before, press disclosures were "unpleasant, unfortunate." Now, the media would be praised:

> The media plays a key role in the process by keeping the public informed. We believe it has performed this role well and with a high sense of responsibility. If the Commission effectively performs its duties and the media performs its role of accurately reporting the facts as they develop, the public will be well-served.

Alan McDonald was the first to testify. After interminable questions and answers—one of which involved the location of the Marshall Space Flight Center (McDonald answered correctly that "Marshall is located in Huntsville, Alabama.")—McDonald finally got to the topic at hand. He said that he got a call the afternoon of January 27 from Bob Ebeling, a Thiokol manager in Utah who had been alerted by NASA officials at Marshall of the predicted low temperatures that night and the next day in Florida. Ebeling asked McDonald for data on the forecast, which McDonald and Carver Kennedy, another Thiokol manager at KSC, provided. They told Ebeling that the low temperature would be around twenty-two degrees F. at six a.m. and twenty-six degrees at the intended launch time of 9:38 a.m. McDonald said:

> I took that data and called back to the plant and sent it to Bob Ebeling and relayed that to him, and told him he ought to use this temperature data for his predictions, and that I thought this was very serious and to make sure that he had the vice president for engineering [Bob Lund] involved in this and all his people; that I wanted them to put together some calculations and a presentation of material.

McDonald also said that he told Ebeling, "This decision should be an engineering decision, not a program management decision." He did not define a "program management decision," though it must have had some questionable connotations for him. He also said he wanted a "recommended launch temperature," not just a go/no-go recommendation.

McDonald wanted the Thiokol presentation to be ready for a teleconference at 8:15 that evening. He did not mention in his testimony that there had already been a teleconference that afternoon that he did not participate in. The Commission had already heard that it was after the earlier teleconference that Judson Lovingood of Marshall told his boss Stanley Reinartz that it looked like a launch delay.

McDonald said that during the teleconference he had been in the same room at Kennedy as Larry Mulloy and Stanley Reinartz from Marshall, as well as Cecil Houston, Marshall's resident manager at Kennedy, and Jack Buchanan, Thiokol's counterpart to Houston.

McDonald then talked about the recommendation against launching below fifty-three degrees presented by Bob Lund, and George Hardy's statement that he was appalled but "wouldn't fly without Thiokol's concurrence." McDonald said that the temperature recommendations "brought a lot of strong comments and reaction from NASA."

But he now introduced a striking new element that had not come up during the closed meeting of the Commission on February 14th, one that no one asked him about, and that never appeared in the news or the Commission's report. He said:

> And other comments were made about whether we could ever fly out of Vandenberg twenty-four flights a year, because it wasn't uncommon to have fifty-three degrees in the early morning hours where a lot of launches occur.

McDonald had broached the enormously significant topic of flight schedule pressure coming from NASA's commitment to fly military missions for the Department of Defense. Later I learned that this had been why Larry Mulloy had told Thiokol engineers after the Level III flight readiness review for flight 51-E a year earlier that he didn't want a launch commit criterion for O-ring temperatures. Now McDonald had brought it up as a factor in the pre-launch pressure applied by

NASA on Thiokol's management before the Challenger disaster. Remarkably, no one else now said a word about it.

McDonald said he had been told to make his evaluation on the basis of a 9:38 launch, with a predicted temperature of twenty-six degrees F. He repeated a point he had made in closed session on the 14th, that he had suggested a launch later that afternoon. He was concerned about the low temperatures. He was told that that option had been considered but rejected "because of some problem either with visibility or weather at one of the trans-Atlantic abort sites. I think it was Dakar or Casablanca, one of those."

Of course, if NASA were trying to get Challenger into orbit in time for the astronauts to be settled before the president's State of the Union address, the earlier in the day the launch took place the better. The Commission made no attempt to verify what McDonald said he was told about visibility or weather at Dakar or Casablanca.

McDonald reiterated that he was "absolutely" surprised NASA would launch below forty degrees. He also repeated overhearing the phone conversation between Mulloy and Aldrich and assuming the O-rings had been discussed. He said he was "absolutely positive and sure" it would have been discussed at the next management levels. He added, "The issue is so controversial I thought that I'm sure that they were aware of it. I have a hard time believing they didn't."

Chairman Rogers then asked McDonald whether he felt NASA was pressuring Thiokol to change its recommendation.

Chairman Rogers: One other question. Dr. Keel asked at the conclusion of your testimony in executive session whether you felt that you were under pressure or had been under pressure or the company had been under pressure to reverse its decision, and I think your answer was yes. Do you remember that?

Mr. McDonald: Yes, definitely. There was no doubt in my mind I felt some pressure. I feel that I have a responsible management position, and I felt pressure.

Chairman Rogers: Would you explain the reasons for feeling pressure?

Mr. McDonald: Well, I have been in many flight readiness reviews, probably as many as anyone, in the past year and a half at Thiokol, and I have had to get up and stand before, I think, a very critical audience at Marshall, and a very good one, justifying why our hardware was ready to fly. I have to get up and explain every major defect and why we can fly with that defect.

And for the most part they are very minor, very, very minor. And I have been hassled about how I'm sure that that is okay to fly with. You know, such things as losing vacuum in carbon cloth in the nozzle while the part's basically cured. It is a critical process.

There are a lot of those critical processes, and I have to address every one of those in great detail as to why I am sure that that part has not been compromised. And it has been that way through all of the reviews I've ever had, and that is the way it should be. And it is not pleasant, but that is the way it should be.

And I was surprised here at this particular meeting that the tone of the meeting was just the opposite of that. I didn't have to prove that I was ready to fly. In fact, I think Bob Crippen made the most accurate statement I ever heard. His conclusion from that meeting was the philosophy seemed to have changed, because he had the same impression I did, that the contractor always had to get up and stand up and prove that his hardware was safe to fly. In this case, we had to prove that it wasn't, and that is a big difference. I felt that was pressure.

Chairman Rogers: And can you explain a little more what source the pressure came from in your mind?

Mr. McDonald: Well, I think the strong statements were made by Mr. Mulloy, and even some of those, the people at Marshall that were on there—Mr. Hardy—were I think fairly strong statements that I took as pressure about when we will ever fly this thing and the launch commit criteria that we can't generate at the last minute, and appalled by our recommendation to fly at temperatures as high as fifty-three degrees. And that, to me, that was pressure to me. It may not have been interpreted by others, but it was pressure to me.

Perhaps the key issue of the entire investigation was why did NASA's managers apply that pressure to get Thiokol to change their minds. But in its report, the Commission never said one word to answer that question. All it said was:

The Commission concluded that the Thiokol management reversed its position and recommended the launch of 51-L, at the urging of Marshall and contrary to the views of its engineers in order to accommodate a major customer.

This statement trivialized the issue into a business relationship—"a major customer." But it was not as a "customer" NASA was pressuring Thiokol that night.

Roger Boisjoly's testimony on February 25 also tracked closely to what he had told the Commission behind closed doors at Kennedy on February 14. He made a point of how much the 51-C cold-weather launch in January 1985 escalated concerns about the O-rings. Boisjoly said:

> SRM-15 actually increased that concern because that was the first time we had actually penetrated a primary O-ring on a field joint with hot gas, and we had a witness of that event, because the grease between the O-rings was blackened just like coal for those arc lengths that were described in the charts, and that was so much more significant than had ever been seen before on any blow-by on any joint.

Later in the hearing, Thiokol engineer Arnie Thompson referred to this instance of O-ring erosion and blow-by as "disastrous," even though it did not cause a shuttle explosion at that time.

Chairman Rogers asked Boisjoly to recite the details of the teleconference the night before the launch. Boisjoly said, "I expressed deep concern about launching at low temperature." His concern was:

> We would have higher O-ring actuation time, in my opinion, and that is what I presented. It was action time—and these are the two [charts]. They are the sum and substance of what I just presented. If action time increases, then the threshold of secondary seal pressurization capability is approached. That was my fear. If the threshold is reached, then the secondary seal may not be capable of being pressurized, and that was the bottom line of everything that had been presented up to that point.

By mentioning the "threshold of secondary seal pressurization," Boisjoly was referring to the loss of redundancy cited in the 1982–1983 waiver, again showing the importance of the "Death Document," as revealed to the Commission and the public through my February 9 news leaks. Boisjoly also forcefully took issue with statements by Thiokol managers that the engineers were divided in their opinion on whether to launch:

> There was never one positive, pro-launch statement ever made by anybody. There have been some feelings since then that folks have expressed that they would support the decision, but there was not one positive statement for launch ever made in that room.

Boisjoly said that the engineers at the time were stunned that their recommendation "was going to be reversed." Referring to a written statement he had submitted after the February 14th Commission meeting, he now said:

> I left the room feeling badly defeated, but I felt I really did all I could to stop the launch. I felt personally that management was under a lot of pressure to launch and that they made a very tough decision, but I didn't agree with it.
>
> One of my colleagues that was in the meeting summed it up best. This was a meeting where the determination was to launch, and it was up to us to prove beyond a shadow of a doubt that it was not safe to do so. This is in total reverse to what the position usually is in a preflight conversation or a flight readiness review. It is usually exactly opposite that.
>
> Mr. Walker: Do you know the source of the pressure on management that you alluded to?
>
> Mr. Boisjoly: Well, the comments made over the net is what I felt, I can't speak for them, but I felt it—I felt the tone of the meeting exactly as I summed up, that we were being put in a position to prove that we should not launch rather than being put in the position and prove that we had enough data to launch. And I felt that very real.

Boisjoly had no way of knowing why NASA's officials were acting the way they were. He also provided some new information about how concerned Marshall had been during mid-to-late 1985 that Thiokol move more quickly on solving the problems with the O-ring joints. He said that NASA was just as concerned as Thiokol about the issue. "We had status reviews going on all the time," he said. "In fact, when any time we would hit a situation where they felt we weren't going quick enough, we ended up having a visit, and they would just be there and watch over our shoulders and make darned sure that we were proceeding in a timely manner."

Earlier in the hearing, Alan McDonald had pointed out that Thiokol even once made a presentation on the SRB seals to a meeting of the Society of Automotive Engineers, asking for help in solving the seal problem.

———

THE THIOKOL MANAGERS also testified. Jerry Mason, senior vice president, Wasatch Division, Morton Thiokol, Inc., tried to explain why the company reversed its recommendation. It was Mason who said that Thiokol needed "to make a management decision," and who told Vice President for Engineering Bob Lund to "take off your engineering hat and put on your management hat."

> Mr. Mason: Well, let's say the request to reassess [i.e., NASA's request to reassess the data after the initial no-fly recommendation] was not a major factor in my view. The fact that we were picking a temperature based purely on the one test or the one flight, and we had had static tests at other temperatures, and Mr. McDonald explained why we didn't consider those conclusive—but it was difficult to say that fifty-three degrees was exactly the temperature that you ought to fly at. . . . Now, the discussion was a free and open discussion with all of the people there, and I believe that it was not—well, at that point it was clear to me we were not going to get a unanimous decision. And so the question was, did we have a reasonable position to go to fifty-three degrees or did we have confidence that we could fly with a twenty-nine degree O-ring?
>
> And the people who were there had heard all of the discussion, and so I concluded that it was appropriate to talk, to get a poll of the chief engineer and the chief program manager, and Mr. Wiggins, who has the division responsibility, to see how they felt, whether they felt that we could safely fly with all of the information that had been presented.
>
> And we did conduct that poll, and we did conclude that it was safe to launch.

Vice President for Engineering Bob Lund had presented Thiokol's initial written recommendation not to launch. This was what prompted Larry Mulloy to say, "When do you want me to launch, Thiokol, next April?"

Mr. Lund: We have dealt with Marshall for a long time and have always been in the position of defending our position to make sure that we were ready to fly, and I guess I didn't realize until after that meeting and after several days that we had absolutely changed our position from what we had been before. But that evening, I guess I had never had those kinds of things come from the people at Marshall that we had to prove to them that we weren't ready. . . . And so we got ourselves into the thought process that we were trying to find some way to prove to them it wouldn't work, and we were unable to do that. We couldn't prove absolutely that that motor wouldn't work . . . and so after listening to the verbal presentation in the afternoon, they [i.e., Marshall] asked what Thiokol's position was, and I looked around the room, and I was the senior person, and I said I don't want to fly. It looks to me like the story says fifty-three degrees is about it.

Yet after Mason told him to "take off your engineering hat and put on your management hat," Lund voted to launch.

The Thiokol manager for the solid rocket booster project, Joseph Kilminster, signed the telefax that Mulloy directed to be sent to Kennedy approving the launch.

Chairman Rogers: Mr. Kilminster, did you have any feeling of pressure being put on you by NASA, or were you just calmly reassessing?

Mr. Kilminster: I felt that the pressure that was put on us was to go back and look at the data, look at the detailed information that had been presented to see if there was something that we were not seeing that we were not representing on the phone.

Chairman Rogers: You didn't feel they were trying to get you to change your mind?

Mr. Kilminster: I did not feel a significant amount of pressure in that regard.

After the candor, openness, and raw human emotion of McDonald and Boisjoly, along with another Thiokol engineer, Brian Russell, who testified briefly on February 25, both the Thiokol managers and the NASA officials who took the stand the next two days seemed like creatures from a strange, faraway, and perhaps ice-shrouded planet.

Essentially, every one of these men was attempting to justify their role in a terribly mistaken decision. Not one admitted he was wrong. For all any of them might have known at the time, a criminal indictment or wrongful death lawsuit might have been their reward for candor, because the Commission did not think to offer anyone immunity from prosecution. Nor did any pursue the simple expedient of taking the Fifth Amendment.

Rogers had told the company attorneys he was going to stage a performance with the aim of creating one hero—McDonald—and multiple scapegoats—Mulloy and the Thiokol managers. As reflected in media reports, this is exactly what he did. Rogers created a public spectacle to defuse a politically sensitive situation, and it was for this he was praised by the press and most of the members of the Senate Commerce Committee and the House Committee on Science and Technology after he delivered his final report.

Why didn't Rogers bring William Graham to the stage? He was the man who started the whole sequence of events rolling on Saturday, January 25, when he cancelled the scheduled Sunday launch. How about Philip Culbertson, Graham's representative at Kennedy when Challenger blew up?

Next, Larry Mulloy discussed with Rogers whether he pressured Thiokol to reverse their recommendation not to launch.

Chairman Rogers: Didn't you take that to be a negative recommendation?

Mr. Mulloy: Yes, sir. That was an engineering conclusion, which I found this conclusion without basis and challenged its logic. Now, that had been interpreted by some people as applying pressure. I certainly don't consider it to be applying pressure.

Any time that one of my contractors or, for that matter, some of Mr. Hardy's people who come to me with a recommendation or a conclusion that is based on engineering data, I probe the basis for their conclusion to assure that it is sound and that it is logical. . . . And this was a rather surprising conclusion, based upon data that didn't seem to hang together, and so I challenged that. And I assure you, sir, that there was no reversal of the tradition of NASA which says prove to me why you can't fly versus prove to me why you can.

Mulloy wanted to be sure that the Commission understood it was not just him or not just Marshall that wanted the space shuttle to fly with what Commission member Sutter had called the previous day a "tender" joint. Mulloy said the joints had long been a "known condition" "accepted by all levels of NASA management." He argued that the rationale for proceeding on that basis was a matter of record.

The Presidential Commission concluded, on page 203 of its report, "The decision to launch the Challenger was flawed. Those who made the decision were unaware of the recent history of problems concerning the O-rings and the joint. . . ." I personally believe this statement was untrue. The recent history was known, especially at Level I under Jesse Moore at NASA headquarters. Mulloy made it clear that joint problems were a topic at flight readiness reviews involving James Beggs, Jesse Moore, Arnold Aldrich, and other top NASA managers. The problem was one of recognition and action. The exception was what may have been concealment by Marshall of the issue of cold weather effects. The Commission never got to the bottom of that.

Following is another exchange between the Commission and Larry Mulloy from February 26:

Dr. Walker: Could you also, as you proceed with your narrative, tell us about any conversations you had with Mr. McDonald during the thirty or thirty-five-minute caucus? . . .

Mr. Hotz: . . . It figures quite prominently in the discussion that you were quoted as saying, do you expect us to "wait 'til April to launch.". . . Is that an accurate statement or not?

Mr. Mulloy: It is certainly a statement that is out of context, and the way I read the quote, sir—and I have seen it many times, too many times—the quote I read was: "My God, Thiokol, when do you want me to launch, next April?" The total context, I think, in which those words may have been used is, there are currently no launch commit criteria for joint temperature. What you are proposing to do is generate a new launch commit criteria on the eve of launch, after we have successfully flown with the existing launch commit criteria twenty-four times. With this LCC, i.e., do not launch with a temperature greater than fifty-three degrees, we may not be able to launch until next April. We need to consider this carefully before we jump to any conclusions. . . . It is all in the context, again, with challenging your interpretation of the data, what does it mean and is it logical, is it truly logical that we really have a system that has to be fifty-three degrees to fly.

Next, General Kutyna asked why the O-ring issue was not of more concern within NASA the night before the launch:

General Kutyna: Larry, let me follow through on that, and I am kind of aware of the launch decision process, and you said you made the decision at your level on this thing. If this were an airplane, an airliner, and I just had a two-hour argument with Boeing on whether the wing was going to fall off or not, I think I would tell the pilot, at least mention it. Why didn't we escalate a decision of this importance?

Mr. Mulloy: I did, sir.

General Kutyna: You did?

Mr. Mulloy: Yes, sir.

General Kutyna: Tell me what levels above you.

Mr. Mulloy: As I stated earlier, Mr. Reinartz, who is my manager, was at the meeting and on the morning, about five a.m. in the operations support room where we all are, I informed Dr. Lucas of the content of the discussion.

General Kutyna: But Dr. Lucas is not in the launch decision chain.

Mr. Mulloy: No, sir. But Mr. Reinartz is in the launch decision chain though.

General Kutyna: And is he the highest level in the chain?

Mr. Mulloy: No. Normally it would go from me to Mr. Reinartz to Mr. Aldrich to Mr. Moore.

This was an important statement by Mulloy. Alan McDonald had already told the Commission he couldn't believe the O-ring concern had not been conveyed to Aldrich. Mulloy now said that "normally" it would go from him to Stanley Reinartz, the manager of the Shuttle Projects Office at Marshall, to Aldrich to Moore. At this critical point in the discussion, Chairman Rogers cut in and changed the subject to something brought up earlier by Sally Ride on another topic. He said, "Could we go back to Dr. Ride's question. . . ?"

The Commission never returned to Mulloy to question him on the subject. Nor did the Commission ask him about the motel room meeting with William Lucas, James Kingsbury, and Stanley Reinartz that preceded the evening teleconference. Remember again that after the afternoon teleconference, Reinartz' deputy, Judson Lovingood, was prepared for a no-launch decision and advised Reinartz to be prepared to inform Aldrich. But after this teleconference and before the evening one, Mulloy and Reinartz went to Lucas's motel room where they talked for an hour. Mulloy did not mention this meeting in his testimony.

Now Reinartz and Lovingood took the stand. Reinartz defended the teleconference with Thiokol as "thorough and professional . . . and in the NASA tradition of full and open participation. . . ."

> During the two-and-a-half hour telecom between Thiokol and Marshall, extended over that time—it was muted for approximately thirty minutes—I would characterize the presentation and associated discussions as deliberate and intense, and a professional engineering examination of the data, and not highly heated or emotional. And no heated protest was injected into the open discussion by the senior Thiokol representative [Al McDonald] at KSC during that two-and-a-half-hour period.

Later in his testimony, Reinartz had an exchange with Chairman Rogers that was widely reported on. It concerned why he didn't forward anything about the teleconference to higher management levels:

> Chairman Rogers: I guess the question that still lingers in my mind is, in the Navy we used to have an expression about going by the book, and I gather you were going by the book. But doesn't the process require some judgment? Don't you have to use common sense? Wouldn't common sense require that you tell the decision makers about this serious problem that was different from everything in the past?

Mr. Reinartz: In looking at that one, Mr. Chairman, together with Mr. Mulloy when we looked at were there any launch commits, any Level II, as I perceived during the telecom, I got no disagreement concerning the Thiokol launch between any of the Level III elements, the contractor, with Mr. McDonald there.

I felt that the Thiokol and Marshall people had fully examined that concern, and that it had been satisfactorily dispositioned based upon the evidence and the data that was supplied to that decision process on that evening, from that material, and not extraneous to what else may have been going on within Thiokol that I had no knowledge of.

Reinartz also said, as had Mulloy, that at a 5:00 a.m. meeting at Kennedy launch control on January 28, they informed Lucas, the Marshall director, of the Thiokol "concerns and engineering recommendations . . . and the full support of the Marshall engineering for the launch recommendation that I felt had led to a successful resolution of this concern."

Again, Commission members wanted to know why Reinartz did not inform Aldrich.

Mr. Hotz: Mr. Reinartz, are you telling us that you in fact are the person who made the decision not to escalate this to a Level II item?

Reinartz: That is correct, sir.

Then came an exchange between Commission members and Judson Lovingood about the afternoon teleconference with Thiokol, when it looked like a launch delay might happen. Note that neither Mulloy, Reinartz, nor McDonald was involved. It was between Marshall personnel at Huntsville, where Lovingood was located, and Thiokol in Utah. Lovingood said that a launch delay looked likely at that point, and that he then suggested they have a later meeting and "go through all the data."

After completing that telecom and then making—and everyone agreeing to meet at certain locations and have the subsequent telecom that evening, I called Stan at the motel and I suggested to him that he go ahead and alert Arnie at that point . . . and that we were going to get together within the center and decide what to do, and then prepare Arnie for getting Level I together and then going up the line.

Why didn't Reinartz follow Lovingood's suggestion and inform Aldrich at this point? Reinartz said that he felt there was not "a full understanding of the situation" and that this was obligatory before going to Level II, although he conceded that "in hindsight" it might have been better to have done as Lovingood recommended. It is difficult to take Reinartz's disclaimer at face value, especially in light of Lovingood's tone, which suggested that the normal procedure would have been to inform Aldrich that afternoon, as well as Reinartz's " hindsight" admission. What was going on at Kennedy that afternoon to keep Reinartz from doing what he knew he should have done? Who had he been talking to? How was this connected with the motel room conversation that would soon take place with Lucas? Of the motel room meeting, Reinartz said:

> Mr. Mulloy was just out of communication for about an hour, and then after that I got in contact with him and we both had a short discussion relating to the general nature of the concerns with Dr. Lucas and Mr. Kingsbury at the motel before we both departed for the telecom that we had set up out at the Cape.

Now Lovingood made a new disclosure. Not only did he recommend to Reinartz that Aldrich be informed of the possibility of a launch delay, he also recommended that Lucas and James Kingsbury, the director of science and engineering at Marshall, who was staying at the same motel as Lucas, take part in the evening teleconference. Reinartz squelched this too. Commission Executive Director Alton Keel asked:

> Mr. Reinartz, you then visited the motel room of Dr. Lucas with Mr. Kingsbury, and also was Mr. Mulloy with you then?
> Mr. Reinartz: Yes, he was, sir. In the first couple of minutes I believe I was there by myself, and then Mr. Mulloy joined us.
> Dr. Keel: And did you discuss with them Mr. Lovingood's recommendation that the two of them, Lucas and Kingsbury, participate?

Mr. Reinartz: No, sir. I don't recall discussing Mr. Lovingood's recommendations. I discussed with them the nature of the telecom, the nature of the concerns raised by Thiokol, and the plans to gather the proper technical support people at Marshall for examination of the data. And I believe that was the essence of the discussion.

Chairman Rogers: But you didn't recommend that the information be given to Level II or Level I?

Mr. Reinartz: I don't recall that I raised that issue with Dr. Lucas. I told him what the plans were for proceeding [with the teleconference]. I don't recall making any statement regarding that [i.e., reporting any information to Level II or Level I].

The next day, February 27, Aldrich and Lucas testified. Rogers asked Aldrich:

At that time, did they [i.e., Mulloy and Reinartz] tell you that there had been serious concerns expressed by Thiokol and Thiokol engineers, and that they had had a long teleconference on the subject, and that first Thiokol had recommended against launch and secondly management, in the person of Mr. Kilminster, had changed its mind and Thiokol then had decided to recommend launch? Did you know any of that sequence at all?

Mr. Aldrich: None of that was discussed, and I did not know until after the 51-L launch that there had been such a meeting.

Later in the hearing on the 27th, Dr. William Lucas took the stand. Chairman Rogers asked him when he had heard about the problem with the O-rings.

Dr. Lucas: . . . It was on the early evening of the 27th, I think about 7 p.m., when I was in my motel room along with Dr. Kingsbury. And about that time, Mr. Reinartz and Mr. Mulloy came to my room and told me that they had heard that some members of Thiokol had raised a concern about the performance of the solid rocket boosters in the low temperature that was anticipated for the next day, specifically on the seals, and that they were going out to the Kennedy Space Center to engage in a telecom with the appropriate engineers back at Marshall

Space Flight Center in Huntsville and with corresponding people back at the Wasatch Division of Thiokol in Utah. And we discussed it a few moments, and I said, fine, keep me informed, let me know what happens.

Chairman Rogers: And when was the next time you heard something about that?

Dr. Lucas: The next time was about five a.m. on the following morning, when I went to the Kennedy Space Center and went to the launch control center. I immediately saw Mr. Reinartz and Mr. Mulloy and asked them how the matter of the previous evening was dispositioned.

At this point in the hearing, Rogers did not question Lucas further about what was said in the motel room meeting. Yet surely this was a critical moment both in the sequence of events leading up to the launch and in the investigation itself. Before the motel room meeting, Thiokol was recommending against the launch, and Marshall managers in Huntsville were preparing mentally for a launch delay. After the motel room meeting, Mulloy, with Reinartz, drove across the ocean sound to Kennedy, got on the phone, and pressured Thiokol into approving the launch. The Commission, as I pointed out in a later article in the *Washington Monthly*, failed to investigate or explain this key turning point in the events leading to the disaster.

Instead, Rogers changed the subject to discuss what Lucas knew of the history of O-ring joint problems. Lucas said, "I did not think it was a problem sufficient to ground the fleet." Rogers then jumped back to the topic of what did Reinartz tell him when he saw him the next morning at Kennedy.

Dr. Lucas: He told me, as I testified, when I went into the control room, that an issue had been resolved, that there were some people at Thiokol who had a concern about the weather, that that had been discussed very thoroughly by the Thiokol people and by the Marshall Space Flight Center people, and it had been concluded agreeably that there was no problem, that he had a recommendation by Thiokol to launch and our most knowledgeable people and engineering talent agreed with that. So from my perspective, I didn't have—I didn't see that as an issue.

Chairman Rogers: And if you had known that Thiokol engineers almost to a man opposed the flight, would that have changed your view?

Dr. Lucas: I'm certain that it would.

Chairman Rogers: So your testimony is the same as Mr. Hardy's. Had he known, he would not have recommended the flight be launched on that day?

Dr. Lucas: I didn't make a recommendation one way or the other. But had I known that, I would have interposed an objection, yes.

Chairman Rogers: I gathered you didn't tell Mr. Aldrich or Mr. Moore what Mr. Reinartz had told you?

Dr. Lucas: No, sir. That is not the reporting channel. Mr. Reinartz reports directly to Mr. Aldrich. In a sense, Mr. Reinartz informs me as the institutional manager of the progress that he is making in implementing his program, but I have never on any occasion reported to Mr. Aldrich.

Lucas was presenting an absurdity. He was not in the reporting chain between Level III—Reinartz—and Level II—Aldrich. Yet he was the one with whom Reinartz and Mulloy had the motel room meeting between the two teleconferences. Why then didn't Reinartz have a meeting with Aldrich? It made no sense. Also, Lucas may never have reported to Aldrich, but he was, with Aldrich, a member of the mission management team. Lucas was in fact a launch official, not a bystander.

What appears to have been happening here was that the NASA witnesses were again sealing off the higher-ups from responsibility by focusing attention on Reinartz as the point where critical information stopped moving up the line. If so, Reinartz had become the willing fall guy.

Now, after Lucas took his ritual verbal beating from Rogers, Jesse Moore, Arnold Aldrich, Richard Smith, and Gene Thomas took the stand. Smith was the director of the Kennedy Space Center, and Thomas was the launch director at Kennedy. Rogers asked them:

Chairman Rogers: By way of a question, could I ask, did any of you gentlemen prior to launch know about the objections of Thiokol to the launch?

Mr. Smith: I did not.

Mr. Thomas: No, sir,

Mr. Aldrich: I did not.

Mr. Moore: I did not.

Chairman Rogers: So the four, certainly four of the key people who made the decision about the launch were not aware of the history that we have been unfolding here before the Commission.

Mr. Moore: That is correct.

We shall now consider statements made during the February 25–27 hearings with regard to the issue of ice on the launch tower. Even before the Commission met for the first time, reports had appeared in the press that Rockwell, the orbiter contractor, did not want to launch because of the ice situation. At its February 10 closed hearing, Rogers said:

If Rockwell comes up in a public session and says, "We advised NASA not to launch and they went ahead anyway," then we have a hell of a problem.

This was, of course, before NASA's story collapsed and its top managers were dismissed from the investigation. Then, at the closed hearings on February 13–14, the Commission focused mainly on the Thiokol situation. The same was the case on February 25, so finally, on the 26th, at the end of the day, the issue of ice on the tower was addressed.

Testifying for NASA was Charles Stevenson, who had made a brief appearance on February 13, and who now gave more detail about the ice inspections the night of January 27 and the morning of the 28th. Stevenson read a statement:

Two actions within the plan were intended to limit the ice debris which could potentially cause damage to the shuttle vehicle during the launch. The first action involved adding 1,450 gallons of antifreeze into the overpressure water troughs [i.e., the sound suppression water troughs for the SRBs].

The second action involved the draining, where practical, of all water systems. Several systems, such as the flex, the deluge, the emergency shower and eye wash were not drained. These systems were opened slightly and allowed to trickle into the drains. The trickling water was found to cause the drains to overflow, and the high wind gusts spread the water over large areas, and it then froze.

Based on these conditions, when we came into the firing room on the day of launch and had a call to stations, the ice, frost, TPS [i.e., orbiter thermal protection system], and debris team observed the icing conditions which were on the FSS [fixed service structure] and notified our upper management. A decision was made at that time to send the ice/frost team to the pad for an assessment of the facility icing conditions.

But Stevenson did not disclose a key fact that later came out during the congressional investigations. It was not, in fact, NASA's standard operating procedure to let the water drip in the launch pad water systems. The normal procedure was to drain these systems to assure that the pipes would not burst. Of course draining and refilling them would take more time than running them at a trickle. Nor could refilling begin until temperatures on the launch pad were above freezing. This was yet another departure NASA made from its usual behavior in order to be able to launch early in the day on January 28.

In his testimony before the Commission, Stevenson did not repeat the statements made by members of the ice team and by Rockwell contractors that were recorded and later reported in the report of the House Science and Technology Committee. One comment was, "Looks like something out of Dr. Zhivago." And Stevenson himself said, "Well, I'd say the only choice you got today is not to go. We're just taking a chance of hitting the vehicle."

The head of the NASA ice team had said "not to go." It was not just Rockwell. But the Commission did not hear about it at this hearing and did not include the fact in its report. In his testimony that day Stevenson repeated the party line that:

> Once the management had assessed that problem [i.e., the danger of ice falling on the orbiter], and had decided that it was not a safety of flight issue for the conditions we had described, then we really didn't have any problem with launching.

Stevenson was back to testify the next morning, Thursday, February 27. He did not mention, as was disclosed in the House committee report, that during the night before launch NASA waived the thirty-one degree minimum launch temperature for the entire shuttle system and waived the constraint on external tank instrumentation down to ten degrees. Stevenson would likely have known about both of these waivers, which indicated NASA was prepared to launch no matter how cold it was that morning.

The Commission determined that the ice on the launch pad the morning of January 28, 1986, was the worst for any shuttle launch. It was so bad that there was a thick sheet of ice on the platform the astronauts would have had to use to escape down the slide-wire baskets in a pre-lift-off emergency. Moreover, the astronauts had not been told about this sheet of ice. Stevenson showed a photo of this platform at the hearing, and the Commission said in its final report that because of it, "greater consideration should have been given to delaying the launch."

Stevenson said that during the ten hours prior to launch, the ice team spent four hours on the pad and another "three or four hours" discussing the problem with management. Chairman Rogers asked whom on the management team he talked to. Stevenson said, "Jesse and Arnie." Billy Davis, another member of the ice team was asked the same thing. He said:

> Yes, it was [i.e., Jesse Moore and Arnold Aldrich]. In fact, my suggestion that if we were going to fly, that we should do it as early as possible, was picked up. Mr. Moore specifically stated that he felt that that was true, too, and they proceeded that way.

Davis was saying that because of the ice, the earlier in the day you launched the better, because once the sun came up and the ice on the tower began to loosen, more would be dislodged at shuttle lift-off. So an early launch would minimize ice debris. Of course an early launch would also mean colder O-rings. The launch actually took place at 11:38, with ice raining down all around. It had been postponed from 9:38, a delay of exactly two hours.

Next to testify was Dr. Rocco Petrone, president of Space Transportation Systems for Rockwell, the orbiter contractor. Petrone, the director of Marshall after Wernher von Braun, was a NASA veteran.

He had been at Kennedy in Florida for the Monday launch scrub but on Tuesday was at Rockwell's support room in Downey, California, looking at the TV monitors of ice on the pad. He told the Commission:

> I then called my program managers in Florida at 5:45 a.m. [Pacific Time] and said we could not recommend launching from here, from what we see. We think the tiles would be endangered, and we had a very short conversation. They had a meeting to go to, and I said let's make sure that NASA understands that Rockwell feels it is not safe to launch, and that was the end of my conversation.

Representing Petrone at Kennedy for the January 28 launch was Robert Glaysher, who then went to a meeting of the NASA launch team and said, "Rockwell cannot assure that it is safe to fly." Interestingly, as with the Thiokol teleconference, NASA also quizzed Rockwell on its data for making a no-launch recommendation. As with Thiokol, Rockwell did not have data readily available. But Glaysher said:

> We actually discussed our position, and I stated more than once during the meeting Rockwell's position that we could not assure that it was safe to fly. It was stated when I first was asked to give our position, and it was also my last statement at that meeting, as the meeting wound up. I also reiterated the statement several times.

Like Thiokol, Rockwell was evidently being pressured to fly. Leading this meeting for NASA was Arnold Aldrich. He told the Commission, "Mr. Glaysher did not ask or insist that we did not launch. . . ." Somebody seemed to have been shading the truth, as Glaysher sounded insistent. He said he "reiterated" his statement "several times." According to testimony from Stevenson and Davis, they spoke directly to Jesse Moore about the ice conditions they had observed, but Moore did not attend the final 9:00 a.m. meeting where Glaysher spoke. Aldrich, however, reported to Moore on the meeting. He said:

> At this point, I returned to the operations support room in the launch complex, where I reviewed the context of this meeting with Mr.

Jesse Moore, the associate administrator for space flight, who was seated at that time with Mr. Philip Culbertson, the NASA general manager. In that summary, I clearly indicated the qualified position taken by Rockwell International, and recommended that the launch proceed unless the ice team identified a significant change in launch pad condition on their final visit to the pad.

After a lengthy discussion of various tangential issues, Aldrich then told Rogers:

If Rockwell had told me that they were "no go," I would have reported to you in the same manner that George Hardy reported in discussion. I would not have overruled a "no go" discussion from the Rockwell team.

So now, as with Thiokol, it was Rockwell's fault. Writing this, I once again thought back to Paul Herr's statement to me the day after Challenger blew up, when he said that they were called from the Cape the night before with word that two contractors opposed the launch. What Herr should have said, I suppose, was that the two contractors should have opposed it even more vigorously than they did and maybe the disaster would not have happened.

At the end of Aldrich's testimony, Vice Chairman Neil Armstrong was interested in the issue of the abort landing site at Dakar in Senegal. Supposedly, bad weather at Dakar caused Mulloy to tell Alan McDonald the launch couldn't be shifted to the afternoon of January 28. Now Armstrong asked Aldrich:

If I could get back to the launch window, was there a requirement to have Dakar in daylight, and what set the thing to be 9:30 to 11:30?

Mr. Aldrich: I think it was crew duration and crew day. We had lights at Dakar and that was go, but we could not go later in the day because of the schedule we had set the launch crew and the flight crew on. There is a limit of the amount of time that we agree that they will stay in the cockpit in the position they were in, and I think that is what ended at 12:30.

Vice Chairman Armstrong: I guess what I'm getting at is, couldn't it have been twelve to three?

Mr. Aldrich: It could have been if we had planned it much earlier in the day. The launch team, of course, plans the countdown. They are in the countdown. They are in the countdown with a series of holds, but they pick up the count and proceed to tank the launch vehicle based on a given launch time.

And also, several days before launch we put the flight crew on the sleep-wake cycle that supports them to be in the right configuration for launch that day and do a full day in orbit. We would have been able to go a three hour launch window in the afternoon if we had set that in motion several days prior to that time. But you couldn't change in the middle of the night and say, well, we will just adjust them around by same number of hours because there are too many constraints and additional problems that creates.

So what Mulloy said to McDonald about dust storms at Dakar was wrong. But did Aldrich really have an answer for Armstrong? Certainly they could have adjusted the astronauts' cycle for that day by a few hours to preserve safety. Besides, McDonald said earlier that when he first appeared at the Cape for the Challenger launch it was to be an afternoon lift-off. Again, the possibility might have arisen that the astronauts had to be settled in orbit in time for the State of the Union. There was no follow-up to Armstrong's question, because Chairman Rogers again changed the subject, as he often seemed to do.

On whether Jesse Moore knew that Rockwell opposed the launch:

Dr. Keel: Mr. Moore, did you know that consistent with the testimony this morning, that Rockwell had apparently said that, "Rockwell cannot assure it was safe to fly?"

Mr. Moore: Yes, sir, I had some indication of that from a report that Mr. Aldrich had given me.

But then Moore changed his emphasis.

Mr. Moore: [Aldrich] did not indicate that that was a safety of flight concern, and it was more indicated in the thermal protection system which might have some damage that it might have to be repaired and cause some delays to turnaround, and he said that he had tagged up with everybody and he felt that it was all go, and he recommended that we launch, and I accepted his recommendation.

Then Moore added.

> But the thought did not cross my mind that, for example, Rockwell
> was saying "no go." No.

The Commission concluded that Rockwell's position was "ambiguous." Rocco Petrone said that Rockwell thought it was "not safe to fly." NASA's launch officials, including Richard Smith, KSC director, said this was not a "no-go."

It is true that ice on the launch tower and pad did not cause the Challenger disaster. However, the Commission's report did not indicate whether it was possible to examine the remnants of Challenger to determine whether ice had damaged the thermal protection system to the degree that there would have been problems on reentry. Contrary to Moore's statements, potential damage to the tiles was a safety of flight issue. Later it was damage to the thermal protection system from external tank insulation falling at launch that destroyed Columbia during reentry on February 1, 2003.

The Commission's report was not conclusive about the import of the ice issue. Nevertheless, the report stated:

> The Commission believes that the severe cold and presence of so
> much ice on the fixed service structure made it inadvisable to launch
> on the morning of January 28, and that margins of safety were whittled
> down too far.

Finally, Moore addressed the issue of whether external pressure had been brought to bear to launch Challenger—sort of. David Acheson, head of the Commission's team on mission planning and operations, asked, in a question which came with a very vague answer:

> Mr. Acheson: Mr. Moore, there have been some implications in the
> press, and I am sure you have seen them, that there might have been an
> unusual degree of eagerness to get on with the launch schedule in the
> case of 51-L that might or might have not changed the balance of cau-
> tion. Would you comment on that please?

Mr. Moore: Yes, sir, I would be happy to comment on that. As a matter of fact, I would like to review, with the permission of the chairman, some of my thoughts on the evening or so leading up to the launch, a couple of evenings, which will get into the question of pressure.

In fact Moore said nothing about his "thoughts on the evening or so leading up to the launch." What he said was:

As we have talked about before, we held our normal launch minus one day review on the 25th of January, I think about eleven o'clock in the morning. We were all go. Everybody polled said they were ready to support the launch. We did have a concern about weather, and that evening we met to discuss weather for the next morning, which was on the 26th. It was a launch opportunity, and that happened to be a Sunday morning. As you heard from the Air Force person talking about the weather, we did not get a very positive forecast, and I think our mission management team was unanimous in saying we probably should not try a launch because of the weather problems that were likely to occur on Sunday morning.

Also, we were told that afternoon that we had an awful lot of dignitaries in to watch the launch. We had people here from the People's Republic of China and several congressmen, and a large number of other outsiders, as well as we understood that afternoon that the vice president was possibly going to stop over on Sunday morning to view the launch, and so forth, and that was on Saturday afternoon.

Nevertheless, we decided to scrub the launch as a result of the weather forecast at 9:30 p.m. that night, and as a matter of fact, to my knowledge, no one had any political pressure whatsoever to try to get the launch off, and that was the case through the entire sequence on this flight, and that has been the case on every flight that I have been associated with.

We have got roundly criticized in the press as a result of the flight just prior to this about all of the multitude of delays starting in the December 20 attempt, I guess. We shut down the week of the holidays to give our team a rest and so forth, and then we had four or five additional scrubs before we finally got it launched, and we also waved off three times at the Kennedy Space Center trying to get it landed at Kennedy.

Moore did not mention that it was Acting Administrator William Graham who made the decision not to launch Challenger after the meeting of the mission management team on the evening of January 25th. The launch was called off just before NASA would have begun to fill the external tank with liquid hydrogen and oxygen fuel.

Moore continued:

So we have not been under any political pressure. This program operates on a launch-by-launch basis. We try to make sure all launches are safe, all issues are put to bed, and worry about downstream schedules later. You always have to lay out downstream schedules.

I have got schedules going into the early '90s, but you take them one at a time, and that is the philosophy by which the shuttle team operates, and you worry about how you adjust your downstream schedules after you have safely launched and safely landed the particular mission you are concerned about.

William Rogers then asked a question which was deleted from the Commission's public record but which I heard in the CNN broadcast. He said, "And there wasn't any political pressure to get this launch up, was there?"

Moore said, "No."

At this point in the February 27 hearing, Vice Chairman Neil Armstrong then changed the subject by asking KSC Director Richard Smith a question about the Kennedy freeze protection plan. Thus ended the Commission's public inquiry into launch schedule pressure.

The three days of public hearings closed with brief testimony from a man named Ben Powers. He was an engineer from Marshall who had agreed with the recommendation of the Thiokol engineers not to launch and who did not change his position after the Thiokol managers overruled their engineers. Later there were press reports that people in his church back in Alabama were praying that he would not be fired for talking honestly to the Commission.

The news stories on the February 25–27 hearings were worldwide and explosive and were the high point of public interest in the Presidential Commission. The problem seemed solved: NASA launched Challenger because warnings from below did not reach the top. That was the official theory of the disaster. It was problems with management systems and communications and spawned a deluge of books and articles over the coming years.

And of course there was an element of truth to this interpretation. It was true that top management did not want to hear bad news, but not because of problems with systems and communications. NASA had all the systems and communications you could possibly desire. They were the world leader in systems and communications.

Rather the problem was that top management likely had other things in mind than safety. What they had in mind was political expediency of many kinds and at many levels. Some of this expediency had to do with launch schedule pressure, especially the increasing military flight rate. Some, in the case of Challenger, probably had to do with the Teacher-in-Space.

At least one Commission member knew that the hearings did not get to the bottom of why NASA applied so much pressure to launch. This member said privately to Roger Boisjoly, "Nothing you could have argued would have stopped them from launching that day." Another Thiokol engineer said, "They told me the decision to launch was political and to go home and not to worry." They said, "If something goes wrong, you won't be blamed."

What was the extraordinary urgency—which apparently the Challenger crew was not even told about—that made this particular launch so unique? That evidently made midlevel officials at Marshall so certain that this launch was a "go," regardless of what contractor experts said, that it was not worthwhile or essential to inform Aldrich or Moore? The key to the Commission's entire approach to the launch decision was that it ignored this question. Instead, it treated the extraordinary events of January 25–28 as normal, as a variation on NASA's modus operandi, as a process issue.

It was not a process issue. It was a violation-of-process issue, a corruption-of-process issue. It was a mystery that someone needed to penetrate but that no one did. And no one ever had any intention of penetrating it. During the aftermath of the disaster, I had several conversations with Jonathan A. Bennett, a reporter for the weekly newspaper The Guardian. He showed me a quote he had gotten from an unnamed employee at the Kennedy Space Center:

We made a bad call when we said [Challenger] was go, but there was something weird going on here that night. . . . Right from the beginning, we always erred on the side of safety. But on Monday night everything was different. It was too cold; it was blowing a gale in the SRB recovery area; there was ice, foot-long icicles all over the pad. Any of those things would have been enough to postpone the launch. When McDonald wouldn't sign off, we did something we had never done before, going over his head to a Thiokol executive in Brigham City. I don't know why everyone was so gung-ho, but "no" was not what people wanted to hear that night.

The public investigation of launch circumstances by the Presidential Commission now ended. The FBI was called in, but not for an independent investigation. Several FBI agents and other Justice Department staff members were assigned to the Commission to conduct interviews with NASA and contractor employees, including interviews on the issue of launch pressure. But these agents reported to the Commission's executive director, Alton Keel, who reported to Chairman Rogers. Rogers, in turn, was working for Donald Regan. At no time was there a separate FBI inquiry, except for an early determination by the FBI's antiterrorism unit that ruled out sabotage as a cause of the disaster.

After the Commission completed its work, I read the interviews with NASA officials on the launch process. These were largely pro forma affairs conducted by staff attorneys and young FBI agents. Their questions were superficial. The transcripts of the interviews showed no apparent mandate to press for meaningful answers to the more puzzling aspects of the event chain. Sometimes the interviews even gave the impression that the NASA officials were reading prepared statements.

I personally did not expect more from the Commission. Marshall was in fact blamed—scapegoated, as Rogers told the Thiokol attorneys Mulloy would be. As Paul Herr predicted, it was the little guys—Mulloy and Reinartz—who were "fried." And it seemed that the Commission expected that Marshall would show contrition in exchange for lenient treatment; i.e., a public scolding from William Rogers.

But they went down swinging. At a press conference back home in

Huntsville on February 28, Director William Lucas accepted Marshall's responsibility:

> The Marshall Space Flight Center, being a very important element of NASA and a very important element of the space shuttle, feels responsible for the loss of Challenger.

But that's about as far as he intended to go. Of the launch process, Lucas said:

> I do not view the process to be flawed. We have one of the most careful flight readiness reviews of any NASA center. This center is more diligent in pursuing flight readiness than any center in the agency.

Lucas was not even ready to say it was an SRB failure. Though he admitted there was a burnthrough, "There is no evidence yet whether the SRB was the root cause in what gave rise to the failure." He added:

> You could question, in the light of what happened, the judgments that were made, but I don't think you can question the process. You could fault the judgment, if you chose to. But I don't fault it. I think that the judgment was correct.

Lucas was saying that Marshall made the right decision in allowing Challenger to be launched. Larry Mulloy also spoke at the press conference. He said:

> I think the launch decision process is sound. I think the launch decision process in this case was sound. . . . I don't think the NASA internal communications system is flawed at all. There are established reporting channels. There are established levels.

In a March 4 interview with the *Huntsville Times*, Mulloy said:

> I know I did my job with the same dedication I've done it for the last twenty-six years. I have nothing to apologize for.

The statements coming out of Huntsville were bizarre, especially Mulloy's vehement defense of the launch decision process. Maybe that was the only way Mulloy, Lucas, Reinartz, and others were able to justify to themselves their participation in the process that led to flying a solid rocket booster which came in third in technical merit when it was originally bid in the mid-1970s. Maybe the Thiokol SRB really was substandard, foisted on Marshall by the politics of space shuttle procurement. So what do you do if you are a professional aerospace engineer with a normal amount of ambition and a family to support?

The Marshall managers spoke of "acceptable risk." Earlier, I cited the 1984 study, which said that the chance of an SRB explosion was one in thirty-five launches, dismal odds.

From a practical standpoint, "acceptable risk" meant that sometimes people would die. And it was true that everyone in the NASA system, including the astronauts, bought into this system. So mentally you could justify it. If, according to the "acceptable risk" logic, you "lost one," and some astronauts were killed, that was "data" in the risk equation. If some excitement resulted from the mishap, that was "the press," just another difficulty to be managed. Of course having a Presidential Commission coming out of left field with its public hearings, well, that was "politics."

Marshall had a strategy for dealing with the press, the public, Congress, and the Commission. This was shown by the "Apocalypse" letter.

This was a lengthy typewritten letter sent to newspapers and TV networks after Lucas, Mulloy, Reinartz, and the other Marshall managers returned to Huntsville from Kennedy after the disaster. The letter said that Lucas called a number of Marshall officials into a large conference room at the Huntsville Operations Support Center and told everyone that any statements to the press had to go through him.

The letter was signed, "God Help Us All—Apocalypse." The letter was accepted as authentic by the Presidential Commission, though Alton Keel, the Commission's Executive Director, followed the Commission's typical practice of trying to disparage any and all internal NASA critics by labeling the author "a disgruntled employee." Yet Apocalypse was high enough up in the Marshall chain of command to have attended all the flight readiness reviews for shuttle launches before Challenger.

Apocalypse said there was a cover-up plan:

Under Phase I of the cover-up, information was to [be] withheld for as long as possible, then fed to the press piecemeal. It was reasoned that the longer the information could be covered up the better, as the course of events would eventually tend to dilute the initial shock and public reactions. . . . Once data could no longer be held back, Phase II would be to present as much highly technical data as possible, letting the situation in the general public's mind be diluted by various conflicting theories which were sure to result. Stories were to be planted which would serve to shift the blame away from [Marshall] to Thiokol and the contractors doing the processing at the Cape.

At the time of this meeting, William Lucas was on Jesse Moore's board and had the job of investigating everything that had to do with the SRB which everyone at NASA knew had failed. There was as yet no Presidential Commission, so Lucas had to assume he was in the driver's seat.

The Apocalypse letter also described the fear felt by Marshall employees in the presence of Lucas, who had a nifty way, it seemed, of cutting them down in meetings in front of their colleagues. The result was that no one brought him information unless he was absolutely sure of his position. It was Lucas, Apocalypse wrote, who made most of the detailed decisions about space hardware, including the main engines and the SRBs. Lucas told his managers that whatever happened, Marshall would not be the center blamed for any launch delays.

The NASA IG ran ads in the *Huntsville Times* asking Apocalypse to contact them. Maybe he did. In any case, Lucas went into retirement in July 1986.

In fact, the Apocalypse letter documented a precise blueprint of the actions of NASA's top officials after the disaster. Phyllis and I intuitively knew something like this was going on from the day Challenger blew up. Marshall and the other NASA top managers tried their strategy on the Presidential Commission. Things went awry with the *New York Times* article of February 9, Dr. Richard Feynman's determination to penetrate the smokescreen, Al McDonald's interview with the *New York Times* about his objections to the launch, and Roger Boisjoly's candor when speaking to the Commission both behind closed doors and before the public.

Perhaps the best commentary on how the Marshall managers conducted themselves came from a March 15 letter to the editor in the *Huntsville Times*:

To the *Times*:

I have been in the aerospace industry for twenty-five years. After seeing the NASA officials on TV and reading your account of the press conference of February 28, I am now convinced that:

a) The NASA decision-making process is flawless.

b) The Morton-Thiokol engineers who said there was a temperature-related problem with the O-rings were illogical.

c) "The launch process is sound," as Mr. Mulloy said.

d) The Rockwell engineers and management didn't really mean it when they advised against launch.

e) There never was a disaster on January 28 as claimed by the investigating Commission. It must have been a figment of their imaginations.

I also believe the tooth fairy will leave a dollar under my pillow tonight.

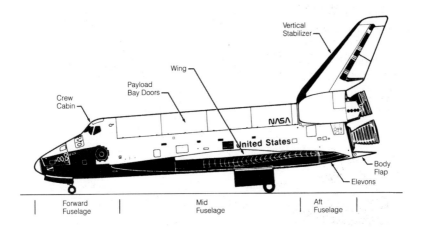

Space shuttle orbiter in landing configuration. The shuttle was the world's first reusable spacecraft. Two of the orbiters, Challenger and Columbia, have been lost through mishaps. (Presidential Commission report.)

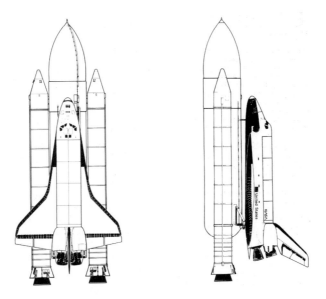

Space shuttle stacked for launch showing the orbiter mated to the external tank with the two solid rocket boosters attached to external tank by struts. The external tank is the only part of the shuttle that is not reused. The solid rocket boosters are built in segments which are assembled prior to flight. (Presidential Commission report.)

MORTON THIOKOL, INC.
Wasatch Division

Interoffice Memo

31 July 1985
2870:FY86:073

TO: R. K. Lund
               Vice President, Engineering

CC: B. C. Brinton, A. J. McDonald, L. H. Sayer, J. R. Kapp

FROM: R. M. Boisjoly
               Applied Mechanics - Ext. 3525

SUBJECT: SRM O-Ring Erosion/Potential Failure Criticality

This letter is written to insure that management is fully aware of the seriousness of the current O-Ring erosion problem in the SRM joints from an engineering standpoint.

The mistakenly accepted position on the joint problem was to fly without fear of failure and to run a series of design evaluations which would ultimately lead to a solution or at least a significant reduction of the erosion problem. This position is now drastically changed as a result of the SRM 16A nozzle joint erosion which eroded a secondary O-Ring with the primary O-Ring never sealing.

If the same scenario should occur in a field joint (and it could), then it is a jump ball as to the success or failure of the joint because the secondary O-Ring cannot respond to the clevis opening rate and may not be capable of pressurization. The result would be a catastrophe of the highest order - loss of human life.

An unofficial team (a memo defining the team and its purpose was never published) with leader was formed on 19 July 1985 and was tasked with solving the problem for both the short and long term. This unofficial team is essentially nonexistent at this time. In my opinion, the team must be officially given the responsibility and the authority to execute the work that needs to be done on a non-interference basis (full time assignment until completed).

It is my honest and very real fear that if we do not take immediate action to dedicate a team to solve the problem, with the field joint having the number one priority, then we stand in jeopardy of losing a flight along with all the launch pad facilities.

R. M. Boisjoly

Concurred by:

J. R. Kapp, Manger
Applied Mechanics

Roger Boisjoly's July 31, 1986, memo warning of potential "catastrophe of the highest order—loss of human life." Boisjoly was concerned that his employer, Morton Thiokol, Inc., the manufacturer of the solid rocket boosters, was not giving sufficient support to the task force which had been formed to resolve the problems with the O-ring seals. He left the company after the disaster. (Presidential Commission report.)

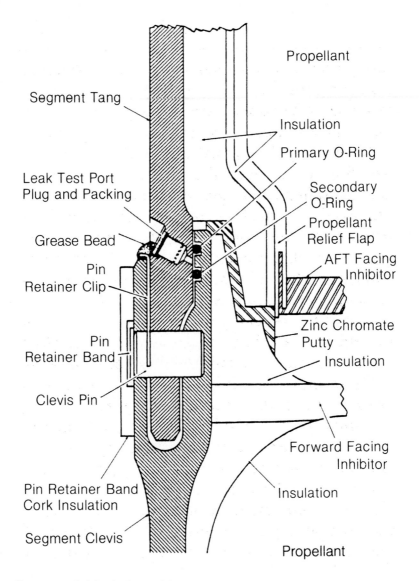

Propellant

Segment Tang

Insulation

Primary O-Ring

Leak Test Port
Plug and Packing

Secondary
O-Ring

Propellant
Relief Flap

Grease Bead

Pin
Retainer Clip

AFT Facing
Inhibitor

Pin
Retainer Band

Zinc Chromate
Putty

Insulation

Clevis Pin

Forward Facing
Inhibitor

Pin Retainer Band
Cork Insulation

Insulation

Segment Clevis

Propellant

Cross section of solid rocket booster field joint showing position of tang, clevis, O-rings, and putty. Engineers had learned that the putty was forming blow holes that allowed flames from the propellant to impinge on the O-rings through a blowtorch effect. This was particularly dangerous because the force of ignition was causing the metal casings of the mated booster segments to spread apart through a phenomenon known as "rotation." In cold temperatures the O-rings lacked the resiliency to follow the moving metal, leaving a gap through which flames could penetrate. (Presidential Commission report.)

MEMORANDUM   7/23/85

TO: BRC/M.Mann

FROM: BRC/R.Cook

SUBJECT: Problem with SRB Seals

Earlier this week you asked me to investigate reported
problems with the charring of seals between SRB motor segments
during flight operations. Discussions with program engineers
show this to be a potentially major problem affecting both
flight safety and program costs.

Presently three seals between SRB segments use double O-rings
sealed with putty. In recent Shuttle flights, charring of
these rings has occurred. The O-rings are designed so that if
one fails, the other will hold against the pressure of firing.
However, at least in the joint between the nozzle and the aft
segment, not only has the first O-ring been destroyed, but the
second has been partially eaten away.

Engineers have not yet determined the cause of the problem.
Candidates include the use of a new type of putty (the putty
formerly in use was removed from the market by EPA because it
contained asbestos), failure of the second ring to slip into
the groove which must engage it for it to work properly, or
new, and as yet unidentified, assembly procedures at Thiokol.
MSC is trying to identify the cause of the problem, including
on-site investigation at Thiokol, and OSF hopes to have some
results from their analysis within 30 days. There is little
question, however, that flight safety has been and is still
being compromised by potential failure of the seals, and it is
acknowledged that failure during launch would certainly be
catastrophic. There is also indication that staff personnel
knew of this problem sometime in advance of management's
becoming apprised of what was going on.

The potential impact of the problem depends on the as yet
undiscovered cause. If the cause is minor, there should be
little or no impact on budget or flight rate. A worse case

scenario, however, would lead to the suspension of Shuttle
flights, redesign of the SRB, and scrapping of existing
stockpiled hardware. The impact on the FY 1987-8 budget could
be immense.

It should be pointed out that Code M management is viewing the
situation with the utmost seriousness. From a budgetary
standpoint, I would think that any NASA budget submitted this
year for FY 1987 and beyond should certainly be based on a
reliable judgment as to the cause of the SRB seal problem and
a corresponding decision as to budgetary action needed to
provide for its solution.

*Author's July 23, 1986, memo warning that "flight safety has been and is still being compro-
mised . . . , and it is acknowledged that failure during launch would certainly be catastrophic."
The memo was written following interviews with the lead solid rocket booster engineers at NASA
headquarters. (NASA, reproduced in Presidential Commission report.)*

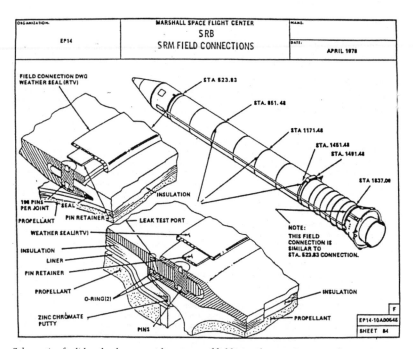

ORGANIZATION: EP14	MARSHALL SPACE FLIGHT CENTER SRB SRM FIELD CONNECTIONS	NAME:
		DATE: APRIL 1978

FIELD CONNECTION DWG
WEATHER SEAL (RTV)

STA 523.83

STA. 851.48

STA 1171.48

STA. 1451.48
STA. 1491.48

STA 1837.00

INSULATION

196 PINS PER JOINT
SEAL
PIN RETAINER
PROPELLANT
LEAK TEST PORT

NOTE:
THIS FIELD
CONNECTION IS
SIMILAR TO
STA. 523.83 CONNECTION.

WEATHER SEAL (RTV)
INSULATION
LINER
PIN RETAINER
PROPELLANT
O-RING (2)
INSULATION
ZINC CHROMATE PUTTY
PROPELLANT
PINS

F

EP14-10AD0645

SHEET 84

Schematic of solid rocket booster with cutaway of field joint showing O-rings and putty. Starting with the second space shuttle mission, the O-rings began to show signs of heat distress from the burning propellant leaking into the joints between segments. It was a burnthrough at one of these joints that destroyed the shuttle Challenger, killing its seven-member crew. (NASA, reproduced in Presidential Commission report.)

The Challenger astronauts. Front, left to right: Pilot Michael Smith, Commander Francis (Dick) Scobee, Mission Specialist Ronald McNair; Rear, left to right: Mission Specialist Ellison Onizuka, Payload Specialist Christa McAuliffe, Payload Specialist Gregory Jarvis, Mission Specialist Judith Resnik. According to official transcripts, the main topic of conversation among the astronauts as they sat in the Challenger orbiter awaiting launch on January 28, 1986, was the unusually cold weather. (NASA, reproduced in Presidential Commission report.)

Challenger on pad 39B, Kennedy Space Center. This was the first time 39B had been used since the Apollo program. The Vehicle Assembly Building where the shuttle components are stacked is visible in the distance. Challenger sits awaiting launch on the giant mobile launch platform. (NASA, reproduced in Presidential Commission report.)

Challenger on the launch pad in the early morning of January 28, 1986, with inset showing thick ice in a water trough. Personnel from NASA and Rockwell spent hours inspecting the ice and trying to clear it out of the sound suppression troughs. A year earlier, NASA had cancelled a launch with ice build-up not as severe as with the Challenger launch. (NASA, reproduced in Presidential Commission report.)

Heavy ice on the launch tower the morning of January 28, 1986, with foot-long icicles. One of the Rockwell contractors said, "Looks like something out of Dr. Zhivago." The head of the NASA ice team told launch controllers, "I'd say your only choice is not to go." (NASA, reproduced in Presidential Commission report.)

"Black puff of smoke" appearing at the field joint of the right-hand solid rocket booster at ignition as hot gases penetrate the O-ring seal. NASA disclosed these photographs to the Presidential Commission at a hearing on February 14, 1986, at the Kennedy Space Center. (NASA, reproduced in Presidential Commission report.)

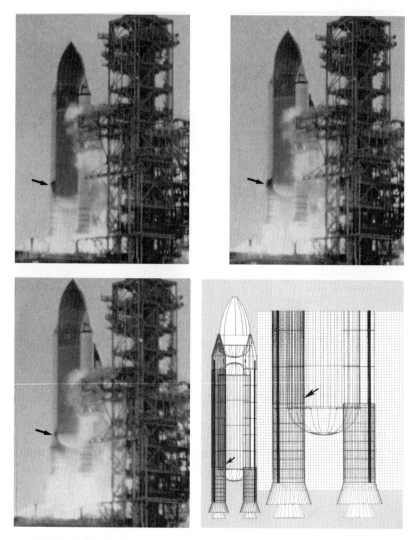

The "black puff of smoke" continues as Challenger lifts off. Investigators concluded that the hole in the solid rocket booster joint through which the smoke emerged re-sealed with debris from burning putty and O-rings. Later in the flight, the hole broke open, possibly due to the forces from high-altitude wind shear. (NASA, reproduced in Presidential Commission report.)

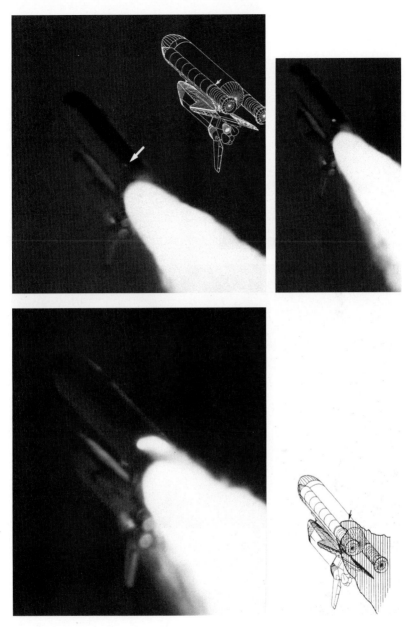

"Plume" of flame appears at the booster rocket joint fifty-eight seconds into flight. At this point the fate of Challenger was sealed. The flame leak rapidly expanded, burning through the strut that attached the solid rocket booster to the external tank. (NASA, reproduced in Presidential Commission report.)

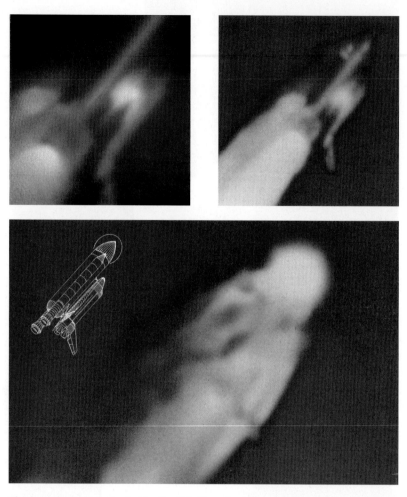

The shuttle begins to shatter, igniting liquid fuel from the external tank as the tank starts to break up at seventy-three seconds into the flight. (NASA, reproduced in Presidential Commission report.)

The Challenger orbiter breaks into pieces from dynamic forces with the crew cabin intact, as the solid rocket boosters fly away from the debris. The orbiter itself did not explode. The crew cabin hit the ocean surface at 200 miles per hour. Three of the astronauts' emergency air packs had been activated after the orbiter broke up. (NASA, reproduced in Presidential Commission report.)

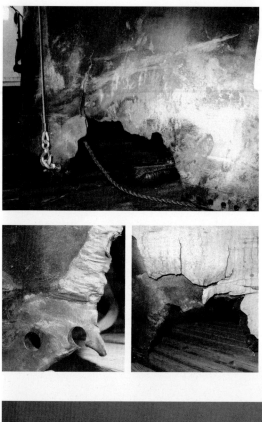

Recovered segments of the right-hand solid rocket booster show a burnthrough "large enough for a man to pass through." After the shuttle broke up, the errant boosters were destroyed by the range safety office by activating built-in explosive charges. The burned-through segments were found and raised from the ocean floor. (NASA, reproduced in Presidential Commission report.)

The author with Roger Boisjoly at a 1991 symposium at SUNY Binghamton sponsored by Dr. Mark Maier. The author had met Boisjoly a year earlier when they jointly received the Cavallo Foundation Award for Moral Courage in Business and Government. (Courtesy Dr. Mark Maier.)

"AFRAID THAT THE MESSENGER MAY BE SLAIN"

—The Commission Moves Ahead—Sort of

AFTER THE FEBRUARY 25–27 hearings, there was a flood of news articles, editorials, and political cartoons about the public spectacle of NASA and its contractors seeming to point the finger of blame at each other. More attentive observers waited in vain for further revelations that would resolve the unconvincing testimony and penetrate the deeper mysteries of the calamitous launch decision.

It should be remembered that few of the disclosures had been initiated by NASA or the Presidential Commission. Rather they began as leaks or testimony by participants in the events, primarily myself at headquarters and Alan McDonald and Roger Boisjoly at Thiokol. The Commission's public hearings mainly covered topics that had already appeared in the press.

The hearings were obviously aimed at containment and damage control. Even so, I felt that William Rogers was sincerely astonished and appalled by the glimpse he got of NASA's attitudes and actions. Now, as time passed, more disclosures dribbled out that showed even more vividly how concerned NASA and Thiokol had been about the O-ring flaws, how no one was willing to suspend flights to fix them, and what an extraordinary state of alert NASA was in because of the cold weather on the evening of January 27 and the morning of January 28, 1986.

The Commission now shifted to the technical issues involved in the accident scenario. With Jesse Moore gone, his successor, Rear Admiral Richard Truly, organized the design and data analysis task force. Former NASA manager James R. Thompson, who had been Marshall's associate director of engineering in charge of space shuttle main engine development, now returned from his current job as deputy director for technical operations at Princeton University's Plasma Physics Laboratory. Thompson was named Truly's deputy for the task force to oversee the technical review that eventually reproduced the SRB burnthrough in laboratory tests. Later, Thompson succeeded William Lucas as Marshall's director after Lucas retired.

On March 6, the White House announced that President Reagan had asked Dr. James Fletcher to return to NASA to serve again as administrator. After leaving NASA at the end of the Ford administration, Fletcher had stayed in the Washington, D.C., area as a business consultant and part-time professor for the University of Pittsburgh. Fletcher had headed the Defense Technologies Study Team, also known as the Fletcher Commission, which laid much of the theoretical foundation for the Strategic Defense Initiative.

Fletcher was part of the mainstream defense establishment, and William Graham now slipped back into the relative obscurity from whence he came. After Challenger, he was never in the running for the top job. Fletcher himself said that NASA needed strong leadership and that Graham "has three strikes against him" and "didn't really know what was going on." An unnamed House staff member said Graham " . . . is like a waterbug on top of the water. He has no idea what was going on underneath."

Graham had also lost the confidence of several important senators and congressmen with his refusal to allow James Beggs to fly on the NASA jet to the January 31 Houston memorial service for the dead Challenger astronauts. Reportedly among those who opposed him as permanent administrator were Senator Jake Garn, himself a shuttle passenger, and the chairman of the Senate space subcommittee, Slade Gorton.

But Graham got off lightly. If NASA had in fact blown up Challenger trying to get it into orbit in time for the president's State of the Union speech, Graham would have had to have been closely involved in implementing the decision. But he was never asked a single question about his role in any of the Commission's open or closed hearings.

Graham's term at NASA ended when President Reagan named him to be White House science adviser and head of the Office of Science and Technology Policy. He succeeded George Keyworth, one of Graham's main sponsors for the NASA job, who had left his White House position in 1985. After a delay of several weeks, Graham's appointment was confirmed by the Senate on October 1. His main function as what was called the nation's "top scientist" would be to pick up where Keyworth left off in selling SDI to Congress and the academic community.

Graham did make one notable decision, which was to inform Admiral Truly in a March 1986 memo that NASA would shift to a mixed fleet of shuttle and unmanned launches to deploy commercial satellites. Later in the year, President Reagan issued an order that took NASA out of the commercial launch business altogether. Regarding military flights, the shuttle launch complex at Vandenberg was abandoned. When the shuttle resumed flights in 1988, NASA continued to fly military missions for DoD, but these ended early in the first Clinton administration, with the last dedicated military flight being launched in December 1992. So the "operational" Space Transportation System, intended to be used for all U.S. space launches, was dead. This was the main institutional result of the Challenger disaster. NASA would return to its original and proper calling as a scientific, research, and exploratory agency.

James Beggs resigned as administrator to clear the way for Fletcher, who had complained that the Presidential Commission was starting to seem like a "witch hunt." On the eve of his Senate confirmation hearing, the *New York Times* published an editorial entitled, "Escape the NASA Nightmare," saying that Fletcher belonged to an era of NASA that had failed. But the only senator to vote against Fletcher's confirmation was Al Gore, who found similarities in Fletcher's "Star Wars" study to his earlier claims of huge numbers of shuttle flights and amazingly low unit costs.

On March 7, the Presidential Commission conducted another public hearing at the Kennedy Space Center. The topic was a presentation by Marshall of its scenarios on why the Challenger accident might have occurred. Jack Lee, Marshall's deputy director, carried the burden of the testimony.

Lee admitted to the Commission, "We know the SRB is the failure." He did not mention that every informed person at NASA knew this within twenty-four hours of the disaster. But of the six possible SRB failure scenarios Lee presented, none had to do with loss of O-ring resiliency due to cold temperatures.

A few days earlier, Marshall had conducted a test by forcing cold gas through a four-inch cylinder with simulated O-ring seals. When the seals held, Marshall announced that cold weather had played no part in the Challenger disaster. Their hometown newspaper, the *Huntsville Times*, even railed in an editorial that the Presidential Commission had prematurely judged Marshall's embattled brass.

Roger Boisjoly later commented:

I wasn't pleased with the way MSFC management was diligently attempting to find a condition other than low temperature which caused the disaster. For example, I witnessed NASA spend a two- to three-week side effort to prove that a Challenger joint close-out photo showed a twisted O-ring prior to mating. This was after I told them that the photo was only showing a track of smeared grease and not a twist, because I had run a desktop test myself some time before to show that the O-ring could not twist as they were contending. I was proved right after their efforts failed to produce a twist in the O-ring, and they finally admitted that the photo showed a smeared grease track.

The Marshall scenarios had one thing in common. They all shifted attention away from the Marshall/Thiokol pre-launch teleconference. The testimony matched Apocalypse's description of the Marshall cover-up, which was to "present as much highly technical data as possible, letting the situation in the general public's mind be diluted by various conflicting theories which were sure to result."

But it was far too late for these kinds of games to succeed. Twice during the March 7 hearing, Chairman Rogers said, "some other outside independent source" might be better qualified to do the testing than Marshall. A Commission source told the Associated Press that, "The Presidential Commission believes much of the testimony it is hearing from NASA and its contractors is self-serving," and that "the Commission is especially irritated with testimony from officials at Huntsville's Marshall Space Flight Center."

Some members of the public, though, were impressed by Marshall's March 7 performance. One bystander who attended the hearing told the *Orlando Sentinel*, "We are observing geniuses at work."

This was Marshall's last shot at downplaying the issue of O-ring resiliency in the cold weather. They seemed to be raising every spurious possibility they could think of. But by late April, tests conducted for the Commission by NASA engineers and outside experts showed that the SRB field joint could start to fail at a temperature as low as fifty degrees F. The tests were supervised by General Kutyna, who told the *New York Times*:

> The bottom line is that temperature is the key variable, but temperature alone didn't cause it. . . . Even on a warm day, I wouldn't fly that rocket.

The working group that conducted the tests came to several other conclusions:

- After Challenger broke apart, a second joint failed on the right SRB and another plume appeared. This was further proof of the fragility of the SRB joints.
- After each flight, the SRB segments ballooned slightly during subsequent testing and never regained their shape. This raised new questions about the reusability of the segments. NASA had never discovered this effect.
- The external tank broke from the bottom up when the SRB attachment strut failed. Earlier speculation had focused on a failure from the SRB wheeling and striking the ET with its nose cone.
- The shuttle did not "explode." The smoke seen in videos was hydrogen and oxygen burning in the atmosphere. The orbiter was ripped apart by aerodynamic forces.

———

HAVING BECOME AN actor in the public drama of the Challenger aftermath, I was not ready to fade away, especially as it became clear that the Commission would never attempt to discover the real reasons for the launch decision. Except for my new supervisor at Treasury, who soon would be leaving for another job, no one else there seemed to want to stand in my way. Being at almost the bottom rung of the general schedule pay grades, I had little more to lose, and I was ready to fight any attempt to remove me altogether from the federal service. At home at night I was working on a paper analyzing the causes of the Challenger disaster. It had three parts: the NASA budget, the organizational atmosphere, and the politics of the space program, including the shift in NASA's priorities to a military orientation.

Around this time, Kathy Sawyer, the space reporter for the *Washington Post*, phoned me for an interview. She was researching the political history of the space shuttle, and, when we met, I mentioned my paper to her. She discussed it with David Ignatius, who was editor of the *Post*'s Sunday "Outlook" section.

Ignatius was enthusiastic and wanted to publish the segment on organizational factors within NASA that contributed to the tragedy. The article appeared on Sunday, March 16, as the lead "Outlook" story, with the title, "Why I Blew the Whistle on NASA's O-ring Woes." The title was invented by a *Post* headline writer without my knowledge. I didn't like the label of "whistleblower," but I guess I was stuck with it.

Looking back years later, my statements may seem obvious. But at the time, less than three weeks after the details of the Thiokol prelaunch teleconference became public, I was the only participant in the events who was saying these things. I wrote:

> At the February 27 hearing of the Presidential Commission, Marshall and headquarters top managers gave the impression that they never saw the O-rings as a flight safety issue or as a serious concern. From my own experience I can say that at both locations people understood completely the implications of a possible O-ring failure. It's just that it was viewed as "no problem."
>
> . . . In their testimony and comments to the press, some seemed almost proud that they could claim not to have been overly concerned or not to have been informed. But in their justifications for not taking action, they overlooked the fact that the shuttle did blow up because of problems that were known and not corrected. Yet in their testimony, people actually seemed to believe they were excused by saying they didn't see the problem as all that serious.

This apparent blindness might seem even more astonishing except that it may relate to the fact that NASA's strong self-image works against any impulse by its personnel to admit to major problems or mistakes.

Unfortunately at NASA, the agency's achievements have been elevated by many to a plane approaching idolatry, shown by countless posters and photographs of the space shuttle and other pieces of machinery that adorn the walls of hallways and offices. With many employees, this overwhelming presence of the agency's image—sometimes mistaken for "morale"—was such that the impact of the Challenger disaster scarcely penetrated. To me the explosion was a tragedy of unfathomable proportions from the hour it happened. But it was quite natural for many of NASA's staff to believe that once the problem was solved and the screw tightened to fix it, the shuttle would be back in the air again, with teachers and who-knows-what-else on board. Some dreamers were even predicting a June launch, an estimate I could not then believe and which has since proved wrong.

I was also continuing my conversations with Christine Dolan of CNN. She was delving into the right-wing plot carried out in 1985 to maneuver William Graham into the administrator's job at NASA. It was Dolan who identified the Heritage Foundation, Attorney General Edwin Meese, and White House personnel director John Herrington as parties to this intrigue and who pointed out the dubious circumstances under which Beggs was indicted. The purpose of the enterprise? "The whole thing at NASA was military," she told me, which accorded with my own observations. It had been clear to me and others at NASA that Graham's arrival signified a major shift toward use of the shuttle to support SDI.

The Commission now conducted a series of private interviews with NASA managers, engineers, and technicians. These interviews were carried out by staff investigators on detail from the FBI or Justice Department who reported to Executive Director Alton Keel.

I was interviewed three times by Commission investigators, but before that, NASA's Office of Inspector General wanted to talk to me. I had been called by Frank Curran, head of the IG's office at Goddard Space Flight Center, located just outside the capital beltway in Greenbelt, Maryland. On Tuesday, March 18, two days after my *Washington*

Post article, Curran came downtown with a woman colleague for a morning meeting.

Much of the interview concerned my memos on the O-rings. Curran asked, "Why didn't you come to us with your concerns when you were writing memos?"

I said, "I didn't know you guys got involved. I thought you did contract financial problems."

Curran answered, "Oh yeah, that's what people think of us."

Not once did the idea enter my head, during the time I worked for NASA, of going to the IG. I was documenting my findings and filing them in writing through the appropriate management channels. I was not playing the role of whistleblower within the organization.

Curran took copious notes, until I began to talk about the Graham/Meese/Beggs scenario. Then he put down his pen. I saw that I was speaking on this topic in vain. I then told Curran about my concerns for safety in the Centaur program, but without mentioning the history that I had written. He seemed to know nothing about Centaur or problems in that area. There the interview ended.

A few weeks later, Curran phoned me for a second meeting and came back downtown. His first question was, "What about Centaur?" I felt some fear in exposing myself as having left NASA with a major piece of analysis that I had never submitted to my superiors, but I felt it was in the public interest to give him my history and did so. On June 19, 1986, NASA canceled the shuttle-Centaur program. It was a wise decision in light of the unresolved safety issues.

Of course, if NASA had moved ahead with Centaur and the type of disaster that was possible occurred, publication of my history would have been a shocker, probably exceeding the impact of the O-ring memos. I was glad that I had given Curran the study and felt I made my greatest contribution to the space program by writing it. At this point, the IG was clearly the right audience.

On March 28, I was interviewed by Commission investigators Randy Kehrli and Pat Maley. Kehrli was a Justice Department attorney and Maley an FBI agent. Neither of these young men seemed to have much experience within the government. We met at the Commission's offices on Sixth Street, S.W., across from NASA. Kehrli said they were interviewing me because of my testimony to the commission, my *Washington Post* article, and two letters I had sent Rogers.

The first letter was the one I gave the Commission at the February 18 Senate hearing, providing them with the Manifest Bingo documents. The second was a shorter one, dated March 20, in which I wrote:

> I believe there is sufficient evidence for the Commission to include the following in its investigation:
>
> The real possibility that Dr. William Graham was involved in the decision to launch Challenger;
>
> Launch pressure from the shift in NASA's highest priority from civilian to military flights;
>
> Whether William Lucas was involved in any political pressure to launch [i.e., via the motel room conversation with Mulloy and Reinartz];
>
> The possibility that individuals within the administration approved the decision to seek an indictment of James M. Beggs in order to remove him from the leadership of NASA because of his known opposition to Dr. Graham's appointment and to making military flights NASA's highest priority. Mr. Beggs was indicted for alleged actions which in all previous cases had been resolved through administrative procedures;
>
> Whether in flying military missions NASA is in violation of the National Aeronautics and Space Act of 1958 and whether the Defense Department should have its own manned spaceflight capability under the terms of the act;
>
> Whether Mr. Beggs might have been able to stop the launch of Challenger had he not had to leave office under whatever circumstances he did leave.
>
> In my opinion, these matters should be explored at the staff level prior to hearings. I shall be glad to participate in any staff review. . . . I have also discussed most of these matters with NASA's Office of Inspector General.

The first half of the interview concerned the sources of the statements I had made in my O-ring memos. I also made the point that there were many other problems besides O-rings in the solid rocket booster program, including Thiokol quality control, the loss of SRB cases through attrition, shuttle processing turnaround times at KSC, and the filament wound case. These were issues I had also spoken about at the Commission's February 11 public hearing.

Kehrli and Maley then asked me to explain my statement that the Commission should investigate "launch pressure coming from the shift in NASA's highest priority from civilian to military flights."

> Mr. Cook: . . . . It was known to me, and expressed to me, that the military flight schedule was an urgent flight schedule, that, first of all, just in terms of numbers, the SDI depended on NASA's flying.
>
> On the 23rd of July of 1985, Abrahamson told the House that the projected flight schedule for SDI flights would exceed the projected NASA launch capability. That wasn't even to mention Kutyna's flights that he was going to fly out of Vandenberg [i.e., for military satellite launches].
>
> We were looking at—when the filament wound case wasn't going to make it—we thought the first Vandenberg flight was going to slip and probably steel [SRB] cases were going to have to be diverted from the Kennedy launch schedule to meet the military flight schedule.
>
> This was a clear indication of a priority for the military schedule and of the urgency of supplying equipment to meet that. NASA's budget depended upon military reimbursements. NASA could not meet that flight rate on its own budget. It required commercial reimbursements, which was a declining factor because we were nowhere near meeting the commercial flight rate. In fact, we were cutting back on [commercial] reimbursements in our budget iterations as we went through them.
>
> The budget was growing more and more to depend on DoD [Department of Defense] flights. You couldn't meet your payroll, you couldn't pay your contractors, unless that money was coming in and unless that flight rate was met. And so the programming—and it was a very tightly interlocked program—was coming more and more to depend on meeting the military flight rate and on the urgency of doing so.
>
> Mr. Kehrli: I guess that is from a budgetary angle?
>
> Mr. Cook: It is not just a budgetary angle. It is a scheduling angle and equipment availability angle. That involves all of these other variables, attrition and turnaround time, I mean the whole thing.
>
> And when you have a national security requirement, you can simply say, "Okay guys, look, we're sorry, we have to fly your Jupiter [scientific] probe a year from now." It's one thing to say that, and the scientists do it and they put the thing in mothballs for a year. It's another thing to say,

"We're sorry, we can't do military reconnaissance for a year." It is a totally different atmosphere.

Even though the Commission devoted Chapter VIII of its final report to "Pressures on the System," it did not mention pressures from the military flight rate. In its section on "The Space Shuttle Design," it did not mention that major design decisions had been made to accommodate Air Force requirements. It did not mention the likelihood that Marshall suppressed the issue of cold temperatures on the O-rings at least in part because it did not want to interfere with military flights out of Vandenberg. It did not mention the agreement which Jesse Moore signed with Secretary of the Air Force Aldridge just a few days before the Challenger disaster, cited in Chapter 10 of this book, which would have led to half or more of all shuttle flights being dedicated to military missions by 1991. It did not mention that the shuttle was to become the primary testing platform for SDI weapons. Finally, it did not mention the issue I raised in writing and interviews about whether it was even legal, under the National Aeronautics and Space Act of 1958, for NASA to be flying DoD payloads at all. During the Commission's investigation, I was the only person to raise these issues, but I was ignored.

At the end of the interview, Kehrli asked me for any other memos I had written on the space shuttle program. I mentioned the ones that are cited in early chapters of this book, as well as others, and gave him copies. These included my report on the flightworthiness review for the filament wound case. Kehrli also asked me if I had sold NASA documents to any press sources, which I had not. The Commission did not cite any of these memos in its final report, probably because they indicated a much higher awareness of problems with the solid rocket boosters at headquarters than the Commission cared to convey in a study that was a whitewash of the high degree of knowledge of top headquarters officials.

Around this time, solid rocket motor engineer Paul Herr, the source of much of the information in my memos and some of the documents I gave to the New York Times, was being interviewed by Commission investigator Emily Trapnell. I read the transcripts of Herr's interviews several months later, after the Commission had completed its work and shipped its documents to the National Archives.

In the two interviews, Herr corroborated the views I have ascribed to him throughout this book. In contrast to the representations made by NASA managers to the Commission at various points that they did not view the O-ring joints as a "safety of flight" issue, Herr said that in 1984, "I became very concerned about it," as a "potentially lethal problem area."

Herr explained how the Marshall engineers had come to him with their concerns about the O-rings and how he raised the issue in Code M meetings. He said, "I kept bringing it up every time I could . . . that we really need to be working this problem."

In its final report, the Commission wrote a thirty-two-page chapter entitled, "An Accident Rooted in History." The chapter covered the history of the O-ring joints from the initial design to the Challenger disaster. It did not mention Herr's statements or interviews, which contributed to evidence of the high degree of knowledge of joint problems at NASA headquarters.

Herr noted that the former director of the Propulsion Division—David Winterhalter's predecessor—had been reluctant to raise such issues. This director, Herr said, was:

> . . . not totally responsive—and I'm trying to be fair about it—to—to problem areas for one reason or another, which I could never really put my finger on. . . . I guess he was just afraid that the messenger may be slain if he carried bad news to the front office.

In his second interview, Herr described how the safety program fit in.

> Mr. Herr: Well, I don't want to sound like a smarty, but let me tell you, at the moment, in the last couple or three years, it has been very meager and infrequent, I think could best describe it. At one time there was a strong quality and reliability group within the shuttle program office until I guess it was about 1983. It was deemed by upper management that we didn't need that program.
>
> The shuttle was becoming operational, so it was divorced, and therefore each time we had any kind of a quality problem we had to go

through another organization to get their attention, and usually what I got was that, hey, things are in great shape, quit sweating it. Yet we were responsible for the hardware that had to be flightworthy, and I thought it was not only an unfair situation, but untenable, and I think that has proven to be true.

Ms. Trapnell: How about the way that the SR&QA [safety, reliability, and quality assurance] organizations function at the centers? Do you think there is any more effectiveness of those organizations on the center level?

Mr. Herr: Well, I would say there is a little more effectiveness, because they have a greater depth and . . . more staff, which is good and bad, and a lot of their normal reviews are perfunctory.

They set up a system, and there again, the project office has to rely on their judgment to provide the hardware manufacturing quality coverage that is acceptable to the center director and not to the program office, and there again, that is a double-edged sword.

The program office wants good quality. They have to go through the center director, and if they, of course, needless to say, if they want to cover something up, why, they don't have to work very hard at it. So is it—the whole quality office in my opinion needs to be looked at again and maybe reassessed as far as how it is implemented.

Herr was talking about how things worked at the Marshall Space Flight Center, where the director was William Lucas and the head of the SRB program office was Larry Mulloy. The implication was that Marshall's managers were covering certain things up, though Herr did not identify specifics. Herr concluded this part of the interview by saying:

In an operational program like this, the quality of the hardware is paramount, and I guess I have been concerned about that. In this O-ring thing, whether it is quality or design or negligence or whatever hasn't been firmly established, but any one of the three can cause a lot of trouble.

What may have been the most valuable part of Herr's testimony has been lost to the record. In the April 7 interview, he told Emily Trapnell that in 1985 he prepared a "package" of documentation on the O-ring joint problem for a management official at NASA headquarters. When I read the transcript on file at the National Archives, the transcript stated that the interview tape was "inaudible" the several times Herr mentioned the official's name. This section of the transcript read as follows:

> Ms. Trapnell: 51-C?
>
> Mr. Herr: 51-C, correct. (Inaudible) 51-C was severe erosion, which triggered (inaudible) put together a package of what went on, I think I did, and submitted it to him. And that was like in the timeframe of— oh, I don't know, May or June—and the reason it took that long is because it came up as an FRR item for the next launch in June. So I (inaudible) correspondence (inaudible). And also (inaudible).
>
> Ms. Trapnell: And that was in the package you put together for Mr. (inaudible)?
>
> Mr. Herr: That's right. And I put a note in there. And I told him that we needed some (inaudible) some office help (inaudible).

The transcript continued like this for two more pages, then closed with the statement, "At this point, the balance of the tape is untranscribable."

Herr's "package" was not in the Commission's records at the National Archives. This was an astonishing omission. Commission investigators had searched the files at Marshall for pertinent documents, but evidently not at headquarters. Or if they did find it at headquarters, they did not mention it in their report or send it to the archives with the rest of their records.

If they did find the package, why didn't they mention it? Was it to protect the management official for whom Herr had prepared it? The critical nature of this discussion related to the fact that 51-C was the cold weather launch of January 1985, which caused severe O-ring blow-by and the massive presence of dark soot.

This was the flight that set the alarms ringing at Thiokol and Marshall about the effects of cold temperature on the O-rings. The question must therefore be raised whether Herr's package contained such references. If so, this would further undermine the attempt by the Commission to portray NASA's top managers as being uninformed. Herr, after all, was in close touch with the engineers at Marshall, where this concern had registered in the Science and Engineering Directorate and the SRB program office.

When I read the transcripts of the Herr interviews at the National Archives, I asked the archivist-in-charge to direct me to the interview tape, which was listed as having been turned over by the Commission when it deposited its files. The tape was supposedly being held in the archives' audio collection, and I wanted to listen for myself to determine if the official's name and other details about Herr's package were truly inaudible. Herr's package might have cast further doubt on the already dubious assertion in the Commission's final report that those who launched Challenger were unfamiliar with the recent history of the O-rings.

But the tape was blank.

The archivist had no explanation and said she would look into the matter and let me know. At a later visit, she said that technicians had examined the tape under a microscope and ascertained that nothing had ever been recorded on it—it was a blank original. She said that "three or four" other tapes were blank as well. But despite my request, the archives never contacted me with a further explanation. Apparently, these key pieces of evidence, important parts of the official U.S. government record, had been tampered with. And they certainly would not have been tampered with by the staff of the National Archives.

The NASA astronauts were the next to be heard from, when the Commission conducted another hearing on April 2 in Washington, D.C. By now, it was evident what a dangerous piece of hardware the space shuttle really was and what a poor job NASA's men-in-suits had done in managing it. The Commission's sympathies lay with the astronaut corps, not the least because two of its members—Neil Armstrong and Sally Ride—were space celebrities.

Criticism of NASA had been fueled by the emergence of senior astronaut John Young's memo dated March 4, which appeared in the *Houston Post* before being released publicly by the new Associate Administrator for Space Flight Richard Truly. In the memo, Young wrote:

> From watching the Presidential Commission's open session interviews on television, it is clear that none of the direct participants have

the faintest doubt that they did anything but absolutely the correct thing in launching 51-L at every step of the way. While it is difficult to believe that any humans had such complete and total confidence, it is even more difficult to understand a management system that allows us to fly a solid rocket booster single-seal design that explosively, dynamically verifies its Criticality 1 performance in its application. . . . There is only one driving reason that such a potentially dangerous system would ever be allowed to fly—launch schedule pressure.

Testifying at the April 2 hearing were Young, who was director of the Astronaut Office; Paul Weitz, his deputy, who flew on STS-6; Robert Crippen, a four-time shuttle veteran; and three-flight veteran Henry Hartsfield. Also on the dais was Young's supervisor, George Abbey, JSC's flight crew director, but not an astronaut. Later in the day, Arnold Aldrich, the Level II manager from Houston, returned to the stand to testify on NASA's "communication" problems.

It was an event never before seen in Washington, D.C.—the cream of America's active astronautical talent on a public stage, testifying before a Presidential Commission, without, moreover, the presence of NASA's politicized managers to muffle their opinions. The hearing provided a clear picture of how the 1985 regime of nine shuttle missions had been pushing their capacity to support the program to the maximum.

John Young said that the qualities required of an astronaut were "desire, dedication, determination, drive, and the ability to work with others," and that in 1985 they were "working as hard as the system can work." He said the system broke down when the astronauts were not informed about the flawed O-ring joints. Richard Truly, pilot for the second shuttle mission back in 1981, had already said that he was not told of the first appearance of O-ring erosion on that flight until after the Challenger disaster.

Robert Crippen, who had attended flight readiness reviews where O-ring erosion had been presented by managers from Marshall, spoke next. He talked about the 51-E flight readiness review that followed the January 1985 51-C cold weather flight. The fact of the 51-C erosion had been discussed, but "it really wasn't that big of a deal."

Crippen also said he was not aware that redundancy on the joint had been waived. He added that the shuttle was so complex that the astronauts had to rely on the people who operated the systems. Young then said that the system "should have taken care of the process long before it got to an FRR."

Young also said that the astronauts had wanted to get rid of the explosive devices on the external tank and SRBs, since, if the shuttle system was as safe as it supposedly was, these weren't needed. But, he added, "We just got some data saying it's not as reliable as it should be."

Other problems were discussed, including brake and landing problems, lack of adequate training time in the shuttle simulators, disruption from last-minute changes in the shuttle cargo manifest, the need for an independent internal safety panel at NASA, and a lack of orbiter spare parts, leading to frequent cannibalization.

There was a memorable moment during the hearing when astronaut Henry Hartsfield said that even though the shuttle was in no way an operational system, "Nobody has a machine like this." It was "a magnificent machine."

Commissioner Richard Feynman answered that it was also "a risky machine . . . with flaws." He said that at flight readiness reviews officials "agonize whether they can go," even though the SRB seals eroded on the previous flight. But they go and nothing happens, so they lower their standards because "they got away with it last time." He called this "a kind of Russian roulette," "a perpetual movement heading for trouble."

By this point in their investigation, the Commission seemed to have convinced itself and the public that the chief cause of the Challenger accident was poor communications among the various management levels at NASA. In this vein, Arnold Aldrich now stated that there were at least three other breakdowns, besides the fact that the problem with the joint seals was "not brought through my office in either direction." The other breakdowns, he said, were that he was not informed of objections by the Thiokol engineers to the Challenger launch, that funds were being programmed for a joint redesign, and that at flight readiness reviews the problem was presented as of "limited concern" or "not a concern."

But "communication" is a two-way street. In my opinion, Jesse Moore was correct when he said in an April 24 interview with Commission investigators:

Level II [i.e., Aldrich as national Space Transportation System manager], with appropriate penetration, should have been aware of this. I mean, I think they should have been interacting with Marshall enough to know about this particular problem.

Moore's comment showed how a focus on "communications" glossed over the fact that it was people, not systems, who were at fault for not utilizing the extensive mechanisms for interaction available at NASA. The O-ring flaws were the skeleton in NASA's closet. Dozens of people knew about the problem. The real question was why people failed to comprehend, if not facts, at least their import. At the April 2 hearing, Henry Hartsfield said bluntly, "The system obviously depends upon people. I mean the people are the weak link."

———

WHEN CHALLENGER BLEW up, there was so much debris that pieces rained down on the ocean surface for nearly an hour. That afternoon, NASA's booster rocket recovery ships, along with Coast Guard and Navy vessels, began to move into the impact area to retrieve floating fragments, mainly sections of the lightweight aluminum external tank.

Over the next few days, currents from the Gulf Stream carried detritus up the Atlantic Coast, so that the search area eventually extended ninety miles out to sea and as far north as Cape Hatteras, North Carolina. By February 7, the search for surface wreckage was complete. The more difficult job lay ahead of raising the pieces that sank to the ocean floor.

It would seem that the most urgent part of the task would be that of recovering the crew remains. President Reagan had eulogized the astronauts as "our seven Challenger heroes." He spoke of their "brave sacrifice." Throughout history, the timely burial of those who had fallen in the line of duty has been an emblem of decent, civilized society and part of the honor owed by the living to the dead.

This now might have seemed a manageable task, as photos of Challenger's breakup released on April 23 showed the crew compartment from the shattered orbiter emerging intact from the fireball.

Thus there had been reason to believe that by plotting the module's trajectory, the point of ocean impact could be readily determined and the compartment located. Timely retrieval of the bodies would allow meaningful autopsies to be performed. This might allow forensic investigators to determine the precise time and cause of death, which could aid in the design of a safer shuttle. But this could also show that NASA might have been wrong in the claim it made initially that the astronauts died immediately when the shuttle blew up.

Another reason for timely recovery of the crew capsule might have been to gain access to tapes of crew conversations over the internal audio system that were not tracked by Houston ground controllers. Observers were shocked, therefore, when NASA gave recovery of the crew remains a low priority.

With the aid of computers, the recovery team used photographs and telemetry data to establish the probable point of ocean impact of major shuttle fragments. Covering only a few square miles a day, surface vessels then scanned the seabed with sonar, while submarines took video images of likely wreckage.

NASA had decided not to attempt the recovery of all debris, but to concentrate on what seemed essential to analyzing the accident. By the end of April, this comprised thirty percent of the total shuttle, including pieces of the orbiter, external tank, and solid rocket boosters.

NASA claimed that the crew cabin was not found until March 7, almost six weeks after the disaster. It had shattered at water impact but was held together by a web of electrical wire. The cabin was resting at a relatively shallow depth of 90–100 feet, fifteen miles offshore.

The Presidential Commission did nothing to urge the recovery of the remains, despite the potential importance of an autopsy to a complete accident analysis. Finally, during the first week in April, the remains were raised by divers from the Navy ship Preserver. The area had been sealed off from the press and other observers. The remains were unloaded at night and taken for autopsy to the Life Sciences Support Facility at Patrick Air Force Base on Cape Canaveral.

Three bodies were brought to shore in bags and taken to the base in thirty-gallon plastic garbage cans in the back of a Navy pick-up truck. The rest were transported in aluminum coffins. According to the January/February 1989 *Space Age Times*:

> In the last of its dubious actions, NASA officials asked Brevard County, Florida, medical examiners to sign death certificates, even though they had never seen the bodies. When they refused, the remains

were taken onto federal property where the state has no jurisdiction, and NASA typed up their own death certificates.

Three weeks later, NASA carried the bodies by hearse to KSC's shuttle landing strip. On April 29 they were flown to the Air Force Military Mortuary at Dover, Delaware, for release to the families.

Why did NASA wait so long to bring up the remains? William Shannon, columnist for the *Boston Globe* and former U.S. ambassador to Ireland, speculated on August 6 "that NASA deliberately prolonged the search in the hope that the warm waters of the Gulf Stream would decompose the bodies and make an autopsy by pathologists much more difficult."

Recovery of wreckage from the right-hand solid rocket booster confirmed the burnthrough. In early April, the Navy's research submarine NR-1 located a piece of the rocket's aft-center segment with a 15 x 28-inch semicircular hole burned through it along the rim where the O-ring joint had been. The hole could not have been in a worse location —only two feet from the surface of the external tank.

Soon the salvagers pulled up the adjoining piece of the booster's aft segment, also with a charred hole, and on April 28, the ship recovered the final piece of the burnthrough area. A total of six square feet of the booster's casing had burned away along twenty-eight inches of joint circumference. What likely had started as a tiny blow hole through the layer of putty inside the joint had, in seventy-three seconds, grown large enough to destroy Challenger and its crew and change the U.S. manned space program forever.

PART IV

RESPONSIBILITY

"SHOCKINGLY SPARSE CONCERNS FOR HUMAN LIFE"

—The Commission's Flawed Report

AS APOCALYPSE SAID Marshall's managers were hoping, the attention of the news media was shifting to other topics, such as allegations of illegal influence-peddling by a former Reagan aide and alleged involvement of the Libyan government in a terrorist bombing in West Germany. This led to the April 14–15 U.S. Air Force and Naval air attacks against Libyan leader Muammer al-Gaddafi. The incident drowned out the news of NASA's raising the astronauts' remains and the locating of the burned-through SRB segment on the ocean floor.

The press now fell under attack for its coverage of the Challenger tragedy. In mid-March, Kennedy Space Center Director Richard Smith accused the press of negatively reporting shuttle launch delays. "I don't think it's caused us to do anything foolish," he told the *New York Times* on March 16, 1986, "but that's where the pressure is. It's not from anywhere else." Smith also claimed that the Presidential Commission had "gotten off on a bad foot" by questioning the actions of NASA's officials before they understood the cause of the accident. He said, "There's too much headline hunting, and this is distorting the picture and causing potential long-term damage to the agency."

In an April 2 *Wall Street Journal* article, staff writers Laurie McGinley and Bryan Burrough sided with complaints that criticism, whether from the Commission, the press, or other outsiders, or internally between NASA centers, "may linger for years and hamper the space program's recovery." The *Wall Street Journal* had also complained that CNN's live coverage of the hearings had been excessive and unnecessary.

After James Fletcher returned to NASA as administrator, he took up the attack. In a speech on May 22, Fletcher said NASA was not "just another government agency," but a "vital national asset." Addressing a group of aerospace industry executives, he said:

> The NASA you and I know made mistakes in the past, corrected them, and moved on. . . . but sometimes I wonder if the NASA you and I know is the same organization that some in the media portray since the Challenger accident.

Fletcher added that some reporters "have acquired a deep and unwarranted suspicion of NASA" that could do "irreparable damage" to the space program. One result, he said, could be morale problems and resignations. Another could be a decline in public and congressional support. Of course this type of complaining about media exposure could also encourage the forces of reaction within NASA and prevent the lessons from Challenger from being assimilated.

There was one NASA official who spoke clearly and forthrightly, providing an exception to the joke going around among newsmen that NASA stood for "Never a Straight Answer." This was James R. Thompson, deputy head of the internal task force investigating Challenger.

On April 8, 1986, Thompson confirmed that the accident had been caused by failure of the shuttle's right-hand solid rocket booster and that the field joint that erupted had "several shortcomings" that should have been repaired. As reported in the *Washington Post*, he said the design was "quite marginal" and that prior flight anomalies "just really weren't taken seriously."

The Challenger news was buried even deeper when on April 26 a nuclear reactor blew up at Chernobyl in the Soviet Ukraine, forcing the evacuation of 92,000 people and sending radioactive clouds over much of Europe. It took a while for Soviet authorities to tell the world what had happened, prompting outrage from the West.

It was clear, however, that as far as technological disasters were concerned, government officials behaved pretty much alike. The statement by Soviet Deputy Prime Minister Shcherbina that the Chernobyl accident was the result of "the coincidence of several highly improbable and therefore unforeseen failures" was similar to those of NASA officials after the Challenger tragedy.

After the astronauts spoke at the April 2 hearing, news reports emerged that additional O-ring documents at Marshall had been destroyed. At Marshall, there was an internal publication called "Weekly Notes" that was issued by the Science and Engineering Directorate under James Kingsbury. According to the Commission's records that I later read in the National Archives, there had been an entry in "Weekly Notes" that cited the effects of cold weather on the O-rings.

Marshall viewed "Weekly Notes" as a basis for internal discussions among engineers and had a policy that they were to be discarded after each use. Still, engineers retained copies for reference. Mike Tackett of the *Chicago Tribune* told me that at a spring 1986 meeting of the S&E Directorate, Marshall's engineers were "reminded" of the policy that all copies of "Weekly Notes" were to be destroyed.

Despite the fate of the "Weekly Notes," other documents from Marshall were found during the investigation that showed how the O-ring joints had been a subject of concern among NASA's engineers from the earliest design stages. The documents included a February 6, 1979, memorandum written by William Ray, stating that the Parker Seal Company, manufacturer of the O-rings, believed "that the O-ring was being asked to perform beyond its intended design and that a different type of seal should be considered."

There was also a January 18, 1984, memorandum from Associate Administrator for Space Flight James Abrahamson to Marshall Director William Lucas that expressed a "growing concern" about "solid rocket motor failures and anomalies across a broad range of NASA, DoD, and U.S. industry programs." Abrahamson wrote, "I also realize that we are now flying motors where basic design and test results are not well understood."

Another document was a February 28, 1984, "routing slip" written by John Miller that raised "urgent" concern about the field joint putty, noting that:

. . . . ZCP [putty] failure to provide a thermal barrier can lead to burning both O-rings and subsequent catastrophic failure.

The Commission conducted one more hearing before it started getting ready to deliver its report to the president. This was on May 2 at a U.S. Department of Transportation conference room near NASA in Washington, D.C. It was a closed meeting, but the Commission released a transcript eight days later.

Just before the hearing, on April 30, an unnamed NASA official told the *Chicago Tribune* that the May 2 meeting was to reinterview some of the witnesses, "especially from Marshall" to discuss discrepancies in their testimony, specifically about the O-rings.

The hearing was triggered when Commission investigator John R. Molesworth of the FBI found some alarming documents as he was searching filing cabinets at Marshall. These showed that Larry Mulloy had imposed, then waived, a "launch constraint," due to the O-ring problem, which applied to each shuttle launch after 51-B in April 1985, when the secondary O-ring had eroded. A launch constraint meant that the shuttle would not be allowed to fly until the problem was fixed. A waiver meant that, yes, it could "fly as is." Neither Mulloy nor anyone else from Marshall had mentioned the launch constraint at any subsequent flight readiness reviews, nor had they told the Commission about it.

Rogers asked Mulloy why the Commission had not been informed of the launch constraint. He also asked why the constraint had been "closed out" in mid-December 1985, so was not even mentioned as a problem in the flight readiness review for the Challenger 51-L mission.

Mulloy responded that closing out the launch constraint was an error. He said that Marshall had received a letter from Alan McDonald of Thiokol "which proposed that this problem be dropped from the problem assessment system," but that it was still "going through the review cycle" at Marshall. He added that dropping the O-ring joint from the problem assessment system was "unfortunate."

But Mulloy was the one to cover the solid rocket boosters in the flight readiness review for Challenger. How could he not wonder why the O-rings were missing from the problem list? Evidently he said nothing about it at the time. But he now told the Commission that, even if the O-ring problem had been covered in the Challenger flight readiness review, it would have made no difference in how he conducted himself in the pre-launch teleconference with Thiokol.

Treatment of the O-ring problem at NASA headquarters had been touched on in the Commission's hearings but not treated extensively. It now came up on May 2. This time, Michael Weeks, Jesse Moore's deputy for technical issues, said of Moore's monthly meetings:

> The O-ring was actively brought into those monthly meetings during the—well, during the entire last couple of years, where, as you well know, there were many of those erosion cases. There was nothing hidden in the flight readiness reviews. There was nothing hidden in the associate administrator monthly reviews that didn't bring forward that there was a significant O-ring erosion problem. And then when the first case of the secondary O-ring being eroded to the tune of about 32/1000 inch, that caused a number of reviews.

Chairman Rogers responded that, "Mr. Aldrich said quite the opposite. . . . Your testimony is, it seemed to contradict that." Rogers expressed his exasperation that NASA and Thiokol had failed to take the many warnings about the O-rings more seriously. One witness answered by saying, "In this case, the train ran down the man waving the red flag."

It had been three months since the Commission was created. From its first hearing, when even the existence of O-rings was so unknown that the New York Times referred to them in a hearing transcript as "old rings," to the explosive leaks of my July 23 memo and the "Death Document" on February 9, to disclosures of the incredible drama of the Thiokol teleconference, and now to the hemorrhage of incriminating records from the Marshall files, the Commission had presided over perhaps the most staggering unveiling of official blundering and concealment in American history.

It was almost inconceivable that such a thing could have happened inside an agency which our culture had come to revere almost as working magic. No one had been able to explain it, and no one tried now.

When the May 2 hearing transcript was released, Mulloy defended himself to the press as he had done after his February 11 and 26 appearances before the Commission. He claimed he had not "intentionally" omitted information during his earlier testimony and that he had not told the Commission about the launch constraint because he did not consider it "significant."

At the February 11 public hearing, before I took the stand, Mulloy had told the Commission there had been "no anomalous erosion" of the O-rings in 1985. When I testified, I said there had been, and Mulloy corrected himself when he resumed his testimony later in the day. He now continued:

> I did not mention that we had an internal tracking system that was dealt with in flight readiness reviews. I didn't feel it needed to be dispositioned.

On Sunday, May 11, the *Washington Post* reported that on the previous Friday:

> Mulloy was transferred . . . from his job as head of the rocket booster project to a newly-created post as assistant to the director of science and technology at Marshall. The new position has no defined responsibilities.

Then on June 5, Marshall Director William Lucas announced that he would retire from NASA in July. That day, the *New York Times* reported that Congressman James H. Scheuer (D-NY) called for a "thorough house cleaning of the whole group of decision makers that led us into this awful tragedy." By the end of 1986, Larry Mulloy, George Hardy, Stanley Reinartz, and James Kingsbury, all of Marshall, had also retired.

The May 2 hearing was the Commission's last. Whether it even should have had public hearings—the transcript of the May 2 event was released so soon after the fact that it was, in effect, public—will always be controversial. Clearly, William Rogers was trying to achieve an effect, and long after the disaster died down, many in NASA had come to believe that his purpose was to deflect attention from the Reagan administration for its politically-contrived flight rate. But the Commission can also be credited for giving those who had something to say the opportunity to speak.

Now the Commission retired into the shadows, while the staff, under Alton Keel, wrote its report. Dr. Richard Feynman complained that the deliberative process was mere " 'wordsmithing'—correcting punctuation, refining phrases, and so on. We never had a real discussion of ideas."

"Besides the wordsmithing," Feynman wrote later, "we discussed the typography and the color of the cover. At each meeting we were asked to vote, so I thought it would be efficient to vote for the same color we had decided on in the meeting before—but it turned out I was always in the minority. We finally chose red. It came out blue."

Rogers wanted to add a recommendation stating, "The Commission strongly recommends that NASA continue to receive the support of the administration and the nation." Feynman viewed the recommendation as "inappropriate."

Finally, Feynman sent Rogers a telegram:

> PLEASE TAKE MY SIGNATURE OFF THE FRONT PAGE OF THE REPORT UNLESS TWO THINGS OCCUR: 1) THERE IS NO TENTH RECOMMENDATION; AND 2) MY REPORT APPEARS AS AN APPENDIX WITHOUT MODIFICATION FROM VERSION #23 OF MR. HANSEN.

Feynman said that the Commission threatened that if he didn't go along, the story would be spread that he was a publicity hound who was trying to sell more copies of the book he was writing. "That one made me smile," he said, "because I could imagine the laughter it would produce from my friends at home."

Finally, there was a compromise. Rogers agreed to print an analysis Feynman wrote of decision making at NASA as an appendix to the report to the president, though Alton Keel crossed out many sections, including a statement that NASA overestimated the safety of the shuttle "through their stupidity or their habits of dissembling." On the other hand, Rogers' tenth recommendation would become a "concluding thought," with the wording changed from "strongly recommends" to "urges." At the last minute, Alton Keel called Feynman to ask how he felt about "strongly urges," but Feynman wouldn't budge.

Most of what the Presidential Commission was expected to say in its report had already appeared in the press during the days before it was released. It was clear that lower- and mid-level officials would continue to be scapegoated.

The Presidential Commission's findings were contained in a 256-page document with nine chapters and four large volumes of appendices. The Commission determined that Challenger was destroyed by a burnthrough of the aft field joint of the right-hand solid rocket booster. The "contributing cause" was the failure to heed the warnings of the Thiokol engineers who recommended not launching in the cold temperatures of the morning of January 28, 1986.

The report made nine recommendations, covering the areas of 1) solid rocket booster joint redesign, including independent oversight by the National Research Council; 2) shuttle management, including management structure, placing more astronauts in management positions, and establishing a new shuttle safety panel; 3) a criticality review and hazard analysis of all shuttle components; 4) establishing a new safety organization within NASA; 5) improving communications; 6) improving shuttle landing safety; 7) improving launch abort and crew escape options, though excluding any possibility that the crew could escape to safety during the two-minute SRB burn; 8) establishing a shuttle flight rate consistent with NASA's resources and no longer relying on the shuttle for all of the nation's space launch needs; and 9) better shuttle maintenance.

As part of its "Concluding Thought," the Commission hailed "NASA's spectacular achievements of the past and anticipates impressive achievements to come." As expected, the report gave the overwhelming impression that the fault lay mainly with the Marshall Space Flight Center. Jesse Moore and Arnold Aldrich were portrayed through quotations and by implication as being essentially uninformed. The report also quoted James Beggs as saying, "I had no specific concerns with the joint, the O-rings, and the putty." If he had no concerns, it was not because he had not been told. Former Deputy Administrator Dr. Hans Mark said he had briefed Beggs on the O-rings and told *IEEE Spectrum*:

The only criticism I have of the report is that they laid more blame on the lower level engineers and less blame on the upper level management than they should have. As with most of those commissions, the guys on the bottom took the rap. They quote Moore and Beggs and a few others saying they didn't know about the O-ring problems, which I find awfully hard to believe. I mean, hell, I knew about it two years before the accident and even wrote a memo about it. So, I mean, I just find it very hard to believe.

The Commission's report did not fault any policies, practices, or actions of the Reagan administration, nor did it trace any decisions leading to the accident back to the White House. This included the broad policy of militarizing the shuttle program.

And the Commission never got to the bottom of why the flawed launch decision was made or who really was responsible. On the issue of whether the White House pressured NASA to launch, the report stated, "The Commission concluded that the decision to launch the Challenger was made solely by the appropriate NASA officials without any outside intervention or pressure."

Finally, while the Commission traced the O-ring problems back to the original design in its chapter on "An Accident Rooted in History," it downplayed the extent of NASA's awareness that cold temperatures seriously degraded O-ring and joint performance.

The Commission's final report contained a section on "STS 51-C and Cold Temperature." The section stated:

On January 24, 1985, STS 51-C was launched. The temperature of the O-rings at launch was fifty-three degrees, the coldest to that date. O-ring erosion occurred in both solid boosters. The right and left nozzle joint showed evidence of blow-by between the primary and secondary O-rings. The primary O-ring in the left booster's forward field joint was eroded and had blow-by or soot behind the ring. The right booster's damage was in the center field joint—the first time that field joint seal was damaged. Both its primary and secondary O-rings were affected by heat, and the primary ring also had evidence of blow-by of soot behind it. This was also the first flight where a secondary O-ring showed the effect of heat.

The report stated that one week later, Larry Mulloy sent Marshall's Larry Wear an "urgent message" ordering that the flight readiness review for the next flight:

> ... should recap all incidents of O-ring erosion, whether nozzle or case joint, and all incidents where there is evidence of flow past the primary O-ring.

This set up what was one of the most critical meetings during the history of the O-ring problem prior to the fateful teleconference the night before Challenger was lost. This was the Level III flight readiness review between Thiokol and Marshall conducted in Huntsville on February 8, 1985, for shuttle mission 51-E, a mission that was postponed, with the designation later changed to 51-D. The Commission's report stated:

> Thiokol presented test results showing "maximum expected erosion" and "maximum erosion experienced" for both primary and secondary O-rings for the field and nozzle joints. Accepting damage to the primary O-ring was being justified in part, based on an assumption of the secondary O-ring working even with erosion. However, the criticality classification indicated the primary seal was a "single point failure" [i.e., the "Death Document"].
>
> During this flight readiness assessment at Marshall, for the first time Thiokol mentioned temperature as a factor in O-ring erosion and blow-by. Thiokol said in its conclusions that "low temperature enhanced probability of blow-by—51-C experienced worst case temperature change in Florida history." Thiokol concluded that the next shuttle flight "could exhibit same behavior." Nonetheless, "The condition is not desirable but is acceptable."

Thiokol also presented a report at this meeting which stated that while the 51-C experience caused a concern that the O-ring seal could be lost, its resolution to this concern was to "accept risk." Thiokol did not present any analysis or rationale at the meeting for this conclusion. Indeed, it really should not have been Thiokol's role to make such a judgment. It was NASA that flew the space shuttle with its astronauts on board. Over the course of my federal career, I have managed many contracts. It is the place of the customer, not the contractor, to decide whether or not to "accept risk."

But there were other references to the effect of cold temperatures on the O-rings at the Level III flight readiness review embedded in the charts for the 51-E FRR in the Commission report's appendices. For instance, there was a statement that during the primary O-ring seating phase following engine ignition, "Low Temperature Shrinks O-ring and Increases Durometer." This statement was repeated in a later chart as well. "Durometer" is a measure of hardness. This statement referred to conditions present for all shuttle launches. Everyone present for the FRR from Marshall and Thiokol now had this information.

Also buried in an appendix to the Commission's report was the fact that the Level III FRR briefing package for 51-E had an entire chart entitled "Temperature Effects." The chart stated,"Thermal Analysis Shows that the SRM Follows Daily Temperatures to a Depth of Five Inches." This referred to the mean bulk temperature of the propellant. Another item on the chart referred to the putty, stating, "Putty Becomes Stiffer and Less Tacky." The Commission concluded in its report that stiffness of the putty, along with the O-rings, can also be a factor in preventing the proper sealing of the joint and so may have contributed to the disaster.

Finally, the chart on "Temperature Effects" had a separate item that stated, "O-ring Becomes Harder." Under this item were three additional statements:

A Viton O-ring with 70 Durometer at 70 degrees Can Increase to 85 Durometer at 20 degrees F.
Temperature Prior to Flight Dropped to 17 degrees F.
Temperature Squeeze Reduced by 1% Due to a 4 degree F. Delta

Thus not only did the Level III FRR contain qualitative statements about the effects of temperature on the O-rings, it contained actual durometer data. The Presidential Commission noted in its report that data on O-ring hardness was developed later in 1985 through bench testing at Thiokol. But this chart proves that similar data was actually available several weeks earlier.

A Level III flight readiness review was only a preliminary step in preparing for a shuttle launch. A similar review would be conducted for the other two major shuttle components—the orbiter and external tank. The next step was to pull the critical data together for the final pre-launch meeting, the Level I flight readiness review. Actually, this would have included both Level I—the associate administrator for space flight from headquarters, Jesse Moore—and Level II—the STS program manager from Houston, Arnold Aldrich, along with mission control and launch control managers from Johnson and Kennedy. Usually the NASA administrator also attended.

The question for Marshall thus became whether they would present Thiokol's concern about the effects of cold temperatures on the O-rings at the Level I flight readiness review for 51-E. This meeting took place at Kennedy on February 21, 1985. James Beggs, Jesse Moore, and Arnold Aldrich were there. But the temperature issue was not discussed.

The question, which the Commission did not answer, was whether Marshall was deliberately concealing critical information from the larger NASA group, which would have included, most particularly, representatives from Houston with ties to the astronaut community. Roger Boisjoly explained the omission in a written statement to the Commission in connection with his testimony at the February 26 public hearing. He wrote:

> I remember as clear as if it were yesterday, that Larry Mulloy did not want us, Al McDonald and I, to make a big deal about temperature effects on STS 51-C in our discussions during the STS 51-E FRR [flight readiness review]. He was afraid it would establish launch commit criteria based on temperature.

Later Roger Boisjoly told me that Mulloy told them he did not want the temperature issue to come up because it might interfere with planned military launches from Vandenberg when that facility came on-line in 1986. Also according to statements by Alan McDonald to the Commission on February 25, NASA said the same thing to him about wanting to avoid interfering with Vandenberg flights the night of the Challenger pre-launch teleconference.

The Commission did not address this issue in its report, yet it clearly supports the argument that there were major compromises with safety due to the government's policy of militarizing the shuttle program.

Deciding not to make O-ring temperature a launch commit criterion in order not to interfere with launches from Vandenberg is not something Larry Mulloy could have done on his own. Such a decision would have had to involve higher management officials at Marshall. Would it have involved anyone at headquarters, or was Marshall a "rogue" organization making its own decisions not to interfere with military flights?

A document in the Commission's records that might have provided a clue to what headquarters management knew at the time about O-ring temperatures was Paul Herr's "package" that was missing from the Commission's records at the National Archives. It was notable that Herr prepared this package after 51-C, the January 1985 cold weather flight. He would likely have gathered information for his package from engineers at Marshall who would have been in attendance at the Level III flight readiness review on February 8, when Thiokol presented the temperature issue and the "fly as is" recommendation.

After the pattern was set with the deliberate suppression of cold temperature considerations at the Level I flight readiness review for 51-E, events marched to their January 28, 1986, denouement.

The next alarming event was flight 51-B launched on April 29, 1985. This was the flight where a primary O-ring on a nozzle joint failed to seal at all and where, for the first time, a secondary O-ring was eroded. This was the flight which Thiokol engineers found "terrifying" and which led to the flurry of activity at Thiokol and Marshall, including formation of a seal task force, the now-infamous August 19 meeting at headquarters, and imposition and waiving by Larry Mulloy of the O-ring launch constraint.

The Commission documented these events in its report, but what it did not state was that the flight readiness review after this mission also referred to the adverse effects of cold temperature on the O-rings. In a chart for the July 1, 1985, 51-F Level III FRR entitled, "STS-51B Nozzle Joint Erosion Scenario," was the statement, "Primary O-Ring Does Not Completely Seal at 54-degrees and Part of Gas Jet Continues Past Primary Seal to Secondary O-ring." As with flight 51-E, the reference to temperature was again deleted when the briefing got to Level I for the FRR on July 2.

Regarding O-ring temperature testing, the Commission report stated:

> In response to the apparent negative effect of cold leading to the extensive O-ring problems on flight 51-C in January, Thiokol conducted some O-ring resiliency tests in early 1985. The tests were conducted to quantify the seal timing function of the secondary O-ring and the effect of joint rotation on its ability to back up the primary ring. The key variable was temperature.

These bench tests were the ones Feynman learned about early in the deliberations, leading to his ice water experiment. The tests, as documented in a June 3 report by Thiokol, showed serious degradation of O-ring performance. On August 9, ten days before Thiokol was to present its analysis of the O-ring problems and possible solutions at NASA headquarters, Brian Russell, a Thiokol engineering manager, wrote in a letter to Marshall's Jim Thomas:

> Bench test data indicate that the O-ring resiliency (its capability to follow the metal) is a function of temperature and rate of case expansion. [Thiokol] measured the force of the O-ring against Instron platens, which simulated the nominal squeeze on the O-ring and approximated the case expansion distance and rate.
>
> At 100 degrees, the O-ring maintained contact. At seventy-five degrees the O-ring lost contact for 2.4 seconds. At fifty degrees the O-ring did not reestablish contact in ten minutes at which time the test was terminated.

The resiliency test results were discussed at Marshall. Center Director William Lucas was known to have attended at least one of these meetings. Though the Commission report did not discuss the issue further, key personnel at Marshall, all the way to the top, knew about the bench test data. This was still almost six months before the Challenger disaster. Later, the House Science and Technology Committee showed in its report a memo containing the exact wording of the Brian Russell memo that was addressed from Marshall engineer Jim Thomas to William Hamby, one of Jesse Moore's Code M engineers. It was Hamby, as stated earlier in this book, who accompanied Irv Davids on his July trip to Marshall, leading to Davids' memo on the history of O-ring erosion that was part of the February 9 *New York Times* disclosures. Without any discussion or proof, the House Committee claimed that the memo to Hamby was not sent, but this again raises the question of what headquarters knew or whether Marshall was a rogue center.

Finally, there was the issue of the "General Conclusions" chart for the August 19 briefing by Thiokol and Marshall at NASA headquarters. I have already pointed out that there were two versions of this chart in the Commission's records at the National Archives. The one appearing in the Commission's report contained the statement, "The primary O-ring in the field joint should not erode through, but if it leaks due to erosion or lack of sealing the secondary seal may not seal the motor." The other version which I found in the archives had the statement added in bold print, "Data obtained on the resiliency of the O-rings indicate that lower temperatures aggravate this problem." If the bold print statement was actually part of the August 19 briefing this would prove beyond any doubt that NASA headquarters was fully aware of the problem.

The Commission downplayed the prior knowledge within NASA. It stated:

> A careful analysis of the flight history of O-ring performance would have revealed the correlation of O-ring damage and low temperature. Neither NASA nor Thiokol carried out such an analysis; consequently, they were unprepared to properly evaluate the risks of launching the 51-L mission in conditions more extreme than they had encountered before.

This statement was central to the Commission's obfuscations. On the night of January 27, 1986, Larry Mulloy told Thiokol that they couldn't come up with a new launch commit criterion at that late date. But NASA's procedures permitted a new launch commit criterion to be instituted whenever it was warranted. What made Mulloy's statement particularly troublesome was that the argument with Thiokol's engineers was a replay of the one that took place a year earlier with the 51-E flight readiness review. That was when Mulloy told Roger Boisjoly the launch commit criterion could not be instituted as a matter of policy because of the Vandenberg flights.

And it was not that NASA was "unprepared to properly evaluate the risks of launching the 51-L mission in conditions more extreme than they had encountered before." A year earlier they had said that the conditions for 51-C were "the worst temperature change in Florida history," so conditions for Challenger were not in fact "more extreme than they had encountered before." Rather they were similar. The truth is that NASA was prepared to accept the risks of launching 51-L, rather than being "unprepared to properly evaluate them." Once again, the question is why?

The action of cold temperatures on O-ring resiliency was thoroughly established. It was established through the experience of 51-C launched in January 1985. It was established through the Thiokol durometer data and bench tests. The entire Marshall hierarchy was familiar with the data.

There were other documents buried in the records at the National Archives indicating that NASA knew about the possibly harmful effects of cold temperatures on the SRB joints even prior to the January 1985 cold weather flight. Document PC102350, for example, was a report from the Certification/Verification Process Committee of July 11, 1980, recommending that NASA "perform additional verification at temperature extremes" of the solid rocket motor, because "O-ring hardness variations up to 20% are common."

Mulloy's statement that in the pre-launch conference with Thiokol he was challenging the "logic" of the Thiokol engineers was puzzling to me. He was seeing data he was familiar with and that Marshall had accepted. And the Commission knew it. Why then was he making this claim?

Were there people within NASA willing for astronauts to die in order for policy objectives to be met? In a general sense, the answer to that question had to be in the affirmative. Without a doubt, the shuttle flight rate was politically motivated. Without a doubt, there was "accepted risk." In a military environment, such an equation can be justifiable, which is yet another indication that the shuttle program had in fact become militarized—in this case in its values. These were more issues the Commission ignored. But even this did not explain what Mulloy and Marshall did the night of January 27, 1986.

———

CHAIRMAN WILLIAM ROGERS, Vice Chairman Neil Armstrong, and the other members of the Commission, along with Executive Director Alton Keel, presented their findings to President Ronald Reagan on June 9, 1986. Following a brief White House ceremony, Rogers held a press conference, where he said that the Commission had found "the exact cause" of the disaster. He was referring to the technical cause—the burnthrough of an SRB O-ring joint.

The question had come up of what was now being called "blame." The concept of "blame," of course, was a far cry from "responsibility." The U.S. system of governance provides many instances of judicial and non-judicial proceedings where responsibility is investigated, identified, and consequences determined. By defining the issue through use of the word "blame," Rogers trivialized an important legal and ethical concept and cast aspersions on those who had a reasonable expectation of proper closure of what clearly had been a preventable disaster. He now told the press:

> We were not asked to assess blame, and we have not assessed blame. . . . I think in a sense this is a kind of national tragedy that a lot of us are to blame for. . . . I think in a sense the administration, Congress, the press—all of us were too optimistic, too willing to accept the fact that this [i.e., the shuttle] is operational. I don't think there's anything to be gained by trying to assess blame.

Rogers and the Commission were praised in the press. The *New York Times* wrote that the "Rogers Commission and its chairman have performed with unusual thoroughness and speed. Their report is a model of rigor, clarity, and fairness." The *Washington Post* wrote, "The Rogers Commission—the Presidential Commission on the Space Shuttle Challenger Accident—has served the country well." *USA Today* wrote that Rogers was "a leader who measured up to the tough job."

On June 6, the *Washington Post* had run a feature story in its "Style" section entitled, "The Public Rebirth of William Rogers: Nixon's Quiet Negotiator Taking Charge in the Shuttle Hearing." The article said:

> Sometimes William Rogers comes on like a prosecuting attorney in his job as chairman of the Presidential Commission on the Space Shuttle Challenger Accident.
>
> This is not surprising. With an entire nation looking over his shoulder, the pressures for a truly soul-searching investigation were enormous. Pressure from President Reagan who picked him. Pressure from industry and the military. Pressure from the media. Pressure from the millions who saw the thing blow up on TV.
>
> Why did it happen? Who is responsible? What is the future of the space program? And, most important, how to keep this from becoming another Warren Commission?

But the Commission did not answer these questions. One or two Marshall managers screwing up did not cause Challenger to explode, the U.S. manned space program to come crashing down with it, and NASA to lose its standing as the world's premier technical institution, as the report implied. And by getting rid of these managers and fixing the SRB O-ring joint, NASA did not address the issues. The situation was more complex.

Despite the shortcomings of the Commission's report, one shudders to think what might have happened had NASA been left to its own devices. NASA had become a flawed institution—flawed in conduct, flawed in intention, flawed in science. But even the relatively mild criticism of NASA by the Commission was resented by many within the agency, who believed from beginning to end that the agency they worshipped could do no wrong. Maybe this was why, when Columbia was destroyed at atmospheric reentry on February 1, 2003, another commission described NASA's culture seventeen years later in terms almost identical to the Challenger Commission's report.

This mindset was expressed at the most human level by Jane Smith, widow of shuttle pilot Michael Smith. In a statement reported in the June 17 *New York Times*, she said of the Commission's report that it:

> . . . reflects incredibly terrible judgments, shockingly sparse concerns

for human life, instances of officials lacking the courage to exercise the responsibilities of their office, and some very bewildering thought processes. . . .

I hope from this tragedy we have learned above all to hold allegiance to the sacredness of human life, to have the courage to place safety first, and to honor those who have the strength to honor truth.

"IT IS NOT GOING TO FAIL BECAUSE OF ME"

—The Senate and House Hearings

AFTER THE PRESIDENTIAL Commission finished its work, both the Senate and the House held hearings.

The Senate conducted only two days of hearings, one on June 10, 1986, the day after the Commission reported to the President, and the other a week later on June 17. On June 10, the senators seemed to be competing to see who could wax the most eloquent in singing the praises of William Rogers and his Commission.

The only one who did not join the chorus was Senator Ernest Hollings (D-SC), who, after thanking Rogers and the other Commission members for their work, said:

> If every time one of these kind of things occurs, and no one is responsible, you can put in twelve more safety commissions, eight more review boards, and nine more other safety groups, and if there is no responsibility to it, it won't be safe. I just feel someone should be accountable, and there has been an indication to me that there has been [i.e., the flurry of retirements and reassignments at NASA and Thiokol].

Hollings now expressed the crucial difference between his interpretation of the disaster and the one presented by the Commission. He said:

As your report indicates, there were some safety procedures. That's another area where you and I differ a little. You say that the process was flawed. I find the process and safety procedures violated.

But the real question that Hollings was interested in was whether there were outside pressures. Senator John D. Rockefeller (D-WV) also touched on the question of pressure. He said:

At the beginning of the space program there was an extraordinary degree of national urgency and consensus and, really, there was a degree of excitement in putting a man on the moon. . . . . Then times pass. The launches go up. People relax a bit. Funding seems to be secure. Then it potentially turns into bureaucracy as you have essentially said in your report. Then there are cozy relationships, the question of pressures, pressure to militarize, pressures of budget, pressures of new competition with the Europeans and Ariane, with the Chinese and the Japanese, the pressure of decreasing budgets from the Congress, the pressures to put politicians and others into space, all kinds of pressures.

This was the first time the militarization of NASA had been mentioned in any of the official deliberations.

But it was political pressure involving the White House that Hollings wanted to talk about. He started by saying, "Well, let us talk about that pressure then for a minute."

He then read the text which had appeared in the news several weeks earlier that NASA had submitted to the White House for inclusion in the president's State of the Union speech the night Challenger was launched. This text appeared in a memo from William Graham that was signed for him by General Manager Philip Culbertson and addressed to Alfred Kingon, White House cabinet secretary, that read:

Tonight while I am speaking to you, a young elementary school teacher from Concord, New Hampshire, is taking us all on the ultimate field trip, as she orbits the Earth as the first citizen-passenger on the space shuttle.

Mrs. McAuliffe's week in space is just one of the achievements in space which we have planned for the coming year. The United States Voyager spacecraft has just this week visited the planet Uranus and sent back striking images of this distant world, after a two-and-a-half billion mile trip in space. Later we will participate in a worldwide study of Halley's Comet, launch the Hubble Space Telescope, launch the Galileo spaceship on its way to Jupiter, and participate with our European partners in sending the Ulysses spacecraft to explore the poles of the sun.

Our commitment to continuation of a strong civil space program, through such projects as the space station, the Space Transportation System, and space science and the technology required for the program of the 1990s are an investment in the future of America's greatness in space and the young men and women of this nation who will be the leaders of tomorrow.

Hollings noted that after the disaster, the White House denied that Challenger or Christa McAuliffe were to be mentioned in the speech. He said:

Now, what leaves us to wonder and still pursue this, is the action, of course, of the White House itself. The White House first denied any reference or any thought or any tinge that the president would refer to the Teacher-in-Space. As we congressmen and senators know, the president always has a pleasant gimmick at the end of his talks. He usually refers to an individual, such as the graduate from West Point that came from Vietnam and was the number one honors graduate, or the one that was saving people down here, the Air Florida crash in the Potomac, Lenny Skutnick.

As we all know, any time the president makes a State of the Union message, we can count on some pleasant wonderful approach that brings everybody in America together and makes us proud of ourselves and what have you. And yet they had us believe that there was no idea whatsoever or any submission whatsoever concerning the Teacher-in-Space program. The fact of the matter is, it was denied that any submission was made to the White House.

Hollings said that not only did the White House deny that Challenger or the Teacher-in-Space was to be mentioned in the speech, but they refused to provide him with a copy of the speech draft. He continued:

And then when we got a copy of the speech, it left off the last page. And then we noted that, and then it came in and we found out, oh yes, the last page did include a reference to the shuttle. But what we find is something that is very difficult for this senator to believe. And you are not the appropriate witness, in a sense, to confirm or deny, and I am not asking that you do. But we see that the president at the time of the Challenger explosion was ready to say that evening, "We see the dream coming true and the spirit of discovery of 21-year-old Richard Cavoli. All his life he has followed the path of science and medicine. Today the science experiment he began in high school was launched on the shuttle Challenger."

Now, obviously there is no question in this senator's mind that the president was going to talk about the Challenger. It is equally obvious to this senator that if he ever was going to refer to the Challenger he was going to refer to Christa McAuliffe.

I cannot understand the reluctance of the Commission to ask people at the White House about it. Were any of the witnesses from the White House asked about that?

Rogers replied that they asked everyone at NASA who was involved in the launch "if there was ever any intervention." He said, "Everyone said no such thing happened."

Hollings asked again if the Commission asked anyone at the White House. Rogers replied that they "did inquire from the White House," though he said no individual interviews were conducted. Rogers then said:

> I sat down with two people who were most involved—that is Jesse Moore and Arnold Aldrich—and asked them man-to-man if anything like that happened. And I said, "I know you have testified and you have testified in public. Did it happen at all?" And they said, "Mr. Rogers, I promise you it never happened." Jesse Moore said, "I was so busy, I did not even know the State of the Union message was on." He said, "That is a Washington phenomenon. I did not know it." He said, "We were involved in this for three days, and I assure you nothing like that ever happened."

Rogers then said that the Commission "got the telephone records of all the people we could get and checked them out, and we could not find any call that suggested this at all." He said a launch/speech link was also denied by Larry Mulloy. Rogers continued:

All of these people, it would have been the most natural thing to say, sure, I blame so-and-so.

It did not happen, and so I am convinced it did not. And I hope that the rumor dies. I hope it dies. . . . And of course, in this case, because it was the juxtaposition of the president's State of the Union and the launch, which was not prearranged, it is natural for the rumor to start. But I am absolutely convinced that it is a rumor, and I just hope it does not continue to live on.

Hollings asked why the Commission did not interview anyone at the White House. Rogers answered:

We did not get involved in that, and I do not think we should, because the White House assured us, and the president said so in public in his television program, nothing like that happened. And I certainly did not feel, and I do not feel now, that we should go around summoning people from the White House, because there just was not anything like that that happened.

It is a little bit like trying to investigate a paternity case, going around asking people who is responsible, but there is no baby. It never happened. There is no baby in this case.

You have got to have somebody who says, I think there may be some evidence. There is no evidence in this case, and if people keep talking about it, some people out there in the public are going to say, maybe there is something to it. There is not. There is not one scintilla of evidence.

Hollings replied, "The baby in this case, Mr. Chairman, again most respectfully, is the explosion itself."

Rogers said, "That is not the baby. That is not the baby."

Hollings:

The baby in this case is the explosion itself, and you found pressure. In addition to the O-ring defect, the scientific or technical fault, there was also the human fault. You expressed it by way of communications. You express it by way of procedures of safety and everything else.

Hollings asked again why the Commission did not interview anyone at the White House. Rogers then surprised everyone by pulling out a letter written by Jay Stevens, deputy counsel to President Reagan, to John R. Molesworth, the FBI investigator assigned to the Commission. The letter said that the State of the Union was not to have mentioned Christa McAuliffe, there was never any plan for a phone connection between President Reagan and Challenger during the speech, and several phone calls, which the letter acknowledged took place between Acting Administrator William Graham and White House officials prior to Challenger, had nothing to do with the launch. The exception, said the letter, was a call from Graham to White House staff member Ann Foreman, inviting her to attend the shuttle launch.

Rogers then tried to conclude the discussion by saying:

> I do not think there is a bit of evidence that anybody tried to influence this launch, and if we keep talking about it a lot of people will believe it happened. It did not happen. If you can prove it, I will apologize to you. I will come back here and apologize if you can prove anything like that happened.

But Hollings was not done. The name of William Graham had now come up through the Jay Stevens White House letter. Hollings went on:

> Let us go to Dr. Graham and bring in his own pressure. Now, if I am the head of NASA, and I have made this particular submission to the White House, what about Dr. Graham and Phil Culbertson? I am Phil Culbertson, the number one man at the Kennedy Space Center on the day of launch. I know I have signed off on a recommendation that starts off saying, "Tonight while I am speaking to you . . . " [i.e., referring to the NASA submission for the State of the Union].

Hollings continued, referring to the likely mindset of Graham and Culbertson:

> Now, I know, trying to get that off—I've already submitted it. I do not know whether the White House is going to do it or not. I do not have any idea. I have not received any calls, as you indicate, or anything else like that, and no individual to call.
>
> But is it not natural for me to assume that, having made that submission to the White House, I would like to be able to carry it out? And

so, like the press jumps on NASA and blames them for an unlatched door [on the Monday, January 27 launch cancellation], necessarily the White House would jump on me and say, "Look, you had us all ready to go and you delayed it again."

So I brought really pressure on myself, is that not correct?

Rogers only replied that he did not object to the question, but that he had "nothing more to say about it." But Hollings had more to say. He asked:

> What did you ask Phil Culbertson? Did you ask Phil Culbertson or Dr. Graham if they had that in their statements?
>
> Mr. Rogers: Sure.
>
> Senator Hollings: Well, you did think to ask them. So the question is not totally unfounded.
>
> Mr. Rogers: No. We asked everybody we could find about whether anything like this happened, and everyone says, no.
>
> Senator Hollings: And you do have a statement from Phil Culbertson, and you do have a statement from Dr. Graham?
>
> Mr. Rogers: Yes, we do.

Here Rogers was referring to the series of interviews that Commission investigators conducted with NASA officials on the issue of outside pressure to launch. Graham and Culbertson were among those interviewed. But I read those interviews, and as I indicated earlier, they seemed to be mainly opportunities for the officials to make ritualistic denials that anything happened. Hollings now closed the trap:

> Now, with respect to your logic, which intrigues me, that somebody would come out and indicate blame [i.e., that Rogers would criticize anyone who believed individual responsibility for the tragedy should be affixed], is it not also logical that if no one is fired, no one is dismissed, then there is no one to blame? It is a sort of a sweetheart deal. Everybody goes their way, and everybody is responsible, and nobody is responsible.
>
> I believe if I had dismissed two or three down the line, then if there had been pressure, logically they would have come forward and said, "Wait a minute. Do not set me aside. I was asked to."

No one says that, and you say, I do not have any evidence of that. But is that part of the lack of finding of any individual responsibility in this Commission's report?

Rogers answered with one word: "No." And there the discussion ended. The Senate committee did not publish a report on the Challenger disaster. Its only record was the transcript of the two days of hearings.

———

THE REVIEW BY the Science and Technology Committee of the U.S. House of Representatives was based mainly on its study of the Presidential Commission's investigation and of its own hearings. The committee wrote its own 442-page report.

The House report had strengths and weaknesses, but since it was not published until the end of October 1986, I will confine the present discussion to the hearings that took place in June and July and discuss the report later. From the start of the hearings, Acting Committee Chairman Robert Roe (D-NJ) made it clear that the committee would not be challenging the conclusions or interpretations of the Presidential Commission. He said:

The Presidential Commission on the Space Shuttle Challenger Accident has made its report to the American people. The distinguished chairman of the Commission, the Honorable William P. Rogers, whom we will hear from shortly, has done an outstanding job in presenting to the nation a remarkable document which fully, truly details the entire story of the failures in technology and human error that ultimately led to the shuttle disaster.

During the hearings the question of militarization of the shuttle came up through a question asked of Rogers by Congressman Harris Fawell (R-IL).

Do you believe . . . the growing entry of the military into the use of shuttles, do you believe that this had anything to do with the increased pressure more than perhaps it should? Have you discussed—what about the future now that the military is certain, banging at the gates and very impatient about moving ahead?

Rogers replied:

Well, we discussed, of course, the idea that—the fact that the military payloads which were included in the space shuttle increased the pressure for launches. And we pointed out that having sort of total reliance on the shuttle was not a wise judgment, and that will be changed in the future, because there are going to be a lot more ELVs [expendable launch vehicles] now in the picture. So, to that extent, the answer to your question is, yes, we did consider that, and we think that will be changed now.

Perhaps the Commission "discussed" and "considered" the issue, but nothing about the militarization of the shuttle had appeared in their report.

The August 19, 1985, meeting at NASA headquarters, where Thiokol and Marshall presented the history of O-ring erosion and their plans to fix the flawed joint design, became a major topic of the House hearings. Despite NASA's contention that the O-rings were not viewed as a "safety of flight" concern, according to a written statement provided by NASA to the House committee, forty engineers from Marshall and Thiokol were working on the problem.

The information developed through the House hearings and report make it possible to reconstruct the August 19 meeting in greater detail and explain its critical significance in the history of the Challenger disaster. During the House hearings, it was Congressman James Scheuer who was the most persistent in trying to penetrate NASA's veil of reticence around how much top officials at headquarters knew about the O-ring problems.

In the June 12 hearing, Scheuer asked Michael Weeks whether in the August 19 meeting Thiokol or Marshall had said anything about the cold temperature issue. Weeks answered:

When the briefing was presented to us on August 19, 1985—as you will look in the briefing that was provided to the Commission on February 10—there was no temperature data presented that showed the resiliency was such a critical factor. It wasn't until after the disaster of

51-L that I actually saw the resiliency data that showed that Viton, which is the O-ring material that we've been using, is so slow to recover at very low temperatures.

Weeks was Jesse Moore's deputy for technical matters, the highest-ranking technical engineer in the office of space flight. But O-ring resiliency was in fact mentioned in the Thiokol briefing document for the August 19 meeting. It was highlighted on the page of the briefing entitled "Primary Concerns," which stated as the first item, "Field joint-joint deflection [i.e., rotation] and secondary O-ring resiliency." Resiliency referred, of course, to the effect of low temperatures.

During the Presidential Commission hearings, this briefing chart was discussed in an exchange between Kutyna and Thiokol's Alan McDonald, who made the presentation to NASA headquarters on August 19. The exchange was also cited in the House report and went as follows:

> General Kutyna: . . . . there has been some question that people understood that there was a temperature problem. I remember your conclusions chart, . . . and the very first bullet of that chart had the word "resiliency" in it. Do you feel when you talked about resiliency at that meeting people got the connection between resiliency and temperature, that resiliency was a function of temperature, or was that lost?
>
> Mr. McDonald: It may have gotten lost because we hadn't run a very long range of temperatures when we got that data.
>
> General Kutyna: So it is possible that people at headquarters from that briefing did not understand temperature was a concern?
>
> Mr. McDonald: I guess it is possible they could have.
>
> General Kutyna: Is it probable?
>
> Mr. McDonald: I don't know if it is probable, because we put it as the first bullet of why we thought that was our highest concern, and if that hadn't have happened, we wouldn't have had that concern.

Further evidence that the August 19 meeting covered O-ring temperature effects and resiliency was provided during the House hearings by Larry Mulloy, who said:

> The temperature data that was presented that night [i.e., January 27, 1986] was the same data that existed back in July, and was discussed,

as I say on August 19, three test data points, one at 100 degrees, one at seventy-five degrees, and one at fifty degrees, and what the discussion centered around was what does that mean in terms of the capability to make a seal in that joint.

Mulloy, who was at the August 19 meeting, flatly contradicted Weeks. He said that the bench test resiliency data was discussed. Weeks said it was not. NASA headquarters also provided evidence that Mulloy was right and Weeks wrong. On August 5, 1986, Lynn W. Heninger, NASA's director of the Congressional Liaison Division, sent a letter to committee chairman Roe to "clarify" matters with respect to the August 19 meeting. Heninger wrote, "It was because of this O-ring resiliency data that Morton Thiokol concluded that the field joint was most critical and that was highlighted on page C-1 of the August 19, 1985, presentation."

So according to Heninger, a headquarters official, the resiliency of the O-rings; i.e., the effects of cold temperatures, was "highlighted" on August 19.

Due to the apparent differences between what Weeks and the others were saying, the committee asked Weeks for a sworn affidavit on what was said at the August 19 briefing. In this affidavit, Weeks revealed for the first time that he had visited the Morton Thiokol plant in Utah only a month earlier. He stated, "I personally reviewed the problem in Utah on July 17 and 18, 1985, and, as a result, set up the August 19, 1985, presentation."

Weeks was there for two days, July 17 and 18, as was headquarters engineer Russ Bardos. This was where the bench testing on O-ring resiliency was conducted and where it was a current topic. Roger Boisjoly, who helped conduct the bench tests, would have been at the Thiokol plant when Weeks and Bardos visited . Did he talk to Weeks? Did Boisjoly or anyone else at Thiokol discuss the resiliency data with Weeks? Or were the Thiokol managers and engineers on high alert, with orders to conceal and cover-up? In other words, was Weeks totally conned? Unfortunately, no one on the Presidential Commission or House committee asked. But all available evidence and testimony indicates that Weeks, the top headquarters managing engineer, had at least some indication that cold temperatures degraded O-ring performance. This would answer the question I posed earlier of whether Marshall was a "rogue" center. If a top manager at headquarters knew cold temperatures had this effect, then flying with that condition as an "acceptable risk" could be viewed as official NASA policy.

House members also wanted to know whether Weeks briefed Jesse Moore on the August 19 meeting. The following exchange took place between Moore and Scheuer:

> Mr. Scheuer: Let me read to you Mr. Weeks' testimony.
>
> Mr. Moore: Yes, sir.
>
> Mr. Scheuer: His testimony before this committee in this very room, "I did brief Mr. Moore that evening of August 19 as we were wont to do in the early mornings and evenings. I briefed him on the results of that"—that is the meeting—"and told him about the briefing and showed him the briefing." Presumably, that is the briefing document. . . .
>
> Mr. Moore: If that was the situation, that certainly is not commensurate with my recollection of the situation. Mr. Weeks did say he had attended the briefing, that he did review the situation with Morton Thiokol and the Marshall people, and he felt at that time that his judgment was that it was okay to proceed in terms of our course of action. That is the extent of my knowledge of the August 19 briefing, and the first time I saw the briefing was actually after the Challenger accident on January 28.
>
> Mr. Scheuer: Well, now, the Rogers Commission concluded in their report—and I am quoting—"The O-ring erosion history presented to Level I at NASA headquarters in August 1985 was sufficiently detailed to require corrective action prior to the next flight."
>
> Mr. Moore: Right.
>
> Mr. Scheuer: Do you agree with the Rogers Commission's conclusion that headquarters should have corrected the problem prior to the next flight?
>
> Mr. Moore: In our hindsight and looking at the August 19 briefing and knowing what we know today, I would say yes, we should have corrected all the O-ring problems before the next flight. Yes, sir, I would agree with you.
>
> Mr. Scheuer: Did Mr. Weeks tell you that Thiokol was calling for an accelerated pace to eliminate SRM seal erosion?
>
> Mr. Moore: To my recollection, no.
>
> Mr. Scheuer: There seems to be a very serious conflict.
>
> Mr. Moore: I understand.

This was devastating testimony for Jesse Moore, who had been reassigned to head the Johnson Space Center, the home of the astronauts, and perhaps the most prestigious space facility in the world. The August 19 briefing package was the most important document covering what everyone knew by now was one of the most critical technical problems facing NASA and the space shuttle program. Now, Moore said he never saw the August 19 briefing document. Within three more months Moore had left NASA.

Moore told Scheuer that Weeks had "felt comfortable with the overall conclusions." He therefore concurred in Weeks' and Marshall's recommendation that the shuttle "fly as is" with the O-ring flaws with the redesign underway. He thus made one of the most important decisions in the history of world spaceflight evidently without looking at the briefing document. But is a manager ever excused by saying he followed a subordinate's recommendation, when he didn't do his own homework?

> Mr. Scheuer: We had a very serious failure, in fact, a total breakdown in communications at Level I and NASA in Washington. Is that correct?
>
> Mr. Moore: I am not sure I want to call it a very serious breakdown of communications. Mr. Weeks, as I said, did tell me the night after the August 19 briefing that he had met with the people, and he talked about who all was there and listened to the Thiokol briefing with the Marshall people, and in his judgment he said I don't think we have overly concern to stop or accelerate the flights. He had one more concern that he said he wanted to talk to one of his people that he trusted. He did talk to George Hardy, I believe, at the Marshall Space Flight Center and came back and said he thought the situation was acceptable.

As the questioning progressed, Moore continued to insist that the fault lay with his subordinates. Scheuer gave up his questioning of Moore in apparent frustration and never got a satisfying answer as to why NASA kept flying after August 19, 1985.

On June 25, the House Science and Technology Committee brought before it a group of astronauts. These were Major Donald Slayton, who had been one of the seven original Mercury astronauts, along with General James McDivitt, Captain John Young, Colonel Henry Hartsfield, Commander Robert Gibson, and Lieutenant General Thomas Stafford.

One of the most disturbing things the Presidential Commission had discovered about NASA was that its astronauts had been as far removed as they were from management decisions with life or death import.

At the House hearing, Donald "Deke" Slayton was the first to address the committee. Though Slayton had been selected as a Mercury astronaut, he had been grounded due to a heart problem, so was designated manager of the astronaut corps. Eventually he flew on a Skylab mission, but most of his career took place on the ground. Now he told the committee that during the Mercury program in the early 1960s:

We had a very strong voice directly into the engineering system. There were some things we didn't like when we came on-board. The design was fairly well set, and we were able to influence the change in those and make them happen. Management listened to us. We had a lot of changes we proposed that were not adopted, because somebody in the management chain has to make a management judgment in many cases.

The astronauts' organization grew as NASA moved into the Gemini and Apollo phases. The high status the astronauts enjoyed was shown by the fact that Slayton reported directly to the director of the Johnson Space Center. He worked through the tragedy of the Apollo 1 fire and the harrowing rescue of the Apollo 13 crew, heading the Astronaut Office through 1982. During this time:

I had the option at any point of saying, hey, I don't think this flight is ready to go, and we don't want to go. It was my job to deliver the crew to the pad for the flight, and I surely would never have taken one down there if I thought it was unreasonably unsafe, recognizing that none of them are ever safe.

Slayton said that one time in the Gemini program the Astronaut Office and the crew felt more training was needed, so on their own they delayed a flight for five weeks. Slayton said:

We were told by people in headquarters, "You can't do that," but we did it anyway, because we were not going to go until we were ready.

A large measure of discretion was given to the crew and commander. Slayton said:

> The crew always had a direct input to whatever we did, and under no conditions would I have ever committed a flight either to approach a landing test or the orbital flight I was responsible for, without having the crew's concurrence in it. The crew commanders always had a strong voice in whatever we did.

By the time of the Challenger mission, the shuttle commander no longer had a real choice. To launch or not was becoming totally a management decision.

James McDivitt, a former Apollo commander and program director, then spoke. McDivitt was head of the Apollo configuration control board for three years, which included members of the ground crew, the astronaut flight crew, the hardware program managers, a safety manager, contractor representatives, and a secretary to keep track of it all. McDivitt said:

> If we had a safety of flight issue, we would get it resolved very quickly. We never flew with open issues on the spacecraft, and we had a method through that configuration control board of dealing with all the issues that came up in the program.

John Young was next, and he answered the question of what had changed. He said:

> I think there is probably one difference of what we used to do in the old days and what we did prior to the 51-L accident. That is because people started, I believe, and some in the agency believe the space shuttle was operational in the sense that you really didn't have to think as much about issues involving safety as we really should have thought about it.

It was the definition of the space shuttle as "operational" that was at fault. While the man who tried to implement the operational concept at NASA was James Beggs, the idea was inherent in the original notion of the shuttle as a "space truck" that would service all the nation's launch needs. This policy was bought into by successive presidential administrations from Nixon/Ford, through Carter, into the Reagan years. This is what caused the power shift at NASA from the men in blue spacesuits to the ones in dark suits and ties, from the ones who did the work and took the risks, to the ones who made the decisions and took the credit, all the way up to the top, the administrator of the agency and ultimately, the president of the United States. And yes, these were the ones who shaded the truth when the system blew up in their faces, because that's what managers who are divorced from the work of the men and women in the trenches often do.

At the June 25 hearing, the astronauts told how their status had diminished. Slayton said that since he retired:

> I think maybe the [astronaut] corps has submerged another level or two down in the hierarchy from what it used to be. . . . So where we used to be able to talk directly to the center director and even to the NASA administrator . . . [now] they have to go through about three or four different people to get to that same level.

And when you have to go through three or four different people, the original message never survives. Commander Robert "Hoot" Gibson said that if John Young had comments or concerns:

> he carries them forward, but again, he is reporting through another chain that we weren't reporting through before, and it seems like each time perhaps that we report through a different level, it gets filtered. . . .

One characteristic of a top-down, command-and-control organization, is that an ordinary person in the system can never talk to the managers directly. There are procedures that prevent it and that "filter" the messages. The managers live in their own penthouse culture, surrounded by trappings of status and protected by underlings and communications "firewalls." At NASA the situation was getting worse. As Henry Hartsfield told the committee:

Since I have been at the Johnson Space Center, we have had two major reorganizations, and in each of those, the Astronaut Office was pushed to a deeper level.

So the astronauts became mere employees in what was, in effect, a government-operated corporation. This was shown by another statement Young made in the hearing, that there had been talk of doing away with flight readiness reviews, and:

> We were going to do away with the crew reporting of their mission. In fact, we had done away with it. Several crews did not report up the chain of command, to report on what they did on their missions.

This was an astonishing admission. It showed that agency management cared only about the input side of operations—meeting the schedule and getting the shuttle into orbit and back again, not about what the astronauts did when they were up there. Again John Young described the situation by using the analogy NASA's brass liked to throw around, that the shuttle was like an airliner:

> It is not an airliner, and can never be an airliner. . . . You start treating it like an airliner and start treating your astronauts like airline pilots down in the airline system, that is how we did things before the accident, in quite a few areas, and therefore, operational or safety issues from the crews were not a matter of concern to management.

Remember that when Challenger lifted off, the astronauts had not even been told that the platform by which they could exit the orbiter during an emergency and reach the slide-wire baskets that would take them to the explosion-proof bunker was covered with a thick sheet of ice. John Young said:

> The egress path we found out later was covered with ice, and from a crew standpoint, I don't think you would have wanted to launch from where you can't, you know, where your path to the slot was covered with ice.

So the astronauts would likely have called off the Challenger launch for this reason alone, not to mention all the other horrors with the O-rings, foot-long icicles on the launch tower, redline waivers, etc. But they couldn't. They weren't even told about most of it.

At one point in the hearing, astronaut Henry Hartsfield told an anecdote that vividly illustrated the difference between NASA in the old days and the NASA of the mid-1980s:

> I am reminded of a story that Ken Mattingly used to tell when he was getting ready to fly on Apollo 16. He went out to the pad and was climbing around the Saturn 5 out there and went into an inner area and there was a workman back there with a wrench, and Ken spoke to him and asked him how he was doing. He said, "Doing fine." And he told Ken, "I don't know how this complex machine works, and I don't know too much about your job, except I admire you. But I will tell you one thing, it is not going to fail because of me."

The achievements of NASA during the Apollo era were those of a great democratic culture, where the people at the highest level could mingle and talk as one man to another with those of the lowest, where everyone chipped in to the best of their ability to get the job done. But NASA of the 1980s was an authoritarian bureaucracy, where the managers isolated themselves when making life or death decisions affecting others, because that's the way the political bosses wanted it.

"THEY THINK YOU'RE CLOSE TO THE TRUTH"

—My Work with Senator Ernest Hollings

I N LATE MAY, before the Presidential Commission reported to President Reagan, I sent a letter to Senator Ernest Hollings agreeing with his statements in the press that there likely was a link between the Challenger launch and the president's State of the Union address. He answered, saying he shared my concern "about launch pressure and [did] not feel this issue has been adequately addressed by the Rogers Commission."

Soon after I received the letter, I got a call from Hollings' office saying that the senator would like to talk to me. This was after the two days of Senate hearings in June, where Hollings questioned William Rogers on the possibility of a launch/speech link, and where Rogers told him that no one from the White House had been interviewed by the Commission on the subject.

I went to Capitol Hill to visit Senator Hollings on June 15. When I arrived, I was taken into his office, and he stood up from behind his desk. I was surprised at how short and slender he was. He wore a dark, neatly-pressed suit and a white dress shirt with a heavily starched collar and cuffs. We shook hands.

"When you testified to the Rogers Commission," he told me, "I was watching closely. It was clear that you were the one who was telling the truth."

We talked for a few minutes, as he explained his views on the disaster. "That very night," he said, "the president was to speak. He had to be planning to mention the Teacher-in-Space. NASA and the White House had to have been in touch. And the men from Marshall had to have been influenced by either overt or implied pressure."

Hollings spoke about the close professional ties between William Rogers and White House Chief of Staff Donald Regan. He also spoke of the fact that Vice President George Bush had been the one to designate Christa McAuliffe as the Teacher-in-Space and that Bush had planned to attend the Challenger launch on Sunday, January 26, before it was postponed. McAuliffe was a resident of Concord, New Hampshire, and Hollings said Bush was trying to associate himself with her in preparation for the New Hampshire primary in the 1988 presidential campaign.

I said that I agreed with all he was saying.

"Do you have any proof?" Hollings asked.

"No," I replied. "The evidence seems circumstantial. But I think it's enough to be worth looking at."

"If you had the proof," he said, "we'd go on national TV right now. You know, Jesse Moore sat in the same chair you are now sitting in. He came on his own initiative and said there was no pressure to launch."

"I'm writing something about it," I continued. I told him about an article I was planning for the *Washington Monthly*.

"When will this be coming out?" Hollings asked.

"Probably September," I said.

"That's too late! One of us has to publish something now," he said with a tone of urgency. I hadn't thought about this beforehand but decided to volunteer my services. "I'll write something for you," I said.

"Good!" he replied.

Hollings then called his administrative assistant into the office. He was a man about my age named Ashley Thrift. Hollings said to Thrift, "Mr. Cook will be writing an article for me on Challenger. He is to have all the help he needs. Get Kress on this too."

Hollings gave me a forthright look and shook my hand firmly. "Thank you, sir," he said, and I followed Thrift through a side door into an adjacent office.

Thrift and I talked for a few minutes about the article. Thrift was talkative and respectful, but I was surprised to see that he knew almost nothing about the Challenger disaster and investigation. It made me realize that even intelligent, educated people had a hard time following what had happened.

Thrift asked me to go over to the Russell Office Building, where the Senate Commerce Committee staff was located, and talk to Marty Kress, the staff member who covered space issues for the Democrats. Thrift said he would also speak to the minority staff director, Ralph Dupree, who would arrange for a secretary to type the article.

Kress was working at a cluttered desk in a large office that he shared with a couple of other staff members. Just now he happened to be alone. Next to his desk on a table was a large model of the space shuttle.

I was surprised when Kress told me there were no other committee minority staff members who worked on space issues. He knew some of the NASA managers who had testified before the Commission. He mentioned Stanley Reinartz, referring to him as "Stan," indicating that he was on a first-name basis with people from Marshall. He also said that, like me, he had been planning to attend the QM-5 firing at Thiokol in February 1986, when the capture feature was to have been tested on the SRBs.

"So what brings you here?" Kress asked.

"Senator Hollings has asked me to write an article for him on the possibility that NASA launched Challenger so it would be up for the president's State of the Union speech," I replied.

After a long pause, Kress continued. "Look," he said. "I don't think NASA launched because of the speech. It was because they didn't want a launch commit criterion on the O-rings that would interfere with launching at Vandenberg. It's a lot colder there than in Florida."

This was jaw-dropping news. I had not heard anything about Vandenberg before this talk with Marty Kress.

I now said to him, "That's interesting. Maybe that had something to do with it. But there is circumstantial evidence connecting the launch to the speech that is too strong to ignore."

I then went to speak to Ralph Dupree, who introduced me to the secretary who would be doing the typing. He said that Senator Hollings viewed this project as having a very high priority. I then left the office and went back to my job at the Treasury Annex.

I did the writing for the article at home. I was unhappy that I had allowed myself to displace my own work for a piece of ghost writing but felt that the article would have greater public impact if it came from Hollings rather than me. I was intrigued by the Vandenberg connection. It seemed to me that it certainly could be a factor that would predispose NASA to take extra risks. It also seemed possible that this could have been one reason Mulloy pressured Thiokol to change its recommendation the night of January 27, while the rest of the NASA team was pushing ahead so strongly for other reasons. It made me feel even more convinced that the motel room conversation among Lucas, Kingsbury, Mulloy, and Reinartz, which the Commission failed to penetrate, was a key.

Within a few days, I had completed a fifteen-page draft. Ashley Thrift then convened a meeting attended by Hollings, himself, Kress, the senator's press secretary Mike Fernandez, and me.

During the meeting, I told Hollings and his aides that when Randy Kehrli, the Commission investigator, interviewed me on March 28, he told me that when the Commission finished its work it planned to withhold "sensitive" information. One of the aides then said he had talked to John R. Molesworth, another Commission investigator, the one who was in charge of looking at the issue of White House pressure. Molesworth had told him that there were in fact interviews with White House staff members, but that they were "too sensitive" to be released. This contradicted what William Rogers had told Hollings in the Senate hearing.

Hollings said he wanted to proceed with my draft, but that he had made some comments for us to look at. In the draft, I had faulted President Reagan for his lackadaisical handling of the manned space program. Hollings wanted this statement removed. "I don't want to go after the president," he said. "My opponent is William Rogers. Besides, if you got into the president's car and said, 'Mr. President, please take me to NASA,' he wouldn't know where to go!"

Hollings said that the *New York Times* or *Washington Post* were the places we should try to place the article. He said, "Our thesis is that there was enough to link the speech and the launch that more investigation is needed."

He asked me to continue to work on the article with help from the staff. After sitting silently throughout the meeting, Marty Kress now spoke up. "Most of what you are saying," he said, "has already been in the newspapers." He continued, "I have looked at the Challenger schedule and the postponements, and there isn't anything unusual there. The more I think about it the more I think that Marshall simply realized that with the launch schedule adding more flights they couldn't allow cold weather to stop them."

Hollings thought about it for a few moments. "I want the article to go ahead," he said and left the room.

Later, as I pondered what Kress had said about the Vandenberg connection, I realized that part of the mystery of why NASA did not stop flights to fix the O-ring joints was solved by this information. But was that the key to the Challenger launch? Even with this in their minds, Mulloy and the other Marshall managers still could have done the prudent thing and waited a few more hours, or even a day or two, to launch Challenger. That would not have compromised the Vandenberg launches or the 1986 flight rate. Besides, when NASA ignored the warnings of Rockwell about ice on the launch pad, that had nothing to do with Vandenberg. So more than one factor had to be at work. There were multiple layers of pressure and multiple layers of cover-up.

Suppose, for instance, that William Graham had let it be known before he departed Florida for Washington on Sunday the 26th that even though they had missed the Sunday launch opportunity, they would try for Monday and Tuesday without fail. Suppose the overriding objective was to have Challenger in orbit in time for the president's speech. It is possible that Graham could have been the link between the White House and NASA's launch managers. In my mind, it was also possible that Graham could have conveyed that message to the managers at Kennedy and left it to them to get it done.

Suppose then that the Marshall managers got that message. Prior to the January 27 evening teleconference, Lucas had Mulloy and Reinartz in his motel room along with James Kingsbury, the science and engineering director at Marshall. There had been a teleconference in the afternoon, when Thiokol gave its initial recommendation not to launch. Judson Lovingood, back in Huntsville, thought it looked like the launch would be delayed and said as much to Reinartz.

In the motel room meeting, Marshall as an institution reversed itself. There had to have been a reason. What if they communicated among themselves that there was no option, and that Thiokol had to go along with the decision? If that's the way it happened, the rest was history.

I wasn't ready to suggest all this in the article for Hollings. So I just raised the questions, pointing out that NASA's managers were evidently being protected by the Commission and that the Commission never showed why NASA launched.

As I continued to study the scheduling of the launch, one peculiar fact that stood out was a one-day delay in the initial launch date for the Challenger mission that NASA had introduced into the schedule on December 23, 1985. One day—it made no sense.

By then, Graham had replaced Beggs as agency head. The one-day change was made about two weeks before Graham and Culbertson sent the material to the White House for the State of the Union address that talked about Christa McAuliffe. Originally, Challenger had been scheduled to lift off on January 22 and return on January 28. So with the old schedule, it would have been back on the ground when the president spoke that night.

The one-day delay changed the flight schedule to January 23–29. These dates were noted at the bottom of the memo to the White House that contained the speech material. Typed below the signature line, where Culbertson signed for Graham, was the statement, "Mrs. McAuliffe's flight is currently scheduled for the period of January 23 through 29." This statement is marked with an asterisk, referring to the opening sentence of the speech material at the beginning of the memo, which stated:

> Tonight, while I am speaking to you, a young elementary school teacher from Concord, New Hampshire, is taking us all on the ultimate field trip as she orbits the Earth as the first citizen passenger on the space shuttle.

Could it be that Graham changed the schedule for Challenger so it would still be in orbit when Reagan gave his speech? This would have made Challenger and Christa McAuliffe much more dramatic as props than if Challenger had landed and the mission was over. It would also have made it possible for the president to be on the phone with

Challenger during the speech, especially since it took NASA only about three minutes to make a connection between the shuttle and any phone on the ground.

The second peculiarity involved the still-unclear question of why NASA canceled the launch attempt for Sunday, January 26. William Graham was at the Kennedy Space Center for the Saturday meeting of the mission management team. Also present were Culbertson, Moore, Aldrich, Lucas, Mulloy, Reinartz, and many others. Supposedly, NASA canceled the Sunday launch because of an approaching weather front. But at lift-off time Sunday morning, the weather was sunny, clear, and warm.

NASA did not like to launch the shuttle in the rain, because of possible damage to the heat-resistant tiles which could result in a catastrophic burnthrough during reentry at the end of a mission. But as the fair weather on the morning of Sunday the 26th indicated, the weather at Cape Canaveral is notoriously fickle. Storms come and go almost without warning.

Thus for all previous launches, it had been NASA's practice for the astronauts to board the shuttle and await a possible break in the weather. Here is yet another instance where NASA broke with precedent for Challenger, one which neither the Commission nor Congress examined.

Richard Smith, director of the Kennedy Space Center, was present at the 9:30 p.m. mission management team meeting when Graham cancelled the Sunday launch. Later he said that the weather forecast was "for the worst weather we'd ever had for a shuttle launch."

But while I was doing my research for Hollings, I called the Kennedy Space Center and spoke to a man named Jim Ball in the public affairs office who had been present for briefings on the weather on Saturday the 26th. I told him what Smith had said, but Ball answered, "I wouldn't characterize it as that. It was not as bad or worse than other occasions. We've launched in some pretty dismal weather."

On a previous launch, Ball said, "It rained so hard we couldn't see the lights on the pad," during the countdown. Ball added that he had not been privy to all the meetings where weather was discussed during previous launches, but that for Challenger on Sunday the 26th, "The forecast was just for unacceptable weather conditions. We have had that before and tried to launch." Ball summarized NASA's practice by saying the agency's view was "not to make judgments on whether to launch based on a weather forecast."

Ball's comments puzzled me. He sounded honest and experienced, with no political agenda. Yet his perspective was the opposite of that expressed by Smith and Graham. What was going on here? Given the precedents, it was inconceivable that NASA would have thrown away a launch opportunity on Sunday the 26th.

If NASA had followed its past practices, the astronauts would have boarded on Sunday to await a launch opportunity. But they did not. If they had, given the fine weather, and in the absence of some other impediment, a successful launch likely would have been achieved because the O-rings would not have been frozen.

NASA's professional launch managers did not make the decision to postpone. I learned that Graham had told Congressman Donald Fuqua that he was the one who had decided. Fuqua had been at the Cape, flying around the launch site on Sunday with John Young, looking at the clear skies. Back in Washington that night, as Joseph Trento reported in his book, *Prescription for Disaster*, Fuqua asked Graham who had made the "stupid decision" to cancel, and Graham said, "I did."

Was it really because of uncertainty about the weather report, or for other reasons? Could it have been as superficial as not wanting to have the next day's Super Bowl game between the Chicago Bears and the New England Patriots upstage the Teacher-in-Space mission, or to maximize the publicity from the Teacher-in-Space launch by having lift-off occur on Monday when schools were in session?

Or were there deeper reasons? In a pause in the conversation, Jim Ball decided to give me a hint. He advised me to look at the "ovality rule."

Buried in the appendices to the Presidential Commission's report was a statement that by the time of the mission management team meeting the night of Saturday, January 25, NASA had made a decision to proceed with the Sunday launch. The public affairs office of the Kennedy Space Center confirmed to me by phone that preparations for filling the shuttle's external tank with its liquid hydrogen and oxygen fuel were already underway. At the 9:30 p.m. meeting, Graham reversed these preparations, so that, in the Commission's words, "early count-down activities that had already started were terminated."

The ovality rule has already been discussed in the account in this book of the Centaur program.

Each time NASA attempts to launch the shuttle, the external tank must be filled with liquid hydrogen and oxygen for the orbiter's main engines. If a launch is cancelled, the external tank must be drained and returned to a safe, inert condition. The procedure is then repeated for the next launch attempt the following day.

But this loading and unloading can only be done on two successive days. The reason is that during filling and draining, the shuttle's main propulsion system—MPS—has ductwork that undergoes severe stress from alternate periods of supercooling, followed by the return to atmospheric temperatures. Such stressing can cause the ductwork insulation to crack, resulting in condensation on the fuel lines, which can then drip moisture onto sensitive pieces of equipment. The ductwork can also assume an out-of-roundness condition—ovality. So after back-to-back delays the ductwork must be inspected for damage and repaired if necessary. This takes a full day. Then the next day, another launch can be attempted.

The ironclad rule is that the shuttle can never be loaded with cryogenic fuel for a launch attempt on three successive days. Such a series of events took place during the August 1985 launch of Discovery. On Saturday, August 24, the launch was canceled with full tanks due to threatening weather. The external tank had been loaded and the astronauts strapped in. On Sunday, August 25, another delay occurred because of a computer malfunction. Again, the external tank was full, and the astronauts sat in the orbiter. So after two successive days of cancellations, Monday the 26th was an off-day while checkouts were done. On Tuesday the 27th, the external tank was refilled and the launch took place.

Esoteric as this procedure may appear, for NASA's launch managers it was routine. In the case of the Challenger mission, those who were making the decisions may have reasoned that if a launch were attempted on Sunday, but, as appeared possible, had to be cancelled because of rain, then a second postponement on Monday, for whatever reason, would keep NASA from making a third attempt until Wednesday. But the president's State of the Union message was scheduled for Tuesday.

It seemed to me that Graham's objective on Saturday, January 25, was not to launch Challenger as soon as possible. It was to assure that Challenger was in orbit when the president spoke Tuesday night. A Sunday cancellation may have improved the odds with the ovality rule and the weather report taken into account together. This was because Monday and Tuesday both looked more promising for launch than Sunday, at least when NASA's managers assessed the situation with Graham on Saturday night. The decision would not have to have been made in front of the entire mission management team . It could have been made among Graham and a small number of insiders, then passed on to the larger group. That this may have been the scenario was indicated by the fact that the cancellation took place just before the external tank began to be filled.

When I thought all this through, I became excited and called Ashley Thrift. He couldn't have cared less. He repeated, with some exasperation, that Marty Kress had found nothing unusual about the Challenger launch schedule.

A couple of days later, when I was in Hollings's office with the most recent draft of the article, including a discussion of the ovality rule, Mike Fernandez said that CNN had called them and said that during the weekend before the Challenger launch, William Graham had made a large number of phone calls to White House officials from his motel room.

I called Christine Dolan to verify this. She knew I was working with Hollings and said, "That's right. The information comes from someone here who's writing a book on Challenger." This was Joseph Trento, who published *Prescription for Disaster* a few months later.

She continued, "Graham's motel room phone records are being held by Dick Smith, the center director at KSC. There were 161 calls. Some were to the White House, and others were to the home phones of White House staff members."

She mentioned Alfred Kingon, the White House cabinet secretary, and his deputy, Richard Davis. Both would have been liaisons with NASA in any discussions of the State of the Union speech.

My mouth hung open as she talked. "This should be all you guys need," Dolan said, then hung up. The situation had become high drama. We were going to break the case wide open.

Thrift drafted a letter for Hollings to send to Smith, asking for the phone records. I suggested that Hollings simply call Smith, and Thrift said he would suggest that to the senator.

But nothing happened. A few weeks later, my editor at the *Washington Monthly*, Steve Waldman, phoned Smith to ask him about the phone records. Smith said he had turned the records over to Hollings, but I was never shown them.

I met with Hollings once more to discuss the article, but he didn't mention the Graham phone records. Hollings had been writing some material himself and asked me to elaborate certain points and identify my sources of information. I urged him to contact Stanley Reinartz and others at Marshall and ask them to come clean about why they pressured Thiokol. Hollings did not seem to want to do this.

I continued to write, but by now the article was thirty-six draft pages. Thrift gave it to Hollings, who didn't respond. One time he passed me as I was waiting in the outer office to talk to Thrift and said, simply, "Good morning, America."

Hollings had no further comment, and time was moving on. Thrift tried to arrange another meeting for me with Hollings, but when I showed up, Hollings had gone to the Capitol rotunda to have videotapes made for his upcoming reelection campaign.

Thrift's patience with the shuttle issue now seemed to have run out, and it was clear that something was wrong. One day he said to me, "Richard, if the big boys aren't going to fight, there's nothing you and I can do."

I felt that if the big boys won't fight, then a little one would have to. I told Thrift that unless Hollings published the article, I was going to take it to the *Washington Monthly* under my own name. "I don't blame you," he said. He congratulated me when the article was accepted, but I never saw him or Hollings again.

The episode with Hollings was a bitter disappointment. He was the one senator with the understanding and power to have exposed the Reagan administration's cover-up, especially with the evidence of the 161 Graham phone calls. Yet at the crucial moment, he backed off.

A Washington, D.C., attorney I knew named Bob Levin asked Hollings why he did not act. "History is history," Hollings said. John Holliman of CNN told me he asked Ashley Thrift why the senator had dropped the issue. Thrift replied, "In the interest of national unity." There were also rumors that the new Senate Democratic Majority Leader Robert Byrd had pressured Hollings to back off, as had defense contractors from South Carolina.

I felt in a lonely position. With Hollings having retreated, I was the only person left who had been involved in the Challenger disaster and aftermath still willing to probe the unanswered questions. I began to look around again for help and wondered whether the Reagan administration would try to stop me.

The easiest thing for me to have done would have been to go back to being a Treasury bureaucrat and forget what I had seen, thought, and felt about the Challenger disaster. My involvement in the Challenger aftermath started because of a memo I had written on July 23, 1985, now over a year ago. When I leaked the memo, along with the other O-ring documents, I felt that my personal integrity was at stake. Now the issue was much broader; i.e., whether the government had conducted an honest investigation and whether the Challenger incident really should simply be laid to rest in the mind of the public.

I had no clear answer. With Senator Hollings retreating, I was again, as I had been in the days after the disaster, the only government insider with any knowledge of the matter who seemed inclined to speak up. But leaking NASA documents was one thing. Accusing the president of the United States of a major cover-up was another. Even at Treasury I might not be immune from retaliation.

As I had realized months before, my only protection would be publicity. The louder I shouted, the less likely it seemed that the White House or political officials in Treasury would be able to attack me. A principle seemed to be involved here: if you are going to hit, hit hard. That is what I did with the O-ring leaks, and that was what I decided to do now.

I would carry out a three-pronged attack. The first would be the *Washington Monthly* article, which began to take shape with the help of editor Steve Waldman. The second would be a longer critique of the Presidential Commission and its report, which I would deliver to Attorney General Edwin Meese with a request for a new investigation. The third would be a press conference, where I would release the critique, which I was calling "The Challenger Report," to the public.

I realized that I could not act alone to publish "The Challenger Report." For one thing, it was in the days before widespread use of home personal computers, so I needed access to a word processing system. I also needed to find an organization that would sponsor the press conference, since I had no money, no facility, and no access to publicity.

I phoned several non-profit groups in Washington, D.C. Among these was the Institute for Space and Security Studies, located in Chesapeake Beach, Maryland, on the Chesapeake Bay. The president of ISSS was Dr. Robert Bowman, the retired Air Force officer who is mentioned prominently in earlier chapters of this book as one of the foremost opponents of President Reagan's "Star Wars" program.

Bowman was an ideal sponsor. He had headed the Air Force office that studied possible missile defense options during the Carter administration, but he regarded "Star Wars," as conceived by the Reagan administration, as lunacy. He also believed it had no place in the space shuttle program. He knew a lot about NASA and the shuttle, because he had done the study for James Beggs that foresaw a much lower flight rate than NASA had been projecting. Now he spent much of his time traveling around the U.S. making speeches and publishing a newsletter called "Space and Security News."

Bowman was a smart, gregarious man who agreed immediately to the press conference. He saw that my analysis of how William Graham was brought into NASA to militarize the shuttle was an issue that might help him publicize his own concerns. Bowman asked me to work with his public affairs director, Thomond O'Brien, and allowed me to use his word processing system at the ISSS office in Chesapeake Beach. I spent a couple of weekends traveling from my home in King George to Bowman's house on the bay to type the manuscript.

After a couple of marathon sessions, I had a final product. I also wrote a condensed version of the report that Bowman printed in the October edition of his monthly newsletter, *Space and Security News*. He prefaced my article with an "Editor's Note," which said:

> Mr. Cook's article presents a point of view which should not only be aired, but examined. We have attempted to verify independently the allegations in his article. In many cases we have been successful. In others we have not. Yet, neither have we been able to disprove them. In those

cases where independent verification is not yet available, we felt that Mr. Cook's credibility (which is considerable) was sufficient justification for publication.

My article was entitled, "Unanswered (And Often Unasked) Questions about Challenger." I viewed it as the best thing I had yet written about the Challenger disaster. I had come a long way in my thinking since those anxious days in early February when Phyllis and I agonized over whether to leak the O-ring documents. I called for further investigation of possibly criminally negligent activities:

> ... If these mid-level managers really made the decisions ascribed to them, and if they failed to let their superiors know what the issues were *as they were directed to do and as the "system" required them to do,* then they are criminally liable. Yet some of these people were given early retirement—in essence a reward for their part in all this. Why were they treated so leniently? Or were they really being rewarded for taking the blame for the higher-ups who were really responsible? Were they just scapegoats? Who arranged the payoffs?
>
> If William Graham is implicated in the launch decision—and the Commission never questioned him on this point—it should also be asked what he was doing at NASA in the first place. Indications are that Graham, a nuclear effects expert with no space program experience, was forced on the agency over the strenuous objections of Administrator James Beggs. . . . Soon afterwards, NASA signed an agreement with the Department of Defense for a military flight rate significantly higher than what NASA ever reported to the public or Congress. The Commission ignored all these circumstances. Why, and on whose orders?
>
> These and many other unresolved issues cry out for explanation. They indicate that either the Commission was incredibly incompetent or was itself part of a massive cover-up. Indeed, there is evidence that not only did NASA personnel perjure themselves before the Commission, but that in closed sessions the Commission actually advised them to do so and helped them to concoct their stories. The implications are serious enough to require investigation by the U.S. Senate and the establishment of a special prosecutor. Some of the possible charges could be malfeasance and dereliction of duty on the part of NASA officials and conspiracy

on the part of members of the Rogers Commission, members of the White House staff, and perhaps even those in the Senate responsible for blocking the Senate's own investigation. Depending on the outcome of such investigations, Florida state authorities might also consider charges of negligent homicide against some of those involved.

During the last week of October, my *Washington Monthly* article came out with the title, "The Rogers Commission Failed." It was no small thing to appear in print in this important progressive magazine that was run by Charles Peters, one of the most meticulous and trustworthy publishers in Washington. My editor Steve Waldman told me, "Charley sees this as a very important article. He wouldn't print it without confirmation, which he got on background from one of his White House contacts."

The article described how the Commission's report failed to explain why NASA launched in the face of so many contraindications and did not identify who was really responsible. Soon after the article appeared, I got a call at home from former Commission member General Donald Kutyna. He was quite gracious and apologized to me for the treatment I had received at the hands of Chairman Rogers at the public hearing when I appeared on February 11. Kutyna said he agreed with everything in the *Washington Monthly* article except where I characterized him as part of Rogers' planning at the closed hearing on the 10th to rig the next day's session to cover up NASA's prior O-ring safety concerns.

I thanked Kutyna for calling. It was obviously significant for the only military officer on the Commission and one of the nation's leading experts on space flight to concur with what I was saying. Kutyna agreed that the Commission did not say why NASA launched.

William Shannon of the *Boston Globe* had written several columns about the Challenger disaster and on October 29 wrote of my article:

> In an article for the November issue of the *Washington Monthly*, Cook again blows the whistle, this time on the Rogers Commission and its elaborate avoidance of the question of responsibility, particularly with regard to Acting Administrator Graham.
>
> The Commission's report correctly cited the O-ring failure as the cause of the disaster, but it stated an outright falsehood in assessing

responsibility. It declared that top-level officials who made the decision to launch on that January day "were unaware of the recent history of problems concerning the O-rings and the joint."

The truth is the exact opposite. Testimony before the Commission—and NASA's own records—proved that knowledge of the O-ring erosion danger was widespread in NASA and known at every administrative level. There was not, as the Commission report suggests, a failure of communications.

On October 30, Thomond O'Brien, Bob Bowman's assistant at the Institute of Space and Security Studies, drove me to the Justice Department on Constitution Avenue in Washington. While he waited in his car, I went inside, took the elevator to the top floor, and gave a secretary "The Challenger Report," along with a letter to Attorney General Edwin Meese. The letter read, in part:

> I have reached the conclusion that several officials of the National Aeronautics and Space Administration may be guilty of malfeasance and dereliction of duty with respect to the decision to launch Challenger. It also appears that crimes may have been committed by high government officials in covering up the reasons NASA did not launch Challenger on January 26, 1986, and did launch over the objections of contractor engineers on January 28, 1986. . . .
>
> Therefore I respectfully request that you determine whether a new investigation is in order; whether such investigation should include the formation and conduct of the Presidential Commission; and whether a special prosecutor should be appointed.

O'Brien and I then drove to the nearby National Press Building on F Street, where our press conference was to take place. Bob Bowman was there with his wife and son, who also worked for the institute. Bowman had rented a room near the National Press Club dining room on the top floor, and TV crews were starting to set up cameras. "I've been covering the Challenger for months," said one cameraman. "I knew this story was out there somewhere."

I was nervous, wondering how the people at Treasury would react. I was about to go before TV cameras and accuse the Reagan administration of crimes. Before the press conference started, we handed out a prepared statement:

By late 1985, NASA was undergoing a disturbing change. The agency was passing under the increasing control of those who wanted it to become above all a military program supporting Star Wars testing. Leading this takeover was a nuclear weapons specialist, Dr. William Graham. In November 1985, Graham was made deputy administrator of NASA by President Reagan over the strenuous objections of Administrator James Beggs. Soon afterwards, Beggs was indicted on what now appear to be dubious charges, and was forced by the White House to take a leave of absence. Two months later, NASA signed an agreement with the Defense Department for a military flight rate significantly higher than what had been reported previously to Congress and the public. Many of these would be Star Wars–related missions.

Then, on January 28, 1986, Challenger blew up. Seven astronauts died, including Christa McAuliffe, the Teacher-in-Space and the first ordinary citizen to ride on the shuttle. Clearly the administration viewed the Teacher-in-Space and similar public relations programs as a means to allay public anxiety about the shift in NASA's emphasis to military priorities. There is little question that the Teacher-in-Space figured in the president's State of the Union speech to be given the night of the disaster. And it appears probable that at least twice prior to January 28, Challenger's launch schedule had been rearranged to provide a backdrop for the president's address. There was contact between NASA and the White House during this period and extensive involvement by Acting Administrator Graham in the Challenger launch decision. In launching Challenger, NASA followed procedures different from any previous shuttle mission. The reason could only have been manipulation from the top. NASA was intent that Challenger would be launched no later than the morning of January 28.

After the explosion, the White House raced to set up a Presidential Commission, which consisted mostly of political loyalists and space program celebrities. The Commission was selected mainly by Acting Administrator Graham. In turn, the Commission never investigated Graham's role in the Challenger launch. Instead, it focused on the actions of mid-level managers, who became, in effect, scapegoats. The

Commission created a myth of flawed communications, exonerated top management officials from any responsibility for the accident, and failed to explain why NASA overrode the objections to the cold-weather launch by contractor engineers. In its early days, the Commission worked with NASA to prevent key information from reaching the public, then later refused to examine seriously the many indications of political manipulation of the launch decision. The conclusion is inescapable: the Commission was formed to protect NASA and the White House from real scrutiny. Now, new investigations are needed.

The room was packed with dozens of men and women from the media, including the local Washington, D.C., TV stations and the national networks. As we began, Bowman spoke first and gave a short introduction. I then did the same. Bowman tied in the Challenger launch with his opposition to "Star Wars," and I focused my remarks on the need for a new investigation that would answer the question of why did NASA launch when they shouldn't have.

Suddenly, someone started to shout at us from the audience. "But they denied it! They denied it! The White House denied it!" They were talking about the launch/speech link. The shouts came over and over again. They seemed to have started from one of the networks' national news teams. Others in the crowd had picked it up. The atmosphere had become angry and hostile.

I was not prepared for this. Until now, my contacts with the press over the last nine months had been positive. I'd had dozens of media interviews, been called a "folk hero," and had met and gotten to know scores of journalists. Without exception, they had been sympathetic. Suddenly I had the thought, "We're being sabotaged!"

Bob Bowman was flustered. He had not expected this either. We tried to hold our ground. I started to explain the ovality rule about filling the external tank with cryogenics, but gave up. No one was able to follow what we were saying in an atmosphere that had become near-pandemonium.

At one point I said that despite White House denials, it was clear that Christa McAuliffe would be featured in the President's speech. "So what?" someone in the audience shouted. "What's wrong with that?"

"Larry Speakes lied about it," I said. "He said there was no such plan."

"Big deal!" said the voice.

I saw that the battle was lost. There was not a single question about the militarization of NASA and the shuttle, the connection with "Star Wars," or any interest in how Graham got to NASA. I guessed that these subjects must have been taboo for the American media. I felt badly for Bowman, who had such high hopes.

Bowman quickly wrapped things up, and we gave out the copies of "The Challenger Report." The press conference was exhausting and was not reported by any of the major TV networks, though it appeared on the local news in the Washington, D.C., area. The *New York Times* and *Washington Post* ignored it. CBS offered me a two-minute interview on the CBS Morning News, but I turned it down because I felt that wasn't enough time to do justice to the topic. How could I explain in two minutes what it had taken me nine months to figure out?

There was also an article in *USA Today* written by Jack Kelley. He quoted me as saying of the Challenger aftermath, "This is the biggest government cover-up that I'm aware of. I've never been able in good conscience to walk away from it." Kelly later told me that after the press conference he had gotten a call from a friend who worked for the White House and was traveling with President Reagan on a political trip in North Carolina. This was just before the congressional elections that would take place the following Tuesday. Kelley said, "My friend says they think you're close to the truth and that they're scared."

I was exhausted and discouraged by the events of the last nine months. What I wasn't sure about was where I stood at Treasury, though I was prepared to fight any attempt to fire me. A few days after the press conference, my division director took me aside. He said that an official of Main Treasury had spoken to the commissioner of the Financial Management Service, Ernie Douglas, and told Douglas to "shut you up." The division director said, "The department was very upset about this, and I mean very." Then he smiled. He said, "Ernie told him that you hadn't broken any Treasury regulation, so there was nothing he could do."

Douglas, a former IRS regional director, had a reputation of being a very tough person who did what he felt was right, no matter what you thought of him. The U.S. career civil service, as personified by Douglas and the division director, had stood by me.

Still, a journalist told me, "You know, they have killed people for less than what you have done."

This was also a hard time for Phyllis. Money was scarce, and I spent most of my nights and weekends writing about Challenger. We had been living in King George for a year, and had begun to develop our property. In the spring we had converted the shed into a chicken house and ordered a flock of day-old chicks. Later in the year we began to raise turkeys. We had started our vegetable garden and finished fencing the two-acre property. We also planted raspberries, blueberries, and fruit trees.

During the past year I had experienced federal government service at its hardest and most absurd. It was an ordeal that I would never forget and maybe never get over. But every night, my two-hour commute in the vanpool took me to another world of woods, grass, farms, fields, and firewood that made me realize the vanity of most of mankind's desires and dreams.

"NO ONE EXPECTED CHALLENGER TO BE LAUNCHED"

—The House Report Closes the Government's Book on Challenger

THE REPORT OF the House Committee on Science and Technology, entitled *Investigation of the Challenger Accident*, was dated October 29, 1986. It was the last government report on the disaster. The report was impressive in its documentation of technical issues but presented a vastly over-generalized theory of why the disaster took place. The report conspicuously avoided the White House pressure issue. And it watered down the impression of NASA's malfeasance in overriding the Thiokol engineers.

The committee had access to tapes of conversations in the KSC firing rooms and to other sources of information about the Challenger launch that the Presidential Commission did not mention or disclose in its report. Thus the committee was able to cite additional factors in its report that alone, or in combination with other factors, showed how far NASA departed from its normal procedures or failed to heed unusual conditions in launching Challenger on January 28, 1986.

Following is my best attempt at a complete list of these factors:

- written recommendation by Thiokol's vice-president for engineering after the first January 27 teleconference that Challenger not be launched below a calculated O-ring temperature of fifty-three degrees;

- notification of Marshall management by Judson Lovingood in Huntsville that because of the Thiokol written recommendation, Aldrich and Moore should be informed that a launch delay appeared likely;
- arguments by Thiokol engineers in Utah that the recommendation not to launch be upheld after being challenged by Mulloy;
- concurrence in the Thiokol engineering position by Ben Powers and possibly other Marshall staff engineers;
- transmittal of a launch approval telefax by Thiokol management that actually contained reasons not to launch;
- violation of flight readiness review policy directives by Marshall management in not informing Level I and II of the Thiokol teleconference;
- documentation by Thiokol of adverse impacts of low temperatures on the O-rings through analysis of flight 51-C, bench tests, meetings on the subject at Marshall, and the August 19 briefing at headquarters;
- potential loss of booster rockets due to high seas in the recovery area;
- use of a faulty procedure of letting water pipes on the launch pad drip, rather than drain, in order to save time in preparing to launch the morning of January 28;
- huge build-up of ice on the launch pad as a result of using the flawed drip procedure;
- heavy ice formation in the SRB sound-suppression water troughs;
- statements by Rockwell that because of ice they could not assure a safe launch;
- statements by NASA ice team personnel and Rockwell contractors that they could not predict the post-ignition behavior of ice and how it might damage the orbiter's thermal protection system;
- sheet of ice on the astronauts' escape platform outside orbiter and no attempt to clear this ice during launch countdown;

- recommendation by the NASA ice team leader, Charles Stevenson, that the launch be scrubbed;
- measurements by the ice team that the air temperature in the vicinity of the right-hand SRB was nine degrees F. [actually 16 degrees, as determined later due to instrument recalibration];
- greater high altitude wind shear than for any previous shuttle launch;
- waiver of launch commit criteria for external tank nose cone temperatures that, according to the House report, "justified using lower temperatures on the basis of a back-up procedure that was invalid." [The minimum "redline" temperature for the external tank nose cone was forty-five degrees F. There were actually two waivers processed through launch control at KSC. The first dropped the redline temperature to twenty-eight degrees, and when it looked as though that would not be low enough, it was reduced to ten degrees.]
- House report: ". . . . criteria requiring an eight-hour period between tanking cycles may have been violated. This is significant in that, had the tanking cycles been carried out as required, launch of STS 51-L would have taken place in the afternoon of January 28."
- House report: " . . . the morning of the scheduled launch of STS 51-L, the mission evaluation room (MER) manager requested a waiver of the launch commit criteria lower limit of thirty-one degrees F."
- House report: " . . . violations of launch redlines may also have occurred on the auxiliary power unit (APU) gearbox lube oil (minimum redline temperature forty-two degrees F.) and the fuel test lines (minimum temperature forty-one degrees F.). . . ."

These circumstances fully justified Senator Hollings's statement to Chairman Rogers: "You say that the process was flawed. I find the process and safety procedures violated." In fact, the NASA system was screaming not to launch.

Like the Presidential Commission before it, the House report cited the pressure of the launch schedule. But as with the Commission, the House failed to make the connection with the huge military commitment mandated by the Reagan administration. The report also cited "pressures within NASA to attempt to evolve from an R&D agency into a quasi-competitive business operation . . . at the cost of safety." This was correct, but the report failed to note the declining budget for dealing with design problems with the SRBs and other shuttle components. The House of Representatives is the originator of all revenue bills within the federal government, so had responsibility along with NASA for underfunding the shuttle's design needs.

The House report departed from the Presidential Commission primarily in disagreeing that the culprit was NASA's "poor communication or inadequate procedures as implied by the Rogers Commission conclusion. Rather, the fundamental problem was poor technical decision-making over a period of years by top NASA and contractor personnel, who failed to act decisively to solve the increasingly serious anomalies in the solid rocket booster joints." Actually, there were multiple overlapping causes of the disaster, of which "poor technical decision-making" was the lowest common denominator.

The committee admitted that, notwithstanding all that they had said about poor technical decision making, the launch of Challenger essentially was unexplained. It also blamed "operating pressures"—but as stated previously, the 1986 shuttle launch schedule could have been preserved if the 51-L Challenger flight slipped a few hours or even a few days. It was not "operating pressures" that caused NASA to launch Challenger in unsafe conditions that morning.

While more critical of NASA than the Commission's, the House report was riddled with errors. Among its off-the-mark observations were the following: ". . . the committee could find no evidence that astronauts are denied the opportunity to enter management if they so choose. On the other hand, prior to the STS 51-L accident, astronauts were not encouraged to enter management."

Not a single astronaut raised the issue of not having "the opportunity to enter management." What they were talking about was the fact that the Astronaut Office had been pushed down so far in the NASA bureaucracy that they no longer had the organizational standing to make independent safety judgments or to delay flights if they felt there had been insufficient preparation or attention to safety issues. During this hearing, Congressman Scheuer said that the astronauts should have been able to attend emergency pre-launch meetings such as the tele-conference with Thiokol before the Challenger disaster.

NASA's disregard for the astronauts was shown vividly by the fact that NASA launched Challenger even though their escape platform for launch pad egress was covered with ice. Later, when Columbia was destroyed at atmospheric reentry on February 1, 2003, the astronaut crew had not even been told how seriously engineers on the ground were concerned that the orbiter had sustained severe damage from falling external tank debris. This was the ultimate degradation and insult on the part of NASA to the once-proud American astronaut corps.

And, the House report blandly stated, "The decision to launch STS 51-L [Challenger] was based on a faulty engineering analysis of the SRM field joint behavior." This was incorrect. There was never any engineering analysis done the night of January 27 by anyone that contributed to the decision to launch Challenger. The Thiokol engineers opposed the launch on the basis of a rationale that had already been presented to NASA in meetings up to and including the August 19, 1985, briefing at headquarters. This rationale was that at lower temperatures, loss of resiliency by the primary O-ring could allow hot gas blow-by and that if it continued while joint rotation was unseating the secondary O-ring, there could be a catastrophic burnthrough.

Mulloy and the others at Marshall understood this thoroughly. The Thiokol engineers chose as their benchmark the fifty-three degree O-ring temperature from the 51-C launch in January 1985. In my opinion, Marshall was pressuring Thiokol's management to approve a launch which had to go up for political reasons. The Thiokol telefax that approved the launch contained no engineering analysis. It was a restate-ment of the "General Conclusions" chart from August 19 that actually argued against the launch. The only difference was that at the end, Thiokol asserted that 51-L would be no different from 51-C and that it was safe to launch.

The House report went on:

The information presented to NASA headquarters on August 19, 1985, was sufficient to require immediate and concentrated efforts to remedy the joint design flaws. The fact that NASA did not take stronger action to solve this problem indicates that its top technical staff did not fully accept or understand the seriousness of the joint problem.

This was nonsense. The headquarters engineers "held their breath" with each shuttle launch. They understood the seriousness of the joint problem.

"The committee finds no reason to doubt Mr. Moore's observations that no one within NASA understood the problem with the O-rings. . . ." This was similarly nonsense. Dozens of people understood it clearly enough to stop flights and redesign the joints.

Finally, no mention of the evolution of the O-ring temperature issue during the year before the disaster occurred in the committee report.

In the final analysis, the Committee ultimately said it was clear Challenger shouldn't have been launched and that they didn't know why NASA did so. As William Rogers had said in testimony:

And when you look at the [Commission's] report, you ask yourself, "How could it have happened?" I notice several comments by members of Congress who read this over. They say they just don't understand how it happened, and we don't either for sure.

The House committee wrote:

As a whole, the committee's review of the decision to launch STS 51-L on January 28 indicates a number of questionable practices. It is not clear to the committee why so many warnings went unheeded by NASA personnel that morning.

That was the last word of the U.S. government on the space shuttle Challenger disaster.

———

IN DECEMBER 1986, Malcolm McConnell sent me an advance copy of his book, *Challenger: A Major Malfunction*, that further enhanced the impression of the awful weather conditions at the Kennedy Space

Center on the day of the Challenger disaster. I read the book on the Amtrak metroliner one rainy day as I traveled to New York City to speak on Challenger to graduate students at the John Jay College of Criminal Justice in midtown Manhattan. I'd been invited by Professor Patrick O'Hara, who had published an article on the possible link between the Challenger launch and the president's State of the Union address in *Newsday*.

McConnell wrote of concerns by Challenger pilot Mike Smith about the forecast for freezing weather expected to reach Cape Canaveral and the Kennedy Space Center by Monday, January 27. McConnell's source was North Carolina attorney William Maready. He was a personal friend of Mike and his wife Jane Smith who had flown his private plane to the Cape from his home in North Carolina the weekend before the disaster. I had met Maready myself. In a talk we had in Washington at the Treasury Department cafeteria, he had already told me some of the things I read in McConnell's book. I had also agreed to act as an expert witness in litigation Maready planned to bring on behalf of Jane Smith against either NASA or Thiokol, though the litigation was later settled out of court.

In his book, McConnell wrote that before Mike Smith flew with the astronaut crew to KSC from Houston for the Challenger flight, he phoned Jesse Moore's aide, NASA's shuttle flow director James Harrington, and said:

> Jim, the weather looks terrible for next week. You've got to do everything you possibly can to install those spares and finish out the work on Challenger and get us launched by Saturday, Sunday at the latest.

Maready also told me that Smith asked Harrington for a history of the weather for previous shuttle launches.

As noted, after the Saturday night decision made by William Graham to cancel the launch of Challenger on the following day, the weather that Sunday morning was warm, bright, and clear. In not tanking the shuttle the previous night and boarding the astronauts on Sunday to wait for clear weather, NASA departed from its usual past practices. McConnell later described to me in a phone conversation the anger felt by the astronaut crew at this botched management decision. In his book, McConnell wrote something else Maready had told me, which was that on Sunday night, Smith complained to him, "You know, Bill . . . you've got people making decisions down here who've never even flown an airplane before."

The next day, Monday the 27th, saw the launch scrubbed because of the stuck hatch handle and high crosswinds on the KSC runway that had to be kept safe in case of a post-booster stage launch abort leading to an RTLS [return-to-landing strip]. McConnell disclosed to me an amazing detail—that Mike Smith then advised his mother-in-law, who had come to observe the launch:

> . . . that she could return to her work for at least three days without fear of missing the launch. Given the impending weather, he said, there was no way they'd be able to fly until Thursday.

I had heard from other sources that the crew, when they boarded Challenger the morning of Tuesday the 28th, believed that the launch was going to be scrubbed because it was so cold. I had written in my "Challenger Report" that I delivered to Attorney General Meese that:

> An eyewitness reportedly said the crew was not aware that the decision to launch was certain until a hold in the countdown only a few minutes before lift-off. The Commission's report confirmed that because of concerns with ice on the launch pad, the final "go" was not made until T-minus nine minutes.

But this may just have been the story NASA launch officials were telling the astronauts. What if the decision had already been made to launch that day? What if the top launch managers were covering themselves by pretending there was still a chance the launch would not proceed if the ice team didn't take one last walk around the launch tower? We know that when they did take a final look, the ice was no better. In fact, it was worse. The temperature was now in the mid-thirties, so the ice had started to loosen. This meant that even more would shake loose when the main engines were ignited. The ice conditions on the launch pad were even more dangerous by 11:30 than at the final mission management team meeting at 9:00 a.m.

In November, reporter Nicholas Chriss had written in the *Houston Chronicle*:

Someone in a position to know at the Johnson Space Center, someone who talked to the Challenger crew just before launch, said recently that no one—including the crew—expected the Challenger to be launched in the frigid temperatures of January 28.

NASA had released transcripts of audio tapes where the astronauts joked and remarked about the cold weather. But NASA refused to release the actual tapes that would allow a researcher to see what might have been left out. My perception of the heightened awareness at Kennedy of the weather that day gained further weight when I phoned Eileen O'Hara, a close friend of Christa McAuliffe. O'Hara had spoken to Christa the night of January 28.

O'Hara said that "Christa was well aware of the cold, but she was trying to keep a positive point of view." Christa told O'Hara that the cold might force a scrub of the next day's launch. If this happened, O'Hara said:

The next scheduled flight for Challenger might not be for another week while NASA waited for the weather to warm up, and during the wait, all seven astronauts would fly back to Houston for training exercises.

This was astounding information. It was not farfetched at all to think the astronauts might fly back to Houston. It had happened before, during STS-2, when the astronauts returned for a few days during a delay. Work in the Houston flight simulators was constant for an astronaut crew, and they tended to lose their performance edge after a short layoff. The astronauts flew back and forth in their high-speed jets from runways at Kennedy and Johnson, taking only a couple of hours each way.

This meant that not only was NASA's top management aware of the seriousness of the cold, they had even prepared a contingency plan for a scrub of up to a week. This blew any theory that NASA felt compelled to launch because of schedule pressure from Manifest Bingo and confirmed what I heard in person at Kennedy at the Centaur meetings, that the shuttle launch flow still had up to two weeks of slack. This further gave the lie to suggestions by the Presidential Commission and the House committee that an amorphous and generalized schedule pressure was the cause of the Challenger launch decision.

I discussed these circumstances with Bill Maready in another conversation, this time over the phone when he was at his office in Raleigh, North Carolina. He said that the person who would know about contingency plans for the Challenger crew to return to Houston would be George Abbey, director of Flight Crew Operations, who was at Kennedy when the disaster occurred. When Congressman Bill Nelson published his book, *Mission: An American Congressman's Voyage to Space*, he wrote that before Challenger was launched, Abbey had asked top NASA launch officials if Rocco Petrone of Rockwell had approved the launch. Nelson said they lied and told Abbey that Petrone did approve it.

"NO SUCH THING HAS EVER TAKEN PLACE"

—Did President Reagan Order the Challenger Launch?

THE ONE-YEAR anniversary of the shuttle disaster came and went. For a year, I had spent almost all my spare time researching and writing about the disaster. At Treasury I was struggling to get my career moving again. I was trying to keep our family afloat financially, while doing the constant chores at home that a rural lifestyle entailed. I was disgusted at how both houses of Congress had avoided the inescapable fact that there had to have been White House involvement in the Challenger launch. I was also depressed and discouraged that I had not found any incontrovertible evidence of it.

I wrote one more article on the Challenger disaster, which appeared in the *Houston Post* on February 22, 1987. In the article, in which I felt I was speaking to the NASA astronaut community, I revealed that I had been the one to release the O-ring documents to the press. I felt I had to do this for the sake of the public record.

While writing the article, I had several phone conversations with Roger Boisjoly, whom I had not yet met in person. He was now out of work on a leave of absence. Later he left Thiokol but was able to restart his professional career from a new home in Arizona.

Boisjoly explained to me how, after the January 1985 51-C mission,

Thiokol had begun to look hard at the effects of cold temperatures in making O-ring erosion worse. Boisjoly related to me the key information mentioned previously in this book about why Larry Mulloy deleted references to the effects of the cold weather on the O-rings prior to the 51-E Level I flight readiness review. I reported this publicly for the first time in the *Houston Post* article:

> One lead that investigators seem never to have pursued involved the January 1985 launch of Discovery on a military mission. At fifty-three degrees, the weather was as cold as it had ever been for a shuttle launch. Engineers at the Marshall Space Flight Center found it was no coincidence that a record five instances of thermal distress of O-rings occurred. Yet no mention of temperature was found in data submitted for review by top shuttle officials. The Rogers Commission noted that, but apparently never asked why.
>
> Thiokol engineer Roger Boisjoly told me that he participated in a meeting at which Lawrence Mulloy, the head of the solid rocket booster program at Marshall, ordered the deletion. Mulloy did not want the meeting to result in a launch commit criterion for the O-rings. Such a temperature constraint, Mulloy said, would interfere with the shuttle flight schedule, particularly at Vandenberg Air Force Base, California, the planned launch site of most military missions and a cooler locale than Cape Canaveral.
>
> This suggests the debates over the O-rings before the Challenger launch were essentially a repetition of a battle waged a year earlier and won by Mulloy.
>
> According to Boisjoly, Thiokol engineers consoled themselves with the supposition that before they would see such low temperatures in Florida again, they would have solved the O-ring problem.

Throughout 1987, I spent my spare time working on notes for a book about the Challenger disaster. The Commission had deposited a large file in the National Archives entitled "Political Pressure," which I now began to study.

In examining this topic, we need to go back to the Presidential Commission's public hearings in Washington, D.C. that took place on February 25, 26, and 27, 1986. Thiokol engineers Alan McDonald,

Roger Boisjoly, Arnie Thompson, and Brian Russell told their story at
the Commission's hearing on the 25th. Also testifying were the Thiokol
managers who overruled them. The next day, the Commission heard
from Mulloy, George Hardy, Stanley Reinartz, and Judson Lovingood,
as well as from Charles Stevenson and others on the NASA ice team.
At this point, none of the NASA launch managers who may have been
aware of White House pressure had been called to the stand.

That day, Larry Speakes, President Reagan's press secretary, gave a
press conference at the White House on the Challenger launch:

Q. Does the White House have any involvement in the launching of
Challenger that day—

A. (Speakes) I'm tired of that story. I am really tired of that. I'll bet
you a dollar not a soul in here has gotten that from an official
source. You've gotten it from your press colleagues. It's the most
vicious and distorted rumor I have ever heard.

Q. Nobody's printed it.

A. Nobody's printed it, but what happened was the *New York Times*,
one week ago, Tuesday, heard that CBS News was going to carry
this as their lead story, and it started from that, and it's been
going and going. He came to us and said Regan had called NASA
yesterday—some source over there said Regan had called NASA
and said, "Get that thing up." Absolutely not. I was involved in the
State of the Union.

Q. (Inaudible)

A. I don't believe it. Produce him and let me see him, and let's see
how long he stays in this government.

Q. He's in jail to protect his identity. (Laughter)

A. Produce him, and let's see how long he stays. But I am sick and
tired of that stuff, and I think it is irresponsible on the part of the
press. Ignore it.

Q. Are you denying it?

A. Not only denying it, I'm saying it is a rumor perpetrated by the press.

Q. With no thought given at any time to mention the NASA split
screen cut-off of the space shuttle?

A. That is more of the vicious rumor. Absolutely not. And you really
ought to get off it. You really should.

Q. What you're saying is there was not pressure from anyone at the

White House on NASA about the launch date for this shuttle?

A. Absolutely not. Nor was there any thought of ever putting anything in that, except referring to the kid's experiment on-board, and except referring to the space station. Those two things were in his speech from the start—nothing connected with the shuttle launch. And that story ought to go away. I do appreciate your responsibility in coming to us promptly with rumors which—

Q. The testimony at those [Commission] hearings appears to indicate there was pressure.

A. Not pressure from the White House, no.

Q. Does the president have any idea where that pressure could have come from, or was there any scheme of things, of having a timetable?

A. Well, you're talking about two kinds of pressure. NASA set an ambitious launch schedule. We have nothing to do with that.

Q. It was the national security director that set out an ambitious launch schedule. Wasn't [that] about a year ago?

A. No, I don't think so.

Q. That was reported—

A. I don't know. We didn't establish any schedule for them. Their schedule was consistent with the needs for their program. We didn't tell them when to fly their shuttle. The second thing is, if you're talking about pressure to launch on that day, no, absolutely not. No pressure, period.

Q. Do you have a new NASA administrator?

A. Not yet.

Q. He [i.e., James Beggs] just resigned yesterday [i.e., following his leave of absence].

Q. Any time frame?

A. No time frame. Candy, were you about to speak?

Q. Absent from the split screen and a phone call from the podium in Congress, had there been any—I mean Reagan has frequently called the shuttle astronauts on flights. Had there been a plan that day for him to call that day or were you planning on doing it on a different day?

A. Hadn't planned it. No plan to call, period. As you notice, we have not called. The shuttles were becoming such a regular occurrence that the president hasn't called the last several.

Q. Well, he called someone and asked him to pick up the horses at his ranch or something like that. How many times back was that? Several?

A. A year or so ago. Time flies when you get old.

In answering reporters' questions, Speakes used the full press secretary's bag of tricks—denial, threats, intimidation, humor, persuasion. He was delivering a message to anyone at NASA, the White House, or the press that this subject was taboo. Previously in this book, I cited the instance where at the time of STS-4 on July 4, 1982, NASA sent the shuttle on an extra orbit so the president and his party would not have to arrive so early at Edwards Air Force Base to view the landing. This had been originally reported by Andrea Mitchell of ABC News, who was told she was *persona non grata* at the White House for broadcasting it. Speakes was exercising the same kind of blunt force with the Challenger disaster.

Now that Speakes had made it clear what the party line was, it was probably not an accident that the next day's Commission hearing on Thursday, February 27, addressed the issue of political pressure. The question was broached to Jesse Moore by Rogers who asked, in the exchange that never appeared in the hearing transcript, "And there wasn't any political pressure, was there?"

Moore replied, "No, sir."

But the issue did not go away. It was a few days later when ABC News staffer Nona Snider obtained a copy of the memorandum sent by NASA to White House Cabinet Secretary Alfred Kingon containing the text highlighting Christa McAuliffe and the Teacher-in-Space mission for inclusion in the speech.

After the speech insert appeared, the White House moved swiftly to exercise "damage control," as it obviously called into question Larry Speakes' denials. Now, Patrick Buchanan, the White House director of communications, whose office was in charge of drafting the speech, said the NASA submission was part of a "routine sweep" asking for recommendations for the speech from eighteen federal agencies. He told the *New York Times* on March 12 that Kingon never passed on the NASA submission to White House speechwriters.

Buchanan added that the material suggested by NASA referring to Christa McAuliffe and the 1986 space science flights was inconsistent

with the broad themes of the speech. He said further that the only mention of Challenger was to be a comment on an experiment carried in
the shuttle by the college student, Richard Cavoli. As noted previously, Senator Hollings cited the text referring to Cavoli when he questioned Rogers in the Senate hearing on June 10. Hollings was
incredulous that Cavoli would be mentioned but not Christa McAuliffe.

Now Speakes denied again that Christa McAuliffe was featured in
the speech. He said of the NASA speech submittal, it was "simply a
draft." He said:

> We looked at it, filed it, and forgot it. Every department did it, also.
> It never got into any speech written.

I now located Cavoli myself. He told me that he was at the White
House getting ready to meet the president when Challenger blew up.
How could it be that such attention would be lavished on this unknown
student, while the famous Teacher-in-Space, Christa McAuliffe, was to
be ignored?

Speculation about a launch/speech link had been fueled by an article by *Wall Street Journal* White House correspondent Jane Mayer the
morning of the Challenger disaster. The article carried the headline,
"Hero Hour is Near, and Ronald Reagan is Mum About It." Mayer
wrote:

> The hour of the hero draws near.
> It has become one of Washington's little dramas. Tonight, if all goes
> according to plan, President Reagan will interrupt his State of the
> Union talk on budget and taxes and other issues of the moment. At his
> cue, all eyes—not to mention the television cameras—will turn to the
> gallery of the House of Representatives. And there will be—the Hero.

This year, the article said, the White House was making an unusual
effort to keep the identity of the hero secret.

> Indeed, the identity of this year's hero or heroes may be the most
> painstakingly guarded secret since the invasion of Granada. Drafts of the
> speech have been very narrowly circulated within the administration.

Even so, the drafts have blank lines where the talk of heroes ought to be. Even today, just a handful of officials know, and they aren't telling.

When the president delivered the speech a week late, the following Tuesday, no hero was mentioned. The probable reason, as Hollings had indicated, was that the hero—or heroine—was dead, her body in the shattered Challenger crew cabin at the bottom of the Atlantic Ocean. Christa McAuliffe would have been the ideal theme-figure for a "family values" concept. What better hero than the Teacher-in-Space?

One source who was certain that McAuliffe was to be featured in the speech was the *Washington Post's* White House correspondent Lou Cannon, who later wrote an authorized biography of President Reagan. In an article published on January 29, 1986, the day after the disaster, Cannon wrote:

> The president, described by aides as somber and silent during much of the day, said, "I can't get out of my mind" the husband and children of Christa McAuliffe, the teacher killed yesterday in the Challenger explosion. He had planned to mention her in his State of the Union speech, White House officials said.

Another source was Bill Plante, CBS News White House correspondent, who told me in a personal conversation that McAuliffe "was certainly going to be in the speech." It was also confirmed by NASA General Manager Philip Culbertson, who had signed the speech insert memo to the White House for William Graham. When Dr. Robert Bowman and I were preparing for the press conference sponsored by his institute, Bowman spoke to Culbertson, who told him that White House denials about a launch/speech link were "ridiculous."

For several weeks after the February 25–27 hearings and Larry Speakes' press conference, the subject remained current, including an appearance by Senator Hollings on "This Week with David Brinkley," where he said he had proposed subpoenas and hearings on the White House political pressure issue. His move was blocked by the Senate's Republican leadership.

Also, in response to a letter from Congressman Edward Markey, William Graham had disclosed that he had phone conversations with

White House aides Alfred Kingon and Richard Davis, but he claimed the calls did not concern the Challenger launch.

The question came up again, this time addressed to President Reagan himself at an April 9 press conference. This is the President's only known public statement on the subject:

Q. Mr. President, you're going to have to decide in the next few days whether to fund a fourth shuttle orbiter to replace the Challenger. Do you have a sense now of whether you might agree to do that, and if so how you can fund it, given the restraints of Gramm-Rudman?

A. I'm going to wait until I see what the proposal is and what comes to me. I've heard rumors and talk of this. I would hope that we could continue this. This was the request from every one of the families of those people who lost their lives on the Challenger— that we continue this program. And I said to them that that's what I wanted to do and would hope that we could do.

Q. If I could have a follow-up, sir. The White House has been requested by Senator Hollings to turn over the telephone logs of conversations between NASA officials and White House officials before the Challenger launch to determine whether there was undue pressure put on NASA to launch the Challenger. Do you agree that those logs ought to be given to the senator?

A. I don't know, I'll look into that. But I can tell you this, that all of this attempt to focus on it that somehow they were pressured to go off beginning with myself, no such thing has ever taken place. We don't know enough about that kind of thing to know whether we should advise them to take off or not.

The issue then disappeared from public view until the Senate hearings in June when Hollings raised it again.

But as Rogers told Hollings, the Commission did carry out an investigation of what it called "outside pressure." The lead investigator was FBI agent John R. Molesworth. Other investigators interviewed NASA management officials involved in the launch. I indicated earlier that I read these interviews in the National Archives. They were useless, consisting of *pro forma* denials. Molesworth also obtained affidavits of a similar nature from twenty-eight NASA and contractor officials. He reported his findings in two memoranda to Chairman Rogers that were routed through Executive Director Alton Keel and dated May 5 and 8. The pertinent information from Molesworth's investigation that was available in the National Archives was as follows:

JESSE MOORE INTERVIEW—On April 8, Moore was interviewed by Commission staff member Emily Trapnell, and the "outside pressure" issue was one of the topics. Moore said that he knew on the evening of Saturday, January 25, that Vice President Bush "might stop over on Sunday morning on his way to Nicaragua, I believe." Moore also said he was not aware that the State of the Union speech "was going to be held on that particular night." He denied that there was any outside pressure to launch and said, "The only person I talked to really outside of the normal launch team during that period of time was Phil Culbertson." Moore did not mention that it would have been Culbertson who conveyed any launch pressure coming from William Graham.

WILLIAM GRAHAM INTERVIEW—On April 29, 1986, Molesworth wrote a memorandum to Alton Keel that read as follows:

Dr. William Graham, Acting Administrator, NASA, was interviewed on April 24, 1986. Dr. Graham has been acting administrator since approximately December 7, 1985, and employed as the deputy administrator since approximately mid-November 1985.

WHITE HOUSE PRESSURE TO LAUNCH—Dr. Graham did not receive pressure from anyone at the White House including the president to insure that the 51-L mission was launched in time for the State of the Union message. Dr. Graham is not aware of any calls or personal contacts made to any NASA employee from the White House regarding the timing of the 51-L launch. NASA headquarters was required on January 8, 1986, to prepare a submission to the White House as NASA's input to the State of the Union speech. The assignment was given to Shirley Green, who prepared the submission. Dr. Graham participated in discussions regarding its contents, and the memorandum was prepared by Green. The memorandum was signed out by Phil Culbertson after it was read to Dr. Graham, who was at KSC. Dr. Graham does not recall any discussion or suggestion to include a live communication hook-up with the space shuttle during the State of the Union.

O-Ring History/SR&QA—Dr. Graham was not aware of any problems with SRM field joints or O-rings prior to its disclosure after the accident. Dr. Graham is not familiar with the SR&QA (safety, reliability, and quality assurance) activities at either NASA headquarters or in the field. Dr. Graham intends to study the SR&QA functions for its effectiveness within NASA in the near future.

51-L Accident—Dr. Graham flew from Washington, D.C., to KSC on the afternoon of January 28, 1986. He recalls receiving a briefing the next day which included a film of the accident. During that discussion the possibility of a burnthrough was discussed, however, the O-ring and the field joint were not mentioned. The briefing was conducted by Jesse Moore.

This was at the least a questionable summary of what was supposed to be an investigation. Molesworth transformed Graham's denials into declarative statements of what he did or did not know. As a professional investigator, Moleworth would have known that such a procedure was unusual, and that the value of Graham's unsupported statements was nil.

Of course it would have been absurd to think that Graham would have admitted in this interview a launch/speech link. Graham and the other top NASA officials were fighting for their careers. They all had top secret security clearances, where they had learned the art of professional concealment. And they worked for an administration which, as Larry Speakes wrote in his memoirs, was "obsessed with secrecy."

Karen Ehlers Interview—Karen Ehlers was NASA's flight activity officer for mission 51-L, in charge of coordinating the scheduling of crew activities. She worked in Houston at the Johnson Space Center. On April 24, 1986, she was the "initiator" of a memo from John F. Whiteley, chief, Flight Activities Branch, to NASA's mission planning and operations team, which was a subgroup of the data and design analysis task force on the Challenger disaster. The subject of the memo, which I found in the Commission's records in the National Archives, was "Presidential Phone Call/STS-51-L."

Subsequently, Ehlers was interviewed at Houston by Commission investigator Pat Maley. In his May 8 report to Chairman Rogers, John R. Molesworth wrote:

Karen Ehlers, flight activity officer for 51-L, was interviewed at JSC concerning any plans to make a special communication hook-up between the president and the shuttle. Ehlers advised that she was in a position to coordinate all astronaut flight activities and that at no time during the 51-L planning stages up to the 51-L explosion were there any plans for a communications hook-up between the shuttle and government officials, specifically the White House.

But this wasn't the end of the story. Molesworth continued by stating:

It is a standard procedure to isolate possible points in the astronauts' in-flight schedule that would be convenient times for the shuttle to receive a presidential call.

Three such times had been designated for the Challenger flight. The April 24 memo from Whiteley stated that Ehlers and a representative of the NASA Public Affairs Office:

. . . met to outline the scheduling constraints and opportunities for a presidential phone call in anticipation of such a request. The following three opportunities were identified and are listed in order of priority:
During the crew conference . . . on Day Six;
During the teacher activities on flight Day Four;
During the phase partitioning experiment on Day Five.

Thus it was nonsense for Molesworth to write that there were no "plans for a communications hook-up between the shuttle and government officials, specifically the White House." Identifying and listing three opportunities were "plans."

Moreover, the Commission distorted this information in its report. In the section on "Outside Pressure to Launch," where the Commission concluded that, "the decision to launch the Challenger was made solely by the appropriate NASA officials without any outside intervention or pressure," the three times designated by Karen Ehlers were listed but were identified as "three live telecasts." The report does not mention, as stated in the Whiteley memo, that these were "opportunities for a presidential phone call."

But the discussion of the timing of a presidential phone call had gone further than merely setting aside times. As stated previously in this book, White House aide Richard Davis told CNN that NASA had requested a call.

The Commission's report contained other peculiarities on this subject. The report stated:

> ... to give the crew time to become oriented, NASA does not schedule a communication for at least forty-eight hours after the launch, and no such communication was scheduled in the case of flight 51-L.

But both President Reagan and Vice President Bush had placed phone calls to the space shuttle on numerous missions. Such phone calls had taken place as early as three hours after shuttle lift-off. So much for NASA's forty-eight hour rule. This demonstrates that while NASA set aside "opportunities" for phone calls, they were not "scheduled." Obviously the calls took place at the president or vice president's convenience, with coordination with NASA. So the statement that presidential communication during 51-L was not "scheduled" is also meaningless.

Advance scheduling, moreover, was not required for any technical reason. NASA's ground-to-shuttle communication system was already "wired" for presidential communications. Richard Feynman, who also suspected White House pressure, reported that he asked ground controllers at Johnson how long it would take to complete a president-to-shuttle phone call once it was requested. They said three minutes.

But is there any direct evidence that President Reagan was planning to call Challenger? Consider this: Malcolm McConnell, author of *Challenger: A Major Malfunction*, told me in 1987 that on a visit to NASA's Jet Propulsion Laboratory in Pasadena, California, where he had gone to promote his book, he was " ... told by a staff member that it was 'common knowledge' JPL had been told to clear a communications channel that was being used for the unmanned Voyager spacecraft, so that the president could call Challenger during the State of the Union speech."

This was not a "rumor," which was the way the Presidential Commission and Chairman Rogers characterized anything said by anyone that might suggest a launch/speech link.

There is another detail mentioned in the Karen Ehlers report that may have some bearing on scheduling issues with respect to the Teacher-in-Space aspect of the Challenger mission. This relates to the "teacher activities" scheduled for Day Four. This was to be Christa McAuliffe's nationwide broadcast to millions of school children.

When NASA planned a shuttle mission, its schedule of crew activities was meticulously detailed. Deviations were possible if unexpected conditions arose, but they would be held to a minimum. A multitude of technical planning details and ground operations were oriented to the schedule. If Challenger had been successfully launched on Tuesday, January 28, Christa McAuliffe's presentation on Day Four would have taken place on Friday, while schools were in session, and her program, possibly including a presidential phone call, would have been broadcast to a nationwide audience. But if the launch had slipped even one day, Day Four would have fallen on the weekend. This may have been yet one more circumstance driving NASA to launch that day.

SHIRLEY GREEN INTERVIEW—Shirley Green was NASA's director of public affairs and a political appointee with strong White House connections. She had worked for Vice President Bush for seven years as a press aide and had been at NASA for only a few months. She was NASA's contact with Larry Speakes and Patrick Buchanan and was present at the Kennedy Space Center for the Challenger launch.

In an April interview with the Commission, Green told investigators that she was present in the KSC firing room during the countdown and scrub of the launch attempt on Monday, January 27. After the scrub, she called her White House press office contact, Rusty Brashear, and told him the launch had been rescheduled for 9:38 a.m. the following day.

Green also said that when she had first arrived at the Cape the previous Saturday for the planned weekend launch attempt, she phoned the White House to ask whether NASA would be mentioned in the State of the Union address. She said she could not remember whether she spoke to Rusty Brashear or a man named Denny Grizzly. She described this call as follows:

"Did NASA make the State of the Union?" And I was told, "Yes." And I said, "Good. Did we also get the recommendation on the space station?" He said, "Yes, you did, also space science and the aerospace plane." And I said, "You know, that's terrific. Did they tie it to the Teacher-in-Space being up?" And he said, "No, there's no mention of the teacher." And I said, "I'm sorry to hear that because it's going to be a big media event, I think. But on the other hand, the significant program-matic areas would be in the State of the Union."

Previously, I wrote that White House reporter Lou Cannon, CBS News reporter Bill Plante, and NASA General Manager Phil Culbert-son confirmed that Christa McAuliffe was to be mentioned in President Reagan's State of the Union address. The choice is clear: either those three gentlemen and their sources or Shirley Green was mistaken.

In his report to Chairman Rogers, John R. Molesworth wrote:

> Shirley Green, director, Public Affairs Division, NASA Headquarters, advises that she was at KSC during the weekend prior to the 51-L launch.

Molesworth was distorting the record. Green was not at KSC just "during the weekend." She was there through the disaster on Tuesday. Moleworth continued:

> As part of her regular duties, Green contacts the White House daily. Green did not recall making any specific telephone calls to the White House from KSC; however, it would not be unusual for her to make such calls. Any call made by Green to the White House did not involve the decision process to launch 51-L.

Again, Molesworth was citing disclaimers by a key participant as facts. The Commission's report said nothing about the Shirley Green interview. And obviously it said nothing about William Graham's 161 phone calls from his motel room, some, according to CNN political director Christine Dolan, to the homes and offices of White House aides.

RICHARD COOK INTERVIEW—In late April, Molesworth called and asked to interview me on the subject of the alleged launch/speech link. The interview took place on April 29 at the Commission's offices on 5th Street, S.W., across from NASA headquarters.

Molesworth's manner during the interview was tense and hostile. Before he turned on his tape recorder he said, "The only people who believe this are you, Senator Hollings, and the press."

"I'm trying to understand why NASA launched Challenger," I answered.

"That's what we're trying to find out," he said.

The interview was short and consisted of repeated questions about whether I could give any specific information or refer the Commission to specific people who might be able to verify that a launch/speech link existed. At one point, Molesworth flared up when I asked him who else he had interviewed. He said that was none of my business.

I could only tell him that Christine Dolan of CNN had told me there were pre-launch phone calls between NASA and the White House and that NASA had requested a phone hook-up for Challenger.

At the end of the interview, Molesworth asked me twice not to mention the interview to the press, though he added, "I know I don't have a right to ask you that." In fact I did speak to the press about it. In his May 8 memorandum to Chairman Rogers, Molesworth said of my earlier March 28 interview with Kehrli and Malley:

> Mr. Cook stated that NASA intended to arrange a live communica-
> tion hook-up between the president and the shuttle. He also has knowl-
> edge that a news network has information concerning calls from the
> White House concerning the launch. The interviewers pressed Cook to
> provide specifics concerning these allegations, but he always avoided the
> question or responded with extraneous information.

Molesworth wrote of the April 29 interview that he conducted with me:

> On April 29, 1986, Richard Cook was re-interviewed regarding his
> statements pertaining to White House pressure to launch, a proposed
> live communications hook-up between the president and the shuttle
> during the State of the Union speech, and Dr. Graham's desire to have
> a well-timed launch for political reasons. Cook admitted that his pre-
> vious statements were based solely on press report, rumor, and his
> own scenario of events. Cook could not offer any factual basis for his
> allegations.

Molesworth's description of the two interviews was distorted and seemed part of the same pattern of trying to discredit me that Chairman Rogers had carried out at the Commission's February 11 public hearing. By now I was tired of the bullying and sent the following letter to Rogers:

Dear Mr. Rogers:

I am writing to protest the treatment I received yesterday from Mr. John R. Molesworth of your staff at a meeting he requested which took place at three p.m. on the Commission's premises.

The purpose of the meeting, Mr. Molesworth said, was to investigate whether White House pressure played a part in the launch of space shuttle Challenger.

Mr. Molesworth read from a transcript of testimony I gave to Mr. Randy Kerhrli of the Commission's staff on March 28, 1986. That meeting was also held at the Commission's request. On that occasion, I was invited to raise any additional concerns I had with respect to the launch of Challenger. I then expressed the view that the link between the Challenger launch and the president's State of the Union address made it appear likely that there was pressure on NASA's managers to launch. I elaborated on this surmisal at some length.

At yesterday's meeting with Mr. Molesworth, I indicated that I did not have any further information relating to political pressure beyond what had already appeared publicly in the press and in Commission testimony. I also stated that, to my mind, the launch decision had not yet been explained. The arguments of poor management or a flawed launch decision do more to explain away the decision than to show what factors motivated the decision makers when they acted.

Mr. Molesworth stated that I was the only person who believed there was political pressure, other than Senator Hollings and the press, which is in fact a rather large group. Earlier in the meeting, I had asked Mr. Molesworth who else he had talked to. He answered sharply, "I am the one doing the interviewing!" At the end of this meeting, he said twice, "I would prefer that you didn't discuss this meeting with the press," although he added that he didn't have any right to make that request.

This is the second time the Commission has appeared to try to intimidate me with respect to my testimony. The first was at the February 11, 1986, public hearing. At the same time, while some of the persons responsible for a launch which killed seven people have been questioned sharply, they have also been commended by you for their public service and have been given the opportunity to alter transcripts of their sworn testimony. Further, the individuals through whom political pressure might have been exerted—Dr. William Graham and his assistants—have never, to my knowledge, been required to testify under oath or even to speak on this subject for the public record. I am not the only one to note this astonishing omission.

Instead, it appears, from what Mr. Molesworth told me, that all the disclaimers on this subject have been taken at face value and that this is what has constituted the Commission's investigation. I would be happy to learn, for my own peace of mind, of any details that show a conclusive investigation has been done, but Mr. Molesworth did not share any such information with me. He too was merely generalizing and asserting, and if the investigation had in fact put the matter to rest, I do not understand why I was admonished not to speak to the press. I would think the Commission would be delighted in seeing the matter publicized if a *bona fide* investigation had demonstrated beyond reasonable doubt that political pressure was not present.

I did not give this letter to the press. At this point, I just wanted the Commission off my back and in fact did not receive any further harassment.

APRIL 29 LETTER FROM JAY STEPHENS TO MOLESWORTH—In this letter, which Chairman Rogers disclosed when he was questioned by Senator Hollings on June 10, Jay Stephens, deputy counsel to the president, forwarded earlier correspondence between Senator Hollings and White House Counsel Fred Fielding denying any staff involvement in the Challenger launch. Stephens provided a draft of the State of the Union address without any mention of Christa McAuliffe and stated that "consideration was never given" to having a live hook-up between Challenger and the president during the speech.

Of course these disclaimers were worthless as far as being real evidence. Evidently the Commission wanted something more definite, so on May 12, Stevens sent a short letter to Rogers stating there was "no record, recollection, or indicia of any [White House staff] conversation relating to the decision to launch the shuttle Challenger."

This letter was the entire substance of what was supposed to have been an internal White House investigation. There is no indication that Molesworth interviewed anyone within the White House, though as I indicated earlier, I was told in the meeting with Senator Hollings and his aides that there were such interviews but that they were withheld as being too "sensitive."

OTHER NASA PHONE CALLS—Finally, Molesworth attempted to identify and trace other NASA phone calls either placed to the White House or between top agency officials. The following information resulted:

- A number of calls were identified between top officials at NASA headquarters and the Kennedy Space Center during the week before the Challenger launch. Callers included Jesse Moore, Michael Weeks, William Lucas, Philip Culbertson, and others. Obviously, such calls would be expected as part of the normal course of business.
- Phone calls were placed to the White House by Public Affairs Director Shirley Green, though the record contains no details. These were not mentioned in the Commission's report, though they clearly could be related to political pressure.
- According to Molesworth's report to Chairman Rogers, "additional calls were placed from the [Kennedy] Center to the White House during the pertinent period of time. NASA has provided this information to the Commission. . . . No phone calls to the White House were found during the review of these telephone records which consisted of the twenty-four-hour period from noon January 27, 1986, through noon January 28, 1986."

The nature of these calls was a mystery. Molesworth did not provide any details or describe efforts to identify the parties to the calls or their content. The existence of these calls would appear to undermine the

White House disclaimers of Fred Fielding and Jay Stevens. As these calls were placed from Kennedy to the White House, they would appear to be different from the calls to White House officials by Graham from his motel room. None of these calls was mentioned in the Commission's report.

At this point it was clear that there was significant telephone contact between NASA and the White House prior to the Challenger launch. The fact that Molesworth's record of unspecified "additional calls" included none during the twenty-four hours preceding the Challenger launch did not disprove the existence of pressure. By then, the decision had likely already been made that Challenger had to launch by Tuesday. It was simply a matter of execution. Besides, at that point, it would have been William Graham who was talking to NASA's top launch officials at Kennedy, and in fact Molesworth found such contact. NASA's phone records showed that a call was placed from the KSC center director's office to William Graham at headquarters on January 27, 1986, at 5:30 p.m. This phone call was not disclosed during the Commission's hearings. Molesworth wrote in his report to Rogers:

> This phone call has been discussed with Phil Culbertson, Jesse Moore, Dick Smith, and Dr. Graham. These persons were identified as possible participants in that conversation. None of the participants recalled the conversation; however, both Dick Smith and Jesse Moore stated that it is entirely possible that they called Dr. Graham regarding the status of the launch. Dr. Graham does not recall the conversation.

This was a phone call placed by the top NASA launch managers at Kennedy to the head of the agency in Washington after the word had gone out for everyone involved in the launch to be alert for issues related to the freezing weather blowing in that night. The call was placed by a small group of senior people from the office of Richard Smith, KSC director. Convened by this small group in the director's office, the meeting likely would have been on the order of a near-emergency. The meeting and phone call took place at almost the exact time that Thiokol gave Marshall its initial recommendation not to launch. But not one of these high-level participants, all top space program managers, remembered that the phone call even took place. Of all the absurdities during the investigation, this was among the most glaring. Evidently even the Commission thought so, as their records contained a May 19 follow-up letter from Graham to Molesworth that stated:

> On April 25, 1986, during your visit to my office to interview me in regard to the Challenger accident, you asked a question for which I could not recall the answer. That question concerned the calling party and substance of a telephone call placed to my office from the Kennedy Space Center, as indicated in Kennedy records for 5:37 p.m. on the evening of January 27, 1986, and lasting approximately nine minutes. Records indicate the call was placed from telephone number (305) 867-3333.
>
> That telephone number originates in the office of Mr. Richard Smith, the director of the Kennedy Space Center. Since my interview, I have asked Mr. Smith if he recalled placing such a call or had any information concerning it. He indicated to me that he did remember having called me on the afternoon of January 27 and having talked to me concerning the status of the mission 51-L. Such a call would have been a normal occurrence and not something that I would have a special reason to remember. While I still have no specific recollection of that call or any other call that I can identify with the particular record, I believe it to be quite possible that the call that Mr. Smith remembers is in fact the one indicated in the Kennedy records.

Graham sounded extremely vague in this letter. For one thing, he mentioned Smith, but how about Culbertson and Moore, the other participants in the phone call? But there is no record of any follow-up by the Commission.

What the Commission attempted to do was to document disclaimers by NASA and White House officials that such pressure did not take place, whether those disclaimers were true or not. A real investigation would have torn these disclaimers to shreds and exposed the cover-up and conspiracy that likely existed.

But there is more. In his report to Rogers, Molesworth wrote:

> On April 17, 1986, Joe Rees, Branch Chief, FTS [Federal Telephone System] Sample Program, General Services Administration, provided

a listing of FTS telephone calls made from NASA headquarters and the NASA centers. As a matter of policy, GSA only records a twenty percent sample of all government FTS calls. The search was conducted at the request of the Commission for calls between the centers and NASA headquarters during January 20–27, 1986. GSA was also requested to provide the listing for calls made to White House exchanges.

One printout lists seven calls made from "Kennedy Launch" to NASA headquarters from January 21 to 27. The second lists nine calls to the White House complex from January 25 to 27. Remember, these listings were only a sample.

Molesworth had already indicated that there were "other" calls from Kennedy to NASA headquarters and the White House in addition to those Shirley Green said she made. If the GSA phone records referred to those "other" calls, it may be instructive to review them in more detail.

Four of the seven calls to NASA headquarters were to numbers within the administrator's office, including one to William Graham's personal line, at 9:59 a.m., Monday, January 27. This call took place before that day's launch attempt was scrubbed. Another January 27 call was placed to the administrator's office at 2:37 p.m. This was just after the 2:00 p.m. mission management team meeting, where, as stated in the Commission's report, "Discussion was centered about the temperature at the launch facility and weather considerations predicted for launch at 9:38 a.m. on January 28, 1986."

These two phone calls came at critical times in the event sequence from Monday, January 27. Consider again Graham's 161 personal calls from his motel room over the previous weekend and the fact that he personally made the decision on Saturday night to cancel the launch scheduled for Sunday. Add to this the fact of the phone call from Culbertson, Moore, and Smith from the Kennedy Director's office that afternoon about the time Thiokol was presenting a written recommendation not to launch.

What kind of picture results? At a minimum, we see an image of a NASA acting administrator intimately involved with the Challenger launch decision, in close touch with the top NASA launch officials at the Cape, the contact tracking to key events in the launch sequence, and simultaneous contact with the White House. Meanwhile, Shirley Green is there too in close touch with her own White House counterparts.

As an aside, the other three calls from Kennedy Launch to NASA headquarters were placed to Jesse Moore's office on January 22–23, before Moore would have left Washington for the mission management team meetings at the Cape over the weekend. These calls pointed to nothing unusual.

Of the nine White House calls in the GSA sample, at least three appear to have been connected with Vice President Bush's aborted visit. These are two January 25 calls to the number of Bush's director of scheduling, and another that afternoon to a Secret Service number. A fourth call was to another Secret Service number placed after the cancellation of the Sunday launch.

Two other calls were placed from Kennedy Launch on Saturday, January 25, to the switchboard in the Old Executive Office building. There was no ready explanation for these calls, which were placed before the Sunday, January 26, launch was cancelled.

The seventh White House call was placed to a switchboard number for the National Security Council secretariat on Monday, January 27, at 11:10 a.m., just before the Monday launch was scrubbed.

Two calls are left, neither of which the Commission identified in its records. One of them was placed on Sunday, January 26, at 11:40 a.m. to the main White House switchboard. Thus someone at Kennedy phoned the White House even though the Sunday launch had been canceled.

The second was to President Reagan's scheduling office. The call was placed on Saturday, January 25, at 11:23 in the morning. The call lasted only one minute. The significance of this phone record is that it establishes a link between the Challenger launch and the president's schedule. Again, it is from a sample. Because of the strenuous efforts of the White House and the Commission to deny any conceivable link between the president and Challenger, this record alone constitutes a "smoking gun." (I personally called these numbers to verify their locations.)

There were other calls Molesworth did not mention. In his letter to Congressman Markey, Graham cited calls to and from Philip Culbertson and one he made to Richard Smith, all on Monday, January 27. The call from Graham could be the same as the one from Smith's office that

Molesworth cited, but in his letter to Markey, Graham provided no details. There was also a call on the morning of the disaster that Graham described to Joe Trento for Trento's book, *Prescription for Disaster*:

> [Graham] remembers having a conversation with an official at the space center, probably Center Director Dick Smith. They discussed problems with getting the SRB recovery ships in position for the launch. "I think it is more likely they weren't in position but they were getting in position."

Again, Graham seemed to have memory problems, not a good sign for the head of the world's leading space agency. The point, however, is that this was another call Molesworth failed to discover and raised the obvious question of how many more calls slipped through. In fact, the Commission's investigation of phone calls was incomplete and superficial. Even so, the record points to massive pre-launch telephone contact among various parties at Kennedy, NASA headquarters, and the White House.

My examination of the Commission's records took place during 1987, long after I had worked with Senator Hollings, published the *Washington Monthly* article, and studied the records of the Commission and House investigations. All this left me excited but frustrated. There certainly was enough information to justify re-opening the Challenger investigation, if anyone wanted to do so. I had gotten enough behind-the-scenes corroboration that the White House played a part in the launch to be certain it happened, and this certainty gained strength as I reviewed past press reports of earlier space shuttle missions with numerous presidential phone calls to the shuttle astronauts.

But I could still not find an eyewitness. For a while I tried to make contact with former NASA officials to find out if anyone was ready to talk. I tried to reach Jesse Moore and William Lucas and wrote to Larry Mulloy and Stanley Reinartz, but none answered. And I had to earn a living for my family, so increasingly devoted myself to advancing my career at Treasury and working on our farm.

Within a couple of years, my bureau had relocated to the refurbished Liberty Loan Building in Southwest Washington. Situated across the street from the Tidal Basin, the famous Washington cherry trees, and the Jefferson Memorial, it was a pleasant location. I had gotten two promotions and was again earning close to a normal living. I had survived, and now Challenger and its aftermath gradually receded as a factor in my life.

In September 1988, the space shuttle returned to flight with the liftoff of Discovery. I watched the launch and was excited to see the astronauts make it to orbit and return safely. I felt keenly aware of how vulnerable the crew members were. There was still no escape during the two-minute booster burn. "Good riddance," I thought, when they separated. "Get rid of those monsters."

Two months later, George Bush was elected president. The Reagan era was over and books were starting to appear about the Reagan administration. One of the first was Larry Speakes' book *Speaking Out*. This is what Speakes wrote about Reagan and the Challenger disaster:

The most emotional I saw Reagan was when he received word that the space shuttle Challenger had exploded on January 28, 1986. . . . George Bush, Pat Buchanan, and John Poindexter, who had been watching a live telecast of the launch, rushed into the Oval Office. Bush started to speak, but Buchanan blurted out, "The Challenger just blew up." Everyone was stunned. All the president could say was, "Oh no," and he cradled his face in his right hand. He had very closely followed the selection of the first civilian astronaut to ride on the Challenger, and had announced the selection of New Hampshire schoolteacher Christa McAuliffe months earlier, with all the finalists present in the Roosevelt Room of the White House. [Actually it was Bush who made the announcement.] . . . Somebody said, "Let's turn on the television," and we adjourned to the next room. While we were watching, the president said, "I hope everything is done to track the remains, to track down what happened." There is no question that all seven astronauts had been killed, as the space shuttle had burst into pieces. I said I thought I had better get down to the briefing room, and he said, "Tell them (the press) what we will do is we will fix it (the space program) and we will keep on going. These people were dedicated to this program. We couldn't do more to honor them than to go forward." He had tremendous instincts for saying the right thing at the right time.

When I read this, I went into my files and found a *New York Times* clipping from January 29, 1986. The article cited Patrick Buchanan, who said that he had walked into the Oval Office and said, "Sir, the shuttle blew up." According to Bernard Weinraub, the author of the article:

> Mr. Buchanan recalled later: "The President was stunned. He said something like, 'Isn't that the one with the teacher on it?' "

Buchanan's story did not match that of Larry Speakes. According to Speakes, it was in fact Buchanan who first told the president of the disaster. But Speakes did not mention that the president may have said, "Isn't that the one with the teacher on it?" To the contrary, Speakes was quite clear that all the president did was cradle his face in his hand and say, "Oh no."

Reading these two conflicting accounts by Speakes and Buchanan made me determined to try once more to solve the mystery. Time passed. In early 1990, Patrick O'Hara, the professor I'd gotten to know from the John Jay College of Criminal Studies in New York City, along with the New York City chapter of the American Society for Public Administration, nominated me for a national whistleblower's award. This was one of several awards given annually by the Cavallo Foundation of Boston, Massachusetts. I shared a $10,000 award with Roger Boisjoly. We received it at a ceremony that September at an outdoor garden on Capitol Hill near the Supreme Court in Washington. The foundation paid for Phyllis, Fred, Adele, and me to spend the night at a hotel. This was the first time I had met Roger face-to-face. Pat O'Hara also attended. My supervisor at Treasury gave me annual leave to attend but did not seem happy I had received the award, which was given for "moral courage in business and government." No one at Treasury congratulated me. Rather, it seemed to embarrass them.

Then, over the winter, I received a call from Dr. Mark Maier, a professor at the State University of New York in Binghamton. Mark was an assistant professor and coordinator of the program for leadership and organization studies at the School of Education and Human Development. Mark had gotten a grant to put on a symposium at SUNY-Binghamton on the Challenger disaster. It was entitled "Lessons from Challenger: A Symposium on Management, Organization Decision-

Making, and Social Responsibility." The symposium was to take place April 18, 1991. Also invited were Roger Boisjoly, Kathy Ferguson, a professor at the University of Hawaii and author of *The Feminist Case Against Bureaucracy*, and Paul Shrivastava, professor at Bucknell University and author of *Bhopal—Anatomy of a Crisis*.

Along with the symposium, Mark was producing an elaborate and detailed "instructional module" on Challenger, consisting of a set of three videotapes, a packet of articles, including my *Washington Post* and *Washington Monthly* articles, a written case study with a detailed event chronology, a copy of the Commission's report, a set of overhead transparency masters, copies of internal NASA and Thiokol documents, a facilitator's guide, a Viton rubber O-ring sample, and other teaching materials.

The module included a videotape of flight controllers in the mission control room at Houston watching their video consoles when Challenger blew up. NASA allowed Mark to use it in his production on condition that he never release it to public or commercial television. Mark's production remains in use today and has been shown to dozens of major corporations and is used in presentations on engineering ethics. Today Mark is a professor at Chapman University in Orange, California.

When Mark asked me to participate, I was reluctant to do so. By early 1991, I was tired of the Challenger disaster and never wanted to hear about it again. I had quit writing my book and was sick at heart at never having solved the deepest mystery of the Challenger tragedy—what role had the White House played in the flawed launch decision?

Mark persevered and talked me into becoming a part of his production. He wanted me to come to Binghamton ahead of time to shoot a videotape. Again, I reluctantly agreed, though I saw no point in stating in another public forum that even though I knew the White House had to have been involved in the Challenger launch decision, I had no proof. The prospects of traveling to Binghamton, New York, to say this once again seemed dismally depressing.

Then one day Phyllis told me that she had seen a news report on TV about Kitty Kelley's new book, *Nancy Reagan: The Unauthorized Biography*. Kelley reported that President Reagan and his wife Nancy regularly consulted astrologers for advice. The news story included a short but startling interview with an astrologer from Los Angeles named Ed Helin who had been mentioned in Kelley's book and who said he had advised President Reagan not to launch Challenger.

When Kelley's book was published, her description of the consultation of astrologers by the Reagans produced a sensation in the press. But the sensation was short-lived, viewed merely as a curiosity, and dismissed scornfully as of no real consequence by the sober minds of the mainstream political establishment and news media.

In reality, dependence upon astrological predictions was tightly interwoven with day-to-day White House operations, especially after the distress produced in the mind of Nancy Reagan by the March 30, 1981, attempt on her husband's life by would-be assassin John W. Hinckley Jr. The use of astrology for presidential scheduling had already been elaborated upon by Donald Regan in his memoirs, *For the Record*, published a couple of years earlier. Regan wrote of the role of astrology in the White House daily schedule:

> Virtually every major move and decision the Reagans made during my time as White House Chief of Staff was cleared in advance with a woman in San Francisco who drew up horoscopes to make certain that the planets were in a favorable alignment for the enterprise.

The "woman in San Francisco" was Joan Quigley, who had replaced Jean Dixon as the Reagans' personal consultant. Regan also wrote that he kept a color-coded calendar prominently on his desk to note which days were "good," "bad," or "iffy," according to Quigley's predictions.

Astrology was more than a curiosity in the southern California milieu where the Reagans spent their careers as Hollywood personalities. Los Angeles had long been home to numerous schools of metaphysical teaching, some with ties to Eastern spiritual systems such as Vedanta. Within the Vedantic lore of India, astrology played a predominant and respected role, helping to determine, for example, the compatibility of prospective brides and grooms. American astrologers, with their philosophies rooted in concepts of the synchronicity between the actions of man and the larger planetary and stellar universe, moved easily in the Hollywood environment. Some read the horoscopes of famous movie stars and some, such as Dixon and Carroll Righter, were stars in their own right. Righter and his associate Ed Helin, who had known the Reagans since the late '40s, regularly provided astrological advice to them after they took up residence in the White House in 1981.

According to a statement by Helin cited in *Another Look at Some Presidents* by John Richard Stephens, available at www.ferncanyonpress.com, "As president, he was primarily concerned with the timing of events and how his popularity would be affected by his actions. He called me to determine the best timing for invading Grenada, for bombing Libya, for launching the Challenger, and things like that." Helin was reportedly paid for his services by the Republican National Committee.

I traced Ed Helin to the Carroll Righter Institute in Los Angeles and within a couple of days had him on the phone. I explained to Helin who I was, and he was friendly and talkative. He said that he had advised the White House on astrological matters since the 1940s. He said he had also advised NASA on the astrological acceptability of various launch times since it was created in 1958, including the Apollo lunar program.

"Did you talk to the president before the Challenger launch?" I asked.

"Yes," Helin said.

"Did you talk to him or his aides?"

"Oh, I talked directly to the president," he said. "He had called me."

Helin now explained that he had advised President Reagan that, astrologically speaking, January 28 was not a good day to launch Challenger. He said that the horoscope viewed the weather as a problem.

I was stunned to hear this. Not only were the experts at NASA and its contractors saying not to launch because of the weather, but so was the president's astrologer. Helin now digressed to talk about how he told the president that he saw incompatibilities in horoscopes between him and Chief of Staff Donald Regan. This was interesting, but I wanted to return to Challenger. I asked, "Did the president know that NASA had cold weather concerns?"

"Yes, he did."

"Well, then, who decided to launch?"

"The president."

I wanted to be sure I heard him correctly. "Sir," I said slowly. "You are telling me that the president personally made the decision to launch Challenger in spite of what he knew were NASA's concerns with cold weather. Is that right?"

"Yes," Helin said. "That's correct." Then, after a pause, he continued. "You know," he said, "the reason I think he did that was pressure from the media. The television networks were down there in Florida for the Teacher-in-Space. And they told him that they were spending a million dollars a day keeping their crews and equipment down there."

"Did the networks pressure him directly?"

"Oh yes, they were calling him and pressuring him to launch."

After a long pause I asked, "Sir, do you have any problem with my reporting this conversation publicly or attributing these statements to you?"

"No, no problem at all," Helin replied. I thanked him, and after he gave me a few more details, we hung up.

Any responsible narration of the Reagan presidency must take the use of astrologers by President and Mrs. Reagan as seriously as any other major factor in setting the stage for those eight years. It is part of the history of the times, and if that was their predilection and what gave them confidence to face life, it should be respected. It appears, however, that the ill-fated launch of Challenger may be the only known instance where President Reagan disregarded the astrological advice he sought. This gives compelling testimony to the pressures he must have been feeling to get Challenger into orbit the morning of January 28, 1986.

Helin, while engaged in what to many is an oddball profession, repeated his story about advising against the Challenger launch during TV interviews, and must be taken as a reliable source. As such, his account is a crucial piece of evidence that not only links the White House to the flawed launch decision, but also makes the connection with President Reagan himself. And what about a link with the State of the Union address? Helin indicated that President Reagan gave the launch order after pressure from the TV networks because of the money they were spending. But in his phone conversations, the president may not have told Helin about the State of the Union connection.

My conversation with Ed Helin took place over fifteen years ago, and I have not reported it publicly until now. When I traveled to Binghamton for the video recording session with Dr. Mark Maier, I said only that I had talked to someone who was involved in the Challenger launch and that this person told me President Reagan personally was involved in the launch decision, knowing of NASA's cold weather concerns.

I felt at last that the mystery of the Challenger launch had been largely solved. I knew that the complete story of what happened at the White House during those days could likely fill a book, though mercifully it was a book no one would ever be able to write. For there are things in history that the waters of time simply wash over. We learn what we need to learn, no more and no less. Beyond that point, individuals must be left alone with their privacy, their anguish, and their ultimate redemption. So it has been with the Challenger story.

I had my own pain to contend with. I felt sadness to hear Ed Helin's account. I was sad for my country, sad for the astronauts and their families, and sad for Ronald Reagan. I recalled Larry Speakes' image of him holding his face in his hand, saying "Oh no." Then my mind wandered back, and I recalled conversations with Roger Boisjoly about how hard it was for him to get a hearing within his company on the dangers of the O-rings and how he was pressured to suppress information on the effect of cold temperatures so as not to interfere with military flights. I thought of my weekends at Bob Bowman's institute on the Chesapeake Bay typing the report I gave the Justice Department, and I recalled the press conference at the National Press Club where the news media tried to shout us down. Then I recalled the days I spent in Senator Hollings' office and the certainty we shared that the White House must have had a role. I remembered my meetings with Phil Boffey at the *Times* bureau and the fear I felt for my family's livelihood, and I thought of my desperation to maintain my dignity as I stood on the witness stand that day under the barrage of William Rogers' questioning.

As the memories of the last five years of my life came welling up inside, I lowered my head to my folded arms and wept bitter tears. It had been my fate to live this story, and someday it would be my fate to tell it. Then my children and others of their generation would read my book and look deeply into the soul of our country and see both its littleness and its heroism.

Not yet, though. It was not yet time. I put my account of the Ed Helin interview away with the rest of my Challenger papers in the boxes in the attic of our little country house in King George, Virginia. There they would remain for many years.

POSTSCRIPT

THE PRESIDENTIAL COMMISSION had both strengths and weaknesses, though its political objective was damage control, to be accomplished by minimizing adverse fallout for the Reagan Administration, the White House, and President Reagan himself. Thus, while much of the story of the O-ring flaws reached the public, including the attempt by the Thiokol engineers the night before the launch to delay the flight, the overwhelming impression was that the loss of Challenger was, to use one of NASA's favorite words, an "anomaly."

My hope is that this book has dispelled that impression. The deeper causes of the Challenger disaster were the takeover of the manned space program by those who wanted to militarize NASA, underfunding of government activities, the use of the space shuttle program as a political prop, and top-down management by decree.

Placed in a larger context of what has been going on in the U.S. during the 1980s and since then, the Challenger disaster has much to teach. The hallmarks of this period were the trillion-dollar defense build-up, tax cuts for the upper income brackets, enormous federal budget deficits, the erosion of our public and private infrastructure, and a new era of warfare. The resurgent military industrial complex brought the doctrine of proxy wars fought in such places as Angola, Nicaragua, and Afghanistan. The brief era of peace between the end of the Vietnam War in 1975 and the revolution in Iran four years later was over, and the state of virtually permanent warfare that has become a dominant feature of national life today had been foreshadowed. And, in the midst of the 1980s, as though to symbolize what was going wrong, Challenger blew up and seven astronauts died.

In the early shuttle era, lasting from April 1981 to January 28, 1986, NASA tried, with twenty-five shuttle launches, to carry on its tradition of manned space exploration, but with too little money, fatally-flawed equipment, and a compromised mission. Since then, the manned program has struggled along, with another disaster taking place in 2003 when the shuttle Columbia burned up on atmospheric reentry, and with the partial development of an International Space Station that is still a long way from being finished. As of this writing, there are signs that the government wishes to prepare new plans for weapons in space reminiscent of the Strategic Defense Initiative.

To me, the Challenger disaster is an indicator of trends in modern U.S. history that can lead to a much larger social and political catastrophe. It marked a time when we took a wrong turn in our public life. The errors made then are being repeated, so that the lessons we failed to learn on and after January 28, 1986, we must now learn today. I am confident that in the long run we can and will succeed in doing this. The key is a culture based on respect for human life and peaceful cooperation among nations and peoples. The early manned space program contributed to this ideal by showing that the Earth and those living on it are united in their hopes and dreams. We must now reclaim that vision.

COLLEGE PARK, MARYLAND, AND WASHINGTON, D.C.
OCTOBER 22, 2006

NASA's Shuttle Matrix Organization on January 28, 1986

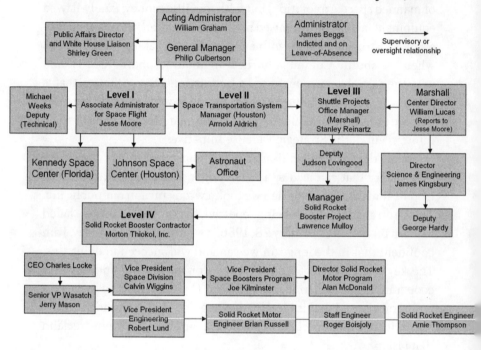

ACKNOWLEDGEMENTS

THE LIST OF people to whom I owe a debt of gratitude in writing this book is long. Let me first go back to 1986 and the immediate aftermath of the Challenger disaster. While Paul Herr, the lead solid rocket motor engineer at NASA headquarters, took no part in my decision to leak the O-ring documents, he freely gave his honest engineering judgments about Challenger, so made it possible for me to have more confidence in my testimony before the Presidential Commission and my writings on the tragedy. I thank Phil Boffey and Bill Kovach at the *New York Times* for listening to a lonely analyst who carried in his briefcase a collection of explosive papers and for representing them fairly and accurately in the pages of their newspaper. Later, Kathy Sawyer and David Ignatius at the *Washington Post* kindly lent their support and skills to getting my article into print on "Why I Blew the Whistle on NASA's O-ring Woes." Then it was Charles Peters, publisher of the *Washington Monthly*, and Dr. Robert Bowman, head of the Institute for Space and Security Studies, who supported me in my criticisms of the Commission. Thanks to the many writers and journalists who provided me information, including Christine Dolan, Joseph Trento, and Malcolm McConnell, and thanks to Congressman Ed Markey for his consideration. I would also like to acknowledge the efforts of the large number of scholars, writers, and interested citizens who, over the years, have studied the Challenger disaster and contributed to the important body of literature on the tragedy. Among these is Diane Vaughan, author of an award-winning book on the subject.

There were two members of the academic community who were strong allies. One was Dr. Patrick O'Hara of the John Jay School of Criminal Justice at the City University of New York, who promoted my nomination by the New York City chapter of the American Society for Public Administration for the Cavallo Foundation Award for Moral Courage in Business and Government. The other was Dr. Mark Maier, now of Chapman University, who invited me to work with him on his industrial training seminar on the Challenger disaster. Mark has remained a friend over the years and helped immensely by acting as a technical adviser for the book. Of course any errors in the book are entirely my own responsibility and should not be attributed to Dr. Maier or any other reviewer.

I finally made the decision to write the final version of the book in the summer of 2005, using notes and drafts that had languished for years. Once the writing began, it went quickly. My ex-wife Phyllis, with whom I shared the Challenger drama and who figures as a major actor in the story, was supportive throughout, as were my children Nat, Tim, Adele, Fred, and Melissa, my parents, Richard E. and Marjorie Cook, and my sisters and their husbands—Christine and Bob Dunbar, and Sandy and Don Hutton. I am grateful to my friend Steve Zarlenga, director of the American Monetary Institute, for his encouragement and assistance, to my talented writing coach, Linda Grover, to my agent, Al Zuckerman of Writer's House, to the staff of Thunder's Mouth Press and Avalon Publishing, and to my original publisher John Oakes.

I am also grateful to my friend Sharon Thomas for her support along the way and to Deborah Robin Croft for believing in me as the project came to fruition. Thanks too to Randi Blank, Mathew and Margaux O'Malley, Carol Beach, and Dr. Lewis Coleman. Finally, I wish to acknowledge the friendship of my many colleagues at the U.S. Treasury Department, where I worked for over twenty years after leaving NASA. Thanks also to many other supportive friends in the Washington, D.C., area and elsewhere and to my teachers and mentors over the years.

GLOSSARY

Abort—One of several modes by which a shuttle flight can be prematurely terminated. An example is RTLS—return to launch site—whereby the shuttle reverses direction over the Atlantic Ocean and attempts to land at the Kennedy Space Center. RTLS cannot be activated until the solid rocket boosters have completed their two-minute burn and are jettisoned.

Actuation Time—The length of time, measured in microseconds, that it took the O-rings to shift position in order to fill the gaps in the solid rocket booster joint seals. Stiffening of the O-rings from cold temperature increased the actuation time, making a burnthrough more likely.

Administrator—The top NASA official; head of the agency, appointed by the president.

Anomaly—An occurrence out-of-the-ordinary on a space vehicle component.

Antiballistic Missile Treaty—ABM Treaty, signed in 1972 to limit development of weapons intended to shoot down enemy ballistic missiles; viewed as obstacle to the Strategic Defense Initiative; unilaterally abrogated by the U.S. in 2002.

Ariane—The French unmanned rocket launched from Guyana in South America and viewed as a competitor with the space shuttle for the commercial and international launch businesses.

Associate Administrator for Space Flight—A career NASA official who headed the space flight program and gave all shuttle launch and landing orders.

Atlantis, Columbia, Challenger, Discovery—The four shuttle orbiters as of January 1986.

Attrition—Rate at which solid rocket booster segments designed for reusability were prematurely lost to future use through mishaps of various kinds.

Bench Tests—Engineering tests conducted in a laboratory. It was bench tests conducted by Thiokol in early 1985 that quantified the degree to which the O-rings lost resiliency and so could fail to seal under lowered temperatures.

Burnthrough—Potentially catastrophic leakage of burning fuel through the side of a rocket.

Capture Feature—Solid rocket booster joint redesign in the planning stages at the time of the Challenger disaster; part of the post-disaster joint reengineering instituted to allow the shuttle to fly again.

Centaur—A cryogenic upper stage rocket utilizing liquid oxygen and hydrogen; adapted from the unmanned Titan- or Atlas-Centaur to be used with the shuttle for interplanetary probes or defense satellites; abandoned after the Challenger disaster.

Centaur Integrated Support Structure—CISS, a cradle-like device that would secure the Centaur upper stage in the orbiter payload bay.

Charring, Erosion, and Blow-By—Varying degrees of damage to the O-Rings in the joints of the space shuttle solid rocket boosters.

Chief Engineer—NASA official with oversight for all technical programs; prior to the Challenger disaster, estimated the chance of a catastrophic shuttle failure at 1 in 100,000 launches.

Codes—NASA symbols for organizational units; Code A = Office of the Administrator; Code B = Comptroller; Code M = Office of Space Flight; Code E = Office of Space Science.

Committee on the Present Danger—Non-governmental group formed to lobby the federal government to increase military expenditures.

Criticality—Designation of risk level of a shuttle component. "Crit-1" indicates that failure could lead to "loss of shuttle, mission, and crew." "1R" indicates that a critical component has a back-up that can be activated in an emergency. "R" stands for redundancy.

Cryogenics—Gases supercooled to their liquid state, including the hydrogen and oxygen used as fuel in the space shuttle main engines and the Centaur upper stage.

Design and Data Analysis Task Force—NASA group set up to investigate the Challenger disaster after the interim review mishap board was abolished by the Presidential Commission.

Edwards Air Force Base—Military facility in California whose expansive desert lakebeds were used as the shuttle's west coast landing site.

Enterprise—Full-scale shuttle model used for manned gliding flights during the early test stages; named after the spacecraft of "Star Trek" TV fame.

Escape Platform—Deck on the launch tower across which the astronauts would run if a pre-launch abort were declared and they had to escape to a blast-proof bunker by means of a basket-slide wire system.

Expendable Launch Vehicle (ELV)—Rocket system that cannot be reused, such as the Atlas-Centaur, Titan-Centaur, Delta, etc.

External Tank (ET)—The large cigar-shaped container that was attached to the underside of the orbiter and held the liquid oxygen and hydrogen that fueled the main engines. The solid rocket boosters were connected to the external tank by metal struts.

Extravehicular Activity (EVA)—A spacewalk done by an astronaut outside the shuttle cabin.

Failure Modes Effects Analysis (FMEA)—NASA system that designated the level of criticality of shuttle components but without quantifying the risk of failure for these components.

Filament Wound Case (FWC)—Lightweight version of the solid rocket booster made from epoxy-resin composites to be used for shuttle launches from Vandenberg; abandoned after the Challenger disaster and never fired on a shuttle mission.

Flight Readiness Review (FRR)—A series of meetings conducted at the NASA centers for each shuttle flight where readiness was assessed and action items assigned to prepare for a shuttle launch.

Fly As Is—NASA term meaning that the shuttle would fly with a substandard or less-than-fully-safe component until it could be redesigned and replaced.

Galileo and Ulysses—Unmanned planetary spacecraft to be launched from the space shuttle by the Centaur upper stage during missions scheduled for 1986.

General Dynamics—Contractor responsible for building the Centaur upper stage.

Geosynchronous Orbit—An orbit usually at 22,500 miles above earth, where the rotation of a satellite is at the same speed as that of the Earth, causing the satellite to remain stationary over a given point on the Earth's surface.

Inertial Upper Stage (IUS)—Solid-fuel upper stage rocket carried in the orbiter's payload bay.

Interim Review Mishap Board—Group set up within NASA immediately after the Challenger disaster to investigate the incident; consisted mainly of NASA officials who participated in the launch decision; terminated by the Presidential Commission after declaration that the launch decision "may have been flawed."

Johnson Space Center (JSC)—NASA facility in Houston, Texas, from which shuttle missions were controlled once the orbiter reached orbital insertion; organizational home of the astronaut corps.

Joints—Connections between the segments of the solid rocket boosters, which were supposed to be sealed by O-rings and heat-resistant putty.

Kennedy Space Center (KSC)—NASA facility at Cape Canaveral in Florida from which the shuttle was launched.

Launch Commit Criteria (LCC)—Environmental or technical conditions that had to be met to permit a shuttle launch to take place.

Launch Tower—The service structure at the shuttle launch pad, which supported fueling, astronaut access, and mechanical supplies and functions.

Level I—Associate administrator for space flight; responsible for overseeing the entire shuttle system and approving each launch.

Level II—Director of the National Space Transportation System at Houston; responsible for integrating all shuttle components.

Level III—Program head for each shuttle component, such as the solid rocket boosters at the Marshall Space Flight Center.

Level IV—The contractor in charge of shuttle components, such as Morton Thiokol for the solid rocket boosters, Martin Marietta for the external tank, Rockwell for the orbiter, and General Dynamics for the Centaur.

Lewis Research Center (LRC)—NASA facility in Cleveland, Ohio, which oversaw the development of the Centaur upper stage.

Manifest Bingo—Humorous designation of a chart created at the Kennedy Space Center to depict the complexities of the 1986 shuttle flight processing schedule.

Marshall Space Flight Center (MSFC)—NASA facility in Huntsville, Alabama, which oversaw shuttle propulsion systems, including the solid rocket boosters, main engines, and external tank.

Michoud—Location in New Orleans where the external tanks were built.

Mission Management Team (MMT)—The group of top NASA managers and engineers who worked together at the Kennedy Space Center to oversee shuttle launches.

Mission Model—Number of shuttle flights planned for a given calendar year.

Mobile Launch Platform (MLP)—The large tractor-like vehicle that transported the shuttle from the Vehicle Assembly Building to the launch pad and from which the shuttle was fired.

Morton-Thiokol Corp.—The company in Utah that manufactured the solid rocket boosters.

NASA One—Jet used to fly executives, VIPs, and other personnel back-and-forth from Washington, D.C. headquarters, to other NASA facilities.

National Aeronautics and Space Act of 1958—NASA's enabling legislation, which declared that the space program "should be devoted to peaceful purposes for the benefit of mankind."

Office of Communications—Unit within the White House responsible for writing speeches for the president, including the 1986 State of the Union speech.

Office of Management and Budget (OMB)—Unit within the Executive Office of the President responsible for overseeing development and implementation of the federal budget.

Office of Science and Technology Policy (OSTP)—Unit within the Executive Office of the President responsible for overseeing NASA and other federal science-related programs; headed by the president's science adviser; after 1983, in charge of promoting the Strategic Defense Initiative to Congress and the scientific community.

Operational—Word used to describe the space shuttle system upon completion of the first four manned "experimental" flights.

Orbiter—The spacecraft for the space shuttle that carried the astronauts and payloads.

O-rings—Circular rubber seals used to seal the joints between solid rocket booster segments. The solid rocket booster joint seals had two O-rings. The one closest to the burning propellant was the primary O-ring. The secondary O-ring was a redundant feature but was susceptible to failure due to joint rotation.

Ovality—Abnormal misshaping of cryogenic fuel lines. The "ovality rule" dictated that NASA attempt to launch the shuttle only on two consecutive days, with the next day taken off to check the lines for ovality, cracks, etc.

Payload Assist Module (PAM)—Solid-fuel upper stage rocket carried in the orbiter's payload bay.

Payload Bay—The compartment in the body of the orbiter, which could be exposed to space by the opening of large double doors and which held shuttle payloads and scientific instruments.

"Pitch"—A NASA briefing designed to convince others to go along with a preferred course of action.

Presidential Commission on the Space Shuttle Challenger Accident—Also known as the Rogers Commission, the group chartered by President Reagan to investigate and report on the disaster.

Propulsion Division—Unit within the Office of Spaceflight at NASA headquarters that was responsible for overseeing all space shuttle rocketry.

Qualification—Process by which a piece of hardware is demonstrated to be ready for use; usually done by testing and analysis. At NASA, hardware that had been qualified was considered flightworthy.

Radioisotope Thermoelectric Generator (RTG)—Plutonium-powered device for long-term electricity-generation in space; to be used on the Galileo and Ulysses spacecraft and launched during the shuttle-Centaur missions.

Redlines—Launch conditions that, if not met, could cause a shuttle launch to be postponed or cancelled.

Redundancy—Engineering feature whereby a component in a system is equipped with a back-up that will operate in case the original fails. In the solid rocket booster joint system, redundancy had been lost due to joint rotation at ignition. When this was discovered, the redundancy requirement was waived by NASA to permit the shuttle to continue to fly.

Resiliency—Ability of the rubber O-rings to resume their rounded shape after being placed under pressure. Loss of resiliency in cold temperatures degraded their ability to fill the gaps in the solid rocket booster joint seals during the microseconds after ignition.

Resources Analysis Division—Unit within the NASA comptroller's office where the author was employed at the time of the Challenger disaster.

Reusability—Indicating that the space shuttle orbiter and solid rocket boosters were the first U.S. rocketry elements designed to be used over again.

Rotation—Phenomenon observed whereby the solid rocket booster joints would expand during rocket ignition, creating a greater possibility of burnthroughs.

Solid Rocket Boosters (SRBs)—The two solid-fuel rockets attached to the external tank, which burned for approximately two minutes and supplemented the main engines in allowing the shuttle orbiter to attain orbital insertion.

Space Transportation System (STS)—The entire NASA complex of space shuttle vehicles, payloads, personnel, contractors, and facilities.

Strategic Defense Initiative (SDI)—Also called "Star Wars," the program announced by President Reagan in 1983 to place weapons in space to counter potential enemy ballistic missile attacks; believed by many to have the capability of deploying offensive weapons as well. The space shuttle was to be the primary testing platform for space weapons technology.

Structural Test Article (STA)—Full-scale model of a hardware unit used for testing. The filament wound case structural test article burst in a test below the designated required margin of safety.

Teacher-in-Space Program—An attempt by NASA to place a nongovernment person on-board a space shuttle mission for educational purposes. The Teacher-in-Space Christa McAuliffe died in the Challenger disaster, after which the program was cancelled.

Thermal Protection System (TPS)—Heat-resistant tiles that coated the surface of the orbiter. A burnthrough of the TPS resulted in the destruction of shuttle Columbia during atmospheric reentry in February 2003.

Tracking Data and Relay Satellites (TDRS)—Space-based communications system that would allow NASA to maintain radio contact between mission control in Houston and the shuttle orbiter and dispense with its expensive network of ground stations; consisted of a network of satellites in geosynchronous orbit.

Turnaround Time—The length of time it took for the shuttle orbiters to be prepared for their next mission after completion of a previous one.

Upper Stage—A rocket carried in the orbiter's payload bay that, when deployed, provided further thrust to transport satellites or scientific payloads into higher orbit or interplanetary space.

Vandenberg Air Force Base—Located in California, Vandenberg was home to the Defense Department's never-used shuttle launch site, which was abandoned as unsafe after the Challenger disaster.

Vehicle Assembly Building (VAB)—Multi-story structure at the Kennedy Space Center where the shuttle orbiter, external tank, solid rocket boosters, and payloads were mated and prepared for launch. The shuttle was then transported to the launch pad by a mobile launch platform.

Viton—Type of synthetic rubber from which the O-rings were manufactured.

Wind Shear—Sudden shifts in wind direction. The wind shear during Challenger's lift-off was the most severe of any shuttle launch and contributed to the solid rocket booster burnthrough.

X-Ray Laser—Space-based nuclear-weapon under development by the Lawrence Livermore Laboratory and contemplated for use by the Strategic Defense Initiative.

NOTES

U.S. government documents cited throughout this book are within the public domain as part of official records and are available under the Freedom of Information Act or other authorities from NASA, the National Archives and Records Administration, or the Library of Congress. In no case have officially classified documents been quoted or referenced.

CHAPTERS 1-6

Sources for these chapters consist of the author's notes, recollections, and memoranda, in addition to internal NASA documents cited in a history of the shuttle-Centaur program provided by the author to the NASA Office of Inspector General in 1986 and available under the Freedom of Information Act.

CHAPTER 3

p. 31. "The shuttle's solid rocket boosters were a large, dangerous experiment. A 1979 NASA publication, *The Space Shuttle at Work*, gave the following description."
Howard Allaway, *The Space Shuttle at Work*, NASA, 1979, p.72.

p. 43. "The next STA is stronger than the first, but based on analysis and coupon testing, only has a probable factor of safety of 1.39."
A coupon is a patch of material cut out for testing.

p. 43. "Tightening of the forward solid rocket booster/external tank attach point tolerance is in progress and will reduce FWC load at the failure point by about two percent, leading to a revised factor of safety of 1.42."
This data meant that, at best, FWC safety would still be marginal.

p. 44. "This removal is complete, but was done with a significant labor cost which should show up in the December cost reports."
Thus NASA would pay for the contractor's mistakes.

CHAPTER 4

p. 51. "Once Galileo was released from the Atlantis, the spacecraft would cruise through the asteroid belt beyond Mars before it settled into orbit around Jupiter. There it would measure and photograph the giant planet for almost eight years."

Delayed by the Challenger disaster and the cancellation of Centaur, Galileo was finally launched on October 18, 1989, on a solid-fuel inertial upper stage. Because the IUS did not have the performance capability of the Centaur, Galileo was deployed around the sun. Then, whipping back into space, it conducted a fly-by of Venus, skirted the Earth, and headed toward Jupiter.

p. 51. "The purpose of Ulysses was to investigate the structure of the sun's magnetic field and the pathways of the solar wind. It was to be inserted into its unusual solar polar orbit by using Jupiter's gravity as a giant slingshot that would allow it to break the plane of the solar system's planetary ecliptic and circle the sun above and beneath its poles."

Ulysses was launched by the shuttle on October 6, 1990. It used two upper stages to escape the planetary ecliptic, an IUS and a payload assist module, PAM-S.

p. 52. "It meant that design changes to the IUS or to the planetary spacecraft, or even variations in launch schedules or mechanics, could push the payload weight out of range."

Launch schedule variations can lead to differing relative planetary positions as the planets swing around the sun in their orbits. This can lead to variations in the thrust needed to reach a given planet. An example of how launch mechanics can affect lift capacities is variations in the time interval between space shuttle main engine firings.

p. 55. "Centaur has demonstrated reliability of ninety-seven percent while IUS has never flown."

Of course this was the unmanned Centaur, not the version to be adapted for the Shuttle.

p. 56. "Centaur has more mission flexibility, including multiple burn/restart and low-thrust capability."

This refers to the fact that with a liquid-fuel engine you can regulate the flow of fuel to the burn chamber, whereas a solid-fuel rocket is like a Roman candle—once ignited, it burns until the fuel is used up.

CHAPTER 6

p. 81. "From 1981 to 1985, there had been five main engine test failures on the ground at Marshall's Bay St. Louis, Mississippi, test facility. All failures were at 109 percent or greater throttle settings, and all would have been catastrophic in flight. Here was another potential 'fly as is' situation, where NASA may have been forced to add to the already uncomfortable risk of main engine failure."

As cited in the report on the Challenger disaster of the House Science and Technology Committee, the five test failures were engine 0204 in September 1981; engine 2013 in April 1982; engine 2208 in August 1982; engine 0108 in February 1984; and engine 2308 in March 1985.

CHAPTER 7

p. 91. "The similarities between von Braun's early conception and NASA's eventual space shuttle were striking."
Robert M. Powers, *The World's First Spaceship Shuttle*, Stackpole Books, 1979, p.44.

p. 92. "Even before the 1969 Apollo 11 moon landing, President Nixon had appointed a Space Task Group to study the future of U.S. manned spaceflight."
Jerry Grey, *Enterprise*, William Morrow and Company, New York, 1979, p.89. The author is indebted to Grey's book and to Richard Lewis's *The Voyages of Columbia: The First True Spaceship*, for much of the detail about shuttle development in this chapter.

p. 92. "In 1988, two years after the Challenger disaster, former NASA administrator and Space Task Group member Thomas Paine would say, 'There's no question that Mars is the great destination of humanity for the 21st century.' "
ABC News, "Beyond the Shuttle," September 18, 1988.

p. 93. "This would be 'a low unit-mission-cost transportation system that would make Earth-moon space easily and economically accessible to man for his use for exploration, applications, science, and technology research.' "
Allaway, op.cit., p.31. Both before and after the Challenger disaster, critics derided NASA for trying to operate experimental spacecraft on a commercial airline model. The report of the Space Task Group showed that the model was part of shuttle planning from the beginning.

p. 94. " 'Mueller knew that would mean changing Max Faget's beloved straight-wing design into a delta wing, but he had no choice. He agreed.' "
Grey, op.cit., p.68.

p. 95. "If the Air Force was to be forced by political and financial pressure to utilize the shuttle, it wanted to launch it into polar orbit from Vandenberg Air Force Base on the California coast."
John M. Logsdon, "The Space Shuttle Program: A Policy Failure?", *Science*, May 30, 1986, p.1101.

p. 95. "Extra demands would also be placed on the propulsion systems."
Ibid, p.1101.

p. 95. "The changes to support military missions also added twenty percent to the cost of shuttle development and operations."
Grey, op.cit., p.67.

p. 96. Dr. James Fletcher's letter to Defense Secretary Packard
Logsdon, op.cit., p.1104.

p. 96. ". . . . OMB agreed to fund $5.5 billion—with a cost per launch of only $6 million."
Ibid, p.1102.

p. 97. "As space scientist, author, and publicist Jerry Grey is reported to have said, 'First you have to get the horse, then you decide where to ride him.' "
Gregg Easterbrook, "The Spruce Goose of Outer Space," *Washington Monthly*, November 1980, p.34.

p. 97. "This would have meant a smaller orbiter with a 14 x 45 foot payload bay, an option Administrator Fletcher seemed willing to accept."
Logsdon, op.cit., p.1103.

p. 97. "The Air Force, for instance, would have to retain the unmanned Titan 2 to launch its largest reconnaissance satellites."
Ibid, p.1103.

p. 97. "Later, Ehrlichman recalled that 'a strong influence was what the military could do with the larger bay in terms of the uses of satellites,' and 'the capability of capturing satellites or recovering them.'"
Ibid, p.1104.

p. 99. "The engine's high-pressure pumps would be capable of emptying an Olympic-size swimming pool in twenty-five seconds."
Grey, op.cit., p.63.

p. 100. "NASA wrote in a 1979 publication, 'in the face of tight budgets, the decision seemed obvious.'"
Allaway, op.cit., p.33.

p. 103. "By September 1975, NASA had completed only 13 of the 964 engine tests required for flight certification."
Ibid, p.129.

p. 103. "From March 24, 1977, to November 4, 1979, there were fourteen engine test failures. The engines had problems with faulty seals, uneven bearing loads, cracked turbine blades, cracked fuel injector posts, broken heat exchangers, valve failures, and hydrogen line ruptures. In several cases, engines exploded. Eight failures resulted in fires on the test stand. The first time three engines were fired together, they all blew up. NASA had to double the number of test engines it ordered from Rocketdyne."
Richard Lewis, *The Voyages of Columbia: The First True Spaceship*, Columbia University Press, New York, 1984, p.142.

p. 105. "It was found that these engines also had the smaller welding wire. They had to be removed from Columbia's tail section, shipped back to Rocketdyne in California, and repaired."
Ibid, p.96.

p. 107. "The 100,000 square-foot CSOC facility would be encased in steel so the Soviet Union could not intercept its computer signals."
David Sanger, "Control Center for Space Shuttle is Dropped from Pentagon Budget," *New York Times*, January 26, 1987.

p. 107. "The peacetime nature of our space assets was reinforced by the decision to compel the Air Force to design all its new satellites for launch on the space shuttle. . . . "
Dr. Robert Bowman, *Star Wars: Defense or Death Star?*, Institute for Space and Security Studies, 1984, p.148.

CHAPTER 8

p. 109. "And when a man left the professional or technical ranks to 'put on a management hat,' funny things could and did happen."
This refers to the incident the night before the Challenger disaster when the ranking Thiokol executive directed the engineering manager to "put on your management hat" in voting to overturn the company's engineers who recommended against the launch.

p. 110. "Remarkably, the actual number was twenty-three and would have been twenty-four had mission 61-C, the flight preceding Challenger, been launched on time instead of slipping for a month."
Dr. Robert Bowman, "How a Tight Budget Overloaded Shuttle," *Baltimore Sun*, May 7, 1986.

p. 111. "According to CBS News reporter Robert Schakne, Beggs' last instruction to his managers at NASA before he left was that the goal of twenty-four flights per year must be achieved."
As told by Schakne to the author.

p. 112. "Fuqua told the *Washington Post* that he knew the shuttle really wasn't operational. 'Every time Beggs said that to me,' he said, 'I chuckled.'"
Kathy Sawyer, "Oversight Was Blurred," *Washington Post*, April 17, 1986.

p. 112. "'. . . create a bounty of new jobs, technologies, and medical breakthroughs surpassing anything we have ever dreamed and imagined . . . if the doubting Thomases would just stand aside and get out of our way.'"
Jim Heaphy, "Challenger's Trail of Blame," *In These Times*, June 25–July 8, 1986, p.3.

p. 113. "From 1980 to 1985, employment at headquarters was cut more than ten percent, and the number of NASA scientists and engineers dropped twenty percent."
R. Jeffrey Smith, "Experts Ponder the Effects of Pressures on Shuttle Blowup, *Science*, March 12, 1986, p.1496.

p. 114. "NASA also tried to pattern shuttle payload bookings after the management of charter airline flights and used the American Airlines organization chart as a model in creating its headquarters customer service operation."
Grey, op.cit., p.160.

p. 117. "Dr. Hans Mark, who was a former secretary of the Air Force and NASA's deputy administrator under Beggs from 1981 to 1984, said after the Challenger disaster that 'NASA is a first-class engineering development organization, but it was never

intended to be the agency for the long-term operation of a Space Transportation System.'"
Dr. Hans Mark, "The Future of NASA," *International Security*, Spring 1987, p.177.

p. 118. "At times, more than $750 million in work was being done without price agreements, and one audit report stated, 'The budget and planning cost estimates prepared by Rockwell International Corporation are often inaccurate and unreliable.'"
Stuart Diamond, "NASA Cut or Delayed Safety Spending," *New York Times*, April 24, 1986. The IG reports were also observed first-hand by the author at NASA.

p. 120. "The senator wanted to hear about a report by three NASA consultants who recommended that President Carter be informed of 'narrower-than-Apollo' safety margins, because 'the shuttle bears the burden of being a significant part of the image of U.S. technical capability.' "
These and other Proxmire quotes from Kathy Sawyer, op.cit.

p. 121. "If the shuttle blew up on the pad, it would have the force of 3.15 kilotons, or 630,000 pounds of TNT."
Lewis, op.cit., p.122.

p. 121. "'We feel one of the important safety considerations is the effect of the schedule driving technical people to make 'fixes' rather than engineer a solution to the problem.'"
Smith, op.cit., p.1497.

p. 122. "There were at least seventy-eight instances of anomalous behavior of the orbiters' communications and tracking equipment, including an unexplained three-channel shutdown on STS-3 that was 'the worst communications failure in the history of U.S. manned spaceflight.'"
Lewis, op.cit., p.173.

CHAPTER 9

p. 129. "In an article in *Foreign Policy*, Colin S. Gray and Keith Payne wrote that with the proper strategy, U.S. losses would be 'maybe as few as twenty million deaths.' "
Colin S. Gray and Keith Payne, *Foreign Policy*, Summer 1980.

p. 129. "'He was almost technically ignorant. Not quite, but almost. He grasps a few of the broader concepts, but when you start talking in any kind of detail about the broader aspects of the program, his eyes glaze over.'"
Joseph J. Trento and Susan B. Trento, *Los Angeles Times Magazine*, January 18, 1987.

p. 130. "'Whatever else the shuttle does and whatever other purposes it will have, the priority, the emphasis, and the driving momentum now has to be those satellite systems which are important to national security.'"
From internal NASA documents.

p. 130. "As early as 1982, the General Accounting Office reported that at least one-fourth of NASA's budget was devoted to military projects."

"The Militarization of NASA," *St. Louis Post-Dispatch*, December 16, 1986.

p. 130. Quotations from the September 1982 Air Force Association National Convention are from *Air Force Magazine*, November 1982, p.8ff.

p. 132. "Keyworth viewed Teller as his 'intellectual father.' In fact, in an interview with *Barron's*, he referred to Teller as 'my dad. He is sort of a second father.'"
Barrons's, December 6, 1982.

p. 132. "He also favored greater involvement of the private sector in space ventures, a position that was supported by such conservative groups as the Heritage Foundation, which criticized NASA for trying to be the 'sole arbiter of space.'"
National Journal, March 22, 1986, p.692.

p. 135. "On May 6, 1981, Dr. Hans Mark, NASA's newly-appointed deputy administrator, told the students and faculty of the Naval War College, 'One could create a long list of things in which the United State enjoys a technological lead that could be exploited to enhance its position in the world.' "
Dr. Hans Mark, "Technology and the Strategic Balance," *Technology in Society*, Vol. 4, pp.15–32.

p. 136. "Others went well beyond Mark in envisioning weapons in space. One of these was Allan D. Simon, a Washington, D.C. consultant who had been director of air warfare in the Office of the Secretary of Defense and a member of numerous Pentagon advisory boards."
Allan D. Simon, "The Coming Weapons," *Astronautics and Aeronautics*, November 1982, p.40ff.

p. 138. "For many years, there had been a few on the 'lunatic fringe' who warned of the imminent deployment of Soviet laser battle stations and urged us to go beyond our prudent research program into a crash development of our own 'Star Wars' system."
Bowman, op.cit., p.50.

p. 138. "Reagan was briefed on the laboratory's programs, including 'an upcoming test in Alaska of a large, ground-launched nuclear weapon that was designed to destroy incoming Soviet missiles.' According to Teller, Reagan asked 'maybe a dozen questions' and 'got along with everybody.'"
James Chace and Caleb Carr, *America Invulnerable*, Summit Books, New York, 1988, p.295.

p. 140. "The goal of the Kitchen Cabinet—extraordinary for a non-official body—was, in the words of William Broad, writing in his 1985 book *Star Warriors*, 'to formulate a plan for creating a national system of defense and to convey that plan to the newly elected president.'"
William Broad, *Star Warriors*, Touchstone Books, New York, 1986, p.122.

p. 142. "Later in 1983 he said he wanted the U.S. to develop a larger anti-satellite (ASAT) capability, 'not because that is the best way to do the ASAT mission, but

because it will give us the technology to do the ABM mission.'"
Bowman, op.cit., p.46.

p. 143. "'The traditional defense budget clearly isn't going to grow much in the near future. Every company is on notice that, if they want to be a long-term player, they can't let SDI get away.'"
Anthony Lewis, "The Military-Industrial Complex," *New York Times*, November 21, 1985.

p. 143. "As Robert Bowman wrote, Fletcher's panel: '... attempted to identify the technology hurdles to be overcome in pursuing a "Star Wars" system capable of intercepting 99.9% of ICBMs launched against us. The fifty-person panel worked for four and a half months and produced a voluminous classified report which included a good bit of skepticism.'"
Bowman, op.cit., p.68.

p. 144. "As Jerome Wiesner and Kosta Tsipis wrote in the *New York Times*: 'In an effort to counter the incredulity generated by [the president's March 23, 1983, speech], the White House appointed a committee of experts under James Fletcher . . . to decide ex post facto whether Star Wars would be technically feasible. . . .'"
Jerome B. Weisner and Kosta Tsipis, "Put 'Star Wars' Before a Panel," *New York Times*, November 11, 1985.

p. 146. "He said, 'We can get any amount of money out of General Abrahamson we want to invest in survivability for anybody who's got a good idea.'"
Washington Post, April 22, 1986.

CHAPTER 10

p. 150. "According to Dr. Robert Bowman, who directed the project while with the Air Force: 'The end result of the restructured Talon Gold program will be a pointer-tracker system that can be combined with the other two elements of the DARPA triad to form a prototype laser battle station. The import of this program is that it represents the first publicly acknowledged use of the space shuttle for large-scale space weapons tests.'"
Bowman, *Star Wars: Defense or Death Star*, op.cit., p.68–69.

p. 155. "Alumni of the committee are sprinkled throughout the highest levels of the government, amounting to a virtual takeover of the nation's national security apparatus.'"
This and other information on the Conservative Movement influence within the Reagan Administration is derived largely from 1981 *Washington Post* reports, including a major article in the November 23, 1981, issue.

p. 155. "The CPD also said, 'The U.S. should reconstitute its lost capabilities for industrial mobilization.' In other words, the CPD wanted to place the U.S. economy and government on a full wartime footing."
This and other quotes are from CPD literature derived from public documents acquired by the author from a visit to CPD headquarters in Washington. With respect to CPD lobbying for the Reagan military build-up: "For more than a third of a century,

assertions of Soviet superiority created calls for the United States to 'rearm.' In the 1980s, the call was heeded so thoroughly that the United States embarked on a trillion-dollar defense buildup. As a result, the country neglected its schools, cities, roads and bridges, and health care system. From the world's greatest creditor nation, the United States became the world's greatest debtor—in order to pay for arms to counter the threat of a nation that was collapsing." Anne Hessing Cahn, "The Trillion Dollar Experiment," *Bulletin of the Atomic Scientists*, April 1993.

p. 156. "According to conversations I had after the Challenger disaster with Christine Dolan, political news director of the Cable News Network, a group was set up that included Edwin Meese, John Herrington, and figures with the Heritage Foundation." Christine Dolan was also a resource for Joseph Trento's book on the Challenger disaster, *Prescription for Disaster*.

p. 158. "He told Beggs that Graham had support from the 'west coast.'" Joseph J. Trento, *Prescription for Disaster*, Random House, New York, 1987, p.256.

p. 159. "On December 4, the day after the indictment, spokesman Larry Speakes said President Reagan believed Beggs 'will do the right and proper thing . . . whether it is to continue or not to continue—whatever he does, in our view, will be the right and proper thing.'" Author's notes from television news reports.

p. 161. "In an article entitled, 'New NASA Chief is on Top of the World,' Richard Corrigan of the *National Journal* reported three days before Challenger was lost: 'They say you can tell the age of the boy by the price of the toy. William R. Graham suddenly finds himself in charge of billions of dollars' worth of high technology gear as acting chief of the nation's space agency, and, at age forty-eight, he's as giddy as a kid at Disney World." Richard Corrigan, "New NASA Chief is on Top of the World," *National Journal*, January 25, 1986, p.229.

p. 161. "Graham also told Jesse Moore's Office of Space Flight to accept no more commercial customers on the shuttle. This reversed one of Beggs' most cherished policies, opened the door to the privatization of spaceflight by encouraging private companies to enter the launch business, and fueled speculation that a higher degree of military utilization of the shuttle was on the way." Internal NASA discussions.

p. 161. "Though Graham's name did not appear on the document, this was the first major agreement signed between NASA and the Air Force during his tenure. It represented a major departure from Beggs' balanced program of equal shuttle utilization for science, commerce, and defense." I read this document while at NASA. It was non-classified from a national security standpoint but was nevertheless being kept secret from Congress and the press.

p. 162. "Thus on the eve of the Challenger launch, it is a fact, which was not generally recognized in the literature on the disaster, that NASA was in the throes of the greatest leadership crisis in its history."

The exception was the book by Joseph Trento, *Prescription for Disaster,* which provided an outstanding history of the politics of the manned space program.

p. 163. "'There has been a lot of infighting. One reason for that is that the president doesn't give strong direction. He lets every issue ventilate until it bubbles up and forces a decision. On the other hand, there hasn't been a disaster, so maybe Reagan's system works.'"

James McCartney, "Administration is at War with Itself, Officials Say," *San Jose Mercury-News,* January 28, 1986.

CHAPTER 12

Boisjoly quotes in this chapter and elsewhere:

Roger M. Boisjoly, "Ethical Decisions—Morton Thiokol and the Space shuttle Challenger Disaster," The American Society of Mechanical Engineers Report #87-WA/TS-4, presented at the ASME Winter Annual Meeting, Boston, MA, December 13-18, 1987.

p. 190. "Within two hours of the tragedy, Graham had been informed it was an SRB O-ring joint."

Joseph Trento, op. cit., p.293.

p. 197. "Later I read in the *New York Times* that they were saying the same things at Thiokol in Utah, where a former plant worker said, 'It isn't fair! Why does the media come up with these things and try to place blame? They want to attack and find guilt.'"

New York Times, February 13, 1986.

p. 204. "'The effects of environmental and weather factors on the putty and O-rings may have design implications which require further investigation.'"

While Paul Herr said that weather conditions could aversely affect the O-rings, he did not say anything about cold temperatures, and I had not yet heard that the Thiokol engineers had argued against the Challenger launch for this reason.

CHAPTER 13

p. 209. Regan quote: "Plainly an investigation of the tragedy would be necessary. . . ."

Donald T. Regan, *For the Record: From Wall Street to Washington,* 1988, p.333.

p. 211. Rogers quote: "I think we're going to work very closely with [NASA]. We're not going to rely solely on that investigation . . . ."

Quotations from author's notes.

CHAPTER 14

Feynman references in this and later chapters are from his article, "An Outsider's Inside View of the Challenger Inquiry," *Physics Today,* February 1988, and his book, *What Do You Care What Other People Think? Further Adventures of a Curious Character.*

p. 234. "Rogers then made a statement that was deleted from the official transcript and is being printed here for the first time."
A journalist obtained a copy of material the Commission deleted from its published hearing transcripts and shared it with me.

CHAPTER 16

p. 311. "'It was clear,' an unnamed Commission member said, that what happened the night of January 27 'did not conform to any previous NASA flight procedures.'"
Washington Post, February 19, 1986.

CHAPTER 17

p. 321. "NPR reported on February 20 that the night before launch, Larry Mulloy had reacted to the cold weather warnings of the Thiokol engineers by exclaiming, 'My God, Thiokol, when do you want me to launch, next April?' This was a detail the Commission had not yet heard."
NPR had been called immediately after the disaster by a group of wives of the Thiokol engineers to tell them how upset their husbands were and how they had been overruled in the launch decision. They asked NPR to keep the information confidential at the time, saying they just wanted to go on record.

p. 322. Boisjoly's account of encounter with General Donald Kutyna: Boisjoly, op.cit., p. 9. Boisjoly eventually left the company.

p. 323. Anecdote of McDonald locking himself in Senate conference room:
Sen. Hollings personally told me the story of McDonald's visit to Washington.

p. 326. "Dribin told him that the night before the start of the February 25–27 open hearings:
'Chairman Rogers summoned the contractor lawyers to his hotel room that evening and blandly asserted, "I have an American hero in Alan McDonald"'. . . . . "
Dr. Mark Maier, "Ten Years After A Major Malfunction . . . Reflections on 'The Challenger Syndrome'," *Journal of Management Inquiry*, Vol. 11, No. 3, September 2002, pp.283–4.

p. 353. "At least one Commission member knew that the hearings did not get to the bottom of why NASA applied so much pressure to launch. This member said privately to Roger Boisjoly, 'Nothing you could have argued would have stopped them from launching that day.' Another Thiokol engineer said, 'They told me the decision to launch was political and to go home and not to worry.' They said, 'If something goes wrong, you won't be blamed.' "
As told to the author.

p. 378. In describing the salvage operation, I am indebted to Richard Lewis and his account in *Challenger, The Final Voyage*, Columbia University Press, New York, 1988.

CHAPTER 18

p. 360. "Fletcher himself said that NASA needed strong leadership and that Graham 'has three strikes against him' and 'didn't really know what was going on.' An unnamed House staff member said Graham '... is like a waterbug on top of the water. He has no idea what was going on underneath.'"
National Journal, March 22, 1989, p.688.

CHAPTER 19

p. 382. "There was one NASA official who spoke clearly and forthrightly, providing an exception to the joke going around among newsmen that NASA stood for 'Never a Straight Answer.'"
The joke being told in my son's elementary school was that NASA stood for "Need Another Seven Astronauts."

p. 386. "The May 2 hearing was the Commission's last. Whether it even should have had public hearings—the transcript of the May 2 event was released so soon after the fact that it was, in effect, public—will always be controversial. Clearly, William Rogers was trying to achieve an effect, and long after the disaster died down, many in NASA had come to believe that his purpose was to deflect attention from the Reagan administration for its politically-contrived flight rate."
See the NASA publication, *Power to Explore: History of MSFC.*

p. 386. The additional information on the 51-E flight readiness review on O-ring temperature was contained in Volume II, Section H of the Commission's report.

CHAPTER 21

p. 420. "This was jaw-dropping news. I had not heard anything about Vandenberg before this talk with Marty Kress."
Marshall's suppression of information about the effect of cold temperature on the O-rings in order not to interfere with Vandenberg flights is cited several times in this book, but I did not hear about it until the discussion with Kress. I later learned that Alan McDonald had mentioned the Vandenberg connection in his testimony to the Commission and that Marshall had insisted to Thiokol that the information not be mentioned at the Level I flight readiness review for mission 51-E. Thus three separate sources confirmed this critical information that connected NASA's failure to adequately address the O-ring problem to their commitment to fly military missions for the Department of Defense.

p. 432. "'Depending on the outcome of such investigations, Florida state authorities might also consider charges of negligent homicide against some of those involved.'"
Later I received a request to provide possible topics for a review of the Challenger disaster by the House Criminal Justice Subcommittee. In a March 3, 1987, letter to Julian Epstein, I listed forty-two possible topics of inquiry, including, "Whether NASA coerced local authorities in Alabama to suppress information pertaining to the suicide death of William Clemens, a Marshall employee who studied the effects of cold

temperature on the O-rings." The subcommittee also asked whether I thought there was a need for new legislation, to which I responded, "I have not had a chance to think much about the need for new legislation; however, it does seem to me that some kind of provision should exist for an immediate criminal review of any incident involving death to a federal employee or in the operation of federally-owned equipment. I think there should also be penalties where death results from negligence growing out of mismanagement. . . . In a technological age where safety depends on good, honest management, the laws have not kept pace."

CHAPTER 22

p. 442. "Later, when Columbia was destroyed at atmospheric reentry on February 1, 2003, the astronaut crew had not even been told how seriously engineers on the ground were concerned that the orbiter had sustained severe damage from falling external tank debris."

In an e-mail, Dr. Mark Maier of Chapman University wrote me:

"The ground controllers—in prepping the crew for a media link-up—told the Columbia astronauts that there had been some concern with foam coming off at liftoff, but that they had examined it and everything was fine, that there was nothing for the astronauts to worry about, that they were just passing the information along 'fyi' in case it came up during the press conference from space."

CHAPTER 23

p. 450. Transcript of Larry Speakes press conference is printed courtesy Federal News Service.

Larry Speakes published his memoirs, *Speaking Out*, in 1989. I also had a phone conversation with Speakes after his book was published where he said that it was the Teacher-in-Space mission that caused NASA to launch Challenger when it did. But he would not comment on any White House involvement in the decision.

p. 452. "This had been originally reported by Andrea Mitchell of ABC News, who was told she was *persona non grata* at the White House for broadcasting it."

Andrea Mitchell, *Talking Back . . . To Presidents, Dictators, and Assorted Scoundrels*, Viking Adult, New York, 2005, p.167. Mitchell said a whistleblower told her that NASA sent Columbia on an extra orbit to accommodate the president's schedule.

p. 469. Regarding the phone calls from the Kennedy Space Center to the Executive Office of the President and the White House, the author personally verified each by calling the number and asking what office he had contacted.

INDEX

Abbey, George, 447
ABM research, 135–36, 139, 141–45.
  See also Strategic Defense Initiative
ABM Treaty, 129, 141–42, 145
Abrahamson, James, 110, 111, 144–45,
  149, 383
acceptable risk (fly-as-is)
  anomalies as, 75–76, 125
  Centaur and shuttle issues, 288–89
  defining, 243, 356, 396–97
  O-ring problem as, 179, 242–43,
    390–91, 410–11
  risk estimates and measures,
    125–27, 243
  Rockwell's assessment of, 119
  SSMEs at 109% thrust as, 80–81,
    492n
Acheson, David, 155, 217, 350
Air Force
  Aldridge and, 58, 130, 161–62, 369
  CSOC facility, 107
  and IUS program, 52, 54–55
  NASA and, 58, 94–97, 107–8,
    161–62, 369
  Titan 34D-7 order, 134, 152, 162
  See also militarization of shuttle
    program; Vandenberg Air Force
    Base
Air Force Space Command, 129–30
Aldrich, Arnold

briefing Moore re: Rockwell,
  347–48
on Challenger disaster, 219, 298,
  305
Commission testimony, 294–95,
  310, 341, 343–44, 347–49
as director at Johnson, 24–25
ice team's no launch
  recommendation to, 346
Rockwell's no launch decision, 185
Aldridge, Edward C., Jr., 58, 130,
  161–62, 369
Allen, Lew, 130
antiballistic missile research, 135–36,
  139, 141–45. *See also* Strategic
  Defense Initiative
Antiballistic Missile Treaty, 129
anti-satellite (ASAT) capability, 142
"Apocalypse" letter from MSFC,
  356–57, 362
Apollo lunar missions, 92
Appropriations Subcommittee on HUD
  and Independent Agencies, House,
  52–53
APUs (auxiliary power units), 123
Armstrong, Neil, 210, 211, 239–40,
  279, 305, 319, 348–49
ASAT (anti-satellite) capability, 142
astronauts
  Commission testimony, 373–76

dangerous situation information withheld from, 185, 238–39, 244, 293, 305, 374, 413–17, 442, 503n
escape plan for launch pad, 101–2, 120–21, 185, 293, 442
House Committee interviews and findings, 412–17, 441–42
JSC concern versus Marshall disregard, 43
memorial service for, 201
military officers as, 150
on NASA internal investigation board, 196–97
recovery of crew remains, 376–78
training requirements, 117
See also specific astronauts
Atlantis orbiter, 75, 81, 176–78, 492n
Atlas-Centaur, 53–54
auxiliary power units (APUs), 123
Aviation Week and Space Technology (magazine), 121, 149

Ball, Jim, 424–25
Bardos, Russ, 32, 410
Beggs, James
on Air Force upper stage needs, 57
career of, 110, 160
on Centaur cost overruns, 66–67
flight rate goal of, 111–12
GD and, 158–59
indictment of, 85, 158–60, 367
knowledge of O-ring design flaw, 37, 388–89
on NASA's business policies, 131
opposition to Graham, 157, 158
plan for space transport, 20
on Reagan and technology, 129
resignation of, 361
and SDI, 153
at shuttle launch meetings, 24
Bennett, Jonathan A., 353–54
Boeing Aerospace Co., 51, 296. *See also* Inertial Upper Stage
Boffey, Phil, 213–16, 221–23, 284–85
Boisjoly, Roger
on cold weather issues with O-rings, 448–49
Commission testimony, 297, 301–2, 331–33
on MSFC cover-up, 362
on NASA's chicanery, 322
on omission of temperature concerns, 392
O-ring rubber resiliency tests by, 244, 306–7, 391, 394–95, 409–10
recommendation against launch, 181, 182
on SRB seal issues, 322–23
watching launch with Ebeling, 189–90
Boston Globe, 378, 432–33
Bowman, Robert
The Challenger Report and, 430, 431, 433–36
on Fletcher Commission, 143–44
flight rate projections of, 110
on Star Wars and shuttle, 107–8, 138, 145–46
on Talon Gold program, 150
Brackett, Elizabeth, 287
Braden, Bill, 195
brake damage, 123–24
briefing chart for O-ring issues, 229–30, 284, 395, 442
Brier, Jim, 18–19, 207–8
Broad, William, 140
Brown, George, 42–43
Buchanan, Patrick, 452–53, 472
budgets
Centaur cost overruns, 62–68, 71–72
design freeze related to, 37, 113–15, 441
FWC cost overruns, 40, 44–45
manipulation of, 21, 32–33
pricing policy and cost overruns, 111
schedule pressures and safety versus, 119–27
SSME cost overruns, 33
Stockman's cancellation of Centaur, 57–59
budget threat, O-ring joint redesign as, 37, 227, 237–41, 266–67
Burrough, Bryan, 381–82
Byrd, Robert, 429

Califano, Joseph, 213
Cannon, Lou, 454

capture feature for O-ring redesign, 36–37, 176, 179–80, 201, 204–5, 205, 237–38, 270
Casey, William, 128
Centaur
    cancellation of, 26, 49, 57, 366
    challenges related to, 54, 62–65, 72–73, 82
    competition with IUS, 51–59
    cost overruns, 62–68, 71–72
    cryogenic fuel in, 26, 50, 61–62
    filament wound case for, 26, 38–45, 491n
    for Galileo and Ulysses launches, 50–53, 57–58, 61, 70
    GD performance issues, 67–68, 70–71
    NASA contracts for, 61, 64–65
    NASA Jan., 1986, meeting on, 76–83, 165–66
    overview, 4–5, 19, 49, 61, 62, 492n
Centaur integrated support system (CISS), 61, 62, 70–71, 74
Challenger disaster
    Cook's memo on, 203–8
    debris from, 376–78
    effect on SDI, 147–48
    experience at Thiokol, 189–90
    "General Conclusions" briefing chart, 229–30, 284, 395, 442
    interim review mishap board, 196–97, 219
    lessons appropriate to present situations, 478–79
    NASA cover-up, 194–99, 202, 203, 208, 222, 356–57
    organizational factors related to, 364–65
    O-ring joint design and, 189–91
    overview, 186
    response at NASA D.C. office, 190–94
    smoke from SRB/ET area, 186, 190, 296–97, 363
Challenger (Lewis), 190–91
Challenger orbiter
    flight readiness review, 179
    launch schedule anomalies, 167–68, 180, 351, 424–27, 444–45, 468–69

    mechanical problems with, 5, 175–76
    O-ring damage incidents, 170–71, 172, 173, 175
    preparation for one week delay in pre-disaster launch, 446–47
Chernobyl accident, 382–83
Chriss, Nicholas, 446
CIRRIS (cryogenic infrared radiation instrument for shuttle), 170, 177
CISS (Centaur integrated support system), 61, 62, 70–71, 74
CNN, 325
Cold War, 39, 95, 129, 130–31, 135, 138–39, 141. See also Strategic Defense Initiative
Columbia orbiter
    Commission report on, 398
    descent problems, 172
    Jan. 1986 postponements, 166–67
    missions, 57, 170
    Reagan's politicizing and, 171
    reentry destruction of, 29, 105, 124, 350, 442, 503n
    TPS design and, 105
commercial customers, 96, 112–13, 161
Commission. See Presidential Commission on Challenger
Committee on the Present Danger (CPD), 154–55, 498n
communication equipment, 122–23
computing units (CUs), 72–73, 122, 172
comsat launchings, 96, 112–13, 161
Conservative Movement, 137–38, 153–62, 365
consolidated space operations center (CSOC), 107
contractor issues, 118–20. See also specific contractors
Cook, Richard C.
    biographical info, 7–11, 12–15
    Challenger disaster memo, 203–8
    The Challenger Report, 429–36
    Commission testimony, 265–79
    media interviews, 213–16, 221–27, 284–89, 315
    Molesworth's interview of, 461–64
    national whistleblower's award, 472
    qualifications, ix–xi, 4, 15, 265–66
    Rogers, letter to, 317

SRB memo, 6–7, 38, 191–92, 196, 198, 225–26, 234–35, 271–72, 276–77
Corrigan, Richard, 161
cost overruns. *See* budgets
coupon testing, 43, 491n
Covert, Eugene, 217, 237
CPD (Committee on the Present Danger), 154–55, 498n
Criminal Justice Subcommittee, House, 502n
Crippen, Robert, 304–5, 374–75
cryogenic infrared radiation instrument for shuttle (CIRRIS), 170, 177
CSOC (consolidated space operations center), 107
Culbertson, Philip, 290, 454, 456
Curran, Frank, 365–66
CUs (computing units), 72–73, 122, 172

Dakar, Senegal, abort site, 180, 329, 348–49
Danforth, John, 316
Davids, Irv, 32, 197–98, 237
Defense Contract Audit Service (DCAS), 68
defense satellite communication system (DSCS), 177
Demisch, Wolfgang H., 143
Department of Defense (DoD)
    Centaur and, 58
    dependence on NASA and shuttle program, 106–7, 131
    NASA, SDI, and, 150–53
    NASA/DoD study of Centaur, 56–57
    plans for weapons in space, 150–53
    RTG clearance for shuttles, 82
    secret orbiter missions, 170, 173–74, 176–77
    support for STS, 216–17
    See also Air Force; militarization of shuttle program
design and data analysis task force, 321, 360
Directors and Boards (journal), 131
Discovery orbiter, 29, 119, 134, 173–76
DoD. *See* Department of Defense
Dolan, Anthony, 156

Dolan, Christine, 156, 325, 365, 427, 499n
Douglas, Ernie, 436
DSCS (defense satellite communication system), 177
Duke, George, 47
dump valve, 72, 77–78
Dupree, Ralph, 420

Easterbrook, Greg, 102
Ebeling, Robert, 181, 189–90, 327–28
Ehlers, Karen, 457–59, 460
Ehrlichman, John, 97
electromagnetic railgun, 136
ELVs (expendable launch vehicles), 50, 53–54, 134, 152, 162
Enterprise orbiter, 102–6
environmental impact statements, 83, 126–27
escape plan for launch pad, 101–2, 120–21, 185, 293, 442
ET. *See* external tank
EVAs (extravehicular activities), 62, 178
expendable launch vehicles (ELVs), 50, 53–54, 134, 152, 162
external tank (ET)
    challenges related to, 27–29
    foam insulation on, 29, 174
    ovality rule, 81, 425–27, 435–36
    overview, 19–20
    strut failure theory, 193
    waiver of launch commit criteria, 346, 440
    worker error involving, 119–20
extravehicular activities (EVAs), 62, 178

Failure Modes Effects Analysis (FMEA), 125, 243
failure probability studies, 126–27
Fairchild cryogenic dump valve, 72, 77–78
FBI role in investigation, 354, 365, 366–73
Federal of American Scientists, 176
Feynman, Richard
    biographical info, 228
    on Commission report-writing process, 387–88

on flight rate goals, 96–97
on flight readiness reviews, 375
investigation of NASA by, 228–32, 322
on NASA decision making, 387
on O-rings and temperature, 247, 249, 254–55, 261–65, 279–80
field joints, 172
Field School, Washington, D.C., 10
filament wound case (FWC), 26, 38–45, 491n
Financial Management Service, U.S. Treasury Department, 314–16, 436
Fletcher, James, 95–98, 360, 361, 382
Fletcher Commission, 143–44
flight control system on shuttles, 101
flight rate goal
    Beggs's 24-per year goal, 111–12
    Bowman's projections, 110
    ET production for, 27, 28
    failure to attain, 29, 32–33
    importance of, 17
    increase in military usage, 161–62
    militarization of shuttle program and, 368–69
    1986 schedule, 165–67
    obtaining funding and, 98
    original plan, 20, 96–97
    pressure to meet, 40–41, 47
    shortcuts as result of, 116–17
flight readiness reviews, 24, 48, 179, 336, 375, 390–92, 393–94
fly-as-is. See acceptable risk; waivers of safety standards
FMEA (Failure Modes Effects Analysis), 125, 243
foam insulation on ET, 29, 174
For the Record (Regan), 209–10
fraud, 119
Frosch, Robert, 52–53, 54, 103, 120–21
fuel dump for Centaur abort, 61–62, 80
Fuqua, Donald, 112
FWC (filament wound case), 26, 38–45, 491n

Galileo, 50–53, 57–58, 61, 70, 82, 167, 492n
General Accounting Office (GAO), 56, 103, 115, 118–19, 130

General Dynamics (GD), 25, 26, 38–45, 53–55, 67–68, 70–71, 74, 158–59, 491n. See also Centaur
Glaysher, Robert, 184–85, 347
Glenn, John, 4
Gore, Al, 318, 361
Gorton, Slade, 316, 319
Graham, William
    career of, 85, 156–62
    on Challenger disaster, 194, 195–96, 202, 203
    Commission testimony, 218, 258–60
    CPD, Heritage Foundation, and, 154–56
    Culbertson firing, 290
    leaving NASA for White House position, 360–61
    lobbying in D.C., 185
    Molesworth's interview of, 456–57
    on New York Times story, 233–34
    phone calls (161) to D.C. before launch, 427–28, 468–70
    postponement of Challenger launch, 179
    Rogers and, 258–60
    on SRB O-ring issue, 318–19, 457
    Teacher-in-Space program and, 164–65, 291
    text for Reagan's STOUA, 401–2
Green, Shirley, 460–61
Grey, Jerry, 287–88
Grier, Herbert, 121

Hamby, William, 198, 237, 393–94, 395
Hardy, George, 294, 299, 307, 321
Hartmann, Erich, 101
Hartsfield, Henry, 375, 416, 417
Helin, Ed, 475–77
Heninger, Lynn W., 410
Henry, Richard C., 130–31
Hercules Corporation, 36
Heritage Foundation, 140, 154–56
Herr, Paul
    on Challenger disaster, 193–94, 197
    Commission interview of, 369–73, 393
    Cook on information from, 285–86
    O-ring concerns, 35, 207

position at NASA, 32
Herrington, John, 154
Hess, George M., Jr., 146
Hollings, Ernest, 316, 318–19, 323–24, 400–407, 418–19, 421–22, 428–29, 454
Honegger, Barbara, 129
Hotz, Robert B., 217, 236, 320, 336
House Appropriations Subcommittee on HUD and Independent Agencies, 52–53
House Criminal Justice Subcommittee, 502n
House Science and Technology Committee, 56, 123, 395n, 407–17, 438–43, 492n
House Subcommittee on Space Science and Applications, 65–67
Houston Post, 373–74, 448–49
Huntsville Times, 101, 357–58

ice, tile damage from, 105, 124, 183–84, 350
ice on tower issue, 174, 183–86, 194–95, 218, 293–95, 344–50, 445
IEEE Spectrum, 388–89
IG (Inspector General) Office, 365–66
inertial upper stage (IUS), 51–59, 117–18, 492n
Inspector General (IG) Office, 365–66
interim review mishap board, 196–97, 219, 312, 321
International Solar Polar Mission (ISPM), 51, 53, 57. *See also* Ulysses spacecraft
Investigation of the Challenger Accident (House Committee on Science and Technology), 438–43
ISPM (International Solar Polar Mission), 51, 53, 57. *See also* Ulysses spacecraft
IUS (inertial upper stage), 51–59, 117–18, 492n

Jane's Spaceflight Directory, 112–13, 171, 177
Jarvis, Gregory, 179
Jet Propulsion Laboratory, 130
Johnson Space Center (JSC)
about, 17–18
Centaur and, 75
centralization of shuttle ops, 115
concern for astronauts, 43
exclusion from O-ring info, 283
load alleviation for FWC, 43–45
temperature issues withheld from, 305
water hammer effect issue, 81
joint rotation issue, 171, 226–27, 267, 284
JSC. *See* Johnson Space Center

Kearney Mesa, San Diego, CA. *See* Centaur
Keel, Alton, 297, 311, 340–41, 349, 387–88, 392
Kehrli, Randy, 366–69
Kelley, Jack, 436
Kelley, Kitty, 473–74
Kennedy Space Center (KSC)
Commission hearings at, 291–312, 361–63
flight schedule and shuttle shuffles, 165–67, 180
freezing temperatures at, 173–74, 181–85
ice on tower issue, 174, 183–86, 194–95, 218, 293–95, 344–50, 445
Lockheed processing contract, 114–15, 119–20
schedule pressures at, 79–80
shuttle-Centaur meetings at, 76–79
shuttle landing issues, 124
SRB handling at, 18, 19, 46–47, 79, 85–86, 166, 172
Keyworth, George, III, 131–33, 142
Kilminster, Joe, 182–83, 299–300, 321, 334
Kingon, Albert, 325, 452
Kingsbury, James, 181
Kitchen Cabinet, Reagan's, 139–40
Kohl, Helmut, 171
Kohrs, Dick, 292–93, 296
Kovach, Bill, 223, 286
Kress, Marty, 420, 421–22
Krupp, Leo, 6
KSC. *See* Kennedy Space Center
Kutyna, Donald
agreement with Cook, 432

as Commission member, 217, 219–21, 294
Feynman and, 264
on military payloads, 152
on O-ring joints, 230–31, 241–42, 337, 363
on temperature issues, 409–10

Lamberth, Horace, 293, 295–96
landing problems, 124, 172, 174, 175
Langley Air Force Base, 40–41
lasers in space, 135–36, 139, 146, 150, 154
launch commit criteria (LCC), 182–83, 243–44, 294–95, 336–37, 393, 395–96, 440, 449
Lee, Jack, 361–63
Lehrer, Jim, 287–89
Level I flight readiness reviews, 24
Lewis, Flora, 146–47
Lewis, Richard, 190–91
Lewis Research Center, 55–56, 68–69. See also Centaur
Lilly, William, 52
load reduction measures for FWC, 43–45
Lockheed, 114–15, 119–20, 174
looking for "quick fix," 270
Lovelace, Alan, 55, 68
Lovingood, Judson, 219–21, 226, 298–99, 339–40
Lucas, William
    Commission testimony, 341–43
    on freeze of shuttle design, 114, 117
    management style, 357
    motel room meeting with Mulloy and Reinartz, 181, 182, 338, 340–43, 422–23
    on MSFC cover-up, 356–57
    as MSFC director, 22, 25
    on O-ring joint design flaws, 244
    on responsibility for Challenger launch, 354–55
    retirement of, 386
Lund, Bob, 291, 298–99, 302, 306, 327–28, 334, 495n

Maier, Mark, 325–26, 472–73
main engines. See space shuttle main engines

main propulsion system (MPS), 105, 426
Maley, Pat, 366–69
management
    Mulloy's style of, 41–42, 182, 309–10, 321, 336–37
    NASA's communication issues, 25, 352–53, 355, 375–76, 412, 434–35
    responsibility of, 502–3n
    top-down, by objectives, 109, 114, 415–16
Manifest Bingo, 79–80, 165–66
Maready, William, 444–45
Mark, Hans, 117, 130, 135–36, 388–89
Markey, Edward, 324
Mars flights, 92–93
Marshall Space Flight Center (MSFC)
    about, 18
    "Apocalypse" letter, 356–57, 362
    destruction of documents, 383
    directors of, 21–22
    flight safety issues, 206, 277–78
    on FWC, 41–42, 43
    O-ring redesign and, 179, 181
    and O-ring/temperature relationship, 104–5, 174, 362
    program operating plan (POP), 22
    shuttle design freeze by, 113–15
    See also external tank; Lucas, William; Mulloy, Larry; solid rocket boosters
Martin Marietta, 25, 27, 28
Mason, Jerry, 299, 300–301, 302, 333
Mattingly, Ken, 417
McAuliffe, Christa
    about, 3, 87
    on cold weather, 446
    on NASA's determination to launch, 168
    planned presentations from space, 179
    Reagan's STOUA and, 401–7, 452–53
    training and PR, 164
McCarty, Bill, 203
McConnell, Malcolm, 443–45, 459
McDivitt, James, 414
McDonald, Alan, 247–51, 308–11, 319–20, 327–30, 409–10

McFarland, Robert "Bud," 140
McGinley, Laurie, 381–82
Meese, Edwin, 153–54, 160, 433
militarization of shuttle program
  Commission's failure to address,
    389
  early signs of, 45, 51
  and flight rate goal, 368–69
  NASA and DoD/Air Force
    collaboration, 45, 94–97, 107–8,
    156–62
  as Reagan's policy, 93–94, 106,
    132–33, 149
  right-wing influence on, 137–38,
    153–62, 365
  Rogers on, 407–8
  safety as victim of, 121, 289, 502n
  See also Air Force; Vandenberg Air
    Force Base
military-industrial complex, 128,
  129–31, 156. See also Strategic
  Defense Initiative
military shuttle flights, 26, 45, 50, 170,
  173–74, 176–77, 361. See also
  Vandenberg Air Force Base
military specification for O-ring rubber,
  244, 300
Miller, John, 383–84
mission model. See flight rate goal
MLPs (mobile launch platforms), 79,
  167
mobile launch platforms (MLPs), 79,
  167
Molesworth, John R., 190, 455–70
Moore, Gilbert, 201
Moore, Jesse
  agreement with Air Force, 161–62
  Aldrich's report on ice issues,
    347–48
  on capture feature, 237–38
  on Category 1 items in program, 292
  on Challenger disaster, 195–96,
    218–19
  Commission protection of, 320
  Commission testimony, 218–19,
    234–40, 244–45, 261, 291–92,
    343–44, 349–52
  as director of JSC, 321
  on explosion, 5–6
  FWC and, 43, 45

ice team's no launch
  recommendation to, 346
  on lack of safety of flight concerns,
    238–39
  Molesworth's interview of, 456
  on NASA manager communications,
    375–76
  on NASA's investigative intent,
    260–61
  on NASA's pressure for launch,
    350–52
  optimism of, 84
  O-ring issues and, 36, 411–12
  position at NASA, 17, 23–25, 412
  on Reagan's STOUA, 403
  review of Centaur, 75–76
  at Senate hearings, 319
Morton Thiokol. See Thiokol
MPS (main propulsion system), 105,
  426
MSFC. See Marshall Space Flight
  Center
MTI. See Thiokol
Mulloy, Larry
  Commission testimony, 241–44,
    261–65, 335–38, 383–84,
    385–86
  denying Thiokol engineer's
    objections, 291
  on events leading to Challenger
    disaster, 298–99
  launch commit criteria and, 182,
    243–44, 308, 449
  on launch decision process, 355
  management style, 41–42, 182,
    309–10, 321, 336–37
  motel room meeting with Lucas and
    Reinartz, 181, 182, 338, 340–43,
    422–23
  on O-rings, 242–43, 244, 245–46,
    261–65
  position at NASA, 386
  on resiliency tests, 409–10
  waiver of launch constraints,
    327–28, 384
Mutch, Thomas, 52

NASA
  Air Force and, 58, 94–97, 107–8,
    161–62, 369

commercial customers, 96, 112–13, 161
competitors, 112, 153, 401
Conservative Movement takeover, 156–62
design and data analysis task force, 321, 360
establishment of, 93–94
interim review mishap board, 196–97, 219, 312, 321
management communication issues, 25, 352–53, 355, 375–76, 412, 434–35
O-ring joint defect awareness, 25–26, 176, 229–30, 283–84, 288, 395, 408–12, 442–43
ovality rule, 81, 425–27, 435–36
phone calls between White House and, 427–28, 465–70, 468–70
procedures sacrificed for Challenger launch, 438–40
publicity for, 163–65
public relations of, 115–16
recovery of crew remains as low priority, 376–78
reorganization of, 113–15
response to Challenger disaster, 190–94
self-image, 364–65
shuttle matrix organization, 481
subdivisions of, 16–17
See also Space Transportation System
NASA field centers, 17–18
NASA's Aerospace Advisory Panel, 116
NASA's Aerospace Safety Advisory Board, 121–22
NASA Select (TV station), 115
National Aeronautics and Space Act (1958), 57–58, 91, 93–94, 367, 369
National Public Radio (NPR), 321, 501n
National Security Council (NSC), 140
Nelson, Bill, 65, 166, 447
Newman, Thomas, 18, 216–17
"New NASA Chief is on Top of the World" (Corrigan), 161
news media
    Cook interviews, 213–16, 221–23, 284–89, 315
    Fletcher on, 382
    praise for Rogers and Commission, 397–98
    pressuring NASA and Reagan, 381, 476
    response to Bowman/Cook press conference, 435–36
    Rogers on, 233, 327
    TV news on Challenger disaster, 3–4, 6, 87
    See also specific media organizations
New York Times
    on Beggs' indictment, 159
    Boffey's interviews of Cook, 213–16, 221–23, 284–85
    Challenger disaster exposé, 213–16, 221–27
    editorial on Fletcher, 361
    on "fly-as-is" reasoning, 119
    McDonald interview, 319–20
    on NASA house cleaning, 386
    on Rogers and Commission, 397
    on SRB drop in power, 202
    on Star Wars, 144, 146
Nixon, Richard M., 92, 93
NPR (National Public Radio), 321, 501n
NSC (National Security Council), 140
nuclear weapons. See weapons in space

O'Brien, Thomond, 157
Office of Comptroller (Code B), 18
Office of Inspector General (IG), 118–19
Office of Management and Budget (OMB), 57–59
Office of the Administrator (Code A), 17
O'Hara, Eileen, 446
O'Hara, Patrick, 472
OMB (Office of Management and Budget), 57–59
operational management instructions (OMIs), 80
orbital maneuvering system pod damage, 175
orbiters
    Atlantis, 75, 81, 176–78, 492n
    design freeze, 37, 113–15, 441
    Discovery, 29, 119, 134, 173–76

diversity of problems, 122–25
DoD secret missions, 170, 173–74, 176–77
Enterprise, 102–6
fuel reloading compromise, 81
launch system, 24
parts shuffle between, 166
pre-Challenger disaster problematic missions, 169–86
redesign for Galileo/Ulysses, 80
Rockwell as contractor, 102–6, 118–19
See also Challenger orbiter; Columbia orbiter
O-ring
damage in multiple shuttle flights, 5, 6–7, 35–36, 170–71, 172, 173, 175, 176, 178, 221
mil spec on rubber, 244, 300
rubber resiliency tests, 244, 306, 391, 394–95, 409–10
O-ring joint design
astronauts ignorance of problems, 238–39, 374
cold weather issues, 172, 174, 194–95, 243–44, 284, 293–96, 300–302, 389–97, 409–10, 448–49
Commission on, 218–21, 388, 389–97
conferences about, 25–26, 33
joint rotation issue, 171, 226–27, 267, 284
military launches from Vandenberg and, 174, 289, 328, 369, 392–93, 420–21, 422, 502n
NASA's awareness of problems, 6–7, 35–36, 70, 190–92, 197–98, 198–99, 204–6, 332–33, 336, 389–90, 394–96
pre-launch leak check issues, 299–300
putty problem, 7, 38, 170, 172, 204, 243, 383–84
redesignation of funds for, 40
secondary seals, 26, 36–37, 104–5, 175, 220, 267, 284, 331–32, 393–94
Thiokol's awareness of problems, 168, 179, 182, 189–90

waiver of safety standards, 26, 38, 179, 204–5, 207, 242–43, 267, 284, 287–88, 303, 305, 331–32
O-ring joint redesign
as budget threat, 37, 227, 237–41, 266–67
capture feature "quick fix," 36–37, 176, 179–80, 201, 204–5, 205, 237–38, 270
Orlando Sentinel, 286–87
Orr, Vern, 134
ovality rule, 81, 425–27, 435–36

Paine, Thomas, 92–93, 95
PAMs (payload assist modules), 172, 492n
Parker Seal Co., 383
payload assist modules (PAMs), 172, 492n
payload bay size, 39, 50, 95, 97
payload bookings, 115
Perle, Richard, 163
Perry, William J., 106–7
Peterson, Mal, 67, 69, 84
Petrone, Rocco, 22, 184, 346–47
planetary probes, 102
Plante, Bill, 454
polar orbits, 39, 95
politics
of Challenger launch, 352–56
right-wing influence, 137–38, 153–62, 365
in space shuttle program, 54–59, 111, 171, 289, 356
of Teacher-in-Space program, 164–65, 167–68, 171, 179
in U.S., 1970s–1980s, 11–12
See also Reagan, Ronald
POP (program operating plan), 22
Powers, Ben, 352
Presidential Commission on Challenger
alteration of transcripts, 232, 352
astronauts at open hearings, 373–76
Bowman and Cook's assessment of, 434–36
creation of, 209–10
FBI and Justice interviews, 354, 365, 366–73
findings, 336, 352–53, 369, 370, 372–73, 375, 386–97

KSC hearings, 291–312, 361–63
members of, 210, 217
NASA and, 211
on NASA's management
    communication issues, 352–53,
    355, 375–76, 412, 434–35
on O-ring joint design, 218–21,
    283–84, 388, 389–97
overview, 359
"Political Pressure" file, 449–70
public hearings, 217–21, 325–52,
    361–63
recommendations, 388
Roe on results of, 407
on safety of flight concerns, 34,
    239–43, 345, 350
sessions on Cook's disclosures,
    231–51, 257–81
testimony from NASA and Thiokol,
    34–35
See also Feynman, Richard; Rogers,
    William
Presidential Commission testimony
of Aldrich, 294–95, 310, 341,
    343–44, 347–49
of astronauts, 373–76
of Boisjoly, 297, 301–2, 331–33
of Cook, 265–79
of Graham, 218, 258–60
of Herr, 369–73, 393
of Lovingood, 339–40
of Lucas, 341–43
of McDonald, 247–51, 308–11,
    327–30, 409–10
of Moore, 218–19, 234–40, 244–45,
    261, 291–92, 343–44, 349–52
of Mulloy, 241–44, 261–65, 335–38,
    383–84, 385–86
of Petrone, 346–47
of Reinartz, 338–39, 340–41
of Smith, 343–44
of Thomas, 343–44
of Thompson, 307–8
of Truly, 374
pressure to approve launch
Commission "Political Pressure" file,
    449–70
Molesworth's investigation of,
    455–70
Reagan's STOUA and, 401–7

on Rockwell, 347–48
on Thiokol, 181–83, 189–90,
    245–46, 303–4, 307, 308–10,
    329–30, 332
See also schedule pressures
program operating plan (POP), 22
Propulsion Division of Code M, 26–27,
    277. See also external tank; solid
    rocket boosters
Proxmire, William, 120–21
public relations, NASA's, 115–16

Quigley, Joan, 474

radioisotope thermoelectric generators
    (RTGs), 82, 126–27
rain, tile damage from, 124, 424
Ray, William, 383
RCS (reaction control system), 123, 124
R&D Associates, 157–58
reaction control system (RCS), 123, 124
Reagan, Ronald
    approach to controversy, 128–29
    at astronauts' memorial service, 201
    economic effect of, 12
    election of, 12
    establishment of Commission on
        Challenger, 209–10
    Graham appointment, 158, 423
    on lack of pressure for launch, 455
    launch order from, 475–76
    launch/speech link, 453–54, 459
    policy on space, 133–34
    pressure on shuttle program, 112
    and SDI, 138–39, 139–42
    space program publicity and,
        163–65, 167–68, 171
    STOUA, launch and, 165, 324–25,
        401–7, 423–24, 452–55
redlines, 82
Regan, Donald, 209–10, 474
Reidy, Chris, 286
Reinartz, Stanley
    Commission testimony, 338–39,
        340–41
    failure to inform Aldrich, 298, 305,
        339–41
    launch order from, 185, 245–46
    McDonald's attempt to prevent
        launch order by, 183

motel room meeting with Lucas and
 Mulloy, 181, 182, 338, 340–43,
 422–23
position at NASA, 25
The Republic (Plato), 8–9
Resources Analysis Division of NASA,
 16–17, 18–20
Ride, Sally, 217, 238–39, 294–95,
 305–6
risk estimates and measures, 125–27, 243
Rockefeller, John D., IV, 152, 401
Rocketdyne, 103–4
Rockwell
 advising against Challenger launch,
 183–84, 185, 246–47, 344, 345,
 346–50
 "fly-as-is" recommendation, 119
 as orbiter contractor, 102–6, 118–19
 STS operations contract, 115
Roe, Robert, 407
Rogers, William
 appointment to Commission,
 209–10
 on blame, 397
 "blame" versus responsibility, 397
 blaming news leaks, 233
 Cook's questioning by, 265–79
 dialogue with Graham, 258–60
 on difficult questions from public,
 242, 293–94
 on full disclosure, 299
 intent of, 211, 280–81
 Moore and, 218–19
 on NASA, 232–33, 329–30, 362,
 386–87
 news media praise of, 397–98
 praise for media, 327
 on Reagan's STOUA as source of
 pressure [not], 403–7
 on Rockwell, 246–47
 scapegoat development process,
 326–27, 335
 at Senate hearings, 319
 on Thiokol's no launch
 recommendation, 248, 249, 250,
 301–3, 306–9
 thwarting investigation attempts,
 228–29
 on waiver of O-ring safety standards,
 291–92

See also Presidential Commission
 on Challenger
Rowley, Storer, 290
RTGs (radioisotope thermoelectric
 generators), 82, 126–27
Rummel, Robert W., 217
Russell, Brian, 394–95

safety
 balancing with schedule and cost,
 76, 119–27
 as casualty of NASA acting as a
 business, 441
 militarization of shuttle program
 versus, 121, 289, 502n
 optimism versus, 84
 STS program, 370–71
 See also acceptable risk; schedule
 pressures; waivers of safety
 standards
safety of flight concerns
 Apollo method for handling, 414–15
 Commission findings, 34, 239–43,
 345, 350
 denial of O-rings as, 238–41, 279,
 345
 O-rings as, 370, 408
 potential for tile damage as, 349–50
Sanger, David, 319–20
Sawyer, Kathy, 364
schedule pressures
 commentary on, 83–84
 equipment issues, 79
 Galileo and planet positions, 73–74,
 78–79
 safety and cost versus, 119–27
 safety as equivalent factor to, 76
 Ulysses spacecraft, 79
 See also flight rate goal; pressure to
 approve launch
Scheuer, James, 126, 386, 408–9,
 411–12
Schmitt, Harrison, 58
Science, Technology, and Space, Senate
 Subcommittee on, 316–19, 400–407
Science and Engineering Directorate,
 42
Science and Technology Committee,
 House, 56, 123, 395n, 407–17,
 438–43, 492n

SDI. *See* Strategic Defense Initiative

SDIO (Strategic Defense Initiative Office), 143, 144–45, 147–48, 368

Senate Subcommittee on Science, Technology, and Space, 316–19, 400–407

sensor malfunctions, 122, 175–76

Shannon, William, 378, 432–33

shuttle-Centaur program. *See* Centaur

Shuttle Projects Office at Marshall, 25

shuttles. *See* orbiters

Simon, Allan D., 136–37

single point failure, 77–78, 173, 242–43, 390

Slayton, Donald "Deke," 413–14, 415

Smart, Tim, 286–87

Smith, Dick, 427–28

Smith, Jane, 398–99

Smith, Mike, 444–45

Smith, Richard, 343–44, 381, 424

Snider, Nona, 452

Solar Max satellite, 172–73

solid rocket boosters (SRBs)
  Abrahamson on, 383
  construction and recycling process, 19, 85–86
  description of, 31–32
  flight readiness reviews, 48
  innovative aspects of, 99–101
  Kutyna's post-explosion findings, 363
  MSFC management of, 20
  power deficit at explosion, 122, 175, 190–91, 202
  "problem-free" testing of, 104–5
  problems with, 33, 47–48
  production costs, 37
  recovery of Challenger's, 378
  segment attrition rate, 45–46, 205–6
  smoke from SRB/ET area, 186, 190, 296–97, 363
  thrust variances, 122, 175, 190–91, 202
  trends leading to, 169–86
  turnaround time, 46–47
  TV news on, 3–4, 6, 87
  wind shear factor, 293, 445
  See also O-ring; O-ring joint design; O-ring joint redesign

Space Age Times, 377–78

space camp for children, 116

Space Flight Office (Code M), 17–18, 19–20, 21, 40–41, 113–15

Spacelab, 171

Space Science and Applications, House Subcommittee on, 65–67

Space Science Office of NASA, 17, 82–83

The Space Shuttle at Work (NASA), 31

space shuttle main engines (SSME)
  budget deficits, 33
  development issues, 103–4, 105–6
  innovative aspects of, 99
  main propulsion system, 105, 426
  at 109% thrust for Galileo/Ulysses, 80–81, 492n
  performance increases, 114
  premature shut down in flight, 175–76
  problems noted and ignored, 122–25

space shuttle program. *See* Space Transportation System

space shuttles. *See* orbiters

space station, 18, 91, 92–93, 132

Space Task Group, Nixon's, 92–93, 493n

Space Transportation System (STS)
  astronauts' Commission testimony, 373–76
  contractor issues, 118–20
  DoD plans for, 150–53
  early missions, 57, 109–10, 113
  hierarchical levels of, 24–25
  launch commit criteria, 182–83, 243–44, 294–95, 336–37, 440
  Nixon's introduction of, 97–98
  pricing policy versus cost recovery, 111
  result of disasters, 83–84
  safety program, 370–71
  scheduling issues, 117–18
  shuttle-borne upper stage program, 50–59
  trends leading to Challenger disaster, 169–86
  weight minimization, 39
  See also militarization of shuttle program; orbiters

Speakes, Larry, 450–53, 471–72

SRBs. *See* solid rocket boosters
SSME. *See* space shuttle main engines
Star Warriors (Broad), 140
Star Wars. *See* Strategic Defense
  Initiative
Star Wars (Bowman), 138
STA (structural test article), 39–40
State of the Union Address (STOUA),
  165, 324–25, 401–7, 423–24,
  452–55
Stephens, Jay, 464–65
Stevenson, Charles, 184, 344–46
Stockman, David, 57, 59
STOUA (State of the Union Address),
  165, 324–25, 401–7, 423–24, 452–55
Strategic Defense Initiative Office
  (SDIO), 143, 144–45, 147–48, 368
Strategic Defense Initiative (SDI)
  ABM research, 135–36, 139, 141–45
  Abrahamson and, 144–45, 149
  aerospace beneficiaries of, 143, 145
  ASAT capability, 142
  Challenger disaster effect on,
    147–48
  and Cold War, 141
  launches required for, 151–53
  NSC planning of, 140
  purpose of, 134–38
  Reagan and, 132, 139–42
  Soviet response to plan, 143
  technical critique, 145–46
  test failures, 146–47, 150
  weapons in space aspect of, 83,
    135–37, 139–40, 144–46,
    150–54, 157–58
structural test article (STA), 39–40
STS. *See* Space Transportation System
Sutter, Joseph, 217, 296, 308

Taft, William Howard, IV, 83
Talon Gold program, 150
TAOS (thrust-assisted orbital shuttle),
  96
TDRS (Tracking and Data Relay
  Satellites), 51–52, 166
Teacher-in-Space program, 163–66,
  167–68, 171, 179, 434–35. *See also*
  McAuliffe, Christa
Teller, Edward, 131–32, 138, 139,
  146–47, 155

thermal protection system (TPS), 95,
  101, 105, 124, 349–50
Thiokol
  advising against Challenger launch,
    168, 179, 182, 189–90, 247–51,
    289–90, 298–99
  bench tests on O-ring rubber, 244,
    306, 391, 394–95
  Commission testimony, 34, 327–35
  failure investigation team, 201
  Marshall's pressure to approve
    launch, 181–83, 189–90, 245–46,
    303–4, 307, 308–10, 329–30, 332
  and O-ring problem, 7
  pre-Commission instructions to
    engineers, 297
  SRB bid of, 100
  in STS hierarchy, 25
  See also O-ring joint design; solid
    rocket boosters
Thomas, Gene, 343–44
Thompson, Arnie, 183, 297, 307–8
Thompson, James R., 360, 382
Thrift, Ashley, 419–20, 427, 428–29
thrust-assisted orbital shuttle (TAOS),
  96
thrust variances, 122, 175, 190–91, 202
tile damage, 105, 124, 173–74, 183–84,
  350, 424
Titan-Centaur, 53, 54
TPS (thermal protection system), 95,
  101, 105, 124, 349–50
Tracking and Data Relay Satellites
  (TDRS), 51–52, 166
tracking equipment, 122–23
Trapnell, Emily, 369–73, 456
Trento, Joseph, 425, 427, 470, 499n
Truly, Richard, 321, 374
TRW, 13–14, 143
Tsipis, Kosta, 144

Ulysses (ISPM)
  Centaur required for launch, 51, 53,
    57, 61
  launch of, 492n
  nuclear energy source clearances,
    82–83, 86
  purpose of, 51
  schedule pressures and, 73–75, 79,
    84, 166

"Unanswered (And Often Unasked) Questions about Challenger" (Cook), 430–32
upper stage programs, 50–59
Urgent Supplemental Appropriations Act (1982), 58
U.S. Booster Industries (USBI), 32
USA Today, 397, 436
USBI (U.S. Booster Industries), 32

VAB (Vehicle Assembly Building), 19, 79, 166, 172
Vandenberg Air Force Base
    cold weather at, 174, 289, 328, 369, 392–93, 420–21, 422, 502n
    FWC for launches from, 26, 38–45, 491n
    plan to launch shuttles from, 39, 94–95, 150, 166, 361, 420–21
    See also Air Force; militarization of shuttle program
Vehicle Assembly Building (VAB), 19, 79, 166, 172
verification completion notice, 109–10
Vietnam War, 92
Volcker, Paul, 12
von Braun, Wernher, 21–22, 91, 100–101

waivers of safety standards
    for brake design, 123–24
    for Centaur, 75–78
    defining acceptable risk, 243
    FMEA versus thorough testing, 125
    freeze on shuttle design, 113–15
    main engine at 109% power, 80–81, 492n
    for meeting flight rate goal, 116–17
    for O-ring joint design, 26, 38, 179, 204–5, 207, 242–43, 267, 284, 287–88, 303, 305, 331–32

shuttle's fuel reloading process, 81
temperature launch constraints, 183–84, 195, 295, 328–29, 345–46, 440
    See also flight rate goal
Walker, Arthur B. C., Jr., 217, 336
Walker, Robert S., 65–67, 242–43
Wall Street Journal, 381–82
Washington Monthly, 429, 432
Washington Post, 321, 324, 364–65, 397, 398
water hammer effect, 81
weapons in space, 83, 135–37, 139–40, 144–46, 150–54, 157–58
"Weekly Notes" (MSFC), 383
Weeks, Michael
    decisions made by, 25–26
    on FWC STA, 43
    on July 23rd memo, 234–37
    on O-ring erosion, 385
    on O-ring joint design, 229–30, 241–42
    on temperature data, lack of, 408–9, 410
    Thiokol visit and resiliency data, 410–11
Weinberger, Caspar, 129–30
Wetzel, Paul, 6, 32, 35–37, 45–46, 285–86
Wheelon, Albert D., 217
Wiesner, Jerome, 144
Wiggins Group, 126
Williams, Walter, 196
Winterhalter, David, 32, 240–41, 279

X-ray laser, 135–36, 139, 146, 150, 154

Yardley, John, 55
Yarymovych, Mike, 94–95
Yeager, Charles "Chuck," 217–18
Young, John, 123, 373–74, 414, 416